Organizational Behaviour

SECOND EDITION

Dipak Kumar Bhattacharyya

Professor
Xavier Institute of Management (XIMB)
Bhubaneswar

OXFORD
UNIVERSITY PRESS

Oxford University Press is a department of the University of Oxford.
It furthers the University's objective of excellence in research, scholarship,
and education by publishing worldwide. Oxford is a registered trade mark of
Oxford University Press in the UK and in certain other countries.

Published in India by
Oxford University Press
22 Workspace, 2nd Floor, 1/22 Asaf Ali Road, New Delhi 110002, India

First Edition published in 2009
Second Edition published in 2014
Digitally Printed in 2023

ISBN-13: 978-0-19-945116-6
ISBN-10: 0-19-945116-8

Typeset in Times New Roman
by Cameo Corporate Services Limited, Chennai
Printed at Manipal Technologies Limited, Manipal

Dedicated to

Sutapa, Sudip, and Tapodeep,

managing whose behaviour
while I was developing this manuscript seemed to be more difficult than
organizational behaviour

Features of the Book

Learning Objectives

A bulleted outline of the main concepts and ideas indicates what you can expect to learn from each chapter

Opening Case

Chapter-opening cases highlight the importance of the topic on which the chapter is based in the organizational context

CASE STUDY

The Unfortunate Director

nt of an organization is examining the of a report submitted by one of his he director had prepared an excel- but it was way behind schedule.

holidays. Despite these efforts, he fail the deadlines.

Even though the director has prepa lent report, his president is unhappy b

Organizational behaviour is the analysis of an organization's structure and functions and the behaviour of its people.

People started working in groups to accompl sible for individuals or individual households understanding of management and organizatio coordinating the efforts of individuals working

With increasing global competition and cont role of managers is becoming more and more cuss the definition and concept of management principles of management are closely related to

Side Bars

Facilitate easy retention of core concepts

Exhibits

Help build on the concepts discussed in chapters and facilitate better understanding of the theories

EXHIBIT 1.1   Management: Science or Art?

ce is defined as a body of knowledge system- through the application of scientific meth- any department of enquiry. Thus, chemistry cience refers to a systematic body of knowl- accumulated through the application of sci- methods in this area. Science is systematic sense that certain relationships and princi- well as their limitations have been discov-

to emphasize that management is still a growli science.

The function of art is to effect change or accor plish goals by deliberate efforts. Art is reflecte in the practical application of theoretical know edge. In this sense, management is an art as we Management principles are being evolved not f the sake of knowledge alone but also for the

Practitioner Speak 1.1   **Why American Management Rules the World**

After a decade of painstaking research, we have average the best managed in the world. This is not what expected to find. But while Americans are bad at football (

Practitioner Speak

Experiences of seminal brains from the academia and industry are shared and links given for further study

---------- **SUMMARY** ----------

e have defined man-
ectives and discussed
and importance. We

importance of manage
the contemporary focu
as strategy, social resp

Summary

A recapitulation of key ideas and concepts that are discussed in each section is given for easy retention

Key Definitions

A list of all important terms has been given at the end of every chapter for easy recapitulation

KEY DEFINITIONS ----------

Decision-making orientation   The view that dec
   making is the primary function of manageme

CONCEPT-REVIEW QUESTIONS ----

1.1   Define management. Which approach to r
      agement do you consider more relevan

Concept-review Questions

Questions that test the level of understanding of the core themes discussed in each chapter

Critical Thinking Questions

Stimulating questions are provided to help develop further understanding of the concepts given in the book

CRITICAL THINKING QUESTIONS –

1.1   Organizational behaviour studies basically a
      two areas—deciding the appropriate str

CASE STUDY

Excellence at Macquarie Bank[1]

Bank is an excellent example of how a
cessful organization was able to main-
ccess using an incremental adjustment
hile operating in a rapidly changing

environment. During the 1980s and 1990s, ch
occurred in the environment of Australian fi
institutions. These included rapid deregula
the financial services sector by the Australian

extract is from *Blackwell Cases in Human Resource and Change Management*, edited by John Storey (2

Case Studies

Case studies at the end of chapters elaborate on various organizational problems and give students a chance to use their learnings from the chapter to solve them

Preface to the Second Edition

Human behaviour has always been difficult to comprehend. Theories, explanations, and treatises often fall short of explaining human motives. Behavioural scientists have tried for ages to record and interpret human behaviour and motives. With the advent of industrialization and its subsequent proliferation, the need to understand human behaviour in the organizational context arose. Consequently, the study of organizational behaviour has gained momentum with time and has become one of the most fundamental subjects in various disciplines.

Organizational behaviour as a subject is now taught in management, engineering, psychology, and various other professional programmes. The rapidly changing organizational landscape has prompted the course contents of organizational behaviour to adapt and change accordingly. Since the publication of the first edition of this book in 2009, many changes have taken place in the corporate world, leading to renewed focus and attention on organizational behaviour. However, Indian students have been compelled to read and understand this core subject by referring primarily to international texts that obviously lack Indian focus. This second edition takes into account more relevant and timely changes and improves the richness of the content by including a chapter on organizational change, balancing theory with practical examples through more exhibits, illustrations, and features such as practitioner speak, and tailoring the subject to the Indian context.

ABOUT THE BOOK

The second edition of *Organizational Behaviour* caters to the syllabi requirements of students pursuing courses in the management stream. Since the publication of the first edition of the text, I have been receiving encouraging feedback about the book from students as well as faculty members. This edition improves upon the coverage of the original edition, and makes the text much more comprehensive and better structured. The focus of this edition has been on striking a better balance between the theory of organizational behaviour and its applications. I hope that it will further aid students in understanding the basic principles of this subject.

KEY FEATURES

- Provides a thorough understanding of the basic concepts of organizational behaviour
- Covers topics such as the use and abuse of emotional intelligence at workplace, value analysis, globalization, total quality management, six sigma practices, strategic knowledge management in Indian organizations, and catalysts for knowledge management practices in organizations
- Includes pedagogical features such as sidebars, exhibits, practitioners speak, end-chapter questions and problems, and a recapitulation of the topics covered

NEW TO THIS EDITION

- A new chapter on introduction to organizational change
- New sections such as attitude–behaviour relationships, emotional labour, affective events theory, factors of organizational politics, dependence–power relationship, organizational politics and defensive behaviour, and the impact of globalization on organizational behaviour
- Improved explanations and coverage
- New exhibits and illustrations
- A feature called 'Practitioner Speak' containing experiences of practitioners and academicians to acquaint students with real-life problems and solutions pertaining to organizational behaviour

ONLINE RESOURCES

The companion website of the book, http://oupinheonline.com/, provides the following resources:

For faculty
- Instructor's manual
- PowerPoint slides

For students
- Multiple-choice questions

EXTENDED CHAPTER MATERIAL

The following additional sections have been introduced in this edition of the book:

Chapter 6
- Attitude–behaviour relationship

Chapter 7
- Emotional labour
- Affective events theory (AET)

Chapter 11
- Attribution theory and locus of control

Chapter 13
- Factors of organizational politics
- Dependence–power relationship
- Organizational politics and defensive behaviour

Chapter 15
- Impact of globalization on organizational behaviour

Chapter 19
- A new chapter titled 'Introduction to Organizational Change'

COVERAGE AND STRUCTURE

With its expanded coverage, the book is now organized into 22 chapters.

Chapter 1 introduces readers to the world of organizational behaviour and management.

Chapter 2 discusses the evolution of organizational behaviour and explores behavioural theories such as neo-classical approach, modern approaches, contemporary school of management thoughts, and management by objectives.

Chapter 3 deals with organizational strategies and policies and strives to develop an understanding of topics such as prescriptive and descriptive schools, strategy and organizational behaviour, aligning strategies to transform people, and operational control systems.

Chapter 4 explains organizational structure and systems.

Chapter 5 discusses personality and its influence on organizational behaviour, and discusses concepts such as determinants of personality, personality types and opposites, phenomenological perspectives on personality, perception and its influence on individual behaviour, and impression management.

Chapter 6 explores concepts such as values and attitudes, attitudes and organizational behaviour, attitude measurement, and human resource development and attitudinal change. This chapter includes sections on attitude survey and accuracy, and reliability and validity scales.

Chapter 7 explains the use and abuse of emotional intelligence at the workplace, emotional intelligence, individual behaviour and performance, and assessment of the emotional intelligence and competence.

Chapter 8 discusses the key concepts of groups, theories of group formation, stages of group development, effectiveness of groups, groupthink, and group dynamics.

Chapter 9 introduces readers to the fundamentals of conflict management and stress in organizations.

Chapter 10 describes the various concepts of organizational behaviour and job design.

Chapter 11 discusses the concepts of employee motivation in detail and highlights the important objectives of motivation, theories of motivation, employee counselling, and designing motivation strategies.

Chapter 12 discusses concepts of leadership in detail. It explores concepts such as formal and informal leaders, significance of leadership, organizational leadership and environment, functions of leadership, leadership and power, leadership styles, and leadership theories.

Chapter 13 deals with power and politics in organizations. It discusses concepts such as organizational power and control, theories of power, sources of power, and organizational politics. New sections on factors of organizational politics, dependence–power relationship, and organizational politics and defensive behaviour have been included.

Chapter 14 discusses communication and negotiation in organizations. It explains concepts such as effective communication, psychological and behavioural influence on communication, group communication, communication barriers, transactional analysis, and negotiation.

Chapter 15 discusses the concepts of globalization and explores topics such as challenges in managing organizational behaviour, changing business practices in India, and international organizational behaviour.

Chapter 16 explains ethics and organizational behaviour and discusses topics such as code of ethics and code of conduct, building ethical culture in organizations, perception versus behavioural issues and ethics, ethics of production, and international business ethics.

Chapter 17 describes learning organizations and explains concepts such as learning cycle, learning orientations, and learning curve.

Chapter 18 covers concepts on organizational culture and discusses topics such as managing corporate culture changes, mergers and acquisitions and their impact on corporate culture, and Hofstede's cultural orientation model.

Chapter 19 is a new chapter that presents an introduction to organizational change.

Chapter 20 explains the concepts of knowledge management.

Chapter 21 discusses the concepts of organizational behaviour research in detail.

Chapter 22 explains advanced topics such as total quality management and organizational behaviour.

ACKNOWLEDGEMENTS

I am grateful to the editorial team of Oxford University Press, India for their extensive help in reviewing the first edition of the book using multiple reviewers across the country, and providing me with valuable inputs for the need-based development of this edition of the book. I express my gratitude to all the external reviewers for their kind suggestions, which immensely helped me in bringing out this book. Oxford University Press also helped in fine-tuning this edition to make it more student-friendly. I also acknowledge the valuable insights that I have received from my students, colleagues, and friends.

Last but not the least, my family members, especially my wife and children, deserve special mention for their timely support during the development of the second edition. Every effort has been made to trace the copyright holders and to obtain their permission for the use of copyright material. I apologize in advance for any inadvertent errors or omissions and would be grateful if notified of any corrections that should be incorporated in the future reprints or editions of this book.

Any suggestions and comments for the second edition would be gratefully acknowledged. You can reach me at dkbhattacharyya@yahoo.co.in or dkb@ximb.ac.in

Dipak Kumar Bhattacharyya

Preface to the First Edition

Management comprises planning, organizing, resourcing, leading, directing, and controlling functions of an organization for the accomplishment of its goals. The goals can be achieved by the effective deployment of human, financial, technological, and natural resources. The modern approach to management largely emphasizes on people as the most important resource of an organization, incorporating practices that lead to organizational excellence. This has led to the emergence of organizational behaviour as an important discipline, which has evolved from the various practices and theories on management and other disciplines, with specific focus on the individual and the group in the organizational environment. The field has contributions from disciplines such as psychology, sociology, social psychology, anthropology, and economics.

Organizational behaviour is the study of the individual and group behaviour within an organization, its effects on the performance of the organization, and the application of this understanding to enhance the productivity and effectiveness of the organization. In simple words, it delves into the behaviour of the people working in an organization to achieve common goals or objectives.

The discipline provides a perspective on the human side of management, emphasizes on interpersonal skills and the ability to work with people, and deliberates on topics such as attitudes, interpersonal relationships, performance, productivity, emotional intelligence, conflict management, job satisfaction, commitment, leadership, power and politics, industrial relations as well as levels of organizational commitment.

In business organizations, the behaviour of people has major ramifications because the effectiveness of an enterprise largely depends on the successful handling of the performance of people, which again is the outcome of multiple individual and group-level behavioural issues. A manager with sound knowledge of organizational behaviour can better handle such issues and deliver the desired results. All these, therefore, make the study of organizational behaviour an important imperative for aspiring managers and practitioners. Organizational behaviour is taught in management, commerce, and social science programmes to gain a deeper understanding of the behavioural pattern of people in organizations.

ABOUT THE BOOK

This comprehensive textbook is designed to meet the requirements of students of graduate and postgraduate management programmes for the course on organizational behaviour. It has been developed to help students appreciate and manage the complexities and challenges of human behavior associated with the working of organizations in today's dynamic business environment. The book covers the basic concepts, theories, and researches in the field and focuses on all levels of analysis, ranging from individual to organizational and inter-organizational behaviour.

The coverage includes unique chapters on emotional intelligence, knowledge management, total quality management, and organizational research, elaborated with various application tools and techniques. It includes discussions on cross-cultural issues and the use of organizational development tools for effecting cultural transformation and change. The influence of globalization, impact of technology, role of governments, challenges for management of organizational behaviour, leadership, and changing business practices in India have also been elaborated upon in the book. The book highlights contemporary organizational behaviour concepts associated with TQM, six sigma practices, empowerment, quality circles, innovation, and creativity.

The book is divided into twenty-one chapters, covering areas that match with the curriculum requirements of various national and international universities and institutes.

PEDAGOGICAL FEATURES

The various pedagogical features of the text are as follows:

- The book has a management and business orientation and also touches upon psychological and sociological issues.
- The book includes case studies from global and Indian companies.
- Each chapter ends with a summary followed by key term definitions.
- The concept review questions and the critical thinking questions would help students to reflect on various issues.
- Each chapter of the book starts with a small case or corporate practice example of Indian or international organizations and ends with a case study.

Faculty members teaching organizational behaviour will find this book comprehensive. All the areas of organizational behaviour have been discussed with multi-disciplinary perspectives to emphasize on the development of holistic knowledge of the students of management and social sciences

Students will find this book interesting to read, as it is presented in a lucid and understandable language, maintaining appropriate sequence. Each chapter is compact and broad in scope, with enough case examples, corporate incidents, and illustrations to develop the managerial acumen of students. The book is insightful, with explanations that are simple yet comprehensive, drawing from the author's over two decades of teaching experience of the subject and incorporating students' classroom feedback.

ACKNOWLEDGEMENTS

I am grateful to all those who have extended timely help in reviewing the chapters and offered critical comments. I gratefully acknowledge Oxford University Press for reposing trust in my authorship and publishing this book. Two of my faculty colleagues—Ms Sutapa Bhattacharyya and Ms Soma De—had taken pains to edit some portions of the manuscripts. I acknowledge with gratitude their help and cooperation. My family members, professional collegues, friends and especially Mr N.R. Datta (Chairman of Camellia Group) deserve special mention.

I would also like to extend my gratitude to the external reviewers, whose comments and suggestions I have found useful and tried to incorporate in the book.

Any suggestions and comments for the book will be gratefully acknowledged.

Dipak Kumar Bhattacharyya

Brief Contents

Detailed Contents

List of Exhibits and Case Studies

Introduction to Organizational Behaviour and Management

LEARNING OBJECTIVES

After studying this chapter, the reader will be able to

- define management and understand its nature and process
- analyse the various dimensions of management
- explain the functions and processes of management
- discuss the important characteristics and features of management
- understand the importance of basic management in the study of organizational behaviour

CASE STUDY

The Unfortunate Director

The president of an organization is examining the key aspects of a report submitted by one of his directors. The director had prepared an excellent report, but it was way behind schedule. The director had virtually collapsed in his chair, as he had spent sleepless nights finalizing the report.

He had to do it all by himself, right from the beginning to the final fine-tuning. None of his subordinates, including his secretary, could assist him because they were either on leave or had fallen ill. Even in the past, they had failed to help him with their inputs. Hence, he preferred to do everything by himself. This resulted in him working long hours in office, and even attending work on Sundays and holidays. Despite these efforts, he failed to honour the deadlines.

Even though the director has prepared an excellent report, his president is unhappy because of the delay in submission. The director is always busy, as he has a lot of work pending on his table, whereas his subordinates have a good time doing nothing. They are pleased with their patronizing director, whose ways they are well aware of. All they have to do is approach him for assistance in having their work done, like obtaining the required data from the appropriate authority, and he completes the task for them!

Put yourself in the shoes of the unfortunate director. What will your approach be?

INTRODUCTION

Organizational behaviour is the analysis of an organization's structure and functions and the behaviour of its people. This behavioural study encompasses both groups and individuals. It is an interdisciplinary field and has its roots in sociology and psychology. Organizational behaviour is based on sociology, as the term organization represents social collectivity. It is also linked to psychology because the subject encompasses the study of people, individually and in groups, at the workplace (essentially, an organization). Individual and group behaviour is again a function of many factors, which extend to other interdisciplinary fields such as economics, political science, social anthropology, engineering, and human resource (HR) management. The scope of organizational behaviour is, therefore, extensive. An organization needs to manage all these aspects to sustain itself in a competitive market.

Theoretically, it is difficult to draw a line between management and organizational behaviour. It can be said that one supplements the other. Some organizational behaviour issues have their roots in various management processes. In fact, the study of management began much before the study of organizational behaviour. Studies in organizational behaviour started in the middle of the 20th century. Organizational behaviour studies, therefore, draw from management theories to understand aspects such as organizational structure, behaviour of people in an organization, and the issues concerning external and internal fit.

Successful management of organizational behaviour largely depends on the management practices that prevail in an organization. Understanding organizational behaviour, therefore, requires a clear understanding of the basics of management. Hence, in the first two chapters of this book, we shall discuss the basics of management and its evolution, in order to lay the foundation for better understanding of organizational behaviour.

Going back in history, we find that before the Industrial Revolution (which took place in Europe in the middle of the 18th century), people used to manage their economic activities through home-centred production systems. They were the owners of labour services and capital. However, as participation was spontaneous (as it was their own work) and the size of activities was small (confined to the family members), management as a significant human activity did not get much recognition in those days. With the advancement of technology, communication, and transportation, the domain of the market expanded beyond the neighbourhood areas. It was at this time that organized production activity in the form of factory-centred production systems began to emerge. People started working in groups to accomplish common goals, as it was not possible for individuals or individual households to achieve these goals on their own. An understanding of management and organizational behaviour then became crucial for coordinating the efforts of individuals working in groups.

> Organizational behaviour is the analysis of an organization's structure and functions and the behaviour of its people.

With increasing global competition and continuous advancements in technology, the role of managers is becoming more and more important. In this chapter, we shall discuss the definition and concept of management, without losing sight of the fact that the principles of management are closely related to the study of organizational behaviour.

NATURE OF MANAGEMENT

Human needs are largely satisfied through economic activities undertaken by organized groups and associations. In their own interest, people should come together and accomplish common

> Management may be defined as a dynamic process concerned with getting things done through and with the efforts of others by harnessing human and other resources of the institution—business or otherwise—and creating an environment favourable for the performance of the people for the accomplishment of desired objectives with a minimum of unsought consequences.

goals through cooperation. However, to be more effective in this pursuit, it is essential that group efforts are properly organized, directed, and coordinated. In other words, there is a need for management. Therefore, management is as old as civilization or organized life. The systematic study of management, however, has evolved only in the last six or seven decades.

The literature on management has grown at an unprecedented rate in recent times, particularly after World War II. This, in turn, has greatly helped in improving research, teaching, and practice of management as a branch of study. However, such a growth has also given rise to differences of opinion and approach. Hence, we have various schools of management thought, such as the operational school, mathematical school, human behaviour school, systems school, and decision theory school. These divergent views relating to management have made the task of defining management extremely difficult. Operationally, management may be defined as a dynamic process concerned with getting things done through and with the efforts of others by harnessing human and other resources of the institution—business or otherwise—and creating an environment favourable for the performance of the people for the accomplishment of desired objectives with a minimum of unsought consequences.

Today, the efficiency of management distinguishes one organization from the other, as it adds to its strength. Different authorities have defined management differently. However, irrespective of the differences in approach and environment, the management process is essentially the same in all organized activities and at all levels in an organization.

MEANING OF MANAGEMENT

Let us first review the definitions of management given by experts in the field. Here, we have arranged the definitions chronologically, and have subsequently categorized them into different approaches.

- F.W. Taylor (1911), the father of scientific management: Management is the art of knowing what you want to do ... in the best and cheapest way.
- R.C. Davis (1951): Management is the function of executive leadership anywhere.
- E.F.L. Brech (1953): Management is concerned with seeing that the job gets done; its tasks all centred on planning and guiding the operations that are going on in the enterprise.
- Peter Drucker (1954), who attempted to narrow the debate: It is a multi-purpose organ that manages a business and manages managers and manages workers and work.
- William Spriegel (1955): Management is that function of an enterprise which concerns itself with the direction and control of various activities to attain the business objectives. Management is essentially an executive function; it deals particularly with the active direction of the human effort ...
- Mary Cushing Niles (1956): Good management, or scientific management, achieves a social objective with the best use of human and material energy and time and with satisfaction for the participants and the public.

- Lawrence A. Appley (1956), who reinforced the logic further: Management is the development of people and not the direction of things … Management is personnel administration.
- Stanley Vance (1959): Management is simply the process of decision making and control over action of human beings for the express purpose of attaining pre-determined goals.
- Harold Koontz (1961): Management is the art of getting things done through and with people in formally organized groups. It is the art of creating the environment in which people can perform and individuals could cooperate towards attaining of group goals. It is the art of removing blocks to such performance, a way of optimizing efficiency in reaching goals.
- John F. Mee (1963): Management is the art of securing maximum results with a minimum of effort so as to secure maximum prosperity and happiness for both employer and employee and give the public the best possible service.
- James L. Lundy (1968): Management is principally the task of planning, coordinating, motivating, and controlling the efforts of others towards a specific objective.
- Prof. A. Dasgupta (1969), the father of Indian management education: Management is the creation and control of technological and human environment of an organization in which human skill and capacities of individuals and groups find full scope for their effective use in order to accomplish the objectives for which an enterprise has been set up. It is involved in the relationships of the individual, group, organization and the environment.
- Dalton E. McFarland (1970): … that process by which managers create, direct, maintain, and operate purposive organizations through systematic, coordinated, cooperative human effort.
- Theo Haimann and William G. Scott (1970): Management is a social and technical process which utilizes resources, influences human action, and facilitates changes in order to accomplish organizational goals.
- Joseph Massie (1973): … the process by which a cooperative group directs action towards common goals.
- Robert L. Trewatha and M. Gene Newport (1976): … the process of planning, organizing, actuating, and controlling an organization's operations in order to achieve a coordination of the human and material resources essential in the effective and efficient attainment of objectives.
- Howard M. Carlisle (1976): … the process by which the elements of a group are integrated, coordinated, and/or utilized so as to effectively and efficiently achieve organizational objective.
- George R. Terry (1977): Management is a distinct process consisting of planning, organizing, actuating, and controlling, performed to determine and accomplish the objectives by the use of people and resources.

DIFFERENT DIMENSIONS OF MANAGEMENT

We can infer from the definitions that management basically aims at accomplishing goals and objectives through the efforts of people. Further review of the definitions reveals the following different dimensions of management:

Productivity orientation   F.W. Taylor and John F. Mee pioneered this concept. Their definitions are primarily concerned with increased productivity.

> Management is the optimization of constraining resources to achieve some intended goals.

Human relations orientation   Lawrence A. Appley and Harold Koontz pioneered this concept. Their definitions of management primarily lay emphasis on the relationships among people.

Decision-making orientation   Definitions under this category focus on decision-making as the primary function of management. Ross Moore and Stanley Vance were the pioneers of this concept.

Leadership orientation   The proponents of this concept have highlighted leadership as the essence of management. Donald J. Clough and Ralph C. Davis were the two pioneers who related management with leadership.

> Fayol divided all activities of organizations into six groups: technical, commercial, financial, security, accounting, and managerial.

Process orientation   Management as a process has been defined by numerous authors such as James L. Lundy, Dalton E. McFarland, Howard M. Carlisle, E.F.L. Brech, Robert L. Trewatha, M. Gene Newport, and George R. Terry.

Until now, we have discussed the various definitions of management and their orientation. Quite obviously, readers might be confused as to what should be the appropriate definition. It is recommended that the definitions are not memorized. Instead, one should try to conceptualize them, so that one's basic concept is clear. Management is the optimization of constraining resources to achieve some intended goals. 'Resources' is a broad term and encompasses everything that we require as inputs, including knowledge and information. Resources are not available in abundance and there are always some constraints in securing them. Every organization tries to achieve its charted goals and objectives through efficient management and proper allocation of scarce resources.

MANAGEMENT FUNCTIONS AND PROCESSES

Functions relating to activities such as production, purchase, sales, advertising, finance, and accounting differ from one enterprise to another. However, the functions of management are common to all business units and non-profit organizations. Henry Fayol (1949), the father of the modern management theory, divided all activities of organizations into six groups (Fig. 1.1):

- *Technical*: Production and manufacturing activities
- *Commercial*: Buying, selling, and exchange activities
- *Financial*: Capital optimization activities
- *Security*: Protecting mutual interests of employees and employers

Figure 1.1 Major organizational activities

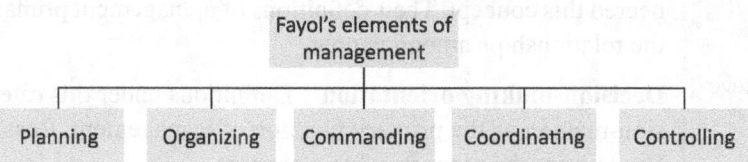

Figure 1.2 Fayol's elements of management

- *Accounting*: Bookkeeping (recording) of profits, costs, and liabilities, and preparing reports like balance sheets
- *Managerial*: Planning, organizing, directing, coordinating, and controlling

Fayol distinguished between the principles and elements of management. Principles are the rules and guidelines, whereas elements are the functions of management. He has grouped the elements into five managerial functions—planning, organizing, commanding, coordinating, and controlling; this is a widely accepted classification (Fig. 1.2).

Luther Gullick used the acronym POSDCORB—the letters of the acronym indicate different management functions, namely planning (P), organizing (O), staffing (S), directing (D), coordinating (CO), reporting (R), and budgeting (B). Reporting is a part of the control function. Budgeting represents both planning and controlling. Newman and Summer also classified management processes into the functions of organizing, planning, leading, and controlling.

The most useful method of classifying managerial functions is to group them around the components of planning, organizing, staffing, directing, and controlling. These functions of management are common to all business and non-business enterprises, but the manner in which they are carried out will not be the same in all organizations. All these functions constitute the job of a manager, and the relative importance of each function varies from time to time. Thus, while tight economic conditions may force a firm to lay more emphasis on control for the time being, a growing concern may have to devote more time to resolve organizational problems.

> Gullick's POSDCORB stands for planning, organizing, staffing, directing, coordinating, reporting, and budgeting.

Another way of describing the functions of management is to consider them as a process. As a process, management refers to a series of interrelated functions, namely planning, organizing, staffing, leading or directing, controlling, and coordinating (Fig. 1.3).

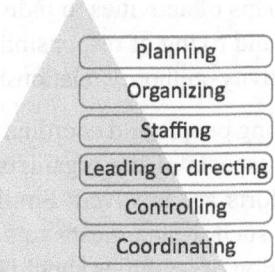

Figure 1.3   Management as a process

Planning

Planning means deciding in advance what, how, and when something is to be done. It involves projecting the future course of action for the business as a whole as well as for the different sections within it. Planning is, thus, the preparatory step for actions and helps in bridging the gap between the present and the future. Since planning is essentially choosing, it is dependent upon the availability of alternatives. It is because of this process of choosing from different alternatives that decision-making is considered an important aspect of planning. Thus, planning is an intellectual process and signifies the use of a rational approach for obtaining solutions to problems. In a more concrete sense, the process comprises determination or laying down of objectives, policies, procedures, rules, programmes, budgets, and strategies. Management planning might be for a short period and/or for the long run. For improved efficiency and better results, short-range plans should be properly coordinated with long-range plans.

> **Planning means deciding in advance what, how, and when something is to be done.**

Planning is a fundamental function of management; all other functions are greatly influenced by the planning process. The increasing interest evinced in planning amply manifests the importance of planning in businesses. Very often, the planning process is erroneously described as the prerogative of the top management. However, the fact is that planning permeates all levels in an organization, and all managers, irrespective of their position in the management hierarchy, must plan within the limits of their authority and the decisions of their seniors.

Organizing

Organizing is the next function of management and involves breaking a plan into activities, grouping those activities, and allocating resources to them. This is done by structuring the functions and duties to be performed by a group of people for the purpose of attaining the objective of the enterprise. The functions and activities of an enterprise depend upon the objectives to be accomplished and are directed towards the fulfilment of such objectives. This necessitates the establishment of activity–authority relationships in the enterprise.

> **Organizing involves breaking a plan into activities, grouping those activities, and allocating resources to them.**

More specifically, organization as a function of management involves the following steps:

- Determination of the activities of the enterprise, keeping in view its objectives
- Classification of such activities into appropriate groups

- Assignment of these groups of activities to individuals
- Delegation of authority and fixing of responsibility for performing such assigned duties
- Coordination of these activity–authority relationships throughout the organization

Thus, division of work among people and coordination of their efforts to achieve specific objectives are the fundamental aspects of the organizing function. Problems related to organizing arise only when group efforts are involved. Similarly, an organization is always intended to achieve objectives, and as such, it is a means to an end and never an end in itself. Therefore, for better results, organization of activities should be based upon practical prudence and sound application of organizational principles.

Staffing

Organization, as a function of management, helps executives to establish positions and lay down their functional relations to one other. However, it is through the staffing function that different positions in the organizational structure are filled. The staffing process, therefore, provides the organization with adequate, competent, and qualified personnel at all levels. Since successful performance by individuals largely determines the success of the structure, it is imperative for the management to pay adequate attention to various aspects of the staffing function. It implies that managers should properly assess the manpower requirements of the organization, consistent with the qualifications required for proper and efficient discharge of duties of the existing and possible jobs in the organization. They should also lay down suitable selection and placement procedures, develop employee skills through training and appraisal schemes, and devise suitable schemes of compensation.

> Staffing refers to how different positions in the organizational structure are manned.

Staffing is a continuous function. A new enterprise needs to employ people to fill up various positions in the organization. In an established concern, the death, resignation, or retirement of employees and the frequent changes in objectives as well as other internal changes make staffing a continuous function of management.

Directing

Mere planning, organizing, and staffing are not sufficient to set the tasks in motion. The management might have well-coordinated plans, properly established duty–authority relations, and able personnel; nevertheless, it is through the function of direction that the manager is able to make the employees accomplish their tasks by synchronizing their individual efforts with the interests and objectives of the enterprise. It calls for properly motivating, communicating with, and leading the subordinates. Motivation induces and inspires the employees to perform better, while through good leadership, a manager is able to make the subordinates work with zeal and confidence.

> Directing involves issuing orders and instructions, guiding and counselling subordinates to improve their performance, and supervising them.

Directing embraces three essential activities:

- Issuing orders and instructions
- Guiding and counselling subordinates in their work to improve their performance
- Supervising the work of subordinates to ensure that it conforms to orders and instructions issued

Controlling

While directing, the manager explains to his/her subordinates the work expected of each of them, thus helping them to perform their respective jobs to the best of their abilities so that the enterprise's objectives can be achieved. However, even then, there is no guarantee that work will always proceed according to plan. It is this possibility of actions deviating from the plan that calls for constant monitoring of the actual performance so that appropriate steps may be taken to make it conform to plans. Thus, the controlling task of management involves compelling the activities to conform to plans. The important steps to be initiated in this direction are as follows:

- Measuring accomplishments against predetermined standards and recording of deviations
- Analysing and probing the reasons for such deviations
- Fixing responsibility in terms of persons responsible for negative deviations
- Bringing improvement in employee performance so that group goals are achieved through effective implementation of preset plans

> **Controlling involves compelling the events to conform to plans.**

Control is thus closely related to the planning aspect of the job of a manager. However, it should not be viewed merely as a post-mortem of past achievements and performances. In fact, a good control system should suggest corrective measures to prevent recurrence of negative deviations in the future. The principle of feedback when incorporated in the control system can be of great use in this direction.

Coordinating

> **Coordination deals with harmonizing work relations and efforts at all levels for achieving some common purpose.**

Coordination has been advocated as a separate function of management by many authorities including Henry Fayol. However, coordination, being all-pervading and encompassing every function of management, is considered more as an important managerial essence than a separate management function. Poor coordination is attributed to the failure of all the management functions.

Practitioner Speak 1.2

Does 'Management' Mean 'Command and Control'?

I read recently that IBM was abandoning the term 'knowledge management' for 'knowledge sharing'. According to an article on the Knowledge Board site (thanks to Chris Johannesson from NBC Universal for suggesting that I blog about it), Chris Cooper, knowledge sharing solutions leader at IBM Global Business Services (GBS), deems it a 'philosophical repositioning'. Cooper notes, 'Management suggests control: control of process and control of environment.' Another GBS knowledge specialist, Luis Suarez, notes in the same article, 'Command and control corporations are no longer going to be there. People need to be freed to share what they know.

Read this insightful blog posted by Davenport on *HBR Blog Network* by accessing the following link: http://blogs.hbr.org/davenport/2008/07/does_management_mean_command_a_2.html.

Coordination deals with harmonizing work relations and efforts at all levels for accomplishing group goals. The whole idea of coordination is to adjust, reconcile, and synchronize individual efforts with group efforts.

Sometimes, coordination is confused with cooperation, and it is considered, though erroneously, that if there is cooperation, coordination will follow automatically. Though cooperation helps to achieve coordination, it is by no means the sole factor. One can take the example of a cricket match. Without coordinated efforts on the part of the players, it is difficult for the team to win a match. Coordination is not spontaneous. Differences in approach, understanding, timing, interest, or efforts have to be reconciled while synchronizing individual efforts.

An important function of a manager is to coordinate the work of his/her subordinates. For better results, the following guidelines are suggested:

- Coordination should be viewed as the responsibility of every manager right from the bottom to the top, and the manager must ensure that every individual knows the dominant goals of the enterprise and also how his/her job contributes towards accomplishing the objectives of the department. Even when a supervisor is able to accomplish these objectives, he/she should be made to realize that the department's achievement is not significant unless combined with the achievements of the other units and it contributes in attaining the dominant objectives of the organization. Thus, every manager should understand and appreciate the hierarchy of objectives.
- Individual efforts are more easily synchronized if coordination is achieved in the early stages of planning and policy-making. Thus, where production and marketing policies are at cross purposes, coordination between the two groups of activities will be a difficult task.
- Coordination is better achieved through the understanding of interpersonal and horizontal rather than vertical relationships of people in the organization or by the issue of orders for coordination.
- Another essential requirement is good communication. As a result of constant changes in the business environment, plans and policies are frequently revised and compromises and adjustments are made. If the required information is not communicated well in advance, unifying individual efforts to accomplish the goals of the enterprise becomes difficult.

IMPORTANT CHARACTERISTICS OF MANAGEMENT

In the context of the various definitions of management and subsequent discussions, we can enumerate the important characteristics of management as follows:

- It is an organized activity.
- It is aligned with organizational objectives.
- It optimizes constraining resources.
- It works with and through people.
- It involves decision-making.
- It is a science as well as an art (Exhibit 1.1).

Practitioner Speak 1.3

It's Time to Invert the Management Pyramid

As time passes by, people and things change. Now, what if time passes by and people change, but things that should change, don't?

Read this insightful blog posted by Nayar on *HBR Blog Network* by accessing the following link: http://blogs.hbr.org/hbr/nayar/2008/10/its-time-to-invert-the-managem.html.

EXHIBIT 1.1 Management: Science or Art?

Science is defined as a body of knowledge systematized through the application of scientific methods in any department of enquiry. Thus, chemistry as a science refers to a systematic body of knowledge accumulated through the application of scientific methods in this area. Science is systematic in the sense that certain relationships and principles as well as their limitations have been discovered, tested, and established. However, it does not mean that the principles and laws so established are immutable. Discovery of new knowledge and phenomena can always change any principle, irrespective of its standing and respect. Management can be described as a science, but it is an inexact science when compared to physical sciences. It is a theory that has a number of principles related to coordination, organization, decision-making, and so on. It is true that we cannot have the same kind of experimentation in management as is possible in natural sciences. Nevertheless, it is also the case with economics, political science, military science, and a number of other studies dealing with the complex structures of group norms and behaviour. It would, however, be appropriate to emphasize that management is still a growing science.

The function of art is to effect change or accomplish goals by deliberate efforts. Art is reflected in the practical application of theoretical knowledge. In this sense, management is an art as well. Management principles are being evolved not for the sake of knowledge alone but also for their application in real-life situations. In fact, skill in the application of principles to work situations is so important to the job of an executive that some authorities regard management to be essentially an art. However, it does not mean that science and art are mutually exclusive. The fact is that science is theoretical, whereas art is practical and both are complementary to each other. Thus, the theory and the practice of management are mutually helpful.

One possible way to address this issue is to argue that whereas learning of management is a science, application of management in practice is more of an art. This is because even though we all learn the same principles of management, our management practices differ.

- It is universal and intangible.
- It is an interdisciplinary approach.
- It is a social process.
- It is a strategic function.
- It is a profession.

Since most of the aforementioned points are self-explanatory, we shall now discuss only management as a profession.

Management as Profession

The corporate form of organization with the separation of ownership from management, growing complexities in managing the organizational activities, and development of an organized body of systematic knowledge of management are the essential factors responsible for raising the status of management to that of a distinct profession. A field is normally characterized as a profession when it exhibits the following special features:

- Systematic body of knowledge
- Need for learning, proper training, and education
- Restricted entry on the basis of examination or education
- Dominance of service motive over profit motive

With the exception of restricted entry, management has all the other qualities required of a profession. It is now backed by a systematic body of knowledge. A number of management principles have been developed, which need proper learning and education. Besides, in a number of countries, management institutes, associations, and universities are now imparting management-related knowledge. Moreover, the current social and moral climate has created new challenges for managements. The present-day managements must be creative rather than adaptive and must be conscious of their ethical and social responsibilities. Another important development in the field of management has been the rapid increase in the number of professional management consultants, whose quality is also improving by the day. However, management fails the test for professionalism because of the absence of restricted entry. Though there is growing awareness in the society to prefer properly educated and trained people for managing business enterprises, self-made managers cannot altogether be eliminated. Thus, management may not strictly be similar to the legal or medical profession, yet professional overtones are very much present in it.

IMPORTANCE OF MANAGEMENT

Readers are not required to separately study the importance or significance of management. All the points discussed until now indicate the importance of management. However, we are listing here some points, which the reader can elaborate on based on the earlier discussion:

- It optimizes the use of scarce resources.
- It ensures effective leadership and motivation.
- It promotes industrial relations and harmony.
- It facilitates the achievement of goals.
- It facilitates change and growth.
- It enhances the quality of life.
- It improves productivity.
- It contributes to organizational competitiveness.
- It develops professionalism.
- It contributes to organizational growth.

MANAGERIAL LEVELS

> There are three managerial levels: strategic, tactical, and operational.

The number of managerial levels in an organization largely depends on its size. In small and medium enterprises (SMEs), management teams may consist of only the owner and his/her own people. However, in large organizations, a three-tier hierarchy of managers is common. The top, middle, and first-line managers are hierarchically arranged with a clear demarcation of their functional domains.

The top level is also known as the corporate or strategic level and consists of those who work as presidents, vice-presidents, chief executive officers, chief operations officers, directors, or general managers. The top-level managers handle the overall responsibility of managing the growth and success of an organization. Some of their key areas of responsibility include planning and strategy framing, overall performance evaluation, selection of key personnel, and facilitating subordinate managers in achieving the results. The middle-level managers are subordinate to the top level and they work as divisional or strategic business unit heads, functional heads, or as operations managers. They are also known as the tactical or business-level managers and are mainly entrusted with implementing and controlling the plans and strategies framed by the top level. Within the ambit of overall plans and strategies framed by the top level, the middle-level managers prepare intermediate plans, frame tactical goals and objectives for the department, develop departmental policies, review reports on progress of sales and production, and also facilitate the first-line managers. The first-line managers are basically involved in operational activities, making use of the subordinates at the grass-roots level. They are subordinates to middle-level managers. The primary nature of their activities involve framing operational plans, achieving output targets, supervising and controlling day-to-day activities, managing inventory and quality control, and controlling labour costs. Figure 1.4 depicts the managerial levels.

Figure 1.4   Managerial levels

Functional and General Managers

Depending on the nature of functions, managers can be classified as marketing, finance, operations, or HR, and so on. Again, general managers in some organizations usually work at the top level. These managers have strong conceptual skills and a holistic understanding of every managerial function.

Line and Staff Managers

Managers can also be classified into two categories—line managers and staff managers. Irrespective of hierarchy, line managers are those who are involved in operational activities and staff managers are those who facilitate line managers in their functioning. However, such a crude classification is an age-old practice and makes organizations more prone to conflict.

MANAGERIAL SKILLS

In order to function successfully, all managers must possess some skill sets. Katz (1974) categorized managerial skills into three categories—technical, human, and conceptual (Fig. 1.5).

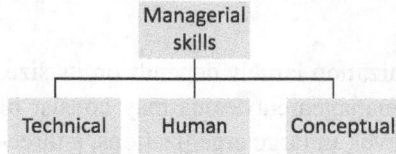

Figure 1.5 Managerial skills

Apart from these skills, managers should also possess design and business skills. Although managers, irrespective of their hierarchical levels, should have all these skills, the degree of their requirement varies depending on their hierarchical levels. Technical skills are specific to a task and the first-level managers must possess high levels of such skills. These include a thorough knowledge of the methods, processes, and procedures. Human skills are interpersonal skills and are equally important for all managerial levels. Interpersonal skill is the ability to work with people or groups and essentially include leadership, motivation, and communication skills, which are needed to accomplish the desired results. Conceptual skills relate to the understanding of abstract situations. Thus, these are holistic in nature and are required more at the top-management levels. Design and business skills are the problem-solving skills of managers. Both the top- and the middle-level managers should have this skill so as to build their capability to resolve organizational problems.

MANAGERIAL ROLES

Managerial role is a position-specific behavioural pattern. Based on his study of five organizations, Henry Mintzberg (1973) identified ten different roles of managers, classifying them into three broad roles, namely interpersonal, informational, and decisional (Fig. 1.6). Interpersonal roles are classified as figurehead, leader, and liaison roles. Informational roles are classified as monitor, disseminator, and spokesperson roles, and decisional roles are classified as entrepreneur, disturbance handler, resource allocator, and negotiator roles. These managerial roles have been elaborated in Table 1.1. Exhibit 1.2 discusses an excerpt on management for the 21st century.

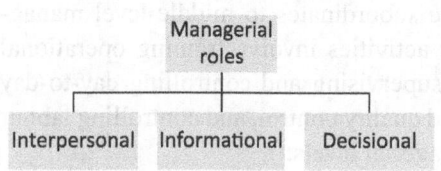

Figure 1.6 Managerial roles

Table 1.1 Mintzberg's managerial roles

Role category	Role type	Role nature
Interpersonal	Figurehead, leader, liaison	Representing an organization and performing ceremonial duties, motivating subordinates to achieve their goals and objectives, and maintaining horizontal chains of communication
Informational	Monitor, disseminator, spokesperson	Collecting information concerning the organization and short-listing relevant information, sharing relevant information with subordinates, and maintaining protocol while sharing information with outsiders
Decisional	Entrepreneur, disturbance handler, resource allocator, negotiator	Focusing on innovation and change within the organization, managing conflicting situations by taking corrective action, optimizing resource allocation for different competing needs within the organization, and representing the organization in all major negotiations

Source: Adapted from Henry Mintzberg, *The Nature of Managerial Work*, Harper and Row, New York, 1973.

EXHIBIT 1.2 Management for the 21st Century

Times are changing and so are we. However, management styles still prefer to keep clinging on to those age-old institutions, which were formulated for companies that were completely different from what modern organizations are—in letter and in spirit. The evolution of the modern organization has indeed rendered these principles of governing companies and people following them redundant. Erika Andersen, a leading management consultant, and a prolific contributor to the much-acclaimed Forbes posts, writes about the need to stay abreast of changes in the working environment of companies and the ways to achieve it.

Management principles, for the most part, were formulated for the late 19th or early 20th century corporations that mostly dealt with labourers who developed skills over time. Most of their jobs required them to work on a set of specific tasks such as cutting dressing materials, welding metals, and the like. Thus, there was not much room for innovation, creativity, or thought.

However, the organizational dynamics for modern companies vary greatly, thereby calling for new managerial styles. Command and control management style, more suitable for managing farm workers and industrial labourers of the 19th century, should be replaced by a much more empathetic managerial styles. However, the biggest problem that organizations have to deal with is to change the way managers manage.

In order to ensure that companies can make optimal use of their employees and keep pace with changing times, Andersen offers two simple suggestions:

- Assume each employee has something unique to contribute and managers have to discover that unique quality in each employee.
- Try to become the manager you yourself would prefer.

An updated management style is the need of the hour. Thus, modern managers should give up age-old management fads and adopt new ones that are more humane and aligned with their organizational objectives.

Source: Andersen, E., 'Why Management is Broken—and Why it Matters', http://www.forbes.com/sites/erikaandersen/2013/01/16/why-management-is-broken-and-why-it-matters/, last accessed on 4 February 2013 (adapted).

SUMMARY

In this introductory chapter, we have defined management from different perspectives and discussed its nature, processes, functions, and importance. We have also examined from a historical perspective the development process of the study of management and its various schools of thought. The basic functions of management have been explained briefly as all these functions are related to organizational behaviour. Two important issues—management as a profession and whether management is a science or an art—have been discussed. While expounding the importance of management, we have also examined the contemporary focus of management on areas such as strategy, social responsibility, and its role as a social process. This being an introductory chapter, which sets the pace for the whole book, it is recommended that the readers understand and conceptualize the contents rather than memorize them. Understanding the basics at this stage will help the readers understand the subject better and develop a thorough knowledge about management, which is essential for the proper understanding of organizational behaviour.

KEY DEFINITIONS

Decision-making orientation   The view that decision-making is the primary function of management

Human relations orientation   The view that management should primarily lay emphasis on people

Leadership orientation   The view that leadership is the essence of management

Process orientation   The view that management is a process

Productivity orientation   The view that management is a means to enhance productivity

CONCEPT-REVIEW QUESTIONS

1.1 Define management. Which approach to management do you consider more relevant in today's organization?

1.2 Elaborate on the different dimensions of management.

1.3 What are the different functions of management?

1.4 Using a diagram, describe the management processes. Explain each process, keeping in view its importance in today's organization.

1.5 Write short notes on the following:
(a) Social audit
(b) Managerial activities
(c) Decision-making
(d) Staffing

CRITICAL THINKING QUESTIONS

1.1 Organizational behaviour studies basically address two areas—deciding the appropriate structure and managing people's behaviour, both individually and in a group. In this context, explain why the basics of management are relevant and why their study should precede the study of organizational behaviour. Justify your answer.

1.2 You are the manager of an organization. You are required to manage the functions of several teams of industrial workers. Elaborate on an action plan for your assignment.

1.3 Critically examine the following statements:
(a) Management is both a science and an art.
(b) Management principles are not universal.
(c) Management lacks in social responsiveness.
(d) Management optimizes the utilization of constraining resources.

SELECT BIBLIOGRAPHY

- Drucker, Peter, *Practice of Management*, HarperCollins Publishers, New York, 1954.
- Koontz, H., 'The Management Theory Jungle', *Academy of Management Journal*, Vol. 4, Issue 3, 1961, pp. 174–88.
- Massie, Joseph L., *Essentials of Management*, Prentice Hall, New Delhi, 1973.

CASE STUDY
Excellence at Macquarie Bank[1]

Macquarie Bank is an excellent example of how a highly successful organization was able to maintain its success using an incremental adjustment process while operating in a rapidly changing environment. During the 1980s and 1990s, changes occurred in the environment of Australian financial institutions. These included rapid deregulation of the financial services sector by the Australian Labour

[1] This case extract is from *Blackwell Cases in Human Resource and Change Management*, edited by John Storey (1995).

government. The critical moves involved were the floating of the Australian dollar; the progressive removal of restrictions on competition among banks, building societies, merchant banks, and other institutions that offered financial services; and the grant of new banking licences, including licences to 16 foreign banks to operate in Australia.

From its inception as Hill Samuel Australia in the early 1970s, the bank's strategic focus was merchant banking (investment banking). However, in 1980, the bank commenced a process of diversification. With deregulation in the 1980s it diversified further, building up strength in specialist markets, particularly in high value-added niches (market segments) such as corporate services, bullion, and commodities. The pace of diversification quickened by the mid-1980s, with the bank entering a range of new areas including retail domestic banking, equity investments, property, and leasing. Growth took place by way of both development and acquisition. Macquarie remains one of Australia's most successful and profitable banks. So, how did Macquarie executives manage the needed organizational change?

Change in Macquarie has been a process of constant adjustment. One executive described it this way: 'We never stay still, but we don't change in quantum leaps—our corporate culture would preclude that. Running a business on partnership concepts means that policy decisions are not dramatic. They evolve.' The rapid growth in Macquarie's product range was accompanied by a quadrupling of staff strength in the 1980s. The number of business product units, or 'clusters', increased to almost 30 by the late 1980s, presenting an increasing problem of coordination in a collegial/partnership system where unit heads nominally report to the managing director.

The obvious answer was to create additional structures, systems, and controls, but this was foreign to the collegial values of the bank, which was staffed mainly by highly qualified professionals. The strategy adopted was to formulate a 'goals and values' statement, that is, an articulation of deeply held values about cultural and business

behaviour, including how the process of change should be managed. The statement is essentially a set of values and norms and internal controls that substitute external control systems. Developing business units into highly autonomous profit centres and then creating cross-functional synergies through a more systematic communication by the management across these centres supplemented the efforts for coordination.

What were the methods adopted at Macquarie to bring about these changes? There was an increasing convergence on a consultative style of management. The consolidation of the style is reflected in the frequent use of the executive committee as a forum for the discussion of major issues and decisions. The collegial style was symbolized by the fact that the managing director shared the same open-plan office.

Interestingly enough, when first-line and middle-level managers were asked for their perceptions of the bank's leadership style, they saw it as substantially more directive than consultative. All fifteen respondents who rated the managerial style this way indicated that they thought this directive style was appropriate. 'We need strength and decisiveness at the top', one commented. Consistently, those who rated the leadership style as consultative believed that the style was not directive enough for the present environment. This is an interesting comment because it challenges one of the basic assumptions of the organizational development movement—that people desire to be consulted on issues related to organizational strategies. In a turbulent external environment, however, they may prefer decisive leadership.

Macquarie does not have the all-encompassing HR systems typical of some organizations. It follows an organic, developmental approach, aptly summarized by one executive as follows: 'We recruit the best from universities and graduate schools, give them on-the-job training and pay them top money. We are a meritocracy. We try to provide a flexible organizational environment where people can achieve.' The policies are well suited to a flat organizational structure, where specialist skills can be developed within small work teams, closely related to the product–market interface. It is not expected that Macquarie will change the basic tenets of the meritocracy system. However, there was sufficient evidence during the study to indicate that the bank may need to consider more systematic approaches to its HR policies in the future.

The following were the priority areas in HR practices:

- Recruitment and selection (corporate image of an employer is important; use of psychological tests and the policy of 'growing our own' from graduate trainees is a key strategy)
- Performance appraisal (an essential mechanism for tracking goal achievement and helping in determining rewards)
- Rewards and compensation ('We pay well')
- Organization and development ('goals and values' statement, team building, monthly newsletter, etc.)

The question that naturally arises is, 'How was the bank able to maintain an incremental strategy and achieve such outstanding results in a dynamic environment?' Its success appears to have been mainly a function of its small size as compared to the other banks and its combination of diversified niche strategies and a loosely linked flexible organization. Its short communication chains and collegial workforce culture led to considerable flexibility in responding to changing market demands. These are the strengths that larger organizations seek to emulate through the formation of decentralized, strategic business units.

Macquarie Bank has been successful in operating this way so far. As the bank grows further, the executives will have to assess whether these strategies continue to prove adequate. Nevertheless, the case demonstrates that participative evolution can be an effective change strategy even in a turbulent environment, at least for a relatively small, highly specialized, and successful niche player such as Macquarie.

Case Analysis

This case study illustrates how the Australia-based Macquarie Bank could achieve success in a rapidly changing environment by making use of the incremental-adjustment process. Between the 1980s and the 1990s, the financial sector reforms in Australia intensified the competition between domestic banks. The competition got further accentuated by the entry of foreign banks into the country. In order to survive in the new highly competitive environment, Macquarie Bank, leveraging the advantage of deregulation, changed its business focus, shifting from core merchant banking operations to value-added, niche-specialist markets such as corporate services, bullion, and commodities. The pace of diversification was further extended to cover new areas such as equity investments, property, and leasing. Such incremental-adjustment processes got a further boost through acquisitions, which helped the bank to become one of the most successful and profitable banks of Australia. Obviously, the experience of Macquarie Bank is now an important example for others to emulate.

Incremental-adjustment process in a changed environment could not have been successful without the strategic management of human resources. It is inevitable in any change process. During the process of adjustment, Macquarie Bank sustained the partnership concept, allowing its policy decisions to evolve slowly. To sustain rapid growth, the bank had to quadruple its staff strength, increase its business product units to 30 clusters, and meet the challenge of increased coordination. Instead of going through the normal process of creating additional structures and systems by taking advantage of qualified professionals, the bank chose to formulate a 'goals and values' statement, which enunciated certain values and norms that aimed at developing a corporate culture and business behaviour for promoting an autonomous internal control. This was further supplemented by developing strategic business units (autonomous profit centres) and cross-functional synergies, that is, switching over to a consultative style from their erstwhile collegial style.

The methods adopted by Macquarie Bank to bring about the changes to keep pace with the changing deregulatory environment can be identified as managing by consultation. This is the opposite of the directive style. This consultative style primarily reflects extensive use of committees for discussions and decisions on major issues. In any process involving organizational change, particularly in a situation such as that of Macquarie Bank, it is quite likely that people would like to implement consultation on organizational strategies. This, however, may not be correct when the external environment is turbulent. In such cases, a decisive leadership may be a better option.

Questions for Discussion

1. To what extent does Macquarie Bank practise strategic HR management (SHRM)? Support your discussion with appropriate evidence.

During the process of change, Macquarie Bank did practise SHRM. It focused not only on sustainability in a changing competitive environment but also on growth. Mahey and Lawlon (1998) argued that there are three challenges that an organization has to withstand in order to sustain and enhance competitive advantages. These are the challenges of managing intangible assets, strategic change, and innovation. Macquarie Bank had to face all these challenges due to the rapidly changing environment of the financial sector in Australia. It could successfully respond to such challenges through the practice of strategic HR management. Increasing convergence on the consultative style of management through the executive committees helped the bank focus on strategic changes through teamwork. We even find traces of the lifecycle model (Kochan and Baroach 1985) being used by the bank during this process of change. The bank defines this as the organic development approach. It not only recruited the best from universities and graduate schools but also gave them on-the-job training and paid them 'top money'. Creating a culture of achievement further reinforced such practices of meritocracy. Flexible organizational environment, flat organizational structure, and small work teams also furthered meritocracy. One of the other models of SHRM, about which we find evidence in Macquarie Bank, is the best practice

view, pioneered by Huselid (1995) and Becker and Gerhart (1996). In this model, 18 key practices are covered, bundles of which help an organization to achieve sustainable, competitive advantages over others. The study by David Guest and Angela Baron (2000) indicates that it pays to pursue the best practice view of SHRM. Some of the best practices, such as induction training, formation of work improvement teams, performance-related pay, regular appraisals, and equitable HR policies, were followed by the bank.

Similarly, we also find the induction of the 'best-fit' model of SHRM, pioneered by Buller (1988) in the bank's HR practices. Macquarie has integrated its HR policy responses with the environmental changes, thus enabling it to derive full benefit from SHRM.

A reflection of the resource-based approach of SHRM, which was pioneered by Prahalad and Hammond (1990), Storey (1995), and Muller (1998), can also be seen in the bank's human resource practices. Macquarie Bank leverages bundles of tangible and intangible resources around its products and services and integrates various skills, technologies, and business processes to achieve competitive advantages.

2. Based upon your findings, make recommendations regarding the next stage of development that can improve the strategic management of people within the bank, keeping in mind the changing business environment.

Despite all the achievements and the successful response to the changed environment, the bank needs to relook its HR practices, as some of them need to be more strategic. The following recommendations are considered appropriate:

(a) During recruitment and selection, corporate branding or image building is very important. The recruitment process needs to be reinforced by introducing psychological tests. Graduate trainees should have reasonably attractive avenues for career progression so as to give the message that they can 'grow adequately in the organization'. Even though it pays top money, there is no indication whether the bank keeps track of the achievement of goals and aligns the same to determine rewards, making use of an effective performance appraisal system. Hence, just saying 'we pay well' does not spell out how strategic their rewards and compensation structure is.

(b) Similarly, organizational development initiatives do not give much information about the creation of a culture of shared values, extension of the scope of consultative decision-making beyond the executive committees (by developing team culture), and introduction of a monthly newsletter. These are some examples of HR strategies that need to be introduced by the bank.

(c) Even though the bank could achieve outstanding performances by implementing the incremental strategy so far, this could be attributed to its relatively small size (as compared to its competitors) and diversified niche strategies in a flexible organization and collegial workforce culture. The bank needs to be more strategic in its HR practices for the strategic management of its people if it wants to sustain itself in the long run.

3. How can an organization such as Macquarie evaluate the success of the personnel and HR management (HRM) interventions?

The best way to evaluate the success of the personnel and HRM interventions is to introduce organizational diagnostic survey, balanced scorecard, HR scorecard, and so on. Right now, there are several other overriding objectives for most HR functions: improving efficiency, adding greater value, and demonstrating this value to the businesses they support. Macquarie Bank could make its HR functions highly effective by defining the goals, analysing the environment, shaping the strategies, and then embedding these processes into the system. Apart from this, the bank can achieve a good measure of success by creating processes to guide internal HR consultation activity; crafting new performance measurement tools for HR; reshaping functional structures to fit activities; analysing and managing stakeholders and relationships; contacting internal customers; contributing to business planning and facilitating decision-making; aligning HR information to key business decision areas; diagnosing business needs and underlying problems; designing interventions that are explicitly business linked; identifying, assessing, and managing risks; creating cost–benefit models for HR interventions; prioritizing interventions and managing resource allocation; managing project implementation; measuring HR interventions and their impact; and measuring internal customer satisfaction. Thus, by following these approaches the bank can evaluate the success of the personnel and HRM interventions in a better way.

Evolution of Organizational Behaviour

Evolution of Organizational
Behaviour

LEARNING OBJECTIVES

After studying this chapter, the reader will be able to

- explain the process of development of various management thoughts
- critically evaluate and differentiate between various management thoughts
- discuss modern management thoughts
- link management thoughts to the evolution of organizational behaviour
- explain the concept of management by objectives

CASE STUDY
MECOM in BHEL

Bharat Heavy Electricals Limited (BHEL) is one of India's most progressive public sector organizations and perhaps the first company in India to develop a corporate plan. The top priority in their corporate plan is the development of people to achieve excellence. In BHEL, organizational behaviour is managed by promoting transparency. This principle is known by the acronym MECOM, which stands for manager–employee communication system. It entitles all cross sections of employees to directly communicate with the senior management of the organization. MECOM welcomes free criticism, appreciation, complaints, and feedback from all employees.

The senior managers first brief the groups about the market position, new challenges, and customer expectations. Thereafter, the groups are informed about what the organization intends to achieve in terms of productivity, efficiency, and quality, which are considered by BHEL as the most important and critical factors that must be addressed to meet the changing expectations of the customers. This initial briefing session is followed by discussions on the roles of individual divisions and groups, where the group or division heads brief the groups about the need for improving productivity, efficiency, and quality at all levels of activities to meet the increasing expectations of the customers.

Later on, an open discussion, on the ways and means to meet the challenges, is held with the employees.

BHEL believes in conducting competitive business, updating employees on a continuous basis, and ensuring a better mutual understanding between the management and the employees. Such unrestricted flow of information not only nurtures harmonious relations between the management and the employees but also facilitates organizational growth, as employees begin to develop an increased sense of responsibility.

INTRODUCTION

Management is as old as civilization, and traces of this field of study can be found even thousands of years ago. It would not have been possible to erect the pyramids of Egypt or construct the Great Wall of China or the Taj Mahal without successfully managing the activities involved. There may not be any documentary evidence of the management principles followed in those days but management practices were certainly used to accomplish these tasks. The earliest evidence of management practices is found in the work of Adam Smith, who advocated the philosophy of division of labour.

As mentioned in Chapter 1, management was influenced by various disciplines such as sociology, economics, political science, anthropology, psychology, and even literature. Due to the prevalence of such multidisciplinary approaches, even authors like Harold Koontz (1961) could be found referring to it as a 'jungle'. There are many differences even in the classification of its approaches. However, Hutchinson's analysis (1971) is considered to be the best basis to classify the various management approaches. He looks at the process of development of management from five different perspectives. Without going into the details of such differences in approaches, this chapter analyses the history of management from the following three different perspectives:

- Classical approach
- Neo-classical approach
- Modern approach

Conventionally, the classical approach is considered as constituting the traditionally accepted views and not those views that have become classical due to time factor (concepts of the past). In other words, classical here does not mean that the concepts and ideas are rooted way back in time and hence very old. The classical approach of management lays emphasis on organizational efficiency as a tool to ensure organizational success. It believes in functional interrelationships, following certain principles based on experience, bureaucratic structure, and the reward–punishment system. Classical thoughts on management developed in three different directions—scientific management, administration theory, and bureaucracy.

The neo-classical approach lays emphasis on human relations, the importance of the man behind the machine, the importance of individual as well as group relationships, social aspects, and so on. This approach was pioneered in 1930 by Elton Mayo and his associates. It further got extended to the behavioural sciences approach, pioneered by Abraham Maslow, Chris Argyris, Douglas McGregor, and Rensis Likert. The quantitative approach (during World War II) and the contingency (situational) approach were also developed and they too form a part of the neo-classical theory.

Modern management thought combines the concepts of the classical approach with those of the social and natural sciences. It emerged from systems analysis.

Table 2.1 Pre-classical thoughts

Contributor	Pioneering ideas
Robert Owen (1771–1858)	He is considered a pioneer in the field of human resource management. He advocated the necessity of having concern for the welfare of the workers.
Charles Babbage (1792–1871)	As an inventor and management scientist, he built the practical mechanical calculator, which is considered the basis of the modern computer. Further, he advocated the idea of specialization of mental work and emphasized the necessity of profit sharing.
Andrew Ure (1778–1857) and Charles Duplin (1784–1873)	They emphasized the necessity for management education, which paved the way for professionals manning the management positions.
Henry Robinson Towne (1844–1924)	He emphasized the significance of business skills in running a business.

PRE-CLASSICAL APPROACH

Most discussions on the evolution of management thoughts start with the classical approach. However, some contributions to pre-classical management have been acknowledged briefly in Table 2.1 to enable a better appreciation of the process of development of management thoughts.

On reviewing the contributions of the pre-classical theorists, it is clear that their emphasis was more on developing some specific techniques to solve the identified problems. Due to their technical background, they could not think of management as a separate field. Therefore, they integrated management with their respective areas of specialization. Andrew Ure, Charles Duplin, and Henry Robinson Towne laid the foundations of the management theories that ultimately shaped the management thoughts we see today.

CLASSICAL SCHOOL OF THOUGHT

The classical school of thought is divided into two different approaches—the scientific school and the administrative school. These theorists laid down certain principles for managing an organization. Exhibit 2.1 briefly highlights their contributions, and the essence of their principles has been discussed later in the chapter.

EXHIBIT 2.1 Classical Thoughts

Scientific management	
Fredrick W. Taylor (1856–1915)	Development of scientific management
Frank B. Gilbreth and Lillian M. Gilbreth (1868–1972)	Time and motion studies
Henry L. Gantt (1861–1919)	The Gantt chart
Administrative theory	
Henry Fayol (1841–1925)	General theory of management
Max Weber (1864–1920)	Rules

Scientific Management

Scientific management is the most pioneering classical approach, and it places emphasis on the scientific study of work methods to improve the employee efficiency of the workers. F.W. Taylor is considered to be the most important contributor to this school of thought. He developed the specific principles of scientific management in 1911, because of which he came to be known as the father of scientific management. He started experimenting with the concept in 1878 at the Midvale Steel Company. During his days at Midvale, he saw that the employees were 'soldiering', that is, 'deliberately working at a pace slower than their capabilities'. He identified that the workers indulged in soldiering primarily for the following three reasons:

- Fear of losing jobs if they increase their output
- Faulty wage systems
- Outdated methods of working

In order to eliminate this problem, Taylor developed the principles of scientific management, mainly emphasizing the five important issues shown in Exhibit 2.2.

In essence, Taylor emphasized the following points to achieve organizational efficiency:

- Develop a scientific way to perform jobs.
- Train and develop workers to perform the job.
- Establish harmonious relations between the management and the workers.

In order to ensure that these objectives are achieved, Taylor suggested two important managerial practices—the piece-rate incentive system and the time and motion study. The piece-rate incentive system rewards the worker who produces the maximum output. The existence of such incentive systems obviously motivates workers to work more to maximize their earnings. This system requires the workers to perform at some pre-decided standard rate to earn their base wages. The standards are decided using the time and motion study. If the workers are able to produce more, then, in addition to their base rate, they get incentives for the number of extra units produced over and above the standard minimum units. This serves the interest of the workers as well as the management, as the workers feel motivated to maximize their earnings while the management gets the benefit of increased productivity.

The time and motion study facilitates the determination of a standard time for performing a job. Time study helps in the determination of the time required, duly defining the art of

---

EXHIBIT 2.2   Principles of Scientific Management

The following are the five important issues of the theories of scientific management formalized by Taylor:

- Lay emphasis on organized knowledge rather than relying on the rule of thumb.
- Obtain harmony in group action.

- Achieve cooperation.
- Work for maximum output rather than restricted output.
- Develop all workers for their self-development as well as for organizational prosperity.

recording, analysing, and synthesizing the time elements of each operation, whereas motion study involves the study of movements while doing a job in parts. It eliminates wasteful movements and retains only the necessary ones, thereby making a job simpler, easier, and better.

The time and motion study concept was developed by Taylor in association with Frank Gilbreth, who is also known as the Father of motion study, and Lillian Gilbreth, who conducted extensive research on motion study. Both the Gilbreths explored ways to reduce fatigue. They classified 17 basic hand motions such as search, select, position, and hold, which they called *therbligs* (spelling the word *Gilbreth* backwards with t and h transposed and including s at the end). Their research has helped to analyse the exact elements of a worker's hand movements. A simple modification of the bricklaying movements following Gilbreth's approach, helped increase the hourly output from 120 to 350 bricks.

Henry Laurence Gantt also worked as a close associate of Taylor at Midvale and subsequently at Bethlehem Steel. His contributions to the scientific management school of thought are the introduction of the task and bonus system and a chart commonly known as the Gantt chart. As per his incentive plan, workers receive their day wages even when they do not perform their jobs completely, but receive a bonus when they complete the work earlier than the normal standard time. Gantt and Taylor also recommended payment of bonus to foremen based on the incremental improvements in the performance of workers under them.

The Gantt chart is used for production planning and for comparing the planned and actual performances. It is a visual device used for production control, indicating the progress of production in terms of time rather than quantity. The concept of programme evaluation and review technique (PERT), which was subsequently developed, is based on the Gantt chart.

Gantt or Bar Charts

Introduced in 1917, the Gantt chart is the oldest and most extensively used method for planning, scheduling, and controlling production. It shows the relationships between different activities over a given time frame. The time frame, expressed either in hours, days, weeks, or months, is shown on the horizontal or *x*-axis and the activities are plotted against the *y*-axis. The time frame or timescale would depend on the nature of the operations and activities, which may be determined by past experiences or by an approximation based on which the activities may be scheduled and monitored. These charts may be in the form of any of the following:

- Scheduling or progress charts, which show the sequence of job progress
- Load charts, which show the work assigned to a work group or allocated to machines
- Record charts, which track the actual time spent and delays, if any

> Gantt charts show the relationships between different activities over a given time frame.

Gantt charts need to be updated at regular intervals—for instance, when work is delayed at the start, when it continues beyond its time schedule, or when the progress of work is not as per the actual plan. If unforeseen eventualities occur, corrective action would have to be taken and the corresponding changes made.

Exhibit 2.3 shows that machine A has been loaded until week 6 for a given job, machine B has been loaded until the first half of week 4, and so on.

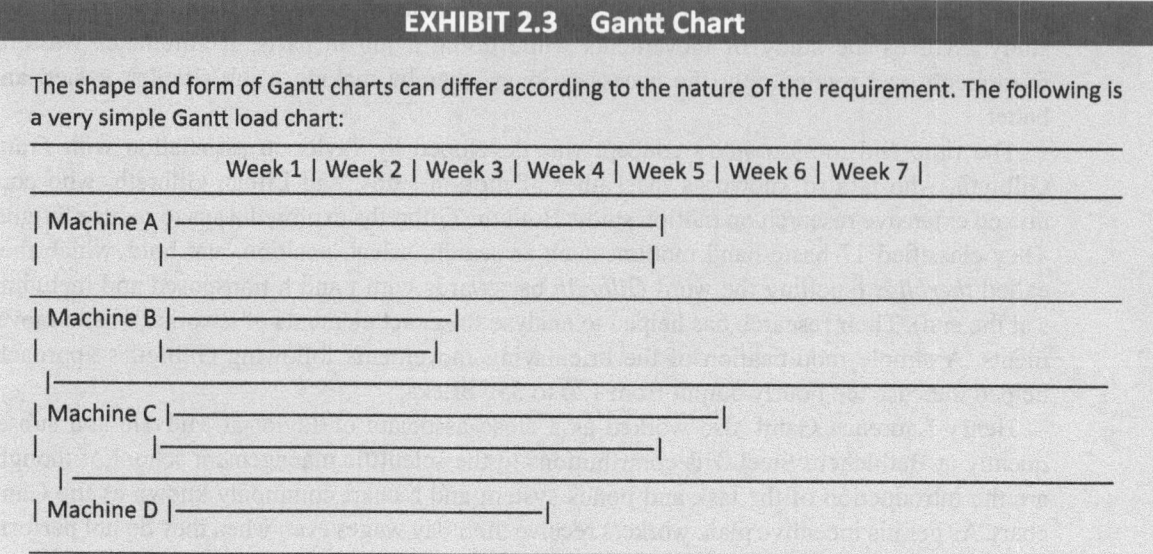

EXHIBIT 2.3   Gantt Chart

The shape and form of Gantt charts can differ according to the nature of the requirement. The following is a very simple Gantt load chart:

Week 1 | Week 2 | Week 3 | Week 4 | Week 5 | Week 6 | Week 7 |

Critical Path Analysis and PERT Chart

The critical path analysis (also known as the critical path method or CPM) or the project evaluation and review technique (PERT) chart helps to schedule and manage complex projects. This chart was developed in the 1950s to control large-scale defence projects. The underlying assumption is that any given task has one or more predecessor as well as successor tasks, except at the start and finish nodes.

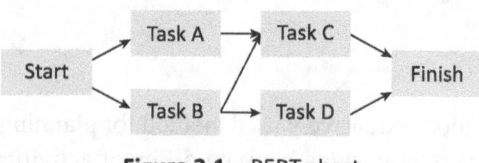

Figure 2.1   PERT chart

Figure 2.1 shows a simple PERT chart. A circle (here, a rectangle) represents a node, that is, an event. An arc (here, an arrow) represents an activity. The total network represents the relationships between the activities.

Drawbacks of Scientific Management School of Thought

The following are the drawbacks of the scientific management school of thought:

- Basic scientific management principles revolve around operation-level problems and do not focus on managerial issues that are essential for managing an organization. Hence, it is often said that they relate more to engineering than to management.
- The principles are based on the assumption that people are rational and are primarily driven by their desire to fulfil material gains. Therefore, emphasis is laid only on the economical and physical needs of the people and not on their social needs.
- This theory ignores the human desire for job satisfaction.

Administrative Theory—General Theory of Management

Administrative theory, the other part of the classical school of thought, focuses on identifying the basic principles to coordinate the internal activities of an organization. Henry Fayol,

Administrative theory focuses on identifying the basic principles to coordinate the internal activities of an organization.

a French industrialist, through his pioneering work on general and industrial management, explained that satisfactory results could be achieved through scientific forecasting and proper methods of management. Fayol classified the business operations of an organization into six activities (explained in Chapter 1) and outlined 14 principles of management, which are shown in Exhibit 2.4.

EXHIBIT 2.4 Principles of Management

Fayol listed the following principles of management:

Division of labour If people are specialists, they can perform their tasks better. It recommends grouping people according to their areas of specialization. The modern assembly line concept is an outcome of this principle.

Authority Managers must have the authority to get things done. However, formal authority alone may not ensure cooperation from the subordinates. They must have the expertise to exert personal authority as well.

Discipline People working in an organization need to comply with the rules and agreements that govern the organization. Results cannot be achieved without discipline. Good discipline is the result of good leadership and together they can create an environment of good work culture.

Unity of command Members in an organization must receive instructions from only one person. Conflicts arise when one receives orders and instructions from multiple bosses. Therefore, ideally an employee should report to a single boss.

Unity of direction All operations of an organization need to be directed towards one objective. Goals cannot be achieved without unity of direction.

Subordination of individual interest to common good Interests of an individual employee should not take precedence over the interests of the organization as a whole.

Remuneration It should be fair to both employees and employers.

Centralization Whereas centralization reduces the role of the subordinates in the process of decision-making, decentralization enhances it. Managers should retain responsibility through centralization but at the same time give their subordinates enough authority to perform their jobs effectively.

Hierarchy There should be a line of authority, illustrated in the form of an organizational chart, clearly showing the hierarchy from the top management down to the lowest level.

Order Men and materials should be in the right place at the right time. Job allocation should be made in a way that suits the employees.

Equity Managers must be fair to their subordinates.

Stability of staff Employee turnover should be as minimal as possible to ensure continuity and efficiency of an organization.

Initiative Subordinates should have the freedom to plan and carry out their tasks even though they may commit mistakes.

Esprit de corps Team spirit should be promoted to develop a culture of unity in an organization. Wherever possible, verbal communication should be used instead of formal written communication as this helps in developing team spirit in an organization.

Source: Fayol, Henry, *General and Industrial Management*, Translated by C. Storrs, Sir Isaac Pitman & Sons, London, 1916 (adapted).

Table 2.2 Characteristics of bureaucratic organization

Characteristics	Description
Specialization of labour	Jobs are broken down into routine, well-defined tasks so that the members of an organization know what is expected from them and can become competent enough to do a particular subset of tasks.
Formal rules and procedures	Written rules and procedures should specify the behaviour desired from the members of the organization, facilitate coordination, and ensure uniformity.
Impersonality	Rules, procedures, and sanctions should be applied uniformly to all individuals.
Well-defined hierarchy	Multiple levels of positions must be designed carefully keeping in mind the reporting relationships among various levels. This should provide for supervision, handling of exceptional situations, and establishment of accountability.
Career advancement based on merit	Selections and promotions should be based on the qualifications and performances of members.

Bureaucratic Organization

Max Weber pioneered the theory of bureaucratic organization, which places emphasis on the authority structures and relations. According to Weber, 'A bureaucracy is a highly structured, formalized, and impersonal organization.' He advocated the necessity of a formal organizational structure with set rules and regulations. The characteristics of bureaucratic organizations, as described by Weber, have been presented in Table 2.2.

Bureaucracy is often criticized for its red tapism and profligacy of rules. However, Weber's concept is intended to remove ambiguity, inefficiencies, and patronage.

Limitations of Administrative Theory

Behavioural theorists of the neo-classical approach have criticized the classical theorists on a number of grounds, the first being that the management principles are not universally applicable in today's complex business situations. Some principles of Fayol are also contradictory. For example, the principle of specialization contradicts the principle of unity of command. Similarly, Weber's bureaucracy also takes away the individual's creativity and flexibility, which dissuades the individual from responding to complex situations in global environments. Further, classical theorists ignore the important aspects of organizational behaviour, such as the problems of leadership, motivation, power, or informal relations. They also fail to consider the influences of internal and external environmental forces affecting an organization and lay more emphasis on achieving higher productivity than on the other aspects.

NEO-CLASSICAL APPROACH

This school of management lays emphasis on the human element in an organization, duly recognizing its importance. It places more stress on individual attitudes and behaviours and on group processes. The major contributors to this school of thought are listed in Table 2.3.

Table 2.3 Contributors to behavioural theories

Contributors	Pioneering ideas
Mary Parker Follet (1868–1933)	Focuses on group influences
Elton Mayo (1880–1949)	Discusses the effect of human motivation on productivity and output
Abraham Maslow (1808–1970)	Relates human motivation to hierarchy of needs
Douglas McGregor (1906–64)	Emphasizes human characteristics—theory X and theory Y—and the corresponding style of leadership
Chris Argyris (1964)	Relates human and organizational development—Model I and Model II

Mary Parker Follet

Follet was the pioneer of the behavioural approach to management. She recognized the significance of the human element and attributed greater significance to the functioning of groups in workplaces. According to Follet, the critical role of managers should be to bring about constructive changes in organizations, following the principle of 'power with' rather than 'power over'. She opined that power should not be based on hierarchical levels but should be collectively developed to foster a cooperative concept that involves the superiors as well as the subordinates and enables them to work together as a team. Hence, the emphasis is more on power-sharing. Organizations need to become democratic to accommodate employees and managers. Employees work harder when their organizations recognize their individual motivating desires.

Elton Mayo

Even though Follet was the pioneer of the behavioural approach to management, it is Elton Mayo who is recognized as the father of the human relations approach. Mayo and his associates conducted a study in the Western Electric Company's Hawthorne plant between 1924 and 1932 to evaluate the attitudes and psychological reactions of workers in on-the-job situations. Their experiments were carried out in the following four phases:

- Illumination experiments
- Relay assembly test room experiments
- Interview phase experiments
- Bank wiring observation room experiments

Illumination Experiments

> Illumination experiments involved the manipulation of illumination for one group of workers (test group) and the comparison of their performance and productivity with another group (control group) for whom the illumination was not manipulated.

The illumination experiments took place between 1924 and 1927 in the Hawthorne plant of Western Electric Company, involving the company's industrial engineers. The experiments involved the manipulation of illumination for one group of workers (test group) and the comparison of their performance and productivity with another group (control group) for whom the illumination was not manipulated. In the first spell of the experiments, the performance and productivity of the test group improved. However, it did not last long. The control group's performance also improved in between, even though there was no change in the light conditions of this group. With such contradicting results, researchers concluded that the intensity of illumination was not related to the productivity of workers and that some factors besides illumination must have influenced the performance of the workers. Hence, Elton Mayo and his associates from Harvard University proceeded to the subsequent phase of the experiments.

Relay Assembly Test Room Experiments

The relay assembly test room experiments were conducted under the guidance of Elton Mayo between 1927 and 1932. At this stage, the researchers were concerned about other working conditions such as working hours, refreshments, and temperatures. They selected six women employees of the relay assembly test room, whose job was to assemble a relay (a small device) using thirty five spare parts. The selected women employees (samples) were placed in a separate room and briefed about the experiments. In the test room, alterations were made to variables, such as increased wages and rest period and shortened workday and workweek. In addition, the selected workers were allowed to leave their workstations without permission and were also given special attention. It was found that productivity increased over the study period. Such results led the researchers to believe that better treatment of subordinates made them more productive. They highlighted the significance of social relations. The researchers were convinced that workers would perform better if the management looked after their welfare and the supervisors paid special attention to them. This syndrome was later labelled as the Hawthorne effect.

Interview Phase Experiments

In the interview phase of experiments, about 21,000 people were interviewed over three years between 1928 and 1930. The purpose of the interview was to explore in depth the attitudes of the workers. On the basis of the results of these interviews, the following conclusions were drawn:

- A complaint may not necessarily be an objective recital of facts. It also reflects personal disturbance, which may arise from some deep-rooted cause.
- All objects, persons, and events carry some social meaning. They relate to the satisfaction or dissatisfaction of the employees.
- The personal situation of the workers is the result of the configuration of their relationships, involving sentiments, desires, and interests. Such relational variables influence the workers' past and present interpersonal relations and result in their personal situations.
- Workers assign meaning to their status in the organization and attach much importance to events, objects, and specific features of their environment, such as hours of work and wages.
- Workers derive satisfaction or dissatisfaction from the social status of their organization. It means they also look for social rewards, in the form of an increase in their personal status, born out of their association with an organization of repute.
- The social demands of the workers are influenced by their social experiences within their groups both inside and outside the workplace.

Bank Wiring Observation Room Experiments

The bank wiring observation room experiments were conducted to test some ideas that had cropped up during the interview phase. It was conducted in 1931 and 1932. The experiment involved 14 participants (samples), including wiremen, solderers, and inspectors. In this phase of the experiment, there was no change in the physical working conditions. Payments to selected workers were based on an incentive pay plan, which related their pay to their output. They had the opportunity to earn more by increasing their output. However, the researchers observed that the output was constant at a certain level. Analysis of the results showed that the group encourages neither too much nor too little work. On their own, the group members enforce 'a fair day's work'. Group norms, therefore, are more important to workers than money. The study thus provided some insights into the workers' informal social relations within their groups.

The Hawthorne experiments thus focused on the importance of human relations and hence contributed immensely to management theories.

Criticism

Despite its brilliant contribution to the theories of management, the behavioural approach was criticized on the following grounds:

- It is believed that the procedures, analysis of the findings, and conclusions drawn therefrom are not rationally linked to each other. In fact, the conclusions are not supported by adequate evidence.
- The relationship between satisfaction or happiness of the workers and productivity was established through simplistic assumptions, whereas in reality, the situation is more complex due to behavioural phenomena.
- All these studies failed to focus on the attitudes of the workers, which played a crucial role in influencing their performance and productivity.

Abraham Maslow, Douglas McGregor, and Chris Argyris have made significant contributions to the behavioural school of thought. Maslow's and McGregor's contributions are in the form of theories of motivation. While Maslow focused on the importance of human needs, which are the major driving forces for human motivation, McGregor made certain assumptions about people, categorizing them under theory X or theory Y. Theory X essentially represents a negative view about people—that they are lazy, have little ambition, dislike work, avoid responsibility, and require directions to work. Theory Y, on the contrary, assumes people are more positive, are capable of self-control, are innovative and creative, and do not inherently dislike work. These theories are not discussed in detail here, though their contributions to the behavioural school of thought are acknowledged.

Chris Argyris's maturity–immaturity theory, integration of individual and organizational goals, and Model I and Model II patterns are important contributions to the behavioural school of thought. According to the maturity–immaturity theory, people progress from a stage of immaturity and dependence to a state of maturity and independence. If organizations keep their employees in a dependent state, they allow them to remain immature, thereby preventing them from achieving their true potential. Further, Argyris also contended that a formal organization develops a rigid structure, compelling people to behave in an immature way. This leads to incongruence between the individual and organizational goals, hinders organizational development, results in failure, and fosters frustration and conflict. People therefore exhibit signs of aggression, regression, and suppression. Model I and Model II patterns involve two different assumptions. Workers in Model I type of organizations are motivated by the desire to manipulate others and protect themselves from others, whereas those in Model II type of organizations are less manipulative and more willing to learn and take risks. Argyris therefore suggested that managers should always try to create a Model II type of organization.

Peter F. Drucker and Rensis Likert also contributed significantly to this school of thought in 1954 and 1967, respectively. Drucker pioneered several modern management concepts in the fields of innovation, creativity, problem-solving, organizational design, management by objectives, and so on. All his principles have been acknowledged in different chapters of this book. Likert, on the other hand, attributes low productivity and poor morale of the employees to a typical job-centred supervision technique. He has suggested some typical leadership styles to ensure better productivity and improve the morale of the workers, which have been discussed in Chapter 12.

MODERN APPROACHES

Some modern approaches such as the quantitative school, systems theory, and contingency theory also played a significant role in the evolution of management theories.

Quantitative School of Thought

The quantitative school of thought emerged during World War II. During the war, managers, government officials, and scientists were brought together to help the army effectively utilize resources. These experts, using some earlier mathematical concepts advocated by F.W. Taylor and Gantt, solved many logistical problems during the war. Subsequent to the war, such techniques were applied by many organizations to solve their business problems. This school of thought extensively utilizes statistics, optimization models, information models, and computer simulations for decision-making and economic effectiveness to solve business problems. The different branches of the quantitative approach are management science, operations management, and management information systems (MIS).

Management Science

The management science approach visualizes management as a logical entity, expressing management in terms of mathematical symbols, relationships, and measurement data. This approach is also known as the operations research approach. It is used in areas such as capital budgeting and cash flow management, production scheduling, development of product strategies, human resource (HR) planning, and inventory management. Various mathematical tools such as queuing theory, linear programming, PERT, CPM, decision theory, simulation, replacement, probability theory and sampling, time series analysis, and index numbers are used to minimize errors in management decisions. Realizing the importance of these tools in modern management, business schools have now included them in the curriculum of management programmes to help develop managerial skills.

Operations Management

Operations management is primarily concerned with production management and its related areas. It is difficult to draw a line between management science and operations management. Most of the mathematical tools mentioned in management science are used in operations management as well. Moreover, this approach helps in decision-making in other functional areas such as finance, marketing, and HR management.

Management Information Systems

The MIS approach focuses on designing and implementing computer-based information systems for use by the management. It converts raw data into information inputs, which are subsequently used by the management for decision-making. Nowadays, MIS helps in enterprise-wide decision-making by integrating the different functions of management. Human resource information systems (HRIS) is an important example of enterprise-wide decision support systems and is used for making critical or strategically important decisions, as it provides valuable inputs.

Systems Theory

The systems theory approach is an extension of the quantitative school of thought. This approach considers organizations as a whole because the interdependent nature of activities requires organizations to interact with the external environmental factors. In the current competitive scenario, organizations cannot function in isolation and have to operate and take decisions as an open system because its decisions are interrelated and interdependent on the environmental situation. Synergy is the phenomenon of open systems of management in which the total system is more than a simple sum of its parts. In other words, if a manager effectively coordinates the efforts of the related subsystems, the result would be greater than the sum total of such independent efforts, that is, two plus two would be greater than four. The systems approach to management is important, also because it helps in avoiding entropy, which is a syndrome wherein systems and processes eventually decay. Further, such a situation can also be averted by relating an organization to its environment.

Contingency Theory

The contingency theory approach, another extension of the modern approach, has also contributed significantly to the evolution of management thoughts. This approach discards the concept of universality of management principles and favours taking managerial decisions after carefully considering the situational factors. According to this theory, the task of a manager is to identify the technique that will, in a particular situation and at a particular point of time, contribute best to achieving the organizational goals. The theory contends that organizational phenomena exist in a logical pattern, which managers can gradually understand by interpreting the various situations. They can thereby frame their managerial styles, which may vary from situation to situation.

Contingency theory and systems theory are together classified as the integrative school of management thought because these two theories integrate the classical, behavioural, and quantitative theories into a framework that uses only the best of each approach in a given situation.

CONTEMPORARY SCHOOL OF MANAGEMENT THOUGHT

The contemporary school of management thought provides a framework of management practices based on more recent trends such as globalization, theory Z concepts, McKinsey's 7-S approach, excellence models, and productivity and quality issues.

With the emergence of global entities such as the World Trade Organization (WTO) and the European Economic Community (EEC), all organizations are now operating in a global economy. Managers now need to think globally even while operating in the domestic market. Companies are losing their market shares even in their domestic markets because of competition from foreign players. Hence, understanding management with a global perspective has now become important.

Theory Z Concepts

Theory Z concepts, pioneered by Ouchi and Jaeger (1978), incorporate the Japanese and American management cultures and emphasize the need to study and adopt appropriate management practices from other countries. The concept can be understood from the information provided in Table 2.4.

McKinsey's 7-S Framework

McKinsey's 7-S framework identifies the following seven independent organizational factors that need to be managed by today's managers:

Strategy   To determine the allocation of scarce resources and to commit the organization to a specific course of action.

Structure   To determine the number of levels (in hierarchy) and authority centres.

Systems   To determine organizational processes, procedures, reports, and routines.

Staff   To determine key HR groups in an organization and describe them demographically.

Style   To determine the manner in which managers should behave to achieve organizational goals

Superordinate goals or shared vision   To determine the guiding concepts that an organization needs to instil in its members

Table 2.4 Theory Z practices

Type A (American)	Type J (Japanese)	Type Z (Modified American)
Short-term employment	Lifetime employment	Long-term employment
Individual decision-making	Consensual decision-making	Consensual decision-making
Individual responsibility	Collective responsibility	Individual responsibility
Rapid evaluation and promotion	Slow evaluation and promotion	Slow evaluation and promotion
Explicit, formalized control	Implicit, informal control	Implicit, informal control with explicit, formalized measures
Specialized career path	Non-specialized career path	Moderately specialized career path
Segmented concern	Holistic concern	Holistic concern, including concern for the employee's family

Skills   To determine the abilities of people in an organization.

The 7-S framework suggests that any change in any S factor may result in the adjustment of the other S factors. Now, however, the concept of 8-S has been introduced by adding one more S—*Streaming*. Streaming includes those areas that either directly or indirectly influence or shape all the other 7-S factors. For example, governmental regulations have an impact on organizational strategy. Competition certainly has an influence on the structure, systems, and even the vision of an organization. The events in the global economy also affect an organization. All these factors exist outside the organization, in an area called the *stream*. In order to ensure alignment and development, companies need to take into account not only the internal components but also the external environment.

Peters and Waterman (1982), in their pioneering work, *In Search of Excellence*, identified some common characteristics of excellent organizations. These characteristics, which have been listed here, have now become important management principles:

Bias for action   They make things happen.

Closeness to customer   They know their customers and their needs.

Autonomy and entrepreneurship   They value these qualities in each employee.

Productivity   They achieve productivity through people, based on trust.

Hands-on, value-driven management   They make such management mandatory.

Stick to the knitting   They always deal from strength.

Simple form, lean staff   They develop cost-effective work teams.

Simultaneous loose–tight properties   They decentralize many decisions but retain firm overall control.

Global competition has also accentuated the need for enhancing quality and productivity, which are the basic requirements of any organization trying to sustain or retain competitive advantages. Hence, management practices should focus on them by developing the HR accordingly.

MANAGEMENT BY OBJECTIVES

> When objectives are set in a systematic manner, consciously directed towards effective and efficient achievement of organizational and individual targets, it is known as management by objectives (MBO).

In 1954, Peter F. Drucker emphasized the organizational need for setting objectives to make performance more measurable. When objectives are set in a systematic manner, consciously directed towards effective and efficient achievement of organizational and individual targets, it is known as management by objectives (MBO). The elements of MBO were first used by General Electric Company, which introduced decentralized decision-making. Management by objectives is mainly required for performance appraisal, as it calls for the active involvement of the subordinates in setting the objective standards. This exerts an enhanced degree of commitment from them to achieve the results. It also acts as a motivating factor for the employees because they can understand their specific objectives and assess the degree of

> **Practitioner Speak 2.1**
>
> **Decision making, Top Gun style**
>
> When Tom Cruise's 'Maverick' inverted his F-14 fighter jet and gave 'the bird' to his Soviet opponent in the opening scene of 1986's *Top Gun*, Cruise assured himself a lighthearted place in the history of the Cold War. What that scene also did, however, was provide one of cinematography's great examples of a key concept of air-to-air combat: the OODA loop. Maverick's uncanny ability to move rapidly through a complex decision cycle, always ending up in a superior position, not only made for great cinema but also represented one of the more complex theories to emerge from 20th Century military thinking.
>
> Read this insightful blog posted by Hagel, Brown, and Davison on *HBR Blog Network* by accessing the following link: http://blogs.hbr.org/2013/09/decision-making-top-gun-style/

their achievement. Thus, MBO improves the clarity in managing an organization, encourages personal commitment, and develops effective controls.

The concept of MBO has paved the way for participative management, involving people in framing objectives and aligning their individual goals with the organizational goals and vice versa.

SUMMARY

Subsequent to the Industrial Revolution, there was an evolution of various theories in management. All these theories were developed in various phases and have relevance in specific areas. The importance of any of these theories cannot be underestimated. These theories can be considered to have laid the foundation on which the edifice of management theory is being built. However, it is found that the systems approach and contingency approach to management are more relevant today. The modern approach to management, therefore, has its roots in past management theories; it largely emphasizes the importance of behavioural issues, which embody certain practices, leading to organizational excellence. All these theoretical management inputs help us understand the basics of organizational behaviour. Organizational behaviour is thus viewed as a configuration of various practices and theories on management, with specific focus on structure and people-related issues. Thus, unless these issues are interpreted in relation to the various approaches to management, organizational behaviour will lose its focus.

KEY DEFINITIONS

Classical approach   The traditional accepted views on management

Contingency theory   The emphasis on manager's learning and interpretation of various situations

Gantt chart   A tool developed by Henry Laurence Gantt to compare the actual and planned performance in production planning

Management by objectives   A process that requires the management of an organization to primarily focus on objectives and then manage the whole organization with the directions set by the objectives

Modern approach   A theory that combines the classical and the neo-classical approaches

Neo-classical approach   A theory that lays emphasis on human relations

PERT   Project evaluation and review technique, a tool used in scheduling and managing complex projects

Scientific management   A theory of management that emphasizes organized knowledge rather than the rule of thumb

Theory Z   A concept that combines the Japanese and American approaches to develop modified management practices

CONCEPT-REVIEW QUESTIONS

2.1 Briefly discuss the various schools of management thought.

2.2 What are the important features of a bureaucratic organization? Point out the merits and demerits of a bureaucratic organization.

2.3 Explain briefly the contributions of F.W. Taylor towards the evolution of management thoughts.

2.4 What are the principles of management as advocated by Henry Fayol? Do you think all these principles are relevant in today's organizations?

2.5 Discuss the major findings of the human relations theory and examine how this theory contributes to organizational effectiveness.

2.6 Distinguish between the neo-classical and classical approaches to management. What are their advantages and disadvantages?

2.7 What are the important characteristics of the modern management thought? How is it different from the earlier approaches?

2.8 Examine the importance of the contingency approach and systems approach to management.

2.9 Discuss the contributions of McKinsey, Drucker, and Waterman to the development of modern management thought.

2.10 Write short notes on the following:
(a) The Hawthorne experiments
(b) The situational approach
(c) Esprit de corps
(d) The contemporary school of management thought
(e) McKinsey's 7-s framework
(f) Theory Z
(g) Characteristics of excellent organizations as identified by Peters and Waterman

CRITICAL THINKING QUESTIONS

2.1 Discuss how theory Z management practices can be relevant for a globally present Indian organization facing an economic turbulence. What possible adjustments would you like to make on people-related issues in theory Z to survive in a competitive market?

2.2 As an expert in organizational behaviour studies, discuss how the basic management theories and approaches can benefit you.

SELECT BIBLIOGRAPHY

- Argyris, C., *Integrating the Individual and the Organization*, Wiley, New York, 1964.
- Becker, B. and B. Gerhart, 'The Impact of Human Resource Management on Organizational Performance Progress', *Academy of Management Journal*, Vol. 39, 1996, pp. 779–801.
- Dale, Ernest, *Management Theory and Practice*, McGraw Hill Book Co., New York, 1965.
- Drucker, Peter, *The Principles of Management*, HarperCollins Publishers, New York, 1954.
- Guest, David and Angela Baron, *The Case for Good People Management*, Chartered Institute of Personnel and Development, London, 2000.
- Huselid, M.A., 'The Impact of Human Resource Management—An Agenda for the 1990s', *International Journal of Human Resource Management*, Vol. 1, Issue 1, 1995, pp. 17–43.
- Koontz, H., 'The Management Theory Jungle', *Academy of Management Journal*, Vol. 4, Issue 3, 1961, pp. 174–88.
- Massie, Joseph L., *Essentials of Management*, Prentice Hall, New Delhi, 1987.
- Ouchi, W.G. and A.M. Jaeger, 'Type Z Organization: Stability in the Midst of Mobility', *Academy of Management Review*, April 1978, pp. 305–14.
- Peters, T.J. and R.H. Waterman, *In Search of Excellence—Lessons from America's Best Run Companies*, Harper and Row, New York, 1982.

CASE STUDY
The HP Way

Stanford University classmates Bill Hewlett and Dave Packard founded Hewlett-Packard (HP) in 1939. HP is a leading global provider of products, technologies, solutions, and services to consumers and businesses. Compaq Computer Corporation was formed after a 1982 meeting at a pie shop in Houston, Texas. The May 2002 merger of HP and Compaq Computer Corporation forged a dynamic, powerful team of 1,40,000 employees with capabilities in 160 countries and doing business in 43 currencies and 15 languages. Revenue of the combined company was $72 billion for the fiscal year that ended on 31 October 2002.

The successful merger of HP and Compaq is attributed to the strategic management of its people by both the organizations. Together, employees in the new HP share a passion for customers; an intense focus on teamwork, speed, and agility; and a commitment to trust and respect for all individuals.

The strategic approach to the management of its people is evident from HP's diversity and inclusion philosophy. How HP makes use of this strategic approach can be understood with the help of some examples. HP considers a diverse, high-achieving workforce as the sustainable competitive advantage that differentiates it from others. To better serve the customers, it attracts, develops, promotes, and retains such a diverse workforce. Strategic use of such diverse workforce is essential to win in the marketplaces, workplaces, and communities around the world. An inclusive, flexible work environment at HP values differences and motivates employees to contribute their best. Trust, mutual respect, and dignity are fundamental beliefs that are reflected in the behaviour and actions of HP's workforce. Accountability for diversity and inclusive goals drive HP's success. This is further reinforced by compliance, equal opportunity, and affirmative action.

Such practices at HP are also evident from their policies and supporting practices that are built upon their core philosophy as well as a set of values that include a strong belief that all employees should be treated with dignity and respect. HP does not discriminate against any employee or applicant for employment on the grounds of race, creed, colour, religion, gender, national origin, disability, and age. It is also the company's policy to comply with all applicable national and local laws pertaining to non-discrimination and equal opportunity.

Strategically, HP emphasizes the equity compensation plans and benefit programmes. The HR department at HP evaluates the employees and compensation strategies and oversees HP's total rewards programme. It reviews the leadership development process, reviews and approves objectives relevant to performance, determines the compensation in accordance with those objectives, approves employment agreements for key executive officers, approves and amends HP's incentive compensation, stock appreciation rights, and stock option programmes, and so on. The HR team at HP also monitors global workforce management programmes. Such strategic focus through HR helps HP to not only recruit and retain a diverse talented workforce globally but also instil confidence in their minds.

According to HP's CEOs, the company's philosophy on rewards is refreshingly simple: 'When excellent performance is acknowledged and rewarded, people are motivated and work smarter.' The strategic compensation and benefits programme at HP encourages and supports actions that enable it to retain its market leadership. This further motivates the employees to strive for exceptional achievements. In addition, when that achievement leads to increased profits, everyone shares the rewards.

Another example of HP's strategic people management practice is evident from the organization's aim to tailor the working hours to the needs of its employees, depending on their personal and business roles, and its active support to its employees to work from home. HP encourages employees to develop their work and life skills so as to help them achieve personal as well as career goals. It supports employees in acquiring additional relevant knowledge and skills as well as ensures that their work projects and assignments complement and accelerate their individual development. A happy and stable working environment also motives HP's employees to perform well.

The company believes that ideas thrive on teamwork. Thus, all cross sections of employees at HP are encouraged to come up with original ideas and to also share them with their co-workers and superiors.

The HP practices are evident from the following excerpt from an advertisement for an HR specialist position in the company:

In view of its global presence, HP has integrated the global environment in its HR policy responses. In fact, it claims that its diversity has helped it follow the inclusion strategy better. For HP, its diverse global manpower is its best strength, as this leverages the competencies of its workforce for managing the organization. It leverages bundles of tangible and intangible resources around its products and services and integrates various skills, technologies, and business processes to gain competitive advantage.

> HP invents. We make ideas happen. And we make great products. Our locations are state-of-the-art, cutting edge, and all over the world. Our HR generalists provide all-round support to an assigned business entity by using their specialist skills to deliver customer-focused HR programmes, services, and consultancy that will improve business and operational performance.

HP's way of managing the organization as a whole follows the 'best practice view', pioneered by Huselid (1995) and Becker and Gerhart (1996). In this model, 18 key practices are covered, bundles of which make an organization achieve sustainable competitive advantage over others. A study by David Guest and Angela Baron (2000) indicates that it pays to pursue the best practice view in managing an organization. Some of the best practices of HP are its feedback on performance, performance-related pay, regular appraisals, multi-skilling, and equitable HR policies.

Recent Developments at HP

(This note is additionally given to help readers appreciate the initial crisis faced by HP post its merger with compaq, which is now over. After successfully handling its crisis, HP continues to enjoy its market position, without any change in its strategies and core values.)

HP began enjoying resurgence under the disciplined leadership of Mark Hurd, validating the controversial merger plan of ex-CEO Carly Fiorina. The company's board of directors dumped her unceremoniously at a time when HP started reaping the benefits of acquisition of Compaq in 2002. Today, however, through aggressive cost-cutting by the present CEO Mark Hurd, HP is back to its glorious past without having had to exit from any business sector or dramatically change its strategy.

Question for Discussion

Read the given case study and critically comment on HP's best practices, listing them priority-wise. Further, discuss why HP's post-merger results were better.

Organizational Strategies and Policies

LEARNING OBJECTIVES

After studying this chapter, the reader will be able to

- understand the concept of strategy and its significance in managing people and organizations
- describe strategy framing
- explain the concept of policy and policy framing
- develop a strategy map
- describe how strategic and organizational controls are implemented in an organization

CASE STUDY
The Ranbaxy Way

A successful organization works like a happy family. It ensures the happiness and well-being of the employees by following the best practices in human resource management (HRM), which aims at inculcating positive organizational behaviour. People in such organizations develop a permanent bonding with the organization and play the role of partners of the organization in the development process. However, this is possible only when the employees understand and are aware of their stakes in the organization. How this is facilitated can be best understood from a study of career planning at Ranbaxy Laboratories Limited, India's largest pharmaceutical company. Most Indian organizations chart a career development path for their employees. However, they fail to provide opportunities for career development to the employees, thereby rendering the career development plan quite ineffective. At Ranbaxy, however, the managers and supervisors document their views on the employees' performances and help them reach their desired growth levels. This ensures increased employee retention, smooth succession plans, and an excellent management of the company's manpower inventory.

At Ranbaxy, another important HRM strategy for career progression focuses on continuous development of employees through mentorship pro-grammes. The company puts all the newly recruited employees under the charge of mentors, who guide them through the work process and help them perform better. This strategy hugely benefits the organization because enhancing employee value through mentorship incubates future leaders within the organization, wins their loyalty, and ensures the contribution of their competencies towards the success of the organization. Ranbaxy's mentorship strategy thus provides opportunities for profes-sional career development to individual employees and makes the organization, in the true sense, a learning organization.

INTRODUCTION

> Strategy is a pattern of decisions con-cerning policies and practices associated with an organiza-tional system.

It is imperative that readers understand the concept of strategy, as this book extensively discusses strategic issues while explaining various areas of organi-zational behaviour. With a basic knowledge of management and strategy, read-ers will be able to comprehend with ease the issues concerning organizational behaviour, from both the academic and professional perspectives.

Strategy is a pattern of decisions concerning policies and practices associ-ated with an organizational system, which encompasses all functional areas. Understanding the organizational system helps in the formulation of organi-zation-wide strategies. Strategies need to be formed in each functional area and also at each level of an organization. For example, the HR function adopts a competence-based approach in framing strategies to develop the people and sustain competitive advantages. Similarly, for managing organizational behaviour, organizations adopt strategies for leadership, motivation, commu-nication, design and structuring, and so on.

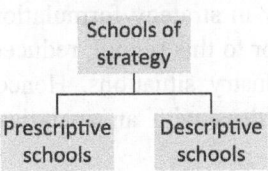

Figure 3.1 Mintzberg's schools of strategy

Mintzberg, et al. (1998) identified 10 schools of strategy, which are broadly classified as prescriptive and descriptive schools (Fig. 3.1). All these schools of thought either directly or indirectly influence organizational behaviour studies.

PRESCRIPTIVE SCHOOLS

The prescriptive schools can be classified into design, planning, and positioning schools (Fig. 3.2), which are discussed in detail here.

Design school This approach views strategy formation as a process of matching the task environment (internal to the organization) to the mega environment (external to the organization). Hence, this school emphasizes the importance of attaining a fit between an organization's strength and weakness (internal) as well as between its opportunities and threats (external) by adopting appropriate strategies. Strategy formulation, as per this school, is the application of a conscious thought. A conscious thought is not analytical (formal) or intuitive (informal), but is the culmination of collective inputs of the members of an organization for informed decisions.

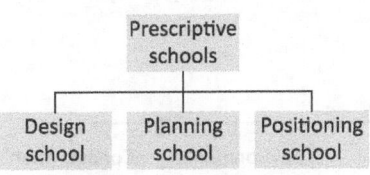

Figure 3.2 Mintzberg's prescriptive schools of strategy

The strengths, weaknesses, opportunities, and threats (SWOT) analysis helps organizations to balance idealism and pragmatism for developing an effective strategy. A successful organization builds on its strengths, removes its weaknesses, protects itself against internal vulnerabilities and external threats, and exploits new opportunities. It does all these by selecting the right strategic fit and implementing it quicker than its competitors.

Planning school Breaking down the process of strategy formation into some distinct and identifiable steps, the *planning school* makes strategy formation more of a formal process than a cerebral one. Thus, in one way, this school reflects most of the design school's assumptions, except that it views the strategy formation process as a formal checklist of logical steps. For organizational behaviour studies, a lot of managerial decisions are formal and are bound by well-defined norms like the standard operating procedure (SOP) to ensure consistency in a series of actions. However, this school of thought suffers from the limitation of rigidity, as organizations may often feel constrained to adopt real-time strategy within the ambit of changing market scenarios.

Positioning school This is largely influenced by the works of Michael Porter. It views strategy formation as an analytical process, placing the business within the context of the industry that it is operating in and looking at how the organization can improve its competitive positioning within that industry. This school was the dominant view in strategy formulation in the 1980s. Sun Tzu, author of *The Art of War*, and noted contributor to this school, reduced strategy to generic positions, based on formalized analysis of industry situations. Hence, this school leverages on value chains, game theories, and other ideas with an analytical view.

The value chain model analyses the process of value addition in an organization right from the stage of receiving raw materials (inputs) to adding value through the various processes within the organization and even extends to selling to customers. The game theory model provides insights into the way players in a market interact in specific circumstances. Such an approach can help participants to not only learn the right way to play, but also understand the competitors' behaviour and what is likely to happen if they alter the rules. Game theory has greatly expanded the scope of analysis of business strategy, sharpening corporate competitiveness, and advancing policy.

DESCRIPTIVE SCHOOLS

Descriptive schools are classified into seven distinct schools of thoughts—entrepreneurial, cognitive, learning, power, cultural, environmental, and configuration schools (Fig. 3.3).

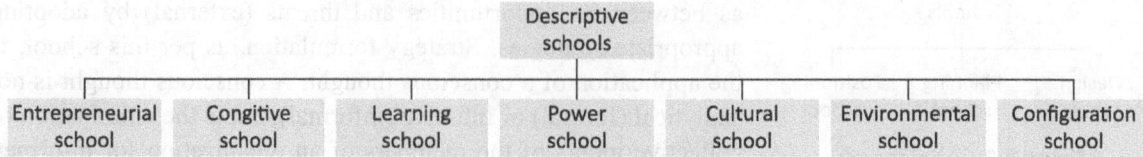

Figure 3.3 Mintzberg's descriptive schools of strategy

Entrepreneurial school   This school emphasizes the central role of the leader and considers strategy formation as a visionary process. Similar to the design school, the entrepreneurial school considers the chief executive as the centre around whom the strategy formation process revolves, as it is deeply rooted in intuition and gut feelings. Hence, this school shifts the strategies from precise designs, plans, or positions to vague visions or perspectives, typically through metaphors. Success or failure of the entrepreneurial school's strategy formation depends on the quality of the vision of the leader.

Cognitive school   This school considers strategy formation as a mental process and analyses how people perceive patterns and process information. It looks inwards into the minds of strategists. This school subscribes to the view that strategies are developed in people's minds as frames, models, or maps. An extension of this school of thought adopts a more subjective, interpretative, or constructive view of the strategy process, that is, cognition is used to construct strategies as creative interpretations rather than to map reality in more or less an objective way.

Learning school   This school regards strategy formation as an emergent process, where the management of an organization pays close attention to strategies that work or do not work over time and incorporates these 'lessons' into the overall plan of action. Hence, according to this school, strategies emerge as and when people come to learn about a particular situation as well as their organization's capability to deal with it. Some of the terms related to this type of strategy formation are instrumentalism, venturing, emerging strategy, and retrospective sense making. Thus, strategies are emergent, they can be found throughout the organization, and their formulation and implementation intertwine with each other.

Power school   This is a process of negotiation between power holders within the company and the external stakeholders or between the company and the external stakeholders. The power school views strategy as emerging out of power games within the organization and outside it. This comparatively small but quite different school has focused on strategy-making rooted in power in two senses—micro and macro. Micro power sees the development of strategies within the organization as essentially political—a process involving bargaining, persuasion, and confrontation among inside actors. Macro power, on the other hand, takes the organization as an entity that uses its power over others including its partners in alliances, joint ventures, and other network relationships to negotiate 'collective' strategies in its interests.

Cultural school   This school views strategy formation as a collective process involving various groups and departments within the company. The strategy developed is thus a reflection of the corporate culture of the organization. As opposed to the power school, which focuses on self-interest and fragmentation, the cultural school focuses on common interest and integration. The theory concentrates on the influence of culture in discouraging significant strategic change. Culture became a major issue in the US and Europe after the impact of Japanese management was fully realized in the 1980s and it became clear that strategic advantage can be the product of unique and difficult-to-imitate cultural factors.

Environmental school   This school sees strategy formation as a reactive process—a response to the challenges imposed by the external environment. This school believes that a firm's strategy depends on events in the environment and the company's reaction to them. In a strict sense, it might not be strategic management if one takes the term 'reaction' to mean how organizations use their degrees of freedom to create strategy. The environmental school, nevertheless, has brought into focus the demands of the environment. Among its most noticeable theories are the *contingency theory*, which considers the responses expected of organizations facing particular environmental conditions, and the *population ecology writings*, which claim severe limits to strategic choice.

Configuration school   This school mandates strategy formation as a process of transforming the organization from one type of decision-making structure into another. It describes the relative stability of strategy, interrupted by the occasional and dramatic leaps to new ones. This school enjoys the most extensive and integrated literature and practice at present. One part of this school, which is more academic and descriptive, sees an organization as a configuration, that is, coherent clusters of characteristics and behaviours, and serves to integrate the claims of the other schools—each configuration, in effect, in its own place. Planning, for example, prevails in machine-type organizations under conditions of relative stability and in entrepreneurship under more dynamic configurations of start-up and turnaround.

After going through the contributions of all these schools, it is evident that the process of strategy formulation is still not clear. Even at this stage, it is not known as to how an individual or a group is able to leap from the collection and analysis of information to the conceptualization of alternative courses of action, although it may be conceded that the cognitive school provides the nearest explanation. Hence, from the organizational behaviour point of view, none of these 10 approaches is complete in itself. Each offers some useful concepts and some strong points to aid understanding but has its disadvantages as well. Hence, it is for the organizations and their leaders to decide as to which school of thought suits them the most for the purpose of framing a strategy. On analysing the strategy formulation process of organizations theoretically, it is seen that they may have been influenced by one or more schools.

From the organizational behaviour perspective, there are many other theories on strategy. The behavioural role theory, pioneered by Katz and Kahn (1978) and Jackson and Schuler (1995), considers employee behaviour as the key to successful strategy implementation. The theory advocates that while framing strategies, an organization should align its policies and practices with its strategy. This will ensure that the expectations of the employees' roles within the organization are fulfilled. The resource-based theory of Barney (1991) and Prahalad and Hamel (1990) suggests that only the employees of an organization can provide sustainable competitive advantage. This is because people are characteristically rare, inimitable (features that cannot be found in any other resource of an organization), and non-substitutable resources for achieving competitive advantage. The human capital theory of Becker (1964) linked the strategic importance of people to other economic assets, arguing that the knowledge, skills, and abilities of the people also have economic values. This concept was later developed into human resource accounting by Flamholtz (1981) and others. The transaction cost theory of Williamson (1981) suggests that by considering people as a strategic resource, organizations can ensure cost minimization, as this will enhance periodic monitoring and governance. The agency theory of Eisenhardt (1989)

> From the organizational behaviour perspective, the behavioural role theory considers employee behaviour as the key to successful strategy implementation.

> Mintzberg's five Ps of strategy describe the characteristics of strategic planning from different perspectives including that of organizational behaviour.

suggests strategic alignment of the interests of the agents (employees) and the principals (employers) in an organization, which would result in streamlining the employee–employer relations and systems.

The common characteristic features of all these theories justify the alignment of people with organization-wide strategy and hence, these are grouped under rational choice theories. Similarly, there are institutional (Meyer and Rowen 1977; Powell and DiMaggio 1991) and dependency (Pfeffer and Salancik 1978) theories on strategy. These theories focus on constituency-based interest, since a strategic approach to people is not empirically proved as a contributor to organizational performance. The institutional theory argues the need for acceptance of strategy by stakeholders, whereas the dependency theory reckons this will unduly enhance the level of influence of the employees over the organizations and will thereby defeat the purpose.

Prima facie, environmental, organizational, institutional, and technological factors are potential influencers of strategy. Potential influencers are factors that directly or indirectly affect the organizational strategy formulation process. The relative importance of each such factor will depend on the organizational characteristics. However, there is a need to give cognizance to each factor or else an organization will not be able to sustain its growth and profitability.

Based on the discussions so far, strategy can be defined as the direction and scope of an organization over the long term, which are to be achieved by matching its resources to its changing environment and, in particular, to its markets, customers, and/or clients so as to meet the expectations of the stakeholders. It is either the plans made or the actions taken to help an organization fulfil its intended purposes. A strategic plan for the future is called the intended strategy and strategic actions are known as realized strategy. Strategic means refer to the plans and policies, whereas strategic ends may be broad (visions and missions) or focused (goals and objectives).

Mintzberg, et al. have provided the five Ps of strategy (Fig. 3.4). Although essentially the five Ps are generally used to describe the characteristics of strategic planning from different perspectives, these are also relevant in organizational behaviour. The five Ps of strategy are as follows:

Plan   Strategy as a plan guides an organization towards different courses of action and provides a path from the current state to the desired future end state.

Pattern   Strategy as a pattern ensures consistent behaviour over time.

Position   Strategy as a position determines the location or positioning of particular products in particular markets or a particular leadership style in a particular situation.

Perspective   Strategy as a perspective represents a philosophy or value system, such as the style of communication or interpersonal relations in an organization.

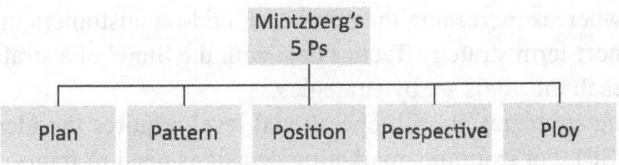

Figure 3.4   Mintzberg's five Ps of strategy

Ploy Strategy as a ploy suggests the means of gaining some advantages through specific manoeuvring, for example, motivating employees in an organization through participative leadership.

STRATEGY ACROSS LEVELS

Strategy is all-encompassing and function-specific. Organizational structure and design, whether hierarchical or non-hierarchical, has three levels, namely corporate, business, and operational (Fig. 3.5). The corporate level is also known as the top level or strategic level. It is considered a strategic level because at this level the senior management formulates the overall organizational strategies. Corporate-level strategies focus on the (a) overall scope of an organization's activities, (b) structural and financial aspects, and (c) resource allocation. These strategies emanate from the organizational mission. The business level is also known as the competitive, middle, or tactical level. Strategies formulated at the corporate level are translated into specific action plans at this middle level. In addition, middle-level managers frame intermediate strategies that are specific to their functions or divisions. Strategies framed at this level deal with issues such as the following:

Figure 3.5 Strategy across organizational levels

- Market competition strategies
- Product or service development strategies matching the market requirements
- Strategies for meeting and satisfying customer needs
- Strategies for achieving the organizational objectives such as long-term profitability, sales growth, and efficiency

> Organizational structure and design, whether hierarchical or non-hierarchical, has three levels, namely corporate, business, and operational.

The operational level is also known as the first level or the execution level. The operational-level managers frame strategies that are necessary for routine day-to-day activities, which include strategies on inventory, quality, and production planning. Even though the corporate level frames strategies for the overall organization, the business- and operational-level managers are also required to frame their specific strategies and action plans within the ambit of the corporate-level strategies. Thus, strategies are framed at every level, but their nature and purpose are different.

STRATEGY AND TACTICS

An organization can have long-term and short-term strategies. A continued focus on product development by investing in the state-of-the-art research facilities is an example of a long-term strategy, whereas increasing the number of add-on customers in a particular quarter is an example of a short-term strategy. Tactics deal with the 'how' of a strategy. It involves deploying the means to reach the goals set by strategies.

Implementing strategies at each operational level requires the identification of critical success factors (CSF). For example, marketing decisions need to focus on product, price, market, and promotion. Financial decisions may focus on capital acquisition, allocation, dividend, and

Demystifying Strategy: The what, who, how, and why

Many leaders I work with struggle with strategy. They know it's important to have strategies in order to align decision making in their businesses. They understand that they can't observe and control everything in their organizations (much as many of them would like to). They earnestly want to develop good strategies and they get the theory. But when it comes down to the nitty-gritty of crafting strategy, they rapidly get bogged down.

Read this insightful blog posted by Watkins on *HBR Blog Network* by accessing the following link: http://blogs.hbr.org/watkins/2007/09/demystifying_strategy_the_what.html.

> Tactics deal with the 'how' of a strategy.

working capital management. Research and development (R&D) decisions focus on basic research, commercial development, lead time, organizational fit, and basic R&D posture (defensive, offensive, innovation, development, etc.). In organizational behaviour, managing cross-cultural issues may require an understanding of the different cultural constructs and identifying the best fit for a cultural synergy. CSF analysis is a method developed at MIT's Sloan School by John Rockart in 1981 to guide businesses in creating and measuring success. It is a top-down methodology especially suitable for designing systems and is a means of identifying the tasks and requirements needed for success and for prioritizing requirements.

After learning strategy formulation and its implementation, it is essential to understand the process of strategy evaluation. Strategy evaluation ensures an understanding of the extent of strategic fit, matching the adopted strategies with the organizational requirements. Among others, it requires (a) internal and external consistency, (b) availability of resources, (c) degree of risk, (d) lead time, and (e) workability.

STRATEGY AND ORGANIZATIONAL BEHAVIOUR

Organizational behaviour plays a crucial role in organizational development. Organizational development is a strategic initiative aimed at bringing the desired changes in an organization so as to achieve the organizational goals. Hence, strategy is closely related to the field of organizational behaviour studies. Strategy encompasses the study of organizations from various perspectives, methods, and levels of analysis. At the micro level, strategic organizational behaviour studies focus on individual and group dynamics in a particular organizational setting. At the macro level, strategy influences the whole organization, such as adapting the organizational culture, designing the structures, and keeping pace with the market requirement.

> Organizational development is a strategic initiative aimed at bringing the desired changes in an organization so as to achieve the organizational goals. Hence, strategy is closely related to the field of organizational behaviour studies.

Strategic human resource management (SHRM) is an extension of the strategic fit analysis, which also encompasses organizational behaviour. SHRM is an HR system that is tailored to meet the demands of business strategies (Miles and Snow 1984). Further, it is also defined as a pattern of planned HR activities intended to enable an organization to achieve its goals (Wright and McMahan 1992). Both the definitions consider SHRM as a reactive management, where

---

EXHIBIT 3.1   Strategic Focus at Dell Computers

To ensure that the HR objectives fulfil both employees' and organizational objectives, Dell Computers actively seeks and cultivates a certain type of employee mindset. With the change in business focus from renting a computer to selling it, Dell required an HR department that could partner the company's business units. To achieve this, Dell divided the HR into two areas—operations and management. Whereas HR operations support Dell employees in general, the management division supports Dell's business. Dell's HRM team identifies its personnel's needs, works out lines of reporting and organizational charts, and defines training needs. It consults the business units on matters relating to strategies. This ensures zero confusion in strategy. At Dell, the issues relating to the roles of the employees and their areas of accountability are very clear, which makes possible a speedy execution of the company's plans. Its strategy starts with an executive team that develops quantitative and measurable key objectives for the coming year. These objectives are articulated and circulated globally. In this way, Dell creates a culture of ownership among its employees and develops 'shared visions' that help fulfil the organizational as well as employees' objectives.

> SHRM is an extension of strategic fit analysis, which also encompasses organizational behaviour.

the behaviour of employees in the organization is used to implement strategy. SHRM becomes proactive when the pattern of prevailing organizational behaviour is considered while framing the strategy of an organization (Sanz-Valle, et al. 1999). A strategic focus on organizational behaviour is beneficial for both the employees and the organization. Exhibit 3.1 explains the issue further.

ALIGNING STRATEGIES TO TRANSFORM PEOPLE

Aligning strategies to people, processes, technology, systems, and relationships and cascading them to every member of the organization is what an organization does to transform people. With the change in technology, the work process changes, as also the required set of competent people working with the organization. Competency development and renewal requires a thrust, not only on the knowledge and skills of the people but also on their attitudes. Thus, strategic alignment requires total involvement and understanding of an organization's vision, mission, goals, and objectives. Strategies provide the direction to achieve the intended objectives through well-charted action plans. All the employees should have a clear understanding of the organization's strategies. One possible way to do this is to develop a strategy map and make all members of the organization understand it. This ensures that all of them relate to critical business drivers and identify the gaps between plans and their execution. An organization translates corporate strategy into operating business units by using some measurement criteria or matrices.

> Strategic planning is the process of thinking through the current mission of the organization, taking into account the current environmental conditions—both external and internal.

In reality, however, strategy formulation may not always be value-driven, that is, it is not rooted only in vision. Market competitiveness often requires companies to adopt a more dynamic portfolio approach, which involves considering the Boston Consulting Group (BCG) matrix, SWOT analysis, or the analysis of competitive forces in line with Michael Porter (1985) to map the current business position. All these help not only in strategy formulation but also in strategy implementation and evaluation. Hence, these can also be used to measure the effectiveness of organizational strategy. However, this is beyond the scope of this book as the focus on value-based strategy formulation is restricted to the basics. For a better understanding of strategies, readers can refer to the case studies given in Chapters 5 and 18.

Framing Strategy

Strategic planning is the process of thinking through the current mission of the organization, taking into account the current environmental conditions—both external and internal. Such plans, therefore, set the guidelines for future decisions and results. The different stages of strategic planning are discussed here. A clear understanding of these will lay the ground for framing a strategy.

Vision

Vision denotes intentions that are broad, all-inclusive, and forward-thinking. The vision of an organization has the following features:

- It describes the aspirations for the future.
- It does not specify the means to be used to achieve the desired ends.
- It must be inspirational.
- It is often unwritten.
- It must be communicated.

Vision can be communicated in the form of a mission statement or through personal selling (e.g., behaviour of the visionary). The attitude towards quality and handling of customer complaints are examples of the vision of an organization. Sample vision and mission statements can be found in the case studies of Chapters 5 and 18.

Mission

A mission statement is the vision in a tangible form. Thus, it articulates the vision. A mission statement of an organization can change from time to time, depending on its change in business focus. Through a mission statement, an organization attempts to answer questions related to the following:

> Vision denotes the intentions that are broad, all-inclusive, and forward-thinking.

- Basic purpose of existence
- Unique or distinctive features of the organization
- Likely difference in business three to five years into the future
- Principal customers, clients, or key market segments
- Principal goods and services, for the present and for the future
- Principal economic concerns
- Basic beliefs, values, aspirations, and philosophical priorities of the firm

> Vision in a tangible form is the mission statement.

Key elements The following are the key elements of a mission statement:

View of future This refers to the anticipated regulatory, competitive, and economic environment. Such perspectives influence the business focus of an organization.

> Goals are attempts to make a mission statement more concrete.

Competitive arenas This refers to the business and the geographic business areas where the organization will compete.

Sources of competitive advantage This refers to the skills that the company will develop for gaining competitive advantage and also the description of how the company intends to succeed.

Benefits By developing a mission statement, an organization primarily decides on a direction for the people working with it. In addition, the statement depicts the company's concerns for meeting the expectations of the different stakeholders. The following are some of the benefits of a mission statement:

- It establishes boundaries to guide strategy formulation.
- It acknowledges the organization's responsibilities towards its various stakeholders and establishes standards for organizational performance.
- It suggests standards of individual behaviour.

Goals A mission statement tries to make a vision more specific, whereas goals are attempts to make a mission statement more concrete. The following are some features of goals:

- They address both financial and non-financial issues.
- They facilitate reasoned trade-off (range of goals should be perfectly consistent with one another).
- They can be reached with a stretch.
- They cut across functional areas.

Objectives Objectives are the operational definitions of goals. They describe in specific measurable terms what the organizations hope to accomplish within a given time frame. The top management of an organization decides the overall objectives, which then cascades to the divisional, departmental, and individual employee-level objectives. Individual employee-level objectives are known as key result areas (KRAs), key performance areas (KPAs), key performance indicators (KPIs), or key sales objectives (KSOs). Such individual-level objectives then become the basis for performance evaluation. Thus, characteristically, objectives can be measured, they have a time dimension, and they reduce conflicts (misunderstandings) by setting a common direction for all employees of the organization.

> Objectives are the operational definitions of goals.

EXAMPLE OF STRATEGY AND ACTION PLAN FOR HUMAN RESOURCE MANAGEMENT

A strategy and action plan for HRM for a hypothetical organization has been discussed here, first by listing the details in the light of vision, mission, goals, objectives, strategies, and action plan (Exhibit 3.2) and then by presenting them in a structured manner in Fig. 3.6.

EXHIBIT 3.2 Details of Strategy and Action Plan for HRM

Vision

- We are committed to provide an enjoyable work environment to our employees to promote teamwork, improvement in quality, and excellence.
- Our employees are our valued customers and the most important stakeholders.
- We are committed to achieve financial growth of our organization by fostering growth and creativity of our valued employees.

Mission

To achieve excellence in human resource management and foster growth and creativity

Goals

- To promote teamwork
- To ensure improvement in quality
- To foster growth and creativity

Objectives

Goal 1

- Achieve group cohesiveness by inculcating participative management.
- Reduce dissonance in managerial decisions.
- Reduce conflict and grievances to achieve zero loss of man-days and increase productivity.

Goal 2

- Achieve higher levels of quality consciousness in the organization.
- Reduce costs of quality to zero within the next five years.
- Provide error-free product and services to customers to increase customer retention levels and to further increase market share.

Goal 3

- Promote creativity in the organization.
- Provide opportunities for growth of employees.
- Increase the retention levels of employees to reduce current employee turnover by 80 per cent in the next five years.

Strategies

Goal 1 Improve participative management.

Goal 2 Initiate organization-wide quality improvement.

Goal 3 Develop in the organization a culture that promotes growth and creativity.

Action Plans

Strategy 1

- Establish small group forums such as quality circles (QCs), self-managed teams (SMTs), value engineering teams (VETs), and total quality management (TQM) clubs in the organization.
- Shift focus from statutory participation to total participation.
- Empower employees by involving them in the decision-making process.
- Implement organization-wide transparent communication network.

Strategy 2

- Implement quality awareness programmes through regular training and development.
- Develop TQM culture by increasing formal and informal interactions with all cross sections of employees.
- Practise TQM philosophy through personal selling (reflected in the behaviour of all).

Strategy 3

- Encourage directed creativity culture and practices with clear documented policy.
- Emphasize in-house talent rather than outsourcing.
- Implement reward system for focused and need-based creative ideas.
- Implement documented promotion policy to provide growth opportunities for employees.

Vision

We are committed to providing an enjoyable work environment to our employees to promote teamwork, improvement in quality, and excellence.

Our employees are our valued customers and the most important stakeholders.

We are committed to achieving financial growth of our organization by fostering growth and creativity of our valued employees.

Action plans

Establish small group forums such as quality circles (QCs), self-managed teams (SMTs), value engineering teams (VETs), and total quality management (TQM) clubs in the organization.

Shift focus from statutory participation to total participation.

Empower employees by involving them in decision-making process.

Implement an organization-wide transparent communication network.

Objectives

Strategies

Goals

To promote teamwork

Achieve group cohesiveness by inculcating participative management.

Reduce dissonance in managerial decisions.

Zero loss of man-days and increased productivity.

Improve participative management.

Mission

To achieve excellence in human resource management and foster growth and creativity

To ensure improvement in quality

Achieve higher levels of quality consciousness in the organization.

Reduce cost of quality to zero within the next five years.

Provide error-fee products and services to customers to further increase market share.

Initiate organization-wide quality improvement.

Implement a quality awareness programme through regular training and development.

Develope TQM culture by increasing formal and informal interactions with all the cross sections of employees.

Practise TQM philosophy through personal selling (reflected through behaviour of all).

To foster growth and creativity

Promote creativity in the organization.

Provide opportunities for growth of the employees.

Increase the levels of employee retention to reduce current employee turnover by 80% in the next five years

Develop in the organization a culture that promotes growth and creativity.

Encourage directed creativity culture and practices with clear documented policy.

Emphasize in-house talent rather than outsourcing.

Implement reward system for focused and need-based creative ideas.

Implement documented promotion policy to provide growth opportunities for employees.

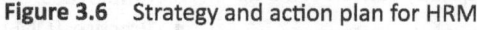

Figure 3.6 Strategy and action plan for HRM

POLICY

A policy is a predetermined and established guideline that aims at the attainment of accepted goals and objectives. Such guidelines facilitate properly designed efforts to accomplish the strategic intent. Policy is not a strategy or tactic. Strategy is a proposed course of action to exert a far-reaching impact on the ability of the enterprise to attain its goals. Strategy relates to means.

A policy can be differentiated from objectives. A policy relates to the fundamental framework of principles and rules, which are used as reference information for decision-making and ensure that there is a constant pattern in the decisions taken. Objectives are specific goals

> A policy is a predetermined and established guideline that aims at the attainment of accepted goals and objectives.

or aims, preferably in quantitative terms, that an individual or group seeks to accomplish. Hence, an objective refers to something that is sought to be accomplished, whereas a policy acts as a guide to accomplish the objective.

A policy is also different from a procedure. A procedure defines the manner or way of accomplishing something, that is, it is a process or a method. A policy refers to a framework of general principles, whereas, a procedure necessarily indicates how to do something and directs employees towards the accomplishment of the desired goals.

Policies are also differentiated from programmes, which are developed on the basis of policies with a view to implement them and accordingly involve one additional step beyond policies. The execution of programmes leads to specific actions including practices and procedures.

Policies are also different from rules. Rules specify what is to be done or not to be done in a particular situation and need to be followed without deviation. Policies, however, can be flexible enough to enable authorities to take circumstance-specific decisions within the overall policy parameters.

Operationally, organizations adopt two types of policies—standing and single use. Standing policies are those used in programmed or recurring decision-making. Procedures, SOPs, and rules are of this nature. Single-use policies are used for programmes, budgets, and projects. Since such policies relate to one-time decision-making, they are scrapped once the goals are achieved. As a sample of a standing policy, the leave policy of Fortune Furnitech is given in Annexure 3.1.

Origins of and Responsibility for Policies

Policies may originate from anywhere inside an organization or from external sources—the community, governmental legislation, changes in the economy, and international developments such as wartime or defence conditions. Internally, policies have their origins in the employees' suggestions or complaints, in collective bargaining, and at any level of management—staff or line.

The approvals for new or changed HR policies ultimately come from the top management. However, the responsibility for administration rests with the line managers. An effective HR department recommends policies that it considers appropriate for the benefit of the organization. It also assists in communicating policies to those who should know them. Some ways of communicating the policies are standing orders, house journals, circulars, and documented policy manuals. The HR department interprets policies, exercises control over policy administration, and periodically reviews the policies to ensure fairness and uniformity.

Considerations in Developing Human Resource Policies

In formulating a policy, the first consideration is its objective or purpose. Operationally, it is also necessary to contemplate the costs and benefits of implementing the proposed policy taking into account the size and complexity of the organization. Then comes the need for determining the acceptability of the policy to the management and employees, and this largely depends on its administrative feasibility and its fairness to employees.

Due to the unfortunate tendency to consider policies as formulae that obviate the need for careful thought, it is necessary to anticipate circumstances that may subsequently arise in

> In policy formulation, first comes the objective or purpose, followed by the calculation of costs and benefits, and lastly the acceptability of the policy to the management and employees.

administering the policy. Here, imagination as well as knowledge of operational problems is required. The supervisors are in a good position to aid in projecting exigencies that may arise under a particular policy.

Unions have had a tremendous impact on policy formulation. They seek the introduction of certain policies and seek to alter certain management policies (e.g., in relation to overtime payment). Their very presence causes managements to address their concerns and proactively make changes in policies so as to act as a defence against unions. The influence of some unions on policy administration appears to be beneficial, whereas that of others is harmful to management–employee relations.

Guidelines for Policy Formulation

The following are some well-established guidelines for policy writing (Fig. 3.7):

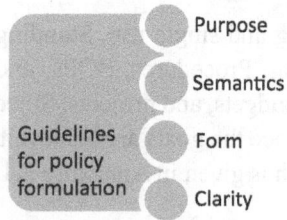

Figure 3.7 Guidelines for formulating policies

Purpose A statement of the purpose or the rationale behind a policy helps others to understand and accept the policy.

Semantics The choice of words should be geared to the educational level of the group for whom the policy is intended. Wordings should avoid irritating expressions that antagonize, humiliate, or cast aspersions. For example, sentences such as 'You are forbidden' ought to be avoided. In other words, the use of legalistic language should be avoided to the extent possible.

Form An outline form may be useful for management reference and application. However, outlines are difficult for employees to follow since they repel reading and are cold and lifeless. Relatively short paragraphs, some use of underlining, and adequate line spacing (double rather than single) encourage reading.

Clarity Short sentences are better than long ones linked together by words such as 'whereas', and 'provided' because simple sentences are easier to read and comprehend than complex or compound sentences.

Practitioner Speak 3.3 **Shape Strategy with Simple Rules, Not Complex Frameworks**

Successful companies shape their high-level strategies by relying not on complicated frameworks but on simple rules of thumb. Managers in these organizations translate corporate objectives into a few straightforward guidelines that help employees make on-the-spot decisions and adapt to constantly shifting environments, while keeping the big picture in mind.

Read this insightful blog posted by Sull and Eisenhardt on *HBR Blog Network* by accessing the following link: http://blogs.hbr.org/cs/2012/09/shape_strategy_with_simple_rul.html.

Communicating Policies

The management has a definite responsibility to ensure that the employees become familiar with all the policies that affect them. Written explanations of changes in policy, reinforced by oral discussions, are usually used for policy communication. Any one or all of the written media found in organizations may be used—employee handbooks, bulletin boards, company periodicals, and so on. In orientation sessions for new and old employees, oral explanations can be accompanied by visual aids such as filmstrips, placards, and funnel boards.

Administering Policies

Uniformity in administration is desirable when the circumstances among the various individuals and groups concerned are similar. Customs, practices that have been in operation for some time, and the needs of different groups of employees influence decisions concerning the degree and extent of uniformity. The questions of fairness and the attitudes of employees towards concessions in specific cases also need to be considered. Long-standing policy differences between office and shop floor, for example, are constantly criticized by the unions.

Questions pertaining to rigidity of administration and consistency or flexibility of interpretation must also be faced. While deciding to give special consideration to an employee or awarding penalty for a violation, many factors must be taken into account—the individual's past work record, demonstrated capability, knowledge at his/her disposal, history of relationships with others, impact of the decision on others and on future situations, past practices, responsibility of the management, nature and frequency of the request or act, obligations of the organization to the employee and to society, respective values, reasons, and ameliorating circumstances are some factors that need to be carefully considered.

STRATEGIC CONTROL

Strategy is selected and implemented over a period of time. Nevertheless, strategies being forward-looking and designed to accomplish future objectives, it is necessary to enforce control over them. Strategic controls can be enforced by certain operational controls, such as the following:

Premise control This is designed to check, systematically and continuously, whether the premises set during the planning and implementation process are still valid. For example, a bank may adopt an aggressive marketing strategy to achieve 15 per cent annual growth, on a planning premise that their non-performing assets would not be more than 10 per cent. Premise control should therefore ensure monitoring the non-performing assets at branch levels on a regular basis.

Implementation control This is designed to assess whether the results of the overall strategy associate with incremental steps and actions. For example, an internationally known fast-food centre decided to maintain the ratio between company-owned outlets and franchisee outlets at 3:1 to ensure control over quality of foods, rates, and so on. However, the growing

---

EXHIBIT 3.3   Embedding Strategy into Workforce: An HROB Perspective

Strategic decisions, as a rule, are left to the top management of organizations. However, the people formulating organizational strategies are not necessarily the people who execute them. Thus, it becomes necessary for the top management to ensure that the strategies formulated by them are communicated and executed properly to reach the desired outcomes.

In this regard, Professor Charles Galunic of INSEAD insists on ensuring that the top management of companies embeds strategies into the workforce. There are two chief considerations for the senior management—whether employees understand the strategy and whether they accept it. Thus, the concept of strategic embeddedness revolves around the understanding and acceptance of strategies.

Employees are not likely to have much idea about strategies. Thus, it is the responsibility of the management to communicate them effectively and ensure that employees work towards achieving them. The top management and managers have to act according to the organizational structure that a company may have or the level of the employees who have to be addressed. Most senior-level managers devise strategies and want their subordinates to pass it on to their next levels. Many times, this passing on of strategy results in junior employees receiving garbled messages. On the other hand, what is required is the personal involvement of the senior management. It has been found that the top management is perceived to be more trustworthy when they engage more with employees. Thus, engaging with employees to talk about the strategies help embed the strategies in them.

Source: Galunic, C., 'Disseminating Strategy: A User's Guide', *Fortune*, 24 May 2013, http://forbesindia.com/article/insead/disseminating-strategy-a-users-guide/35157/1, last accessed on 4 June 2013 (adapted).

---

competition in this business later forced it to reverse the ratio to enable it to open outlets at new locations.

Strategic surveillance   This is designed to monitor a broad range of events inside and outside the company that are likely to threaten the course of the firm's strategy. For example, in the early years of its attempt to sell the CFA courses, the Institute of Chartered Financial Analysts of India (ICFAI) made its course more finance oriented, covering all conceivable finance papers, targeting the financial services sector as the prospective employers of their students. Later on, since the financial services sector became highly unstable and volatile, ICFAI felt the need to target other sectors as prospective employers of their students. It therefore shifted its focus to business administration and included papers such as marketing, human resources development, information technology, and strategic management. While marketing its large expensive mainframe computers, IBM adopted a similar shift in focus, from corporate houses to libraries, worldwide.

Special alert control   This is the need to thoroughly, and often rapidly, reconsider the firm's basic strategy based on a sudden event. For instance, a likely political coup or internal disturbances in a country will create pressure on exporters to that particular country, who may have to thoroughly reconsider their export market strategy. Similarly, a sudden incident such as a major air crash could have a devastating effect on the concerned airline company. Exhibit 3.3 discusses points on integrating strategy into the workforce from the perspective of human resource management and organizational behaviour (HROB).

OPERATIONAL CONTROL SYSTEMS

Strategic controls are useful to the top management for monitoring and steering the basic strategic direction of the company. However, operating managers also need control methods appropriate to their level of strategy implementation. The primary concern at the operating level is the allocation and use of the company's resources. Operational control systems guide, monitor, and evaluate progress in meeting the annual objectives. Usually, the following steps are taken for effecting operational control:

- Set standards of performance.
- Measure actual performance.
- Identify deviations from standards.
- Initiate corrective action or adjustments.

There are three types of operational control systems, namely budgets, schedules, and key success factors. A *budget* is an item-wise summarization of estimated expenditures and it charts the means of financing them in a given time frame. Hence, it can be defined as a systematic plan for expenditure over a specific period with given resources. A budget is also known as a single-use plan, as it ceases to exist after the expiry of the specified time period.

> Strategic controls are useful to the top management for monitoring and steering the basic strategic direction of the company.

A *schedule* is a documented plan or procedure for each item or operation for achieving a defined objective within a given time frame. Usually, managers working at operational levels prepare documented schedules in the form of a series of activities to be done or of events to occur over a particular time period.

Key success factors are those, which can achieve the performance goals of the organizations. These key success factors are also known as key performance indicators.

SUMMARY

Framing an appropriate strategy and aligning it with the people and the organizational structure form an essential part of organizational behaviour studies. This chapter discusses the issues related to strategy, emphasizing people-related issues, since managing people is considered the most crucial factor for the achievement of corporate goals in organizational behaviour. Organizations develop their objectives and accordingly bring about changes in organizational behaviour by performing a situation analysis, self-evaluation, and competitor analysis at the internal and external levels as well as at micro and macro levels. Organizations craft their vision and mission statements after carefully evaluating the market situation. The vision statement provides a long-term view of a possible future, whereas the mission statement defines the role of the organization by translating the vision statement into action statements. By aligning people—the most important resource support—with the vision and mission statements, an organization decides its overall objectives in financial and strategic terms. It then reduces them to tactical objectives and action plans, which contain details of the ways in which the objectives are to be achieved. Organizational behaviour studies provide very important inputs for strategy formulation, its implementation, and the process of evaluation of the effectiveness of the strategy.

After discussing the various schools of thought on strategies and understanding how these schools of thought encompass organizational behaviour studies, in this chapter we have elaborated on strategy framing, duly identifying vision and mission statements of organizations. We have also examined the strategy implementation process with various resource supports, including people, emphasizing the need for deciding a suitable organizational structure.

In addition, a brief introduction to the strategic control and evaluation process has been provided to enable student managers understand how strategic management as a whole influences the organizational behaviour in an organization.

Framing goals and objectives based on the organizational mission and then developing strategies and action plans to achieve these goals and objectives require hands-on practice. Accordingly, a tentative strategy map has been illustrated with hypothetical assumptions on people-related issues. We have also discussed the various types and levels of strategies.

The chapter has also focused on policy framing techniques, because many managerial decision-making powers need to be delegated to the lower levels, which again require separate policy guidelines. A sample policy statement has been appended at the end to help students understand the process of policy framing. The chapter starts with a brief note on the HR management practices of an Indian pharmaceutical company and ends with an Indian FMCG company's case, illustrating how these companies could attain the highest level of performance in a fiercely competitive market by adopting people-centric strategies.

KEY DEFINITIONS

Business strategy The strategies framed at the middle or business level

Corporate strategy The strategies formulated at the corporate level, which give the overall direction to an organization

Functional strategies The strategies limited to the domain of each department's functional responsibility, which includes marketing strategies, new product-development strategies, HR strategies, financial strategies, legal strategies, and information technology management strategies

Goals The specific aims of a company, usually prepared in subjective terms

Grand strategies The overall strategies of an organization, focusing on core issues such as growth, market development, product development, innovation, horizontal integration, vertical integration, concentric diversification, conglomerate diversification, turnaround, divestiture, liquidation, and bankruptcy

Human resource planning The process to assess future manpower requirement for an organization

Human resource strategy The strategies for the human resource management function

Mission The focus on current business purpose, verbalizing the vision statement

Objectives The specific targets in measurable terms for a given time frame

Operational strategy The strategies formulated at the first level to carry out day-to-day activities

Policy The guidelines for programmed decision-making

Strategic control The practice of reviewing strategies with premise control exercise

Strategic human resource management A branch of human resource management that requires management of people in an organization strategically

Strategic intent An organization's overall strategies, mainly focusing on key result areas

Vision The overall organizational philosophy, beliefs, values, and culture

CONCEPT-REVIEW QUESTIONS

3.1 Discuss the importance of human resource (HR) strategies. Can HR strategies be independent of corporate strategies?

3.2 How can you align human resource planning with the HR strategies of an organization? Explain with examples.

3.3 What are the implications of policies and procedures on strategies?

3.4 Develop a personnel policy for an organization, selecting at least four important areas of human resource management (HRM).

3.5 What is the significance of strategy in organizational behaviour studies? Explain by highlighting specific areas.

3.6 Write short notes on the following:
   (a) Vision and mission

(b) Strategic control

(c) Grand strategies

(d) Strategy and action plan

(e) Operation strategy factors

CRITICAL THINKING QUESTIONS

3.1 Consider yourself the chief of an organization. You have recently acquired two units located in two different countries, whereas your area of operation is in India. Critically state the types of strategies that you would like to adopt to align the employees of the newly acquired units, who are very different from the Indian employees, with the culture, vision, and mission of your organization. What structural changes in the organization would be necessary to integrate these newly acquired units and why?

3.2 In managing organizational behaviour, what are the strategic issues that are important for us to study? Your answer should relate to both structural and behavioural issues.

SELECT BIBLIOGRAPHY

- Barney, J., 'Firm Resources and Sustained Competitive Advantage', *Journal of Management*, Vol. 17, 1991, pp. 99–120.
- Becker, B.E. and M.A. Huselid, 'High Performance Work Systems and Firm Performance: A Synthesis of Research and Managerial Implications', *Research in Personnel and Human Resources Journal*, Vol. 16, Issue 1, 1998, pp. 53–101.
- Becker, Gary S., *Human Capital: A Theoretical and Empirical Analysis, with Special Reference to Education*, Columbia University Press, New York, 1964.
- Bhattacharyya, D.K., *Human Resource Research Methods*, Oxford University Press, New Delhi, 2007.
- Eisenhardt, K.M., 'Agency Theory: An Assessment and Review', *Academy of Management Review*, Vol. 14, Issue 4, 1989, pp. 57–74.
- Flamholtz, Eric, *Personnel Management, Human Capital Theory and Human Resource Accounting*, Institute of Industrial Relations, University of California, 1981.
- Hamel, G. and C.K. Prahalad, *Competing for the Future*, Harvard Business School Press, Boston, 1994.
- Jackson, S.E. and R.S. Schuler, 'Understanding Human Resource Management in the Context of Organisations and Their Environments', *Annual Review of Psychology*, Vol. 46, 1995, pp. 237–64.
- Katz, D. and R.L. Kahn, *The Social Psychology of Organizations*, Wiley, New York, 1978.
- Meyer, John W. and Brian Rowen, 'Institutionalised Organizations: Formal Structure as Myth and Ceremony', *American Journal of Sociology*, Vol. 83, No. 2, 1977, pp. 340–363.
- Miles, R.H. and C.C. Snow, 'Designing Strategic Human Resource Systems', *Organisational Dynamics*, Vol. 13, Issue 1, 1984, pp. 36–52.
- Mintzberg, H., B. Ahlstrand, and J. Lampel, *Strategy Safari: A Guided Tour through the Wilds of Strategic Management*, Free Press, New York, 1998.
- Pfeffer, J. and G.R. Salancik, *The External Control of Organizations—A Resource Dependence Perspective*, Harper & Row, New York, 1978.
- Porter, M., *Competitive Advantage: Creating and Sustaining Superior*, Free Press, New York, 1985.
- Powel, Walter W. and Paul J. DiMaggio, *The New Institutionalism in Organizational Analysis*, University of Chicago Press, Chicago, 1991.
- Prahalad, C.K. and G. Hamel, 'The Core Competence of the Corporation', *Harvard Business Review*, Vol. 68, Issue 3, 1990, pp. 79–91.
- Sanz-Valle, R., R. Sabater-Sanchez, and A. Aragon-Sanchex, 'Human Resource Management and Business Strategy Links: An Empirical Study', *International Journal of Human Resource Management*, Vol. 10, Issue 4, 1999, pp. 655–71.
- Williamson, Oliver, E, 'Economics of Organisations—The Transaction Cost Approach', *American Journal of Sociology*, Vol. 87, 1981, pp. 548–77.

- Wright, P. and G. McMahan, 'Theoretical Perspectives for Strategic Human Resource Management', *Journal of Management*, Vol. 18, 1992, pp. 295–320.

CASE STUDY

Marico—Surviving a Fiercely Competitive Industry[1]

From a humble sales turnover of ₹105.9 million in 1991, Marico, a leading consumer products and services company in India, could reach a sales turnover of ₹10,128 million in 2005. This impeccable growth rate in less than 15 years placed Marico on India's corporate map and made it an interesting case to study for management students. Today, Marico manages 12 brands in its seven factories and some sub-contracting facilities, with more than 1000 employees on its payroll. It has already created a niche in hair care, skin care, and health foods through brands such as Parachute, Saffola, Sweekar, Hair & Care, Nihar, Shanti, Mediker, Revive, Kaya Sundari, Aromatic Fiancee, and Hair Code. Marico's branded products are exported to all the SAARC countries, including Bangladesh, and the Middle East and Egypt. The overseas sales of Marico are managed either by exporting from India or by developing local operations in the respective foreign countries. Whatever may be the route, today Marico is successful in positioning Indian brands widely across the neighbouring SAARC countries and in the Arab world. Every month, over 70 million consumer packs of Marico reach 130 million consumers spread over 23 million households, through a widespread distribution network of 2.5 million outlets in India and overseas. With its consistent dividend payout in every quarter, Marico is now considered investor friendly as well.

Marico's Values

Marico's business growth is backed by its own set of well-articulated values. Unlike other organizations, the corporate values are revisited and improved upon at regular intervals. This set of values is their primary guiding force to help them keep pace with the competitive world. The company believes that this set of values has a cascading effect on their preferred organizational practices and culture, which facilitates the pursuit of their business goals. Marico's value statements encompass the following:

Opportunity Seeking

Marico seeks to convert every opportunity into a new growth option. For Marico, opportunities are inherent not only in the unfulfilled needs of the consumers, but also in the attitudes and habits of the people. It converts every opportunity into a business growth possibility.

Bias for action Marico subscribes to the need for quick action rather than a delayed well thought out action. In the true sense, it follows the non-rational model of decision-making, strongly believing that 100 per cent availability of information that could enable a carefully planned decision is more a myth than a reality in a globally competitive market.

Consumer-centric approach Partnering with the consumer to create and deliver is what Marico believes in. The company designs its value-added goods and services after carefully understanding the needs and preferences of the consumers and thus succeeds in winning their trust.

Excellence Marico is able to sustain world-class standards by striving to be better than the best with continuous benchmarking, improvement in performance, and additions to the capabilities of the organization.

Innovation Fostering a culture of innovation and creativity with beway for employees to commit mistakes, Marico has forged ahead of others in

[1] This case study has been developed by the author based on inputs collected from www.maricoindia.com, last accessed on 12 March 2007.

achieving quantum results. Incubating new ideas on a small scale and then cascading their success in large projects helps Marico to hedge the risk of failure involved in institutionalizing innovation.

Openness and transparency Marico allows diversity of opinion. Listening to all without bias and promoting openness promotes mutual respect and trust in Marico. It helps the company to harvest collective wisdom and paves the way for developing a learning organization.

Global outlook Sensitivity and adaptability to diverse issues, more specifically to gender and cultural issues, make Marico, in the true sense, a global player with a strong understanding of global markets.

Lack of boundaries Leveraging collective wisdom with cross-functional inputs and encouraging openness in discussion among employees, irrespective of their functional areas, make Marico a truly interdependent organization.

Organizational Structure

To achieve its business goals, Marico has adopted the following organizational structure.

Flat structure Marico has only five levels of reporting structure from the managing director to the level of shop floor operator. This has helped it to be more responsive to the environmental eventualities and members of the organization can provide their best, keeping pace with the changing business needs. Each member in the structure is adequately informed about his/her role and supporting relationships between the levels. In the process, Marico remains dynamic and is continuously evolving with market situations.

Profit centres Creating profit centres to enhance focus in business operations further helped Marico to be more proactive in inculcating a sense of ownership among its employees. Marico's profit centres are organized in relation to product lines. Accordingly, they have created the following product lines:

Consumer products This comprises the operations of Marico Ltd and Marico Bangladesh Ltd. This division manufactures and markets Marico's 10 leading consumer product brands including Parachute and Saffola.

Aesthetics services This comprises the operations of Kaya Skin Clinics under the banner of Kaya Skin Care Ltd. Kaya Skin Clinics offer US FDA-approved scientific dermatological procedures that are customized to suit the Indian skin.

Global Ayurvedics This comprises the operation of Sundari LLC in the US. Sundari markets the Sundari range of Ayurvedic skin care products in the US and other parts of the world.

All these profit centres have their dedicated marketing teams, distribution channels, sales force, and backroom facilities. The creation of profit centres has led to higher business orientation and improved cross-functional coordination. It has ensured that organizational structure supports the overall company strategy and business direction. Each business unit has a business head supported by a team of professionals. A common finance division and HR department provides support to the employees in the pursuit of their professional goals.

Finance The finance division handles the legal, treasury, tax, control systems, and management information support. In addition, every profit centre has its own dedicated finance cell.

HR The HR department formulates and builds strategies to sustain a stable and high-talent organization. Addressing the market needs, it also fosters a culture of innovation in the workplace.

Business Direction

Marico has spelt out its business direction in 2010 as follows:

- Improving the quality of peoples' lives in several parts of the world through fast-moving consumer products and services in personal and health care sectors

- Offering brands that enhance the appeal and nourishment of hair and skin
- Making available brands that contribute to healthy living, through products drawn from agriculture and offered in natural or processed forms
- Developing, in parts of the world beyond the Indian subcontinent, a franchise for branded products and services
- Aiming to be the leader in each of the businesses through heightened sensitivity to consumer needs
- Setting up of new standards in the delivery and quality of products and services and processes of continuous learning and improvement
- Sharing prosperity among members, shareholders, and associates who contribute in improving equity and market value

Business Model and Orientation

Marico's business model is to focus on growth, improve value addition for its customers, and widen its retail reach. This involves market expansion of all its brands in all the territories with enhanced standards of quality and delivery, leveraging the unique ethnicity of India and stimulating a work culture that promotes empowerment, teamwork, and innovation. Marico wants to grow and consolidate its position in the global market.

Questions for Discussion

1. Read the case carefully and develop a strategy map for Marico.
2. Enumerate your self-charted strategies that can help Marico achieve its business direction of 2010. Provide the action plans that you have developed in the light of your strategies.
3. Do you think Marico can achieve its strategic intent (as envisaged by you) with its present organizational structure? Give reasons for your answer.

ANNEXURE 3.1
Employee Leave Policy

Policy Number: _____
Coverage: All employees of Fortune Furnitech including the managerial level and executive directors
Board's Approval: _____
Effective Date: _____

Policy

It is the endeavour of Fortune Furnitech to establish and maintain an orderly system of administration, and towards that end, the company's policy with regard to the various forms of leave available to employees of the company is laid down as follows:

1.0 Specific Objectives

1.1 Objectives of the Policy
- Ensure uniform standards and procedures for administration of leave within the company.
- Provide an employee leave programme that will facilitate monitoring the various forms of leave, ensure accurate application, detect potential abuses, and keep a full record of the leave system.
- Ensure that employees, supervisors, and departmental heads are familiar with the company's leave programme.

2.0 Responsibilities

2.1 Board (or the Designated Committee)
- Review, amend, and adopt changes in the Employee Leave Policy.
- Approve changes in the actual leave benefits, as considered appropriate.

2.2 Chief Executive Officer (or the Designate)
- Provide for administration of the procedures outlined in the Employee Leave Policy.
- Assist department heads, supervisors, and employees in the implementation and administration of the Employee Leave Policy.

- Recommend to the board changes in the Employee Leave Policy or changes in the actual benefits and leave granted to employees, where considered appropriate.

2.3 Department Heads and Supervisors
- Ensure the completion of all required forms and records regarding the Employee Leave Policy.
- Ensure that employees are aware of the Employee Leave Policy.
- Ensure that employees provide complete information and all necessary documentation for required forms, in accordance with the Employee Leave Policy.
- Assist employees by clarifying their eligibility for leave programmes and helping them complete the necessary documentation.
- Recommend changes to the Employee Leave Policy, where considered appropriate.

2.4 Employees
- Become familiar with the Employee Leave Policy.
- Comply with all regulations and procedures as outlined in the Employee Leave Policy.

3.0 General Provisions

3.1 Leave Rules of the Company
- Employees eligible for leave will complete the application for leave in accordance with the policy outlined herein. This application will be forwarded to the supervisor and/or department head for consideration and, where necessary, forwarded to the chief executive officer for consideration.
- The leave will be approved or denied as appropriate and the employee will be notified of the decision in writing.
- The individual(s) responsible for payroll will be notified as necessary.
- The employee's personal file will be updated.

3.2 Specific Procedures
The following are the various types of leave included in the leave programme of the company:
(a) Leave without pay
(b) Annual leave
(c) Medical or sick leave
(d) Statutory holidays
(e) Casual leave

4.0 Leave without Pay

4.1 Eligibility
Leave without pay is not normally granted unless all leave to which the employee is entitled has been completely availed prior to the application. Upon application by an employee, leave without pay may be granted to an employee as per the following stipulations:

- Employee having completed less than one year of service is to be granted up to 10 working days.
- Employee having completed one to five years of service is granted up to 20 working days in a year.
- Employee having completed more than five years of service is granted up to 45 working days in a year.

Up to one week of leave (five working days) Applications are to be submitted in writing to the appropriate superior, who may grant up to five working days leave without pay when grant of this leave will not involve extra expenses for the company in the form of overtime payments or hiring of additional staff.

Longer than one week of leave Applications are to be referred by the department head through the HR Department to the chief executive officer.

Payroll staff is to be advised of all leaves as and when granted and also immediately when the employee returns to work. A copy each of the application and authorization is to be added to the employees' personal files.

4.2 Effect of Leave without Pay on Employee Benefits
The following clause would be applicable to all leave without pay exceeding 15 days.

During the period of leave without pay, no employee will be eligible for any benefits. The company can recover the actual cost of any benefit payable to the employee as terminal benefit such as insurance contribution and gratuity. For leave of absence less than 15 days, however, the company will accommodate such cost, provided the leave of absence granted to the employee did not cause any pecuniary loss to the company by way of the need for engaging extra hand to complete the assigned tasks of the employee. No pay will be granted for any statutory holidays if such holidays fall within the period of leave.

5.0 Annual Leave
- On satisfactory completion of the period of probation, all employees will be entitled for annual leave.

- The period of the annual leave calendar year is 1 January to 31 December.
- After satisfactory completion of the period of probation, all employees will receive a maximum of 30 days annual leave in a calendar year and such leave would be credited at 2½ days for each completed month. For availing annual leave during the year, the period of annual leave would be restricted to the number of days credited in the account of the employee taking into account the number of months served. However, the company can grant annual leave in advance, taking into consideration the merits of the individual cases.
- A maximum of 180 days can be accumulated as annual leave.
- Unavailed portion of annual leave (subject to the limit of 180 days) can be encashed by an employee during normal retirement. In cases of resignation, encashment of annual leave will be subject to the acceptance of resignation of the employee by the company.
- Under no circumstances can an employee be granted annual leave exceeding 15 consecutive days at a time.

All annual leave applications are to be routed through the departmental heads to the chief executive officer for prior sanction under intimation to the HR department.

6.0 Medical or Sick Leave

- The company will provide medical or sick leave to all its employees on their satisfactory completion of the period of probation. The period of medical leave shall be restricted to 15 days (half-pay) in a calendar year. Hence, an employee can commute such medical leave with full pay for a maximum period of 7½ days in a calendar year.
- Medical leave is given to an employee for giving protection of loss of wages due to illness. Hence, employees who intend to avail medical leave should intimate their respective heads of the department during the period of absence on grounds of illness, enclosing a certificate from a registered medical practitioner. After joining, the employee should also produce a certificate of fitness to his/her head of the department to regularize his/her period of absence. The head of the department will accordingly forward the documents with due recommendation to the HR department.

7.0 Statutory Holidays

The list of statutory holidays is prepared during every calendar year and varies as per the declaration of the statutory bodies.

8.0 Casual Leave

- All employees, including those who are on probation, shall be entitled to get maximum six days casual leave in a calendar year. For availing casual leave, it is mandatory to obtain prior approval from the head of the department. However, if an employee suddenly requires casual leave to meet any exigency, and if the period exceeds one working day, the employee must ensure that his head of the department has been informed or else his period of absence shall be treated as unauthorized absence and he will be liable to face disciplinary action.
- Unavailed casual leave expires on completion of the calendar year. Hence, it cannot be accumulated and encashed.

Organizational Structure and Systems

LEARNING OBJECTIVES

After studying this chapter, the reader will be able to

- identify the methods and processes involved in organizing
- describe the various types and forms of organizational structure
- discuss line and staff management issues
- explain the process of delegation of authority
- understand the issues of centralization and decentralization
- discuss issues related to span of management

CASE STUDY

What Made Xerox Restructure?

In order to meet the demands of changing conditions, Xerox reorganized its document in the early 1990s processing business into three geographical customer units—desktop document systems, office document products, and personal document products—and nine business divisions. All these divisions were small and responsive divisions, organized around products and customers. Previously, Xerox was organized into huge divisions centred on sales, marketing, manufacturing, service, and engineering. Since then, the company went on adding to its product mix and this necessitated the need for horizontal organization, focusing on the following essential elements:

- Building the organization around processes rather than functions
- Having few levels of management above a process
- Using a multidisciplinary team in the process
- Using customer satisfaction as input to assess performance
- Rewarding team and individual performance
- Having regular meetings of team members with customers and suppliers
- Training team members
- Disseminating information with transparency

Xerox was working with other companies and was introducing new technologies; hence, such changes became necessary.

INTRODUCTION

In order to optimize the use of resources available in an organization, a manager has to prepare a clear plan of action and then implement it effectively. Such initiatives by the manager create appropriate conditions for the people in the organization to work such that it is possible to achieve the intended goals and objectives. Pooling together resources and people and making everybody understand the importance of cooperation for accomplishing a job are the twin functions of organizing. Planning decides what to do, whereas organizing focuses on how to do it properly by forming appropriate groups. Therefore, similar to planning, organizing is also an important function of management. Behavioural scientists and sociologists view an organization as comprising human relationships in group activities. In an operational sense, however, organizations are entities of people who are divided into groups based on the distinct nature of their work. Each group is expected to coordinate their activities to achieve the common objectives.

Organizational behaviour (OB) focuses on organizational situations. It has now acquired different dimensions due to the influence of several factors. Global competition requires many organizations to redefine their structure and even relocate, taking advantage of the state-of-the-art technology and communication support. With reduced trade barriers under the World Trade Organization (WTO) regime, the first priority of many organizations is to become global players. Proximity to the market, 24×7 customer support, and economies of scale in operations have led many organizations to redefine their structure. Even global majors such as IBM, Ford, DuPont, and Siemens are globally spreading their organizational structures. Global competition has also accentuated organizational turbulence, which always prompts organizations to revisit their existing structures and people relationships. Use of e-commerce, workplace diversity, and ethical issues are also prompting organizations to reconsider their established processes and systems and restructure from time to time to remain up to date.

DEFINITIONS AND PRINCIPLES OF ORGANIZATION

Stephen P. Robbins and Mary Coulter (2002) defined organizing as 'determining what tasks are to be done, who is to do them, how the tasks are to be grouped, who reports to whom, and where decisions are to be made'. L.A. Allen (1958), on the other hand, defined organizing as 'the process of identifying and grouping the work to be performed, defining and delegating responsibility and authority, and establishing relationships for the purpose of enabling people to work most effectively together in accomplishing objectives'. Alvin Brown (1945) defined organizing as 'the part each member of an enterprise is expected to perform and the relations between such members, to the end that their concerted endeavour shall be most effective for the purpose of the enterprise'. Koontz and O'Donnell (1982) considered organizing as 'the establishment of authority relationships with provision for coordination between them, both vertically and horizontally in the enterprise structure'. An organization is essentially a formal structure of people that is set up to achieve some defined goals. A business unit or a manufacturing unit may be termed a business organization or a manufacturing organization because these are essentially formal structures of persons who strive to achieve some defined goals.

> Organizing is defined as determining what tasks are to be done, who is to do them, how the tasks are to be grouped, who reports to whom, and where decisions are to be made.

> Organization is used to refer to a social group that is deliberately created and maintained to achieve some intended goals.

It is evident from the definitions that different authorities have defined the word organizing in different ways. The most common definitions are as follows:

- An organization is a *group of people* who are organized to achieve a common purpose.
- It is an *entity*, a unit, or an establishment that utilizes resources to achieve some common purpose.
- It shows a *structure of relationship* in an enterprise.
- It is a *process* that facilitates the alignment of tasks and facilities of people working in an enterprise, to achieve the intended goals.

As per Arthur Young, organizing involves the following:

- Grouping of activities
- Establishing authority and responsibility
- Describing working relationships

Organization, organizing, and organizational structure are related terms. *Organization* is used to refer to a social group that is deliberately created and maintained to achieve some intended goals. More specifically, it is defined as a formal social group. In addition, it is also referred to as a process of determining the activities that are required to achieve the intended goals, creating various roles, and ensuring effective operation of the total system. *Organizing*, on the other hand, is defined as a management process that corroborates with our earlier definition of organization as a process of identifying, classifying, grouping, and assigning various activities to groups of people with adequately defined authority relationships for achieving some intended goals. *Organizational structure*, on the other hand, is an outcome of the organizing process. It is the framework of a decision-making authority, that is, a system of relationships that govern the activities of the people working in an organization to achieve some intended goals. All these principles have emerged from the definitions of organization given by various authorities listed at the beginning of this section.

THEORIES OF ORGANIZATION

From a historical perspective, the theories of organization can be grouped into the following three major heads:

- Classical theory
- Neo-classical theory
- Systems theory

The classical school of thought was mostly concerned with the micro aspects of an organization, that is, in one way their approaches were divorced from societal issues, which in reality interact with an organization. The neo-classical approach is the process of relating to the psychological variables of people. It gives importance to the social aspects—if not directly, at least indirectly. The systems approach takes a macro view of an organization. This approach ultimately recognized that organization is a dynamic process and exists only by interacting with the environment.

BASIC PRINCIPLES OF ORGANIZING

As there are diverse managerial styles, there are no universal principles of organizing. However, the following principles are widely followed:

- Every person should be immediately responsible to only one superior and not to several superiors. This does not mean that work cannot be performed if directions come from several superiors. It only emphasizes that in such cases, the subordinates get confused and ultimately the common goals are not achieved. It is always better to organize people in such a way that for each employee there is only one superior who gives orders to him/her and to whom he/she is ultimately responsible.
- The authority granted should match the responsibility given. If this is not done, there may be a decline in the subordinates' desire to take initiatives.
- The span of control should be appropriate to the circumstances so that it is neither too wide nor too narrow.
- The best use should be made of specialization.
- The number of levels of management should be kept as low as possible because too many levels lead to bureaucracy and distortion or loss of communication.
- The degree of centralization should be appropriate. Too much of centralization may lead to delay in decision-making and implementation of those decisions. This cripples organizations because they fail to respond quickly to both internal and external changes.
- There should be an equitable distribution of work, in terms of both variety and volume.
- Duties and responsibilities should be distributed in a manner that ensures maximum utilization of the abilities of the employees.
- Duties, authorities, and responsibilities should be clearly defined; otherwise, it may lead to empire-building.
- The organization should be flexible enough to accommodate change, cutting across hierarchical barriers. Too much rigidity may weaken the competitive strength of the organization.

HUMAN FACTORS IN ORGANIZING

Many modern writers on management stress the need to consider the human factors in an organization, which are certainly as important as the formal factors. Although there is no empirical evidence to justify such views, many organizations do emphasize these points. They include factors such as grouping of male and female employees and grouping of employees as per age group, marital status, race, religion, and other such factors. It is suggested that as far as possible an equilibrium among these factors be maintained while grouping people in organization. However, it may be difficult for a relatively small organization to maintain such an equilibrium. In such cases, proper coordination needs to be ensured.

IMPORTANT STEPS IN ORGANIZING

Based on the principles of organizing, the important steps involved in organizing can be enumerated as follows:

- Enumerating and grouping the activities of the enterprise consistent with its objectives
- Assigning activities to different executives

- Delegating authority and placing responsibility for carrying out the assigned duties
- Making provision for effective coordination and establishment of definite lines of supervision

IMPORTANCE AND BENEFITS OF ORGANIZATION

A sound organization facilitates the management process, encourages growth and diversification, ensures optimum use of technological improvements, encourages genial treatment of human resources, and stimulates creativity.

Facilitating management   A properly designed organization facilitates both the management and operation of the enterprise. The management functions can be performed with certainty and continuity only if appropriate functional groups are provided to help the managers. The grouping and arrangement of activities directly affect the operating results. If important activities are overlooked or subordinated, the results would be dissatisfactory. Successful managers always try to develop a good organizational structure by carrying out an organizational analysis.

Encouraging growth   The organizational structure is the framework within which an enterprise grows. This requires a flexible structure that allows easier incorporation of changes. Moreover, a sound organizational structure facilitates growth by increasing the efficiency of the organization.

Optimum use of technological improvement   The advantages of new technological improvements can be best realized by having a suitable organizational structure. For instance, the use of computer involves costs, but it processes information very quickly. Hence, the organizational structure should be such that it easily integrates new technology into its systems.

> Organizing comprises enumerating and grouping activities, assigning activities, delegating authority and placing responsibility, and making provision for effective coordination and establishing definite lines of supervision.

Encouraging genial treatment of human resources   This is referred to as providing psychological satisfaction to individuals in the organization because an individual contributes best when the satisfaction is the highest. Most of the psychological satisfaction is derived from one's work, relationships, and working environment, for which a good organizational structure is necessary. It leads to development of employees by creating avenues for training and promotion.

Stimulating creativity   A sound organization based on specialization stimulates creative thinking and initiative by providing well-defined areas of work with scope for the development of new and improved ways of functioning.

Practitioner Speak 4.1

The Importance of Organizational Design and Structure

One of the wonderful things about being a coach is that I meet hundreds of executives who freely share their business and leadership challenges with me. As well as helping me understand how hard it is to run an organization, they show me how they are managing to adapt or—not—to changing organizational structures.

Read this insightful blog posted by Corkindale on *HBR Blog Network* by accessing the following link: http://blogs.hbr.org/corkindale/2011/02/the_importance_of_organization.html.

Better coordination   A sound organizational structure facilitates better coordination and control in the enterprise.

TYPES OF ORGANIZATION

Different Companies follow different types of organization. What may be successful in one case may not work well in another. The basis for classification of organizational types is many. Following different approaches, there can be a closed or an open system of organization. In organizations with closed systems, 'interacting elements operate without any exchange with the environment'. It means that such organizations require no inputs (human, knowledge, informational, or technological) from the external environment in which they operate. The primary characteristics of these organizations are that they are perfectly deterministic and there is no exchange between the system and the external environment. However, today no organization can be truly closed. Hence, totally closed systems of organization exist only in theory.

The open systems of organization stress on the need for flexibility and adaptability in the organizational structure and also on the interdependence of the organization with its external environment. Louis E. Boone and David L. Kurtz (1992) defined open systems of organization as 'a set of elements that interact with each other and the environment and whose structure evolves over time as a result of interaction'.

Organizations can also be classified as formal and informal. A formal organization is a group of people working together in close cooperation under a common authority towards goals that benefit the employees as well as the organization. In formal organizations, jobs as well as official positions are well defined with a definite measure of authority, responsibility, and accountability. An informal organization, on the other hand, is a network of personal and social relations, which arise spontaneously as people associate with one another. It lays emphasis on people and their relationships. Informal organizations, therefore, may or may not support the formal goals and objectives. Managers need to understand and recognize the informal as well as formal relationships and integrate both the forms to achieve the intended goals.

Thus, organizational types can be broadly categorized on the basis of two perspectives: closed and open organizations, and formal and informal organizations. However, modern organizational theories emphasize various other types as well, which have been discussed while explaining the organizational structure.

ORGANIZATIONAL STRUCTURE

Organization as a structure is the particular system of arrangements and the pattern of network relations in an enterprise between various positions. It is characterized by activity–authority relationships. The structure is not accidental. The key executives determine the structure, creating relationships and defining exercise of authority.

> Organization as a structure is the particular system of arrangements and the pattern of network relations in an enterprise between various positions. It is characterized by activity–authority relationships.

The organizational chart is a useful static model of this formal structure. As an organization is a system of human relationships, a social system, or the total system comprising a number of interacting subsystems, it is essential for the organizer to take into account the mechanistic and humanistic aspects while designing the structure. The organization should be structured such that personnel encounter minimum obstacles and derive maximum satisfaction while striving to accomplish departmental or enterprise objectives within the environment furnished by it.

The organizational structure is a means to an end, that is, business performance and results. Hence, it should be so designed as to help accomplish business objectives. Peter F. Drucker (1954) suggested the following three ways to determine the kind of structure needed to attain a given set of objectives:

- Activity analysis
- Decision analysis
- Relation analysis

Drucker has criticized the traditional approach of classifying business functions into the categories of production, marketing, and so on. He has emphasized the need for segregating each of these functions into many activities and understanding their contribution in attaining the objectives of the business.

There is another way of looking at objectives in relation to an organization. Some writers describe organization as a type of 'open system' constantly interacting with the environment for its survival and growth. It receives input from its environment. The organization as an open system must therefore define its objectives in relation to the environment and constantly adapt to changes.

WHAT COMES FIRST—STRATEGY OR STRUCTURE

Quite often, there are debates on questions such as what comes first—strategy or structure. There exists opposing views. Based on the success stories of world-class organizations such as Sears, General Motors, DuPont, and Standard Oil, it can be argued that strategy development comes first followed by organizational structure. Again, this has been proved wrong in the case of some organizations. For example, in Kodak, changes in structure preceded changes in strategy. However, this did not work well. In fact, Kodak lost its business worth $3.5 million between 1981 and 1985 due to the mismatch between strategy and structure. A particular organizational structure, in fact, influences strategy. A given structure develops a particular mindset among people working in an organization. Changes in the structure effected with a view to keep pace with changes in strategy may not work as found in the case of Kodak. Hence, while framing a strategy, an organization has to consider the pros and cons of the prevailing structure. Changing structure requires change in organizational culture and climate. Organizational culture is a complex mix of assumptions, behaviours, myths, and metaphors, whereas organizational climate sets the basic style of functioning of an organization. Certain other

> Organizational structure influences strategy. Hence, while framing a strategy, an organization has to consider the pros and cons of the prevailing structure.

contingency factors such as the size of the organization, the nature of technology, and the type of employees (knowledge workers or not) also influence organizational design. The most pioneering work in this case was undertaken by Alfred D. Chandler (1962), who suggested that a mismatch between strategy and structure could adversely affect organizational performance.

DEVELOPING ORGANIZATIONAL STRUCTURE OR DESIGN

Designing a new organizational structure or reorganizing an existing one requires careful consideration of the current practices and principles of organization. There are no rules that can lead to the development of the best organizational structure. However, the following steps of designing or reorganizing a structure are found to be effective in achieving an enterprise's objectives.

Clear definition of objectives   The first step is to lay down the objectives in very clear terms. This will help in determining the basic characteristics of the organization.

Identifying activities and grouping them into convenient classes   The next important step is enumerating the activities necessary to achieve the objectives, grouping them in a systematic manner, assigning activities to groups of personnel, and providing for their coordination. As far as possible, similar functions should be combined into one position.

Determining structure   The organizer has to decide about the span of supervision, types of organizations, basis of departmentation, and the pattern of the authority structure.

Revising systems based on assessment of personnel and funds   The last step is to assess the capacities and abilities of the people available to man different positions in the organization, along with other resources at the disposal of the enterprise. The ideal organization should then be adapted to fit the reality of the situation.

These are the general guidelines to be followed. Each enterprise should be viewed as a separate case and developed accordingly. It is unwise to follow a particular structural form because it proved effective in one instance. Local conditions, business objectives and policies, scale of operation, nature of work, and above all the character and abilities of the personnel available are important factors to be considered while developing an organizational structure.

DYNAMIC ORGANIZATIONAL STRUCTURE AND DEPARTMENTATION

Organizational structure should not be static. An enterprise operates under a highly dynamic environment, where the technology, social, political, and economic setting in which it operates and the people managing the organization are continually in a flux. This calls for adapting the organizational structure to the changing conditions so that it can survive and grow. Accommodating changes in the organization requires that the structure be partly modified so as to adjust it to the changes in the attitudes, ambitions, and abilities of the people. Exhibit 4.1 discusses the role of organizational structure in creating successful organizations.

EXHIBIT 4.1   Role of Organizational Structure in Creating Successful Organizations

Organizational structure can prove to be a key differentiator in helping organizations become successful. To be precise, adapting the organizational structure to meet the set objectives and remaining flexible to change without compromising goals is what characterizes the best global enterprises. Moreover, a jointly conducted survey by Fortune and the Hay Group has concluded that the most important factor in common between the best performers across industries is that they do not have too many aspects about organizational structures and practices in common.

The report elaborates on how organizations pertaining to the same industry can choose to structure themselves differently. Medtronics, for example, has been structured as per its product line. In addition to dividing the company into different lines of business such as health care, security tools, and office supplies, functional units such as legal, strategy, and human resources have also been deployed at the top level. On the other hand, 3M, an organization having similar business interests, has been structured on the basis of lines of business alone. What is actually common among these much-revered organizations is that the core blueprints of organizational structure seldom change.

In terms of adapting to changing business environments without altering their organizational structures, experts feel that the operating models of these organizations help them to remain dynamic. The fact that such organizations can bend without breaking is what makes them successful. Again, companies such as John Deere train employees to work on cross-border projects. Successful companies are also highly agile. Lastly, the organizational structure is complemented by recruiting the best talents from the job market.

Source: Kimes, M., 'What Admired Firms Don't Have in Common', *CNN Money*, 6 March 2013, http://money.cnn.com/2009/03/06/news/companies/hay.survey.fortune/, last accessed on 17 June 2013 (adapted).

Principles

The different bases of grouping activities provide only general guidelines. While grouping, the manager must consider the advantages and disadvantages of each method of departmentation along with the basic factors involved in grouping the activities of the enterprise. Only after such evaluation should one contemplate determining the kind of composite departmental structure best suited to the requirements of the organization.

The following are the basic factors in grouping activities:

Specialization   The organizational structure should divide and group the activities of the concern in such a way that similar and allied activities are, on all occasions, placed under one department. Specialization leads to more and better work with the same effort.

Control   Departmentation should be done so as to facilitate control.

Coordination   If objectives are to be accomplished effectively, departmentation should also help in coordination.

Balance   Departmentation should also allow adequate attention to each of the functions of the enterprise so that different activities are properly balanced.

Duplication of sections   Departmentation should, as far as possible, avoid duplication of sections.

Human side   Departmentation should not overlook the human side of an organization. The impact of structure on the human factor should be given due consideration.

Reduction of cost   Activities should also be grouped in a manner that will best contribute to achieving enterprise objectives and reducing its operational cost.

Recognition of local conditions   The pattern of grouping should be evolved in a way that local conditions are given due recognition.

Apart from these basic factors, the following principles should also be given due consideration, as per the requirement, in departmentalizing the activities or functions:

- Ease of direction
- Flexibility
- Optimum utilization of manpower
- Opportunities for the application of individual talent
- Uniform and consistent policy of operation
- Functional efficiency in production, distribution, and finance
- Clear and comprehensive channels of communication
- Contribution to the survival and prosperity of the business

Process

The process of departmentation may be divided into the following three stages:

Primary departmentation   This is achieved by initial break-up of functions into basic activities.

Intermediate departmentation   This is achieved by creating departments in the middle levels of the organization.

Ultimate departmentation   This is accomplished by dividing activities into separate units at the lower levels.

Based on the prevalent practices, organizational structure can be of the following four major types:

- Functional structure
- Divisional structure
- Hybrid structure
- Matrix structure

Patterns Used

The most common patterns are grouping by functions, products, territories, processes, customers, and time. Apart from these, departmentation by simple numbers was an important method in the organization of tribes and armies. (Simple numbers, in the army, are numbers assigned to each unit or division. Some tribes also have simple numbers assigned to them.)

Departmentation by Functions

Deparmentation by functions refers to the grouping of activities of an enterprise into major functional departments such as production, sales, and finance. The other commonly recognized

> Departmentation by functions refers to the grouping of organizational activities by functional departments such as production, sales, and finance.

functions requiring separate grouping are buying, accounting, personnel, and research. However, these functions vary according to the organization.

Departmentation by functions is the most widely used basis for grouping activities into administrative units and is found in almost all enterprises at some level or the other. Figure 4.1 illustrates a functional organizational structure of a multi-product company having both institutional and retail sales; only the depths of marketing and HR are shown.

Advantages The following are the advantages of departmentation by functions:

- Functional departmentation represents a very natural and logical way of grouping the different activities of an enterprise.
- Such grouping ensures specialization. By concentrating on similar activities, specialized knowledge and skill are acquired, which can be utilized for the efficient management of the departments. This leads to economy in operations and efficiency in the use of manpower and other resources.
- It facilitates coordination within the function. It is easier for a manager in charge of a particular function to synchronize activities and unify efforts of the personnel engaged in that particular function than to coordinate activities pertaining to different functions.
- Direct and adequate attention to basic activities guarantees the availability and effective utilization of the capabilities of the human resource.
- Functional departmentation is a time-tested method and can easily be justified by the management.

Disadvantages The following are the disadvantages of departmentation by functions:

- There is a tendency towards too much centralization, which causes delay in decision-making and flow of information. Decisions on problems covering two or more functions can be made only at the higher levels in the organization. Further, the communication of the decision to the lowest level and its subsequent implementation takes a lot of time.
- Functional departmentation tends to make the functional executives obsessed with their respective functional areas that they lose sight of the business as a whole and its objectives. Thus, a need arises for emphasizing the mission of the enterprise to all functional executives, which consumes a good amount of time. It makes coordination between different functional areas difficult.

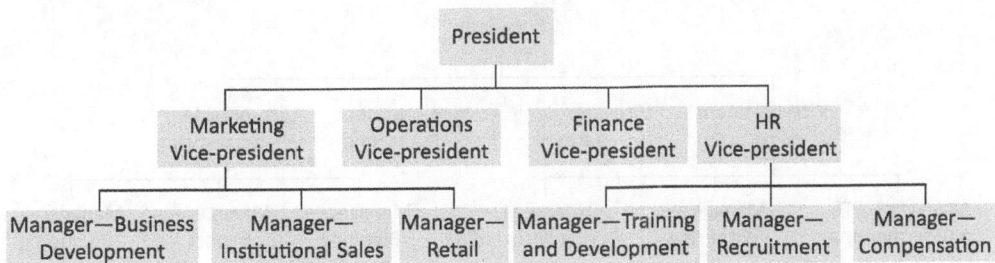

Figure 4.1 Functional organization structure

• A company that is functionally organized does not offer a good training ground for developing managers who are all-rounders. A manager supervising a particular function more often remains confined to being an expert in handling problems of that particular function alone.

Departmentation by Products or Services

When the activities associated with each product or a group of closely related products are combined into relatively autonomous and integrated units within the overall framework of a company, the organization has product departmentation. Under this arrangement, an executive is placed in charge of all the activities relating to a product or product line and enjoys extensive authority over production, sales, development, service, and other functions pertaining to that particular product. The place or location of the product unit is irrelevant here. Figure 4.2 illustrates a process-centric divisional structure of a tea-manufacturing company.

Product or process departmentation enjoys the advantage of specialized product knowledge and promotes the coordination of different activities connected with a particular product. Since the responsibility for the result of each product is fixed, the executive who is in charge of the product is motivated for expansion, improvement, and diversification of the product. It helps an organization compare one product line with another, drop unprofitable product lines, and expand the profitable ones. The formation of autonomous units also enables the organization to gain the advantages of better coordination, better customer services, and better control of resources.

> Departmentation by products and services refers to the grouping of activities of closely related products or services into combinations of relatively autonomous and integrated units within the overall framework of a company.

The system has its disadvantages too. Such an arrangement can at times lead to difficulties in coordination. Managers who have been successful in running their departments may well be prompted to allocate more powers to themselves. However, these can be remedied through centralization of certain key activities and major policy decisions at the top level of the organization. The system also requires that the organizations hire persons with general managerial abilities, which raises the managerial cost. Costs are also increased due to duplication of centralized services and staff activities. The top management level may also face problems in controlling and monitoring the activities of various product departments. Problems may also be faced at the level of decision-making in such organizations because the top management may not like to delegate crucial decision-making powers to the departmental heads.

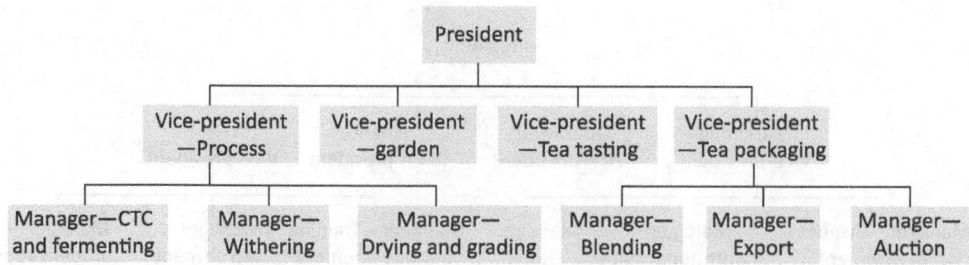

Figure 4.2 Divisional organizational structure

Departmentation by Locations or Territories

When the activities of an enterprise are physically or geographically dispersed, providing each such separate unit with powers and facilities for running its local administration by itself is highly desirable to ensure efficiency and economy in operations. This is known as territorial departmentation. Koontz and O'Donnell have put forth two valid reasons favouring territorial departmentation:

- It ensures that the managers do not ignore local factors in decision-making.
- It helps take advantage of certain economies of the localized operations.

Grouping by locations signifies adaptation to local needs and facilitates prompt actions. Activities within the scope of one's area or authority can be more effectively coordinated and controlled. Such departmentation also offers opportunity to the top management to allow employees to gain experience with minimum risks to the firm. However, communication gaps and delays in decision-making are its major disadvantages.

Departmentation by Time

When operations extend far beyond the normal work period of an individual, it may be spread over certain shifts. Such a grouping is frequently termed as departmentation by time. In enterprises engaged in continuous processes such as public utilities and restaurants, departmentalization by time is a normal practice. Units created on the basis of time perform similar operations. However, decisions need to be taken regarding the extent to which each shift can be self-contained and the kind of relationships that should exist between specialized activities at normal times and during extra hours. Grouping by time is more common in the production function of enterprises.

> Territorial departmentation refers to the grouping of activities of an enterprise when they are physically or geographically dispersed, providing each such separate unit with powers and facilities for running its local administration by itself.

> Departmentation by time refers to the grouping of organizational activities where work extends far beyond normal work periods and spreads over certain shifts.

Departmentation by Process and Equipment

Activities may also be grouped into different departments on the basis of the processes involved or the equipment used. Such groupings are usually formed by the manufacturing concerns. Thus, a cotton textile unit may have separate units for spinning, weaving, dyeing, inspection, and shipping. Better supervision, optimal use of equipment, specialization, and avoidance of duplication of investment are the advantages of such departmentation. The same pattern of departmentation as illustrated in Figure 4.2 is followed here as well.

Departmentation by Customers

Grouping by customers is more popular in the sales activities of an enterprise. It is usually followed when the welfare and interests of the customers are the top priority. Customers may be classified on the basis of age, sex, income, and taste. Customer departmentation assures full attention to different customer groups and helps in enhancing the company's image and goodwill. Since customers are divided into identifiable groups, the pattern permits the use of specialized knowledge for each of these groups.

Hybrid form of departmentation combines both functional and divisional structures. It is generally adopted by large organizations that seek to gain the advantages of both these structures.

Hybrid Structure

Hybrid structure is a form of departmentation that combines both functional and divisional structures. It is generally adopted by large organizations that seek to gain the advantages of both these structures. Functional structures give the benefits of economies of scale, in-depth expertise, and resource utilization efficiencies, whereas divisional structures give the benefits of specialization of products, services, and markets. In India, most of the public sector units and departmental undertakings (like the Indian Railways) follow this structure. A typical hybrid structure of an organization is illustrated in Figure 4.3.

The hybrid structure offers the benefit of specialized expertise and economies of scale in prime functional areas. It facilitates adaptability and flexibility in handling diverse products or service lines, territories, differing needs of customers, alignment of divisional and corporate goals, and so on because of its partial divisional nature. However, this structure requires the hiring of several staff members at both the corporate and functional (operational) levels. Control is also difficult because of the huge organizational structure and it leads to conflict as well. Coordination between a division and a corporate functional department is time consuming, which further creates organizational imbalance.

Matrix form of departmentation superimposes a horizontal set of divisional reporting relationships on the hierarchical functional structure. It is also known as grid organization or project/product management organization.

Matrix Structure

The matrix type of departmentalization superimposes a horizontal set of divisional reporting relationships on the hierarchical functional structure. It is also known as grid organization or project/product management organization. It is a combination of both functional and divisional organizations. Therefore, it enjoys two chains of command—vertical and horizontal. A typical matrix structure is illustrated in Figure 4.4.

Decentralized decision-making, better project or product coordination, improved environment monitoring and the resultant response to change, and flexible utilization of manpower and other resources (including support services) are some of the advantages of matrix structure. On the other hand, this structure requires high administrative costs, creates confusion over authority and responsibility, enhances interpersonal conflicts, and overemphasizes group decision-making.

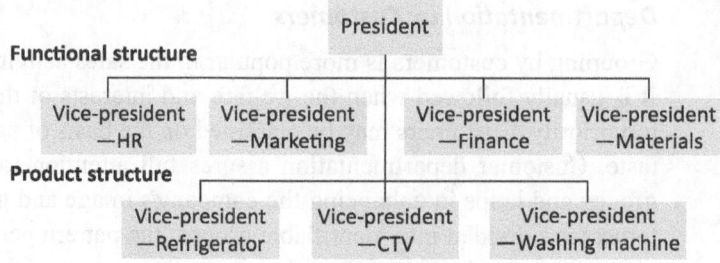

Figure 4.3 Hybrid organizational structure

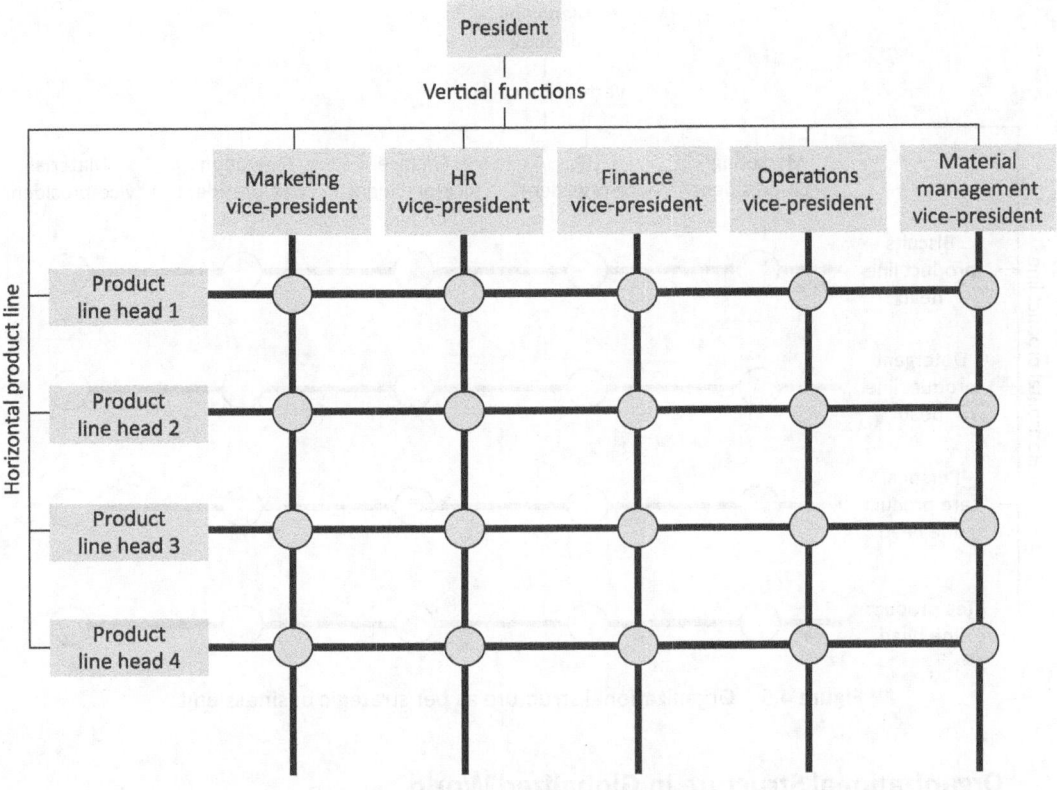

Figure 4.4 Matrix structure

Despite potential disadvantages, the matrix structure is now widely used to cope with the increased environmental pressure and to develop a competitive strategy. Unless the whole process is efficiently managed, it is not likely to benefit an organization.

Recently, it was also observed that organizations are being structured following the *strategic business units* (SBUs) or *independent business units* (IBUs) concept. SBUs/IBUs are set up as distinct business units to ensure that some products or product lines are promoted as independent businesses. The General Electric Company was the first to use this method of structuring. Figure 4.5 illustrates an SBU structure.

Practitioner Speak 4.2

Hierarchy and Network: Two Structures, One Organization

Almost all companies organize people in a hierarchy, and then run well known managerial processes (planning, budgeting, staffing, measuring, etc) with it. We have all seen so many hierarchical org charts—sprawling boxes of letters and arrows arranged in inverted pyramids—and have been through so many budget, planning, and problem solving meetings, that we take all of this as a given, as if it had existed forever. In fact, it hasn't.

Read this insightful blog posted by Kotter on HBR Blog Network by accessing the following link: http://blogs.hbr.org/kotter/2011/05/two-structures-one-organizatio.html.

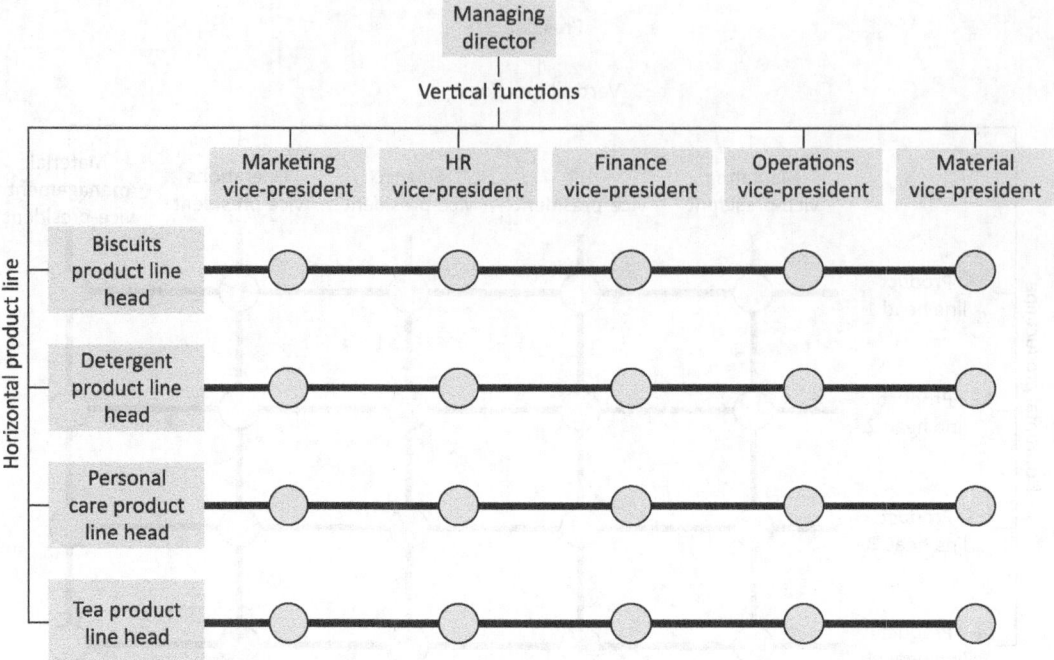

Figure 4.5 Organizational structure as per strategic business unit

Organizational Structure in Globalized World

For business reasons, organizations today operate globally. To suit the global business require-ments, organizations nowadays frame different structures such as global, international, multi-domestic, transnational, informated, cellular, and networked.

Global organization A global organizational structure is not locally responsive. It does not believe in optimal sourcing and concentrates instead on work activities in one locale, that is, in the country of its origin, and follows a centralized approach. It believes in home-based operations, even though it does business globally. Strategically, this type of organization offers similar products or services worldwide, irrespective of its acceptance or otherwise in various global markets.

International organization An international organization goes beyond home-based operations. It creates separate hubs for its various products or service mix, locating such hubs in those countries where it can get the benefit of optimal sourcing. These hubs in different countries work as 'centres of excellence' and cater to the world market.

Multi-domestic organizations These organizations follow a decentralized geography-based approach to customize their operations, specific to the requirements of the countries where they intend to do business. They develop specific products and services acceptable to local markets.

Transnational organizations These organizations blend the international and multi-domestic approaches to optimize their locational advantages and also to reap the benefits of

Practitioner Speak 4.3

How IBM's Sam Palmisano Redefined the Global Corporation

In the 20th century, a select group of leaders—General Motor's Alfred Sloan, HP's David Packard and Bill Hewlett, and GE's Jack Welch—set the standard for the way corporations are run. In the 21st century only IBM's Sam Palmisano has done so.

Read this insightful blog posted by George on HBR Blog Network by accessing the following link: http://blogs.hbr.org/hbsfaculty/2012/01/how-ibms-sam-palmisano-redefin.html.

optimal sourcing. They customize their products and service mix on a regional basis and at the same time benefit from their worldwide centres of operations. Unilever, Proctor and Gamble, and NEC are good examples of this type of organization (Bartlett and Ghoshal 2000).

Informated organizations These organizations manage information up and down in the organization, making extensive use of computers and other related supports. They are low in virtualization and high in information technology (IT) infusion (Zuboff 1988).

Cellular organizations These organizations are characterized by small, autonomous work groups or business units, which are self-governed and can grow, reproduce, and form relations as per their needs (Miles and Snow 1984). They are different from the earlier discussed SBUs or IBUs in the sense that they can operate more independently, even crossing the boundary of cells.

Networked organizations These organizations develop active linkages between internal and external organizations to meet the knowledge needs. They are a mix of virtualizations and IT infusion and are active in making strategic alliances.

Organizing as Part of Total Management Tasks

Organizing is closely related to the other phases of management. This can be better understood when the changes in the organizational structure and the project effects of such changes on the other tasks of management are taken into consideration. In fact, changes in organizational structure must be matched with suitable changes in the planning, staffing, and controlling phases of management. It is to be remembered that an organization comes to life only in association with other tasks of management. Thus, the function of organizing should always be viewed as a part of the total management tasks.

DELEGATION OF AUTHORITY

Authority delegation is one of the most important organizational activities. No organization is possible without delegation, because it presumes the non-existence of subordinates in the organization with one person doing all the tasks. While establishing the organizational structure, managers must group activities, assign them to different individuals in the organization, and delegate authority necessary for their effective and efficient functioning to achieve the mission of the enterprise. Delegation is thus an essential process indispensable to all organizations. The principle of span of management also requires authority to be delegated to subordinates. When a manager delegates authority, he/she creates subordinate positions and thereby makes the organization possible. While delegating authority, the manager must know what is to be delegated

While establishing the organizational structure, managers must group activities, assign them to different individuals in the organization, and delegate authority necessary for their effective and efficient functioning to achieve the mission of the enterprise.

and up to what limit. Managers cannot delegate authority that they do not have, nor can they delegate all their authority without sacrificing their position as a manager.

Features

Delegation of authority involves the following three basic features, irrespective of the level at which authority is passed on to the subordinates:

Assignment of tasks and duties   The subordinates must be given a clear indication of the work to be done.

Granting of authority   The executive who is delegating authority must transfer sufficient rights or permissions to the subordinates to accomplish the assigned tasks.

Creating obligations   Once duties have been assigned and authority delegated, the responsibility for accomplishment of tasks is spontaneously fixed. According to Fayol, this is exaction of responsibility from the subordinates for accomplishing the assigned tasks.

Thus, duties, authority, and obligations constitute three important ingredients of delegation. All these aspects are interrelated and a change in one is bound to call for adjustment in the others.

Barriers

Delegation in organizations often becomes difficult for multiple reasons, most of them being perceptual. In fact, such barriers can be attributed to both—the one who delegates (managers or executives) and to the delegate (employees to whom the authority is delegated).

From Executives

The following are the barriers to delegation from the executive's side:

- Some managers prefer to withhold a larger part of their authority under the pretext that despite delegation they would still continue to remain responsible for the accomplishment of the tasks. Such an attitude is self-defeating and causes real limits to delegation.
- Certain personal attitudes are also important in making real delegation. Every delegation must involve a degree of authority or discretion. The decision of a subordinate is not likely to be exactly similar to that of the delegator; hence, successful delegation requires a manager to be receptive to the ideas of other individuals. Similarly, in order to make delegation realistic and effective, a manager must not only be willing to push decision-making power down the levels of organizational structure but also be prepared to allow others to make mistakes. It is even more essential that the manager must believe and trust his/her subordinates.
- Lack of ability to direct well is still another barrier to successful delegation on the part of top executives.

From Staff Members

The following are the barriers to delegation from the staff members' side:

- There are also obstacles to a subordinate accepting delegation. Even when the manager is willing to delegate a part of his/her authority, some subordinates are more comfortable with following directions and referring to their superior, rather than being involved in the creative process of decision-making.
- Fear of criticism may also deter the subordinate from accepting delegation. Lack of confidence is yet another serious problem.
- In addition, lack of necessary information and resources to do the assigned duties also make subordinates feel hesitant in accepting delegation.

DELEGATION VS DECENTRALIZATION

Delegation primarily refers to the creation of responsibility and the entrustment of authority the from one individual to another. Decentralization refers to systematic delegation of authority in an organization-wide context. Delegation can take place from one individual to another. However, decentralization is complete only when the maximum possible delegation is made to all or most of the people and they are delegated a specific kind of authority.

> Delegation primarily refers to the creation of responsibility and entrustment of authority from one individual to another. Decentralization applies to systematic delegation of authority in an organization-wide context.

Thus, delegation is the process, whereas decentralization is the result. Delegation is from person to person, whereas decentralization is usually complete en block. Delegation is a necessity where organizational structure is present, whereas decentralization may be optional. In delegation, control is at the top, but in decentralization, it is at the decentralized unit. An organization can delegate well without enough decentralization, but this does not mean decentralization can be totally absent in an organization. It always exists in a large or small degree in all organizations.

From an organizational point of view, there is no absolute centralization or absolute delegation. The existence of the former may be conceptually possible in a one-man organization.

Delegation involves sharing of either managerial or operating work between managers and subordinates, whether the subordinates are managers or non-managers. In contrast, decentralization is concerned with the sharing of managerial work between two managers.

PRINCIPLES OF DELEGATION

The following are some important guides, rules, and principles, which help make delegation more effective:

Clarity of delegation Whether specific or general, written or unwritten, delegation of authority must be clear in terms of its contents, functional relations, scope, and assignments. Ambiguity leads to poor results and tends to make the delegation less effective.

The principle of clarity of delegation also implies defining in clear terms the horizontal and vertical relationships of the position of each subordinate to other positions in the organization. Every subordinate must know his/her own position in the organizational structure and should also know how his/her position fits in the overall management hierarchy. Every manager must know all the employees working under him/her and also those occupying positions higher than him/her in the organization. This helps in seeking guidance and also in providing guidance in terms of scalar chain established in the organization.

Specific written delegations help both the manager and the recipient of authority. However, such specific delegations become more and more difficult in the higher echelons of organizational structure.

The principle of clarity should not be taken to mean that authority relations between the subordinates and the seniors, once established, become immutable. With the changes in work, authority delegation should be suitably modified.

Consistency with results expected   Before proceeding with the actual delegation of authority to a subordinate, a manager should know the jobs and results expected of such a delegation. Only that amount of authority sufficient to accomplish the results should be delegated. This principle operates on the premise that goals are set, plans are made, and jobs are set up to accomplish or implement those goals. This principle also helps to minimize the dangers of delegating too much or too little authority.

Responsibility cannot be delegated   The obligation to accomplish the assigned task is absolute and is not partitioned when authority is delegated to a subordinate. Even after delegation, the chief executive remains accountable to the board of directors for management and supervision of the entire enterprise. If this principle is violated, three important consequences would follow:

* The rule of single chain of command will be violated.
* Management at the top shall have great responsibility and yet would not be accountable for the results.
* If would become difficult to determine who is accountable for what.

Thus, when authority is delegated, obligations are not passed down the organization; instead, new responsibilities are created at each level.

Parity of authority and responsibility   Whenever authority is delegated, responsibility steps in and coexists with authority. Subordinates can be held accountable for the tasks assigned to them to the extent of the authority delegated to accomplish those tasks. Accordingly, a sales manager cannot be held responsible for production failures for which he/she was given no authority. Similarly, a store clerk cannot be held responsible for issue of materials against wrong indents received from the store manager. Hence, authority and responsibility should relate to the same assignment.

Exception principle   Authority is delegated to push down the process of decision-making as near the source of information and action as possible. The recipients of authority should make proper use of it and take all decisions falling within the scope of authority. Only in exceptional cases, when they cannot take a decision at their own level, should they refer them upwards for consideration and decision by superiors.

Practitioner Speak 4.4

Encouraging Managers to Update

Managers' common reluctance to delegate responsibility is a topic that has long intrigued Jeffrey Pfeffer, coauthor, with Charles O'Reilly, of *Hidden Value: How Great Companies Achieve Extraordinary Results with Ordinary People* (Harvard Business School Press, 2000). Pfeffer says that there is mounting evidence that giving people more responsibility for making decisions in their jobs generates greater productivity, morale, and commitment. Yet despite these benefits, many managers are reluctant to cede control. We recently asked Pfeffer, whose research helps explain the reasons for such reluctance, what companies can do to overcome it.

Read this insightful blog posted by Harvard Management Update on *HBR Blog Network* by accessing the following link: http://blogs.hbr.org/hmu/2008/02/encouraging-managers-to-delega.html.

By delegating authority, a manager does not absolve himself/herself of his/her responsibility. It is, therefore, essential for a manager to devise suitable techniques of control so as to ensure that the authority delegated is properly used and results are achieved as per expectations.

Pooling together of the authority of two or more managers before a problem can be solved or a decision made is described as splintered authority.

Shared authority   A superior seeking the cooperation of his/her subordinates for making a decision is known as shared authority.

CENTRALIZATION VS DECENTRALIZATION

Staiger (1964) has suggested that the following should not be decentralized:

- Responsibility for objective determination
- Responsibility of developing a comprehensive business plan and policy
- Final responsibility for business control
- Responsibility for quality design and quality standards
- Final approval of the budget and other financial plans
- Decision on the manner of raising of capital and its utilization
- Responsibility for deciding various capital projects such as large-scale and long-term commitments of the financial project

However, with the emergence of participative approach, some of Staiger's observations do not hold good in today's competitive business environment. For example, to ensure enhanced commitment to deliver the results, nowadays determination of the objectives of the business is made more through a participative or distributed decision-making rather than a centralized decision at the top.

Criteria for Decentralization or Measurement of Degree of Decentralization

Ernest Dale (1965) through his research has listed the following criteria for decentralization:

Number of decisions   The greater is the number of decisions made lower down the management hierarchy, the more is the decentralization.

Importance and significance of decisions The more important and costlier is the decision made lower down the management hierarchy, the more is the degree of decentralization.

Effects of decisions The more the functions are affected by the decisions made at the lower levels and the more that such decisions affect the importance of the organizational structure, the greater will be the degree of decentralization.

Checking decisions The lesser is the checking required for decisions made lower down the management hierarchy, the higher is the decentralization.

No change Decentralization is at its maximum where no change has to be made.

W.H. Newman (1951) has indicated the various degrees of decentralization as follows:

- Complete reservation of authority or total absence of decentralization will be called a case of total centralization.
- If plans, policies, and decisions are made at the top, the degree of decentralization will be considered very low.
- If full authority for taking operational decisions is delegated to the lower levels without any reservation or limitation, it is considered a good amount of decentralization, though it cannot be called total decentralization.
- Where plans, policies, and authorities are pushed down to the lower levels, the organization will be called a bottom-up organization.

Need for Decentralization

Despite different observations about decentralization, as pointed out earlier, organizations may be required to decentralize or distribute authority in certain circumstances. Even though theoretically arguments might differ, many experts appreciate the need for decentralization.

According to Allen (1958), the need for decentralization arises in the following situations:

- To reduce or ease the burden of the top executives
- To provide opportunities for greater diversification of product lines
- To pay special attention towards particular product lines or product markets
- To promote development of future managerial talent for business
- To increase the morale of the members of the organization
- To keep pace with technological developments in some industries (e.g., electronics industry)

Advantages of Decentralization

The following are the advantages of decentralization:

- Decentralization reduces the burden on the top executives.
- It motivates subordinates to take initiatives and shoulder responsibilities for higher performance.
- It boosts the morale of the members in the organization.
- It develops the managerial potential among employees.
- It ensures product line diversification.
- It ensures division of work.
- It establishes better coordination and operation.

- It ensures effective control.
- It ensures quicker decisions.
- It facilitates management by objective (MBO).

Disadvantages of Decentralization

The following are the disadvantages of decentralization:

- Excessive operational cost
- Lack of divisibility
- Non-availability of good executives
- Wastage of staff service
- Challenges in policy control because different decentralized units may adopt different policy approaches
- Obstacles and difficulties faced by the central office in taking immediate decisions in emergency situations
- Potential loss of control of the central office over the decentralized units

Ways to Achieve Decentralization

Achieving decentralization in organizations is not easy. Executives and subordinates are always in conflict on decentralization issues. Subordinates allege that by decentralization the management wants to get part of their job done through them. On the other hand, some executives opine that decentralization will only add to their problems as the subordinates always need to be guided. In their view, decentralization will reduce the effective time available with them for other managerial work. The following are the main obstacles to delegation:

Self-sycophant attitudes Executives nurture self-sycophant attitudes like 'I can do it better myself' and, therefore, are unwilling to delegate.

Lack of ability to direct others Some executives do not possess the ability to direct and get work done by the subordinates.

Lack of confidence and faith in subordinates This problem can be solved by training the subordinates or bringing in new subordinates. A manager's opinion of his/her sub-ordinates can be subjective and be manifested even unconsciously. Though the superior accepts decentralization, he/she is afraid of losing position and hence does not let the subordinate to learn or perform his/her job well. Such a tendency is more prevalent among promotee executives.

Absence of executive control Executives may fear being overpowered if subordinates grow and show development.

Temperamental aversion Executives may be handicapped by temperamental aversion to taking chances, notwithstanding the clarity of delegation. The greater the number of subordinates, the higher the chances of decentralization and more likely are the troubles. To delegate is to take a calculated risk.

The foregoing five problems can be addressed through attitudinal changes or modifications. The reasons for the executives' reluctance to delegate must be ascertained. Sometimes, though

> **Practitioner Speak 4.5**
>
> **4 Reasons Why Bosses Need Bosses**
>
> Exxon Mobil Shareholders vote May 28 on a resolution that would prohibit one person from holding the titles of both CEO and chairman. Backers say that Exxon needs a visionary independent chairman who, undistracted by the demands of running the largest U.S. public company and unconstrained by its conservative corporate culture, can craft a bold strategy for tomorrow's uncertain energy environment.
>
> Read this insightful blog posted by Hemp on *HBR Blog Network* by accessing the following link: http://blogs.hbr.org/hbr/hbreditors/2008/05/4_reasons_why_bosses_need_boss.html.

the superiors give orders to subordinates, the latter are hesitant to take up responsibilities. Their reluctance can be attributed to the following reasons:

- Lack of faith in self and a sense of dependence can make some subordinates refer the work back to their superiors. They tend to avoid taking up responsibilities.
- There is a fear of criticism. If something goes wrong and the superior publicly criticizes it, there could be a negative effect on the morale of the subordinates who not only resent negative criticism but also react to them.
- Lack of necessary information and resources can sometimes result in subordinates refusing to take up responsibilities.
- Subordinates avoid taking up responsibilities because they are overloaded with work.
- Lack of adequate positive incentives and inducements is another reason.

Enthusiasts of decentralization have to remember that its application requires the social and administrative adjustment of attitudes and behavioural patterns of specific individuals. In a dynamic society, such adjustments are a common occurrence. Even the best plans will not work unless personal adjustments are made. Thus, decentralization has a behavioural dimension.

LINE AND STAFF RELATIONS

Irrespective of their structures, organizations are basically tightly knotted together by the cord of authority relationships. Such relationships act as a cohesive force and integrate the whole organization. The types and degrees of authority vary with the decision-making levels. Different authority relationships basically revolve around line and staff relationships. Line functions directly influence the accomplishment of objectives of an organization, whereas staff functions help the line members to work effectively and accomplish the organizational objectives. However, in reality it is difficult to separate direct and supportive functions. In fact, functions are based on the nature of the organization. Hence, such categorization of line and staff functions varies from organization to organization. For instance, in a manufacturing organization, production and sales are considered line functions, whereas finance, purchase, personnel, maintenance, and quality control are considered staff functions. Line and staff distinctions are made on the basis of two viewpoints—functional viewpoint and authority relationships viewpoint. Allen defined line and staff functions as—'Line functions are those which have

> Line functions directly influence the accomplishment of objectives of an organization, whereas staff functions help the line staff to work effectively and accomplish organizational objectives.

direct responsibility for accomplishing the objectives of the enterprise and staff refers to those elements of the organization that help the line to work more effectively in accomplishing the primary objectives of the enterprise.' Since organizational objectives determine the line and staff functions, any change in objectives may also result in changes in the line and staff functions. The principal distinctions between the line and staff are given in Table 4.1.

Conflicts

Though line and staff managers are supposed to work harmoniously to achieve the organizational goals, their relationship is usually, one of the major sources of conflict in most organizations. Since such conflicts lead to loss of time and organizational effectiveness, it is always desirable to identify the sources of such conflicts and initiate necessary action to overcome them. Theoretically, it is impossible to differentiate between line and staff functions, and hence, conflicts cannot be avoided. However, line and staff conflicts can be grouped into three categories—conflicts due to line viewpoint, conflicts due to staff viewpoint, and conflicts due to the nature of line and staff relationships.

Due to Line Viewpoint

The following conflicts arise due to the views held by the line managers:

Lack of accountability Line managers generally perceive that staff managers are not accountable for their actions. Such lack of accountability makes the staff ignore the overall organizational objectives. Staff takes the credit for achieving the results, which is actually achieved by the line, but if a problem occurs, the line is then blamed. Such perception among the line managers is one of the most important sources of line and staff conflict.

Encroachment on line authority Line managers often allege that staff managers encroach upon their authority by giving recommendations on matters that come within their purview. Such encroachments influence the working of line departments and often lead to hostility, resentment, and reluctance to accept staff recommendations.

Dilution of authority Staff managers often dilute the authority and belittle the responsibilities of line managers. Line managers fear that their responsibilities may be reduced and they even suffer from a feeling of insecurity.

Table 4.1 Distinctions between line and staff managers

Line authority	Staff authority
They are generalists.	They are myopic.
They direct others.	They assist others.
They delegate authority.	They serve authority.
They train subordinates.	They investigate the problems.
They use sanctions.	They solve special problems.
They exert control over subordinates.	They make plans.
They have veto power.	They support the line.
They take operating decisions.	They provide ideas to the line.
They have the final responsibility.	They possess special expertise.

Theoretical basis Staff managers being specialists, generally think within the ambit of their specialization. They fail to relate their suggestions to the actual reality and are unable to understand the actual dimensions of the problems. This is because the staff are cut off from the day-to-day operations. This results in impractical suggestions, making it difficult to achieve organizational goals.

Due to Staff Viewpoint

The following conflicts arise due to the views held by the staff managers:

Lack of proper use of staff Staff managers allege that line managers often take decisions without any input from them. They inform staff only after taking decisions, which makes staff managers feel unwanted. However, if anything goes wrong, staff managers are made responsible for decisions taken by line without the consultation of staff.

Resistance to new ideas Line managers resist new ideas as they feel implementing new ideas implies that there is some fault with the present way of working. Such rigidity of line managers dissuades staff from implementing new ideas in the organization and adds to their frustration.

Lack of proper authority Staff managers often allege that despite having the best solutions to the problems being faced in their areas of specialization, they fail to contribute to organizational goals. This is because they lack the authority to implement the solutions and are unable to persuade the line managers (who have the authority) to implement them.

Due to Nature of Line and Staff Relationships

The following conflicts arise due to the relationship between the line and staff managers:

Different backgrounds Line and staff managers are usually from different backgrounds. In general, line managers are seniors to staff in terms of organizational hierarchy and levels. On the contrary, staff managers are relatively younger and better educated. Staff managers often look down upon the line. Such complexes create an atmosphere of mistrust and hatred between the line and staff.

Lack of demarcation between line and staff authority In practice, it is difficult to make a distinction between line and staff authority. Overlapping and duplication of work creates a gap between the authority and responsibility of line and staff. Each tries to shift the blame on the other.

Lack of proper understanding of authority Failure to understand authority causes misunderstandings between the line and staff. This leads to encroachment of the decision-making space and creates conflict.

Resolution

To overcome the line and staff conflict, it is necessary for an organization to follow certain approaches:

Clarity in relationships Duties and responsibilities of both line and staff should be clearly laid down. Relationships of staff with the line and their scope of authority need to be clearly defined. Similarly, line managers should also be made responsible for decision-making and they should have the necessary authority. Line should enjoy the freedom to modify, accept, or reject the recommendations or advice of the staff.

Proper use of staff   Line managers must know how to maximize organizational efficacy by optimizing the expertise of staff managers. They need to be trained on it. Similarly, staff managers should also help the line to understand how they can improve their activities.

Completed staff work   Completed staff work denotes careful study of the problem, identifying possible alternatives for the problem, and providing recommendations based on the compiled facts. This will result in more staff work and pragmatic suggestions.

Holding staff accountable for results   Once staff managers become accountable, they would be cautious about their recommendations. The line would also have confidence on staff recommendations, as the staff would also be accountable for the results.

SPAN OF MANAGEMENT

Span of management is the limitation of the number of subordinates who can be effectively supervised by a manager in the discharge of his/her management duties. The incapacity of human beings restricts the number of persons who can be managed effectively. Actual spans in business organization indicate that there is no single best number that can be universally applied. However, all management experts agree that there is a definite span limiting the number of subordinates who can be managed effectively by one executive. There are various approaches in determining the ideal span of management.

Classical Approach

The classical approach has dealt with generalizations embodying specific number of subordinates for an effective span. Classicists have suggested the span for upper and top level to be from three to eight subordinates. However, a recent operational approach has suggested that there are too many variables in management and no exact number can be fixed.

Graicunas' Theory on Superior–Subordinate Relationships

A.V. Graicunas (1933), a French management consultant, analysed superior–subordinate relations and classified these relationships into three forms. His study was based upon theoretical projection by mathematics rather than on empirical observation. His formula was based on a geometric increase in the complexities of managing as the number of subordinates increase. The three types of superior–subordinate relationships as identified by him are as follows:

> Span of management is the limitation of the number of subordinates who can be effectively supervised by a manager in the discharge of his/her management duties.

Direct single relationships   Such relationships arise from the direct and individual contacts of the superior with the subordinates. Thus if A as a superior has three subordinates X, Y, and Z, there would be three direct single relationships.

Direct group relationships   These arise between the superior and the subordinates in all possible combinations. Thus, a superior may consult a subordinate with a second in attendance, with all the subordinates, or with various combinations of them. Depending upon the possible combinations, there would be nine relationships such as X with Y, Y with Z, and X with Y.

Cross-relationships   These are the mutual relationships among the subordinates necessary for working under a common superior, such as X and Y and Y and X. The two relationships are different because in the first case

Y consults X and in the second case X consults Y, and in both cases the situations may be different. There are six cross-relationships for the subordinates.

On the basis of analysis of these relationships, Graicunas developed the following formula.

$$\text{Direct single relationships} = n$$

$$\text{Direct group relationships} = n\left(\frac{2^n}{2} - 1\right)$$

$$\text{Cross-relationships} = n(n-1)$$

$$\text{Total relationships} = n\left(\frac{2^n}{2} + n - 1\right)$$

where, n = number of subordinates.

On the basis of this formula, the possible relationships with variable number of subordinates increase rapidly.

Where there are four subordinates under one superior, the number of relationships will be as follows:

$$4\left(\frac{2^4}{2} + 4 - 1\right) = 44$$

When the number of subordinates is increased by one, that is, from four to five, the number of relationships will be as follows:

$$5\left(\frac{2^5}{2} + 5 - 1\right) = 100$$

Wide vs Narrow Spans

The span of management directly affects the number of levels in an organization. Wider spans of management lead to flat organizations, whereas narrow spans of management result in tall organizational structures.

A narrow span, which results in many levels in the organization, creates problems in terms of both cost and efficiency. First, the levels are very expensive because more supervisory staff are needed, which leads to higher expenditure in the form of executive remuneration. Expense is further increased on account of additional subordinates for more number of managers. Hence, cost increases in both executive and operative levels. Secondly, communication in a tall organization has several limitations. Communication through scalar chain has to travel through various levels; this not only delays the reach of communication at the appropriate points but also leads to it getting distorted or sometimes missed altogether. Thirdly, a narrow span (tall structure) presents problems in coordination and control as the top management is far away from the operatives where the actual work is performed. Encouraging lower-level managers to develop cross-relationships, however, can eliminate this problem. Fourthly, a narrow span also adversely affects employee morale. A subordinate who finds himself/herself submerged at the bottom of the organization pyramid feels sensitive about the fact that he/she hears nothing from the top organization (leadership). Due to such a placement, he/she gets very few opportunities to gain self-reliance and take initiative and therefore hardly enjoys any feeling of belongingness. Hence, the employee may be less enthusiastic about the job.

Finally, narrow spans also reduce opportunities for management development. Too many levels hardly allow for delegation of any real authority and greatly limit the supervision to very few activities at lower levels. The result is that the subordinate is deprived of the benefit of managing a larger number of related activities.

However, tall structures have certain advantages such as reinforcing the authority relationships through emphasis on status, placing burden on cross-communication, which sometimes becomes a problem, and providing opportunities for promotion because of availability of many positions.

A wide span or flat structure calls for supervision of too many people. Supervision will become less effective because the manager will not have sufficient time and energy to attend to each subordinate. Large number of contacts may also distract the manager from important questions of policy.

Advantages of the flat structure are that the communication chain is shorter and is free from hierarchical control. Subordinates feel more autonomous and develop an independent spirit. The flat structure also reduces cost as a lesser number of executives are required.

The factors responsible for a wide span may be identified as follows:

- Prevailing trend towards decentralization
- Improving communication technology
- Increasing size of organizations
- Evolving a new pattern of leadership from a growing acceptance of group processes

While deciding the span, the advantages and disadvantages of these two situations should be carefully examined in terms of tangible as well as intangible factors. The actual span should be determined keeping in view all the pertinent factors in a particular situation and at a given time.

Factors Determining Span

The determination of span depends upon the number of relationships that can be managed by a superior. As such, an important determinant is the manager's ability to reduce the frequency and time impact of superior–subordinate relationships, though this ability itself is determined by several other factors. The factors that determine the optimum span may be stated as follows:

Ability of executives The supervisory ability of executives comprises the capacity to comprehend problems quickly, to get along well with people, and to command respect and loyalty from subordinates. In addition, the communicative skill, decision-making, leadership ability, and controlling power are important determinants of supervisory ability. Accordingly, executives differ from each other in their ability to supervise others. When the ability is high, a larger number of subordinates can be supervised. In contrast, a poor ability limits the span of supervision.

Capacity of subordinates Efficient and trained subordinates can discharge their duties satisfactorily without much help and direction from the superiors. In such a case, the span may be larger because a superior will be required to devote less time in managing them. However, changes in subordinates make the span narrower.

Nature of work When the work involves routine, repeated efforts or when the executive manages similar functions, he/she becomes well versed with jobs and can handle a larger number of subordinates. On the contrary, activities and functions with a degree of variability and more complexity in nature increase interrelationships and consume more time of the executive and thus reduce the span of the supervisor.

Time available for supervision Every manager needs time for contacting or attending to various persons, for doing administrative jobs of planning and policy-making, and also for other processes. These functions are not directly related to guiding the subordinates. Hence, the span to a great extent depends on the availability of time for supervision.

Delegation of authority Ambiguous or inadequate authority delegation consumes a disproportionate time of the manager in counselling and guiding subordinates. Where subordinates are delegated with clearly defined authority sufficient to carry out the assigned duties, it would considerably reduce the time and attention of the senior and thus increase his/her span provided the subordinates are trained enough.

Degree of decentralization An executive operating under a decentralized set-up is relieved of much of the burden of making programmed decisions and can afford to supervise a relatively larger number of subordinates.

Use of objective standards Reviewing the performance of subordinates can be done either by personal observation or through the use of objective standards. In the latter case, a manager is saved of many time-consuming relationships and can therefore concentrate on points of strategic importance, thus widening the span of supervision.

Territorial continuity of functions supervised Where the functions are geographically separated, supervision of components and personnel becomes more difficult and time-consuming. The manager must spend considerable time in visiting the separate units and make use of a more time-consuming formal means of communication. Geographic continuity of functions supervised by the manager, therefore, reduces the span of control.

Availability of staff assistance When an organization is equipped with staff services, subordinates gain much of their guidance on methods, schedules, and personnel problems from staff experts and, thus, require fewer contacts with line managers. The manager normally gets involved when the staff fails to run the show. Thus, provision of staff assistance helps the executives to supervise a large number of subordinates.

According to Allen, the following points determine spans:

- Diversity
- Dispersion
- Complexity
- Volume
- Attitude towards delegation

Additional factors that determine span in an organization can be listed as follows:

- Training of the manager
- Capacity and mindset of the subordinates
- Dynamic and complex nature of activities

EXHIBIT 4.2   Qualifying the Quantifying Aspects of Span of Control

The definition of span of management or control relies on the number of people who can be effectively managed by a manager. However, is span of control all about numbers or are there qualitative aspects underlying the final number arrived at? A recent post by Harwell has elaborated on how various factors influence the number of subordinates who can be effectively managed. More importantly, it is essential that the management understands the dynamics underlying the number crunching that goes in determining the right span of control.

Any particular managerial job is different from any other. Thus, the nature of job determines the right span of control one can exert over one's subordinates. Ideally, the main determinants of the right span of control are as follows:

- Nature of tasks to be performed by subordinates

- Tenure of the subordinates in the job
- Rate of change in job conditions
- Variety in jobs to be performed by the manager
- Ratio of investment in technology per employee in the organization

Apart from these, it is also important to consider that some managers have to get involved and work along with their employees. This too considerably reduces their ability to manage a large team. In some cases, managing a larger team of subordinates may be possible. However, one also needs to consider the trade-off between a larger number of employees to be managed and the tasks that the manager would have to delegate to others in that case. The trade-off should ideally result in more effective management and cost reduction for the organization.

Source: Harwell, 'The Right Span of Management isn't a Number', 8 July 2008, http://blog.makingitclear.com/2008/07/08/soc/, last accessed on 25 June 2013 (adapted).

- Degree to which objective standards are established
- Extent and clarity of delegation
- Existence of a good communication system
- Degree of decentralization

Exhibit 4.2 discusses more points about span of control.

VIRTUAL OR NETWORKED ORGANIZATIONS

Information systems have now changed the world of business and also the way people work. Traditionally, organizational structures were based on location-specific activities and face-to-face communication. With the advancement of information systems, organizations now operate in a distributive environment, with flexibility in the nature and way of work. Such organizations are called e-organizations or virtual organizations. They do not have a central geographical location and interact essentially through computer networks. By nature, these organizations outsource most of their functions because of their borderless operations and market network. Most of the global consulting and high technology organizations operate by creating a virtual organization, leveraging the information systems. In these organizations, which may be either temporary or permanent, virtual teams and virtual projects are developed.

> Organizations that operate in a distributive environment, and are flexible in nature and way of work, are called e-organizations or virtual organizations. Such organizations interact essentially through computer networks.

Rosabeth Moss Kanter (2001) referred to the radically transformative nature of the global network, that is, the new e-world that connects everyone with everyone else. This requires a new operating environment and new forms of business, working, and organization. To survive in this era of e-revolution, organizations need to be innovative, shifting away from traditional hierarchical bureaucratic systems and structures.

Kanter identifies four key elements of an effective organizational e-culture. These are improved strategy to develop new products and services, urge to grow in size through partnerships and collaborations, operate as integrated communities by removing the internal barriers, and, finally, being talent-dependent or driven.

E-organizations have the following three important characteristic features:

- Management of production process, encompassing procurement, stock replenishment, payment processing, vendor control, and production control activities through electronic links
- Management of customer-centric activities, encompassing marketing, selling, processing of customers' orders, and extending support to customers through electronic information systems
- Managing internal processes, encompassing employee services, training, information sharing, and even recruiting through electronic applications

DESIGNING ORGANIZATIONS FOR UNCERTAIN ENVIRONMENTS

Organizational design depends on two core aspects: (a) the vision and philosophy of the founders of the organization and (b) the environmental interface. Organizational founders initially design their organizations from business and operational perspectives, but the changes of operating environment requires rebuilding the structure and integrating the strategies, business interests, and environmental uncertainties. Environmental pressures on organizations are diverse and may include the competitors, suppliers, customers, trade unions, technological changes, and governmental regulations. Katz and Khan (1970), while emphasizing the need for organizations to align with the environment, said that organizations should be able to develop a mechanism to cope with environmental influences. Environmental uncertainty and flexibility in organizational design was also advocated by Burns and Stalker (1961) and Lawrence and Lorsch (1967), particularly for the lifestyle products industry. The 24×7 customer services, like the mobile customer services, are examples. Exide Battery in India has the largest market share in the automobile battery segment. Yet it has introduced BATMOBILE (Battery Mobile) services to enable customers get a stand-by battery within 10 to 15 minutes of getting stranded on the road due to battery failure. This required Exide to scale up its service department structure with more marketing orientation to ensure that competitors hardly get any opportunity to find any lapse in its services to enter its market domain. For many products, on-time availability is an important determinant of success. Competitors step in when the organization fails to supply its products to retail outlets on time. Asian Paints, the number one in the low-price segment, does not any opportunity to Berger Paints and others to be visible in the outlets selling paints—it has made its order booking system online. Earlier, a retail outlet had to wait for a week to get supply of paints after it placed its orders. With the redesigning of sales and marketing operations, Asian Paints is now able to reach its products within hours of online order booking. Using the effectual logic of organizational design, it can be understood that effects (uncertain in nature) not only force the organizations to adopt transformational approaches to design but also design the environment per se. The demand for many lifestyle products is the consequential effect of environmental redesign by new-generation entrepreneurs. Male fairness cream is one such example. Here, its demand has been created by organizations by introducing the concept that even young males like to look fair and attractive.

Environmental uncertainties affecting organizational design are difficult to calculate or assume. Organizations may not be very clear about their focus areas. It is for these reasons that organizations often become proactive in designing their structure by leveraging their strategic intent. Such strategic options encompass the following four areas:

- The environment is beyond control and unpredictable. Hence, it is better to use some predictive techniques to develop a favourable design for an organization. This is the planning approach to organizational design in an uncertain environment.
- Unpredictability of the environment reduces the planning horizons, and therefore, it is better to develop a flexible organizational design by using adaptive approaches.
- Adopt a visionary approach, considering that environment is unpredictable. Design the organization in a way that facilitates accomplishment of the desired outcomes.
- Believe in effectual transformation. Influence the environmental changes through organizational redesign. Assume future environmental factors that are largely non-existent and seek to create them through an approach of interactive goal creation with others including imagining new futures arising out of current means. This is called the effectual transformation approach.

SUMMARY

In this chapter, we discussed the basic issues of organizing activities. The success of an organization largely depends on the way it organizes its activities. While organizing, it is necessary to follow certain basic principles. What may be good for one organization may not be so for another. While there are many forms of organizational structures, selecting an appropriate structure for an organization largely depends on its style of managing activities and priorities. A manager has to study all facets of the organizational life before finalizing a structure. The structure sets the culture of an organization. Often, it creates an organizational climate. Hence, changing an existing structure requires careful study of the problems encountered. Quite often, changing the strategies of an organization influences the structure. Globalization has now intensified competition for organizations. It has also led to various new issues that organizations worldwide now need to deal with. One major issue is market consolidation by mergers and acquisitions. Cross-border mergers require compliance with multicultural issues, diversity issues, corporate governance issues, and so on. For business reasons as well, organizations are now required to achieve economies of scale by locating their manufacturing and back office jobs in competitive wage-cost countries. All these factors require organizations to experiment with their structures and identify the best fit.

However, it is important to recognize that despite globalization, global competition, deregulation, change of technology, and new generation of knowledge workers as an organization's manpower, the knowledge about fundamental concepts of organizational structure and design has become most important for managers, irrespective of their functional areas. This is because every manager has to organize his/her activities to get the best from his/her team. It is always desirable that an organization's design is chosen based on consideration of multidimensional aspects. Any organizational design has two primary contexts—structural and human. Structural contexts focus on goals, strategies, and structures, whereas human contexts include work processes, people, coordination and control, and incentive mechanism. These two contexts together help an executive to design an organization from a more holistic perspective.

KEY DEFINITIONS

Delegation   Entrustment of authority and creation of responsibility by one individual to another

Diversity   The differences in culture, race, gender, age, and so on, which lead to diversity issues and are applicable to both the employees and the customers

Matrix structure   Type of organization that superimposes a horizontal set of divisional reporting relationships on the hierarchical functional structure; also known as grid organization

Span of management   Limitation of the number of subordinates who can be effectively supervised by a manager in the discharge of his/her management duties

Strategic business unit   Departmentation of an organization, based on product line or product mix, wherein one business head manages the activities independently; each SBU's competitor groups are different.

Virtual organizations   Such organizations operate in a distributive environment and also are known as e-organizations

CONCEPT-REVIEW QUESTIONS

4.1 What are the important sources of conflict between line and staff? How can such conflicts be reduced?

4.2 Describe the advantages and disadvantages of departmentalization by functions and departmentalization by products and services.

4.3 What is the main basis of departmentalization?

4.4 Define organizing. Explain the term organization. Differentiate between organization and organization structure.

4.5 What are the essential elements of organizing?

4.6 Define span of management. Why is it so important for structuring an organization?

4.7 What is delegation? List the major benefits of delegation of authority.

4.8 Explain the difference between delegation and decentralization. How can we decide the degree of decentralization?

4.9 Explain the meaning and scope of authority, responsibility, and accountability.

4.10 Write short notes on the following:
   (a) Matrix organization
   (b) Hybrid structure
   (c) Strategic business unit
   (d) Wide versus narrow span
   (e) Decentralization
   (f) Departmentation by time
   (g) Barriers to delegation
   (h) Formal and informal organizations
   (i) Human behaviour in organizing
   (j) Systems theory in organization

CRITICAL THINKING QUESTIONS

4.1 Design an organizational chart for an integrated steel plant that maintains a very thin corporate layer, but has staff support along with the line at the operational level. Further, name your proposed organizational structure, justifying why you have selected such a structure.

4.2 A company has retained you to study their existing structure and reporting relationship. The company believes that since they are operating with the state-of-the-art technology and their core business is to extend technical support to telecom majors, there is no merit in retaining their brick-and-mortar organizational structures in all the countries of their operation. Instead, they prefer to follow a networked structure, with their controlling office in India. Suggest the right course of action they should take.

4.3 If we want to switch over from a functional structure to a matrix structure, what are the immediate problems we are likely to face and how should we solve those problems?

SELECT BIBLIOGRAPHY

- Allen, Louis A., *Management and Organization*, McGraw-Hill, New York, 1958.
- Allen, Louis A., *Professional Management*, McGraw-Hill Book Co., New York, 1973.
- Bartlett, C.A. and S. Ghoshal, *Transnational Management—Text, Cases and Readings in Cross-Border Management*, 3rd ed., McGraw-Hill/Irwin, Boston, 2000.
- Bloom, B., *Stability and Change in Human Characteristics*, John Wiley and Sons, New York, 1964.
- Boone, Louis, E. and David L. Kurtz, *Management*, McGraw-Hill Inc, New York, 1992.
- Brown, Alvin, *Organisation: A Formulation of Principle*, Herbarter PR, New York, 1945.
- Burns, Tom and G. Stalker, *The Management of Innovation*, Tavistock, London, 1961.
- Burton, Richard, M. Gerardine DeSanctis, and Obel Borge, *Organizational Design: A Step-by-Step Approach*, Cambridge University Press, Cambridge, 2006.
- Chandler, Alfred D., *Strategy and Structure*, MIT, Mass, 1962.
- Dale, Ernest (ed.), *Management Theory and Practice*, McGraw-Hill Book Co., New York, 1973.
- Dale, Ernest, *Readings in Management: Landmarks and New Frontiers*, McGraw-Hill Book Co., New York, 1965.
- Drucker, Peter, *The Practice of Management*, Harper and Brothers, New York, 1954.
- Graicunas, A.V., 'Relations in Organizations', *Bulletin of the International Management Institute*, 7 March 1933, pp. 39–42.
- Kanter, R.M., *Evolve! Succeeding in the Digital Culture of Tomorrow*, Harvard Business, Boston, 2001.
- Kanter, R.M., *When Giants Learn to Dance*, Simon and Schuster, New York, 1989.
- Katz, D. and R.L. Kahn (eds), *The Social Psychology of Organisations*, Wiley, New York, 1978.
- Koontz, Harold and Cyril O'Donnell, *Essentials of Management*, Tata McGraw-Hill Publishing Company Limited, New Delhi, 1982.
- Lawrence, Paul and Lorsch Jay, *Organisation and Environment*, Irwin, Homewood, Illinois, 1967.
- Miles, R.E. and C.C. Snow, 'Designing Strategic Human Resource Systems', *Organisational Dynamics*, Vol. 13, Issue 1, 1984, pp. 36–52.
- Newman, W.H., *Administrative Action*, Prentice-Hall, Englewood Cliff, 1951.
- Robbins, Stephen P. and Mary Coulter (eds), *Management*, Prentice Hall, New York, 2002.
- Sarasvathy, S., *Effectuation: The Logic of Entrepreneurial Expertise*, Routledge, Cheltenham, 2007.
- Zuboff, Shoshana, *The Age of the Smart Machine: The Future of Work and Power*, Basic Books, New York, 1988.

CASE STUDY

The Chinese Dragon and a New Organizational Structure

Since the reform initiative in 1979, the Chinese government has promoted an aggressive policy of export-led growth that has resulted in an annual average of double-digit growth rate. The transition of the Chinese economy from an administratively controlled regime to a market-oriented one was under the close observation of international trading bodies. Many member countries of the World Trade Organization (WTO) were apprehensive about the possible impact of Chinese accession to the WTO. China's internal economic strength led the world to believe that the 21st century will be dominated by China. Despite such apprehensions, many however believed that the immediate imbalance in the foreign trade of many countries, created because of China grabbing the world market, will get offset by the world consumers' gain in the long run. It was also expected that this will also place China under pressure to comply with the changing global norms, tastes, and preferences. After an effort over a decade, China ultimately became a member of the WTO in the Doha Ministerial Conference (2001). For many, China's entry into the WTO is still a source of anxiety. Low labour cost and devaluation of the Chinese currency are imminent in China. This will spark job losses in domestic markets. Many even subscribe to the feeling that China will destroy the basic fabric of free trade under the WTO regime as it still largely follows its regulated economic practices, violating the principles of free market. Some believe that China's accession to WTO is a deliberate political move to sort out its disputes with trade partners subscribing to commonly agreed principles of the WTO.

Impact on India

On the positive side, China's entry into WTO may provide some relief to the Indian industry. As a member of the WTO, China will have to abide by the multilateral rules and agreements and make its policies transparent. All these may lessen the anxieties of the Indian industry about infiltration of exceptionally low-cost products from China into the Indian market. China is likely to lose several of its existing advantages in the process of being WTO-compliant. Substantial lowering of tariffs, reduction of subsidies, and so on should provide significant opportunities for accessing the Chinese market. Removal of quantitative restrictions (since China is not a country with balance of payment difficulty)

is also expected to widen export opportunities. Moreover, with transparent economic and trade policies, it should be easier for Indian companies to understand this complicated and vast market, establish their presence, and develop long-term strategies.

On the negative side, China's accession the WTO has created new challenges for India in the sphere of trade and foreign policy. India will come under increased pressure to further liberalize, particularly because China's offers on trade liberalization go well beyond India.

Chinese entry into WTO is also likely to create an impact on some sectors of the Indian industry as follows:

- In the manufacturing sector, China has developed an excellent edge over the Indian industries. Further, India cannot impose anti-dumping duties on Chinese imports without discretion.
- In the textile sector, China will capture India's market share in the European Union and other countries because of its higher productivity.
- The Indian auto industry, more particularly the two-wheeler industry, will also get adversely affected due to China's relative cost advantage. For example, China can manufacture scooters for as little as $100.

In order to reap the advantages arising post the Doha conference and China's subsequent accession to WTO, the following Indian companies decided to set up joint ventures with Chinese companies: (a) Bajaj Auto Ltd, (b) Ajanta Clocks, and (c) Videocon.

Various trade associations and the Confederation of Indian Industry feel that, on the whole, trade between China and India will increase after China's accession to the WTO.

Questions for Discussion

1. On reading the news about accession of China to the WTO, your organization, an internationally well-known name in manufacturing of bicycles, which had just two years ago started operations in India, decides to relocate its manufacturing base to China, while retaining other service and

corporate support in India. Discuss what should be the likely structure of your organization. (To help you understand the bicycle manufacturing and support services of the company, a brief outline of the product- and process-oriented activities is given here.

2. Explain the logic behind your suggested structure. What advantage can be reaped from this move? What are the likely problems your organization may encounter as a result of such a move?

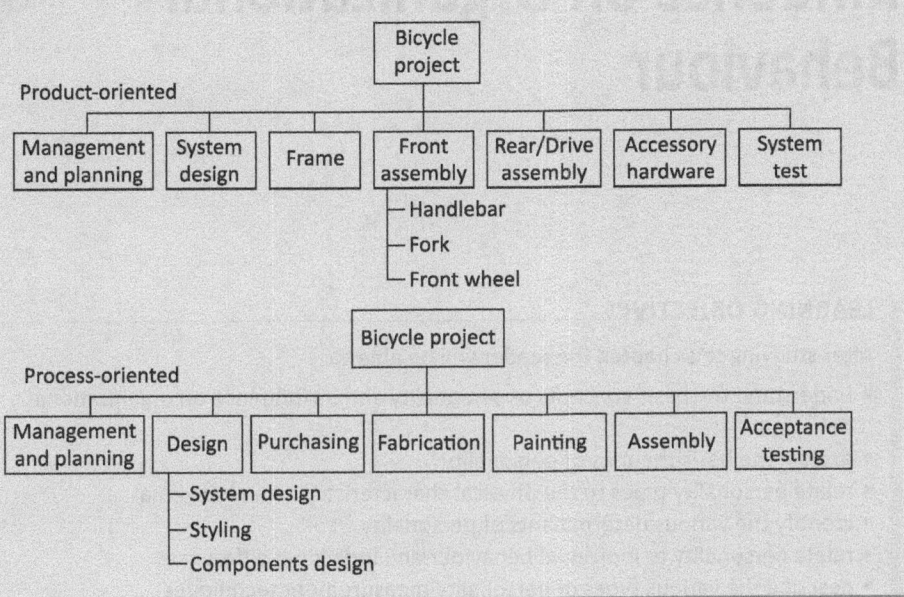

Personality and its Influence on Organizational Behaviour

LEARNING OBJECTIVES

After studying this chapter, the reader will be able to

- understand the basic concepts of personality and its influence on organizational behaviour
- explain the basic theories of personality
- relate personality types to the physical characteristics of an individual
- identify the various determinants of personality
- relate personality to individual behaviour and individual differences
- describe the various types of personality measurement techniques
- understand the different perspectives on personality
- relate personality to individual behaviour
- understand personality and the decision-making process

CASE STUDY

To Cooperate or to Defect!

Though the employees of an organization try to achieve success by means of cooperation, situations at times may compel them to defect, that is, to desert. The Princeton University's Institute of Advanced Science had elaborated this in the 1950s as the prisoner's dilemma. In the basic scenario, from which the theory has gained its name, two prisoners who the police know to have committed crime A, but whom they also wish to convict for the more serious crime B, are held in separate cells and offered the following deal:

- The one who testifies implicating the other in crime B will go free, whereas the other will receive three years in prison (the 'sucker's payoff').
- If they both testify against each other, each will receive two years.
- If they both remain silent, they will both be convicted of crime A and serve one year.

Thus, there are two choices. The first is to remain silent—to cooperate with the partner and not the police. The second option is to confess—to defect.

However, when there is no scope of communicating with the partner, as he/she is held in a separate cell, as a rational player a prisoner will choose to defect, that is, confess to implicate the other convict with the more serious crime and go free. This enables him/her to maximize the upside (zero years) and minimize the downside (two years instead of three years). The prisoner's dilemma, therefore, teaches how in a situation of crisis people compromise their personal values to exercise a rational choice.

Personality is the supreme realization of the innate idiosyncrasy of a living being. It is an act of high courage flung in the face of life, the absolute affirmation of all that constitutes the individual, the most successful adaptation to the universal condition of existence coupled with the greatest possible freedom for self-determination.

—Carl Gustav Jung 1934

INTRODUCTION

To understand organizational behaviour, it is essential to understand individual behaviour. The nature and personality of individual human beings determine their behaviour. The word 'personality' is derived from the Latin word *persona*, which denotes the masks that used to be worn by theatrical players in ancient Greek dramas. Hence, personality is the superficial social image that an individual adopts. Further, personality can also be viewed as a reflection of the most dominant characteristics that are observable in the behaviour of an individual (namely aggressiveness or shyness). It is through personality that an individual makes an overall impression on others in various social settings. A quick comparison of behaviour, character, and personality can be made as follows. Behaviour is the external appearance and not the exposition of the true feelings of the mind. Character is the index of the mind and feelings, that is, behaviour that is endorsed and directed by the mind, whereas personality is self-directed behaviour. The components of personality, therefore, are the mind (clarity and understanding), the will (steadiness and equality), the heart (conservation, warmth, expansiveness, and magnetism), the vitality (energy), and the physique (perseverance and endurance for work).

Personality is defined as some structured patterns of thoughts, feelings, and behaviour of a person. Personality patterns help us in understanding, and predicting the characteristics of a person. In organizational behaviour studies, individual personality is important because the individual personalities of the employees refer to their dynamic mental structures and coordinated processes of the mind, which determine their emotional and behavioural adjustments to the organization. Personality is dynamic because the mental structures of the individual employees continuously develop over their lifetime. Further, in organizational behaviour studies, personality and the individual behavioural pattern of the employees become an important construct to adjust and succeed in work situations. Particularly in a changing business environment, to get the right fit, employers make use of personality tests in selection and recruitment decisions. Moreover, interest in personality assessment is also important for cultural transformation in an organization. With the understanding of cognitive and emotional bases of human behaviour, personality assessment has gained further importance.

The word 'personality' is derived from the Latin word *persona*.

> In organizations, a limited view of a person is often taken, focusing more on the degree of willingness (or otherwise) to pursue organizational goals.

In this backdrop, personality studies are focusing on personality differences such as types and traits, that is, some characteristics of people that can differ from each other. Even though traditionally these are considered from a psychological point of view, understanding them holistically requires the consideration of biology (with more focus on neurology), evolution and genetics, sensation and perception, motivation and emotion, learning and memory, developmental psychology, psychopathology, and psychotherapy. There are various personality theories, but there is no unified approach.

PERSONALITY AND ORGANIZATIONAL BEHAVIOUR

The work-related behaviour of the people in an organization stems from both the environmental and individual factors. From the environmental approach, interpersonal, group, and societal influences and individual factors extend across cognitive abilities, acquired expertise, personality styles, motivation, and physical attributes.

A common aspect of personality is the manner in which one thinks of its effect on behaviour. One tends to think of personality in terms of a particular set of traits. For example, an aggressive, impatient person is thought of as one who is likely to act in an aggressive manner. The direction of the relationship is thought to stem from the personality trait and move to the behaviour. That is to say, an individual's personality greatly influences how he/she behaves and not the other way around—that the behaviour would explain the personality. For example, it is usually assumed that a shy person is not likely to go to parties, but it could also be assumed that someone who does not go to parties or other social occasions is likely to become shy. The assumed relationship between personality and work-related behaviour is one of the key reasons why it is of interest to those studying and managing organizations.

One of the fundamental issues in the understanding of people's behaviour is how a person is understood in an organizational setting. Jackson and Carter (2000) pointed out that in work organizations, a limited view of a person is often taken, focusing more on the degree of willingness (or otherwise) to pursue organizational goals. However, experience shows that in work organizations, people are more complex in their behavioural patterns. In organizational contexts, such complex behavioural syndromes can be accounted for from social and psychological standpoints. For example, one can think of people in the context of role, identity, personality, or self.

Practitioner Speak 5.1   **Companies have Split Personalities**

If companies are individuals, they often seem to have dissociative identity disorder. For many organizations, each division, function and channel has its own personality. And, frequently, there are no core corporate values consistently reflected from communications across the enterprise, so that various departments have no common ground from which to work.

Read this insightful blog posted by Ford on *HBR Blog Network* by accessing the following link: http://blogs.hbr.org/cs/2013/02/speaking_with_one_voice.html.

PERSONALITY THEORIES

According to Sigmund Freud (1856–1939), the conscious mind refers to the present perceptions, memories, thoughts, fantasies, and feelings of people. This is what people in an organization tend to be, that is, they have a propensity to be preconscious. However, Freud argues that these are not the real reflections of their minds. The largest part of the mind of a person is the state of the unconscious mind. This state of mind is not easily seen in the behaviour of the people in an organization, but is the source of their drives, instincts, and motivations. Freud's classification of the id, ego, and superego states of mind largely influences or shapes one's personality. The primary process of a mind is the id state, which translates the needs into motivational forces, that is, instincts or drives. This state of mind elevates to the ego state, relating to reality without a state of consciousness. With the influence of the ego state of mind, people develop the capability of problem-solving. This is what is called the secondary process of the mind. The primary state of the mind, that is, the id state, meets with obstacles in the world in attaining goals. Such experiences shape the superego state of the mind. Personality disorders are seen in people when they fail to keep record of such experiences and frame strategies to avoid them. They become a problem for the organization. There are two aspects of the superego—the conscience (internalization of punishments and warnings) and the ego ideal (derived from rewards and positive experiences).

Anna Freud (1895–1982), Freud's daughter, furthered Freud's research on psychoanalysis. While examining the dynamics of the psyche, she said that ego is the 'seat of observation', from which one observes the work of id and superego.

Erik Erickson (1902–94), another Freudian ego-psychologist, focused more on society and culture-related issues. According to his principle, people develop their personalities through certain stages. Progress through each stage is, in part, determined by the success or failure in all the previous stages. Each stage involves certain developmental tasks that are psychosocial in nature, and also has certain virtues or psychosocial strengths that help them through the rest of the stages of their lives.

Carl Jung (1875–1961), also a Freudian, developed the theory of collective unconscious of humanity. Jung's theory divides the psyche into three parts: ego (conscious mind), personal unconscious (not presently conscious but can be), and collective unconscious (psychic inheritance). Collective unconscious is the reservoir of our experiences and it influences our behaviour, especially the emotions.

Alfred Adler (1870–1937) postulated a single 'drive' or motivating force behind all our behaviour and experience. He calls that motivating force the 'striving for perfection'. It is our common desire to fulfil our potentials and to come closer to our ideals. It is very similar to the more popular idea of self-actualization.

Albert Ellis (1957) developed the rational emotive behavioural therapy (REBT). REBT begins with ABC. 'A' is for activating experiences, such as family troubles, unsatisfying work, early childhood traumas, and all other factors pointed to as the sources of our unhappiness. 'B' stands for beliefs, especially the irrational, self-defeating beliefs that are the actual sources of our unhappiness. 'C' denotes consequences, neurotic symptoms, and negative emotions such as depression, panic, and rage that stem from our beliefs. Although the activating experiences may be quite real and may have caused real pain, it is our irrational beliefs that create long-term disabling problems. Ellis adds D and E to ABC; 'D' indicates discussion and 'E' is the effect, which further encompasses three effects—'Ea' (emotional effect), 'Ec' (behavioural effect), and 'Eg' (mental effect).

Aaron Beck developed a form of therapy called cognitive therapy (CT—also known as CBT or cognitive behavioural therapy), which has many common features with Albert Ellis' REBT. CT is based on the idea that many psychological problems ultimately arise from cognitive 'errors', especially regarding one's self, one's world, and one's future. In an organization, managers need to help employees explore and test their beliefs and thought processes and develop better approaches to life's problems. Beck discovered that the original thinking errors are overgeneralization, minimization of positives, and maximization of negatives.

The theory postulated by Erich Fromm (1900–80) is a rather unique blend of Freud and Marx. Freud emphasized the unconscious, biological drives and repression, postulating that our characters are determined by biology. Marx, on the other hand, saw people as determined by their society and more specifically by their economic systems. Fromm added to this mix of two deterministic systems a third factor—the idea of freedom. He suggested that people tend to transcend the determinisms that Freud and Marx attributed to them. In fact, Fromm made freedom the central characteristic of human nature.

The entire system developed by B.F. Skinner (1904–90) is based on operant conditioning. An organism is in the process of 'operating' on the environment, which in ordinary terms means that it is bouncing around its world, doing what it does. During this operating process, the organism encounters a special kind of stimulus, called the reinforcing stimulus or the reinforcer. This special stimulus has the effect of increasing the operant, that is, the behaviour occurring just before the reinforcer. This is operant conditioning. The behaviour is followed by a consequence, and the nature of the consequence modifies the organism's tendency to repeat the behaviour in the future.

A behaviour followed by a reinforcing stimulus results in an increased probability of that behaviour occurring in the future. A behaviour no longer followed by the reinforcing stimulus results in a decreased probability of that behaviour occurring in the future.

Hans Eysenck (1916–97) developed the theories of temperament. Temperament in our personalities is genetic and in-born. However, it is wrong to construe that personality cannot be learned. Through the process of upbringing, people develop temperament, based on their interaction with nature. Personality types, which get influenced by temperament, are also evident in ancient Greek philosophy. This theory became popular during the middle ages. Eysenck's theory is primarily based on physiology and genetics. Although he was a behaviourist who gave great importance to learned habits, he considered personality differences as growing out of our genetic inheritance. He was, therefore, primarily interested in what is usually called temperament.

William Sheldon (1949), based on the work of Ernst Kretschmer (1930), developed a model of matching the physical types with the psychology types or personality of people. In Table 5.1, the physical types and their corresponding personality constructs are illustrated. According to Sheldon, the connection between the three physical types and the three personality types was embryonic development.

Table 5.1   Personality constructs with matching physical types

Physical type	Physical characteristics	Psychology type	Psychological characteristics
Ectomorphs	Slender, often tall people, with long arms and legs, and fine features	Cerebrotonics	Nervous types, relatively shy, often intellectual
Mesomorphs	Stockier people, with broad shoulders and good musculature	Somatotonics	Active types, physically fit and energetic
Endomorphs	Chubby people, tending to be 'pear-shaped'	Viscerotonics	Sociable types, lovers of food and physical comforts

Albert Bandura (1973) opined that behaviourism, with its emphasis on experimental methods, focuses on variables that can be observed, measured, and manipulated, and avoids whatever is subjective, internal, and unavailable, that is, mental. In the experimental method, the standard procedure is to manipulate one variable and then measure its effects on another. All this leads to a theory of personality that says that one's environment causes one's behaviour. Bandura suggested that it is true that the environment causes the behaviour, but it is also true that the behaviour causes the environment. He labelled this concept *reciprocal determinism*: the world and a person's behaviour cause each other.

The study carried out by Gordon Allport (1897–1967) indicated that one factor that motivates human beings is the tendency to satisfy biological survival needs, which he referred to as opportunistic functioning. He noted that opportunistic functioning could be characterized as reactive, past-oriented, and biological. However, Allport felt that opportunistic functioning was relatively unimportant for understanding most human behaviour, which he believed is motivated by something very different—functioning in a manner expressive of the self—which he called *propriate functioning*. Most of what people do in life is a matter of being who they are. Propriate functioning can be characterized as proactive, future-oriented, and psychological.

The theory formulated by George Kelly (1905–67) begins with his *fruitful metaphor*. He had noticed long before that scientists and therapists often displayed a peculiar attitude towards people. His fundamental postulate says this:[1] 'A person's processes are psychologically channelized by the ways in which he anticipates events.' This is the central movement in the scientific process: from hypothesis to experiment or observation, that is, from anticipation to experience and behaviour.

Donald Snygg (1904–67) and Arthur W. Combs (1912–99) said, 'All behaviour, without exception, is completely determined by and pertinent to the phenomenal field of the behaving organism.' The phenomenal field is our subjective reality, the world we are aware of, including physical objects and people, and our behaviours, thoughts, images, fantasies, feelings, and ideas such as justice, freedom, and equality. Snygg and Combs emphasize that this phenomenal field is the true subject matter for psychology.

Abraham Maslow (1908–70), through his pioneering theory on the hierarchy of needs, illustrated that the behaviours of people are primarily aimed at satisfying their unfulfilled needs, based on their priority on primary needs first, followed by subsequent need factors, which he has arranged in five orders.

---

[1] This and all subsequent quotations are from Kelly's *The Psychology of Personal Constructs* (1955).

Carl Roger (1902–87) saw people as basically good or healthy—or at the very least, not bad or ill. In other words, he saw mental health as the normal progression of life, and he saw mental illness, criminality, and other human problems as distortions of that natural tendency. Moreover, Rogers' theory is a relatively simple one when compared to that of Freud. The entire theory is built on a single 'force of life', which he calls the actualizing tendency. It can be defined as the built-in motivation present in every life form to develop its potentials to the fullest extent possible.

From the review of all these theories, it is evident that personality is not easily defined. Basically, personality refers to our attempts to capture or summarize an individual's *essence*. It is the science of describing and understanding persons and is a core area of study in psychology. Together with intelligence, the topic of personality constitutes the most significant area of study of differences in the personalities of individuals.

No two people are exactly the same—not even identical twins. Such issues of differences are fundamental to the study of personality. Even though such differences come from intelligence, the influence of personality is also found to be an important determinant.

Intelligence influences the different aspects of personality in many different ways. In fact, intelligence is sometimes considered a part of personality, though it will probably always be debated. The point to bear in mind is that both intelligence and personality are prominent individual differences.

The study of personality can be made from different perspectives such as the following:

- Trait perspective
- Biological perspective
- Psychoanalytic perspective
- Learning perspective
- Phenomenological perspective
- Cognitive perspective

DEFINITIONS OF PERSONALITY

The following are some well-known definitions of personality given by different authors.

Personality is self—an organized, permanent, subjectively perceived entity, which is at the very heart of all our experiences.

—Carl Rogers

Personality is something which guides and directs all human activities.

—Gordon Allport

Personality is the outcome of a series of psychological crisis.

—Erickson

> Luthans has defined personality as how people affect others and how they understand and view themselves, as well as their pattern of inner and outer measurable traits, and the person–situation interaction.

According to Freud, the structure of personality is composed of three elements—id, ego, and superego.

Salvatore Maddi (quoted by Boeree 2006) defined personality as a stable set of characteristics and tendencies that determine those commonalities and differences in the psychological behaviour (thoughts, feelings, and actions) of people that have continuity in time and that may not be easily understood as the sole result of the social and biological pressures of the moment.

Blanchard and Johnson (1992) say, 'As individuals mature, they develop habit patterns, or conditioned responses, to various stimuli. The sum of these habit patterns, as perceived by others, determines their personality.' It can be shown as follows:

$$\text{Habit } a + \text{habit } b + \text{habit } c + \cdots + \text{habit } n = \text{Personality}$$

Fred Luthans (1995) gives the following definition: 'Personality would mean how people affect others and how they understand and view themselves, as well as their pattern of inner and outer measurable traits, and the person–situation interaction.' He further stresses on the importance of personality traits in organizational behaviour. According to him, there are the following five personality traits that especially relate to job performance:

- *Extraversion*: Sociable, talkative, and assertive
- *Agreeableness*: Good natured, cooperative, and trusting
- *Conscientiousness*: Responsible, dependable, persistent, and achievement-oriented
- *Emotional stability*: Tense, insecure, and nervous
- *Openness to experience*: Imaginative, artistically sensitive, intellectual

Carver and Scheier (2000) provide us with a more contemporary definition of personality: 'Personality is a dynamic organization, inside the person, of psychophysical systems that create a person's characteristic patterns of behaviour, thoughts, and feelings.' Dynamic organization suggests ongoing readjustments, adaptation to experience, continual upgrading, and maintaining. Personality does not just lie there—it follows a process and is organized.

CHARACTERISTICS OF PERSONALITY

On review of the foregoing definitions, the characteristics of personality can be identified as follows:

Stability Stable personality characteristics develop consistent patterns of behaviour. Characteristics such as warm, friendly, cold, hostile, aggressive, and emotional are often found to be stable in some individuals, which influence their personalities.

Commonalities and differences in behaviour Personality characteristics may be either common or different. Hence, to understand what an individual has in common with and what is different from others, it is necessary to assess certain aspects such as the following:

- Like all other people
- Like some other people
- Like no other people

Personality induces people to behave in a manner as required by social and biological pressures. It is an abstraction based on inferences that are derived from behavioural observation.

Personality is often some uniqueness in characteristics that differentiates one individual from another. It is an evolving process, and it develops through internal and external influences, which include genetic and biological influences, social experiences, and changing environmental stimulus.

DETERMINANTS OF PERSONALITY

Several factors influence the shaping of an individual's personality. By observing the behaviour of a person, it is possible to understand the influence of specific types of behaviour on the personality characteristics of an individual. Such personality characteristics are briefly reviewed here.

Heredity   Some characteristics of our behaviour are genetic, which are inherited. Some of the traits such as physical height, slimness, dexterity, intellectual capacity, ability to learn, and logical power are also inherited. All these have a significant influence on our behavioural patterns.

Family background   The socio-economic status of the family and the education of the parents and other family members shape the personality of an individual to a considerable extent. In fact, family members try to influence the behaviour of children in a desperate attempt to personify their own values, roles, and so on.

Nature of interacting people   People influence each other and such influences shape the personality. Hence, it is often said that one's personality is constantly evolving throughout one's life.

Culture   Culture shapes our personal values and predispositions. It is the unique characteristic of a social group. The values and norms shared by the group's members set it apart from other social groups. The essence of culture is the collective programming of the mind. According to anthropological concepts, culture relates to a shared system of beliefs, attitudes, possessions, attributes, customs, and values that define group behaviour. Values are assumptions about 'how things ought to be' in the group. Thus, culture plays a significant role in influencing the behaviour of an individual.

PERSONALITY AND INDIVIDUAL DIFFERENCES

Individual difference variables explain how people are similar or different in their behaviour and how this influences their thinking and feeling. People can be classified based on their intelligence and personality attributes. In organizations, it is essential to study the psychological differences of employees because of a wide variability in their personality characteristics. The similarity or dissimilarity of the employees should be understood through the study of individual differences. Such a study of differences, using psychological and personality attributes, helps us to explain and predict individual behaviour and performance.

EXHIBIT 5.1   Personality for Employment: A Deterrent or a Determinant?

Personality plays an important role in the recruitment and selection of employees. Despite having the requisite skills, knowledge, and experience, one's candidature may be rejected because of one's personality. Employers are increasingly looking for a better cultural fit among organizations and employees. Thus, prospective employees should know what employers expect of them. A recent study by Forbes has revealed that five personality traits are regarded as highly important by most multinational companies.

Among the most sought-after personality traits for organizations, the first in line is *professionalism*. Then comes *high energy* and *confidence*. These three traits considerably influence the first impression of candidates during interviews. The way an interviewee carries himself/herself, dresses, greets the interviewer(s), and talks, wins or loses half the battle during the first 30 seconds of the interview. *Self-monitoring* is another personality trait that lends credibility to prospective candidates. A candidate's ability to perform without guidance and lead others is credited highly. Thus, candidates who can share experiences wherein they have excelled through self-motivation may be seen in better light by interviewers than others. Lastly, *intellectual curiosity* is another personality trait that can seal the deal for prospective employees. Hence, candidates whose interests are aligned with continuously learning new technologies are better placed to adapt to rapidly changing organizational environments.

Selection of employees based on personality traits has emerged as an important tool for many organizations. At least 40 per cent of the Fortune 100 companies resort to psychological testing as part of their employment procedure. Thus, with the growing importance of personality testing for employment, candidates need to be extra careful about the impression they make during interviews.

Sources: Casserly, 'Top Five Personality Traits Employers Hire Most', 4 April 2012, http://www.forbes.com/sites/meghancasserly/2012/10/04/top-five-personality-traits-employers-hire-most/, last accessed on 9 July 2013; Shaffer and Schmidt, 'Personality Testing in Employment', September–October 1999, http://www.hiringstrategies.com/personality_testing.htm, last accessed on 9 July 2013 (adapted).

People psychologically differ from each other. Some of the prevailing thoughts of differences among individuals can be attributed to the following:

- *Gender differences*: Hunters (men), gatherers (women)
- *Intelligence differences*: Caste, class, education, etc.
- *Personality differences*: Job specialization

The importance of personality in the recruitment of a candidate is shown in Exhibit 5.1.

PERSONALITY TYPES

The theory of personality types categorizes people into either distinct or discontinuous types. It is synonymous with personality styles, but is different from the personality trait theory. To illustrate the difference, introversion is a personality type, whereas a continuum of introversion to extroversion, which clusters people in the categories of middle or extremes, is a personality trait. The trait approach tries to synthesize and formalize these traits in order to explain and predict behaviour. Traits are the distinguishing qualities or characteristics of a person. They include a readiness to think or act in response to a variety of different stimuli or situations. Figure 5.1 shows the various personality types along with their dominant traits.

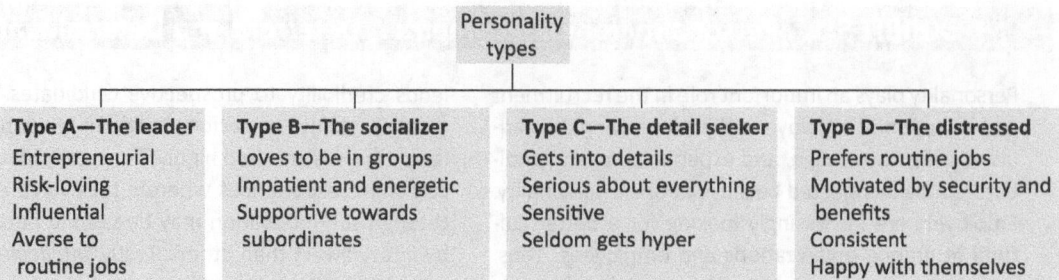

Figure 5.1 Personality types and their dominant traits

Type A Personality—Leader

People with type A personality have an entrepreneurial streak and are willing to take risks to receive the rewards that go along with their work. They are usually very independent, direct, and to the point. A manager with type A personality will always try to influence the subordinates to get to the bottom line. Type A personalities dislike routine work and get their subordinates involved (through delegation) in performing routine jobs. They enjoy change and fear routine, repetitive, protocol-bound jobs. They are focused on what they do, sometimes even remaining insensitive to others. This personality construct is evident in entrepreneurs, business owners, managers, and sales people, or in those involved in any other challenging jobs that require direct handling.

Type B Personality—Socializer

People with type B personality love to be a part of groups, and in an organization, they become the centre of attention. They love excitement and are often impatient, demanding, and highly energetic. As they want to be in the limelight, they do very well in sales, advertising, marketing, public speaking, party planning, travel, and other similar positions. Type B personalities are supportive of their subordinates and enjoy being around while the subordinates perform. Since they prefer being liked by others, if others neglect them, they take it rather personally.

Type C Personality—Detail Seeker

People with type C personality thrive on details and accuracy and are serious about everything. Accountants, engineers, computer programmers, and analysts are of this type. They are usually very neat, dress fashionably, and are very calculated and precise in just about everything they do. They do not like hype and prefer to depend on verifiable facts for decision-making. Being consistent in their actions, type C personalities follow a charted procedure and their actions are reliable. Being sensitive, they also become good customer-relation executives.

Type D Personality—Distressed

People with type D personality do not like change and prefer doing the same thing repeatedly within a set of guidelines. They are easily motivated by security and benefits. They are punctual, consistent, and supportive of others and usually feel happy and content with themselves.

PERSONALITY OPPOSITES

Personality clashes take place in an organization that has personality opposites. However, in general, personality opposites attract each other.

Practitioner Speak 5.3

The Right CEO Personality for Process Improvement

I recently argued that in industries such as distribution and logistics (Amazon, FedEx, UPS), process manufacturing (Exxon), insurance (Aetna), restaurants (McDonald's), and retail banking (Bank of America, Citibank, Wells Fargo), continuous process improvement is essential. I also argued in my last post that the CEO has a critical and unique role to play in process improvement, enabling a company's activities to be redesigned across functions and divisions. If the CEO doesn't play this role, process improvement stays comfortably within functional boundaries. For example, marketing optimizes its activities for its own benefit and the sales and customer service functions do likewise. The end-to-end process of customer acquisition and retention—getting rid of duplicate activities and information across marketing, sales and customer service—isn't touched.

Read this insightful blog posted by Power on *HBR Blog Network* by accessing the following link: http://blogs.hbr.org/cs/2010/11/the_right_ceo_personality_for.html.

Types A and D are opposites. Similarly, types C and B are opposites. Opposite personalities can complement each other when they try to understand each other's perspectives. However, in an organization, the opposites need to be properly identified and managed so as to avoid conflicts.

Jungian Types, Myers-Briggs, and Keirsey's Four Temperaments

Jungian psychology is the most widely used classification of personality. It emerges from Jung's holistic philosophy and psychology about an individual. Jung's typology, however, is not considered in the mainstream of personality, as it is not empirically driven. His perceived process of individualism is based on the strengths and weaknesses of psychological types.

Myers–Briggs developed the Myers–Briggs Type Indicator (MBTI), a commercially available questionnaire, which is widely used in business and training. It provides information and exercises for a better understanding of one's own personality type and that of others with whom the individual interacts and works.

Keirsey has renamed and reconceptualized the Jungian types; however, they relate very closely to the Jungian types. Keirsey's four temperaments refer to 'temperaments' rather than personality.

MEASUREMENT OF PERSONALITY TRAITS

Many psychologists have tried to reduce the numerous traits to a few essential ones. Among the best-known essential trait approaches are the following:

- Murray (20+ needs): 20 psychogenic needs
- Cattell (16 traits): 16 personality factors questionnaire
- Eysenck (3 traits): Eysenck personality questionnaire (EPQ)—extraversion, neuroticism, and psychoticism
- Costa and McCrae (5 traits): NEO—neuroticism, extraversion, openness to experience, agreeableness, and conscientiousness

Needs as Personality—Henry Murray

Henry Murray (1893–1988) was active in developing a theory of motivation from the 1930s to the 1960s. He believed that a need is a potentiality or readiness to respond in a certain way under certain given circumstances. It is a noun that stands for the fact that a certain trend is apt to recur (Murray 1938).

A major assumption of Murray's theory was that behaviour is driven by an internal state of disequilibrium. In other words, people lack something and this drives them. Else, they are dissatisfied and they desire something. Murray classified needs as follows:

The primary (biological) needs are food, water, air, sex, and avoidance of pain.

The following are the secondary needs (either derived from the biological needs or inherent in the psychological nature):

- Achievement, recognition, acquisition
- Dominance, aggression, autonomy
- Affiliation, rejection
- Nurturance, play, cognizance (knowledge of something)

Murray believed that stronger needs are expressed more often over time and lead to more intense behaviour.

Murray's main contribution was that he understood personality as being driven by the secondary needs: achievement, dominance, affiliation, and nurturance. The extent to which each of these needs was felt by an individual shaped his/her personality and behaviour. Since the 1960s and the 1970s, the main needs studies have also examined achievement, power, affiliation, and intimacy.

For example, the need for achievement (or achievement motivation) was studied extensively by David McLelland in the 1970s and is the most-researched need. It refers to the desire to do things well and overcome obstacles to do things better. People possessing high achievement motivation tend to choose more difficult tasks than people with low achievement motivation. This is because they want to find out more about their ability to achieve.

The need for power was studied intensely by David Winter in the 1970s. It is the desire to have dominance, impact on others, prestige, position, and influence over others. Those who have the need for power are often concerned about controlling their image that is portrayed to others. If the need for power can be combined with taking on responsibility, then 'acceptable' displays of power can be experienced.

> Murray has noted that a need is a potentiality or readiness to respond in a certain way under certain given circumstances.

The need for affiliation was studied by McAdam in the 1980s. It refers to the desire to spend time with other people. It can be more useful to look at the subcomponents, such as social comparison, emotional support, positive stimulation, and attention from others.

The need for intimacy is the desire to experience warm, close, and communicative exchanges with another person. Ultimately, it is the desire to merge oneself with another. The need for intimacy correlates (medium correlation) with the need for affiliation but focuses more on one-to-one interactions, particularly self-disclosure and listening.

Murray's needs theory is sometimes studied as a part of the trait perspective, as needs are considered akin to traits. However, it can be seen that the needs theory is studied more often within the psychoanalytic perspective because it is seen as the driving theory of personality.

Cattell's 16 Personality Factors

Cattell (1905) viewed language as a useful source of information about personality. A quality described by many words, he figured, was likely to be a more important part of personality. He used this lexical criterion in determining his original list of trait names.

Cattell narrowed Allport and Odbert's (1936) listing of over 17,000 words down to 4500 words and then narrowed these down further to 171 trait names. He then collected self-ratings on these words and conducted a factor analysis. He used both observer and behavioural data. The result was his 16 personality factors (16 PF):

- Reserved versus warm
- Concrete reasoning versus abstract reasoning
- Reactive versus emotionally stable
- Deferential versus dominant
- Serious versus lively
- Expedient versus rule conscious
- Shy versus socially bold
- Utilitarian versus sensitive
- Trusting versus vigilant
- Practical versus imaginative
- Forthright versus private
- Self-assured versus apprehensive
- Traditional versus open to change
- Group-oriented versus self-reliant
- Tolerates disorder versus perfectionist
- Relaxed versus tense

Super Traits—Hans Eysenck

Hans Eysenck (1916–97) initially thought that all people could be described in terms of two super traits, which he believed had a biological basis:

- Introversion–Extraversion (continuum of sociability, dominance, liveliness, etc.)
- Emotionality–Stability (neuroticism—continuum of being upset and distressed)
- Psychoticism (added later, less researched), a predisposition towards becoming either psychotic or sociopathic (psychologically unattached to other people); in addition, a tendency to be hostile, manipulative, and impulsive

Eysenck designed the Eysenck personality questionnaire (EPQ). A second-order factor analysis of Cattell's 16 PF shows two factors— introversion/extraversion and anxiety. Hence, the underlying factors of Cattell's scales are very similar to those of Eysenck.

An example of the research supporting the super traits was a 1968 study by Giese and Schmidt with a group of college students over the age of 19 years (reported by Eysenck 1973), in which extraversion strongly predicted the age at which the students experienced their first coitus.

There are many studies on primary personality traits, but an effective measurement of personality traits for identification and classification is widely done using the MBTI and the Big Five Model. MBTI is essentially a 100-question personality test to understand from people their feelings and actions in a given situation. The responses are then classified into four major types, namely extroverted versus introverted, sensing versus intuitive, thinking versus feeling, and judging versus perceiving. These are then combined into 16 personality types—ESTJ, INFP, ESFP, INTJ, ESFJ, INTP, ENFP, ISTJ, ESTP, INFJ, ENFJ, ISTP, ENTJ, ISFP, ENTP, and ISFJ. The attributes of some of the types are as follows:

ESTJ

The ESTJ personality types prefer dealing with facts and the present and make decisions using logic. They are organized on a logical basis and are therefore practical. They like to solve problems in a businesslike and impartial manner. They take care of details before considering any strategies.

INFP

People with INFP personality type are more focused on their inner world and therefore are driven by thoughts and emotions. They give more importance to personal values, are flexible and open to new insights, and are adaptable. They take fancy to new ideas and sometimes make very creative contributions. They like to grow and feel that others should grow too. They undertake work that has a meaningful purpose.

ESFP

People with ESFP personality type derive their energy from the outside world of actions and spoken words. They prefer dealing with facts, enjoy friendship, and are often impulsive. They tend to take part in firefighting and troubleshooting and come out with practical solutions to problems involving people.

INTJ

People with INTJ type of personality derive their energy from the inner world and more from their emotions. They deal with the patterns and possibilities for the future, making impersonal decisions. They are strategists, capable of identifying long-term goals and achieving them. However, they are also a bit sceptical and critical, both about themselves and about others. They have a keen sense of deficiencies in quality and competence.

ESFJ

The ESFJ personality types take their energy from the outer world of actions and spoken words. They deal with facts and people and make decisions based on personal values. They are very warm and seek to maintain harmonious relationships with colleagues and friends. They have a strong sense of duty and loyalty.

INTP

The INTP types take their energy from the inner world of thoughts and emotions. They make decisions based on logic. Their life is flexible and they follow new insights and possibilities. They are quiet, detached, and adaptable only when there is a clear principle. They are not interested in routine and they will often experiment or change things to see if they can be improved. They operate best when solving complex problems that require the application of intellect.

It is important to mention that the MBTI questionnaire cannot be printed here for the obvious lack of copyright. However, interested researchers can obtain this from available websites to assess the personality types of employees.

Big Five Model

Despite the wide popularity of the MBTI, its results are not always foolproof. Many researchers recommend its use only for self-awareness. The Big Five Model, in contrast, has a strong application support and often researchers feel that it is a better alternative.

A strong consensus emerged in the mid-1980s about the number and nature of personality traits. Five superordinate factors emerged, often referred to as the 'Big Five' or the five-factor model. The presence of these five factors is well supported by a wide variety of research. The following are the Big Five personality factors:

- Extroversion
- Conscientiousness
- Openness to stability
- Emotional stability
- Agreeableness

In 1949, Fiske published early evidence supporting the five-factor model. During the 1980s and 1990s, a vast array of research was combined to support the five-factor model. Not everyone, however, agrees on the nomenclature of the five super traits.

The five-factor model is commonly measured by the NEO personality inventory by Costa and McCrae (1992). The Big Five, according to the NEO are as follows (remember OCEAN or NEOAC):

- Neuroticism (emotional stability)
- Extraversion (introversion)
- Openness to experience (closeness to experiences)
- Agreeableness (disagreeableness)
- Conscientiousness (lack of conscientiousness)

Each super trait is measured by six facets (or subordinate traits). These are displayed in Table 5.2.

Table 5.2 Super traits

N	E	O	A	C
Anxiety	Warmth	Fantasy	Trust	Competence
Angry hostility	Gregariousness	Aesthetics	Straightforwardness	Order
Depression	Assertiveness	Feelings	Altruism	Dutifulness
Self-consciousness	Activity	Actions	Compliance	Achievement-striving
Impulsiveness	Excitement-seeking	Ideas	Modesty	Self-discipline
Vulnerability	Positive emotion	Values	Tender-mindedness	Deliberation

SITUATION VS PERSONALITY DEBATE

It is often believed that our personality is influenced by the circumstances and situations that surround us. Such a debate on our behaviour can be situation-specific and not based on our personality. However, since our personality also guides our behaviour, it is important for us to understand the interface between the situation and the personality, that is, how an individual's personality transcends the situation and guides the action.

In a crisis, a human resource (HR) manager needs to be more aggressive than normal. Similarly, a submissive and obedient employee can become very aggressive once provoked. Hence, it is appropriate for us to trace the behaviour of a person not only to personality factors but also to the environmental issues that perhaps act as stimuli. As a result of such assumptions, the concept of situational personality has emerged. The concept of dispositional approach to personality identifies some of the important psychological characteristics that are stable, whereas some change as per situations.

Walter Mischel (1968) challenged the assumption of personality-determined behaviour and established that our behaviour is situation-specific. Hence, the unresolved debate, whether personality is situation-specific or not, balances with the widely acceptable assumption that personality factors are characteristics held for a long time and remain consistent in their disposition, independent of situational cues.

Other common psychological tests to measure personality factors include 16 PF, DISC (drive, influence, steadiness, compliance), Thomas Profiling, FIRO-B, and Belbin Team Role Profiling. Here, some of the personality measurement tools that are used for organizational change and development have been detailed.

Japanese scientists have recently made some observations relating blood groups with personality types. However, there is not enough adequate research information to validate it. This research body of Japan does its research on blood types. The findings are reproduced in Table 5.3.

Table 5.3 Blood groups and personality

Blood group	Personality
O	They are persuasive leaders, achieve goals, trendsetters, loyal, passionate, and self-confident. The weaknesses, however, are vanity, a jealous nature, and a propensity to be competitive.
A	They like harmony and peace in organization, gel well with others, and are sensitive, patient, and affectionate. Their weaknesses, however, are stubbornness and inability to relax.

(Contd)

Table 5.3   *(Contd)*

Blood group	Personality
B	They are individualistic, creative, easily adaptable to new situations, straightforward, and prefer to do things in their own perceived way. However, being independent, they often go too far.
AB	They are cool and controlled, liked by others, and always endeavour to put people at ease. They tend to be natural entertainers, tactful, and fair. Often, however, they appear to be blunt and face difficulties in making decisions.

BIOLOGICAL PERSPECTIVES OF PERSONALITY

The biological approach is most closely linked to the dispositional perspective. Since both attempt to identify the underlying, consistent individual differences, the main areas of investigation are as follows:

- The relationship between genetics and personality
- The evolutionary explanations and evidences for the origins of personality
- Neuropsychology and personality
- Other biological functions and processes that influence human psychology and personality

LEARNING PERSPECTIVES OF PERSONALITY

Carver and Scheier (2000) examined personality from the accumulated set of learned experiences over the lifetime of individuals. Learning perspectives have their roots in the traditions of behaviourism as well as social psychology. According to Carver and Scheier, personality is 'susceptible to moulding, grinding, and polishing by the events that are from the person's unique and individual history'. Our behaviour is learnt through our experiences while interacting with the environmental forces, although the assumptions do not discard the instincts and pre-set responses to stimuli. The theory, however, discards the assumption of the innate nature of personality structure, that is, temperament, traits, instincts, and so on. Hence, for learning theorists, personality essentially is the function of learning experiences, which mould persons, making them different from one another.

PHENOMENOLOGICAL PERSPECTIVES OF PERSONALITY

Phenomenology, existentialism, and humanism are the basic fabrics of phenomenological perspectives of personality. This perspective views people as intrinsically good and self-perfecting, and they grow and evolve towards greater manifestation of their completeness, making them unique. Such uniqueness of individuals makes them different from each other and they develop their personalities as per their own potentiality. Phenomenological people, therefore, are unpredictable in their behavioural pattern and personality constructs. Organizations dislike their presence in a team, but they can do wonders in jobs that require challenge and creative inputs. Table 5.4 integrates the main theoretical perspectives on personality.

> Personality is susceptible to moulding, grinding, and polishing by the events that form the person's unique and individual history.

Table 5.4   Integration and review of main theoretical perspectives on personality

Overview of personality		
Perspectives	**Strengths**	**Weaknesses**
Biological	Testable theories with increasing validity and efficacy	Does not grapple with 'personhood' and sense of personal self
Psychoanalytic	Attention to the unconscious	Unverifiable? Sexist?
Dispositional	Good individual assessment techniques; trait-vs-type approach	May label people on basis of scores; overly-reliant on self-report instruments
Learning	Scientific analysis and practical application	Overlooks IDs present from birth
Humanistic	Optimistic, growth-oriented	Ignores scientific method
Cognitive	Captures active nature of human thought	Ignores the unconscious

PERSONALITY MEASUREMENT

Measurement of personality is done by focusing on traits, such as extraversion, to test if the scores on a test of a particular trait either relate to or predict aspects of organizational behaviour such as work commitment, job satisfaction, and employee honesty. Organizations identify such personality traits while recruiting and matching the profile of prospective employees. A primary assumption is that a particular personality trait is related to a particular work behaviour. Recruiting people based on this assumption establishes a link between interrelating complex behavioural variables with organizational and societal variables. Personality measurement seeks to identify the circumstances in which personality predicts or does not predict particular behaviours.

Three separate influences are being examined: those arising from logical, judgemental, and statistical processes. The degree of logical overlap between a personality attribute and a specific behaviour is the principal determinant of the predictiveness of a personality scale. Personality traits are not expected to be associated with behaviours unless the two are logically overlapping. Second, judgemental processes are important in the measured validity of a personality scale, since most assessments of behaviour are based on judgements made by a supervisor or another colleague. Judgements about a person's behaviour may be influenced by the aspects of the judge (his/her motivation to contribute assessments, perspicacity, etc.), characteristics of the trait or behaviour being judged (its observability, evaluativeness, etc.), and aspects of the relationship between the judge and the target person (familiarity, friendship patterns, etc.). Third, statistical influences on criterion-related validity include the reliability of scales, the variance of scores, and so on. One statistical impact arises from the pattern of correlations between a focal personality trait and other traits, which are themselves associated with the behaviour under investigation; the focal trait sometimes predicts behaviour indirectly through other personality features.

A range of instruments is used to define and assess personality traits, which may be one trait or multiple traits. The widely used measuring instruments for personality traits are those developed by Eysenck and Cattell and the Big Five Model of Costa and McCrae.

> Measurement of personality is done by focusing on traits to test if the scores on a test of a particular trait either relate to or predict aspects of organizational behaviour.

RELATING PERSONALITY TO BEHAVIOUR

Barrick and Mount (1991) using a meta-analysis of studies examined the relationship between the scores on the 'Big Five' and the measures of job performance. They suggested that personality traits could predict some types of work-related behaviour, but the correlation between a person's score on the test and his/her job performance rating (often taken from the supervisor's appraisals) was usually small. That is, there could be some relationship between the scores on a personality test and some measures of job performance, but it is not a strong relationship. More generally, Furnham (1997) points out that the research evidence on the relationship between a person's score on a personality test and the subsequent measures of job performance have not been conclusive. On looking across a range of research studies, he estimates that personality traits can account for between 15 and 30 per cent of the variance in explaining work behaviour. That leaves between 70 and 85 per cent of the variance in people's work behaviour to be explained by factors other than personality traits. These would include organizational issues such as the organizational structure, activities, norms, and other individual variables such as the attitude to work and the behaviour at work.

The relationship between personality and organizational behaviour can be seen as bidirectional, that is, organizations are as likely to shape and influence the formation of individual personalities as the individual personalities are likely to shape the personalities of organizations. Thus, through particular patterns of reward in organizations, individuals are socialized into particular forms of personality functioning. A critique of the concept of personality is outlined here.

Personality research typically examines the employees' responses to the scales of a personality inventory in relation to other people's judgements of them on behavioural criteria. Investigations are based on the measurement of logical, statistical, and judgemental attributes of the personality traits and behaviours under investigation. How well can different personality–behaviour correlations be predicted by these three sets of features? Each set has been found to be important. For example, it has been shown that criterion-related validity is directly proportional to the degree of logical overlap between the aspects of personality and behaviour under investigation.

> The relationship between personality and organizational behaviour can be seen as bidirectional, that is, organizations are as likely to shape and influence the formation of individual personalities as the individual personalities are likely to shape the personalities of organizations.

Recent investigations have focused on the Big Five methodology and on the sales performance. It has been shown that relationships between the Big Five personality factors and employee behaviour can be underestimated by the common practice of averaging correlations from separate components of a factor. Effective sales performance has been found, sometimes, to be linked with levels of agreeableness that are low rather than high, contrary to common expectations. Other studies are examining how criterion-related validity can depend on the source of criterion ratings. Although an employee's boss prefers to use a published framework for assessing employees' behaviour, personality can be better predicted when the assessment also considers inputs from the employees' peers and subordinates. These issues are being investigated in a number of job settings.

Causes of Human Behaviour

Human behaviour is broadly classified into two characteristics—inherited characteristics and learned characteristics. External forces usually do not influence inherited characteristics and these may not be the determinants of performance. Physical characteristics are one of the inherited characteristics. Such characteristics relate to height, vision, and stamina. Another inherited characteristic is intelligence, and the degree of intelligence determines behaviour. For example, intelligent people are more responsive to change. They can be easily convinced and their behaviour is more stable and predictable. Likewise, sex, age, and religion are also inherited characteristics, which have some influence on the behaviour of an individual.

Learned characteristics, on the contrary, result in a permanent change in behaviour. Learning is the result of interactions with the environment. It involves an individual's attitudes, values, and perceptions and the environment around the individual. Perception is a process of receiving, selecting, organizing, interpreting, checking, and reacting to sensory stimuli. Through perception, one processes a piece of information and then interprets it to deduce a sensible meaning.

> Perception is a generic term for the complex sensory control of behaviour.

Attitude, on the other hand, is a perception with a frame of reference. It is a stable way of thinking, perceiving, and acting towards a situation or object. Personality is a set of traits and characteristics that form the habit, strength, and a static response pattern to a certain stimuli. Values are the basic convictions that depict an individual's moral structure and help to determine what is right and what is wrong.

PERCEPTION AND ITS INFLUENCE ON INDIVIDUAL BEHAVIOUR

Perception is the result of processing of information received by individuals regarding various events around them. It involves the organization of inputs through a dynamic inner process, which shapes all that comes in from the outside environment. This information-processing approach rests on the assumption that a person's perceptions of another are based on the information available about the other person and how one uses this information. Various researches on perception revealed that quite often a perceiver uses his/her own race or gender biases to make certain assumptions about another person. The individual, while perceiving the world, provides a picture that expresses his/her own individual view. This may differ from the reality. The study of the difference between the perceptual world and the real world is of great significance in organizational behaviour. Since the behaviour of an individual at work is the product of the individual's perceptions, it is important for a manager to understand not only his/her own perceptions but also the perceptions of his/her subordinates to create a situation under which their behaviour might improve.

Perceptual Set

Perception is a generic term for the complex sensory control of behaviour. It is inferred from a hypothetical internal event of an unspecified nature, controlled largely by external stimulation and variables such as habit and drive. Therefore, it is appropriate to state that people tend to perceive what they expect to perceive. This is the primary reason why different individuals perceive the same situation in different ways. An understanding of the perceptual process helps us

EXHIBIT 5.2   Perceiving Perception at the Workplace

According to the great Chinese philosopher Lao Tse, 'Knowing others is wisdom; knowing yourself is enlightenment.' Awareness about oneself can be vastly beneficial, especially in the organizational context. On the one hand, it helps realize better one's potential to the hilt, and on the other, it helps control what others perceive of you.

Perceptions can be helpful as well as detrimental, especially at the workplace. The way one is perceived is hard to understand since very few people come up with real feedback on enquiry. However, it is important to know how one is seen by others and understand if there is a gap in one's intent and the way it is perceived.

There are times when perceptions become reality unless they are managed properly. Managing perceptions can be an uphill task since it is concerned with controlling what others think of us. Moreover, even if one manages to get feedback, most of the times it is hardly constructive. Thus, ideally one should look for people who take keen interest in observing his/her behaviour and is ready to give feedback worth paying heed to.

Subsequently, one should work on changing the negative perception. This may take time and can happen only when a person is conscious of how he/she is being perceived by others. In this regard,

Scott Eblin, a noted management consultant, has come up with a three-step approach:

- *One should bring in some difference in one's behaviour.* This is necessary since there must be some truth in others' perceptions. One should understand that there is obviously something wrong with the way one behaves in the workplace and that has generated the negative perception. Thus, some changes become necessary for turning around perceptions.
- *One should help people take note of one's behavioural changes.* Colleagues and superiors at the workplace are too preoccupied with their problems and work pressure. Thus, they may fail to take note of the conscious efforts one is putting in to change others' perceptions. Therefore, at times, one should enquire if others notice any difference in his/her behaviour. Even if they have not noticed it earlier, they may then think and recognize the difference.
- *Patience is the key.* One cannot expect radical changes in perception overnight. It takes time and continuous conscious efforts from the concerned individual to bring about a difference in the way people see him/her. So, one has to keep trying until such time people change their perceptions.

Sources: Fortner, 'Manage Perceptions in the Workplace', 13 October 2010, http://thebusinesstimes.com/manage-perceptions-in-the-workplace/, last accessed on 10 July 2013; Eblin, 'Their Perception is Your Reality', 5 July 2012, http://eblingroup.com/2012/07/their-perception-is-your-reality-2.html, last accessed on 11 July 2013 (adapted).

to understand why individuals behave in the way they do. Exhibit 5.2 talks about the importance of managing perceptions at the workplace.

INDIVIDUAL BEHAVIOUR AND PERFORMANCE

Let us examine the correlation between the influences of individual behaviour on the performance. Individual performance is primarily the result of three important characteristics, which are an individual's capacity to perform, his/her willingness to perform, and organizational support. Due to the influence of behaviour on the performance of an individual, organizational behaviour as a subject has started receiving much importance and has now become a core area of study for management students.

> Individual performance primarily includes an individual's capacity to perform, his/her willingness to perform, and organizational support.

The following are the most important personality attributes that may influence organizational behaviour:

Locus of control   This means both internal and external controlling power.

Machiavellianism   This is an individual's propensity to manipulate people to satisfy their personal interests. With high machiavellianism, an individual tends to be cool, logical, and pragmatic, maintains emotional distance, and tries to control people, events, and situations.

Self-esteem   This too determines the behaviour of the people in an organization. People with high self-esteem like more challenging assignments, whereas people with low self-esteem tend to show susceptibility to external influences.

Self-monitoring   The power of self-monitoring enables individuals to adjust their behaviours to external factors and situations and makes them adaptable to situations.

Risk-taking   This propensity also reflects on managerial behaviour in decision-making. Managers with a disposition towards high risk-taking tend to take more rapid decisions and do not make use of elaborate information in making a decisional choice. Those who tend to take fewer risks, on the other hand, believe in routine decisions that may lead to known outcomes.

THINKING AND DECISION-MAKING PROCESS

Due to differences in individual personalities, perceptions, attitudes, and thinking, the decision-making process differs from manager to manager. For obvious behavioural significance in decision-making, one needs to understand the behavioural implications and the differences in information processing that ultimately lead to decision-making.

Of the three different roles of managers, namely interpersonal, informational, and decisional, the decision-making role is very significant and is in fact the real test of a manager. Information processing is essentially a cognitive process. Pre-existing systems of knowledge and experiences, which also include beliefs, propositions, schemes, and theories, develop our interpretative capability to attach meaning to any information. These processes follow three major approaches.

Normative approach   Lens model of information processing is a normative approach. It develops a response capability in an individual to achieve some intended objectives (associated with a task).

Cognitive approach   This approach uses expectancy, demand, and incentives that drive an individual to process information and is often referred to as cerebral competency.

Process-tracing approach   This approach obtains measures of event (processes) between information input and output stages, that is, between the information received from the task environment and the end result.

IMPRESSION MANAGEMENT

Impression management is a process by which people try to control or manage the perception others hold about them. At the workplace, people try to present themselves in a way that impresses others. Impression has implications in customer relations, interpersonal relations, and

> Impression management is a process by which people try to control or manage the perception others hold about them.

the overall performance management of individuals. Similar to other cognitive processes (perception), impression management also follows a defined process. It is studied in relation to aggression, attitude change, and attributions. The following are the two major components of impression management:

Impression motivation   Impression motivation in organizations motivates the subordinates, because they realize that their boss perceives them positively and values their goals.

Impression construction   This is a form of a specific type of impression that the superiors nurture using self-respect, identity images, role constraints, target's values, and current social image. These five factors create the influence in impression construction.

Impression management strategies in organizations are twofold: demotion prevention and promotion enhancement. Demotion preventive strategies are adopted in negative events, to ensure that one is not perceived in a negative manner. Such strategies make use of excuses, apologies, and even, at times, disassociation. Disassociation strategy is relevant in those cases wherein people realize that their participation in decision-making will lead to failure (based on their past experience). Promotion enhancement strategies involve entitlements, enhancements, and association.

William Gardner (1992) suggests that while managing impression, an individual should not try to make use of an image that is not compatible with him/her. This may make the boss appear unconvincing to the subordinates. For example, if a manager asks the subordinates to follow certain norms that he/she does not follow, it may have a negative impact on the impression. Thus, in managing organizational behaviour, managers need to practise impression management by protecting their self-image with a deliberate attempt to influence the positive perception of their subordinates. Non-verbal cues like smiles or eye contacts and verbal cues like appreciation (even for small achievements) work better in impression management.

SUMMARY

In this chapter, we discussed the different aspects of individual behaviour and their influence on organizational behaviour. Organizational behaviour studies help us to understand the individual, interpersonal, small group, and intergroup behaviour of people. The important variables in organizational behaviour are people, structure, technology, and environment. Understanding such behavioural issues is important to achieve organizational goals and objectives. Individual behaviour is the outcome of personality. Hence, personality and its constructs have been explained to scientifically determine

what constitutes the personality of an individual. Similarly, perception and its influence on human behaviour have also been examined, and finally behaviour and its influence on performance have been dealt with to lay the foundation for our discussion on organizational behaviour. Individual personality, perception, attitude, thinking, and the decision-making process differ from manager to manager. Thus, organizational behaviour can be defined as the analysis of the structure and functions of organizations and of the behaviour of the groups and individuals within them.

KEY DEFINITIONS

Decision-making process   Due to the differences in individual personalities, perception, attitude, and

thinking, the decision-making process differs from manager to manager. For obvious behavioural significance in decision-making, one needs to understand the behavioural implications and the differences in information processing that ultimately leads to decision-making.

Operant conditioning   This process was developed by B.F. Skinner. An organism is in the process of 'operating' on the environment, which in ordinary terms means that it is bouncing around its world, doing what it does. During this operating process, the organism encounters a special kind of stimulus called the reinforcing stimulus or the reinforcer. This special stimulus has the effect of increasing the operant—that is, the behaviour occurring just before the reinforcer.

Perceptual set   Perception is the generic term for the complex sensory control of behaviour. It is inferred from a hypothetical internal event of an unspecified nature, largely controlled by external stimulation and variables such as habit and drive. Therefore, it is appropriate to state that people tend to perceive what they expect to perceive. This is the primary reason why different individuals perceive the same situation in different ways.

Phenomenological perspective   Phenomenological perspective believes that people 'introspect', that

is, concentrate and report on subjective conscious experiences. Introspection was seen as lacking in scientific rigour and as not having any particular application. Then psychoanalysis, which emphasized the unconscious mind, was developed and became more dominant.

Rational emotive behavioural therapy   This was developed by Albert Ellis and it begins with ABC. A is for activating experiences, such as family troubles, unsatisfying work, early childhood traumas, and all other things pointed to as the sources of our unhappiness. B stands for beliefs, especially irrational, self-defeating beliefs that are the actual sources of our unhappiness. C stands for consequences, neurotic symptoms, and negative emotions such as depression, panic, and rage that stem from our beliefs.

Socializer—Type B personality   People of this type love to be part of groups and organizations. They become the centre of attention. They love excitement, are often impatient and demanding, and possess high energy levels. As they want to be in the limelight, they do very well in sales, advertising, marketing, public speaking, party planning, travel, and other similar positions.

CONCEPT-REVIEW QUESTIONS

5.1   Define the term personality and explain its various characteristics.

5.2   Explain the various theories of personality and distinguish between descriptive and predictive theories.

5.3   Explain the influence of behaviour and personality on decision-making.

5.4   What is perception? Explain the factors influencing the perceptual process.

5.5   Explain the significance of organizational behaviour. What are the main variables of organizational behaviour?

5.6   Write short notes on the following:
   (a) Perception
   (b) Perceptual set
   (c) Individual behaviour versus organizational behaviour
   (d) Lens model

CRITICAL THINKING QUESTIONS

5.1   For the recruitment of customer care executives for an automobile manufacturing organization riddled with customer complaints, you have been asked to suggest some personality assessment tools. Accordingly select the tools and also

recommend how the use of such tools will benefit the recruitment and selection process keeping in mind the unique nature of this job.

5.2   Many organizations still believe that the individual behaviours of the people in the workplace largely get influenced by group norms. One such organization, engaged in software development, recruited the best talent from different campuses. The selection process was based on technical tests and the innovativeness of the applicants. As the company develops ERP solutions, every programmer is required to collect inputs from different cross-functional team members. Of late, the company identified gap areas in coordination between different cross-functional team members, resulting in delays in developmental work. Understand this situation and comment on how the company can avoid such a situation, duly addressing personality issues.

SELECT BIBLIOGRAPHY

- Allport, G.W. and H.S. Odbert, 'Trait Names—A Psycholexical Study', *Psychological Monograph*, Vol. 47, 1936.
- Barrick, M.R. and M.K. Mount, 'The Big Five Personality Dimensions and Job Performance: A Meta Analysis', *Personnel Psychology*, Vol. 44, Issue 1, 1991, pp. 1–26.
- Bhattacharyya, Dipak Kumar, *Human Resource Research Methods*, Oxford University Press, New Delhi, 2007.
- Boeree, George, *Personality Theories: Introduction*, www.social.psychology.de/cc/click.php?Td=25, last accessed on 24 July 2007.
- Carver, C.S. and M.F. Scheier, *Perspectives on Personality*, 4th ed., Simon and Schuster, Needham Heights, 2000.
- Costa P.T. and R.R. McCrae, 'Revised NEO Personality Inventory and NEO Five-factor Inventory: Professional Manual', *Psychological Assessment Resources*, Odessa, 1992.
- Ellis, Albert, 'Outcome of Employing the Techniques of Psychology', *Journal of Clinical Psychology*, Vol. 13, 1957, pp. 344–50.
- Eysenck, H.J., *The Structure of Human Personality*, Methuen, London, 1953.
- Feist, J., *Theories of Personality*, 3rd ed., Harper San Francisco, New York, 1985.
- Funder, D.C., *The Personality Puzzle*, W.W. Norton and Company, New York, 1997.
- Furnham, A., *Personality and Demographic Determinants of Leisure and Sports Performance*, www.sportsscience.ro/htm/reviste_2004_38.5.html, last accessed on 24 July 2007.
- Hersey, Paul, Kenneth H. Blanchard, and Dewey E. Johnson, *Management of Organisational Behaviour—Leading Human Resources*, 8th ed., Pearson Education, Inc., Delhi, 2002.
- Jackson, Norman, and Pippa Carter, *Rethinking Organisational Behaviour*, 4th ed., Prentice Hall, New York, 2000.
- Jung, C., *Psychological Types,* Routledge and Kegan Paul, London, 1923.
- Kelly, George, *The Psychology of Personal Constructs, Routledge*, London, 1955.
- Luft, J., 'The Johari Window', *Human Relations Training News*, Vol. 5, Issue 1, 1961, pp. 6–7.
- Luthans, Fred, *Organizational Behaviour*, 7th ed., McGraw-Hill International, New York, 1995.
- Murray, H.A., *Exploration in Personality*, Oxford University Press, New York, 1938, pp. 124.
- Myers, I.B. and M.H. McCaulley, *A Guide to the Development and Use of Myers-Briggs Type Indicator*, Consulting Psychologist Press, Palo Alto, 1985.
- Sheldon, William, *Varieties of Delinquent Youth*, Harper and Row, New York, 1949.
- Walter, Mischel, *Personality and Assessment*, Wiley, New York, 1968.
- Warr, P.B., D. Bartram, and A. Brown, 'Big Five Validity: Aggregation Method Matters', *Journal of Occupational and Organizational Psychology*, Vol. 78, 2006, pp. 377–86.
- Warr, P.B., D. Bartram, and T. Martin, 'Personality and Sales Performance: Situational Variation and Interactions between Traits', *International Journal of Selection and Assessment*, Vol. 13, 2005, pp. 87–91.
- Warr, P.B. and S. Hoare, 'Personality, Gender, Age and Logical Overlap in Multi-source Ratings', *International Journal of Selection and Assessment*, Vol. 10, 2002, pp. 279–91.

CASE STUDY

Dabur India Limited—Success Story of a Century-old Indian Conglomerate

Dabur India Limited is a leading Indian consumer goods company with diversified interests in health care, personal care, and foods. Dabur commenced its operations in 1884 and today it is a multi-location, multi-product enterprise. The company has gone a long way in popularizing a whole range of products based on the traditional science of Ayurveda and making them easily available to people in more than 50 countries, including the Middle East, Southeast Asia, Africa, the European Union, and the American continents. It has collaborated with leaders in their fields to set up joint ventures in India.

The present organizational structure of Dabur is divided into two major small business units (SBUs)—Consumer Care Division (CCD) and Consumer Health Division (CHD)—and three subsidiary group companies—Dabur Foods, Dabur Nepal, and Dabur International. Dabur International again has three step-down subsidiaries—Asian Consumer Care in Bangladesh, African Consumer Care in Nigeria, and Dabur Egypt. Dabur today has 17 ultra-modern manufacturing units spread across the globe. It markets its products in 60 countries with 50 C&F agents, 5000 distributors, and 3.4 million retail outlets in India alone.

CCD, which can be categorized into fast-moving consumer group (FMCG) products, has two product lines: personal care and health care. Leading brands under this category are Dabur Vatika, Anmol, Hajmola, Dabur Amla Chyawanprash, and Lal Dant Manjan. The company has successfully positioned honey as a food product.

CHD of Dabur deals with more than 250 classical Ayurvedic medicines. These are sold both through prescriptions and over the counter. Some of the major categories are Asav Arishtas, Ras Rasayanas, Churnas, and medicated oils. Some of the proprietary Ayurvedic medicines are Nature Care Isabgol, Madhuvaani, and Trifgol.

Vision

Dabur is driven by its vision statement: Dedicated to the health and well-being of every household.

Its strategic intents have their roots in its vision. Though the company primarily works to 'significantly accelerate profitable growth' focusing on its core brands by leveraging its state-of-the-art technology and spreading market reach to new geographical areas, some of the intents indicate that Dabur is more a value-driven company. Whether such strategic intents have their roots in its traditional Ayurvedic product-mix or not is a matter of debate. However, the company's strategic intents are certainly visible in some of its internal practices. The following are some of its strategic intents:

- Provide the consumers with innovative products that are within easy reach.
- Build a platform to enable the company to become a global Ayurvedic leader.
- Be a professionally managed employer of choice, attracting, developing, and retaining quality personnel.
- Be responsible citizens with a commitment to environmental protection.
- Provide superior returns, relative to the peer group, to the shareholders.

Strategic Intents of Dabur

Dabur has successfully translated its strategic intents to its internal practices, as mentioned earlier. The core values are ownership, passion for winning, development of people, consumer focus, teamwork, innovation, and integrity.

New initiatives have also come forth in the field of HR mobilization. Being the fourth-largest FMCG in the country, Dabur India Limited's unique module in this field gives a whole new dimension to evolving HR practices. A newly incorporated module at Dabur is the e-learning programme, termed as Employee Orientation on Web for Engagement and Reference (EMPOWER).

The primary aim of this plan is to enable all employees to get accustomed to the Dabur culture instantaneously with the aid of daburnet. The plan is self-based and is available on the intranet. This practice is the foundation for transparency and open communication for growth, which form the pillars of its success.

Through EMPOWER, Dabur is trying to build a sense of belonging among its employees. This new web-based module is aimed at bringing about an atmosphere conducive to its organizational culture in today's growing and competitive age. The company recognizes the growing importance of its human asset to sustain itself in this competitive race and, therefore, strives to revamp its HR perspective right from the organization's lowest level. Dabur intends to build a cohesive work environment, where people will take pride in what they do, not just because it is valuable work but also because they want to work for the good of the organization.

Today, a job is no longer measured merely in terms of its pay scale, but there are many more dimensions attached to it, which make it valuable. Therefore, organizations like Dabur have resorted to building up a culture for themselves, which will attract employees not only by means of good pay packages but also by promising useful work and a good work environment that is sensitive to employee needs.

One of the important strategies of Dabur is to 'be the most sought out employer'. To achieve this strategy, Dabur focuses on the following action plan:

- Career development of employees to be planned
- Career mapping and management development with organizational development initiatives to be carried out
- Delegation and decentralization to be made
- Identification of training needs of the employees to be done more frequently and followed more diligently
- Innovativeness and creativity of employees to be given more weightage, given proper recognition, and suitably rewarded
- A system of flexible rewards and choosing of incentives to be introduced

Integration of Business Strategy with Human Resources Strategy

The HR at Dabur plays a vital role in strategy formulation. It ensures the right amount of personnel at the right time. By using various tools, the HR ensures job-fit candidates in accordance with the competencies required for carrying out the job. It calculates the future manpower requirements, thus ensuring the requisite strength of manpower for future assignments. It also visualizes the future manpower's competency requirements.

With its humble beginning in the year 1884, Dabur boasts of having crossed a market capitalization figure of $5 billion in the year 2013. Dabur India Limited has marked its presence with some very significant achievements and today commands a market leadership. Its story of success is based on dedication to nature, corporate and process hygiene, dynamic leadership, and commitment to its partners and stakeholders. The results of its policies and initiatives speak for themselves.

Work Environment in Dabur

To support the strategic intent, which translates its vision into action, and its core values, Dabur's internal practices emphasize the following:

People development 'People are our most important asset. We add value through result-driven training, and we encourage and reward excellence.' This is the basis of employee relationship, and Dabur strongly feels this focus helped it to achieve its current status. The company takes special care of its employees by recognizing and rewarding good performance and focusing on continuous employee development, by keeping pace with changing requirements, without rendering people obsolescent and junk, by focussing on continuous skill development, and by strengthening familial bonds. Dabur truly addresses the need for the Indian *gurukul* system. To further ensure that the organization does not suffer from geriatric problems, in view of Dabur's more than 100 years of existence, Dabur continuously recruits young and dynamic professionals, inducting them either laterally (in case of those who are experienced) or as management/engineer trainees by visiting campuses. Newly recruited employees are continuously upgraded, exposing them to new learning experiences and rigorous functional and conceptual inputs, backed by an efficient performance management system.

Career path On joining Dabur, one becomes part of a committed team. Performance-driven career development opportunities provide scope for those who have abilities to rise up the ladder. An example of the career path in sales and marketing is shown in the figure.

Internal control Through its 'direct touch team' programme (launched in 2002), Dabur maintains a platform for its employees and business associates in their 'whistle blowing' campaign to eliminate malpractices in its systems. Its principal objectives are to look into unethical behaviour, malpractices, wrongful conduct, fraud, and violation of the company's policies, code of ethics, and laws. This platform allows quick and transparent action, without prejudicing the interests of the complainant.

Questions for Discussion

1. Critically evaluate Dabur's approach to align people with the organization.
2. How are century-old organizations like Dabur, which focus on a traditional product line, still able to sustain in a competitive market?
3. Can you relate any core competency of Dabur that, perhaps, benefited Dabur to get its distinct identity?
4. Identify some of the wrong human relations approaches of Dabur, if any, that you feel could be a deterrent for its long-term growth.

Attitude and its Measurement

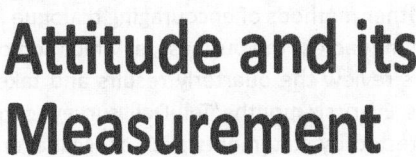

LEARNING OBJECTIVES

After studying this chapter, the reader will be able to

- understand the meaning and concept of attitude
- describe how employees' attitudes relate to organizational behaviour
- appreciate the importance of employees' attitude to support organizational business plans
- explain the process of attitude development
- measure the attitudes of employees by developing relevant questionnaires and selecting appropriate scales

CASE STUDY

Dell—A Great Place to Work

Dell Computers of the US is ranked the third most admired company by *Fortune* magazine. The company delivers value to customers through its direct business model by focusing on the customer's experience. Primarily data-driven, in Dell, the managers report the achievements of their targets on a day-to-day basis. The attitude of Dell's employees is strongly influenced by their aspirations to be a 'great company and a great place to work' through the adoption of a 'winning culture'. Dell's primary focus is on its teams and on individual contributions to the teams. People or line managers are expected to interact with individuals, and their performance

in this area is closely monitored. Both people managers and individual contributors are evaluated on the way in which they deal with people as well as on their technical proficiency. There is consistent emphasis on how people do their jobs, and not just on what they do, including, for example, support for colleagues and behaving ethically.

The company makes a conscious effort to recruit people who have a good *fit* with its values—people who are open, direct, and focus on getting the jobs done rather than engaging in office politics. Each year, the company conducts a leadership programme, which focuses on personal development planning.

Employee engagement is driven by the relationship between individuals and their managers. The expectations of people managers are clearly defined as follows:

- Set a performance plan.
- Work on individual development plans in each team.
- Undertake mid-year review.
- Undertake year-end review.
- Undertake monthly review with each individual (thirty minutes to one hour).
- Give feedback to improve performance.

Dell evaluates its people managers' compliance with their performance management targets, tracking the achievements at each stage. In addition, senior managers are expected to take opportunities to regularly engage with the junior staff, for example, at 'brown bag' lunches with different groups or while visiting operations in other countries, to help embed a common culture.

Other methods of encouraging dialogue include meetings across the business, at which senior managers review the quarterly results and take questions. Every six months 'Tell-Dell' surveys core areas suggested by statements such as 'Management is doing a good job positioning the company to win in the marketplace', 'My manager is effective at managing people', 'I receive ongoing feedback that helps me improve my performance', 'My manager sets a good example of ethical business behaviour', and 'I would recommend Dell as a great place to work'. The surveys provide a broad measure of employee engagement.

The data is analysed to identify trends. Managers are then provided with the task of sharing the results with their teams and developing team action plans to address issues and drive improvements.

INTRODUCTION

Attitude is an enduring evaluation—positive or negative—of people, objects, and ideas. Thus, attitudes are evaluative statements or judgements concerning objects, people, or events. Attitude has three components—cognition, affection, and behaviour of people. A particular attitude of a person can be based on any of these components. Cognition-based attitude is primarily based on the beliefs and properties of an attitudinal object. Affection-based attitude stems from people's feelings (e.g., attitudes towards political candidates). Behaviour-based attitude is based on the self-perception of one's own behaviour when the initial attitude is weak or ambiguous. The affection–behaviour (A–B) relationship comprises moderating variables (i.e., importance, specificity, accessibility, social pressures, and direct experience). The self-perception theory uses the attitudes after an event to make sense out of an action taken.

For organizational behaviour, the attitude of the employees is especially significant, as job satisfaction, job involvement, and organizational commitment largely stem from an individual employee's attitude. Job satisfaction refers to the general attitude of the employees towards their jobs. Job involvement helps in the psychological identification of people with their jobs; whereas organizational commitment is the degree to which an employee identifies with a particular organization and its goals and wishes to maintain membership in the organization. In an organization, people seek consistency among their attitudes and seek to reconcile with divergent attitudes in order to appear rational and consistent.

> Attitudes are evaluative statements or judgements concerning objects, people, or events.

An attitudinal change in a person takes place with a change in the behaviour. The cognitive dissonance theory facilitates the change of attitude through behavioural reinforcement. Persuasive communication and focus on a particular issue facilitate such change of attitude. Hovland, et al. (1953) proposed the Yale Attitude Change Model, which suggests the study of conditions under which people are most likely to change their attitudes. (The Yale Attitude Change Model focuses on the effectiveness of persuasive communication, which depends on the credibility and attractiveness of the speakers.) These conditions are the source of communication (i.e., credible speaker), nature of communication, and nature of audience. The communication between a doctor and a patient on a medical issue (credible source), communication that does not intend to influence people (nature of communication), and persuasive communication to distract an audience within the age group of 18–25 years are likely to yield better results in attitudinal changes. Elaboration-likelihood Model (Petty and Cacioppo 1981), on the other hand, shows that people change their attitudes in two ways—concept (central route to persuasion) and conditions for the central route to persuasion (motivation). The central route to persuasion motivates people to pay attention to the facts in a communicated message. When the facts are logical and compelling, attitudinal changes take place promptly. Therefore, the contents of the messages are especially important. On the contrary, when the facts are not compelling, people are swayed only by peripheral cues such as the mood, emotion, and attractiveness of the speaker. Such peripheral cues may facilitate to enhance motivation but not attitudinal changes. The conditions for the central route to persuasion reinforce motivation by focusing on personal relevance so that people can pay attention to the arguments.

The influence of emotion on attitude changes depends on the routes to persuasion. Emotion or mood manipulation is effective only for the peripheral route to persuasion.

People pay more attention to a speech when the argument is strong and effective in changing their attitudes. People in a sad mood take the central route to persuasion, whereas in a happy mood they take the peripheral route to persuasion. Therefore, attitudinal changes take place when people take the central route to persuasion, such as fear and possibility of harm, which gives better results in inducing attitudinal changes. Hence, managers should use the central route to persuasion, duly inducing the arousal of fear and combining it with a persuasive and appealing message.

In managing organizational behaviour, it should be noted that similar to personality and emotional intelligence, individual employees differ in terms of attitude as well. Eagly and Chaiken (1993) defined attitude as 'a psychological tendency that is expressed by evaluating a particular entity with some degree of favour or disfavour'. Yet, from another perspective, attitude is defined as the way we reflect our values. For example, the innate value systems of the employees may make them optimistic, always looking at the brighter side and working smartly to get a positive outcome. They not only nurture such value-laden attitudes in their own behaviour but also view others from the same perspective. The concept of attitude has a rich history (Fleming 1967). Once used to describe the spatial orientation of physical objects such as statues, the concept has evolved to refer to a person's mental and neural state of readiness (Allport 1935).

DEFINITION AND CONCEPTS

Attitude is the mental state of individuals that tends to act or respond, or is ready to respond for or against objects, situations, and so on, with which their vested feelings, effects, interests,

> Attitude is the mental state of individuals that tends to act or respond, or is ready to respond for or against objects, situations, and so on, with which their vested feelings, effects, interests, liking, desires, and so on are directly or indirectly linked or associated.

liking, desires, and so on are directly or indirectly linked or associated. During the course of development, a person acquires tendencies to respond to objects. These learned cognitive mechanisms are called attitudes. Changes in knowledge are followed by a change in attitudes. Attitudes are different from knowledge in the sense that attitudes are emotion-laden. Knowledge reinforces attitudes and the reinforced attitudes eventually reinforce individual and group behaviour. Hence, attitude is neither behaviour nor the cause of behaviour, but it relates to an intervening predisposition or a frame of reference that influences the behaviour of an individual.

When the interests or feelings of individuals are not connected in any way with the object or situation, their responses (towards the said object or situation) will then constitute their opinions and not their attitudes.

In many research works, especially by the Chartered Institute of Personnel and Development (CIPD) UK, employee attitudes and commitments were found to be strongly associated with business performance, and managers saw the employee voice as contributing to the performance via better employee contributions and productivity gains. The informal climate of involvement and consultation appears to be more strongly associated with employee satisfaction and commitment than the collective machinery for negotiation and consultation. The mechanisms in use for employee voice include two-way communications, project teams, and joint consultation, but there is growing interest in electronic media, attitude surveys, and partnership schemes. The major constraints on employee voice are the lack of skills and enthusiasm on the part of the managers and employees. The Psychological Contract Model, validated by successive employee attitude surveys, suggests that human resource (HR) practices strongly affect the way people feel about their work. Employees' trust in the organization, their sense of being fairly treated, and the extent to which they believe their employer has delivered on the implicit deal between them affect their attitudes towards job satisfaction, commitment, work–life balance, and the state of employee relations.

Attitude theory and research deals with the structure, function, formation, and change of attitudes and is concerned with the relationship between attitudes and behaviour. For example, the model of reasoned action (Fishbein and Ajzen 1975) provides a comprehensive approach to all of these aspects. In this model, the internal structure of an attitude is described in terms of beliefs (expectations), which relate the attitude object (a behavioural alternative) to the evaluated attributes. The function of attitudes is to guide the formation of behavioural intentions. Attitude formation and change is viewed as a process of deliberative evaluation and updating of belief. Attitudes are thought to indirectly impact behaviour via behavioural intentions. Recent approaches, however, assume that a deliberative calculation of expectancy and values is not a necessary condition for either intention formation or attitude formation and change. According to a study conducted by Zajonc in 1980, there is ample evidence to suggest that the liking of an attitude object can be enhanced by increasing its presentation frequency. Furthermore, attitudes, if they are frequently activated from memory, tend to become activated automatically in the presence of the attitude object and then directly impact behavioural decisions (Fazio 1990).

ATTITUDE–BEHAVIOUR RELATIONSHIP

Attitude is a predisposed state of mind of individuals to respond to a given object. Responses may be either favourable or unfavourable. Fazio (1989) observed that attitude establishes an association between a given object and given evaluation. Fishbein and Ajzen (1975) described attitude as a latent variable that impacts behaviour. Many researchers have empirically tested attitude–behaviour relations in the organizational context. However, they are more specific about the relations, using the term behavioural intentions rather than behaviour per se. Behavioural intention is conceptualized as the intention for a specific behaviour (Perloff 2003). Such cautious analysis is attributable to the fact that attitudes, in truth, can only partially determine the behaviour. However, through sustained training and education, organizations can bring about positive attitudinal change, reducing the cognitive dissonance or negative attitudes of employees. This helps employees re-perceive their mental blocks by identifying the possible reasons for such blocks. As a result, employees can understand their desired role in the organizations and change their behavioural intentions.

Subsequent researches by Ajzen and Fishbein led to the development of the concept of theory of reasoned action (TRA) and the theory of planned behaviour (TPB). TRA helps us understand the discrepancy between attitude and behaviour, relating it to our voluntary behaviour. TPB, on the other hand, extends the argument that our behaviour can also be under control, and therefore, it can be deliberate and planned. TRA is viewed as a function of individuals' attitude towards their intentions of behaviour. TPA is a reflection of specific attitudes towards the behaviour; hence, it helps in predicting the behaviour of individuals. With training and education reinforcement, we can bring about positive attitudinal change, which in turn can influence the individual's intention to enhance his/her behaviour.

Values are reflected in the way we treat people, in our approach towards our work, and in our basic work ethics.

The attitude of employees towards their job is influenced by their beliefs about the job, and in the process, they develop their behavioural intentions about the job itself. Fishbein (1967) developed the Job Attitude Model suggesting the belief–evaluation (attitude)–behavioural intention continuum. For example, employees' positive belief about the job aspects leads them to evaluate the job positively (reflection of positive attitude) and develop their positive behavioural intention to perform the job. The effect would be reversed in case the employees are influenced by a negative belief. However, such simple attitude towards the job relationship is not accepted by the proponents of cognitive psychology. They believe attitude to be essentially cognitive and not emotional reactions (affective). Job attitudes are developed by employees while they work for the organization and depend on the job characteristics and the overall work conditions in the organization. Positive job attitude of employees enhances their job involvement, commitment toward organization, and engagement.

VALUES AND ATTITUDES

Values are reflected in the way we treat people, in our approach towards our work, and in our basic work ethics. They are relatively stable over time. Research has taught us that most of our values are formed at about the age of five or six years. We have some terminal values and some instrumental values. We develop terminal values through the process of our upbringing, with cues from our happiness, freedom, and friendship. Since the cycle of our upbringing, by default, does not guarantee happiness every time, we also develop some instrumental values that guide and shape our existing values and help us be cheerful, responsible, and exhibit self-control. Cultural differences also lead to major differences in people's values. Americans want everything immediately, have little patience with waiting, and are pushy. Japanese workers tend to be more patient in waiting for job promotions and are willing to stay with the company for a long period. Germans believe more in analytical decision-making, with less interest in brainstorming and quick decision-making.

Attitude is the way we reflect our values. An optimistic employee always tends to look at the brighter side of an organization and is always positive in his/her approach. Value systems are largely developed through education. The cognitive part is developed through our knowledge, knowing what is right and what is wrong. The affective part, being the emotional side, is developed through our experience. The behavioural part is a blend of knowledge and emotions.

ATTITUDES AND ORGANIZATIONAL BEHAVIOUR

Similar to personality and emotional intelligence, managing the attitude and value systems of employees is very important. Mismatch of value systems and attitudes of employees towards the organization affects their efficiency and performance, which, in turn, forces the organization to experience competitive disadvantages. Some reflections of attitudes at work are listed here:

Job satisfaction—overall positive or negative This is most often looked at in terms of the long run. For example, one may be having a bad day (or even a bad week), but that does not mean one's job satisfaction is bad. This refers to the general attitude of individuals towards their jobs.

Job involvement This is not about being involved in decision-making on the job but about the importance attached to our job or work. Does it help to define us? If losing our job would make us feel less of a person, it means we have a high degree of job involvement. Job involvement measures the degree to which individuals psychologically identify with their jobs and consider their perceived performance levels as important for self-worth.

EXHIBIT 6.1   Scenario Analysis

We know that for effective HR management we need to be flexible but not at the cost of ethics and values. Keeping this in mind, suggest how we can deal with the following dilemmas:

- You are a financial analyst heading the finance department of a large organization. An employee in your department approaches you and tells you that several employees in your department are involved in fraudulent activities. He begs not to be quoted because he fears for his own safety if the leader of the group discovers that he has discussed the matter with you.

- You are the assistant vice-president for financial operations in a large manufacturing firm. After working late one night, you discover that your boss, the vice-president (Finance), and the chief accountant, are providing inside information to several wealthy investors about your company's planned merger with another large manufacturer.
- After a business trip, you begin to file an expense report. A co-worker who accompanied you on the trip files a report that is nearly twice the amount of the expenses actually incurred. He asks you to file a similar report and tells you, 'Everybody here pads their travel expenses bill.'

Organizational commitment   This refers to how committed we feel to meet the goals of the company we work for. Most employees of McDonald's are committed to the quality of their burgers. Similarly, most of the employees of EMC (a US-based computer data storage device company) are committed to customer service. Thus, the degree to which the employees identify themselves with particular organizations and the organizational goals, and wish to maintain their membership in the organizations, decides their attitude towards organizational commitment.

Due to the importance of attitude and value systems, which largely influence the behaviour of individual employees, companies always try to check these aspects before the recruitment process. This is done primarily through reference checking and during the interview. There are many standard psychometric tools for the measurement of attitudes, personalities, and emotions. Apart from these, we can measure the degree of fit, keeping in view the organizational requirements, by using scenario analysis (with an ethical bent), in-basket exercises, role-playing, and so on. The focus of all these exercises is to predict the on-the-job responses and behavioural patterns of employees. See Exhibit 6.1.

One of the attitudinal change exercises used by organizations is modelling the desired behavioural standards with instructions to employees to emulate them. For example, a good customer relationship model can be developed and shown to the employees with instructions to practise it in their dealings with customers. One of the critical attitudinal problems faced by organizations worldwide is managing diversity. The underlying attitude of employees may not warrant belief in diversity, which may be cross-cultural, racial, religious, or gender-based. A mere legal stricture cannot ease this attitudinal problem. It is important for the organization to highlight some of the best roles within the organization or even outside the organization. Organizations can place someone from a minority group in the manager's seat. Cognitive dissonance of employees also stems from attitudinal incongruence. It is the incompatibility between two or more attitudes or between behaviour and attitudes. Since attitudes are largely formed through our habits, strengths, and values, employees often experience discrepancies between what they feel is right and what is actually going on in the organization. By nature, people always seek consistency

Practitioner Speak 6.2

Hiring for Intangibles

The two candidates for the position of CFO at a prominent Silicon Valley firm seemed nearly identical: their education, job experience, and promotion history were remarkably similar. Then someone on the search committee noticed that one candidate graduated from college with honors and the other had not.

Read this insightful blog posted by Harvard Management Update on *HBR Blog Network* by accessing the following link: http://blogs.hbr.org/hmu/2008/02/hiring-for-intangibles-1.html.

among their attitudes and behaviour so as to be rational and consistent in their relationship with the organization. Information transparency and building of mutual trust can ease such mismatches.

ATTITUDE MEASUREMENT

It is not possible to observe one's attitude or psyche because psychological variables are dormant or latent. Being covert, attitude measurement is difficult. Inference, prediction from behaviour data, and interviews conducted with structured questionnaire and scales are the usual tools used for attitude measurement.

The following are the popular methods of measuring attitudes:

- Thurstone scales
- Likert scales
- Semantic differentials

These measuring tools are discussed in detail later.

It is our basic assumption that a person's attitude can be measured by asking questions about his/her thoughts, feelings, and likely actions towards the attitude object. Attitudes can also be measured by a quantitative technique; that is, each person's opinion can be represented by a numerical score. A particular test item or any other behaviour indicating an attitude has the same meaning for all respondents, so that a given response is scored identically for everyone making it. In a typical attitude measurement questionnaire, respondents are asked to indicate whether they agree or disagree with each of a series of belief statements about an attitude object. Attitudes are arranged along an evaluative continuum ranging from the favourable to the unfavourable. Why not have just one belief statement? In most cases, one question will not be enough to address all the likely domains of an attitude (e.g., Cannabis causes as much damage to our health as tobacco). Using only one question significantly increases the likelihood of errors created by irrelevant factors such as the wording of the question. If the responses are summed up over a number of questions, then it is a more valid measure because the error associated with the individual items tends to cancel out over a number of items. Each attitude statement should represent a different and independent view about the attitude object and should cover both the favourable and unfavourable attitudes so that the nature of the response to one item will not affect the response to another item. We assume that more extreme scale positions represent more important or more strongly held attitudes.

> Being covert, attitude measurement is difficult. Inference, prediction from behaviour data, and interviews conducted with structured questionnaire and scales are the tools used for attitude measurement.

Thurstone Scales

It is the first major technique of attitude measurement. The following are its basic assumptions:

- Attitudes lie along an evaluative continuum ranging from favourable to unfavourable.
- The order of attitude statements should be such that there appears to be an equal distance between adjacent statements on the continuum; that is, judgements can be made about the degree of discrepancy among the attitudes of different people.

Method of Equal-appearing Intervals—Method 1

The following are the steps involved in this method:

- Initially, construct an item pool, that is, large amounts of statements of opinions, about an issue.
- Assemble a group of 'judges' (100–150 statements, 40–60 judges).
- Develop a hypothetical scale running from the most favourable, through a neutral point, to the least favourable.
- Allow the judges to consider each item and sort it into piles (categories)—usually 11. Intervals between categories should be regarded as subjectively equal.

Thurstone Scales—Method 2

The following are the features of this method:

- Statements selected for use in the final scale are those that have high inter-judge agreement (low spread) and are at relatively equally spaced intervals along the continuum.
- There should be a desired number of items for the final scale. For example, the 20–20 scale values should be evenly spread across the continuum.
- Respondents score the scale value of each item agreed upon.
- Respondents should agree with very few items (perhaps two or three).

Example of Scoring—Issue of Equal Opportunities

The following are some examples of scoring in the issue of equal opportunities:

- Women are less reliable employees because they are likely to leave after childbirth (2.1).[1]
- Interview panels should scrutinize all the questions before the interview to ensure that none are discriminating (5.8).
- Companies should provide more crèche facilities (8.7).

Likert Scales

Instead of judges, respondents place themselves on an attitude continuum as indicated.

Strongly agree	Agree	Uncertain	Disagree	Strongly disagree
1	2	3	4	5

---

[1] Figures in parenthesis show uneven spread of sample response.

The obtained scores can be summed up and the resulting total used as an index of that person's attitude.

Semantic Differential Scales

The semantic differential scales (Osgood, et al. 1957) focus on the meaning people give to a word or concept. Words have two meanings:

- Semantic or dictionary meaning
- Connotative meaning (what a word suggests apart from the thing it explicitly denotes or names)

Dimensions

The following are the major dimensions of a hypothetical semantic space of an unknown number of dimensions, in which the meaning of any word or concept can be represented at a particular point:

- Evaluation (how good?) (e.g., healthy/unhealthy)
- Potency (how powerful?) (e.g., weak/strong)
- Activity (how active?) (e.g., static/dynamic)
- Midpoint of neutrality
- Social representations
- Social construction

The ideas and opinions that we hold are moulded by what other people believe and say. 'Our reactions to events, our responses to stimuli, are related to a given definition, common to all the members of the community to which we belong', that is, similarity and difference (individuality) of group members (Moscovici 1983). According to Augoustinos (1991), if social representations are cognitive structures shared on a group basis, the agreement between the members of that group should increase with age.

Other Measures

The following are the physiological measures of attitude:

- Skin resistance
- Heart rate
- Pupil dilation, that is, the attitude inferred by comparing a participant's response in the presence of a neutral object and the presence of the attitude object

The following are the problems associated with physiological measures of attitudes (overt behaviour):

- These measures indicate intensity and not direction.
- These measures are sensitive to variables other than attitudes (Petty and Cacioppo 1981); for example, vigilant tasks lower the heart rate and the skin response changes in the presence of novel or incongruous stimuli.
- Sensitive issues—bogus pipeline technique (Jones and Sigall 1971). Bogus pipeline is a method of overcoming social desirability bias.

Using a fake machine, participants are told to measure the strength and direction of their emotional responses. Participants in such cases are less likely to conceal socially undesirable attitudes (e.g., Allen 1973).

Problems with Attitude Measurement

The following are the problems associated with attitude measurement:

- Lack of consensus in different theories regarding the definition of attitude
- Lack of common methods of attitude measurement
- Operationalization of outcome measures
- Self-report

According to Vaughan and Hogg (1995), it is still more common to measure the changes in knowledge and attitudes than the changes in behaviours, for example, in relation to attitude change.

ATTITUDE SURVEY

Attitude survey is indispensable for recruiting new incumbents and for evaluating the human relations in factories, industries, and different organizations. The study of attitude is also important in designing a training programme, which is a core HR department (HRD) function.

Attitude surveys focus on the feelings and motives of the employees about their working environments. There are three basic purposes for conducting attitude surveys:

- To compare the results with other survey results
- To measure the effect of the change that occurs
- To determine the nature and extent of employees' feelings regarding specific organizational issues and the organization in general

Attitude surveys are usually carried out by interviewing a person with a structured close-ended questionnaire. The skill of the interviewer is very important here for the correct measurement of attitude. While framing the questionnaire, the interviewer should be cautious, as simple opinion-laden questionnaire items will not depict the attitude of the interviewee. It is important to include value-laden questionnaire items, use behaviourally anchored statements, and ask the respondents to rank any myth statements. A sample list of such myth statements and value-laden questionnaire items is provided here:

> Attitude surveys focus on the feelings and motives of the employees about their working environments.

- Hard work ensures better results.
- Link to work with subordinates for prompt results.
- Never say no to anyone; listen to everybody's problems.
- One who is indispensable is efficient.
- Maintain the hierarchical structure while taking decisions very rigidly.

Sample Questionnaire Items

The following are some sample questionnaire items for attitude measurement:

- Do you think the expenditure on training is wasteful? (Give your answer by selecting any one from the given alternatives.)

(a) To a large extent

(b) To some extent

(c) To a very little extent

(d) Not at all

- What, to your knowledge, are the major barriers to effective implementation of flexible working hours in India? (Please arrange the factors in order of your perceived preference.)
  (a) Lack of awareness
  (b) Difficulty in implementation
  (c) Supervisory problems
  (d) Lack of support from workers
  (e) Lack of support from unions
  (f) Production problems
  (g) Any other (please specify)

The first questionnaire item (which reflects the attitude of a person regarding training) can be evaluated by adding the weighted value of individual responses. The method to give weight for the questionnaire items has been explained earlier in this chapter.

Let us consider an example. Let the number of respondents be 15. Assume they have given the following responses to the four alternatives of the first question.

Alternatives	No. of respondents
(a) To a large extent	4
(b) To some extent	4
(c) To a very little extent	5
(d) Not at all	2
Total	15

Weighted Average Attitude

Alternatives	No.	Weighted	Attitude
(a)	4	4	16
(b)	4	3	12
(c)	5	2	10
(d)	2	1	2

Alternative (a), 'To a large extent', is the group attitude.

The second questionnaire item allows the respondents to answer the question by selecting all the alternatives in order of their perceived priority. This requires the use of the factorial method for the quantification of all responses.

Let us consider an example to illustrate the matter.

Suppose there are 15 respondents, they have responded by giving ranks to alternative (a) as follows:

Respondent	1	2	3	4	5	6	7	
Rank of (a)	1	3	5	7	1	4	3	
Respondent	8	9	10	11	12	13	14	15
Rank of (a)	2	6	5	1	2	3	4	5

From this, we get the following:

Priority/Rank	1	2	3	4	5	6	7
Number of respondents (Tr)	3	2	3	2	3	1	1

[Total no. of respondents = 15, no. of priorities/ranks = 7, that is, (a) to (g)]

Weighted score value (WSV) is calculated as follows:

Priority	1	2	3	4	5	6	7
Total value	3	2	3	2	3	1	1
Weights (factorial)	7	6	5	4	3	2	1
WSV	21	12	15	8	9	2	1

In the same way, the total WSVs for the other alternatives can be calculated from the responses obtained against each one. Suppose they are as follows:

Alternative	(b)	(c)	(d)	(e)	(f)	(g)
Total WSV	65	30	70	55	60	40

The total WSV of alternative (d) is the highest. Therefore, alternative (d), that is, 'Lack of support from workers', should be the attitude or opinion of the group of respondents.

Similarly, sample behaviourally anchored statements can also be used for attitude measurement.

Various statistical tools can be used for the measurement of attitudes. Since attitudes are psychological or qualitative variables, the first and foremost task for the rater is to assign numerals to objects, events, or persons. The use of the Likert Scale, Thurstone Scale, and so on helps the interviewer to assign numbers, either discrete or continuous. Analysis of variance, correlation, chi-square test, and Kendal's coefficient of concordance test are some useful statistical tools for attitude measurement. A few types of statistical measurements are shown in Table 6.1.

Table 6.1 Types of statistical measurements

Type	Basic empirical operations	Typical usage	Typical statistics	
			Descriptive	Inferential
Nominal	Determination of equality	Classification of male/female, smoker/non-smoker	Percentage mode	Chi-square, binomial
Ordinal	Determination of greater or less	Rankings: Preference data, market position, attitude measurement, many other psychological measures	Median	Rank-order correlation
Interval	Determination of equality of intervals	Index numbers, attitude measurement	Mean, range, standard deviation	Product–Moment correlation, T-test, factor analysis
Ratio	Determination of equality of ratios	Sales, units produced, number of customers, costs, age, etc.	Geometric mean	Coefficient of variation

HUMAN RESOURCES DEPARTMENT AND ATTITUDINAL CHANGE

Changing attitudes, values, and motivations are now the major issues faced by organizations. Through appropriate HRD interventions, organizations can turn such changes into advantages, ensuring quality of work-life balance and keeping pace with the changing human expectations. The following areas of attitudinal changes require HRD intervention:

- Attitudes towards perceived threats to trade union legality and other large-scale efforts to reduce trade union power or cohesion
- Attitudes towards methods of wage negotiations, whether by collective or local bargaining
- Attitudes towards the working conditions and any administrative machinery for the discussion or regulation of such conditions
- Attitudes towards worker training or promotion and towards education in general as a means of improving management and industrial skills

As explained earlier, economic restructuring, market globalization, international quality system standards, and so on have, inter alia, prompted Indian organizations to go for radical organizational restructuring, which, among others, calls for the adoption of total quality management (TQM) principles in managing HR. TQM requires total employee involvement (TEI), employee empowerment, development of small group activities (quality circle forums), and value engineering teams. Translating the TQM requirements into corporate practices, therefore, requires many attitudinal changes at the top, such as developing flatter type of organizations, delayering delegation and information, and developing an organizational culture where every employee needs to be considered a member of a well-integrated family. To infuse attitudinal changes at both the top and bottom levels, it is necessary to adopt the following HRD strategies:

Ensuring employee empowerment   Empowerment is to give everyone—instead of only people with certain positions or certain job titles—the legitimate right to make judgements, form conclusions, or reach decisions, and then act. Empowerment, therefore, calls for employee participation in day-to-day problem-solving and innovation. Traditional participative forums (works committee, joint consultative machinery, etc.) restrict employee participation in operational areas. However, empowerment demands employee participation in each corporate function in order to accept that the employee is not a mere seller of time and labour for a contracted sum of money. The empowered employees acquire the necessary skills and authority needed to make decisions concerning quality and productivity. They initiate changes on their own.

Empowerment changes the attitude of the employee, as it develops employee ownership and employee commitment.

Promoting quality circles and developing culture of total participation This strategy is used to infuse attitudinal changes and to facilitate personal involvement of employees. Quality circles (QCs) were originally coordinated by the Japanese Union of Scientists and Engineers (JUSE). A QC is a small group of workers voluntarily performing quality control activities within the workshop to which they belong. These small groups, with the voluntary participation of every member of the organization, continuously engage themselves in promoting quality control activities because of the total participation of the members of the organization, irrespective of their hierarchical levels. QCs, in reality, encompass the concepts of self-development and mutual development and, at the same time, reinforce quality control techniques. Even though the concept of QCs originated in Japan to help survive under competing circumstances, it has now expanded worldwide, cutting across cultural and ideological barriers. Gradually, it gained popularity in most of the industrialized nations and among the developing nations of the world. India being one of the fast developing nations is no exception. QC can be related to increased employee motivation and productivity, and hence, it is used as an important HRD tool in the organization. Total knowledge, skill, creative abilities, talents, and aptitudes together with values, attitudes, and beliefs of the workers and/or individuals of the organization represent HR in more aggressive terms. QCs ensure the total involvement of employees through a number of small group forums. Experience shows that many organizations have succeeded in improving their productivity by QC activities. Increased productivity can be achieved by increased employee motivation, which QCs can better ensure than any other methods such as complex planning and rigorous execution.

Imparting knowledge and value-laden attitudinal changes in training Organizations need to focus on imparting training to employees on human relations areas such as leadership, communication, and motivation. Such knowledge inputs gradually reinforce the attitude of the employees.

Focusing more on team spirit to integrate employees with organization This initiative is further strengthened when we simultaneously ensure a sense of belongingness among the employees.

ACCURACY, RELIABILITY, AND VALIDITY

> The reliability measure yields the same results in repeated applications to the same respondents or events and the validity measurement measures the degree of freedom from variable errors.

Accuracy is the extent to which a measurement is free from systematic and variable errors. Freedom from variable errors is known as the validity of a measurement. The reliability measure yields the same results in repeated applications to the same respondents or events. The validity measure is consistent because it is free from systematic errors and measures what it purports to measure.

Likert scales are generally more reliable than Thurstone scales. However, validity remains a contested issue; is what is being measured an attitude? Critics would say that what is actually being measured is demand characteristics.

As per Glick and Fiske (1996), measuring attitudes and their relationship to behaviour is a complex and subtle business.

SCALES

A scale is an instrument with the help of which a concept is measured. It is used in all types of data collection techniques such as observation, interviews, and projective techniques. Broadly, there are two types of scales—rating scales and attitude scales.

Attitude Scales

Attitude scales measure one or more aspects of an individual's or group's attitude towards some object. The individual's responses to the various scales may be aggregated or summed up to provide a single attitude for the individual. Similarly, group responses to the various scales may be aggregated or summed up to provide a single attitude for the group.

> Attitude scales measure one or more aspects of an individual's or group's attitude towards some object.

These scales are of three types:

- Likert's summated rating scale
- Thurstone's equal-appearing intervals scale
- Guttaman's cumulative scale

Likert's Summated Rating Scale

A summated rating scale is a set of attitude statements of which all are considered or approximated as having equal attitude value and to each of which the subjects respond with a degree of agreement or disagreement (intensity) carrying different scores. These scores are summed and averaged to yield an individual's attitude score. Under this method, each respondent's ranking is determined by totalling the scores on all the statements (usually five). To illustrate this, let us look at the following example:

This procedure, however, suffers from the following drawbacks:

- Ties in ranks occur quite frequently. There may be several respondents with total scores of 0, 1, 2, 3, 4, 5, and so on, which cannot be ordered in relation to one another.
- It does not throw light on the different ways in which the given scores may be obtained. Different combinations of the scores imply the differences among individuals, which are not revealed by this procedure.
- It is not possible to determine whether the scale is unidimensional or multidimensional, that is, whether the statements are measuring only one property or several properties of an attitude.
- In this scale, all statements are deemed to be of equal attitude value. This is not a scale of statements as such. This method orders the individuals based on their total scores and not the statements.

S. no.	Statement	Agree	Disagree
1.	Advertising promotes sales.	1	0
2.	HRD is exploitation of people.	1	0
3.	Hard work increases productivity.	1	0
4.	Effective time management reduces idle hours.	1	0
5.	Money and other physical benefits are the only motivations.	1	0

Likert's Item Analysis

In Likert's item analysis procedure, the respondents are asked to respond to a certain number of statements (which is usually restricted to 15). The reply to each statement is given in terms of five degrees of agreement or disagreement, namely Strongly agree (SA), Agree (A), Undecided (U), Disagree (D), and Strongly disagree (SD). Each statement, thus, becomes a scale in itself with five points on it. At one end of this scale is strong approval and at the other end is strong disapproval, with many intermediate points between them. The respondents indicate, with reference to each statement, where they stand on this scale. The total of their scores on all statements is taken as the measurement of their attitude. The statements may be either favourable or unfavourable. For favourable statements, the values given are 5, 4, 3, 2, 1, and for unfavourable statements, the values are 1, 2, 3, 4, 5.

The following example illustrates this:

Statement	SA	A	U	D	S
Management is a science	5	4	3	2	1
Management is not a science	1	2	3	4	5

Thurstone's Equal-appearing Intervals Scale

Thurstone's scale attempts to represent the attitudes of a group on a specified issue in the form of frequency distribution. The various opinions or items on a scale are allocated to different positions in accordance with the attitudes they express. The following steps are necessary to construct a Thurstone attitude scale.

- Brief statements expressing attitudes about a particular issue are gathered from current literature or are especially prepared for this purpose. The statements should cover different ranges of attitudes, from the extremely favourable to the extremely unfavourable and also include neutral statements.
- Statements are given an arbitrary number for identification and a group of judges are asked to sort those into several piles.
- After sorting, a complete tabulation is made to determine the number of times each statement is included in the piles.
- The scale values for each statement are determined graphically in the form of an ogive or cumulative frequency curve.
- The final scale is then made, selecting 15 to 20 statements (preferably those on which the judges have had the least disagreement).
- Respondents are then asked to check only those statements with which they agree.

As the construction of this scale is very cumbersome and time consuming, it is usually avoided. Moreover, the scale values assigned to the statements are influenced by the attitudes, backgrounds, and intelligence of the judges who may see things differently from the actual respondents. This scale also does not allow subjects to express the intensity of the feelings of the respondents because they have the choice to indicate their agreement with only the finally selected statements.

Guttaman's Cumulative Scale

Guttaman's cumulative scale is made up of a relatively small number of statements that have been tested for their unidimensionality. A unidimensional scale measures only one variable. The scale is known as cumulative, as respondents agreeing with the most favourable statements are theoretically presumed to agree with all other statements expressing *lesser* degree of favourability. The use of this scale is also avoided because of its complexity.

Another scale for measuring attitudes is the social distance technique of Bogardus, which is normally used to measure highly subjective attitudes.

COMPONENTS OF ATTITUDES

The three components of attitudes are cognitive, affective, and conative or behavioural.

Cognitive component   Cognitive attitudes are based on our thoughts, beliefs, and ideas. The cognitive aspects of an attitude are generally measured by surveys, interviews, and other reporting methods. When a human being is the object of an attitude, the cognitive component is frequently a stereotype; for example, fat people are lazy.

Affective component   This component of an attitude involves the feelings and evaluation assessed by monitoring physiological signs (e.g., heart rate). It is the feelings or emotions that something evokes, such as fear, sympathy, and hatred.

Behavioural component   This component of an attitude consists of the ways of acting towards the attitude object and is assessed by direct observation. It is the tendency or disposition to act in certain ways towards something. The emphasis is on the tendency to act and not the actual acting.

Behaviour does not always conform to a person's feelings and beliefs. Behaviour that reflects a given attitude may be suppressed because of a competing attitude or in deference to the views of others who disagree with it. A classic theory that addresses inconsistencies in behaviour and

> The three components of attitudes are cognitive, affective, and conative or behavioural.

attitudes is Leon Festinger's theory of cognitive dissonance, which is based on the principle that people prefer their cognitions or beliefs to be consistent with each other and with their own behaviour. Inconsistency or dissonance among their own ideas makes people uneasy enough to alter these ideas so that they will agree with each other. An alternative explanation of attitude change is provided by Daryl Bem's self-perception theory, which asserts that people adjust their attitudes to match their own previous behaviour.

Practitioner Speak 6.4

Obama and the Peace Prize: 'A' for Attitude

Beyond the obvious snub to the Bush administration, what was the Nobel committee's goal in awarding President Obama the Peace Prize? Certainly this is not an 'A' for accomplishment, as it will take years, if not decades, to discern whether the Obama administration's international overtures and embrace of the UN system will bear fruit. (Let's remember to acknowledge the hard work of Hilary Clinton here too.)

Read this insightful blog posted by Watkins on *HBR Blog Network by* accessing the following link: http://blogs.hbr.org/watkins/2009/10/obama_and_the_peace_prize_a_fo.html.

INTERPERSONAL RELATIONSHIPS

Interpersonal relationships are built through social associations, connections, or affiliations between two or more people. Such relationships may be either overt or covert, or may even be virtual. At times, it could be the body language or dialogue. Interpersonal relationships often mix the explicit and implicit interaction modes, which may be focused or unfocused. Marketing people try to develop focused interpersonal relationships with the customers. Accounts and administration people try to remain unfocused in their interpersonal relationships with the employees of other departments because of the confidentiality involved in their work. Through interpersonal relationships, we make self-disclosure, provide feedback, exert power, and show respect. Culture and language define the extent of interpersonal relationships. For example, China's share in global trade before their accession to the World Trade Organization in Doha in 2001 was minimal. Back then, China's greatest barrier was its language. Today, China uses English as its official communication language, which enhances its interpersonal relationships with international communities, many of whom today operate in China. Variation in interpersonal relationships is also possible because of the extent of questioning and challenge. Power differentials greatly influence interpersonal relationships. In addition, these relationships vary with respect to intimacy and sharing. They may or may not centre on things shared in common.

> Interpersonal relationships are built through social associations, connections, or affiliations between two or more people. Such relationships may be overt, covert, or virtual.

Stages of Interpersonal Relationships

There are several stages in interpersonal relationships:

Contact   This may be perceptual, a result of interactional cues, invitational, or simply an avoidance strategy. Perceptual contact is the way interacting parties look at each other and their body language. Interactional cues come from nodding, maintaining eye contact, and so on. Invitational contact takes place when either of the interacting parties tries to encourage potential interpersonal relations. Finally, contact for avoidance strategies takes place for lack of disclosure and eye contact.

Involvement   This comes from feelers (like some hints or questions), from deliberate strategies for furthering relationships, or from the urge to get together (like renewing some old relationships).

Intimacy   Intimacy develops out of the urge to get close (for some reason or the other).

Deterioration   This stage is reached when interpersonal relationships fall apart.

Johari window   The Johari window, derived from the work of Joseph Luft and Harry Ingham (1955), is a graphical representation of the relationship between individuals and understanding oneself. Luft and Ingham called this model *Johari*, after their first names, Joe and Harry. It is called a window because of its four quadrants. It is also referred to as a disclosure/feedback model of self-awareness and by some people as an information-processing tool. The Johari window actually represents information—feelings, experience, views, attitudes, skills, intentions, motivation, and so on—within or about a person in relation to his/her group from four perspectives. It is widely used to understand self; achieve personal development; improve communications, interpersonal relations, group dynamics, and team development; and finally, strengthen inter-group relations. This model represents the information for a particular group in relation to other groups and refers to *self* and *others*. The Johari window has four regions—open, blind, hidden, and unknown. What is known by a person about himself/herself and is also known by others is represented by the open area, open self, free area, free self, or *arena*. What is unknown to a person about himself/herself but is known to others is represented by the blind area, blind self, or blind spot. On the other hand, what a person knows about himself/herself but others do not is represented by the hidden area, hidden self, avoided area, avoided self, or *façade*. There may be a situation when neither the person nor do others know about something. This is represented by the unknown area or unknown self. A schematic representation of the model is shown in Fig. 6.1.

Quadrant 1, the open self/area, represents the area of free activity. When we are in this region, either individually or in a group, we are able to be more effective and productive because this space is for good communications and cooperation.

Quadrant 2, the blind self, makes us known to others but unknown to self, which results in our asking for feedback, based on which we try to reduce this area and increase the open area.

Quadrant 3, the hidden self or *facade*, indicates a situation where we know something, but it is unknown to others. This hidden area represents information and feelings, including sensitivities, fears, manipulative intentions, and secrets.

Quadrant 4 contains information, feelings, latent abilities, aptitudes, experiences, and so on that are unknown to the individual as well as to others in the group.

Exhibit 6.2 shows how the Johari window can be used to build trust in teams.

	Information known to self	Information not known to self
Information known to others	1. Open self (public area)	2. Blind self (blind area)
Information not known to others	Hidden self (private area) 3.	Unknown self (dark area) 4.

Figure 6.1 Johari window

EXHIBIT 6.2   Johari Window to Build Trust in Teams

Effective teams can accomplish uphill tasks. Organizations lay stress on close-knit teams for better functioning. However, team building needs time and can become a reality only when the members of a team share the same values, work towards the same goal, and have trust in each other. As the value sets differ from person to person and the goal is set by the management, mutual trust is something that bothers teams from time to time.

In this context, organizations may use the Johari window model to bring in more trust among the team members and therefore, build teams that are more effective. Given the basic premise of the Johari Window, the objective is to increase self-awareness and thus better oneself and build better teams. In this context, certain tips may help attain better bonding among the team members.

- Opening up lets others better understand an individual. However, opening up does not mean over-sharing. Sharing small, trivial, and harmless facts helps bond better without running the risk of disclosing personal information that could diminish one's respect and reputation.
- One should be open to feedback. Paying heed to feedback helps reduce the blind self and expand the open self. This also allows gaining confidence in others and thus connecting better.
- It is always necessary to be cautious while giving feedback. Receiving and giving feedback are two different ball games altogether. While receiving feedback, one should be open and at

(Contd)

EXHIBIT 6.2 (*Contd*)

the same time sieve through the feedback for constructive points. However, while giving feedback, one should make sure that the person on the receiving end is used to receiving feedback and open to receiving it from you.

- Finally, in the context of team building, managers

have a key role to play. They should teach members how to give constructive feedback and help them become more open to receiving feedback. This will help team members expand their open selves vertically, and therefore, build teams that are more effective.

Source: Mindtool, 'The Johari Window: Using self-discovery and communication to build trust', http://www.mindtools.com/CommSkll/JohariWindow.htm, last accessed on 15 July 2013 (adapted).

SUMMARY

Attitudes are learned cognitive mechanisms that can be reinforced by knowledge. Attitude per se is not behaviour but it develops an intervening frame of reference, which influences the behaviour of an individual. Hence, understanding the attitude of employees is essential both at the time of recruitment and during the subsequent periods. Attitudes can be measured using different sets of scales. The right scale will depend on the nature of attitude that is required to be measured. The attitudes of the employees need to be measured at regular intervals because a given attitude may change with new work groups and with the introduction of newly recruited people in the organization. We often try to approximate the

employees' attitudes through various scenario analyses and using myth statements. However, this may not always be correct, as we get only the partial attitudinal reference of employees. Hence, it is always desirable to carefully develop structured value-laden or attitude-laden questions, keeping pace with organizational requirements, and administer them to employees to map their attitudes. Mapping attitudes will alone not suffice the purpose of the organization. Appropriate HR management interventions are required for behavioural modification of employees. Although it is believed that attitudinal change is difficult, it is not impossible. It requires sustained interventions to modify the attitude of employees.

KEY DEFINITIONS

Affection-based attitude   This attitude stems from people's feelings (e.g., attitudes towards political candidates). Affective component is the emotion or feeling segment of an attitude.

Attitude scales   These scales measure one or more aspects of an individual's or group's attitude towards some object.

Behaviour-based attitude   This attitude is based on the self-perception of one's own behaviour.

Cognitive attitude   This attitude is primarily based on

the beliefs and properties of an attitudinal object, which people nurture.

Cognitive dissonance theory   This theory helps us to trace any incompatibility between two or more attitudes or between behaviour and attitudes.

Values and attitudes   Values are reflected in the way we treat people, in our approach to our work, and in our basic work ethics. Attitude is the way we reflect our values.

CONCEPT-REVIEW QUESTIONS

6.1   Define attitude. Why is the study of attitude necessary for organizational behaviour studies?

6.2   What are the different tools for attitudinal measurement? From an organizational point of view, discuss in detail at least two measurement tools with due emphasis on their relative merits or demerits.

6.3 Write short notes on the following:
(a) Equal-appearing intervals scale

(b) Cumulative scale
(c) Summated rating scale
(d) Employee empowerment and attitudinal change

CRITICAL THINKING QUESTIONS

6.1 A company has retained you to study the attitude of 50 employees on the recently introduced pension scheme. Develop at least five structured close-ended questionnaires, using Likert's item analysis scale, and interview the employees. Analyse all the responses using the factorial method and measure the attitudes of the employees.

6.2 A company is assessing the feasibility of developing a Thurstone scale to trace the attitudinal element in the employees' behaviour, which perhaps leads to job dissatisfaction. Suggest detailed methods and also recommend whether this scale should be used at all for such a purpose.

SELECT BIBLIOGRAPHY

- Ackers, P. and A. Wilkinson, *Understanding Work and Employment: Industrial Relations in Transition*, Oxford University Press, Oxford, 2003.
- Allen, Louis A., *Professional Management*, McGraw-Hill Book Co. Inc., New York, 1973.
- Allport, G.W., 'Attitudes', in C.A. Murchinson (ed.), *A Handbook of Social Psychology*, Vol. 2, Clark University Press, Worcester, 1935, pp. 798–844.
- Bhattacharyya, D.K., *Human Resource Research Methods*, Oxford University Press, New Delhi, 2007.
- Budd, J., *Employment with a Human Face: Balancing Efficiency, Equity and Voice*, Cornell University Press, Ithaca, 2004.
- Eagly, A.H. and S. Chaiken, *The Psychology of Attitudes*, Harcourt Brace Jovanovich, Orlando, 1993.
- Fazio, R.H., 'On the Power and Functionality of Attitudes: The Role of Attitude Accessibility', in A.R. Pratkanis, S.J. Breckler, and A.G. Greenwald (eds), *Attitude Structure and Function*, Lawrence Erlbaum Associates, Hillsdale, 1989.
- Fazio, R.H. 'A Practical Guide to the Use of Response Latency in Social Psychological Research', in C. Hendrick and M.S. Clark (eds), *Research Methods in Personality and Social Psychology*, Vol. 2, Sage Publications, Newbury Park, 1990, pp. 74–97.
- Fishbein, M., 'Attitude and the Prediction of Behavior', in M. Fishbein (ed.), *Readings in Attitude Theory and Measurement*, Wiley, New York, 1967.
- Fishbein, M. and I. Ajzen, *Belief, Attitude, Intention, and Behaviour: An Introduction to Theory and Research*, Addison-Wesley, Reading, 1975.
- Glick, P. and S.T. Fiske, 'The Ambivalent Sexism Inventory: Differentiating Hostile and Benevolent Sexism', *Journal of Personality and Social Psychology*, Vol. 70, 1996, pp. 491–512.
- Guest, D. and N. Conway, *Employee Well-being and the Psychological Contract: A Report for the CIPD*, Chartered Institute of Personnel and Development, London, 2004.
- Hovland, C.I., Janis, I.L., and Kelley, H.H., *Communication and Persuasion: Psychological Studies of Opinion Change*, Yale University Press, New Haven, 1953.
- Johnson, M., *The New Rules of Engagement: Life–Work Balance and Employee Commitment*, Chartered Institute of Personnel and Development, London, 2004.
- Jones, Edward E. and Harold Sigall, 'The Bogus Pipeline: A New Paradigm for Measuring Affect and Attitude', *Psychological Bulletin*, Vol. 76. 1971, pp. 349–64.
- Luft, J. and H. Ingham, 'The Johari Window, A Graphic Model of Interpersonal Awareness', *Proceedings of the Western Training Laboratory in Group Development*, Los Angeles: UCLA, 1995.
- Moscovici, S. and M. Hewstone, 'Social Representation from the Name to the Amateur Scientists', in

M. Hewstone (ed.), *Attribution Theory, Social and Functional Extensions*, Basal Blackwell, Oxford, 1983.

- Osgood, C.E., G.J. Suci, and P.H. Tannenbaum, *The Measurement of Meaning*, The University of Illinois Press, Urbana, 1957.
- Perloff, R.M., *The Dynamics of Persuasion: Communication and Attitudes in the 21st Century*, 2nd ed., Lawrence Erlbaum Associates, Mahwah, 2003.
- Petty, R.E. and J.T. Cacioppo, *Attitudes and Persuasion: Classic and Contemporary Approaches*,

Win C. Brown Company Publishers, Dubuque, 1981, pp. 287–365.
- Purcell, J., N. Kinnie, and S. Hutchinson, *Understanding the People and Performance Link: Unlocking the Black Box*, Chartered Institute of Personnel and Development, London, 2003.
- Ulrich, D. and W. Brockbank, *The HR Value Proposition*, Harvard Business School Press, Boston, 2005.
- Vaughan, G. and M. Hogg, *Introduction to Social Psychology*, Prentice Hall, Sydney, 1995.

CASE STUDY

Managing Work Culture Transformation

A legacy-bound multinational electronics major in India had to revisit its business strategies on account of the Korean entry in the business. Being the first in India to produce conventional black-and-white televisions, and later colour televisions, the company took pride in its captive market and, while enjoying all the privileges of such a market, forced its Indian customers to have only what it believed was the best. For years together, it made no changes in variety or models. With the Korean entry, the multinational had to understand the real meaning of competition in the consumer electronics industry. The competition rendered its product prices uneconomical. Again, the availability of multiple models of the Korean products made its own look less attractive to customers. Moreover, the mindset of the employees made them believe that the company could meet their rising demands in salary.

The company was acquired by a traditional Indian electronics major, whose competitive pricing made it successful in the market, next to the Korean manufacturers. The acquisition was legally challenged and even violently opposed by the trade unions. Workers in large numbers decided not to work with the new entity, lesser known than its foreign counterpart. On acquisition, the Indian major first tried to assuage the feelings of the irate employees and the unions stating that their employment is protected with the golden parachute option; that is, service conditions, salary,

and benefits will remain unaltered. Even that did not help them to win the confidence of their employees and the unions. Many employees took early separation and those in the higher age bracket even opted for voluntary retirement, for which their parent company, before selling the stake to the Indian electronics major, had made available separate provisions. Many employees opted to wait and watch.

During the first phase of operations, the Indian electronics major followed rigorous transparency of information and communication with all cross sections of employees. The chief operating officer (COO) was advised to spend more than 80 per cent of his time in meeting and talking to all cross sections of employees, clarifying their doubts and answering their queries, if any. He kept himself busy in moving around the shop floors to meet people without bothering about immediate production loss. The COO also made it a point to meet employees both in groups and individually in his office at designated hours to discuss any issues that otherwise the employees could not share on the shop floors. In between, the COO set an example before the employees, making it clear to all the managers and executives that they need to be on time and be disciplined at the workplace, which was diluted while they were with the multinational entity. After a month, the managers set an example before the workers and then started demanding from them similar behaviour at the workplace. Whenever workers made it an issue that things were not moving at the right pace, they were given the freedom to manage the gang-level activities, deciding on their own, every aspect of their jobs. The management extended full support, facilitated their activities, and even made it a point for any important visitor to the plant to appreciate how the workers could take charge of the shop floor in managing their activities.

The company then identified that there were some common areas of interest for both the workers and the management. A goal congruence model, duly developed in line with these common areas of interest, made it possible for them to assess the results of discussions on mutual interest. The company could see that management issues were not separate from those of the workers. Hence, it took the approach of integrating workers' issues with those of the management, reinforcing workers' attitudes to appreciate the need for change. Initial in-house training support to sell the imperative for change was strengthened by retaining services of expert consultants, which reinforced the thought process of workers and made them realize why they should change to scale up the activities of the organization for mutual interest.

Despite year-long efforts to change the attitude of the workers, it was observed that the company was still ridden with some deadwood, that is, employees who were not only non-performers but also chronic absentees. A list of 22 such employees out of the 300 payroll workers (who were from the erstwhile multinational) was prepared. The list was sent to the unions of their affiliation with a request to suggest what should be the company's standpoint to tackle them. The unions were non-committal at the initial stage, but upon persistent communication, they asked their members to amend their attitudes and behaviour. However, there was hardly any impact. The management then decided to take up the issue at its level, informing the unions that no disciplinary action

will be initiated against anyone, but that external experts will take the employees through rigorous attitudinal change sessions to help them understand the need for change. The unions agreed to this and accordingly the management retained experts to manage the show.

The experts first used successive ice-breaking sessions to allow the erring employees to open their mouth. Some of them started making excuses that they remained absent because of the company's failure to appreciate their achievements. They stated that the company's productivity went up by three times after its acquisition, whereas their wages only marginally increased, which had led to their demotivation.

Indian labour laws allow workers to receive terminal benefits such as gratuity and pension even when they remain absent without pay. This will continue until such time the workers are discharged. Politically conscious workers understand this privilege. Therefore, those who can afford to find better alternative sources of income will opt for it, while remaining on the pay roll of their mother company, with some surprise visits. The elaborate disciplinary procedures take time to discharge the erring workers.

Such employees set a bad precedent for others who are sincere and hardworking. Unions often plead their helplessness, as they fear that agreeing to the views and line of action of the management would reduce their membership, as rival unions can take these members in their group. Political interference is not possible, as everybody is concerned about his/her vote bank. The company is not able to understand how they should tackle these people.

Questions for Discussion

1. As a manager, suggest how you will handle this situation.
2. How was the COO responsible for a positive change in the overall attitude of the employees?

Emotional Intelligence and Organizational Behaviour

LEARNING OBJECTIVES

After studying this chapter, the reader will be able to

- understand the concept of emotional intelligence (EI)
- explain the dynamics of EI and cognitive intelligence
- understand the implications of EI at work
- correlate EI with individual behaviour and performance as well as with leadership and competence
- understand the ways to manage emotions
- explain the various models of EI
- understand neuro-linguistic programming (NLP) and its relationship with EI
- describe the various operational principles of NLP

CASE STUDY

Customer Service with Emotional Intelligence—The Story of EMC Corp.

According to Mike Ruettgers, EMC Corp., 'When a customer believes in you ... they'll stick with you almost no matter what.'

Mike Ruettgers, after joining the EMC Group as vice-president (operations and customer service), found that the failure of the company's product performance was virtually leading the company to bankruptcy. Disk drive, one of their core product lines, was facing a roadblock as customers were against accepting it, although the company enjoyed visible market reputation in product quality and customer services. The company's business had witnessed a serious drop due to product unreliability. As part of the comeback strategy, Mike decided to provide options to customers to either receive a new EMC storage system or take an IBM archival at EMC rate (the price band of IBM was higher). IBM is EMC's major competitor. With IBM traceability, EMC's customers understood that they were buying an IBM product at EMC price.

This move of Mike was criticized at EMC's corporate level, but Mike was convinced that this was the only way to restore the customers' confidence. His assumption was correct. EMC's customers recognized such an extraordinary move, considered it as the company's commitment to its customers, and decided to continue with EMC. With Mike, EMC could turnaround. Technology companies such as Cisco Systems, Sun Microsystems, and Oracle reposed their confidence in EMC data archival products. For EMC, customer service runs like any other business unit and is implanted in the company's DNA. It reads 'continuous innovation with emotional attachment'.

INTRODUCTION

In general, organizations place more emphasis on the verbal and cognitive intelligence of their personnel and accordingly tend to ignore the emotional dimensions of their behaviour. However, the effectiveness of an organization largely depends on the ability of its people to become increasingly self-aware, to develop the language and culture for communicating with others to share information, and to prepare self-defence mechanisms. This is possible not with cognitive intelligence alone but through the self-awareness of people, which prompts them to develop the language and culture required for effective communication of information. Such self-imposed directions of life later got more institutionalized with norms and systems. The human thought process, therefore, evolved through interactions with nature, which incidentally also form a part of the Indian *gurukul* system. Ultimately, however, only those thought processes that were essential for us to persist and that assisted us in our daily lives survived.

Emotional intelligence (EI) has attracted attention because it suggests that emotions convey sensible meanings, which require understanding. It is potentially a useful factor in understanding and predicting individual performances at work. The term *emotional intelligence* was first discussed by John D. Mayer and Peter Salovey (1994). However, their discussions did not evoke much interest among organizations. It was only in 1995 that Daniel Goleman's book *Emotional Intelligence: Why it Can Matter More Than IQ* and his subsequent articles in *USA Weekend* (13–15 March 1998) and *Time* magazine (2 October 1995) evoked a response from organizational behaviour and human resource (HR) management professionals. Goleman's subsequent book, *Working with Emotional Intelligence* (1998), evinced further interest in this subject. Thus, EI is the latest development in understanding the relation between reason and emotion. Human thoughts and emotions are adaptively and intelligently intertwined. Organizations these days integrate EI, personality, and intelligence quotient (IQ) for achieving excellence in employees' performance. They also make use of this integrated approach to recruit the right fit.

HISTORICAL ROOTS OF EMOTIONAL INTELLIGENCE

When psychologists began to think and write about intelligence, they focused on the cognitive aspects such as memory and problem-solving. However, some researchers recognized that the non-cognitive aspects were also important. For instance, David Wechsler defined intelligence as the aggregate or global capacity of an individual to act purposefully, to think rationally, and to deal effectively with his/her environment (Wechsler 1958). As early as 1940, he referred to non-intellective as well as intellective elements, by which he meant the affective, personal, and social factors (Wechsler 1940). Furthermore, in 1943, Wechsler proposed that the non-intellective abilities were essential for predicting one's ability to succeed in life. He wrote the following:

'The main question is whether non-intellective, that is, affective and cognitive abilities are admissible as factors of general intelligence. Such factors are not only admissible but necessary. I have tried to show that in addition to intellective there are also definite non-intellective factors that determine intelligent behaviour. If the foregoing observations are correct, it follows that we cannot expect to measure total intelligence until our tests also include some measures of the non-intellective factors.'

Wechsler was not the only researcher who realized the importance of the non-cognitive aspects of intelligence for adaptation and success. Robert Thorndike, had also written about social intelligence in the late 1930s (Thorndike and Stein 1937). Unfortunately, the works of these early pioneers were largely forgotten or overlooked until 1983, when Howard Gardner began to write about multiple intelligence. Gardner (1993) proposed that intrapersonal and interpersonal intelligences are as important as the type of intelligence typically measured by IQ and related tests. Now let us review the history of industrial–organizational (I/O) psychology. In the 1940s, under the direction of Hemphill (1959), the Ohio State Leadership Studies suggested that consideration is an important aspect of effective leadership. More specifically, this research suggested that leaders who are able to establish mutual trust, respect, and a certain warmth and rapport with members of their group will be more effective (Fleishman and Harris 1962). In 1956, using the assessment-based approach, the American Telephone and Telegraph Company, under Douglas Bray, identified many dimensions of social and emotional competencies such as communication, sensitivity, initiative, and interpersonal skills (Thornton and Byham 1982).

Although most people view EI as being a relatively new field, cognitive intelligence researchers have identified fragments of the concept for over a century. The first book on emotions was published in 1872—Charles Darwin's *The Expression of the Emotions in Man and Animals*. This was the first comprehensive study and written account of the expression of emotions and is still valid. The following are the other researchers who discovered 'something emotional about intelligence':

1920s—Edward Thorndike (social intelligence, emotional factors)

1940s—David Wechsler (non-intellective aspects of general intelligence)

1948—R.W. Leeper (emotional thought)

1993—Howard Gardner (multiple intelligence, interpersonal intelligence—people smart, intrapersonal intelligence—self-smart)

1980s—Reuven Bar-On (emotional quotient—EQ)

1994—Peter Salovey and Jack Mayer (EI)

Daniel Goleman's book *Emotional Intelligence: Why It Can Matter More than IQ* (1995) created a spurt in EI research, books, instruments, and training. In a sense, Goleman's book created a cottage industry for EI. It is doubtful whether any other psychological construct has generated such volume of material in such a short period of time.

As with any emerging field of study, EI is not without critics. In general, people tend to be divided into one of the two camps. In one camp are the academicians, whose approach is to research and thoroughly examine new fields of study prior to their acceptance. This group tends to be critical of the concept of EI as a unique and viable psychological construct. In general, the following are the criticisms of academicians:

- They question the validity of EI, pointing out disagreement on the definition.
- They consider EI to be just a repackaging of well-established personality traits. They point to numerous studies that show what they classify as high correlations among the subscales of EI instruments and those of other personality measures.
- They question the validity of EI actually being intelligence.

Along with its growth, there have been simultaneous efforts to use EI as a means for analysing and improving individual and organizational performance. Business has deemed EI measurement as a tool worthy of being used alongside longstanding assessments such as the Myers–Briggs type indicator (MBTI), the California psychological inventory, and fundamental interpersonal relations orientation-behaviour (FIRO-B), a theory developed during the 1950s (Schutz 1966).

UNDERSTANDING EMOTIONAL INTELLIGENCE

The concept of EI is an umbrella term that captures a broad collection of individual skills and dispositions, usually referred to as soft skills or interpersonal and intrapersonal skills, which are outside the traditional areas of specific knowledge, general intelligence, and technical or professional skills. Most authors on the topic note that in order to be a well-adjusted, fully functioning member of the society (or family member, spouse, employee, etc.), one must possess both traditional intelligence (IQ) and EI (dubbed EQ). Emotional intelligence implies being aware of emotions and the manner in which they can affect and interact with traditional intelligence (e.g., impair or enhance judgement). This view fits well with the commonly held notion that it takes more than just intelligence to succeed in life—one must also be able to develop and maintain healthy interpersonal relationships. When considered from this perspective, EI is not a new concept.

Emotional intelligence is the power of abstract reasoning. Such reasoning power enables an individual to understand the relationships, that is, similarities and differences, among objects and develop the power to study each constituent separately and holistically. Along with the abstract reasoning power, with EI, people can also develop their ideas on input, knowledge base, and strategic abilities. Several constituents of EI, for ease of our understanding, have been explained in Table 7.1.

> The concept of EI captures various individual skills and dispositions that are outside the traditional areas of specific knowledge, general intelligence, and technical or professional studies.

Individual power of abstract reasoning develops with an input function. The inputs vary with the nature and type of intelligence. To illustrate, verbal intelligence requires the inputs of reasoning of language. Similarly, spatial intelligence requires the inputs of reasoning of positioning and movement of objects, whereas EI requires the inputs of reasoning of situation and environment. Expression requires inputs of language, presentation of objects requires inputs of positioning, and response requires inputs of situation. Since abstract reasoning embodies knowledge base and cognitive power, authors like Cattell used the term *crystallized intelligence*.

Table 7.1 Summary overview of parts of intelligence

Constituent	Verbal intelligence	Emotional intelligence
Meta-processing (adjunct)	Knowing that writing something down can help one remember it	Knowing that helping someone may make one feel better
Abstract understanding and reasoning (core)	Being able to identify the protagonist of a story and compare the individual to other people	Being able to analyse an emotion and identify its parts and how they combine
Knowledge base processing (adjunct)	Having knowledge (and remembering analyses) of prior instances of stories	Having knowledge (and remembering analyses) of prior instances of feelings
Input processing (adjunct)	Being able to keep long sentences in memory	Being able to perceive emotions in faces

Source: Mayer and Mitchell 1998

According to Mayer and Salovey (1994), 'Emotional intelligence allows us to think more creatively and to use our emotions to solve problems. Emotional intelligence probably overlaps to some extent with general intelligence. The emotionally intelligent person is skilled in four areas: identifying emotions, using emotions, understanding emotions, and regulating emotions.'

Goleman (1995) defined EI as the 'capacity for reorganizing our own feelings and those of others, for motivating ourselves, for managing emotions well in ourselves and in our relationships'. The underlying belief in Goleman's hypothesis is that rational thinking alone cannot predict success. Thus, high IQ alone cannot ensure success. This is why organizations always endeavour to develop leadership skills and competencies among employees for enhancing their EI.

Another perspective of EI, provided by Dulewicz and Higgs (1999), suggests that it is distinctly associated with the competency models of people. They have identified a set of competencies associated with EI—self-awareness, emotional management, empathy, relationships, communication, and personal style. All these correspond to competencies such as sensitivity, flexibility, adaptability, resilience, impact, listening, leadership, persuasiveness, motivating others, energy, decisiveness, and achievement orientation.

Goleman (1995) takes a somewhat broader position in describing EI in his writings. According to him, EI consists of five factors—knowing one's emotions, managing emotions, motivating oneself, recognizing emotions in others, and handling relationships. Thus, EI can best be defined as the non-cognitive abilities and competencies of people that develop their ability to cope with environmental demands and pressures. Non-cognitive factors are personality, EI, and creativity. Cognitive aspects, on the other hand, are memory and problem-solving ability.

Two Aspects

The essential premise of EQ is that to be successful one requires effective awareness, control, and management of one's own emotions and those of other people. Emotional Quotient (EQ) embraces two aspects of intelligence:

- Understanding self, goals, intentions, responses, and behaviour
- Understanding others and their feelings

Five Domains

Goleman identified the following five domains of EQ:

- Knowing one's emotions
- Managing one's emotions
- Motivating oneself
- Recognizing and understanding other people's emotions
- Managing relationships, that is, managing the emotions of others

Emotional intelligence embraces and draws from numerous other branches of behavioural, emotional, and communications theories, such as neuro-linguistic programming (NLP), transactional analysis, and empathy. By developing one's EI in these areas and the five EQ domains, one can become more productive and successful at what one does and also help others to be more productive and successful. The process and outcomes of EI development also contain many elements known to reduce the stress of individuals and organizations by decreasing conflict, improving relationships and understanding, and increasing stability, continuity, and harmony.

NATURE OF EMOTIONAL INTELLIGENCE

The concept and meaning of EI is still evolving. With every new definition, its nature and contexts are becoming much wider. Thus, it is often difficult to describe the nature of EI in a few points. A refined definition of EI by Salovey and Mayer (1997) extends its meaning as 'the ability to process emotional information, more specifically an ability to recognize the meanings of emotions and their relationships, to reason and problem-solve on the basis of them. In particular, it involves one's capacity to perceive and assimilate emotional feelings, to understand the information of these emotions, and, lastly, the management of them.' Interpreting this definition, Hein (2003) could categorize some of the components of EI as follows:

- Intelligence
- Information processing
- Potential for learning

- Understanding
- Developing
- Growth

With several such extended definitions, the nature of EI now encompasses the following:

- Identification of emotion
- Perception of emotion
- Expression of emotion

- Facilitation of emotional thought
- Understanding of emotion
- Management of emotion

> Emotional intelligence is defined as the ability to process emotional information, more specifically an ability to recognize the meaning of emotions and their relationships, to reason and problem-solve on the basis of them.

Emotional intelligence contains information about relationships, which may be with an object or a person. Any change in the object or person will also change the emotions towards that object or person. To illustrate, we tend to dislike a scary person but like a person with a charismatic personality. Relationships in EI need not always be actual but can even be imaginary. However, irrespective of the actual or imaginary relationships, emotions are accompanied by the felt signals of relationships. EI is our ability to understand and interpret the emotions, and together with the aid of our cognitive intelligence, it can enable us to solve problems.

To minimize the risk of non-performance in the workplace, it would be better to test the EI of the selected candidates before finalizing the recruitment process. Emotional abilities of individual employees strengthen their skills and perceptions on emotion, the appropriate use of emotions to extend the thought process, understanding emotions, and finally managing emotions.

Association with Emotional Processing

According to Hein (1996), a person with EI can distinguish between healthy and unhealthy, and negative and positive feelings. Emotional Intelligence refers to the innate feelings with four major attributes, namely emotional sensitivity, emotional memory, emotional learning ability, and emotional processing ability. Although such innate potential can get damaged with real-life experiences, often the quality of the EI processing abilities of an individual becomes strong enough to override the real-life learning experiences. Thus, the innate emotional processing abilities of an individual become more important than his/her life experiences to shape his/her EI. We can understand this better from Goleman (1995), who considered EI more a skill than a learned one, as emotional processing, which shapes the EI, is a natural and unconscious process.

Emotions and Emotional Information

Even though there is still a difference of opinion about the term emotion, a more generic definition attributes emotion to structured mental processes, to respond to relationships, reinforced with physiological, experimental, and cognitive inputs. To illustrate, our anger is the outcome of our perceived blockage to our goal, and our happiness is the response to our love for others. Employees may feel scared of an autocrat leader, whereas they may show respect to a team leader (who with a participative approach can extract the best out of them).

Emotional information is the information on emotional relationships. Availability of emotional information helps us study not only the cross-cultural variation but also the emotions across animals. However, mere availability of emotional information would not be enough; it requires an ability to interpret it. Cognitive scientists use emotional information as inputs to study emotions in elementary stories.

Correlation with Cognitive Intelligence

In Table 7.2, the correlation between EI and cognitive intelligence has been explained from different theoretical contexts, emphasizing the highest correlation with abstract reasoning. The highest correlation of cognitive intelligence is more evident when we process a situation, a

Table 7.2 Four-branch model of emotional intelligence

Branches	Description of measure	Relation to intelligence and personality
Managing emotion	Ability to manage emotions and emotional relationships for personal and interpersonal growth	Acts as an interface between personality and goals
Understanding emotion	Ability to comprehend emotional information about relationships, transitions from one emotion to another, and linguistic information about emotions	Acts as the central locus of abstract processing and reasoning about emotions and emotional information
Facilitating thought with emotion	Ability to harness emotional information and directionality to enhance thinking	Calibrates and adjusts thinking so that cognitive tasks make use of emotional information
Perceiving emotion	Ability to identify emotions in faces and pictures	Inputs information to intelligence

Source: Mayer and Mitchell 1998 (adapted)

person, or an object, with our abstract reasoning power. In today's globalized world, it is imperative for business to make use of the abstract reasoning power to study cross-cultural issues.

USE OF EMOTIONAL INTELLIGENCE AT WORK

Goleman, while experimenting with EI, applied the concept in a workplace situation to study how an emotionally intelligent worker could make a difference in his/her performance and relationships. Using the emotional competence framework, he could identify the differences between an emotionally intelligent and an ordinary worker on two counts—personal competence and social competence.

Goleman (1995) has explained the details of the emotional competence framework with different subcomponents in his book. Here, however, the gist of the framework is provided to help appreciate how people with emotional competence can benefit an organization.

Personal competence This is the ability to regulate our own behaviour by redirecting disruptive impulses and moods as well as the ability to pursue our goals. Competencies associated with this are self-control, trustworthiness and integrity, initiative and adaptability, comfort with ambiguity, openness to change, and a strong desire to achieve.

Social competence This is the ability to understand others' emotions and develop the requisite skills to tackle people accordingly. It is linked with six competencies—empathy, expertise in building and retaining talent, organizational awareness, cross-cultural sensitivity, valuing diversity, and service to clients and customers.

> Goleman's emotional competence framework is based on personal competence, social competence, self-awareness, and social skills.

Self-awareness This is the ability to understand our own moods, emotions, and drives and their effect on others. The competencies associated with this are self-confidence, realistic self-assessment, and emotional self-awareness.

Social skills This is the ability to manage relationships and build networks to get the desired result from others. The associated competencies are leadership, effectiveness in leading change, conflict management, influence or communication, and expertise in building and leading teams (of internal states, preferences, resources, and intuitions).

Goleman suggested the following steps for developing EI at the workplace:

- Assess job-related emotional skills.
- Determine the available EI of individuals at the workplace. Some organizations make use of 360-degree feedback for this purpose.
- Identify the extent of readiness of the people in the organization to improve their level of EI.
- Assess the level of motivation of the people in the organization to believe in their learning experience to improve EI.
- Make the EI change process self-directed, allowing people to develop their own learning plans, matching their own interests, resources, and goals.
- Help people in organizations focus on their manageable goals, cultivating a feeling that EI development is a gradual process and in pursuing it, they may often be confronted with their old ways of working.
- Help people understand how they can learn through lapses and prevent relapses.
- Provide performance feedback to people.
- Avoid propensity to believe that EI can be developed overnight.
- Make available models of the desired behaviour.
- Introduce rewards for self-improvement to encourage and reinforce a climate of participation for development of EI.
- Develop objective measurement criteria to evaluate the employees' performance against them.

Promotion of EQ in the workplace is summarized as follows:

- Paving the way
- Assessing the organization's needs
- Assessing the individual
- Delivering assessments with care
- Maximizing learning choice
- Encouraging participation
- Linking goals and personal values
- Adjusting individual expectations
- Assessing readiness and motivation for EQ development

To bring about changes in the work through EQ, organizations focus on the following aspects:

- Foster relationships between EQ trainers and learners.
- Self-direct change and learning.
- Set goals.
- Break goals down into achievable steps.
- Provide opportunities for practice.
- Provide feedback.
- Use experiential methods.
- Build support.
- Use models and examples.

- Encourage insight and self-awareness.
- Encourage transfer and maintenance of change (sustainable change).
- Encourage application of new learning in jobs.
- Develop an organizational culture that facilitates learning.

To evaluate the change in the workplace through EQ, organizations need to evaluate individual and organizational effects. Thus, as a rule, the higher a person's EQ, the lesser is the feeling of insecurity and greater the tolerance for openness.

High EQ = Low insecurity = More openness

A person's preparedness to expose feelings, vulnerabilities, thoughts, and so on is a feature of EQ. Again, the converse also holds true. Johari illustrates this very well. Maslow's theory is also relevant—self-actualizers naturally have stronger EQ. People struggling to meet lower-order needs—and arguably even middle-order needs such as esteem needs—tend to have lower EQ than self-actualizers. The original five-stage hierarchy of needs explains that all needs other than self-actualization are deficiency drivers, which suggest some EQ development potential or weakness.

There is a strong thread of EQ in Stephen Covey's *The 7 Habits of Highly Effective Families* (1997). While explaining the seven habits, of highly effective people, Covey first defines a habit as an intersection of knowledge, skill, and desire, and then emphasizes our perceptive view of the world through our emotional bank account, that is, kindness, honesty, keeping promises, managing role expectations, loyalty, and the attitude to admit 'I am sorry'. The seven habits are the culmination of our emotions into a maturity continuum and can be listed as follows:

Habit 1   Be proactive, (the habit of personal vision) recognizing self-freedom and the ability to respond irrespective of situational cues and consequences.

Habit 2   Begin with the end in mind, that is, the habit of personal leadership, knowing where we are going.

Habit 3   Put first things first, that is, the habit of personal management, organizing and executing around priorities.

Habit 4   Think win–win, that is, the habit of mutual benefit, seeking a solution that allows everyone to win. This ensures successful relationships. A win–win character requires three important traits—integrity, maturity, and abundance mentality. With abundance mentality, it is possible to empower people in organizations.

Habit 5   First seek to understand and then to be understood, that is, the habit of communication. Empathic listening ensures this habit.

Habit 6   Synergy, that is, the habit of creative cooperation, can be developed only when we value the differences and believe in alternatives. It makes one plus one greater than two.

Habit 7   Sharpen the saw, that is, the habit of self-renewal, emphasizing physical, mental, social, emotional, and spiritual strength.

Covey's seven habits for highly effective people are, therefore, embedded with EI. Hence, managers with high EI can develop such habits to be effective in their respective areas of work.

Practitioner Speak 7.2

Hiring for Emotional Intelligence

Making a hire can be a hit-or-miss affair. A promising candidate can turn out to be a disaster, leaving frustrated colleagues and tattered client relationships in his wake. Sooner than anyone planned, the new hire and the organization part ways, with recrimination and regret on both sides.

Read this insightful blog posted by Bielaszka-DuVernay on *HBR Blog Network* by accessing the following link: http://blogs.hbr.org/hmu/2008/11/hiring-for-emotional-intellige.html.

Psychologists have identified a variety of intelligences over the years (Gardner 1993). Most of these can be grouped into one of the three clusters—abstract, concrete, and social. Abstract intelligence is the ability to understand and manipulate verbal and mathematical symbols, whereas concrete intelligence is the ability to understand and manipulate objects. Social intelligence, which was first identified by Thorndike in 1920, is the ability to understand and relate to people (Ruisel 1992). Emotional intelligence has its roots in social intelligence (Young 1996).

Exhibit 7.1 discusses the ways to deal with negative emotions at the workplace.

EXHIBIT 7.1 Dealing with Negative Emotions at Workplace

It takes a lot to be poised at work. Many a time, a surge of emotions places barriers to performing to the best of our abilities at the workplace. We all face hard times in life, and not many are able to cope with circumstances such as lay-offs in the company, being overworked, or concentrating while having a tough time at home. In a seminal research, Dr Callahan of Texas A&M University has proposed the concept of four Cs to help better manage emotions at work.

The four Cs in Callahan's framework stand for context, challenges, communication, and community. Callahan has noted that these four Cs indicate the potential causes of emotional responses at the workplace. Thus, organizational actions are categorized into four basic clusters that explain how emotions are triggered, and an understanding of these four Cs would help employees exhibit better control on their actions.

Context

Context refers to the environment in which individuals or organizations operate. Thus, employees should always attempt to adjust to the changing milieu within which they work. Changes are frequently met with resistance and thus changing contexts can trigger various kinds of emotions—both good and bad.

Challenges

Callahan notes that all employees should endeavour to meet organizational objectives by accepting the challenges or goals set for them by the management. Normally, companies organize various activities such as training, strategic planning, and other leadership tasks. However, one common emotion experienced is frustration. It can be frustrating to undertake new challenges without disturbing long-held organizational practices, and it can be equally frustrating if the management is afraid of changing established practices and implementing new ones. In this context, reflection is the key to overcome frustration by thinking about the decision choices in hand.

Communication

Communication is one of the most important tools for management. Established in both formal and informal ways, communication can result in effective management or otherwise. Callahan notes that communication activities are often high

(Contd)

EXHIBIT 7.1 (*Contd*)

on emotion and a large variety of emotions ranging from better employee bonding to jealousy may arise out of these.

Community

All organizations are essentially communities. Some common beliefs and norms bind together all individuals in the organization. Thus, various emotions, which include fear, alienation, and sense of belongingness among others, are evoked from time to time.

Further, Callahan provides some tips to solve emotional problems at the workplace, which include the following:

• Identification of feelings
• Identification of root causes
• Identification of its effect in the future
• Identification of the best option available
• Adoption of the option and acting likewise

Source: Callahan, J., 'The Four C's of Emotion: A Framework for Managing Emotions in Organizations', *Organization Development Journal*, Vol. 26, No. 2, 2008 (adapted).

The positive uses of emotion in an organization include listening with empathy, providing effective feedback and positive climate, ensuring openness and conflict management, and nurturing a no-blame culture. It provides benefits by enhancing trust and commitment, accelerating the pace of performance, inculcating innovation, and providing opportunity to employees to learn through mistakes.

Abuse of EI   Many organizations, because of their ignorance, make inappropriate use of the EI of people, thereby leading to poor performance, high rate of attrition, and increase of conflict in the workplace. Some of the negative uses of EI at the workplace are abuse of power by the superiors, nurturing a climate of exclusion and discrimination, harsh criticism, negative outbursts, and insensitivity to bad news. Managers show such negativity in their behaviour with people primarily because of their lack of emotional control, feelings of fear, and inadequacy. All these negativities significantly cost the organization. For example, harsh criticism inhibits creativity, negative outbursts depress the morale of the employees, and abuse of power leads to employees deviating from the organizational goals.

EMOTIONAL INTELLIGENCE, INDIVIDUAL BEHAVIOUR, AND PERFORMANCE

Emotional intelligence can help in stress resistance, is likely to contribute in managing individual performances, and helps in developing effective leadership.

Does EI influence individual behaviour? Since EI in its present form is a relatively new concept, not many studies are available showing direct linkage between EI and individual behaviour. We shall examine the relationships through linkages between the components of EI and performance. Here, we shall focus on abilities such as being able to motivate oneself, persistence in the face of frustration or failure, controlling one's impulses, monitoring one's own mood, soothing oneself in the face of distressing experiences, empathizing, and hoping for new challenges and opportunities. The various dimensions of EI are shown in Fig. 7.1.

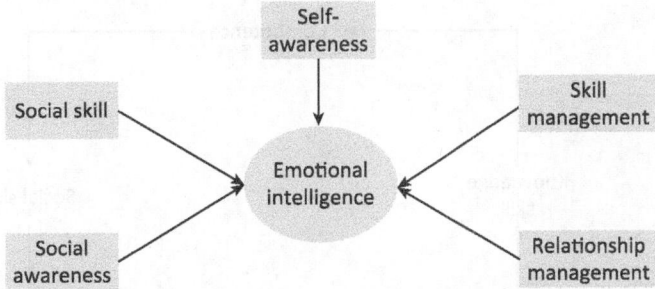

Figure 7.1 Component construct—dimensions of emotional intelligence

Relative Advantage

Emotional intelligence can be a factor in stress resistance, is likely to contribute in managing individual performances, and helps leaders in developing effective leadership. Goleman (1995) treated EI as a personal level independent variable in organizational behaviour. Accordingly, the EI base of each style of leadership as explained by Goleman is illustrated in Table 7.3.

Barring pace-setting and coercive dimensions of leadership style, all others have positive correlation with the overall climate of an organization. People with high EI could have the following characteristics:

- They are more satisfied with work and life.
- They persist longer and work harder than others.
- They adopt to change quickly.
- They demonstrate better organizational citizenship and behaviour.
- They are better suited to jobs that primarily require interpersonal competence.
- They are better team players.
- They are less vulnerable in the face of frustration and stress.
- They contribute more positively to the organizational climate.
- They are able to work with a diverse nature of workforce and are successful at ambiguity management.

Emotional intelligence can be learnt through sustained practice. Mcknight (1991) developed a framework of emotional competence, explaining how organizations can develop this

Table 7.3 Leadership style and emotional intelligence base

Leadership style	Emotional intelligence base
Coercive	Desire to achieve, intuitive, and self-control
Authoritative	Self-confidence, empathy, change catalyst
Affiliative	Empathy, building relationship, communication
Democratic	Collaboration, team leadership, communication
Pace-setting	Conscientiousness, drive to achieve, initiative
Coaching	Developing others, empathy, self-awareness

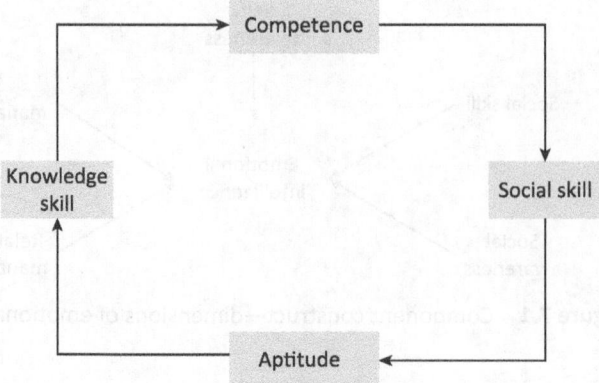

Source: *Mcknight 1991* (adapted)

Figure 7.2 Competence framework

through directed learning and obtain visible results (Fig. 7.2). Competence is a function of training, education, and skills that a person develops over time. It also depends upon some innate qualities that one receives from birth. The innate qualities help people to acquire knowledge, which is necessary for them to become emotionally intelligent. Knowledge also directly influences skills. Thus, competence is the combined result of knowledge, skill, and aptitude. In order to develop emotional competence, learning programmes must be incorporated as practice inputs. Only practice inputs under able guidance help persons in developing skills.

The leadership competencies, which can be enriched through EI, are researched on the following parameters and sub-parameters:

- Self-awareness
  - Emotional self-awareness
  - Accurate self-assessment
  - Self-confidence
- Self-management
  - Self-control
  - Achievement-oriented
  - Initiative
  - Optimism

- Social awareness
  - Empathy
  - Organizational awareness
- Relationship management
  - Inspiration
  - Influencing others
  - Change catalyst
  - Conflict management
- Teamwork and collaboration

ASSESSMENT OF EMOTIONAL INTELLIGENCE AND COMPETENCE

The foregoing discussion establishes the hypothesis that EI is important at the workplace. Now, it is important to understand its assessment and measurement criteria. Although there are various assessment and measurement tools for EI and competence, some of the well-known scales and tools alone are discussed here. Reviewing various existing measures, Davis, et al. (1998) concluded that adequate empirically tested new ideas on EI are not available. A major problem associated with these measures is lack of psychometric properties. Some of the measures also lack predictive validity.

The oldest measure is bar-on emotional quotient inventory (EQ-i). This is a self-report instrument, developed based on clinical trials rather than in any organizational or occupational context. It mainly assesses the personal qualities of people, which helps understand how one person has better 'emotional well-being' than the others. This was used to measure thousands of individuals, with major success achieved on record in the US Air Force recruitment, which supposedly saved nearly $3 million annually.

Multifactor emotional intelligence scale (MEIS) is an instrument that tests the ability of an individual rather than being a self-report measure. It requires the participants to perform a series of tasks especially designed to assess their ability to perceive, identify, understand, and work with emotion. This scale also suffers from the crisis of predictive validity, although it passes construct, convergent, and discriminant validities.

The third measure is the emotional competence inventory (ECI). It is a 360-degree instrument that rates an individual on 20 sets of competencies that link with EI. Goleman used this scale in his research. At present, however, no research evidence is found to test the predictive validity of ECI.

Another measure that has been promoted commercially is the EQ map. Although there is some evidence for convergent and divergent validities, the data has been reported in a rather ambiguous manner.

A 33-item self-report EQ measure was developed by a group of researchers, namely Schutte, Malouff, Hall, Haggerty, Cooper, Golden, and Dornheim, based on Mayer and Salovey's work. This self-report EQ measure has the evidence of convergent and divergent validities and was found to be positively associated with first-year college graduates and supervisor ratings of student counsellors working at various mental health agencies.

Since EQ comprises a large set of abilities, it is also possible to measure it through several tests of specific abilities. One such example is Seligman attibutional style questionnaire, which was designed to measure learned optimism and has been impressive in its ability to identify high-performing students, salespeople, and athletes, to name just a few (Schulman 1995).

MANAGEMENT OF EMOTIONS

In order to understand our emotions, we have to focus on our self-awareness, which helps us to recognize our feelings as we experience them. We also need to increase our ability to monitor feelings to gain psychological insights and better self-understanding. If we fail to notice our true feelings, we may not gain control over our actions. Hence, to manage emotions, we need to handle our feelings appropriately, develop our capacity to soothe ourselves autonomously and resist rampant anxiety, gloom, and irritability. Thus, we have to feel self-motivated and manage our emotions through self-control. Handling relationships requires us to manage the emotions of others as well. This requires leadership qualities and understanding of interpersonal effectiveness. Positive use of emotions requires listening with empathy, providing effective feedback, nurturing a positive climate, openness, no-blame culture, and ability to effectively manage conflict. The five EQ competencies of a leader can be explained using the CARES model, that is, creative tension, active choice, resilience under pressure, empathic relationships, and self-awareness.

> **Practitioner Speak 7.3**
>
> **Change Your Employees' Minds, Change Your Business**
>
> Many business leaders don't care why employees do anything as long as they follow the company's rules, processes, cultural norms and laws. But we've found that leaders can create and sustain stronger business results if they understand—and manage—how employees approach their work every day. When employees' thoughts, feelings, and beliefs are aligned with their daily work, they do that work better. Leaders though can be squeamish about approaching topics many think are better left to psychologists, so they don't even try to create alignment.
>
> Read this insightful blog posted by Keller and Love on *HBR Blog Network* by accessing the following link: http://blogs.hbr.org/cs/2012/03/change_your_employees_minds_ch.html.

When we perceive a threat, our brain reacts to protect us. This is a survival response built into our emotional brain, which is also referred to as the limbic region. The response control mechanism is regulated by the amygdala, an almond-shaped cluster. It is the primary emotional centre in the brain and its core function is to react to perceived danger. It is also the repository for emotional impressions and memories.

The EQ concept argues that IQ, or conventional intelligence, is too narrow and that there are wider areas of EI that dictate and enable how successful we are. Success requires more than IQ, which has been the traditional measure of intelligence that ignores essential behavioural and character elements. It is commonly observed that some people who are academically brilliant are socially and interpersonally inept. It is also known that despite possessing a high IQ rating, success does not automatically follow.

MODELS OF EMOTIONAL INTELLIGENCE

Based on the foregoing discussions, EI models can be categorized into academic and corporate types. The academic model of EI was used in a 1961 book on literary criticism where it was said that certain characters portrayed in Jane Austen's novel *Pride and Prejudice*, possessed EI, an intelligence that 'informs the emotions'. Mayer and Salovey developed the scientific way of measuring emotional abilities, correlating their own feelings with those of others and solving emotional problems. They defined EI as 'a type of social intelligence, which involves the ability to monitor one's own and others' emotions, to discriminate among these emotions, and to use this information to guide one's thinking and actions'. They also argued that EI encompasses both interpersonal and intrapersonal intelligences, with the following five principal features:

- Understanding one's own emotions
- Managing one's own emotions
- Sensitivity to others' emotions
- Ability to negotiate emotionally
- Ability to use emotions for self-motivation

Accordingly, the academic and conceptual models of EI can be illustrated after Salovey and Mayer as shown in Fig. 7.3.

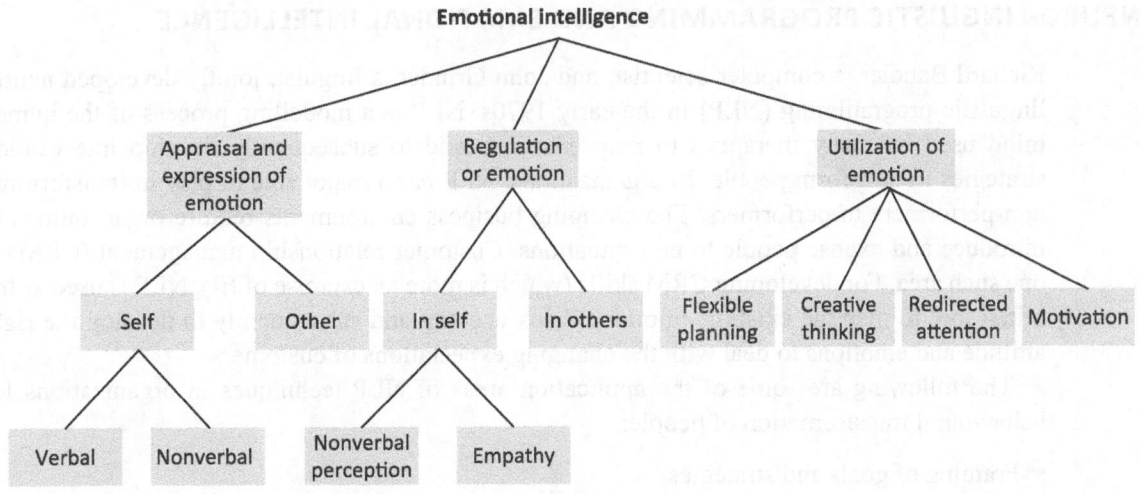

Emotional intelligence

Source: Mayer and Salovey (1994)

Figure 7.3   Conceptual model of emotional intelligence

Emotionally intelligent workers can analyse and express their own emotions, appropriately recognize others' emotions, and thereby effectively manage emotional problems in organizational performance and relationships. Since such workers become empathetic, they also avoid conflict. With socially adaptive behaviour, these workers become good performers with problem-solving abilities and are accepted by their co-workers as well. Being more optimistic, emotionally intelligent persons become more proactive than others.

In contrast to academic or conceptual models of EI, the corporate model, which is drawn after Goleman, encompasses all managerial attributes such as conscientiousness, self-confidence, optimism, communication, leadership, and initiative. After Goleman's thought-provoking study, EI has been recognized as the important ability that managers and leaders need to possess to be effective in teamwork and performance. While technical skills and cognitive intelligence cannot be neglected altogether, employees can become better performers with EI.

A study conducted by Vitello-Cicciu (2002) related the EI of nurses with their leaders. This research documented that emotional awareness of self and others makes managers and leaders emotionally more intelligent. They can be good teamworkers and collaborators and can foster a congenial work environment.

Practitioner Speak 7.4

Make Your Good Team Great

High-functioning teams are what make high-performing companies click. Whether the task is to create an innovative service or implement a new system, groups rather than individuals are shouldering more of the burden than ever before. The ideal team merges individual talents and skills into one super-performing whole with capabilities that surpass those of even its most talented member.

Read this insightful blog posted by Harvard Management Update on *HBR Blog Network* by accessing the following link: http://blogs.hbr.org/hmu/2008/02/make-your-good-team-great-1.html.

NEURO-LINGUISTIC PROGRAMMING AND EMOTIONAL INTELLIGENCE

Richard Bandler, a computer scientist, and John Grinder, a linguist, jointly developed neuro-linguistic programming (NLP) in the early 1970s. NLP is a modelling process of the human mind used by many therapists to map emotions and to subsequently develop intervention strategies to transform people. In organizations, NLP has a major role to play in transforming non-performers to performers. The changing business environments require organizations to introduce and expose people to new situations. Customer relationship management (CRM) is one such area. For developing CRM skills (which is more an exercise of EI), NLP is used as the initial tool to map the existing emotional bank account and subsequently to develop the right attitude and emotions to deal with the changing expectations of customers.

The following are some of the application areas of NLP techniques in organizations for behavioural transformation of people:

- Framing of goals and strategies
- Coaching (both new recruits and the existing ones)
- Helping people to manage stress and conflict
- Improving customer relationship and thereby increasing sales performance
- Improving overall productivity and performance of the organization

> Neuro-linguistic programming is a modelling process of the human mind used by therapists to map emotions and subsequently develop intervention strategies to transform people, that is, non-performers to performers.

Thus, NLP is used as an important tool for calibrating people to achieve the desired goals and objectives of the organization. In a competitive world, organizations can achieve excellence only through the effective use of non-imitable HR. Hence, developing people to meet the changing situations through tools like NLP gives better results.

Some of the important conditions for the success of NLP interventions in organizations are as follows:

- Clearly stating the outcome needs
- Ensuring that outcomes are verifiable through sensory experiences
- Ensuring that the desired outcomes are sensory specific
- Ensuring that the outcomes are appropriately contextualized
- Ensuring that the outcomes preserve the positive aspects of the present state
- Ensuring that the outcomes do not cause harm either to self or to others

Exhibit 7.2 discusses the importance of EI for leadership.

EXHIBIT 7.2 Emotional Intelligence and Leadership

Emotional intelligence can be of immense help for leadership positions. Though the concept of EI does not quite fit into the mould of leaders found in classic historical models of leadership (which focus on military strength and personal might), the rapidly changing world of business now calls for some other qualities as well. Today, leadership qualities are not restricted to being bold, tough, courageous, and firm resolute. This is because employees no longer accept autocratic leadership styles and expect a pro-democratic style of leadership. In addition, they have more avenues to explore than the past.

(Contd)

Thus, leaders have to deal with an empowered workforce and their role goes beyond consultative, cooperative, and democratic styles of managing employees. Prof. Batool (2013) has noted that in recent times the role of EI has increased in identifying modern leaders and developing effective leadership skills. His research outlines the qualities that account for EI in leaders. It also includes ways by which one can use one's EI to improve upon these qualities, which are as follows:

Self-awareness

Self-awareness is a very effective leadership quality. It helps people gauge their strengths and weaknesses and their feelings as well as how their words, gestures, and actions can be perceived by others. Self-awareness can be improved by keeping a record of one's actions on a day-to-day basis. In addition, one may slow down in times of emotional surge to reflect upon the situation and not react in haste. Thus, one can choose to react in a better manner.

Self-regulation

Self-regulation refers to staying under control. One can greatly benefit by regulating oneself since various untoward situations, decisions, and words can be avoided. Using self-regulation, leaders can enhance their flexibility and personal accountability and therefore use EI better. One can enhance self-regulation by developing a better idea about one's values. A close reflection on one's code of ethics gives answers to what one would do and what one would not, thereby facilitating decision-making for leaders. Moreover, increased accountability helps leaders gain the confidence of others

and earn self-respect. The best way of practising self-regulation is by staying calm.

Motivation

Motivated leaders consistently work towards their goals. This is one necessary quality that all great leaders exhibit. Self-motivation can be improved by re-examining one's goals and the reason why one had set such goals. This is likely to renew one's passion for work and result in a highly motivated leader. An optimistic approach always has a positive effect on motivation. A leader should be hopeful about the tasks he/she undertakes and consistently pursue his/her goals until they are attained.

Empathy

Teams and organizational members can be managed successfully by showing empathy towards others. Leaders should possess this quality to be able to place themselves into others' positions and take decisions accordingly. Empathy can be augmented by reading a person's body language and reciprocating accordingly. These measures help leaders gain better respect from employees and provide better leadership.

Social Skills

Social skills can help leaders become effective in many ways. These skills help them forge better rapport with employees, be open to receiving both good and bad news, resolve individual and organizational conflicts, and solve problems diplomatically. Social skills can be mastered by learning the art of conflict resolution, working upon one's communication skills, and knowing how to appreciate others.

Source: Batool, B.F. 'Emotional Intelligence and Effective Leadership', *Journal of Business Studies Quarterly*, Vol. 4, No. 3, 2013, pp. 84–94 (adapted)

EMOTIONAL LABOUR

The concept of emotional labour was developed by sociologist Hochschild (1983) based on her research on service workers. Service workers or employees while rendering customer services need to separate themselves from the work situation to deliver such services. The work situation may require them to answer the same questions from various customers or clients, who often tend to repeatedly ask irritating questions despite the answers given to them. Nevertheless, emotional labourers have to perform their jobs, separating emotionally from the work situation. According to Heery and Noon (2001), emotional workers need to restrain their emotions by 'surface acting' to render customer services, as part of their job requirement. Almost all service workers or employees come under the category of emotional workers. Restraining from emotions is an important prerequisite for the jobs of emotional workers as lack of restraint may result in increased stress in job, job dissatisfaction, and decreased quality of life. Many organizations arrange systematic training programmes for emotional workers to help them gain confidence in their jobs by enforcing self-control on emotions.

AFFECTIVE EVENTS THEORY

Weiss and Cropanzano (1996) are the proponents of the affective events theory (AET). It is called affective events as the theory proposes that employees' workplace emotions are affected by organizational events. Therefore, affective organizational events have a potential influence on the behaviour and attitudes of the employees in their workplace. The AET model helps in assessing the emotions at work by mapping employees' emotions to things at work, which correlates to their performance and job satisfaction. The model describes emotions as responses of individual employees to their work environment. Work environment is the aggregation of a series of work events that encompass employees' day-to-day work life. Such work events may elicit both positive and negative emotions from employees, although the emotional responses of employees get moderated by their personality, feelings, moods, and attitudes. The AET model suggests that employees' job satisfaction is influenced by their emotions, and therefore, their emotions can have a potential effect on their job performances. Briefly, AET acknowledges employees' emotion to be a determinant of their behaviour in job, and thus, emotional imbalance can alter their performance and job satisfaction. Therefore, managing employees' emotions with appropriate work environment is important in organizations.

Based on the foregoing discussion, the following can be identified as the important constructs of AET:

- AET helps in assessing how the emotions of workers or employees can influence their job satisfaction and performance.
- It acknowledges that both positive and negative work events can accumulate and affect the emotions of the workers or employees at the workplace.
- The emotions of workers or employees need to be effectively managed to sustain their motivation at work.

Thus, the AET model links workers' or employees' behaviour at work, emotions, and attitudes. It suggests moderation of adverse work events that may escalate negative emotional responses and affect the performance and productivity of the organization as a whole.

SUMMARY

Emotional intelligence (EI) is based on theories of personality, social intelligence quotient, and psychology. When EI associates with human abilities, it becomes a subject of study of organizational behaviour. With EI, people develop their ability to perceive, identify, and manage emotions and also succeed in developing the requisite competencies to become efficient in their work. In this complex business environment, when organizations are besieged with problems of continuous change, it is imperative to balance the emotional, cognitive, and physical resources for sustaining oneself. Intelligence quotient, per se, can only contribute to one-fifth of the total success of people. It is believed that EI plays a very significant role in the residual four-fifths of individual success, which is classified under non-cognitive abilities and competencies. Non-cognitive factors are important determinants of work behaviour, especially in a rapidly changing work environment. Hogan and Roberts (2000), Hogan and Shelton (1998), and many others have extensively studied the linkages between EI, personality, and workplace performance. Some authors believe that the Big Five personality traits and EI have a direct effect on task and contextual performances.

Task performance relates to behaviours that are directly linked with the job. Contextual performance refers to the interpersonal behaviours or actions that benefit the organization (Borman and Motowidlo 1993). The use of personality measures as a selection tool often suffers from the crisis of low predictive validities. Reasons like job–personality mismatch experienced by organizations are attributed to the use of fixed breadth of dimensions of personality scales. However, in recent years, interest in using personality testing as a selection technique has been renewed after addressing the defects of the common frame of classification of personality traits. Recent meta-analytic results for the influence of personality on performance (Barrick and Mount 1991; Hurtz and Donovan 2000) also establish linkages between personality, task performance, and contextual performance.

KEY DEFINITIONS

Emotional intelligence The ability to recognize and process emotions, their meanings and relationships, and to use this for problem-solving

Emotional processing A process of absorbing emotional disturbances, which focuses on the ability to process emotional information, more particularly the ability to recognize their meanings and relationships, without manipulating the emotions

Multifactor emotional intelligence scale An instrument that tests the ability of an individual rather than being a self-report measure and requires the participants to perform a series of tasks especially designed to assess their ability to perceive, identify, understand, and work with emotions

Neuro-linguistic programming A very powerful concept that contains all the positive and useful aspects of modern psychology and has many beneficial uses in the business environment, for example, CRM (customer relationship management)

Social competence The ability to understand others' emotions and develop the requisite skills to tackle people accordingly and is linked with six competencies—empathy, expertise in building and retaining talent, organizational awareness, cross-cultural sensitivity, valuing diversity, and service to clients and customers

CONCEPT-REVIEW QUESTIONS

7.1 Discuss the historical roots of emotional intelligence (EI). Further, highlight how the EI of people influences their workplace.

7.2 Discuss the differences between EI and cognitive intelligence.

7.3 Explain how an organization can abuse EI at the workplace.

7.4 Discuss how EI correlates with the behaviour and performance of an individual. Further, establish

the relationship between EI and leadership and competence of individual employees.

7.5 Explain the concept of neuro-linguistic programming (NLP) and establish the link between NLP and EI.

7.6 What are the important pre-suppositions of NLP?

7.7 Write short notes on the following:
   (a) Emotional quotient
   (b) Emotional processing
   (c) Social skills

CRITICAL THINKING QUESTIONS

7.1 A company has retained you to recruit HR executives with the prime responsibility of managing the construction workers of a multiplex. The HR executives are required to achieve project completion within fixed timelines and maintain good industrial relations. Suggest how you can use EI and NLP techniques to recruit the right fit for the company.

7.2 In a shopping mall with huge footprints, every single salesperson needs to manage more than 100 queries from visiting customers. However, the conversion rate is only 10 per cent. Suggest how salespersons can visualize the prospects by using their EI.

SELECT BIBLIOGRAPHY

- Barrick, M.R. and M.K. Mount, 'The Big Five Personality Dimensions and Job Performance: A Meta-analysis', *Personnel Psychology*, Vol. 44, 1991, pp. 1–26.
- Covey, Stephen R., *The 7 Habits of Highly Effective Families*, Golden Books, New York, 1997.
- Darwin, C., *The Expressions of Emotions in Man and Animals*, D. Appleton and Company, New York, 1872.
- Davis, M., L. Stankov, and R.D. Roberts, 'Emotional Intelligence: In Search of an Elusive Construct', *Journal of Personality and Social Psychology*, Vol. 75, 1998, pp. 989–1015.
- Dulewicz, V. and M. Higgs, 'The Seven Dimensions of Emotional Intelligence', *People Management*, Vol. 28, 1999, p. 53.
- Fleishman, E. and E.F. Harris, 'Patterns of Leadership Behavior Related to Employee Grievances and Turnover', *Personnel Psychology*, Vol. 15, 1962, pp. 43–56.
- Gardner, Howard., Frames of mind: *The Theory of Multiple Intelligences*, Basic Books, New York, 1993.
- Goleman, D., *Emotional Intelligence: Why it can matter more Than IQ*, Bantam Books, New York, 1995.
- Goleman, D., *Working with Emotional Intelligence*, Bantam Books, New York, 1998.
- Heery, E. and M. Noon, *Dictionary of Human Resource Management*, Oxford University Press, New York, 2001.
- Hein, S., *E. Q. for Everybody: A Practical Guide to Emotional Intelligence*, Aristotle Press, Clear water Florida, 1996.
- Hemphill, J.K., 'Job Description for Executives', *Harvard Business Review*, Vol. 37, Issue 5, 1959, pp. 55–67.
- Hochschild, A.R., *The Managed Heart: Commercialization of Human Feeling*, University of California Press, Berkeley, 1983.
- Hurtz, G.M. and J.J. Donovan, 'Personality and Job Performance: The Big Five Revisited', *Journal of Applied Psychology*, December 2000, pp. 869–879.
- Mayer, J.D. and P. Salovey, 'Some Final Thoughts about Personality and Intelligence', in R.L. Sternberg (ed.), *Personality and Intelligence*, Cambridge University Press, New York, 1994.
- Mayer, J.D. and P. Salovey, 'Emotional Intelligence and the Construction and Regulation of Feelings', *Applied and Preventive Psychology*, Vol. 4, Issue 3, 1995, pp. 197–208.
- McClelland, D.C., 'Testing for Competence Rather than Intelligence', *American Psychologist*, Vol. 28, Issue 1, 1973, pp. 1–14.
- Murray, H.A., *Explorations in Personality*, Oxford University Press, New York, 1938.
- Schutz, W., *The Interpersonal Underworld (FIRO)*, Science and Behaviour Books, Palo Alto, 1966.
- Singh, Shailendra, *Emotional Intelligence for High Performance: High Performance Organizations*, New Age International (Publishers) Pvt. Ltd, New Delhi, 2002.
- Thorndike, R.L. and S. Stein, 'An Evaluation of the Attempts to Measure Social Intelligence', *Psychological Bulletin*, Vol. 36, 1937, pp. 275–285.
- Thornton, G.C. and W.C. Byham, *Assessment Centres and Managerial Performance*, Academic Press, New York, 1982.
- Vitello-Cicciu, J.M., 'Exploring Emotional Intelligence: Implications for Nursing Leaders', *Journal of Nursing Administration*, No. 32, 2002, pp. 203–10.
- Wechsler, D., *The Measurement and Appraisal of Adult Intelligence*, 4th ed., Williams and Wilkins, Baltimore, 1958.
- Weiss, H.M. and R. Cropanzano, 'Affective Events Theory: A Theoretical Discussion of the Structure, Causes, and Consequences of Affective Experiences at Work', in B.M. Staw and L.L. Cummings (eds), *Research in Organizational Behavior*, Vol. 18, JAI Press, Greenwich, 1996, (pp. 1–74).

Emotional Intelligence at the Workplace

A national level management association having its headquarters at New Delhi, India, is headed by a retired major general, to whom four directors looking after four strategic business units (SBUs) report. The retired major general is a non-academic person and manages the show with his administrative acumen, keeping all the directors on their toes. The education director always disagrees with him, whereas the other directors try to appease him by always toeing his line. The other three directors always take his guidance, good or bad, underperform, and give excuses such as 'Sir, you guided us.' The responsible education director often enters into conflicts with the chief to correct the process and help the association grow. In his tenure, the education director could not only increase the business volumes but also contribute significantly to the bottom line, significantly reducing the cost. One such cost control area was curbing unnecessary nationwide air travels, dubbed as marketing visits, by the faculty. The chief considered that this would be counterproductive, as in the long run, this would affect the business prospects of the association. Another major cost control area was restricting the visits to nodal centres for quality check. These centres have been retained by the association to impart classroom training for distance learning students. The education director declared that visits to the nodal centres would be only on the basis of scrutiny of their filled up information and performance records. Within a year such visits came down from 65 to 10.

The association also followed improper pricing of the reading materials, supplied by the publisher, who followed the 8x formula (i.e., pricing eight times higher than the cost). Going through the cost details, it was evident that the publisher kept 40 per cent as marketing cost and gave the association a royalty of 35 per cent, which the association included in its accounts as income from book royalty. The education director felt that since all the publications were customized for the association, the market for the publisher was a captive one; hence, there was no need to allow 40 per cent marketing cost. Similarly, the publisher followed a system of dual pricing for books supplied to the association and books sold to the outsiders. The prices of books sold to outsiders were less than 50 per cent of what was charged to the association.

All these cost-saving exercises resulted in significant savings, leading to an impressive bottom-line effect.

The chief was not satisfied, as all these actions ultimately earned more credibility for the education director. As part of the system of the association, group meetings were held periodically, wherein each director with his senior team members had to sit together and narrate his experiences with the other SBUs, more in a critical manner. In such meetings, the chief acts as only a facilitator. Getting cues from one of the directors of a SBU, which conducts the admission tests for the students who enrol for distance learning programmes, in one such meeting the chief started hurling accusations against the education director and went to the extent of stating that everything under the education director was in a state of stagnation. 'We are in the process of losing our national visibility. Nobody bothers about the future. Students' services are very bad. I did several rounds of random sampling and found that they do not receive proper attention and support. All this rubbish will kill us.' He then wanted the education director to state what remedial actions he proposed to take to solve this impasse. The education director, unperturbed and cool, simply sought to know from his boss whether the conclusions were the results of random or purposive sampling. The complete house suddenly burst into laughter. The irate boss shouted back, asking everyone to stop laughing. Nonetheless, he got the message and kept quiet.

Questions for Discussion

1. Read the case carefully and suggest what emotional therapy you would recommend for the chief, for the education director, and for the organization as a whole.
2. Can you identify the uses and abuses of EI in this case?

Groups and Organizational Behaviour

LEARNING OBJECTIVES

After studying this chapter, the reader will be able to

- Understand the concept of groups
- Identify the different types of groups
- Explain the theories of group formation
- Recognize the effectiveness of groups
- Describe the group decision-making process
- Understand the influence of groups on organizational culture
- Explain the process of team development through group formation
- Develop group roles and norms
- Manage group dynamics and group conflict

CASE STUDY

SonoIndia—A Group Conflict

In SonoIndia, there are frequent conflicts between the work groups and self-constituted employee groups. Such conflicts practically lead to the total disbandment of the group culture philosophy of the organization. Being a Japanese collaborator, SonoIndia has adopted a couple of work culture practices that are followed in Japanese organizations. To promote group work culture, the company has formed teams of employees to achieve the intended objectives. These groups, named as work groups, are divided based on task assignments.

The workers of SonoIndia have also formed their self-constituted employees' groups, mostly under the initiatives of the trade unions. SonoIndia has two recognized unions with membership in the ratio of 60:40. It is often observed that the employer-constituted work group members belong to separate unions, which leads to conflicts and ultimately defeats the very purpose of forming the work groups. A job placement initiative, by deploying all like-minded workers together in a group, went wrong, as the company observed skill mismatch in several groups. The workers' allegiance to their self-constituted groups went to such an extent that the company ultimately decided to negotiate with the union leaders to resolve the impasse. The meeting with the union ended without any fruitful results; instead, it sparked serious differences between the unions. While forming work groups, the unions want the company to select a group leader from the union whose representation among the workers is the highest. The company observed that this would go against their management systems.

In a situation like this, you have been asked to suggest a solution. Explain your charted action plans to achieve group cohesiveness in SonoIndia.

INTRODUCTION

On tracing the origin and development of the social life of human beings, it is evident that right from the beginning people tended to be collective for reasons of survival. This process of collectivism developed mutual interaction, and this, per se, later developed the language and behavioural norms. Extension of such collectivism and subsequent formation of social groups is what is studied today in organizational behaviour. The study of work groups has significant meaning in organizational behaviour because of the behavioural dynamics of collective people. Through the historical process, it has been understood that group formation is a necessity to accomplish tasks, to establish a sense of identity, and to exchange ideas.

Characteristically, groups are studied in two forms—primary and secondary. Primary groups develop an emotional attachment and a culture of their own and make themselves distinctly different from the others by developing their own normative systems. Secondary groups, on the other hand, are developed by detaching personal feelings and attachment to get some specific work done or to achieve a desired level of performance. An example of secondary groups is the work groups in organizations. A primary group is a social group, which can also be an informal group in an organization.

The study of work groups in organizations is important to understand the collective psychology of people when they are in groups. Since the work process in organizations is now managed through work group formation, before fitting an individual to a particular work group, it is essential to assess the degree of compatibility, else the purpose of the organization may be defeated. The failure of Mazda of Japan in the US is attributed to such incompatibility, which forced Mazda to withdraw, despite being the first company (much before Toyota and Honda) to enter the US market. Toyota's current recruitment practices focus more on the assessment of such compatibility, which makes them possible to get the right fit and reduce the attrition rate.

> The study of work groups in organizations is important to understand the collective psychology of people when they are in groups.

Despite such logic behind group formation, a group is often misconstrued as a collection of people. A mere collection of people cannot be called a group because there is no interaction, cohesion, and goal commonality. Therefore, a collection of people (two or more) can be a group only when they have a common purpose or goal, when there exists within the group a stable structure (usually hierarchical with a leader), some established sets of roles, and a standard pattern of interaction, and when the members in the group identify themselves with the group. Many organizations interchangeably use the terms team and group. Although differences between teams and groups in today's organizations hardly exist, the concept of a group is more traditional, as it is the outcome of the principles of division of labour, based on job specialization, and of being placed under one supervisor.

The team concept is more modern because a team does not essentially require functional commonality, but members of groups strive to achieve a common goal. In a team, members interact interdependently and adaptively to achieve specified, shared, and valued objectives. Members in a team believe in shared commitment. In this chapter, however, we will not make any distinction between the terms group and team. However, to keep pace with the organizational practices, teamwork issues have been separately dealt with later in the chapter.

IMPORTANCE OF STUDYING GROUPS

The need to study groups is often questioned. Though the answer is evident from the introductory discussion, the reasons are again recapitulated here. However, as a precursor, it is important to remember that people in a group behave differently, though their individual behaviours may be different. The subject organizational behaviour primarily focuses on the issues of managing people in a group, as organizations essentially represent a form of secondary group (though informal primary groups may exist).

Understanding the group process in organizations helps assess how people in organizations work together and accomplish results. In today's organizations, though adequate time is spent and efforts are made to formulate strategies, the group process and dynamics are neglected, resulting in a failure to achieve the goals. Today's managers must know and appreciate how people behave in an organization, interact among themselves, and share common goals. Understanding these aspects helps the managers integrate the new recruits, prepare them for their job roles, make them aware of the norms, and thus achieve the desired group cohesiveness. Managers need to realize that people not only play their formal roles in organizations but also play different informal roles to develop better understanding among them. In addition, certain normative aspects of groups are also important. Norms need not always be explicit but can also be implicit. The significance of such group norms was recognized in the bank wiring room experiment conducted by Elton Mayo in Western Electric Company, where group norms persuaded workers to contain productivity despite the availability of incentives and opportunities to earn more. Thus, group norms can be both positive and negative. Positive norms bring a sense of order in an organization, whereas negative norms can be against the mutual interest of the people and organizations.

Similarly, the study of group cohesiveness is also important in an organization. Group cohesiveness factors bind all members of the organization to remain together for the purpose of achieving results. It is achieved when group members align their individual needs and goals. This is what Henry Fayol referred to as *esprit de corps*. A cohesive work group is a precursor for an organization's success. The manager, as the leader of the group, must focus on achieving group cohesiveness.

In addition, group development process, group conflict, group decision-making, group think process, and group dynamics are all important aspects to be considered regarding groups in an organization. Organizational success largely depends on the effective management of work groups.

Practitioner Speak 8.1

The Power of Teamwork

Few people realize that a group can accomplish what an individual alone cannot do—even when it comes to individual advancement. If you want the next promotion, you have to elbow that hardworking colleague next to you out of the way, right? Wrong. Here's a true story that shows you why.

Read this insightful blog posted by Craddock on *HBR Blog Network* by accessing the following link: http://blogs.hbr.org/cs/2011/09/the_power_of_teamwork.html.

DEFINITION

From our introductory discussion, it must be clear that in organizations, groups represent a collection of two or more individuals who work for a common goal and are interdependent. They interact with each other to achieve group objectives or goals. Since such interaction among group members entails managing many issues, such as personality, attitude, emotion, and individual interests of the people, the manager's task in managing the group becomes more complex. Managers always need to strive for effective management of group behaviour to achieve the results. Fred Luthans suggests that an effective group in an organization makes its members feel motivated to join, perceive the group as a unified entity, contribute to group processes, and reach agreements and disagreements through various forms of interaction.

Similar to many other managerial terms, the definition of a group is better understood once we explain its essence. This is primarily for reasons of lack of consensus and the interrelationship of the term with various disciplines. In the context of essence, a group can be defined as two or more individuals who share any or all of the following aspects:

Interpersonal interaction   Individuals do not form a group merely by being in the same place. There needs to be interaction between them.

Perceptions of membership   Individuals should be perceptibly aware that they are members of the group.

Interdependency and mutual influence   Any event that affects a group member affects them all; each member influences and is influenced by every other member.

Mutual goals   Individuals come together in pursuit of a mutual goal.

Motivation   Group members seek to satisfy some personal need through their joint association.

Structured relationships   Interactions are structured by a set of role definitions and norms.

As in the case of the definition of group, there is no consensus on the definition of group dynamics, even though Kurt Lewin advocated the term way back in the 1930s. One normative view is that group dynamics describes how a group should be organized and conducted. Democratic leadership, member participation, and overall cooperation are stressed upon. Another view of group dynamics is that it consists of a set of techniques. Here, role-playing, brainstorming,

> In the organizational context, groups represent a collection of two or more individuals who work for a common goal and are interdependent.

the Johari window, transactional analysis, and team building are equated with group dynamics. A third view, which is closest to Lewin's original conception, is that group dynamics is viewed from the perspective of the internal nature of groups, how they form, their structure, and their effect on the organization.

TYPES OF GROUPS

Groups have been briefly categorized into two types—primary and secondary. However, ideally groups can be classified from two dimensions—size and membership cohesiveness. In terms of size, classifications can be made as small or large groups and primary or secondary groups. In terms of cohesiveness, groups can be classified as coalitions, expert groups, and in- and out-groups. The generally accepted theory is that a group to which any person pledges complete membership and loyalty is a primary group; in the event of a conflict of interest, this group's well-being would be paramount. Although there has been no attempt to assign precise numbers to the size of a primary group, the group must be small enough for face-to-face interaction between the members.

Individuals may assume membership of groups other than the primary groups; such membership may be limited by time, task, or location. As an individual's affinity to such a group becomes higher, it is quite possible that this group will move up to become a primary group. In general, however, it is accepted that primary groups are socializing groups and have a very high degree of membership feeling and interdependency among the members.

Based upon an individual's membership status, groups can be classified as membership and reference groups or as in-group and out-group. The criterion here is that the image of the group is very powerful and it attracts individuals to become a part of the group. Until he/she gets full membership of the group, an individual looks to it as a reference group, the values and activities of which have to be imitated.

The Hawthorne studies (conducted in 1924) attempted to examine the relationship between light intensity on the shop floor of manual work sites and employee productivity. A test group and a control group were used. In an early phase, the test group showed no increase or decrease in the output, in proportion to the increase or decrease of illumination. The control group with unchanged illumination increased the output by the same overall amount as the test group. Subsequent phases brought the level of light for the test group down to moonlight intensity; the workers could barely see what they were doing but productivity increased. The results were baffling to the researchers.

> Based on an individual's membership status, groups may be classified as membership and reference groups or as in-group and out-group.

However, those responsible for the Hawthorne studies had enough foresight and spirit to accept the challenge of looking beneath the surface of the apparent failure of the experiments. The unanticipated results of the illumination experiments are generally regarded as the beginning of structured studies of human behaviour at work. Anthropologists had earlier demonstrated the tremendous impact that a primary group (a socializing group such as the family and the peer group) has on individual behaviour, regardless of context or environmental conditions. With the Hawthorne studies came the important recognition that work groups have primary group qualities, even if they were not initially conceptualized as socializing groups.

The Hawthorne studies provided an impetus to the study of human behaviour, specifically the impact that groups have on organizations and individuals. Successive experiments carried out subsequent to the illumination experiments have already been detailed in Chapter 2. From organizational practices, we find the existence of the following types of groups:

Formal groups   These groups are defined by the organizational structure. After the planning process, organizations group the activities and place them under a formal structure, deciding their goals and objectives, and the strategies to achieve them. Formal group members report to their superiors and interact with each other to achieve the common goals. Usually, a formal group comprises those whose nature of job is more or less homogeneous. On a shop floor, people engaged in doing the same job represent a formal group. Similarly, in a call centre, all out-bound callers handling the same customer account represent a formal group. Thus, a formal group is formed based on the job specialization and similarity of skill sets to reap the advantages of division of labour.

Command groups   These groups are also known as task groups. A task is defined as the cross-functional activities carried out by the group members to accomplish a common goal. A team represents the nature of a command group. A command group can be formed by drawing members from various formal groups. For example, to achieve success in new product launches, organizations may form a command group. Once the task is achieved, the group members may be sent back to their specific formal groups.

Committees   To achieve results, organizations often form permanent or temporary committees, drawing members from various formal groups. Committees also represent the presence of cross-functional members. For a command group, goals may be specific, whereas for committees, they are varied. For example, to ensure better transparency and accuracy in purchase decisions, various members drawn from the user sections such as finance, marketing, human resource (HR), and others may represent a tender purchase committee in an organization. Such committees may be permanent in nature. Again, organizations may form temporary committees, whose members may be entrusted with the task of achieving temporary goals. An example is a committee formed to probe into a case of fund embezzlement against a particular member.

Informal groups   Informal groups are formed within a formal organizational structure. Members of these groups primarily meet their social or affiliation needs by sharing their common interests. Thus, informal groups are not organizationally determined; the members themselves form such groups to fulfil their needs for social interaction. In a particular organization, functional proximity primarily determines the formation of informal groups. In addition, like-minded people, that is, those who have the same personality and attitude constructs or those who belong to similar status (in terms of hierarchy or economic status), also form informal groups. The constructive use of informal groups may benefit an organization. However, inefficient management may render informal groups counterproductive.

An informal group may be a friendship group, interest group, reference group, or member-ship group. Friendship groups are formed by like-minded people; those who have common interests form interest groups; reference groups are formed based on the compatibility of deci-sions and opinions; and membership groups are formed for affiliation-related needs.

THEORIES OF GROUP FORMATION

The most basic assumption about group formation is that individuals form groups out of propinquity, meaning spatial or geographical proximity. This may explain why people travelling in the same railway car each day form a weakly bonded group, but it cannot explain the other complexities involved in group formation.

The balance theory of group formation states that people are attracted to one another based on similar attitudes towards commonly relevant objects and goals. Individuals X and Y will interact and form a relationship because of common attitudes and values (Z).

Once this relationship is formed, the participants strive to maintain a symmetrical balance between the attraction and the common attitudes. When an imbalance occurs between the two, organizations make an attempt to restore the balance. If it cannot be restored, the relationship dissolves. Both propinquity and interaction play a role in the balance theory.

> The four stages of group development are forming, storming, norming, and performing.

The exchange theory of groups is based on the outcomes (rewards–cost) of interaction. A minimum positive level (rewards greater than costs) of an outcome must exist for attraction or affiliation to take place. Rewards from interactions gratify needs, whereas costs incur anxiety, frustration, embarrassment, or fatigue. Propinquity, interaction, and common attitudes all have roles in the exchange theory.

STAGES OF GROUP DEVELOPMENT

Being live entities, groups go through a process of evolution, beginning with their birth, maturity, decline, and death. These stages are by no means watertight or even sequential. Figure 8.1 represents the different stages of group formation. A brief explanation of the stages as suggested by Tuckman (1965) is provided here:

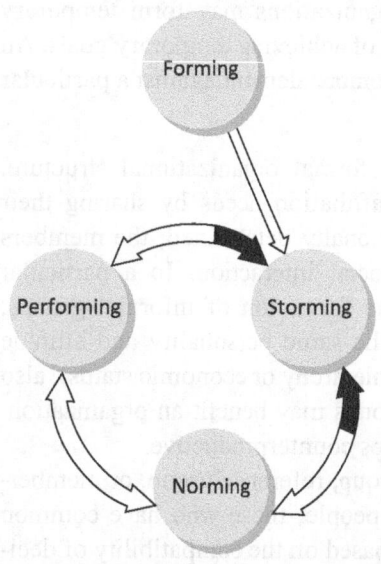

Figure 8.1 Stages of group formation

Forming The group defines the expectations from members, the environment in which it operates, and the reasons for its existence. The members get introduced to each other and share their ideas about what the group is seeking to achieve.

Storming Members contend for influence and positions. They try to be collective but encounter differences on issues such as group structure, agenda, and work allocation. There may be arguments and cross arguments for finalizing a group structure.

Norming Group members recognize the need for mutuality and interdependence. They negotiate their differences and arrive at workable approaches, upholding the interests of the group. Ultimately, they come out with the established norms for the group.

Performing After reaching a consensus on group norms, members start working together to achieve the intended goals.

It is interesting to note here that the first three stages take some time, during which not much progress is made. However, it must

> The effectiveness of any group is measured by the degree of task orientation and the degree of people (or process) orientation.

be understood that these stages lay the foundation for performance. Without these stages, the group will be trapped in trying to come to terms with itself. In addition, effective groups are constantly on the lookout for renewal. As the operating environment or the goals change, the group goes through the first three stages again, thereby rediscovering itself.

Ultimately, the group terminates. This happens when the group is unable to satisfy the needs of the members within the boundaries that it had set for itself. Members look to other groups to satisfy their needs. The group's existence becomes redundant and it fades away.

EFFECTIVENESS OF GROUPS

Two major parameters affect the effectiveness of any group. The first is the degree of task orientation and the second is the degree of people (or process) orientation. The effectiveness of a group depends on its ability to achieve its goals, to maintain itself internally as a cohesive unit, and to change and develop in ways that improve its effectiveness.

The comparison shown in Table 8.1 highlights some differences between effective and ineffective groups.

Table 8.1 Effective and ineffective groups

Effective groups	Ineffective groups
With clarity of goals, congruence between individual goals and group goals is achieved. Hence, goals can be changed depending on the situation.	Goals are imposed and hence get fewer acceptances from group members.
These groups facilitate two-way communication and improve mutual understanding as both sides can avoid confusion.	Communication is one way; hence, individual members' ideas and feelings get subdued, leading to frustration among group members.
They improve participative and distributed leadership among group members, thereby facilitating goal achievement and strengthening internal balance.	Leadership is based on authority; hence, group members' participation is unequal, as authoritative leaders emphasize goal achievements.
Equal sharing of power is possible, thus providing opportunity for individual goal achievement and fulfilment of needs.	Power is mainly derived from role position; hence, group members' participation is more formal and rule-bound. Members' disobedience is considered as violation of discipline.
Flexibility in decision-making, matching with the situation, participative approach, and encouraging group involvement makes the decision-making process more effective.	Decision-making is centralized, which minimizes group members' participation and involvement.
These groups promote positive conflict through group discussions and thus improve the quality of decisions.	Even genuine conflicts are suppressed, leading to increased violence and indiscipline.
Emphasis is placed on group cohesion and thus group members can improve their interpersonal relations, enhancing their level of inclusion and mutual trust.	Rigidity suppresses group cohesion.

Practitioner Speak 8.2

Group Intelligence Correlates More with Social Aptitude than IQ

Considering the complexity and global nature of business today, work is nearly always a team activity, and often those teams are embedded in ever-shifting networks. A new field of study, collective intelligence, is measuring the ability of teams to solve problems. This research is yielding powerful insights into improving the performance of networks, teams, and other collective groups. One breakthrough finding shows that collective intelligence is varied and measurable and—most surprisingly—correlates more with the social abilities of the team members than with the team's aggregate individual IQ.

Read this insightful blog posted by Rice on *HBR Blog Network* by accessing the following link: http://blogs.hbr.org/cs/2012/10/collective_intelligence_and_th.html.

DECISION-MAKING IN GROUPS

Decision-making is the process of selecting a course of action from a number of alternatives. Similar to planning, decision-making is also all-pervasive, and similar to forecasting, it is an important part of planning. Policy documents help organizations in taking managerial decisions. However, these are decisions of routine nature, also called operational decisions. Strategic or important decisions are to be taken after considering different alternatives. In order to be a successful manager, one has to necessarily develop decision-making skills. The decision-making process is similar to strategic planning, which has been explained in Chapter 1, and involves the following:

- Diagnosing, defining, and identifying the source of the problem
- Information gathering and analysis of the facts required to solve the problem
- Developing and evaluating alternative solutions to the problem
- Choosing the best decision from the alternatives
- Communicating the decisions
- Implementing the decisions

Of the various forecasting tools that help us in decision-making, the most important is the decision tree. It is a graphic representation of the sequence of decisions required in determining the expected values of alternative courses of action. Each decision alternative is weighed by developing a pay-off matrix, which depicts the probable value of each of the decision alternatives by quantifying the various outcomes and the probabilities of their occurrence. Probability is the degree of likelihood that a particular event will occur. It varies from zero (no chance of occurring) to one (certain chance of occurring). Outcomes are quantified in terms of expected value (EV), and then based on the EV, decision alternatives are selected.

> Decision-making is the process of selecting a course of action from a number of alternatives.

Apart from the pay-off matrix and decision tree, queuing models, distribution models, inventory models, and game theory are also used as decision tools. Queuing models help reduce waiting time to ensure better service to customers. Distribution models help identify the cost-effective way of distribution of products and services. Inventory models help determine the optimum inventory level for both inputs (raw materials and spares/components) and outputs (finished goods). The game theory helps measure the decision outcomes under different

> Group decision-making involves three major phases—the intelligence activity or the identification phase, the design activity or the development phase, and the choice activity or the selection phase.

situations of uncertainty. In addition, all the decision-making tools discussed earlier in the chapter are also used as important managerial tools. Delphi technique and nominal group technique are examples of group decision-making. Group decisions are also taken by forming various committees.

In a large majority of organizational situations, decision-making is a process of choosing between alternatives. Recently, there has been considerable research on how groups can enhance the effectiveness of decision-making by enlarging the range of alternatives available in order to have a wider choice.

Group decision-making involves three major phases:

Intelligence activity or identification phase It involves searching the environment for conditions calling for decision-making. It is a formal recognition of a problem or an opportunity and a diagnosis is accordingly made. Normally, immediate and severe problems may not have a very systematic and extensive diagnosis, unlike mild problems.

Design activity or development phase Inventing, developing, and analysing possible courses of action take place in this phase. There may be a search for existing standard procedures or solutions or for the design of a new tailor-made solution. At this stage, the decision-makers only have a vague idea of the ideal solution.

Choice activity or selection phase This refers to the actual selection of a particular course of action. This could be based on judgement (intuition or experience), by analysis (logical or systematic), or by bargaining (when some compromise needs to be made for an optimal solution).

Ideally, all members should be able to accept the decision taken by the group. This will be possible only when the group is mature, has a common goal, and has sufficiently strong processes to handle differences of opinion. The time available to the group to arrive at a decision also has a very strong influence on the quality of the decision taken.

Groups use several methods to arrive at a decision. Minority, autocratic decision, majority voting, expert decision, averaging, and consensus are some of the common techniques used. In general, decision-making by consensus is recognized as the most effective method. It satisfies the following five conditions required for an effective decision:

- The resources of the group members are fully utilized.
- Time is well used.
- The decision is correct or of high quality.
- The decision is implemented fully by all the required group members.
- The problem-solving ability of the group is enhanced (or at least not lessened).

Decisions by consensus, however, take a great deal of time and require a very high degree of member-maturity. Nevertheless, in terms of the ability of the group to make high-quality decisions, consensus productively resolves controversies and conflicts—which none of the other methods of decision-making do. Research shows that the more effective groups tend to have designated leaders who allow greater participation and more differences of opinions and express greater acceptance of different decisions than in other groups. Group members who feel that they have had little influence over a decision not only fail to contribute their resources to it, but also are usually less likely to carry it out when actions are required.

Delphi Technique

Delphi is an ancient Greek city. According to Greek mythology, it was here that the oracle of Greek god Apollo delivered messages to those who sought advice or information about the future. The messages were usually ambiguous and could be deciphered only by the priest.

In modern times, the Delphi technique is essentially a group process to achieve a consensus forecast. This method calls for the selection of a panel of experts from either within or outside the organization. The comments of the experts are crystallized from a questionnaire response and are then used as the basis to forecast. A questionnaire is prepared from the responses received from a prior set of questions in a sequencing manner. At every stage, information obtained from the previous questionnaire is shared among the participating members, without, however, disclosing the majority opinion. Otherwise, this may have peer group influence on the minority opinion.

The procedure of the Delphi technique may be enumerated as follows:

- To start with, it requires the selection of a coordinator and a panel of experts from both within and outside the organization.
- The coordinator circulates questions in writing to each expert.
- The experts write their observations.
- The coordinator edits those observations and summarizes them without, however, disclosing the majority opinion in his/her summary.
- Based on the summary, the coordinator develops a new set of questions and circulates it among the experts.
- The experts answer the new set of questions.
- The coordinator repeats the process until he/she is able to synthesize a forecast from the opinions of the experts.

The success of the process again depends on the following factors:

- Experts chosen should have the requisite knowledge and skills to give the best answers.
- Questions should be relevant to the objective.
- Criteria for evaluating responses should be consistent, unbiased, and befitting the objectives. Although there is no universal set of criteria for evaluating responses, it is often considered necessary to adhere to the following guidelines:
  – Consider the assessment made by the experts in terms of their knowledge in the area.
  – Consider the assessment in terms of feasibility, objectives, time, and resource requirement.
  – Consider the assessment in terms of desirability.
  – Consider the assessment in terms of extraneous factors.

Nominal Group Method

Similar to the Delphi method, the nominal group method also involves a panel of experts. However, the major difference between the two is that under the Delphi technique, the experts are not

> **Practitioner Speak 8.3**
>
> ### How to Get the Best Solutions from Your Team
>
> Smart organizations place a premium on group consultation. Studies done by psychologist Patrick Laughlin at the University of Illinois and his colleagues show that the approaches and outcomes of a cooperating group are not just better than those of the average group member, but are better than even the group's best problem solver functioning alone.
>
> Read this insightful blog posted by Harvard Management Update on *HBR Blog Network* by accessing the following link: http://blogs.hbr.org/hmu/2008/02/how-to-get-the-best-solutions-1.html.

allowed to discuss among themselves while assessing the questions, whereas under the nominal group method, they are given the opportunity to discuss among themselves. Under this method, the coordinator assumes the role of a facilitator, allowing the experts to sit together to discuss their ideas; records of these discussions are made on a flip chart. After this round-table discussion on ideas, the experts are asked to rank their ideas according to their perceived priority. The group consensus is then mathematically derived in terms of individual rankings. The process, therefore, affords creativity and facilitates scientific group consensus, unlike consensus by qualification (as the coordinator ultimately decides the best course of action) under the Delphi technique.

GROUPTHINK

Though a high desire for consensus marks a group as being effective, it might become counter-productive for cohesive, mature groups. Having understood the benefits of consensus decision-making, such groups might become so obsessed on reaching a consensus that there will be no realistic appraisal of alternative courses of action in a decision and deviant, minority, or unpopular views go unexpressed. The in-group pressures are so huge that it results in *groupthink*—a deterioration of mental efficiency, reality testing, and moral judgement resulting from in-group pressures.

The groupthink syndrome is defined by Janis (1982) as 'a mode of thinking that people engage in, when the members' striving for unanimity override their motivation to realistically appraise alternative courses of action'. In highly cohesive groups, there is a tendency among group members to try to avoid disagreements or conflicts with one another. Informal group norms are established; these apply pressure on individuals to preserve friendly group relations. As a result, the group avoids disagreements and does not seek out alternatives for critical evaluation. It has been shown (Johnson and Johnson 1994) that individuals try to avoid responsibility for their decisions by procrastinating on a decision or by rationalizing their agreement as group loyalty. The groupthink syndrome produces poor group decisions.

> Groupthink refers to the deterioration of mental efficiency, reality testing, and moral judgement resulting from in-group pressures.

A very formal approach to avoiding the pitfalls of groupthink has been put forward by Dr Edward de Bono, the pioneer of the concept of lateral thinking. Called six thinking hats, this approach formalizes the divergence of thinking processes necessary for high quality decision-making. The following is a brief description of the different modes of thought associated with the six hats:

White hat   Objective look at data and information

Red hat   Feelings, hunches, and intuition

Black hat Logical negative, judgement, and caution

Yellow hat Logical positive, feasibility, and benefits

Green hat New ideas and creative thinking

Blue hat Control of the thinking process

Such categorization allows a legitimate expression of feelings and intuition in a meeting, without apology or justification. In addition, it requires all members to be able to use each type of thinking without sticking to only one type. All the hats used in sequence will be able to bring out the various aspects involved in arriving at a high-quality decision, without having to contend with the pressures of conformance to in-group norms.

The following are some of the characteristics of the groupthink process, as identified by Janis:

- Overestimated group strength
- Illusion of invulnerability
- Unquestioned belief in group's morality
- Narrow-mindedness
- Rationalization
- Stereotyped view of opponent—consider out-group too evil, too weak, or too unintelligent
- Pressure towards uniformity
- Conformity pressure—to avoid disapproval, most people fall into line
- Self-censorship—people withhold their misgivings
- Illusion of unanimity

In the groupthink process, the Abilene paradox occurs when a group takes actions in contradiction to what they really want to do, which means consensus occurs due to pressure from members to preserve group harmony. Moreover, members of the group put in fewer efforts than what they can when they perform the tasks alone. This syndrome is known as *social loafing*. One of the prime reasons for group formation is to enhance productivity. Hence, when the group inhibits individual productivity, due to social loafing, it fails to achieve the results. However, social loafing is minimized when organizations lay emphasis on cohesive teams. Unique and challenging tasks also minimize social loafing.

Using the example of America's invasion of Cuba, Exhibit 8.1 briefly explains how groupthink may lead to poor decision-making.

EXHIBIT 8.1   America's Invasion of Cuba and the Advent of Groupthink

All is not right with collective decision-making. Leaders, even the brightest of them, do take wrong decisions—and with due support from their advisors. Such is the case with former American president John F. Kennedy, whose invasion of Cuba in 1961 is often regarded as America's greatest military debacle. His army was outsmarted and completely routed by Cuban forces, thanks to American overconfidence as well as lack of proper planning and backup air support. Nearly 1200 out of the 1400 soldiers sent to Cuba had to surrender and the rest died. This raised serious questions about the effectiveness of the decision-making processes followed by the JFK government.

Janis (1982), in his analysis of the incident, has come up with the term 'groupthink', referring to the

(Contd)

EXHIBIT 8.1 (*Contd*)

process of reaching a unanimous decision overruling the intent to probe into the alternative courses of action. As for the symptoms of groupthink, Janis (1982) has identified the following factors:

- A sense of being invincible, referring to the illusion of never losing to any force
- A sense of being inherently moral, referring to the illusion of never doing any wrong
- The process of rationalization, meaning that serious drawbacks of the plan are suppressed
- The process of stereotyping the opposition to gain a sense of marked superiority over them
- A sense of unanimity, referring to taking some members' silence for acceptance
- Pressurizing dissenters directly to make them conform to the group
- The process of self-censorship
- Overtly relying upon self-appointed mindguards

However, the following is the heavy price such groups pay for trying to maintain group cohesiveness:

- Reduced mental efficiency of group members
- No proper reality testing
- Biased moral judgement
- Decline in quality decision-making

America's attack on the Bay of Pigs in Cuba is an incident that showcases these symptoms and disastrous results. As expressly admitted later, group members who did not agree remained silent and those who were actively involved in the decision-making assumed that others had accepted the decision.

However, a positive outcome of this incident is that it prompted President Kennedy to revamp the decision-making process by allowing debating and dissent by its members. This helped America avoid a nuclear catastrophe the following year in its conflict with USSR.

Sources: Wright, R. 'JFK and Groupthink: Lessons in Decision-making', 2003, http://www.probe.org/site/c. fdKEIMNsEoG/b.4221087/, last accessed on 29 July 2013; Janis, I.L., *Groupthink*, 1982, Houghton Mifflin, Boston; and Whyte, G., 'Groupthink Reconsidered', *Academy of Management Review*, Vol. 14, Issue 1, 1989, pp. 40–56.

REASONS FOR JOINING GROUPS

With respect to the question regarding why groups are formed, there are a number of general tendencies, some of which are given here:

Similarity-attraction effect   We like people who are similar to us in some way.

Complementarity-of-needs hypothesis   We like people who possess qualities that fulfil our own needs.

Proximity-attraction effect   We like people who are close by.

Exposure   We like people to whom we have been exposed repeatedly.

Reciprocity   We like people who like us.

Basking in reflected glory   We seek to associate with successful, prestigious groups.

Furthermore, we also tend to avoid individuals who possess objectionable characteristics. Yet, from another perspective, the following may be the reasons for joining groups:

> Organizational systems may differ from firm to firm, and because of differing organizational systems and culture, group behaviours also change.

Affiliation   People are sociable by nature. Groups provide a natural way for people to gather to satisfy their social needs.

Goal achievement   In any knowledge-intensive task, groups are more advantageous than individuals. Groups get the benefit of pooled knowledge with numerous alternatives to problem-solving. This is possible because of a greater exchange of information among group members.

Power   Groups enjoy more power than individuals. In individual capacity, people may feel belittled to cope with any relationship where exertion of power becomes necessary. To illustrate, trade unions (example of a group) enjoy more power than the power of an individual employee. Groups enjoy more power than an individual human being fighting for upholding his/her rights. For example, consumer forum (group) enjoys more power than an individual consumer.

Status   Belonging to a group also confers status, such as membership of a club or an association. Some club memberships themselves are indicators of high social status of individual members.

Self-esteem   With group membership, individual group members can nurture self-esteem. With self-esteem, people start thinking of themselves as being a class apart and expect that others should recognize them. Membership of some groups fulfils such desires of self-esteem. Life Insurance Corporation of India maintains different levels of group membership, depending on the business volumes of agents. Obviously, a Chairman Club member enjoys a higher level of self-esteem than a Divisional Manager Club member.

Security   People join groups to feel secure. Some groups are formed exclusively to meet the security needs of members. For instance, to get protection from anti-socials, we tend to form a defence party to unitedly fight them.

GROUPS AND ORGANIZATIONAL CULTURE

It is now accepted that groups are subsets of larger organizational systems, which differ from one organization to another even though they may be in the same trade and in the same nature of activity. Due to differing organizational systems and culture, group behaviours also change. Organizational systems and cultures represent specific values, norms, and cultures unique to different organizations. To illustrate, the attitudes and value systems of the software engineers of IBM and Microsoft differ. Such attitudinal differences influence the change in their behavioural patterns. Some of the behavioural patterns can be traced to collegial culture; major behavioural influences, however, are enforced by the respective organizational cultures. There are many documented evidences of behavioural differences of the same cadre of people in two different organizations. The illustration of Fig. 8.2 can be used to explain the relation between the organization and the group.

The advantages and disadvantages of groups have been listed in Table 8.2.

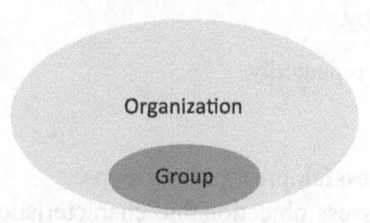

Figure 8.2   Organization and group

Table 8.2 Advantages and disadvantages of groups

Advantages	Disadvantages
Groups can exploit a wide range of knowledge, expertise, and innovative ideas.	Groups may block communication, restricting it to only one person.
Groups can ensure consensus in decision-making.	Groups may have dominant people who may restrict other group members from expressing their views.
Groups can communicate even complex information effectively.	In a group, members may be more status sensitive and may impose self-restriction on participation.
	Bad effect of social loafing, that is, questioning why to work so hard when others also work, may result in members performing less than their potential.

MODEL OF TEAM DEVELOPMENT

Even though the words team and group are interchangeably used in organizations, theoretically both are different. The concept of group has already been clarified earlier. A team is defined as a group that is driven by a common goal. However, it would be wrong for us to consider a team as a subset of a group. A group fulfils the test of homogeneity; that is, group members are involved in activities that are more or less similar in nature. In contrast, a team represents a cross section of people who represent different functions but try to achieve the same goal. To illustrate, the marketing team of a hotel may be represented by the cook, accounts personnel, doormen, stewards, and the room attendants, apart from the core marketing personnel. All these people play an important role in the marketing activities of a hotel.

Conventionally, team formation and development takes place through a sequence of linear phases. Good examples of such team formation are autonomous task or work groups. Team development, per se, does not take place with only a single sequence; it takes place through different stages, which may even be informal.

The stages of team development depend on a number of factors, enumerated as follows:

- Characteristics of the team
- Characteristics of the members of the team
- Background and past experiences of team members
- Nature of tasks and technology
- Environmental dynamics

The team development process can be illustrated in the following eight stages:

Pre-forming stage At this stage, people recognize the need to form a team because of certain external forces. Increased competition may force the employees of an organization to form a strategic team to frame strategies to withstand competition.

Forming It is the stage of team formation and the stage when a team starts its first meeting.

Storming Team members at this stage explore the situation.

Norming Team members now put in efforts to frame certain acceptance codes for accommodation.

Performing   Team members start performing to produce effective results.

Reforming   Team members assess their performance and identify their areas of weaknesses. As per their diagnosis, they redraw their norms to ensure success in achieving their intended goals.

Conforming   Team members, at this stage, achieve their intended goal.

Disbanding   Finally, the team ceases to exist. Members of the team get back to their core areas of job, which may be a particular department, division, or a work group.

Setting of cross-functional teams to develop time-bound goals is quite common in organizations. Working in a team requires that the individual employee must not only have work-related skills but also the attitude required for teamwork. Since a team is driven by a common goal, team members work together even when there may be some absentees in the team; that is, a team of ten members will deliver the results even when four may be absent. This, however, cannot be expected in a group. Since teamwork is now highly emphasized in the corporate world, before recruitment, organizations try to assess the teamwork attitude. Toyota Motors in the US emphasizes this aspect to such an extent that they make the job applicants go through successive hurdles for weeks together. Many organizations now believe more in the teamwork attitude than in individual brilliances.

Thus, team development follows two different activity tracks—task work and teamwork.

Task-oriented behaviour   The first of these tracks involves activities that are tied to the specific task(s) being performed. These activities encompass operational skills and include interactions of the team members with tools and machines, the technical aspects of the job (procedures, policies, etc.), and other task-related activities.

Teamwork-oriented behaviour   The second track of activities is devoted to enhancing the quality of the interactions, interdependencies, relationships, affects, cooperation, and coordination of the team. This track is important for generating group cohesion and organizational commitment and for sustaining the integrity and viability of the team.

A substantial portion of the energies devoted to building better teams can be accounted for in terms of activities that are aimed at people (other team members) and relationships. The coordination demands of a team require the team members to engage in person-to-person activities designed to enhance interpersonal communications, social relationships, and interaction patterns (the maturation and maintenance of the team as a cohesive unit). As the team develops, its ability to communicate, coordinate, and interact should improve, and this contributes to its enhanced viability as a group and to better team performance.

Coordination between Task Work and Teamwork Behaviours

To deliver results through team development, organizations need to develop both the task-related skills and the teamwork skills of individual members. It is important to understand that both are different; hence, development of these two skills needs to be done separately. The cross-functional element in a team integrates both the skills to achieve the common goal. Hence, a team is the real converging point for task and teamwork skills.

Practitioner Speak 8.4

How Will You Make Your Team a Team?

What do you do when the whole of the team you're leading appears to be less than the sum of its parts? Everything seems to be in place: solid people, a demanding but ultimately reasonable plan, sufficient resources. Yet there's still something missing from the effort, and finding a solution to this problem falls squarely on your shoulders. No, leaders can't single-handedly boost performance, but they can guide the tone, the tempo, and the mechanisms that create the opportunity for better things.

Read this insightful blog posted by Harvard Management Update on *HBR Blog Network* by accessing the following link: http://blogs.hbr.org/hmu/2008/02/how-will-you-make-your-team-a.html.

GROUP ROLES AND NORMS

Group norms are the expectations applicable for group members. Group roles, on the other hand, are the situation-specific behavioural expectations from group members. Group norms are usually not documented by the organizations, but these are the agreed-upon behaviours of the members. Hence, norms can also be classified as shared values. Once documented, norms become rules of conduct. To avoid the system of rigid rules of conduct, organizations provide flexibility to group members to develop their own behavioural norms, helping members to align their behaviour with the group.

Similar to group norms, group roles are also shared expectations of group members in a given situation. For example, a front-desk customer relations executive should tackle even an irritated customer while keeping his/her own cool.

> Group norms are the expectations applicable for group members, whereas group roles are the situation-specific behavioural expectations from group members.

Task-oriented, relations-oriented, and self-oriented roles of groups evolve naturally. Organizations, however, may prescribe specific roles to employees. These roles are classified as prescribed roles in a formal organization, which are limited to position title, job description, and organizational directives.

The role of an individual conferred by either the group or the organization may often be the source of problems. Some of these problems may be due to role ambiguity, that is, lack of clarity regarding duties, responsibilities, and/or authority. This may be due to the complexity of the job. Less-capable or less-confident group members may often exhibit role ambiguity.

Role Conflict

Role conflict is the mismatch between the perceived role expectations and the actual role of the individual. It takes place either due to one specific assigned role (internal conflict) or due to the assignment of several simultaneous roles with conflicting expectations (inter-role conflict). Inter-role conflict is 'a case of wearing too many hats'. This can be illustrated by citing examples from the corporate world. Many organizations state that their mission is to grow through customer satisfaction. This requires managers to focus on customer satisfaction and build a corporate image, keeping in view long-term sustainability. However, this role runs into conflict with that of achieving short-term results.

Many Indian organizations still believe in gaining strength in the short run, neglecting the long-term image-building initiatives. Likewise, profit-making and labour welfare often lead to inter-role conflicts. Thus, inter-role conflicts emerge when an individual employee gets too many directives from different bosses or when the employee concerned is required to meet several ends in one go. Thus, apart from wearing 'too many hats', inter-role conflict may also result from having 'too many bosses'.

Group Norms

Group norms may be prescriptive or proscriptive. Prescriptive norms dictate behaviours that should be performed, whereas proscriptive norms dictate behaviours that should be avoided. As already stated, norms differ from rules and hence these are not formal or documented. Norms get intertwined with the organizational practices in such a way that group members remain unaware that they even exist. Organizations may have disciplinary policies (i.e., documented norms) but complying with disciplinary issues may be more the enforcement of group norms. Hence, disciplinary issues document whereas norms indicate what needs to be followed or avoided. Norms thus govern behaviour in many areas. Similar to roles, norms may also be of different types:

- Performance related—relate more to the task of the group
- Appearance—relate more to the attire
- Demonstration of loyalty—internalization of loyalty
- Informal social arrangements—cliques, coalitions
- Allocation of resources—who gets what in a given situation

In organizations, norms develop in a number of ways:

Primacy Adoption of norms to ensure behavioural consistency by minimizing ambiguity

Explicit statements Statements or directives made by a group member

Critical events Evolve over a period of time, some of which may require group members to reassess their existing rules, procedures, processes, or relationships

Carry-over behaviours Carry over the group members' experiences, for example, occupational norms, ethnic norms, and athletic or social group norms

Group norms are established to facilitate group survival. Some critical events may threaten the achievement of group goals. This requires group members to reassess their norms and make adjustments, so that the group can survive and achieve success. Similarly, group norms ensure predictable behaviour of group members, allow members to express the central values of the group (to demonstrate their distinctiveness), and reduce interpersonal problems of group members.

Despite having group norms, group conflicts are often encountered. Group conflicts play a significant role, as some may promote creative decision-making, whereas some may be counterproductive. In terms of the effect, group conflicts may be either cognitive (task-oriented) or affective (relationship-oriented). Cognitive conflict generally plays a positive role, whereas affective conflict, stemming mostly from personality mismatch, may have negative impacts.

Organizations try to avoid group conflicts by setting group norms. Such group norms govern the relationship between group members in a way that hardly allows room for conflict among group members. This, however, can only limit intra-group conflict. Since conflict is also perceived as the most effective way to promote creativity and innovation in organizations, instead of having group norms to avoid conflicts, organizations may adopt openness norms to encourage open discussion.

GROUP DYNAMICS

Group dynamics is an extended thought of Kurt Lewin's concept of action research (1948). Lewin's action research argues against the traditional distinction between basic and applied science by suggesting that scientific understanding will occur most rapidly if the efforts of the researchers and practitioners are unified.

Group dynamics may be defined as the behaviour of a group of people under certain conditions and the way they change with the situation. It can also be defined as a branch of social psychology that studies the dynamics of interaction in a small group.

Group process is followed in almost all organizations. It is the process of understanding how an organization's members work together and get things done. Some of the ways to understand a group process are by studying the group's morale, membership participation, decision-making style, and how the members get along with each other. By developing a group process, organizations can successfully develop self-confidence, refine skills, and make friends. Not everyone in a group has the same expectations, does the same thing, or has the same commitment level. Knowledge about how group members interact, share common goals, and work with one another can help integrate newcomers and prepare them for the roles, norms, and cohesiveness of the group.

> Group dynamics refers to the behaviour of a group of people under certain conditions and the way they change with the situation.

SUMMARY

In this chapter, we have discussed the influence of groups on organizational behaviour. The study of work groups requires thorough understanding of behavioural dynamics of collective people. Although from organizational point of view, we focus more on secondary groups to accomplish the desired level of performance, people in collective form tend to form primary groups more for their emotional attachment. Hence, in organizational behaviour studies, understanding both primary and secondary groups is important.

Apart from the classification of groups into primary and secondary, there are formal groups, command groups, committees, and informal groups in organization. Each type of group has its specific advantages and disadvantages. For group formation, certain defined stages such as forming, storming, norming, and performing are followed. Similarly, decision-making in groups also follows a defined structure to ensure that group activities in organizations are carried out in a scientific manner. It requires diagnosing the decision problem, information gathering, developing and evaluating alternative solutions, choosing the best decision, and, finally, implementing the decision. In addition, in decision-making involving groups, certain decision-making tools such as pay-off matrix, decision tree, queuing models, distribution models, inventory models, and game theory techniques are used. Some qualitative decision-making tools in group such as Delphi techniques and nominal group method are also effectively used by organizations. Groupthink process necessarily requires creativity and innovation. Moreover, in organizational behaviour, the degree of group influence largely depends on the type of organizational culture. Some organizations believe in teamwork; however, style and contexts differ from one organization to another.

The chapter ends with a note on group dynamics, which determines the behaviour of people working in organizations under given conditions and which keeps on changing, depending on the changes in organizational situations.

Effective organizations take a close look at how the members work together, which roles they fill, and whether they are contributing equally. Group process observation and analysis can help early identification of problems, thus alleviating the need for a major overhaul as the year progresses. Being a group member provides a great opportunity to regularly observe how things are proceeding, depending on the frequency of meetings and an understanding of what to look for, one can be instrumental in ensuring group and individual success.

KEY DEFINITIONS

Command group It is a task group where tasks are defined as cross-functional activities and carried out by group members to accomplish a common goal.

Group dynamics It is defined as the behaviour of a group of people under certain conditions and the way they change with the situation.

Groupthink syndrome It is a mode of thinking by group members to strive for a consensus.

Mutual goals Using a goal congruence model, organizations try to set mutual goals.

Role conflict It is the mismatch between the perceived role expectations and the actual role of an individual.

Teamwork-oriented behaviour This type of behaviour enhances the quality of interactions, interdependencies, relationships, affection, cooperation, and coordination of the team.

CONCEPT-REVIEW QUESTIONS

8.1 Explain why people tend to form groups. Is it not possible to survive without forming groups?

8.2 What are the characteristic features of a group? How do such features contribute to the effectiveness of groups?

8.3 Explain the process of group decision-making. What are the problems encountered by an organization in group decision-making?

8.4 Elaborate the concept of group norms. How are group norms decided?

8.5 What are group roles? How do group roles lead to a conflicting situation? In what way is group role conflict resolved?

8.6 Write short notes on the following:
   (a) Tuckman's model
   (b) Socio-emotional or relations-oriented roles
   (c) Team-oriented behaviour
   (d) Task-oriented behaviour
   (e) Self-esteemed group
   (f) Power group

CRITICAL THINKING QUESTIONS

8.1 It is now a corporate practice to achieve success through group formation. However, group formation depends on the organizational culture. In this context, study any organization's autonomous work group system, where people work in a group but remain accountable for their individual tasks.

Prepare your report with the critical assessment of the culture of your sample organization. (Hint: Tata Motors follows this practice in their shop floors.)

8.2 Study the group dynamics of a knowledge-intensive software development company and report its strengths and weaknesses.

SELECT BIBLIOGRAPHY

- Bednar, R.L. and T. Kaul, 'Experiential Group Research: Current Perspectives', in S. Garfield and A. Bergin (eds), *Handbook of Psychotherapy and Behavior Change*, Wiley, New York, 1978.
- Forsyth, D.R., 'Building a Bridge between Basic Social Psychology and the Study of Mental Health', *Contemporary Psychology*, Vol. 38, 1993, pp. 931–93.
- Forsyth, D.R. and M.R. Leary, 'Metatheoretical and Epistemological Issues', in C.R. Snyder and D.R. Forsyth (eds), *Handbook of Social and Clinical Psychology: The Health Perspective*, Pergamon, New York, 1991, pp. 757–73.
- Freud, S., *Group Psychology and the Analysis of the Ego*, Hogarth, London, 1922.
- Hawthorne Studies, *Western Electric Company Hawthorne Studies Collection*, 1924, http://oasis.lib.harvard.edu/oasis/deliver/~book00047, last accessed on 15 July 2007.
- Janis, Irving L., *Groupthink: Psychological Studies of Policy Decisions and Fiascos*, 2nd ed., Houghton Mufflin, New York, 1982.
- Johnson, D.W. and R.T. Johnson, 'Constructive Conflict in Schools', *Journal of Social Issues*, Vol. 50, Issue 10, 1994, pp. 117–37.
- Klein, R.H., *Group Treatment Approaches*, in M. Hersen, A.E. Kazadin, and A.S. Bellack (eds), *The Clinical Psychology Handbook*, Pergamon, New York, 1983, pp. 593–610.
- Le Bon, G., *The Crowd* (translation of *psychologie des foules*), The Viking Press, New York, 1895.
- Lewin, K., *Principles of Topological Psychology*, McGraw-Hill, New York, 1936.
- Lewin, K., *Resolving Social Conflicts: Selected Papers on Group Dynamics*, Harper, New York, 1948.
- Moreno, J.L., *Who Shall Survive?* Nervous and Mental Disease Publishing Co., Washington, 1932.
- Tuckman, B., 'Developmental Sequence in Small Groups', *Psychological Bulletin*, Vol. 63, 1965, pp. 384–99.

CASE STUDY

Group Dynamics at MegaSoft

In network organizations, virtual groups are formed across the globe. This is more important for those who have a global presence and are backed by state-of-the-art technologies. One such information technology-enabled services (ITeS) company is MegaSoft, based in Kolkata, India. The company has formed virtual groups, who work together to achieve a common goal using video conferencing supported computer technology, to communicate and achieve results. The team leader sits at Sector-V of Salt Lake City in Kolkata, whereas his 10 team members are spread across 10 different metropolitan cities of Europe, America, and Japan. They meet at midnight over the computer screen and exchange information about the developments at the various client sites. The team leader, wherever required, suggests the steps to be followed and also apprises the team members of the other courses of actions. By definition, virtual groups do not hold face-to-face meetings. Instead, their communication and interaction is conducted through electronic mail (e-mail) and the Internet. This allows members to witness interaction, develop a visual picture of their group members, and see their reactions.

Team members are allocated their tasks on a weekly basis and the team leader reviews the progress on a daily basis through the Internet. Bob Alexander is the team leader, who operates from Kolkata. Before assigning the tasks to the team members, Bob ensures that all the 10 members understand their jobs, which are highly protocol-bound. Since group members are dispersed globally, each member has to perform individually. However, some tasks require group members to interact and develop group responses that need to be attended by each individual. This is required for commonness of technology support sought by different clients, spread across the globe. In order to ensure interaction among group members, the performance-reporting system of the company gives weightage to the frequency of exchange of thoughts among group members, which can be monitored through computer information available in the main server at Kolkata. This ensures forced interaction and agreement among the group members. Another area of performance assessment, in addition to target or goal achievement, is the degree of consensus while group members exchange their thoughts with their team leader. Each meeting is videotaped and monitored by the HR head to understand the group dynamics.

The results of the group dynamics are then matched with the clients' satisfaction index, which, inter alia, also contains certain performance-related questions about individual group members.

Summarizing the last one-year results, the company could identify the following important issues in the group dynamics:

- Individual group members are not surfacing to the group as a whole. The company could identify this syndrome by mapping the degree of consistency among group members. Customer satisfaction assessment pointed out various technical aspects of development projects about which customers feel that the members do not have adequate knowledge. The team leader wonders why such things should happen when he himself always clarifies their doubts and checks back their understanding over the computer.

- Group members failed to clarify and check back less-understood issues with the team leader on real-time basis because of time mismatch. However, expertise for troubleshooting is adequately available with some group members, who can always be consulted on real-time basis because of common business hours for many clients across the globe.

- Some of the group members hardly interact with others, even informally. Group members mostly interact only with the team leader, although during group meetings all group members virtually remain present.

During the development of the group norms, the company identified telephone calls as the preferred method of communication. Each group member can access the information provided by his/her team leader, even though it may not pertain to him/her. In addition, group members can always call their team leader for any contingencies. The team leader feels that although group members remain isolated from each other, they function within the given protocol to complete their assignments.

Questions for Discussion

1. Carefully go through the case and identify the important areas that MegaSoft should consider strengthening to enhance group cohesiveness.
2. Can you identify the several stages of group development?

Conflict Management and Stress in Organizations

LEARNING OBJECTIVES

After studying this chapter, the reader will be able to

- understand the causes of conflict and stress
- manage conflict and stress in his/her organization
- explain the process of conflict prevention
- describe the different stages of conflict resolution strategies

CASE STUDY

A Case of Three–dimensional Conflict

In the current globalized market, many organizations are trying to optimize their cost on research and development (R&D) work by locating the department in countries such as India and China. This is done to acquire the best talent at a competitive price and to confer more autonomy to R&D work, thereby reducing the interference from the marketing and production departments. This model has also been adopted by the Indian consumer electronics major StarMark India. The company operates in a fiercely competitive market and has already gained cost leadership by acquiring a global major. It deliberately located its R&D wing in Shanghai, China, and recruited the best talents in consumer electronics from across the globe. The R&D people came out with new prototypes, on almost a daily basis, thanks to innovative mar-

ket scanning, and sent those to the production units for development. The marketing and production teams discarded 90 per cent of such prototypes. The marketing team discarded these on the grounds that the designs would not appeal to the customers, whereas the production team refused to accommodate any prototype that required them to restructure their line. At times, the production team even refused to accommodate the designs vetted by the marketing team. This three-dimensional conflict ultimately led the top management of the company to integrate their R&D with production and marketing, forming cross-functional teams. Soon after, the R&D people alleged that such an initiative of the company was counterproductive to R&D work because it had reduced their output level, as no designs could pass through without the mandatory consensus among the cross-functional team members.

As a member of the R&D team, you are in the midst of the crossfire. Suggest how you propose to handle it.

INTRODUCTION

Conflict and stress can prevent individuals from performing at their best. Stress can be caused by a variety of factors and can lead to numerous consequences. Stress is a frequent cause of conflict, and conflict can also increase stress. Conflict mostly occurs whenever people interact. It arises because individuals have different needs, interests, and goals. It can be a highly destructive force if left unchecked and can lead to low productivity and morale.

Conflict is a disagreement between two or more individuals, groups, or organizations. It can be superficial or strong and can be short-lived or exist for long periods of time. Although conflict can be a major problem, certain kinds of conflicts can be beneficial. When handled in a cordial and constructive manner, conflict serves a useful purpose. What constitutes the optimal level of conflict varies according to the situation and the people involved.

DEFINITION AND CONCEPT OF CONFLICT

Conflict is a naturally occurring phenomenon with both positive and negative effects depending on its management (Sheppard 1984). It is a phenomenon inherent in all organizations and arises from the differences in the goals, needs, interests, attitudes, values, and perceptions during the interaction of groups such as management and labour (Bendix 1989). Essentially, organizations function as a 'means for internalizing conflicts, bringing them within a bounded structure so that they can be confronted and acted upon' (Pondy 1992).

Pondy further advocates that conflict is the essence of an organization. This is why an organization cannot be viewed as a purposive and cooperative system. Instead, it is the outcome of inbuilt conflicts, which perpetuate and make organizations adapt to changes by effectively managing the conflicts. By managing organizational behaviour, developing an appropriate organizational structure, and adopting the system and process of cooperative culture, conflict can be effectively managed. Since conflict is inevitable during interaction, its elimination is not possible. Hence, organizational efforts should focus on reducing harmful conflicts while nurturing the positive ones to promote creativity and innovation. Sheppard (1992) also recommended the elimination of destructive conflict.

Fred Luthans (1995) has classified conflicts as intra-individual, interpersonal, intergroup, and organizational.

According to Luthans, conflicts can be classified as intra-individual, interpersonal, intergroup, and organizational.

Intra-individual conflict This type of conflict stems from frustration, which arises from incompatibility between the perceived goals and the actual achievements. In Chapter 11, while explaining motivation, we will be discussing the need–drive–goal model. When individual employees encounter incongruous goals, they become aggressive and frustrated. Ultimately, they decide to either withdraw from the pursuit of their goals or become passive, realizing that nothing is going to be achieved. However, during the final stages of conflict resolution, individual employees may compromise.

Goal conflicts can also be categorized as approach–approach (cognitive dissonance), approach–avoidance (conflict between organizational goals and individual goals), and avoidance–avoidance (perceptive goal congruence). In addition, role conflict and ambiguity are classified under intra-individual conflicts. Role conflict and ambiguity mostly arise from cultural differences.

Interpersonal conflict   This type of conflict arises due to personal differences, information deficiency, role incompatibility, and environmental stress. It can be resolved through negotiation. Organizations adopt the following strategies to deal with interpersonal conflict: avoidance, diffusion, containment, and confrontation. The Johari window can also be used to analyse interpersonal conflict.

Intergroup conflict   This type of conflict arises due to competition for resources, task interdependence, jurisdictional ambiguity, and status struggle.

Organizational conflict   This type of conflict mostly occurs due to structural, hierarchical, functional, line and staff, and formal and informal conflicts.

Functional conflicts are constructive in nature as they help in achieving the intended goals of the organizations through positive disagreements. Thus, functional conflicts help in improving organizational performance. Many organizations strategically encourage functional conflicts, asking employees to play the role of a critic or engaging them in structured debates. Dysfunctional conflicts, however, spark disagreements and negativity and often get personal, resulting in problems in achieving the performance goals of the organization.

Without going into the rigours of theoretical debate, we will now focus on the various causes and the nature of conflict.

CAUSES OF CONFLICT

The causes of conflict can be best understood through the analysis of the sources of conflict. In fact, conflict triggers have already been elaborated, but in this section, we focus on a detailed categorization of those triggers through the classification of the causal factors of conflict.

Needs   Employees differ in their perceived needs; hence, depending on the varied nature of their needs, conflict may be due to multiplicity of needs, incongruity of needs, needs dissatisfaction, and dilemma of choice.

> The causes of conflict are needs, work environment, organizational factors, goals, and individual factors.

Work environment   The work environment can also be a potential source of conflict. The job roles of individual employees, their job interactions, line and staff conflict, and finally the job itself could be the potential sources of conflict.

Organizational factors   Quite often, organizational factors such as authority and responsibility, excessive or low standardization, transfers, communication, and scarcity of resources could be the potential sources of conflicts.

Goals Conflict often arises due to differences in the goals and objectives, both among individuals and between individuals and organizations. It could be a win–win, lose–lose, or win–lose conflict.

Individual factors People also differ from each other in terms of differences in culture, education, status, ideology, attitude, experience, competition, and conflict. Such individual differences could be potential sources of conflict.

TYPES OF CONFLICT

While acknowledging Fred Luthans's contribution to conflict, we have classified conflict into the following types—intra-personal, interpersonal, intergroup, and organization–environment. However, intra-personal conflict issues can be managed through the recruitment and selection process, by not considering candidates with a profile mismatch. Hence, organizations can prevent the occurrence of such conflicts by eliminating those who are attitudinally not compatible. The most commonly observed conflicts in organizations can be classified as follows:

Interpersonal conflict This type of conflict takes place between two or more individuals and is most common in organizations. Differences in perceptions, goals, attitudes and values, personality clashes, and competitiveness are the prime sources of interpersonal conflict.

Intergroup conflict This type of conflict is more evident when an organizational structure increases the interdependence among various groups. Since different groups may have incompatible goals and may compete for common and scarce resources, intergroup conflicts are more visible in organizations.

> The most commonly observed types of conflicts in organizations are interpersonal, intergroup, and organization–environment.

Organization–Environment conflict This refers to the conflict between an organization and the prevailing work environment. To cope with the competitive pressures, organizations often feel compelled to adopt a new work culture deviating from age-old practices. This creates conflict between the organization and the organizational practices, which at its extreme stage leads to major organizational issues such as high rate of attrition, employee unrest, and major problems in industrial relations.

CONFLICT MANAGEMENT

Conflict management is the process of avoiding conflict. However, its avoidance may not be possible in all cases. The conflict management process, in such circumstances, resolves conflicts on a real-time basis. Conflict is often confused with competition. The culture of competition is deliberately created by organizations to extract the best from their personnel. This is an example of friendly competition, sparked with deliberate goals and objectives. Unfriendly competition, on the other hand, leads to conflict. For example, in many organizations, variable pay is linked to individual performance; that is, targets are assigned to individual employees who, on achieving the targets, earn their variable components of pay and incentives. This system reduces their responsibilities towards their groups and the organization as a whole, thus making them selfish.

In organizations, two types of conflicts are visible—conflict over right and conflict over interest.

This is an example of unhealthy or unfriendly competition, which culminates in conflict. On the contrary, professional organizations assign weights to individual, group, and organizational performance, which truly makes it possible for people to deliver their best.

In organizations, two types of conflicts are more visible—conflict over right and conflict over interest.

Conflict over right   This is more related to employer–employee relationship, which is settled through the process of collective bargaining and grievance handling and partially through the enforcement of workplace discipline.

Conflict over interest   This relates to perceptions, attitudes, and opinions, which differ from person to person. Building a proactive organizational culture through shared vision and mission can eliminate this type of conflict.

Conflicts are avoided by organizations by promoting teamwork and cooperation. Teamwork can be possible only through a shared vision, empowerment with stake in decision-making, and transparency in information. Collective bargaining, conciliation (inducing a friendly feeling), negotiation, mediation (when negotiation fails), and arbitration are the most useful examples of conflict resolution tools in organizations. However, use of the appropriate conflict management tool must be situation-specific and need-based. Conflict management requires different levels of interaction between people, which may be basic communication, use of positive body language, or simple evasive tactics. This requires training and opportunity to interact and learn through experiences. To illustrate, collective bargaining or negotiation skills are not possible through theoretical training alone; they also require hands-on exposure to the situation. Learners can be made to understand real-life situations by allowing them to witness the conflict management process with their seniors. Slowly, they gain confidence and start contributing to the solution. During interaction, they learn to escalate and de-escalate the existing situation, depending on the other person's action. In the process, they master the following skill sets:

- Appropriate selection of policies and strategies to handle a conflict
- Proper understanding of their rights and duties, as well as the rights and duties of their peers, to ensure that there exists a proper synergy in actions and interactions
- Understanding of the mechanism of positive response
- Understanding of the process of averting negative behavioural responses
- Recognition of the emotions and feelings of other people
- Understanding of the effects of fear and admiration, and the process of controlling these effects
- Nurture of positive attitude and appearance
- Understanding of the behaviour of people
- Mastery over both verbal and non-verbal communication
- Understanding of the de-escalation strategy, that is, helping people to control their emotions
- Understanding of the process of tackling the effects of an incident, to render effective post-incident support
- Mastery over counselling skills

Practitioner Speak 9.1

Make Conflict Drive Results

Perhaps you've witnessed it: two managers in your organization go head to head in a grab for power, position, or pay. The conflict seeps down into the departments they oversee, as teams become aware of the contest and start backing their respective leaders. Soon communication and collaboration between the opposing departments break down.

Read this insightful blog posted by Harvard Management Update on *HBR Blog Network* by accessing the following link: http://blogs.hbr.org/hmu/2008/02/make-conflict-drive-results-1.html.

CONFLICT MODELS AND STRATEGIES

Organizational conflict is sensitized by a series of events and extends to all interactions among the members, departments, and groups. This makes it unavoidable and inseparable from organizational functioning (Lewicki and Spencer 1992). Organizational conflict represents disagreements, differences, or incompatibility within or between individuals and groups (Rahim 1985). With the effective management of organizational conflict, organizations can reach new heights of creativity, innovation, and competitiveness.

The models of conflict provide a conceptual framework for conflict resolution by elaborating on the process and actions through which conflict is managed in an organization (Patchen 1970). A possible conceptual model of conflict resolution is discussed here.

Stimulating Conflict

Managers in organizations stimulate conflict by nurturing friendly competition. This is, however, an example of a positive conflict to bring about changes in the organizations by harnessing the innovation and creativity of all cross sections of people. At times, organizations stimulate conflict by bringing in new people at very senior level positions (even at the CEO level). These new recruits shake up everything in the organization, including the prevailing systems, procedures, standards, and managerial approaches. Incidentally, it is important to mention that recruiting people at very senior levels is often not liked by organizations, as they prefer to groom people from within, through effective succession planning. However, induction of outsiders is often viewed as a deliberate strategy in some organizations to bring about changes by inducing positive conflict.

Controlling Conflict

In the process of stimulation of conflict, organizations may encounter dysfunctional conflicts that hinder smooth functioning. At this stage, controlling the conflict becomes important. The most dominant strategy of conflict control is to expand the resource base to enhance coordination among interdependent groups. To deviate the employees' attention from dysfunctional conflicts, organizations also set higher goals and try to form work groups with matching personalities and habits.

Resolving and Eliminating Conflict

Strategies for resolving and eliminating conflict are adopted in cases where conflict-related tensions disrupt the activities in the workplace, making it impossible to achieve goals and objectives.

The ways and means to resolve a conflict in such cases include avoidance, smoothing (through lip service by emphasizing that things will improve), and compromising (by bringing together the conflicting parties). Irrespective of the approach taken to resolve a conflict, the core focus of organizations remains the avoidance of destructive conflict.

Resolving Conflicts in Positive Ways

As already explained earlier, conflict cannot be eliminated, and instead, should be effectively managed. At times, organizations need to resolve dysfunctional conflicts by adopting various means. The following are some of the positive ways of resolving a conflict:

Use of 'I' instead of 'you' Managers often tend to use the word 'you'. However, the word 'you' puts the listener on the defence, as it sounds more like an order, emphasizing the point that as a subordinate, one has to carry the order of the superior. Use of 'I' is more personal and non-accusatory.

Power of anticipation Anticipation is a pre-study of the reaction of the listeners to the statements made. This ensures respecting others and thus reduces conflicts.

Selling of self-interest Positive conflict resolution succeeds when managers know the interests of the conflicting persons and then sell the desires and needs. The interests of the conflicting persons or the issues of conflict per se may be money, power, popularity, status, promotion, or security. Hence, managers can effectively sell the interests by appealing to the appropriate needs and desires of the conflicting persons to positively resolve the conflict.

Attitude While resolving a conflict, it is important for managers to understand the attitude of the conflicting persons. Understanding the attitude is difficult, but an incongruity between the verbal responses and the body language often gives clues to managers to help interpret the attitude of the conflicting persons. Accordingly, managers can decide upon the strategies that are suitable for conflict resolution.

Clarity Lack of clarity often sparks conflict. People fail to rationally allocate their priorities and efforts to achieve the goals and objectives when they lack clarity. Hence, eliminating confusion increases positive relationships.

Explanation of adverse consequences This should not be misconstrued as the use of the stick. Instead, it should be seen as an attempt at helping people understand the possible adverse consequences of continuing to nurture dysfunctional conflicts. Through transparent information sharing, by using glass wall management styles, conflicting employees are often transformed into positive contributors to organizational goals and objectives. Hence, it is also a good example of a positive conflict resolution strategy.

Furthermore, to resolve conflicts in a positive way, one needs to first resolve internal conflicts and place oneself in the other person's shoes. Thereafter, one must listen to what the other person needs, set priorities, discuss the situation calmly, come to a mutually agreeable solution, and honestly follow up on the decisions taken.

These techniques can be used together or separately, depending on the conflict. Conflict complaints should always be dealt with on camera (privately or individually), or else it can create tension and aggravate the situation. Through effective negotiations, managers should focus on win–win solutions.

Exhibit 9.1 explains how conflict management can provide opportunities for improvement.

Practitioner Speak 9.2

How to Manage Conflict

Last November, Philippe, a 33-year-old French banker, left Paris for a new challenge in London. He thought that a new job in a fast-growing British investment bank would give him valuable international experience and develop some new skills. The bigger salary and bonus were also a draw.

Read this insightful blog posted by Corkindale on *HBR Blog Network* by accessing the following link: http://blogs.hbr.org/corkindale/2007/11/how_to_manage_conflict.html.

EXHIBIT 9.1   Improvement Through Conflict Management

Conflict management is an uphill task. However, proper management of conflicts is important for organizations to function efficiently. Many of the conflict management techniques can in fact provide opportunities for improvement. Some of these are briefly explained here:

Forcing

Forcing involves pursuing one's viewpoints in spite of resistance from others. This is also known as competing. The following are some positive effects of forcing:

- It may lead to prompt resolution of the conflict.
- It helps augment self-esteem and respect for the person who forces others into taking a decision in times of resistance and indecision.

Collaborating

Win–Win situations can emerge from collaboration. It arises when both parties to a conflict agree to the solution and can come to a mutually beneficial result. The positive effects of collaborating include the following:

- It leads to a resolution that is profitable for both parties involved in the conflict.
- It provides solution to the actual problem.
- It reinforces mutual trust as well as respect.
- The outcome has shared responsibility.
- The outcome is likely to be less stressful for all parties involved.

Compromising

Compromising also involves a mutually acceptable solution that partly satisfies both parties involved in a conflict. Some of the positive effects of compromise are as follows:

- It may lead to prompt resolution of the conflict.
- The final solution is also practical to a large extent.
- It might serve as a temporary solution until such time a win–win solution is obtained.

Withdrawing

Withdrawing occurs when one does not pursue one's stand before the opposing party. It is also known as avoiding. Usually, withdrawing involves not addressing the conflict, postponing, or avoiding. The positive effects of withdrawing include the following:

- Lower level of stress is involved.
- It provides an opportunity to prepare better and then act.
- One can wait for a favourable circumstance under which to act.

Smoothing

Smoothing refers to giving more importance to the other party's concerns rather than pursuing one's own concerns. It is also known as accommodating.

(Contd)

STRESS IN ORGANIZATIONS

Conflict and stress are closely related behavioural phenomena. Conflict may increase stress, which may lead to work-based conflict.

Nature of Stress

Stress is an individual's adaptive response to a stimulus that carries excessive psychological or physical demands. The stressor is the stimulus that induces stress. Stress generally follows a cycle known as the general adaptation syndrome (GAS). According to this idea, individuals have a normal level of resistance to stressful events. Some individuals can tolerate a greater degree of stress, whereas others can handle much less. When a stressor is present, in the first stage, the individual becomes concerned about the stress. During the second stage, the person attempts to resist the effects of the stressor. In many situations, the resistance phase may end the GAS. However, prolonged exposure to a stressor without obtaining a resolution may lead to exhaustion and its incidental consequences. Some stress is necessary for optimal performance, but too much stress can have negative consequences. It is also important to understand that stress can be caused by positive as well as negative incidents.

Stress and Individuals

People handle stress in different ways. Some thrive on pressure; others panic at the slightest pressure and will do anything to avoid stress. Cultural backgrounds can affect a person's response to stressors. Stress can have behavioural, psychological, and medical consequences for individuals. It can lead people to engage in harmful behaviour and can adversely affect an individual. Individual stress has direct consequences on organizations. Too much stress may lead to decline in performance level and withdrawal behaviours such as absenteeism and turnover. People may exhibit poor attitudes when they are under too much stress. This affects their mental health as well as their physiological well-being.

> Stress is an individual's adaptive response to a stimulus that carries excessive psychological or physical demands.

Type A and Type B Personality Profiles

Type A individuals are extremely competitive and very devoted to work. They have a strong sense of timing and urgency. They are likely to be aggressive, impatient, and very work-oriented. It is because of these personality traits that a Type A person is more likely to experience stress than a Type B person.

Type B individuals tend to be less competitive and less devoted to their work. They have a weak sense of timing and urgency. Hence, a Type B person is less likely to experience stress than a Type A person. However, few people are either purely Type A or purely Type B.

Causes of Stress in Organizations

Stress can be caused by a wide variety of factors. Positive stress may result in an increase in energy, enthusiasm, and motivation. Negative stress has more serious consequences. The common causes are organizational stressors and life stressors.

Organizational Stressors

Organizational stressors may relate to task, physical, role, or interpersonal demands.

Task demands   These are stressors associated with the specific task or job being performed by an individual. Some occupations are naturally more stressful than others.

Physical demands   These are stressors associated with the job setting. Environmental temperatures, poorly designed offices, and threats to health can lead to stress.

Role demands   These are stressors associated with a particular position in a group or organization. Examples are role ambiguity and the various role conflicts that people experience in groups.

Interpersonal demands   These are stressors associated with the characteristics of the relationships that confront people in organizations. Examples are group pressure, personality style, and leadership style.

Life Stressors

> Burnout is a general feeling of exhaustion that may develop when an individual simultaneously experiences too much pressure and too few sources of satisfaction.

The causes of stress may reside in events that are not directly connected to people's daily work lives. Any significant change in a person's personal or work situation can lead to stress. The following are the top ten life stressors:

- Death of spouse
- Divorce
- Marital separation
- Jail term
- Death of a close family member
- Personal injury or illness
- Marriage
- Loss of job
- Marital reconciliation
- Retirement

Stress and Burnout

Burnout is a general feeling of exhaustion that may develop when an individual simultaneously experiences too much pressure and too few sources of satisfaction. The effects of burnout are mostly constant fatigue and feelings of frustration and helplessness.

Individual Approaches to Managing Stress

There are various ways of managing stress, for example, exercise and use of relaxation techniques. Time management techniques will help people manage time. Role management can be used to avoid role overload, ambiguity, and conflict. Finally, people can manage stress by developing and maintaining support groups.

Organizational Approaches to Managing Stress

Organizations have a vested interest in helping their employees manage stress. Firms can use institutional and wellness programmes. Institutional efforts to manage stress are based on established organizational mechanisms. Organizations can redesign especially stressful jobs, rearrange work schedules, and eliminate rotating shifts. In addition, the organizational culture can help manage stress. Wellness programmes are specifically created to help individuals deal with stress. Stress management, health promotion, and other such programmes can be made part of an organization's wellness focus.

Career development programmes can help minimize stress by clearly showing managers where they are in their careers at present and where they would like to be. While developing any type of stress management programme, managers need to balance the costs and benefits.

The various types of organizational stress are discussed in Exhibit 9.2.

Practitioner Speak 9.3

How You Can Benefit from All Your Stress

You are stressed—by your deadlines, your responsibilities, your ever-increasing workload, and your life in general. If you are like me, you even stress about how much stress you're feeling—worrying that it is interfering with your performance and possibly taking years off your life.

Read this insightful blog posted by Halvorson on *HBR Blog Network* by accessing the following link: http://blogs.hbr.org/cs/2013/03/how_you_can_benefit_from_all_y.html.

EXHIBIT 9.2   Types of Organizational Stress and Management Techniques

Stress is common among most employees across organizations. Most people have to undergo some level of stress in their jobs. Though the nature and level of stress may vary from one job to another, it is essentially an impediment that employees need to overcome to be more productive in their jobs and to lead a better life.

In the organizational context, Dr Karl Albrecht has classified stress into the following four types:

Time Stress

Time stress relates to an individual's anxiety over time or the lack of it. The usual symptoms are thinking too much about deadlines and rushing through the work to avoid getting late.

(Contd)

EXHIBIT 9.2 (*Contd*)

One can manage time stress by learning time management skills. In addition, one may prepare a to-do list and prioritize as per the urgency or importance of the task.

Anticipatory Stress

Anticipatory stress involves an individual's anxiety about one's future. The usual symptoms are thinking that something might go wrong in the future and an overall sense of anxiety over one's future.

Managing anticipatory stress can be achieved by positive visualization of future events. One may even try meditation in order to focus more on the present and concentrate on other work. In addition, it is important to learn to overcome the fear of failure.

Situational Stress

Situational stress arises from fear of scary situations over which one does not have control and can cause harm to an individual in various ways. Symptoms of situational stress are fear of getting sacked, emergencies, and loss of reputation.

Managing situational stress involves increasing self-awareness and learning to manage one's emotions. Moreover, it helps to improve one's conflict management skills from time to time.

Encounter Stress

Encounter stress involves stress over interacting with too many people or with people in groups. It is typically a result of contact overload. The symptom includes getting drained from talking to too many people or a group of people.

Encounter stress can be managed by improving one's emotional intelligence. Being empathetic also helps curb encounter stress.

Sources: Mind Tools, 'Albrecht's Four Types of Stress', http://www.mindtools.com/pages/article/albrecht-stress.htm, last accessed on 27 August 2013; Albrecht, K., *Stress and the Manager: Making it Work for You*, Simon and Schuster, New York, 1979.

CONFLICT MANAGEMENT PROCESS

Conflict management requires a systematic and structured approach. As mentioned earlier, conflict cannot be eliminated completely and hence needs to be managed. Some of the conflict management strategies commonly used at the organization level are discussed here.

Collective bargaining is of central concern to the process of conflict management. It is the mechanism through which labour and management negotiators try to resolve their disagreements by interacting under formal rules, accepted practices, laws, and conventions (Allen and Keaveny 1983). The purpose of collective bargaining is to regulate relations between unions and management. It has the effect of redistributing power, reallocating resources, rationalizing authority, and changing the psychological climate. Collective bargaining is discussed in detail later in this chapter.

The grievance procedure as a conflict management strategy is an integral part of the total collective bargaining process (remark by Senator John F. Kennedy on 4 August 1954 before the State Federation of Labour Conventions). It serves the general purpose of adjusting disagreements, individual dissatisfaction, and conflict, without recourse to strike threats and use of force. However, the grievance process can also be used to sustain and feed conflict, especially under circumstances where contract bargaining relationships between union and management have not been established (Kennedy 1954).

Within the area of labour management disputes, grievance negotiation and bargaining are key strategies used in the management of conflict. Essentially, negotiation involves the settlement of differences by means of verbal agreements, whereas bargaining also involves many non-verbal actions that are utilized to resolve a controversy (Pruitt and Rubin 1972). Bargaining may, therefore, involve a number of tactics to elicit concessions from the adversary so as to resolve the dispute (Pruitt 1972). The tactics used in the bargaining process, however, depend on the conceptualization of conflict issues. Four types of tactics have been identified in general—coordinating mutually satisfactory outcomes, conceding, breaking off negotiations, and persuading the other party to concede by using positional commitments, persuasive arguments, or threats (Hartley and Kelly 1986).

Employee Discipline and Grievance Handling

The workplace conflict resolution strategy also depends on the enforcement of discipline and grievance handling systems that exist in an organization. In a broad sense, discipline means orderly and systematic behaviour. Every organization, for operative efficiency, frames certain codes of behaviour for employees, under normal practice, contract, statutes, or mutual understanding. Breaking of such behavioural norms creates disciplinary problems.

A typical grievance handling procedure will consist of the following:

- Early intervention
- Identification of problem
- Clear expectations
- Feedback
- Positive reinforcement
- Follow-up

To enforce discipline, organizations adopt various approaches, which may be corrective, positive, or negative. Corrective discipline is ideally suited to solve continual performance problems, rather than isolated ones. Discipline may again be classified as positive discipline and negative discipline. When a person spontaneously abides by the required norms, it is called positive or constructive discipline. However, when he/she is compelled to behave in a desired way under threat or fear of punishment, it is termed negative, punitive, or autocratic discipline. The particular approach that should be followed depends on the respective organization's policies, strategies, and nature of manpower. Positive discipline is achieved through education and training, whereas negative discipline is enforced by punishment.

Indiscipline may be of two types—individual or collective. Individual causes are basically a problem of attitude, whereas problems relating to industrial relations are responsible for collective indiscipline.

Walter Kiechel (1990) recommended the concept of *hot stove rule* to administer discipline in an organization. When we touch a hot stove, we get burnt; thus, we get an immediate response that leaves no question of cause and effect. This analogy keeps the discipline impersonal—it applies to the act of an individual and penalties for a given violation are independent of the personality of the violator.

The approaches followed by an organization to tackle disciplinary problems ultimately focus on individual or collective conflicts.

Theories of Disciplinary Powers

Employers derive their disciplinary power presumably from two theories—institutional and contractual.

Institutional theory   Organizational structure is designed in a hierarchical manner. Employers assume the responsibility of looking after the interests of such an organized community. As such, they feel that they have the power to make regulations, direct operations, and exercise disciplinary control.

Contractual theory   This theory, however, considers that employers' disciplinary powers stem from the contract of employment. Employment contracts subject employees to subordination and thereby vest employers with the necessary authority to ensure performance, which again is possible by the enforcement of disciplinary powers.

Approaches to Discipline

Indiscipline and violence can be diagnosed from the following approaches:

- Legalistic approach
- Humanitarian approach
- Human resource (HR) approach
- Behavioural approach
- Leadership approach

The legalistic approach being too formal and rigid can hardly bring about changes in the workers' minds. This concept is slightly similar to progressive discipline. Other approaches are important because by taking necessary care, it is possible to minimize the recurrence of ill behaviour. These four approaches are interlinked, and therefore, we are not desegregating the approaches. We are rather trying to analyse them from an aggregative angle.

The following are the usual causes of indiscipline:

- Excessive job pressure
- Improper training
- Ignored complaints
- Unfair treatment
- Favouritism
- Poor management–labour relations
- Lack of confident leadership
- Lack of recognition and lack of opportunity for initiative

Looking at it in another way, the reasons for disobedience are identified as follows:

- Ignorance
- Physical or mental incapacity
- Inadequate training
- Dissatisfaction at work
- Misguidance by unions
- Desperate attempts to claim self-leadership by deliberate dissonance
- Absence of standard or uniform disciplinary policy

> There are two major theories of disciplinary powers—institutional theory and contractual theory.

The following are some indicators to identify indiscipline in an organization:

- High rate of absenteeism
- High rate of labour turnover

- High rate of sickness and accidents
- Multiple unresolved grievances
- State of industrial relations
- Low output, faulty out-turn, and low productivity
- Low motivation and morale
- Prevalence of 'we-feeling' in the work group

'We-feeling' means the dominance of individual identity over organizational identity.

Problems Due to Improper Disciplinary Action

Poor handling of disciplinary action may cause serious problems for the organization. Although the nature of problems vary from organization to organization (due to the differences in size, structure, management style, and ownership), the common problems may be summed up as follows:

- Increase in the number of cases of arbitration (including cases hard to defend), thereby raising cost in terms of both arbitration fees and work stoppages (due to loss of working hours of both the aggrieved employees and their witnesses).
- Increase in the cost of training and recruitment due to high labour turnover. Failure of the organization to set right grievances with proper intervention frustrates the employees, and at times, they withdraw from the organization either on their own or on organizational orders. This leads to colossal losses, particularly in terms of training costs, which the organization sustains either in a formal way (through training in outside institutions) or in an informal way (learning while at work).
- Increase in frequent work disruptions causes production loss, creates an adverse impact on market for non-compliance of purchasers' delivery schedules, and thereby affects profitability.
- Increase in hostility and loss of self-respect vitiates the organizational culture and develops mistrust, which in turn seriously impedes productivity.

This necessitates proper handling of employee complaints. A checklist of the actions to be followed by the concerned officer may be devised as follows:

- Put the aggrieved employee at ease.
- Communicate happiness at the employee approaching him/her with the complaint.
- Ask what the employee would like to discuss.
- Listen attentively.
- Sympathize with the employee.
- Explain what he/she (the officer) expects to do.
- Set a follow-up date.

Norms to Ensure Discipline in Organizations

The foregoing discussion must make it clear that to ensure discipline in an organization, a set of norms needs to be followed. The following are the basic prerequisites:

- The goals or objectives should be stated clearly. The rules must be in clear and unambiguous terms, with a special mention of the standards expected of the workmen.

- The rules and regulations should be properly communicated and must be understood.
- The authority to enforce rules must be specified.
- The procedure for appeal by an aggrieved party should be specified.
- The punishment prescribed should be made known.
- The rules of conduct must contain provisions for investigation and settlement of grievances.

Causal Factors of Indiscipline

The problem of indiscipline is the culmination of multiple factors. For precise solutions, we need to consider the exact causal factor responsible for the undisciplined behaviour of the employees. The causal factors may be one or more of the following:

- The employee himself/herself
- The supervisor
- The organization

Employee   Undisciplined employee behaviour largely stems from the organization itself. However, it is not uncommon to see employees who, because of their intrinsic characteristics (which build their habit-strength and personality), are aggrieved easily and nurture indiscipline. Their percentage, though minute, may influence the attitudes of the other members of the organization (at a conscious or an unconscious level) and thereby threaten the smooth functioning of the organization.

Supervisor   The supervisor may be the causal factor for indiscipline because of an inappropriate method of supervision and by giving improper assignments and orders.

To minimize the problems of indiscipline, supervisors should perform the following:

- Avoid inappropriate action in matching offences with sanctions.
- Ensure due adherence to processes and grant equal protection to all employees as a means of creating an organizational culture that supports the employees' dignity and rights.
- Minimize the need for employees to pursue their rights through external channels such as arbitration, government, and courts.

Organization   The organization becomes a causal factor when it uses unsound and unnecessarily restrictive policies and regulations and has improper expectations from the employees. To mitigate this problem, the organization should take the following steps:

- Apply its rules with fair objectivity or uniformity.
- Communicate to the employees the consequences of their actions.
- Adopt fair rules and directives and have reasonable expectations from employees.

Need for Disciplinary Policy

To obviate the problems of indiscipline, every organization should have a well-defined disciplinary policy. This eliminates management inconsistencies and promotes a climate of mutual respect, fair play, and clear standards throughout the organization. Disciplinary policy to a great extent depends on the prevailing norms and legal requirements. However, to make it more effective, the management can lay down its own philosophy, which has a humanitarian approach. Such a step will make the policy flexible and not rigid or formal, which perceives human beings as passive organisms. While framing a disciplinary policy, the management should adhere to the following principles:

- The cause of indiscipline should always be identified.
- Disciplinary rules should be framed after due consultation with the workers or their representatives.
- If any particular rule is infringed upon frequently, its causes should be investigated.
- Rules should be considered as the means and not as an end in themselves.
- Rules should not be rigid.
- Rules should be periodically reviewed to ascertain whether changes are necessary in the light of past experiences.
- Rules should be enforced without any bias.
- Rules should be strictly complied with by the management to set an example before others to emulate.

A sample disciplinary policy is given in Annexure 9.1.

Role of Trade Unions in Discipline

Trade unions are largely responsible for indiscipline and violence, particularly in organizations that have unions and where multiple unions exist. Different philosophies of trade unionism or different schools of thought perceive management differently. At times, they have different expectations. Thus, the economic advantage school believes in the maximization of wage gains. On the other hand, the job security school believes that long-term security of employment is more important than short-run maximization of wages. The Marxist school perceives conflict between capital and labour as inherent. The political school lays emphasis on power conflicts between management and labour over different basic issues such as the recognition of unions and collective concern over power and status. Such divergent schools of thought widely differ in their approaches. Unless the management tries to integrate its own philosophy with those of the trade unions, industrial relations are likely to deteriorate, which subsequently may give rise to indiscipline and violent behaviour.

However, the influence of affiliated trade unions in industrial disputes in India does not seem to be a major problem when we look at the relevant statistical data. On an average, the percentage share of disputes involving unaffiliated unions and others, as compared to the total number of disputes in India, is 85.23 per cent. Similarly, the share of workers involved in such disputes is 84.37 per cent, and finally, the share of total man-days lost due to such disputes is 93.7 per cent.

Steps to Enforce Discipline

A systematic disciplinary procedure is essential to maintain the established standards of work. The following steps are recommended to enforce discipline in an organization:

- Seeking explanation
- Consideration of explanation

- Issue of show cause notice
- Issue of notice for holding the enquiry
- Award of punishment
- Initiating follow-up action

The disciplinary proceedings involved in an internal enquiry are detailed here.

Issue of Complaint

A written complaint from the supervisor about the commission of the act of misconduct is the starting point. The complaint should indicate relevant details such as the time and place of the incident in addition to explaining the incident itself in detail.

Framing of Charge Sheet

The following points need to be ensured when a charge sheet is framed:

- The charge sheet should be drafted in clear and unambiguous language.
- If the charge relates to an incident, the date, time, and place of occurrence should be mentioned.
- The charge sheet, calling upon the employee to submit an explanation, must specify the time by which the employee has to submit his/her explanation.

Suspension Pending Enquiry

If the act of misconduct is very serious, the employee may be suspended pending an enquiry. It has to be made clear that during the period of suspension pending enquiry, the employee will not leave station. Subsistence allowance is payable to him/her under the rules. The employee should give a declaration that he/she is not employed elsewhere during that period.

Issue of Charge Sheet

The charge sheet should be served personally and its receipt must be acknowledged by the recipient. If he/she refuses to accept it, the charge sheet should be sent to his/her local and home address under registered post with acknowledgement due as well as under certificate of posting. If the charge sheet is returned undelivered, the envelope should be kept without being opened. In this situation, a copy of the charge sheet should be displayed on the notice board.

Consideration of Explanation

The employee's response to the charge sheet may be one of the following:

- The chargesheeted employee may admit to the charge and request for mercy.
- The employee may deny the charge and request for enquiry.
- The employee may not reply at all.

Enquiry Proceedings

The following points are to be noted regarding enquiry proceedings:

- If the charge is minor and the employee requests to be excused, no enquiry is required.

- If the misconduct is serious enough to warrant discharge or dismissal, a proper enquiry is to be held before awarding punishment.
- If the employee fails to submit the reply within the specified time limit, steps should be taken to hold the enquiry. While issuing the notice for the enquiry, the employee should be requested to submit his/her explanation.
- The enquiry officer should give full opportunity to the chargesheeted employee to defend himself/herself by cross-examining the witnesses produced by the management.
- It is for the management to prove the charges against the employee and it is not the employee who has to prove his/her innocence.

Co-worker's Assistance

Depending on the provisions of standing orders and service rules, a co-worker may be allowed to help the employee in an internal enquiry.

Ex Parte Enquiry

If the employee fails to turn up for the enquiry after being given sufficient notice, the enquiry officer may conduct the enquiry *ex parte* and gather evidence as required.

Enquiry Report

The enquiry officer, after having gone through the entire records of the proceedings and providing his/her reasons for accepting or rejecting the evidence tendered in the course of enquiry, has to categorically state whether the charges are proved or not proved. He/She has to submit a written report giving the verdict and recommendation together with the reasons.

Final Action

The competent authority will go through the enquiry report and all the relevant papers and exhibits and will have the option to agree or disagree with the findings of the enquiry officer. If he/she does not agree with the findings of the enquiry officer, he/she has to give reasons for doing so. In case the competent authority differs with the findings of the enquiry officer who has exonerated the charged employee and decides to award punishment, he/she has to record reasons for doing so. The employee should be informed in writing of the punishment.

Discipline without Punishment

Disciplinary problems in organizations can also be settled without inflicting punishment. This approach is known as discipline without punishment. John Huberman (1967), a proponent of this approach, spelt out the methodology to handle disciplinary problems in organizations with a positive disciplinary approach. He has suggested the following courses of action to rectify indiscipline among the employees in organizations:

- No disciplinary demotions, suspensions, or other forms of punishment should be applied.
- In case of disciplinary problems that may consequently give rise to unsatisfactory work performance (e.g., carelessness in handling materials, less attention to duty) or breach of discipline (e.g., overstaying rest or lunch periods, absenting from duty), the following action should be taken:

> **Practitioner Speak 9.4**
>
> **The Fatal Flaw with Anger Management Programs**
>
> Handling conflict is one of the most difficult aspects of any manager's job. In the 30 years I've worked with C-level executives, I've noticed that playing King Solomon to warring colleagues has gotten even harder, thanks to the 'anger management' programs designed to eradicate intense emotions in the workplace. Too many of these programs deliver the message: 'Just don't get angry'— usually after someone has already had a bout of rage.
>
> Read this insightful blog posted by Berglas on *HBR Blog Network* by accessing the following link: http://blogs.hbr.org/cs/2013/07/the_fatal_flaw_with_anger_management.html.

- The immediate superior will offer the worker a casual and friendly reminder on the job.
- If the incident continues to recur, the boss will again try to correct it by calling the individual to the office for a serious, but friendly, chat. The boss at this stage will explain the need for and the purpose of the rules to make sure that the employee understands them.
- In case of further repetition of the incident, the earlier step should be repeated with some variation like verifying from the employee whether he/she dislikes the work. If that is the case, the employee may be told that it would be appropriate for him/her to look for some other job or line of work. This conversation may be further confirmed in a letter sent to the employee's home.
- If the employee continues to be indisciplined even after six to eight weeks from this period, he/she should be asked to go home with pay to consider seriously whether he/she does or does not wish to abide by the company standards. At this time, the employee should be informed that recurrence of such behaviour would result in his/her termination.
- If another incident occurs even after this, the employee's services may be terminated.

Huberman contended that this approach, to a significant extent, changes indiscipline among employees, and thus, without directly taking any punitive measures, rectification or correction of the employees behaviour becomes possible.

Opposed to this approach, we have Kiechel's *hot stove rule*, which suggested that infringement of discipline should invite direct punitive measures to rectify the behaviour. Since sufficient studies are not available to authenticate which disciplinary action is more appropriate, it is difficult to suggest a particular approach to handle disciplinary problems in Indian organizations.

GRIEVANCE HANDLING

Similar to managing the problem of discipline, proper grievance handling is also important to manage conflicts. The International Labour Organization (ILO) defines grievance as a 'measure or situation, which concerns the relations between employer and the worker or which affects or may affect the conditions of employment of one or several workers in the undertaking when

> Grievance is defined as the cause for complaints or annoyance.

that measure or situation appears contrary to provisions of an applicable collective agreement or of an individual contract of employment'. It may arise on issues of discipline and dismissal, payment of wages and fringe benefits, working time, overtime, promotion, demotion, transfer, safety, job description, and many other work-related issues.

Grievance is defined as the cause for complaints or annoyance. Initially, grievance handling was a one-step procedure. The worker directly approached the employer and a decision was taken immediately. However, with the development of mass production facilities, an increased number of workers and supervisors, and the complications of multi-tier organizational structure, the number of grievances in organizations has gone up considerably, making it difficult to sustain grievance handling as a one-step procedure.

The best way of handling grievances is to deal with them in the shortest possible time and at the lowest possible level. Unfortunately, not many establishments have a formal laid-out procedure for dealing with grievances. In grievance handling, the role of the personnel manager should be purely advisory, and every effort should be made to induct and train each supervisor in effectively handling the grievances of the subordinates.

Grievance Handling Procedure

The stepladder procedure of grievance handling is a widely used technique. The stages involved in this procedure are as follows:

- The aggrieved employee approaches the immediate supervisor either in person or through a written application in a standard form within a week's time of the occurrence of the grievance. The immediate supervisor (in accordance with the delegated authority and the type of grievance) discusses the grievance with the employee and gives his/her decision. A time limit of two weeks can be given for this stage.
- If the employee is not satisfied with the decision in the first stage, he/she may approach the departmental head, with a written application in a standard form, for reconsidering the case. The employee may be allowed to personally represent the case along with a co-worker. The departmental head should give his or her decision in 15 days' time.
- The appeals at this stage would be handled by a joint committee consisting of an equal number of representatives of the union and management. A secretariat is provided to process the cases at this stage. This committee should also have a time limit for appeals as well as for disposal of the grievance referred to it. This committee shall give its recommendation by consensus and agreement. Unanimous recommendations of the committee shall be accepted by the management, who must issue the orders accordingly. The union and management may also reserve the right to not accept the recommendations. If they do not respond, it should be deemed to have been accepted by both. In the event of non-acceptance of the recommendations by either party or non-unanimity in the committee at this stage, the grievance may be forwarded by the committee to a high-level joint committee.
- At this stage, the joint committee shall consist of the top management and union representatives. Cases spilling over from the previous stage as well as those brought up by either side will be considered and decisions will be taken for implementation. If disagreements still prevail, both the sides may refer it for arbitration.

With a sincerity of purpose and an intention to resolve disagreements across the table, a formalized procedure as indicated here is bound to result in the achievement of industrial harmony.

This model of grievance handling was adopted in the 16th Session of the Indian Labour Conference in 1958 as part of the code of discipline in a voluntary measure. Many progressive organizations have adopted the system with suitable modifications.

PRINCIPLES OF NATURAL JUSTICE

In a series of decisions, the Supreme Court of India has made certain observations while dealing with the delinquent employees. These are known as principles of natural justice, which require the following:

- The employee proceeded against must be informed clearly of the charges levelled against him/her.
- The witness must be examined ordinarily in the presence of the chargesheeted employee with respect to the charges.
- The employee must be given a fair opportunity to cross-examine the witness.
- The enquiry officer has to record his/her findings along with the reasons in the report.

COLLECTIVE BARGAINING AS CONFLICT RESOLUTION STRATEGY

In addition to the enforcement of discipline and maintaining scientific grievance handling systems, organizations make use of collective bargaining, which is a more institutionalized and structured approach in cases involving collective conflict. Collective bargaining is a method to determine the working conditions and terms of employment through negotiations that take place between an employer and one or more workers of an organization. The negotiation process helps the two sides to reach an agreement. Collective bargaining is considered an economic institution, and trade unionism restricts the entry into the trade by forming a labour cartel. Alan Flanders (1975) discarded this concept and advocated that collective bargaining is basically political as it aims to protect an employee's dignity rather than his/her economic interest. The Marxist school considers it as a means of social control. The marketing concept considers the collective bargaining process as a constitutional system to determine the relations between the management and trade unions. Finally, the industrial relations concept views it as a system of 'industrial governance'. In practice, however, we do not take into consideration any of the theoretical distinctions. All these theories converge on three basic

> Collective bargaining is a method to determine the working conditions and terms of employment through negotiations.

issues, which define collective bargaining. It is (a) a means to contract for sale of labour, (b) a form of industrial government, and finally (c) a system of industrial relations.

The ILO (1960) defines the term collective bargaining as 'negotiations about working conditions and terms of employment between an employer, a group of employers or one or more employers' organizations on the one hand and one or more representatives of workers' organizations on the other with a view to reach an agreement'.

In collective bargaining, the objective is to arrive at an agreement on the wages and other conditions of employment about which the parties have divergent viewpoints but ultimately attempt to make a compromise. As soon as the bargain is made, the terms of agreement are put into operation.

Mary Sur (1965) observes that collective bargaining starts with claims advanced by both the sides—demands from the union and statements issued by the management on how far they can concede to these demands and what they want in return. It is similar to the bargaining between a bazaar vendor and a buyer. They start by quoting prices, which are at variance, each knowing that he/she will have to make some accommodation in the end in order to reach a final price they can both agree upon. According to the *Encyclopaedia of Social Sciences*, 'Collective bargaining is a process of discussion and negotiation between two parties, one or both of whom is a group of persons acting in concert. The resulting bargain is an understanding as to the terms and conditions under which a continuing service is to be performed... More specifically, collective bargaining is a procedure by which employers and a group of employees agree upon the conditions of works.'

The most comprehensive definition of collective bargaining has been provided by the Trade Union and Labour Relations (Consolidation) Act 1992 sections 178(1) and (2) of the UK Employment Law programme. It is a negotiation connected with one or more of the following:

- Terms and conditions of employment or the physical conditions in which any worker is required to work
- Engagement or non-engagement, or termination or suspension, of employment or the duties of employment of one or more workers
- Allocation of work or the duties of employment between workers or groups of workers
- Matters of discipline
- A worker's membership or non-membership of a trade union
- Facilities for officials of trade unions
- Machinery for negotiation or consultation and other procedures relating to any of the aforementioned matters, including the recognition by employers or employers' associations of the right of a trade union to represent workers in such negotiation or consultation or in the carrying out of such procedures.

Importance and Need for Collective Bargaining

Collective bargaining is perceived by both employers and employees as an important machinery to settle differences on work-related issues. We have adequately covered the general issues that are usually settled through collective bargaining.

The need for collective bargaining in India arose due to some controversial problems that the Indian industry had to face after the termination of the Second World War. One of the most important among these was that of modernization. The problems of modernization and productivity are to be viewed in the context of industrial development on planned lines. The Indian industry could not compete in foreign markets if it did not follow modern methods of production. Since modernization caused displacement of workers, it naturally invited hostility, and the workers and management, therefore, had to come together in their viewpoint through collective bargaining. The solution to common problems can come from legislative measures.

Collective agreements provide the climate for smooth progress on contentious issues, as there is ample scope for a synthesis between the demands from one side and the concessions from the other. The need for collective bargain arises due to the following reasons:

- In individual bargaining, the workers may be tempted to accept undesirable conditions and may thus bring down the general level of remuneration. Due to immobility of labour, all workers are not in a position to desert a wage-cutting employer. This immobility may be due to ignorance, illiteracy, and industry-specific skill factors.
- Workers who are swift may accept a lower rate of payment, which may yield them a reasonable amount of wages, but such a low rate of wages would yield insufficient earnings to a great majority of workers.
- Sometimes, employers are in a position to control the bulk demands of the labourers and they may, through combined action, force the workers to accept low wages. Collective bargaining is the only way to avert such combined action and prevent the creation of such monopolistic tendencies.
- The market apparatus consisting of the two forces of demand and supply can settle only the problem of determination of wages. Some of the non-wage issues such as the length of a working day, health and safety of the workers, speed operations, introduction of rationalization, and measures for job security have to be settled by personal decisions and not by the forces of demand and supply.
- Collective bargaining also provides some voice in the conduct and management of the industry. Workers now have a definite means for the exercise of real influence in the determination of labour-related matters affecting them every now and then.
- To ensure continuity of production, workers and employers must shake hands and this makes it inevitable to make collective bargaining a regular feature of industrial life.
- The problem of good human relations can be successfully tackled by the collective bargaining process.

Characteristics of Collective Bargaining

Some of the essential characteristics of collective bargaining may be enumerated as follows:

- It is a group action as opposed to individual action and is initiated through the representatives of the workers and delegates of the management at the bargaining table.
- It is flexible and mobile and not fixed or static. It has ample scope for compromise (mutual give and take) before the final agreement.
- It is a two-party process. It can succeed only when both the labour and management want to succeed. There must be a mutual eagerness to develop the collective bargaining procedure, with a view to achieve harmony and progress. It can flourish only in an atmosphere that is free from animosity and reprisal.
- It is a continuous process and provides a mechanism for continuing and organized relationships between the management and the trade unions. The heart of collective bargaining is the process for continuing joint considerations and the adjustments of plans and problems.
- The term itself is dynamic because the concept is growing, expanding, and changing.
- It is industrial democracy at work.

- It is not a competitive process but a complementary process; that is, each party needs something that the other party already has. For example, labour can make a greater productive effort and management has the capacity to pay.
- It is an art, an advanced form of human relations. To get proof of this, one only needs to witness the bluffing, oratory, dramatics, and coyness, which often characterize a bargaining session.

Important Assumptions to Achieve Stable Collective Bargaining

The following are the assumptions made to achieve stable collective bargaining:

- While employers and employees have different interests, these differences are not irreconcilable. Instead, they are rather similar to the differences between buyers and sellers in general. Therefore, through bargaining, a deal can be made, which sets the price and regulates the conditions under which employees sell their labour.
- Each side accepts the legitimacy of the other and its right to survive.
- The sides are roughly equal in strength; otherwise, one side will dominate rather than bargain with the other.
- The union legitimately represents the interests of all those it claims to represent (a claim sometimes questioned by women and members of minority groups).
- Both parties are willing to negotiate seriously with the aim of reaching an agreement.
- If an agreement cannot be reached, it is legitimate for either side to exert economic pressures (in the form of strike or lockouts) in order to induce the other to make concessions. The type of pressure, which is usually regulated by the law or the generally accepted rules of fair play, may differ among countries.
- The government plays only a limited direct role in the bargaining process.

Prerequisites for Collective Bargaining

The success of the collective bargaining machinery largely depends on the attitudes of the workers in general, the unions in particular, and on the attitude of the management. However, if collective bargaining is to successfully exist in the country, the following factors are essential:

- It is necessary for the management to recognize the union and to bargain in more good faith, in the unionized situation. There is also pressure on the union to formulate plans and demands in a systematic manner.
- There should be a change in the attitude of employers and employees. They must realize that the collective bargaining approach does not imply litigation as it does under adjudication. It should be kept in mind by both the sides that the objective of this approach is to resolve their differences on their respective claims quietly and calmly, with their own resources, reducing their dependence on third-party intervention.
- For the purpose of collective bargaining, employers should be represented by the management and workers by their union representatives. Careful thought must be given to the selection of the negotiating team. For the management team, it is better to have a mixed composition, with experts from the fields of production, finance, and industrial relations, headed by an HR expert.

- It is also appreciable to have open minds, listening to others' concerns and points of views, and to have some flexibility in making adjustments to the demands.
- To ensure collective bargaining, unfair labour practices should be avoided and abandoned by both sides. The atmosphere and confidence is vitiated if either side takes advantage of the other by resorting to unfair practices.
- Both sides should avoid placing any irrational or unreasonable demand.
- Negotiations can be successful only when the parties rely on facts and figures to support their points of view. This is why trade unions should be assisted by specialists such as economists and productivity experts.
- Trade unions should encourage internal democracy and conduct periodic consultations with the general rank and file of the union.
- The negotiation results, that is, the terms of contract, should be in writing and embodied in a document. If no agreement is reached, the parties should proceed to conciliation, mediation, or arbitration.
- If no settlement is arrived at, the workers should be free to go in for a strike and the employer for lockout. However, preference should be given to mutually resolve the differences.
- Strikes and lockouts should be the last resort. Periodic discussions may be necessary between the management and the unions to interpret the provisions of the contract and to clarify doubts.
- Trade unions should be equally concerned with the quality of work, leading up to a consistent concern for the viability of the firm and its products and services.
- Once an agreement is reached, it must be honoured and fairly implemented.

Role of Government in Collective Bargaining

The government may influence collective bargaining and employment conditions in ways that differ greatly among countries:

- It may determine employment conditions by law. For example, the government may stipulate the minimum wages and also legislate on issues such as the length of holidays or ethnic discrimination.
- It may directly provide some benefits like pensions.
- It may set the ground rules that govern the parties' conduct, for example, by providing unions the right to bargain, restricting the conditions under which strikes may occur, or determining the scope of bargaining.
- It may settle disputes that the parties are unable to settle themselves, often through mediation or arbitration. In Australia, conciliation and arbitration play major roles in determining the conditions of employment.
- Through its macroeconomic and social policies, it influences the terms of bargaining agreements.
- The government is a major employer itself and often bargains with unions representing its employees, thereby frequently setting a pattern for the entire economy. In fact, in most countries today, trade union density is higher in the public sector than in the private sector.

Furthermore, as the representative of the public, the government is interested in industrial peace, price stability, increased productivity, and non-discriminatory employment patterns.

To achieve these objectives, it can apply pressure on the parties (often through legislation). On the other hand, the parties can pressurize the government (often through political action) as well. Thus, the government is a third party in collective bargaining, combining the conflicting roles of the neutral player and the bargainer.

Three examples illustrate the range of governmental roles. In the US, the government is primarily (and perhaps ineffectively) a referee in collective bargaining. In Latin American countries, where collective bargaining is poorly developed, the parties pressurize the state to obtain conditions that in other countries, including India, might be obtained through bargaining. However, if government participation was high, the collective bargaining process would not be voluntary.

Collective Bargaining in India

There are certain differences in the characteristics of the unions in the developed and developing countries. In the UK, workers are unionized as per their respective trades. Such unionization, which is more concerned with the well-being of the respective trade group, provides the base for bargaining with the management on different employment issues.

The term collective bargaining in fact originated from Great Britain and was coined by Beatrice Potter as evident from her books *The Co-operative Movement* (1891) and *Industrial Democracy* (1897), where it was regarded as the alternative to individual bargaining.

In India, however, collective bargaining is a late development and marked its presence only in 1918 in Ahmedabad. Voluntary collective bargaining in industry and commerce has developed in India since independence. The textile industry in Ahmedabad has the longest history of settlement of disputes by mutual negotiation and voluntary arbitration, which can claim to have paved the way for modern collective bargaining, although this experiment was not directly followed elsewhere.

The inspiration for peaceful settlement of differences between management and labour in Ahmedabad came from Gandhiji, who set out his philosophy of industrial relations in his autobiography. In 1918, Gandhiji was leading the textile workers of Ahmedabad in their demand for better working conditions, but even though he had supported their strike, he was advocating the resolution of conflict by negotiation and mutual discussion between the accredited organizations of labourers and employers. Where negotiations failed, he recommended conciliation by an arbitrator or board of arbitrators whose decision would be binding. In 1918, when the wage disputes were eventually settled on Gandhiji's intervention by reference to an arbitration board representing both employers and workers, he opined that he did not see why all future differences should not be settled in the same way.

Gandhiji was successful in bringing the Ahmedabad Mill Owners' Association around to his point of view, and in 1920, it was agreed that any dispute or difference of opinion that the workplace could not settle itself should be referred to Gandhiji and Seth Mangal Das, the president of the association, as arbitrators. In case they could not reach an agreement, provision was made for reference to an umpire whose award would be final.

In India, collective bargaining started in 1918 at Ahmedabad.

This system prevailed in Ahmedabad until 1939. However, this system of voluntary arbitration could hardly be called collective bargaining. Usually, they were able to come to an agreement, but on several occasions, they had to take recourse to an umpire on some unresolved points. In the first 16 months of its existence, the Arbitration Board gave 23 awards but not all the questions that came before it were the subject of actual disputes.

Just before the Second World War, the system of arbitration in Ahmedabad seemed to be breaking down, and in 1940, under wartime conditions, a reference was made to compulsory adjudication under the Bombay Industrial Regulation Act, 1946.

In 1952, after a lapse of about 14 years, the Ahmedabad Mill Owners' Association and the Textile Labour Union signed two agreements, initially for two years, by which the machinery of voluntary arbitration was revived. This was proper collective bargaining between the two representative organizations, who agreed that in future all disputes between the mills and their employees would be settled out of court.

Collective bargaining in the Ahmedabad textile industry is now carried on at two levels between (a) the Mill Owners' Association and the Textile Labour Association and (b) the individual mills and the Textile Labour Association.

In 1955, a general agreement on the subject of annual bonus was reached for the years 1953–57, covering all the mills. In 1957, a joint productivity council was set up for Ahmedabad textiles.

From the foregoing discussion, it is clear that a continuing collective bargaining process has come into being in the Ahmedabad textile industry.

There was, however, another early instance of an employers' association and an industrial union coming together to solve their problems. This was in the coir industry in Travancore (Kerala). However, in both Ahmedabad and Kerala, collective bargaining process was for the group of employers.

The earliest example of collective bargaining within an individual concern was that of Joint Steamer Companies in Kolkata (then Calcutta). Their first written agreement with Bengal Mariners Union was in 1946. Among the manufacturing enterprises, the earliest record of the post-war collective agreements was that by Dunlop Rubber Company in Shagunge (West Bengal) in 1947. The Bata Shoe Company in West Bengal made its first agreement in 1948. The Indian Aluminium Company (1951), the Imperial Tobacco Company (1952), the Mysore Iron and Steel Company (1953), TISCO, Jamshedpur (1955), and the National Newsprint and Paper Mills in Nepanagar (Madhya Pradesh) (1956) signed their collective agreements with their workmen.

Thus, from 1950 onwards, collective bargaining has acquired importance in India. The new industry groups, such as engineering and chemicals, which have a higher degree of professionalism in management, have developed collective bargaining as an institution. In India, collective bargaining is taking place at various levels, namely plant-level, industry-level, and national-level. We have illustrated certain plant-level and industry-level collective bargaining agreements in the past. The agreements at the national level are generally bipartite agreements and are finalized at conferences of labour and managements convened by the Government of India. The Delhi Agreement of 7 February 1951 and Bonus Agreement for Plantation Workers of January 1956 are examples of such bipartite agreements in the past.

The issues of bargaining in India are generally wages, dearness allowance, retirement benefits, bonus, annual leave, casual leave, and paid holiday. A study by the Employers' Federation of India reveals that the issue of wages is the most prominent among others. Information about collective bargaining settlement has been compiled by the Labour Bureau, Shimla. Politicization of trade unions, failure of both parties to devote adequate time, and third-party interventions are some of the problems of collective bargaining in India. Mary Parker Follet criticized the collective bargaining process, particularly for the absence of workers' rights and privileges, which itself stand against their bargaining power. Workers, being weak bargainers, can never expect to gain from the collective bargaining process.

STRATEGIC CONFLICT MANAGEMENT

In organizations, conflict is created because of differing ideological, philosophical, or strategic orientations. Differences in the ideological and philosophical orientations lead to differing ideas of two conflicting parties, whereas differences in strategic orientations lead to either perceived or actual conflicting interests of the parties involved. Even though in layman's language, conflict is differences of ideas, it may arise for strategic reasons as well. Strategic conflict may either be created or be the outcome of organizational decisions. Schelling (1963) defined strategic conflict as 'essentially bargaining situations in which the ability of one participant to gain his ends is dependent on the choices or decisions that the other participant will make'. Strategic conflicts are substantive in nature, as the involved issues revolve around ideas, decisions, and actions. A manager here prefers conflicting parties to generate their own resolution strategies. Strategic conflict embraces organizations, systems, and processes. Hence, it requires managerial competence to manage strategic conflicts. Some of the competencies required are listed as follows:

> Schelling defined strategic conflict as essentially bargaining situations in which the ability of one participant to gain his/her ends is dependent on the choices or decisions that the other participant will make.

Knowledge This involves the understanding of laws and regulations (relevant to the conflict issues), organizational change process, design and practice of training, conflict resolution principles, and best practices.

Abilities This involves the ability to manage organizational change and conduct, needs assessment, training, design, and evaluation programmes, facilitate consensus building, design conflict management systems, and work in collaboration with others. In addition, assessment of decision-making, mediation, design of communication strategies, and understanding the culture of the organization are important competencies that the managers should acquire for managing strategic conflicts.

SUMMARY

Conflict may provide challenges or opportunities to organizations. At the same time, it may be counter-productive and affect the health of an organization. The most effective way to manage and resolve conflicts in organizations is to negotiate around the issues that cause them and maintain a cooperative process. Inflexibility and non-cooperation are weak defences.

The road to confrontation and bitterness can be prevented if managements realize that negotiating in good faith is the only way to resolve industrial conflicts.

Resolving conflict is best possible through enforcement of discipline, that is, orderly and systematic behaviour. It is an important prerequisite for organizational harmony. Absence of discipline or indisciplined behaviour may stand against the achievement of organizational objectives. To enforce discipline, every organization lays down certain procedures and norms, which employees are required to comply with.

Though approaches to discipline differ from one organization to another, most of them prefer to adopt a legalistic approach. Disciplinary proceedings follow certain well-defined steps. The problem of indiscipline can be avoided by adopting a well-defined grievance redressal mechanism within the organization, or else it can culminate in a collective problem of indiscipline. Principles of natural justice should receive attention while handling grievances or cases of indiscipline in an organization. Handling disciplinary problems requires specialized knowledge and skills.

Collective bargaining is a voluntary process of negotiation between employers and employees to determine the various terms of employment. The process ensures organizational democracy. However, it often proves an ineffective mechanism for reaching an agreement. Over the years, the importance of collective bargaining has been globally receding. Most organizations prefer to have enterprise-wide bargaining rather than industry-wide bargaining. Even industry-wide bargaining agreements are not implemented by many organizations within the same industry group. The example of the banking industry is relevant in this context. In a collective bargaining situation, HR managers need to play a crucial role in striking a win–win deal. To achieve this, they have to improve, their negotiation skills, practising collective bargaining simulation games on a regular basis.

KEY DEFINITIONS

Discipline without punishment This refers to the approach of settling disciplinary problems in organizations without inflicting punishment. John Huberman (1967), a proponent of this approach, spelt out the methodology to handle disciplinary problems in organizations with a positive disciplinary approach.

Ex parte enquiry If the employee fails to turn up for the enquiry after being given sufficient notice, the enquiry officer may conduct the enquiry and gather evidence as required.

Hot stove rule This is a concept developed by Walter Kiechel (1990) to administer discipline in organizations. We get burnt when we touch a hot stove; thus, we get an immediate response and leaves no question of cause and effect. This analogy keeps the discipline impersonal—penalties for a given

violation are independent of the personality of the violator.

Intergroup conflict This typically arises from organizational causes. Increased interdependence among groups increases the potential for conflict. In addition, different groups may have goals that are incompatible. Competition for scarce resources can also lead to intergroup conflict.

Need-based conflicts Employees differ in their perceived needs. Hence, depending on the varied nature of needs, conflicts may arise due to multiplicity of needs, incongruity of needs, needs dissatisfaction, and dilemma of choice.

Power of anticipation Anticipation is a pre-study of the reaction of the listeners to the statements made. This ensures respect for others and thus reduces conflicts.

CONCEPT-REVIEW QUESTIONS

9.1 Explain the causes of conflict and also elaborate upon how workplace stresses add to conflict.

9.2 It is said that conflicts cannot be eliminated but need to be managed. Do you agree with this statement? What types of conflict need to be resolved and what need not be resolved? Elaborate your answer with examples.

9.3 A careful study of workplace-related conflict indicates that many conflicts are the result of organizational environment. If it is so, how can an organization ensure that its organizational environment does not contribute to any conflict?

9.4 What are the steps necessary for corrective discipline? How is a positive discipline approach different from a negative discipline approach? Which approach do you consider the best?

9.5 What are the causes of indiscipline in organizations?

9.6 Briefly describe the common disciplinary problems. Prepare a checklist for resolving such problems.

9.7 Develop a disciplinary policy for an organization covering at least four important areas.

9.8 What are the steps one should follow in initiating disciplinary action against an employee?

9.9 Discuss the stepladder system of grievance handling.

9.10 Define collective bargaining. What are its important characteristics and what are the important prerequisites for its success?

9.11 In the context of the Indian industrial environment, do you think a collective bargaining process is helpful in sustaining good worker–management relations?

9.12 To make collective bargaining process a success, what are the roles of the workers and management representatives?

9.13 Write short notes on the following:
(a) Discipline without punishment
(b) Stepladder system of grievance handling
(c) Burnout
(d) Life stressors
(e) Conflict resolution models

CRITICAL THINKING QUESTIONS

9.1 You have been engaged by an organization to assist in resolving perennial conflict situations, which hinder its growth. The organization is engaged in R&D work in the fields of biomedicine and biotechnology, and every research work requires cross-sectional inputs. Draw your action plan to probe into the problem of conflict. Find out how your line of action can help the organization reduce the conflict.

9.2 Develop a collective bargaining script with imaginary agenda points, assuming you are representing the management side.

SELECT BIBLIOGRAPHY

- Allen, R.E. and T.J. Keaveny, *Contemporary Labour Relations*, Addison-Wesley, New York, 1983.
- Bendix, Reinhard, *Nation Building and Citizenship*, Wiley Eastern, New Delhi, 1989.
- Brown, L.D., 'Normative Conflict Management Theories: Past, Present and Future', *Journal of Organisational Behaviour*, Vol. 13, 1992, pp. 303–09.
- De La Rey, C., 'Intergroup Relations: Theories and Positions', in D. Foster and J. Louw-Potgieter (eds), *Social Psychology in South Africa*, Lexicon Publishers, Johannesburg, 1991.
- Deutsch, M., 'A Theoretical Perspective on Conflict and Conflict Resolution', in D.J.D. Sandole and I. Sandole-Staroste (eds), *Conflict Management and Problem Solving: Interpersonal to International Applications*, New York University Press, New York, 1987.
- Kiechel, Walter III, 'The Organization that Learns', *Fortune*, 12 March, pp. 133–136.
- Kolb, D.M. and L.L. Putnam, 'The Multiple Faces of Conflict in Organisations', *Journal of Organisational Behaviour*, Vol. 13, 1992, pp. 311–24.
- Laue, J., 'The Emergence and Institutionalization of Third Party Roles in Conflict', in D.J.D. Sandole and I. Sandole-Staroste (eds), *Conflict Management and Problem Solving: Interpersonal to International Applications*, New York University Press, New York, 1987.
- Lewicki, R.J. and G. Spencer, 'Conflict and Negotiation in Organisations: Introduction and Overview', *Journal of Organisational Behaviour*, Vol. 13, 1992, pp. 205–07.
- Luthans, Fred, *Organisational Behaviour*, 7th ed., McGraw-Hill International, New York, 1995.
- Patchen, M., 'Models of Cooperation and Conflict: A Critical Review', *Journal of Conflict Resolution*, Vol. 14, Issue 3, 1970, pp. 389–407.
- Pondy, L.R., 'Reflections on Organisational Conflict',

Journal of Organizational Behaviour, Vol. 13, 1992, pp. 257–61.

- Pondy, L.R., 'Organisational Conflict: Concepts and Models', *Administrative Science Quarterly*, Vol. 12, Issue 2, 1967, pp. 296–320.
- Pruitt, Dean, G. and Jeffrey Z. Rubin, *Social Conflict, Escalation, and Settlement*, Random House, New York, 1972.
- Rahim, M.A., 'A Strategy for Managing Conflict in Complex Organisations', *Human Relations*, Vol. 38, Issue 1, 1985, pp. 81–89.

- Schelling, T.C., *The Strategy of Conflict*, Oxford University Press, UK, 1963.
- Sheppard, William, 'Third Party Conflict Intervention: A Procedural Framework,' *Research in Organizational Behaviour*, Vol. 6, 1984, pp. 141–90.
- Sur, Mary, *Collective Bargaining*, Asia Publishing House, Mumbai, 1965.
- Thomas, K., 'Conflict and Conflict Management: Reflections and Updates', *Journal of Organisational Behaviour*, Vol. 13, 1992, pp. 265–74.

CASE STUDY

Conflict Management at Supreme India

Supreme India in New Delhi is a software development company. It has a turnover of ₹2000 crore and has 400 employees. The company is professionally managed. A young dynamic managing director heads the management team. He expects performance of a high order at every level, especially at the supervisory and managerial levels.

Different types of trainees who undergo training in the company fill up the junior-level vacancies. The company offers a one-year training scheme for fresh computer engineers. During the first six months of training, they are exposed to different functional areas. This is considered to be the core training for this category. At the end of this training, the trainees are identified for placement against available or projected vacancies. Then, further training in the next quarter is planned according to individual placement requirements. During the last quarter, the training is on the job. The trainee is required to perform the jobs expected of him/her after he/she is placed there.

The training scheme is broadly structured keeping in mind the training requirements of the computer engineering graduates. The company has a reasonably good system of manpower planning. The intake of trainees is generally planned on the basis of projected requirements.

Naresh Jain joined the company in 2006 after obtaining his B Tech. degree from a reputed institute. He was taken as a trainee against a projected vacancy in the CAD/CAM division.

In Supreme, the areas of interest for a trainee in CAD/CAM are few. Moreover, since Jain specialized in CAD/CAM in his B Tech., his training was planned for the first three months alone. Thereafter, he was provided on-the-job training in the CAD/CAM division. He took interest and showed enthusiasm at work. The report from his divisional head was quite satisfactory.

The performance of the trainees is normally reviewed once at the end of every quarter. During this review, the training manager personally talks to the trainees about their progress, strengths, and shortcomings.

At the end of the second quarter, the training manager called Jain for his performance review. He appreciated his good performance and told him to keep it up. A month later, Jain met the training manager. He requested that his training period be curtailed to seven months and he be absorbed as a regular computer engineer. He argued that he had been performing like a regular employee in the department. He would also gain seniority as well as some monetary benefits as the regular employees are eligible for many allowances such as conveyance, dearness, house rent, and education, which is a substantial amount compared to the stipend paid to him as a trainee.

The training manager turned down his request and informed him that it is not the practice of the company. He told him that any good performance or contribution made by the trainees during the training period would be duly rewarded at the time of placement on completion of one year of training. Further, he told him that it would set a wrong precedent.

Thereafter, Jain's behaviour in the department became different. Initially, his changed attitude did not receive any attention. However, by the end of the third quarter, his behaviour had become erratic and unacceptable. When he was asked by the division head to attend to a particular task, he replied that he was still on training and such tasks should not be assigned to a trainee. According to him, those jobs were meant to be attended by full-time employees and not by trainees.

The divisional head of the CAD/CAM division complained to the training manager about Jain's behaviour and the training manager summoned him. During the discussions, Jain complained that while all the remaining trainees were having a comfortable time as trainees, he was the only one who was put to a lot of stress and strain. The department was expecting too much from him. He felt that he should be duly rewarded for such hard work, or else it was not appropriate to expect such work output from him.

The training manager tried to convince him again that he should not concentrate on rewards, and as a trainee, his sole concern should be to learn as much as possible and improve his abilities. He advised Jain that he should have a long-term perspective rather than such a narrow-minded approach. He also informed that his good performance would be taken into account when the time was right. Furthermore, the manager warned Jain that he was exhibiting a negative attitude. His demand for an earlier placement was illogical and he should forget this as he had already completed eight months and had to wait for only four more months. The manager also advised Jain that the career of an individual had to be seen in the long run and that he should not resort to such childlike behaviour as it would affect his career and image in the company.

Jain apparently seemed to have been convinced by the assurance given by the training manager and remained passive for some time. However, when the feedback was sought after a month, the report stated that he had become more troublesome. He was called again for a counselling session and was given two weeks' time to show improvement. At the end of those two weeks, the training manager met the CAD/CAM division head to discuss Jain's performance. It was decided that he be given a warning letter as per the practice of the company, and accordingly, he was issued one.

This further aggravated the situation rather than bringing about any improvement. Jain felt offended and retaliated by thoroughly disobeying any instruction given to him. This deteriorated the situation further and the relationship between the division head of the department and the trainee was seriously affected.

In cases of rupture in relationships, the normal practice was to shift the trainee from the department where he was not getting along well so that he could be tried in some other department where he could have another lease for striking a better rapport. However, unfortunately, there was no other department to which Jain could be transferred, since that was the only department where his specialization could have been put to proper use. By the time he completed his training, he turned out to be one who was not at all acceptable in the department for placement, because his behaviour and involvement were much below acceptable standards. In view of this, the divisional head recommended that he be removed from that department. When Jain was informed about it, he was thoroughly depressed.

One of the primary objectives of the training department is to recruit fresh graduates who have good potential and train them to be effective workers in different departments. They are taken after a rigorous selection process, which includes a written test, a preliminary interview, and a final interview. During the training period, their aptitudes, strengths, and weaknesses are identified.

Their placements in departments are decided primarily on the basis of their overall effectiveness. Here is a case where the person happened to be hard working at the beginning but turned out to be a failure in the end. The training manager was conscious of this serious lapse and was not inclined to recommend his termination. However, at the same time, it was difficult to retain a person whose track record was not satisfactory. He still felt that a fresh look be given to this case but was unable to identify a solution. He was now faced with a dilemma—whether to terminate or not terminate Jain.

Questions for Discussion

1. Where did things go wrong?
2. Who is responsible for this episode? Is Jain to be blamed?
3. Should the training manager have conceded to his demand for appropriate placement?
4. What options are available for the training manager other than the termination of Jain's services?
5. Did the divisional head of CAD/CAM handle the trainee properly? How could he have got Jain back on the right track?

ANNEXURE 9.1
Sample Disciplinary Policy

Conduct and Discipline

All employees of Fortune Furnitech shall at all times

- maintain absolute integrity
- maintain devotion to duty
- do nothing that is unbecoming of an employee of the company
- abide by and comply with the regulations of the company and all orders and directions of the superiors
- discharge their duty to the best of their abilities in the interest of the company

Taking Part in Political Activities and Elections

No employee shall be a member of or be otherwise associated with any political party or any organization that takes part in political activities nor shall he/she take part in elections, subscribe in aid, or assist in any other manner any political movement or activity. This, however, does not prejudice an employee's right to exercise his/her vote.

Unauthorized Communication of Information

No employee shall, except in accordance with any general or special order of the company or in the performance in good faith of the duties assigned to him, communicate directly or indirectly the contents of any official documents or any part thereof or other information to any other employee or any person to whom he is not authorized to communicate such contents or information.

Gifts

No employee shall accept or permit any member of his/her family or any person acting on behalf of his/her behalf to accept any illegal gratification, pecuniary advantage, or gifts from any person or agent having dealings with the company.

Private Trade or Employment

No employee shall engage directly or indirectly (in the name of his/her family member or relations) in any trade or business or undertake any other employment.

Prohibition to Absence Without Leave

An employee shall not absent himself/herself from his/her duties or from the station of his/her posting without having first obtained the permission of the competent authority.

Acts Constituting Misconduct

- Wilful insubordination or disobedience, whether in alliance with a co-employee or not, of any lawful and reasonable order of superiors
- Wilful avoidance of work or abetment or instigation thereof

- Theft, fraud, misappropriation, or dishonesty in connection with the employer's business or property
- Habitual absence without leave, overstaying the sanctioned leave without sufficient grounds or proper and satisfactory explanation, or habitual late attendance
- Commission of any act that subverts discipline or good behaviour in the premises or establishment such as drunkenness, riotous, disorderly, or indecent behaviour, gambling, taking or giving bribes, or any illegal gratification of any kind whatsoever
- Wilful damage to work, goods in process, or any property of the establishment
- Habitual neglect of work or gross or habitual negligence
- Disclosing to an unauthorized person any information with regard to the establishment, which may come into the possession of the employee in the course of his/her work

- Indulging in scurrilous attacks against the management and other superiors of the employee in his/her official capacity
- Delivering speeches or raising slogans tending to incite workers to violence
- Contempt of regulations and disrespect of authority and general affront to the management, amounting to misconduct
- Impertinent, rude, and disrespectful language, which subverts discipline

Penalties for Violation of Discipline

The CEO-cum-managing director of the company is fully empowered to decide on the penalties for violation of discipline, which may even extend to dismissal from service. However, in all cases, before imposing any penalty, the charged employee will be provided an opportunity to defend himself/herself against the charges levelled at him/her.

Organizational Behaviour and Job Design

LEARNING OBJECTIVES

After studying this chapter, the reader will be able to

- understand the definition and concepts of job design
- list the characteristics of job design
- explain the methods and techniques of job design
- understand the influence of autonomous work groups on job design
- discuss the use of the position analysis questionnaire and job questionnaire for job analysis
- recognize the use of the assessment centres approach for job analysis
- describe job description and job evaluation methods
- appreciate the application of industrial engineering techniques for job design
- understand human engineering value analysis and competency-based approach in job design

CASE STUDY

Effective Job Design and Recruitment Process at McDonald's

McDonald's is one of the Times Top 100 Graduate Employers. Its recruitment process is continuous; one can apply at any time during the year and join the company after successfully getting through their recruitment processes. All candidates have to fill up an online application form, which contains some essay-type questions (mostly related to the job requirements) that are quite easy to answer. After the initial screening of applications, McDonald's responds to an applicant within two days and asks him/her to complete an online personality questionnaire. It is like a psychometric test and is designed to give an idea about the type of personality of the applicant. Once an applicant completes the test, and McDonald's considers the candidate suitable for its organizational requirement, within the next few days the applicant is invited to go through the assessment centre, which

McDonald's refers to as *on job experience* (OJE). The OJE is store-based and takes the candidate through a typical day in a McDonald's restaurant exposing him/her to everything from health and safety, interviews, and group work to experiencing the kitchen, dining, and front counter areas. It is an ideal opportunity for the candidates to assess whether McDonald's is the right place for them to work in. Having gone through this phase, the candidate is invited to a final interview with an operations manager. It is more a chat than a formal interview. Within a week, the offer of employment is issued to eligible candidates. In the intervening period, all the candidates are given periodic feedback about their progress.

McDonald's does all these scientifically because of its well-documented job design and perfect alignment of jobs to its core values—the same level of service and the same level of quality worldwide.

INTRODUCTION

Effective job designs with information and documentation on job analysis, job description, and job evaluation are important prerequisites for managing organizational behaviour. All these processes help in identifying the job requirements, describing the job and job families, determining skill sets, mapping skills, and developing skill inventories in an organization. Traditionally, these critical inputs were used to decide the manpower requirement in organizations to meet the present and future needs. However, behavioural dimensions are critical for effective management of organizational behaviour.

Work systems encompass macrolevel organizational variables such as the personnel subsystem, the technological subsystem, and the external environment. The analysis of work systems is, therefore, essentially an effort to understand the allocation of functions between the worker and the technical outfit as well as the division of labour between people in a socio-technical environment. Such an analysis can assist in making informed decisions to enhance systems safety, efficiency in work, technological development, and the mental and physical well-being of workers.

Researchers examine work systems according to divergent approaches (mechanistic, biological, perceptual/motor, and motivational) with corresponding individual and organizational outcomes (Campion and Thayer 1985). The selection of methods in work systems and analysis is dictated by the specific approaches adopted and the particular objective in view, the organizational context, the job and human characteristics, and the technological complexity of the system under study (Drury 1987). Checklists and questionnaires are the common means of assembling databases for organizational planners in prioritizing action plans in areas of personnel selection and placement, performance appraisal, safety and health management, worker–machine design, and work design or redesign. Inventory methods of checklists, for example, the Position Analysis Questionnaire or PAQ (McCormick 1979), the Job Components Inventory (Banks and Miller 1984), the Job Diagnostic Survey (Hackman and Oldham 1976), and the Multi-method Job Design Questionnaire (Campion 1988), are the more popular instruments and are directed to a variety of objectives.

Job design helps in organizing job tasks; it has a direct impact on the mental and physical health of the employees as well as their performance levels. The physical aspects of jobs require organizations to consider ergonomic issues and help in reducing physical strain, fatigue, and even, at times, boredom (which occurs from doing repetitive tasks). The mental aspects require organizations to address behavioural issues such as developing work systems and cultures, which enable employees to feel relieved from the dehumanizing effects. The compatibility of both the physical and mental aspects leads to employee satisfaction and develops a high performing organization.

To properly address the ergonomic and behavioural issues, job design relates to the organizational structure and style of management. Appropriate management styles, a structural shift from autocratic to democratic decision-making, delegation, and formation of autonomous work groups reorganize the structure by reducing the number and levels of managers, increase the span of control, increase the productivity levels, and boost the motivation of employees.

Thus, the job design principle focuses on the motivational aspects of jobs to make them more interesting and challenging for employees. In the scientific management era, it has been observed that jobs were broken into small independent elements so that workers could repetitively perform the same task. The argument was that in this process, jobs become more scientific and the workers' performances can easily be identified for deciding their financial incentives. However, with the emergence of the human relations school, this argument was negated and the addressing of behavioural issues in job designs started gaining acceptance. Thus, the human aspects of job design now receive more importance in organizations to synergize productivity and employee satisfaction.

The concepts of job design, therefore, suggest incorporating the elements variety, responsibility, and control. Job design ensures that all jobs contain variety; some have responsibility for decision-making and some have control over the way the jobs are done.

PURPOSE OF JOB DESIGN

Breaking down the tasks associated with each component in the system has led to the concept of job design. This concept started gaining importance at the turn of the 20th century when, with rapid technological advancements, mass production and assembly line operations emerged. Since jobs continue to become sophisticated and specialized, the need for an educated and motivated workforce has become indispensable.

The main purpose of job design (or redesign) is to increase both employee motivation and productivity (Rush 1971). Increased productivity can manifest itself in various forms. For example, the focus can be on improving the quality and quantity of goods and services, reducing operation costs, and/or reducing the turnover and training costs.

> The main purpose of job design is to increase both employee motivation and productivity.

On the other hand, increasing employee motivation can be achieved through increased job satisfaction. The Two-Factor Model of Herzberg (1966) shown in Table 10.1 describes two sets of factors, satisfying and dissatisfying, which affect an employee's self-esteem and opportunity for self-actualization in the workplace.

Table 10.1   Job content factors

Dissatisfying factors	Satisfying factors
Administrative policies	Achievement
Supervision	Recognition
Working conditions	Work itself
Interpersonal relations	Responsibility
Salary	Advancement
Status	Growth
Job security	
Personal life	

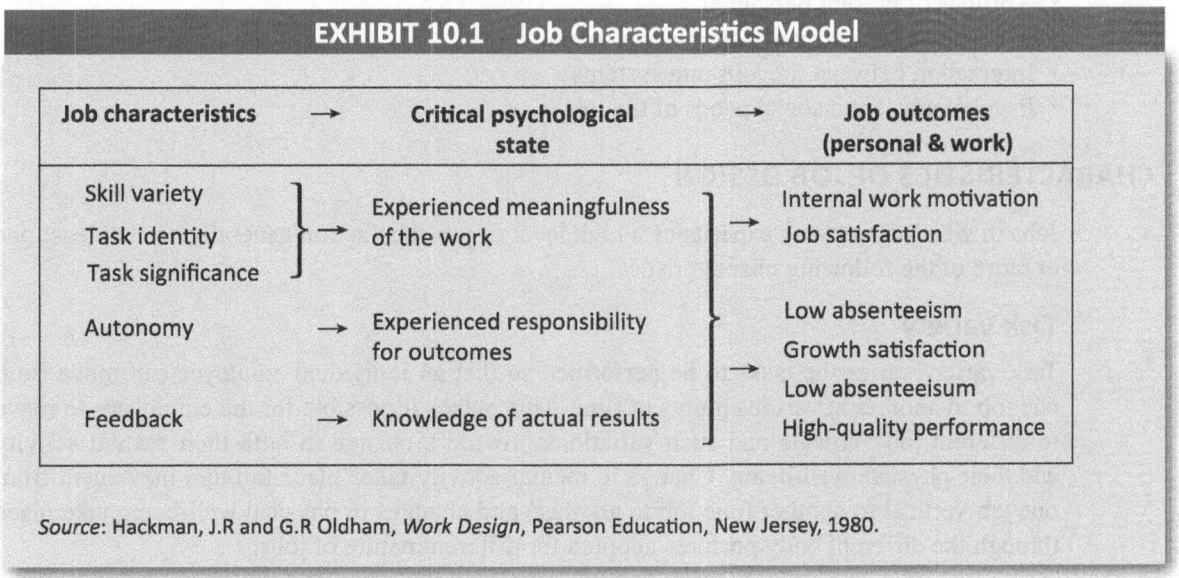

EXHIBIT 10.1   Job Characteristics Model

Source: Hackman, J.R and G.R Oldham, *Work Design*, Pearson Education, New Jersey, 1980.

Herzberg (1966) made a critical distinction between these factors in that a person does not move in a continuum from being dissatisfied to becoming satisfied or vice versa. Rush (1971) tries to explain Herzberg's point by stating that 'the opposite of satisfaction is not dissatisfaction, but no satisfaction; and that the opposite of dissatisfaction is not satisfaction but no dissatisfaction'. In practice, this means that addressing the dissatisfying factors helps in supporting and maintaining the structure of the job, whereas the satisfying factors help the employee reach self-actualization and increase the motivation to continue to do the job (see Exhibit 10.1).

FACTORS AFFECTING JOB DESIGN

Every job undergoes constant modification because of the impact of, mechanization and automation. Some jobs become redundant, whereas others are created, and still others are altered in content. This necessitates different types of education, experience, and other attributes.

> While designing a job, the management must also be concerned with the practical considerations of quantity and quality of the available personnel (both within the organization and in the labour market).

In addition, for effecting job design, the organization needs to respect the unions, who otherwise may stall the move on one ground or the other.

While designing a job, the management must also be concerned with the practical considerations of quantity and quality of the available personnel (both within the organization and in the labour market). Personality conflict and friction, problems of human relations, boredom, obsessive thinking, and so on also need to be taken care of.

Thus, the factors that are likely to affect job design can be enumerated as follows:

- Extent of job specialization and repetitive operations
- Degree of changing technology
- Prevailing labour union policies
- Abilities of present personnel
- Adequate availability of potential personnel
- Interaction between the jobs and systems
- Psychological and social needs of the job

CHARACTERISTICS OF JOB DESIGN

Jobs in which employees experience a high level of job satisfaction generally have at least one or more of the following characteristics:

Task Variety

Task variety varies the tasks to be performed so that an individual employee can move from one job to another at various points of time. This makes it possible for the employees to move to different job verticals and such variations provide a change in both their mental activity and their physical well-being. Change in mental activity takes place through movement from one job vertical to another (one job to another) and changes in physical well-being take place through the different body postures adopted for different nature of jobs.

Task Identity

Wherever possible, tasks should fit together to make a complete job, since this gives the employee a sense of doing a whole job, from the beginning until the end, with a visible output. The important benefit derived from task identity is that it can assist a worker in matching his/her performance with the overall goals of the organization, thus helping him/her in setting reasonable targets. Workers can cultivate their sense of belongingness and can realize that they are partners in the organizational progress.

Task Significance

By establishing task significance, organizations can make workers feel that they have achieved something meaningful in the course of their work. This establishes their importance and enhances their self-esteem. Workers can autonomously contribute to the organizational growth and prosperity once they understand their task significance. This requires organizations to value each task by inculcating a culture of mutual respect.

Autonomy

To ensure autonomy in job design, organizations should, wherever possible, give inputs to their employees on how their jobs should be done—the order of tasks, the speed of work, and so on. Thereafter, the employees should be given a free hand by reducing the extent of supervision and control, so that they realize that they are doing their own jobs and that they are the job owners. However, the process is not so simple. Inculcating a sense of autonomy in workers requires organizational indulgence to allow them to commit mistakes. Organizations should first allow the workers to take decisions independently, knowing well that they may not succeed. However, in the process, they learn through their mistakes and slowly become independent in doing their jobs.

Feedback

The last characteristic of job design is the provision for feedback. Feedback provides an opportunity for the workers to understand their strengths and weaknesses and in the process, helps them mature and achieve greater perfection in future job assignments. Many organizations provide automated feedback systems so that workers can self-assess their extent of performance.

METHODS AND TECHNIQUES OF JOB DESIGN

Robertson and Smith (1985) recommended some strategies for analysing jobs:

- Review literature and other existing data such as prevailing job descriptions and training manuals, and assess job designs from the manuals of technology providers or vendors.
- Interview immediate managers to understand the responsibilities and tasks required for performing the job well.
- Interview the current employees, who are presently doing the job, in the same line and assess the job requirements.
- Observe employees while they do their jobs.
- Encourage employees to do the job individually wherever possible.
- Write job descriptions, detailing all the findings and observations.

In addition, while designing jobs, one needs to refer to the policies, incentives, and feedback systems of an organization as all these factors also affect the efficiency and motivation of the employees.

Some of the important techniques of job design, therefore, can be enumerated as follows:

Job Rotation

Job rotation involves a periodic vertical and horizontal movement of a group of employees between a set of jobs or tasks. It therefore provides some relief from boredom and the monotony of repeatedly doing the same jobs or tasks. However, this requires organizations to initiate multi-skilling of employees through continuous training and learning activities. Some organizations

Job rotation involves a periodic vertical and horizontal movement of a group of employees between a set of jobs or tasks.

provide the opportunity for skill interchangeability because of the commonality of the tasks or jobs. However, in some other organizations, the scope of skill interchangeability may be very little because of the specialized nature of the jobs. In such cases, multi-skilling initiatives can provide the results. Apart from mental satisfaction, job rotation relieves employees from physical strains, as there is a change in the working postures. Employees can reduce their tiredness and muscle strain. Whatever may be the objectives of job rotation, it should not be imposed; instead, employees should be made party to the process, so that they can control the job rotation systems and decide how and when the jobs are to be rotated. This also develops their decisional capability.

Job Enlargement

Job enlargement is the horizontal expansion of jobs and involves the grouping of a variety of jobs within a job rather than between jobs.

Job enlargement is the horizontal expansion of jobs and it involves the grouping of a variety of jobs within a job rather than between jobs. Obviously, the time cycle of the job, that is, the time taken to complete a job, increases. For example, a particular employee may be required to perform a few similar tasks or jobs of several employees in an assembly line. To some extent, it may increase the job load, but employees can autonomously feel satisfied with the variety and develop their sense of responsibility, realizing their importance in the organization. Since, in this process, jobs are horizontally integrated keeping in view skill compatibility, organizations can also derive the benefit of cost optimization by making people work with more responsibility.

Job Enrichment

Job enrichment is another important process of job design or redesign, which reverses the effects of repetitive tasks. Employees develop fatigue by doing repetitive tasks. Boredom and lack of flexibility in jobs make them feel dissatisfied (Leach and Wall 2004). Through the vertical expansion of jobs, job enrichment expands the scope of jobs and employees feel more motivated and self-sufficient. With the wide variety of exposure to jobs or tasks, employees can also groom themselves for future higher positions. For effective succession planning, organizations focus on job enrichment, thus making the employees understand the dynamism of various jobs. All kinds of skills, that is, conceptual, technical, human, and business, are adequately acquired by employees through job enrichment, thus giving them a sense of satisfaction for future growth and development.

In the 1950s and 1960s, Frederick Herzberg developed the basis for job enrichment practices. Hackman and Oldham further refined this in 1975, using the Job Characteristics Model. This model assumes that if five core job characteristics are present, three psychological states critical to motivation are produced, resulting in positive outcomes (Kotila 2001). Exhibit 10.1 illustrates this model.

To ensure that job enrichment produces positive results, Cunningham and Eberle (1990) suggested the use of the questionnaire given in Exhibit 10.2. This can ensure proper alignment between the workers' needs and the organizational needs.

EXHIBIT 10.2   Job Enrichment Questionnaire

- Do employees need jobs that involve responsibility, variety, feedback, challenge, accountability, significance, and opportunities to learn?
- What techniques can be implemented without changing the job classification plan?
- What techniques would require changes in the job classification plan?

Practitioner Speak 10.1

Design Your Top Jobs to Appeal to the Goals of Top Talent

A few leading-edge companies are making real progress in increasing the proportion of women in their executive ranks by turning the problem on its head. Rather than focusing their efforts on fitting the candidates to the jobs (through, say, more mentoring and training), they are taking practical steps to make the positions more attractive to their already high-potential candidates.

Read this insightful blog posted by Martin on *HBR Blog Network* by accessing the following link: http://blogs.hbr.org/cs/2013/08/design_your_top_jobs_to_appeal.html.

AUTONOMOUS WORK GROUPS IN JOB DESIGN

Job design or redesign through the formation of autonomous work groups requires organizations to provide functional autonomy to their employees for their assigned tasks or jobs. This process makes workers self-managing. The group independently decides who has to do what and when. The group members, on their own, select a leader to guide the group. In the corporate world, this approach was first used in Volvo (an automobile manufacturing company) in Sweden. The company allowed work groups to decide the hourly output rate and the level of pay and accordingly organized their activities to achieve results. In these types of organizations, the management plays a supportive and facilitative role. Organizations become bottom-up in nature to support the work group. However, this process still holds the management responsible for the results. It is more a style of management rather than fully empowering employees to feel responsible for the results. However, the process helps in the long run to make employees take responsibility for results when organizations truly invest in the learning and development of workers.

Subcontracting

Subcontracting is another form of an autonomous work group, but in this process, workers no longer remain on the payroll of the organizations. They form their own organizations and become self-employed. Here, workers become fully responsible for the results. Within organizations, such an arrangement can be made by making the work design more specific and measurable for the pricing of jobs and fixing of responsibility.

STEPS IN JOB DESIGN

In designing jobs, we need to follow certain pre-determined steps. This helps in effective job designing. These steps are listed in the following subsections.

Job Information

Job information is an essential input for effective job analysis. It not only facilitates job evaluation for compensation designing, but also helps in disseminating information to employees about their duties and responsibilities. Imperfect knowledge about their duties and responsibilities affects the performance of employees and the overall organizational productivity. Disseminating job information in the letter of appointment may not be adequate. Proper documentation and communication during the induction training is the right approach.

Objectives of Job Information

The first objective of job information is to communicate to the employees the duties and responsibilities attached to a job in order to help them get a clear understanding. This also helps them understand what the organization expects from them.

Another objective of job information is organizational analysis. It helps in workflow analysis with respect to a job and in the identification of redundant work elements in a job. Thus, it facilitates job restructuring.

With respect to organizational behaviour, job information helps in analysing the individual employee's behavioural requirements, so that appropriate action for behavioural improvement can be taken by the organizations for enhancing the competencies of the people to stay competitive in the market. Job information also helps organizations determine the scope of internal hiring and the requirements of external hiring for staffing various positions in the organization.

In setting performance standards and establishing job objectives, job information is essential, both in qualitative and in quantitative terms. This also facilitates in more scientifically appraising the performance of an employee against such set standards.

Job information provides critical inputs for other human resources (HR)-related decisions such as promotion, transfer, relocation, redundancy, and compensation designing.

Job Analysis

Job analysis is the process of gathering information about the job and evaluating the information in terms of what is necessary and relevant. Essentially, job analysis involves three questions: What is a job? What should be analysed? What methods of analysis should be used?

A job is a group of essentially similar activities or tasks performed by a person or a group of persons. However, these tasks or activities of jobs need not be identical. They may be performed in different places, with different equipment, in a different sequence. In addition, some employees may perform certain activities in addition to the main job. Alternatively, some employees may perform a job occasionally or temporarily in place of the persons who are absent. This definition of a job is typically used in compensation designing and for other management practices. However, a more generic description of a job is also used, which is identified by *position* rather than *job*. A position is a family of jobs in which specific duties vary, but some interchangeability of work is possible and the functional nature of the work is similar. Examples include assemblers, clerk-cum-typists, and bookkeepers. The broader definition of a job facilitates the development of accurate job information and this accurately reflects the work of each employee. On the

> Job analysis is the process of gathering information about the job and evaluating the information in terms of what is necessary and relevant.

other hand, the more precise the job definition, the more difficult it is to identify the job differences, which further complicates the management of employees.

Another basic issue for job analysis is whether the organization should measure the work assigned or the work actually performed. Some compensation designing experts argue that unless job analysis considers the work performed, the organization may not give credit to the employees for what they are actually doing. On the other hand, analysing the work performed may imply that employees have been given latitude to assign work to themselves, whereas in reality it is the manager's responsibility to assign a job. The role of an analyst is essentially to gather job information and not to evaluate the logic of work assignments. He/She is primarily responsible for recording those responsibilities that a manager has assigned to an employee.

What Needs to Be Analysed

What the nature of job information for job analysis should be depends upon a number of considerations:

- Is the analysis required for evaluation purposes or for other purposes as well?
- What job level is to be analysed?
- What type of evaluation plan is to be used?
- What is the job knowledge of the analyst conducting the evaluation?

Certain basic areas of information may include the following:

- Fundamental purpose of the job
- Work elements in the job that require a study of specific tasks, areas of responsibility, and examples of work
- General importance of each job element and its relationship to the total operation, that is, the way it is integrated with the total job
- Approximate time spent on each task or specific area of responsibility
- Scope of the job and its impact on the operation
- Inherent authority (not only formal delegation but also latitude of action) and formal or informal audits of work
- Working relationships (including supervision)
- Specific methods, equipment, or techniques that are required for the job
- Job climate, including objectives and work environment
- Job conditions such as physical effort, hazards, discomfort, chasing of deadlines, travel requirement, creativity, and innovations required

What Methods of Analysis Need to Be Used

Job information can be obtained in various ways, either by a staff analyst or by the individual line manager. It is always better to involve the line managers in compiling job information because of functional proximity. One relatively simple and inexpensive method of analysis is collecting job information through questionnaires. Another important method is direct observation of the work performed, which is essential to understand the job role. However, it is expensive and time consuming. Refer to Annexure 10.1 for a sample job analysis data sheet.

Valuable information about jobs can also be obtained from organization manuals, time study reports, former job descriptions, and method studies.

Job Questionnaire

A job questionnaire is a special tool for consolidating job information. It is a printed form in which essential information about the job is listed either by the employee or by his/her supervisors. A major advantage of a job questionnaire is that it uses the knowledge of those who are close to the job. In addition, it gives each employee an opportunity to participate and contribute by giving responses to the questionnaire, which facilitates immediate compilation of job information. Another important advantage is that the compiled information can be used as job descriptions, thus eliminating the need for further writing of job descriptions. Moreover, by using a job questionnaire, organizations also get the benefit of communicating up-to-date job information to the employees.

However, a major disadvantage associated with a job questionnaire is that its success depends on the understanding and writing ability of the individual employees and supervisors. Inconsistencies in the response pattern may arise because of perceptual incongruence, which may multiply further when more cross sections of people participate in the questionnaire response/survey. In addition, compiling job information from the questionnaire response may suffer from the problem of exaggeration.

> A job questionnaire is a printed form in which essential information about the job is listed either by the employee or by his/her supervisors for the purpose of consolidating job information.

To eliminate such inherent disadvantages of compiling job information through job questionnaires, it is always better to obtain information through a combination of direct observation and job questionnaires. This approach may be time-consuming and involve huge costs, but it is more scientific as it eliminates the chance of error by accounting for the perceptive differences between what the employees perceive and what they do.

JOB ANALYSIS METHODS

Of late, there has been an increasing concern about the quantification of the process of job analysis. A structured PAQ can help the process. The PAQ was developed in the early 1970s through the efforts of McCormick and others. It consists of 194 job elements of a *worker-oriented* nature, which are divided into six major categories. The analyst normally rates the job elements on a scale of 0 to 5. However, administering PAQ is not very easy.

The PAQ has six major divisions comprising 189 behavioural items required for the assessment of job performance and seven supplementary items related to monetary compensation. The six major divisions are listed as follows:

- Information input—where and how does one get information on the jobs to be performed (35 items)
- Mental process—information processing and decision-making in performing the job (14 items)
- Work output—physical work done and tools and devices used (50 items)
- Interpersonal relationships (36 items)
- Work situation and job context—physical and social contexts (18 items)
- Other job characteristics—work schedules and job demands (36 items)

Standard job components inventory contains seven sections. The introductory section deals with the details of the organization, job descriptions, and biographical details of the job holder. The other six sections deal with the following:

- Tools and equipment—uses of over 200 tools and equipment (26 items)
- Physical and perceptual requirements—strength, coordination, selective attention (23 items)
- Mathematical requirements—uses of numbers, trigonometry, and practical applications such as working with plans and drawings (127 items)
- Communication requirements—preparation of letters, use of coding systems, and interviewing people (19 items)
- Decision-making and responsibility—decisions about methods, order of work, standards, and related issues (10 items)
- Job conditions and perceived job characteristics

Another approach uses the profile matching methods, which have some common elements, namely (a) a comprehensive set of job factors used to select the range of work, (b) a rating scale that permits the evaluation of job demands, and (c) the weighing of job characteristics based on the organizational structure and socio-technical requirements. *Les profils des postes*, another task profile instrument, developed in Renault (RNUR 1976), contains a table of entries of variables representing working conditions. It provides respondents with a five-point scale on which they can select the value of a variable, which ranges from very satisfactory to very poor, by way of registering standardized responses. The variables cover (a) the design of the workstation, (b) the physical environment, (c) the physical load factors, (d) nervous tension, (e) job autonomy, (f) relations, (g) repetitiveness, and (h) contents of work.

The AET (ergonomic job analysis) was developed by Rohmert and Landau (1985) based on the stress–strain concept. All the 216 items of the AET are coded. One code defines the stressors, indicating whether a work element qualifies or not as a stressor; some codes define the degree of stress associated with a job; and yet some others describe the duration and frequency of stress during the work shift.

The AET consists of three parts:

Part A The man-at-work system (143 items) includes the work objects, tools and equipment, and work environment constituting the physical, organizational, social, and economic conditions of work.

Part B The task analysis (31 items) is classified according to both—the different kinds of work object, such as material and abstract objects, and worker-related tasks.

Part C The work demand analysis (42 items) comprises the elements of perception, decision, and response or activity. (The AET supplement, H-AET, covers body postures and movements in industrial assembling activities.)

In general, the checklists adopt one of the following two approaches: (a) the job-oriented approach (e.g., the AET, *Les profils des postes*) and (b) the worker-oriented approach (e.g., the PAQ). The task inventories and profiles offer a subtle comparison of complex tasks and occupational profiling of jobs and determine the aspects of work that are considered to be high-priority and inevitable factors in improving the working conditions. The emphasis of the PAQ is on classifying job families or clusters (Fleishman and Quaintance 1984; Mossholder and Arvey 1984; Carter and Biersner 1987), inferring job component validity and job stress (Jeanneret 1980; Shaw and Riskind 1983). From the medical point of view, both the AET and profile methods allow comparisons of constraints and aptitudes when required (Wagner 1985). The Nordic questionnaire is an illustrative presentation of an ergonomic workplace analysis (Ahonen, et al. 1989), which covers the following aspects:

- Workspace
- General physical activity
- Lifting activity
- Work postures and movements
- Accident risk
- Job content
- Job restrictiveness
- Decision-making

- Workers' communication and personal contacts
- Repetitiveness of the work
- Attentiveness
- Lighting conditions
- Thermal environment
- Noise

The shortcomings of the general purpose checklist format employed in ergonomic job analysis are as follows:

- With some exceptions (e.g., the AET and the Nordic questionnaire), there is a general lack of ergonomic norms and protocols of evaluation with respect to the different aspects of work and environment.
- There are dissimilarities in the overall construction of the checklists as regards the means of determining the characteristics of working conditions, the quotation form, criteria, and methods of testing.
- The evaluation of physical workload, work postures, and work methods is limited on account of lack of precision in the analysis of work operations with reference to the scale of relative levels of stress.
- The principal criteria for the assessment of the worker's mental load are the degree of complexity of the task, the attention required by the task, and the execution of mental skills. The existing checklists refer less to underuse of abstract thought mechanisms than to overuse of concrete thought mechanisms.
- In most checklists, the methods of analysis attach major importance to the job as a position, as opposed to the analysis of work, worker–machine compatibility, and so on. The psycho-sociological determinants, which are fundamentally subjective are less emphasized in the ergonomics checklists.

A systematically constructed checklist obliges us to investigate the factors of the working conditions that are visible or easy to modify and permits us to engage in social dialogue among the employers, job holders, and others concerned. One should exercise a degree of caution towards the illusion of simplicity and efficiency of the checklists and towards their quantifying and technical approaches as well. Versatility in a checklist or questionnaire can be achieved by including specific modules to suit specific objectives. Therefore, the choice of variables is linked to the purpose for which the work systems are to be analysed and this determines the general approach for the construction of a user-friendly checklist.

The suggested ergonomics checklist may be adopted for various applications. Data collection and computerized processing of the checklist data are relatively straightforward operations and can be done by responding to the primary and secondary statements.

USE OF ASSESSMENT CENTRES APPROACH FOR JOB ANALYSIS

A survey carried out by the Chartered Institute of Personnel and Development (CIPD), UK, indicated that almost 50 per cent of employers are now using the assessment centres approach in the selection of prospective candidates for jobs. Apart from a selection process, assessment centres also help in the job analysis of employees. An effective recruitment process in an organization follows the following sequence:

Attract → Impress → Select → Recruit

Assessment centres assist the whole process by allowing candidates to experience a microcosm of the job while testing them on work-related activities as individuals and in groups. Interviewers can assess the existing performances and predict future job performances.

The design of an assessment centre should reflect the following:

- The ethos of the organization
- The actual skills required to carry out the job
- Potential sources of recruits
- The extent to which recruitment is devolved to line managers
- The HR strategy

Changing organizations should assess the learning ability of candidates, whereas *steady state* organizations should assess their existing skills and abilities, which can be used immediately. Centres that look for potential should be developed differently from those looking for current knowledge and skills.

The assessment centre should reflect the reality of the job and the organization. New recruits have high expectations of their jobs and disappointment can be a destructive influence if the assessment centre has encouraged them to believe that the job or organization fits their values if, in fact, it does not.

The cost of an assessment centre needs to be compared with the potential cost of a recruitment error. To predict job performance, it is important to determine the present and likely future job skills. In addition to the exercises, interviews should be used because they have face validity (they feel *right* to candidates and selectors) but they cannot be used to predict performance (correlation levels from research are very low). Tests are valid only if the candidates for the job match the norm group used to design and validate the test. They should be used as only one piece of evidence and other measures should be compared with them.

Research has shown that well-designed assessment centres with a variety of activities can reach 0.8 predictive validity in assessing future performance. It has also shown that candidates who attend assessment centres that genuinely reflect the job and the organization are impressed by that company even if they are rejected. Attendance at an assessment centre can help the candidate assess the working of the organization. The tasks set should coordinate with the job descriptions and person specification. It must appear fair as a selection process in the time taken, the number of tasks set, and the opportunities for candidates to show different aspects of their abilities.

Essential Job Design Criteria

The essential job design criteria should include the following:

- Duration of the centre (one day might be insufficient for senior posts)
- Location (reality or ideal surroundings and accessibility for candidates with disabilities)
- Number of candidates brought together (five may be too few for comfort under observation and more than eight creates problems in sharing the assessed time)
- Candidates' backgrounds and comparability of past experience
- Number, mix, and experience of assessors

Tasks Involved in Assessment Centres

The essential and desired skills or competencies should be matched to the techniques and tasks that can test them. Depending on the nature of the job, the tasks might include individual or group work, written and/or oral input, written and/or oral output, in-tray, analytical work, individual problem-solving, group discussions, group problem-solving, tasks that match business activities, personal role-play, and functional role-play.

Group exercises should be as real as possible; set goals, have a time limit, encourage candidates to share information and reach decisions, and advise candidates to read the brief very carefully. Assessors can assist in role-playing if they are trained to facilitate discussion and assist in group decision-making. A reasonable preparation time should be offered before these exercises.

The tasks involved should encourage competitiveness or cooperation in order to test for creativity or for building upon the ideas of others in a productive manner. The opportunity to compete with others will motivate some candidates to perform better. In organizations wishing to improve their diversity, elements of competition should be decreased in favour of increased opportunities to cooperate, as these skills are likely to encourage wider participation.

Presentation exercises can be valuable if the job requires this skill and it is beneficial in allowing considerable preparation time for the exercise. If individual work is part of the job, tests can be used. These *psychometric* tests are defined, similar to methods that are used to test skills and abilities, and thus attempt to predict performance through individual tests and exercises.

JOB DESCRIPTION

Compiled job information is translated to job descriptions; these are written records of job duties and responsibilities and provide the factual basis for job evaluation. Job descriptions are recorded on a standard form in a uniform manner.

Many organizations assign the task of preparation of job descriptions to trained and professional job analysts since it requires excellent writing skills. However, this, by itself, cannot guarantee

> Job descriptions are written records of job duties and responsibilities and they provide the factual basis for job evaluation.

flawless job descriptions because a professional job analyst may not have specific job knowledge. Therefore, despite engaging analysts, it is always better to involve in-house people for scientific description of jobs.

In terms of format, the job description should first name the job, using the title that accurately summarizes the duties assigned. While naming a job, it is always better to consider the job family. To illustrate, instead of naming an HR job as HR manager, if the term 'knowledge manager' is used, it may give a contemporary or trendy job title but for others (including members within the organization) it may be a misnomer. Secondly, job description should document in a single form a list of duties assigned. The list should have short sentences or phrases. What is to be included while listing the job duties and how those are to be written will depend on the level of the position and the purpose to be served by the description. For the top management level, a job description may be a description of the business goals and objectives. However, at the operation level, job descriptions may be limited to listing of specific duties performed, equipment used, and procedures followed. The broader the use of the job description information and higher the functional level, the longer the job description. For operational positions, the job description may be about one page, whereas for higher management it may run through several pages.

Job Specifications

In addition to providing information about duties associated with job assignments, job descriptions also outline the basic specifications of jobs. Such specifications include the education or experience required of the candidate and the special knowledge and skill set necessary to carry out the job. In addition, specifications also identify soft skills, such as interpersonal skills, analytical ability, problem-solving skills, or decision-making skills, which are required to perform the duties assigned.

> Job specifications include the education or experience required of the candidate and the special knowledge or skill set necessary to carry out the job.

This exercise of processing the job information is known as developing job specification. It helps in the evaluation of jobs, and at the same time, it defines the attributes required for a job position at the time of recruitment. Therefore, job specifications list out all the attributes required for performing a job, which include education, experience, age, and physical fitness along with other soft skills. This also requires the analyst to have special skills, because any judgemental mistake either by selecting a wrong person for a job or by wrongly evaluating a job, which is directly associated with job pricing, may defeat the purpose. Annexure 10.2 shows a specimen job description and job specification.

Transparency in Job Descriptions

Today's organizations are dynamic and require periodic restructuring, which also necessitates redesigning of jobs. Therefore, it is widely believed that providing a job description to employees may cause controversy because in the future, employees may resist doing work that is not specifically listed in their job descriptions. However, if the job descriptions are well developed, there is nothing wrong in sharing them with the employees, as they spell out the list of duties the employees are expected to perform. Hence, it would be better to include in the job description an all-inclusive statement like 'in addition to the listed duties and responsibilities, your superior may ask you to perform other tasks from time to time'.

By sharing job descriptions with the employees, organizations can make their job evaluation process participative and avoid any dissonance in job evaluation results. This is quite important, as organizations also face employee dissatisfaction on job pricing. Communication of job descriptions enhances their acceptance, as employees will not have any doubts about their duties and responsibilities. Such communication with the employees should be an ongoing exercise, so that employees can understand their changed job duties and responsibilities in the event of the changes taking place.

Management Use of Job Description

Job descriptions help in getting things done through people and they help the management accomplish the following objectives:

- Efficiently organizing the jobs
- Properly recruiting or staffing the organization
- Assigning jobs to people by communicating to them their duties and responsibilities and by setting job standards
- Reviewing performance of the people
- Improving performance through appraisal and training
- Rewarding employees

Therefore, job descriptions play a crucial role in key management activities. However, it is very important for the manager to ensure that job descriptions are correct and whatever jobs have been assigned are essential. He/She must ensure that only essential tasks are grouped into jobs. Since job descriptions have interconnectivity, the manager has to align it to recruitment, performance appraisal, training needs, promotion, transfer, and relocation decisions. From the employees' point of view, it should also show them what is expected of them and how to do the work assigned.

By listing the assigned duties in a job description, a manager can determine reasonable performance standards. Identification of such performance standards facilitates benchmarking of the performance of an employee against the best performer.

Job descriptions also facilitate proper manpower utilization. By periodic reviewing of the listed duties, a manager can identify jobs that are time-consuming but require a lower skill set. He/She can accordingly reassign such jobs to lower-paid employees. In addition, the manager can also study jobs in terms of workload and determine the man-hours required. For low-technology and low-skill jobs, he/she can consider the decision to offload the job to subcontractors. Therefore, the job description process has tremendous implications for effective human resource planning (HRP) in an organization. This can also be called an instrument for proper right-sizing of employee strength in an organization.

Finally, job descriptions, as a basic management tool, also influence operating procedures by identifying duplication of work, indicating a scientific workflow, suggesting better allocation of jobs, and pointing out possible job bottlenecks. Figure 10.1 shows a central peripheral relational model of job analysis.

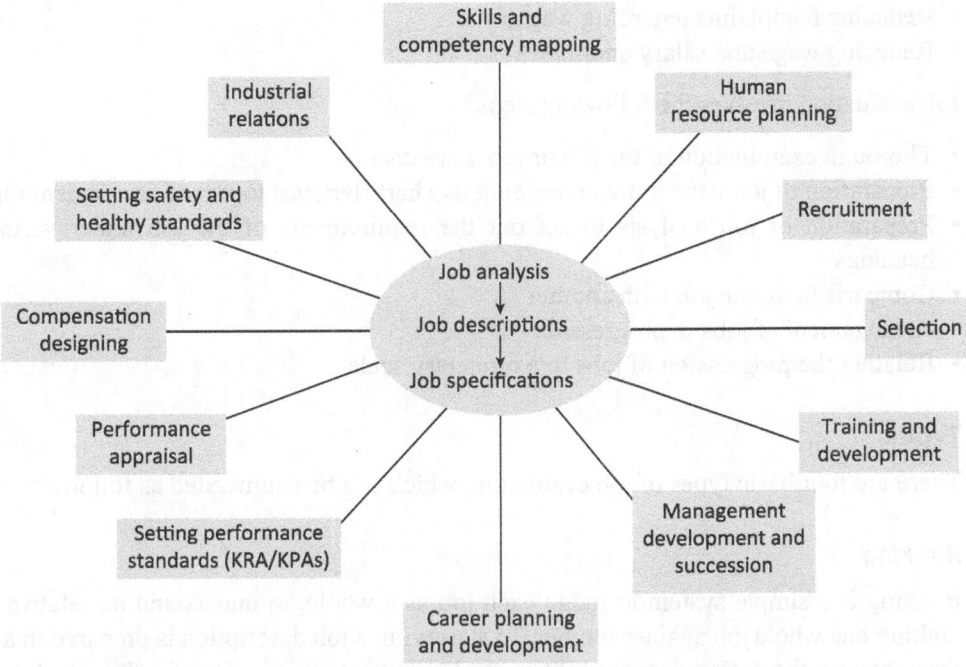

Figure 10.1 Central peripheral relational model of job analysis

JOB EVALUATION

The concept of job evaluation originated in the US in 1971. In 1909, the Civil Service Commission in Chicago and the Commonwealth Edison Company of Chicago pioneered the field. In 1926, Merill R. Lott wrote a book, *Wage Scales and Job Evaluation*, describing the methods used in his company, the Sperry Gyroscope Co., Inc.

Job evaluation is the process of determining the worth of one job in relation to that of another without regard to the personalities. It analyses and assesses the content of jobs to place them in some standard rank order. The end result is used as the basis for a fair and logical remuneration system.

> Job evaluation is the process of determining the worth of one job in relation to that of another without regard to the personalities. It analyses and assesses the content of jobs to place them in some standard rank order.

A properly devised job evaluation scheme provides the management with definite, systematic, and reliable data for working out wage and salary scales. Thus, logical wage negotiation reduces the wage grievances and dissatisfaction with wage differentials and ensures a fair treatment for each employee. It also provides a logical basis for promotion. A survey by the British Institute of Management indicated that job evaluation could be used for the following purposes:

- Reducing layout turnover
- Increasing output
- Improving morale
- Reducing loss of time due to wage negotiation and disputes

- Reducing complaints regarding wages
- Reducing wage and salary anomalies

Job evaluation involves the following steps:

- Thorough examination of the job or job assessment
- Preparation of job description, recording its characteristics to suit of assessment method
- Preparation of job analysis to set out the requirements of the job under various factor headings
- Comparison of one job with another
- Arrangement of jobs in progression
- Relating the progression of jobs to a monetary scale

Types

There are four basic types of job evaluation, which can be enumerated as follows:

Ranking

Ranking is a simple system to judge each job as a whole, to understand its relative worth by ranking one whole job against another. To start with, a job description is prepared in a narrative form, stating the duties, responsibilities, and qualifications required for the job. Jobs are then ranked in order of relative difficulty or value to the company; grade levels are then defined and wage levels are finalized. One of the disadvantages of this method is that the degree of difference between jobs cannot be indicated. Ranking, therefore, may be incorrect and unduly influenced. The relative value of the employees (currently occupying the jobs) may be ranked rather than the jobs. The method may be adequate for easily defined jobs involving a small number of workmen but is regarded as impracticable for complicated jobs where a large number of workmen are involved.

Classification

Classification is different from ranking because grade and wage levels are predetermined before jobs are ranked and descriptions are written defining the type of job that should fall into each group. Under this method, usually a committee allocates jobs to each group using the job descriptions. The system is simple but suffers from limitations similar to those of the ranking system.

Points Rating

Under the points rating system, to achieve a higher level of accuracy, each job is broken down into its component factors or characteristics and then separately evaluated rather than evaluating the job as a whole. A narrative job description is prepared and supplemented by a statement of the various requirements (present in the job). Characteristics such as experience, training, and mental and physical effort common to the jobs are selected and a point value for each characteristic or factor is determined. The factors are defined objectively and points are given to each factor based on its estimated importance. Consolidated point values are finally converted into monetary terms.

Practitioner Speak 10.2

Don't Like Your Job? Change It (Without Quitting)

Sometimes you know your job just isn't right for you. Maybe you're in the wrong field, don't enjoy the work, feel surrounded by untrustworthy coworkers, or have an incompetent boss. Most people would tell you to find something that's a better fit. But that may not be possible. There are many reasons you may not be able to leave: a tough economy, family commitments, or limited opportunities in your field. So what do you do when you're stuck in the wrong job?

Read this insightful blog posted by Gallo on *HBR Blog Network* by accessing the following link: http://blogs.hbr.org/hmu/2012/06/dont-like-your-job-change-it-w.html.

Factor Comparison

The factor comparison method is similar to the points rating system where each job is broken into factors. The only difference is that this method uses five factors—mental requirements, skill requirements, physical requirements, responsibility, and working conditions. After job descriptions, key jobs are judged and related to one another. The jobs are considered one by one and reviewed to understand how much of the current wage rate for the job is paid for each factor. Key jobs are arranged in a scale in order of their value for each factor. The remaining jobs are compared with the key job factors and a comparative monetary value is determined for each factor in each individual job. The total of the factor values so determined for each job represents its rate. This is a complex system, but a higher degree of accuracy can be attained through it.

Limitations

Job evaluation alone cannot establish a wage scale. For wage fixation, it is essential to take into cognizance statutory requirements like Minimum Wages Act, 1948. Similarly, other factors of wage fixation, such as the capacity to pay, inter-industry wage variation, inter-regional wage variation, and collective bargaining agreement, if any, also need to be given importance. Job evaluation is highly subjective (being based on a judgemental estimate). Similarly, it cannot take into account the cyclical effect of the market value of the occupations. For example, finance jobs were once highly priced in the market (now information technology and marketing have taken its place). However, with the failure of non-banking financial companies, finance jobs are not currently that highly priced in the market, even though no material change in the job profile of finance professionals has taken place since then.

Despite such limitations, the job evaluation technique is considered very useful for reasons explained earlier.

JOB ASSESSMENT

At this stage, information about each job is made available to the assessors. Every job, whether manual or not, is closely observed and inspected in actual operation by the assessors. If required, assessors question the operators and their supervisors and ask them to collect further details about the job to clear doubts, if any. To keep pace with the changing job content, due to technological changes, it is necessary to make a periodic reassessment of the job, keeping in view the old job description.

Pricing Job Value

The purpose of job evaluation is to establish the relative job value within the organization in terms of points or rankings and in terms of pay levels. The next step is to translate this data into a pay structure through job correlation. This, therefore, involves first deciding the pay grades and then developing the pay ranges for each grade.

Steps in Job Pricing

The initial process of pricing the job and fitting them into a pay structure calls for translating the points into different job grades. Thereafter, jobs are grouped as per different pay grades and the results are then related with comparable jobs in other companies. However, this may not be possible for jobs that are unique in nature. When jobs are properly grouped, it is not difficult to price each such job group. After pricing, each job group and pay structure can be developed on the mathematical principle that 'things which are equal to the same things are equal to each other'.

From the survey report of other companies, base salaries for each pay grade are established after considering the average paid by the companies surveyed.

The next step in job pricing is to develop pay ranges around the base salaries. Once this is developed, the individual compensation based on performance and other considerations can be worked out. Different pay ranges enable an organization to adopt a flexible approach (within the range) in hiring new employees, taking into cognizance the labour market flexibility.

For instance, for a manufacturing organization, a fitter may have a pay grade ranging between ₹5000–10,000 per month. This pay grade can be broken into different ranges, such as Fitter Grade I—₹8000–10,000 per month, Fitter Grade II—₹6000–8000 per month, and Fitter Grade III—₹5000–6000 per month.

Other Methods of Job Assessment

There are various other methods of job assessment for pricing a job value, which is essential for compensation designing. At the same time, such methods ensure job simplification and humanization of jobs. Even though some of these methods do not directly contribute to job pricing, they are still useful for achieving productivity and efficiency. Such methods are briefly discussed later in the chapter.

Work Study

Work study literally implies the study of human work. British Standard 3138:1969 defines work study as a management service based on the techniques, particularly method study and work measurement, that are used in the examination of human work in all its contexts and lead to the systematic investigation of all the resources and factors that affect the efficiency and economy of the situation being reviewed in order to effect improvement.

Thus, it is a generic term for two interdependent techniques, namely method study and work measurement. In the said British Standard, method study has been defined as 'the systematic recording and critical examination of the factors and resources involved in existing and proposed ways of doing work, as means of developing and applying easier and more effective methods and reducing costs'. Work measurement, on the other hand, is defined as 'the application of techniques designed to establish the time for a qualified worker to carry out a specified job at the defined level of performance'.

Contextual analysis of the agreed definition of work study given by the British Standards Institute, therefore, enables us to define the subject as a procedure for understanding and determining the truth about the activities of the people, plant, and machineries, identifying the factors that affect their efficiency and achieving economy through their optimum utilization. Most of the productivity improvement techniques involve major capital expenditure in plant or equipment. Work study, being a management technique, on the other hand, ensures productivity by using the existing resources. In work study, the human element is emphasized and importance is given to the operation rather than to the technical process. This, therefore, assists the management in the following three major ways, which are actually its primary objectives:

- Effective use of plant and equipment
- Effective use of human effort
- Evaluation of human work

Human Context of Work Study—Trade Union's Response

If work study techniques are not properly applied, they are likely to encounter resistance at all levels. Therefore, it is important to understand human reactions and accordingly design the programme investigation and implementation. Most unions are, by now, aware that work study provides benefits to the workers by eliminating drudgery, frustration, and an unhealthy working environment. It also gives an opportunity to the workers to increase their earnings (at a micro level) and the earnings of the nation as a whole (at the macro level).

However, to satisfy the unions, the following three points need to be considered:

- Workers should be consulted before the introduction of any scheme that is likely to affect their interests in one way or the other.
- There should be a definite policy for those workers who will become redundant after the implementation of the recommendations of the work study team.
- The procedure to deal with the changes in the method of work and for measurement of work should be laid down and communicated to the workers.

The International Labour Organization (ILO) emphasized the importance of such sharing of information with the workers in a resolution concerning consultation and cooperation between employers and workers at the level of the undertaking in its 35th session at Geneva in 1952.

Method Study

Method study is a productivity improvement step that helps to produce the same output using lesser resources or produce more with a proportionately less increase in the inputs. Thus, it reduces, if not eliminates, the waste. Method study ensures creativity, innovativeness, optimal decision-making power, good organizational practices, and better communication. It is essential to keep the following factors in mind while carrying out a method study:

- Economic considerations
- Technical considerations
- Human reactions

Role of Method Study

Summarizing the foregoing discussions, the role of method study can be enunciated as follows:

- To appraise the purpose and objectives of the organization
- To assess the tasks of the organization
- To evaluate the communication and control structure of the organization
- To optimize the use of resources of the organization
- To improve the procedures, methods, and processes of the organization
- To ensure individual and group effectiveness and at the same time satisfaction of work in the organization

Importance and Objectives of Method Study

The objectives of method study are to find better ways of doing things and to contribute to improved efficiency by eliminating unnecessary work, avoidable delays, and other forms of waste. Through a systematic recording, analysis, and critical examination of methods and movements involved in the performance of the existing or proposed ways of doing work, it achieves these objectives. However, the importance or objectives of method study would be clearer once we review its contribution that flows from its said role. The contribution of method study could be indicated as follows:

- Reorientation of the corporate objectives and mission
- Review of plans and programmes
- Evaluation of tasks, targets, and available resources
- Balancing the structure of the organization
- Introduction of a good communication system in the organization
- Better design of plants and equipment
- Simplification of processes and methods
- Standardization of products and procedures
- Improvement of workflow
- Planning and control of work
- Management of resources, inventory control, and replacement of plants and machinery
- Quality and cost control
- Improvement of the layout of the shop floor
- Betterment of working environment and working conditions
- Optimum utilization of resources
- Higher standards of safety, security, and health
- Performance satisfaction

Mechanism of Method Study

The method study technique is flexible enough to accommodate different situations. However, a simple framework for its application in any given circumstance may be designed as shown in Exhibit 10.3.

> ### EXHIBIT 10.3   Framework for the Application of Method Study Technique
>
> *Select* the work to be studied.
> *Record* all the relevant facts of the present (or proposed) method.
> *Examine* facts critically and in sequence.
> *Develop* the most practical, economic, and effective methods, having due regard to all contingent circumstances.
> *Install* that method as the standard practice.
> *Maintain* that standard practice by regular routine checks.

Even though we have indicated six basic steps in a particular order, in actual study, it does not necessarily follow that sequence or pattern. Selection of the subject of study may be preceded by the study of possibility of data collection. Similarly, preliminary critical examination (pilot study) may be needed in order to identify the problem area. During a pilot study, there may be a need for more detailed data. On the other hand, it may be revealed during the preliminary critical examination that the real problem is something other than the selected one. Thus, sticking to a rigid procedure of analysis may often mar the prospect of getting a productive solution.

Transparency is an important feature of method study. Discussion, exchange of views, and efforts at mutual understanding are all part of every basic step of this technique. There are several undefined stages. Before implementation, the final plan has to be discussed with all the concerned employees. Similarly, installing the new system has to be preceded by a plan to familiarize the concerned employees through reorientation programmes. After installation, the system has to be maintained to ensure that this becomes an accepted standard.

The steps of a method study may, therefore, be enumerated as follows:

- Initial data collection
- Preliminary or pilot survey and assessment
- Identification of the problem areas
- Collection and assembly of data concerning the factors
- Determination of their interconnection
- Finalization of the subjects for study
- Definition of the problems or subject for study
- Assessment of their impact or reaction
- Evolution of the alternatives
- Decision on the optimal solutions
- Testing of the solutions
- Preparation of the report
- Presentation of the recommendations
- Decision on the implementation
- Preparation for the implementation
- Installation of the newly evolved system
- Maintenance of the newly installed system
- Evaluation of the improvements achieved

Detailed Procedures

The detailed procedure or steps involved in any method study investigation may be enumerated as follows:

Selection of job   Once the idea of method study is conceived, the first step to be performed is the orientation and determination of objectives. The problem must be defined. The method study investigator faces the following types of problems, which he/she is normally required to solve:

- Bottlenecks that disrupt smooth flow of material and processes
- Products that may be required to be produced economically by application of cost-reducing techniques
- Economic utilization of space, including land and buildings
- Economic utilization of labour, material, and plant
- Elimination of idle items or non-value items, which increase the time involved in a process, due to problems of flow, queues, and congestion

While selecting the subjects for study, it is essential to keep in mind that the ultimate objective of the method study is to improve the levels of achievement by raising the levels of productivity and increasing satisfaction at work. Secondly, the term 'select' should not be taken in a narrow sense, that is, to choose from among others, but it must include a preliminary survey that will enable the investigator to decide on the continuity of the study. Similarly, select does not necessarily mean just the selection of the job but also refers to the selection of the appropriate techniques to achieve the end result.

Recording of facts   Before discarding the existing method or procedure, adequate facts about the present system must be collected. This is required to prepare an objective record of the way the job is carried out. To eliminate the charge of bias, this record is not compiled from second-hand accounts, on the manager's version as to how he/she thinks the job is done, or an operator's description of how the job is done; it is based on direct observation by the concerned investigator.

Critical examination of facts   This is another important stage of method study. The information collected is scrutinized in this stage and each part of the job is critically examined to determine the action to be taken on the part, which includes the following:

- Eliminating it altogether
- Combining it with any other part of the job
- Changing its sequence
- Simplifying it to reduce the content of the work involved

For effective examination of the facts, the following questions are generally asked about the job:

- What is done and why?
- What it does and what that person does?
- Where is it done and why is it done there?
- When is it done and why is it done then?
- How is it done and why is it done in that way?

By rearranging, simplifying, combining, eliminating, or modifying the facts or records, the ground is prepared for devising an improved method.

Development of new method   The alternatives selected are used to reshape and develop the new method, layout, or procedure. These may require test runs to determine their feasibility. Tests of this nature may be preferably carried out at a place away from the work-site, if possible. To ease the problems of acceptance for the new method in the department, it is always advisable to involve the department. The end result must be an improved method and must be acceptable to the departmental staff and workers. It must meet all their practical requirements and technical specifications.

Installation of method   To install the method, a decision must be taken on the ordering of new plants or materials (if any), phasing in changes in the production process, deciding the extent of redeployment and training, introducing new documentation procedures, and setting new quality standards and test procedures. It is good to have a detailed timetable for effecting such changes. The end product of the installation stage is that the new method is in operation at the work-site, the line management is in complete control, and finally all members of the department are fully conversant with the method.

Maintenance of method   When a method has been installed, it tends to slowly change because of small alterations made by the operators or supervisors. A standard reference (job instruction sheet) is needed against which the job can be compared to detect any alterations. Similarly, a corresponding document for an incentive scheme, which also contains details of the standard time for each job, called a job specification, is prepared. With this data, changes in the method can be detected. If changes are considered to be useful, the instruction sheet can be amended to incorporate them; instead, if they are found to be undesirable, they can be removed through line management.

WORK MEASUREMENT

The ILO defines work measurement as 'the application of techniques designed to establish the work content of a specified task by determining the time required for carrying it out at a defined standard of performance by a qualified worker'. Conventionally, it is known as time study, which is primarily carried out to determine the standard time required to perform a specific task. Such time standards are used for planning and scheduling work, for estimating cost, or for controlling labour cost. Otherwise, it may serve as the basis for a wage incentive plan. It has wide applications in deciding a wage incentive plan.

Techniques

Though there are different techniques for work measurement, the following are the principal techniques:

- Time study
- Ratio delay study (statistical sampling technique)
- Synthesis from standard data

> Work measurement is defined as the application of techniques designed to establish the work content of a specified task by determining the time required for carrying it out at a defined standard of performance by a qualified worker.

- Predetermined motion time standard
- Analytic estimating

Of these techniques, time study is the widely used one because others are complicated in nature. This text too discusses only time study in detail, while simply defining the other techniques.

Time Study

The ILO defined time study as 'a technique for determining as accurately as possible, from a limited number of observations, the time necessary to carry out a given activity at a defined standard of performance'. For carrying out a time study, equipment such as a stopwatch, study board, pencils, and slide rule are required. The different types of stopwatches used include the following:

- Stopwatches that record one minute per revolution by intervals of one-fifth of a second with a small hand recording 30 minutes.
- Stopwatches that record one minute per revolution, calibrated in one-hundredth of a minute with a small hand recording 30 minutes.
- Decimal-hour stopwatches recording one-hundredth of an hour with a small hand recording up to one hour in 100 divisions.

The following steps are necessary for carrying out a time study for the measurement of work:

- Collect and complete all available information about the job, which should also include the surrounding conditions and the attributes of the operators that are likely to affect the work.
- Record the details of the methods and also break down different operations into their elements.
- Record the time taken by the operators to perform the operation (element-wise) measuring preferably with a timing device such as a stopwatch.
- Assess the working speed of the operators by comparing it with a predetermined normal speed.
- Convert the observed time to normal time.
- Decide the rate of allowances that may be given over and above the normal time of operation.
- Determine the allowed time for operation.

Other Techniques of Work Measurement

Since carrying out the time study for each job is a time-consuming task, statistical techniques like ratio delay study are often employed. Ratio delay is a sampling technique; hence, in this method, instead of going for the complete job study, a sufficiently large number of readings are taken at random intervals. Similar to all other sampling techniques, there are bound to be some errors in this method as well. However, since the study does not involve much cost, organizations with the necessary expertise prefer this method. Moreover, the method does not encounter any resistance from the workers because the rating is not done and the time is recorded directly using a stopwatch.

Synthesis from standard data method synthesizes time standards that are built or synthesized from element times previously obtained from a direct time study. Most organizations that have an independent work study department build a synthetic table converting the commoner elements. However, some units also use such time records of other organizations as standard data. For non-commonality of technology, skill, process, and working environments, this type of synthesis may not always be correct.

Predetermined motion time standards have been developed for different job elements based on the elementary movement. Usually, for time measurement, work factor, and basic motion, times are recorded in any predetermined time standard. Work study analysts use such time standards as the basis for comparing the observed time of the present workers. This enables the analysts to quickly decide the efficiency or otherwise of the workers and to make decisions accordingly.

Analytical estimation is normally used in plant maintenance and repair work. This is a compromise between straight rate fixing and time study. Since maintenance and repair jobs require adequate planning and also because such jobs, by their very nature, call for creativity and innovativeness, it is difficult to enforce straight rate fixing. Analytical estimation is difficult in nature and is also not always foolproof in case of inexperienced work study analysts.

ERGONOMICS

Ergonomics is derived from two Greek words—*ergon* meaning work and *enomos* meaning laws. It is the study of the effects of a work system on the workers and it aims at fitting the work to the workers to increase their efficiency, comfort, and satisfaction. The ILO defines ergonomics as 'the application of human biological sciences in conjunction with engineering sciences to the worker and his working environment, so as to obtain maximum satisfaction for the work which, at the same time, enhances productivity'.

The contextual analysis of the ILO definition, therefore, provides a more meaningful basis for understanding ergonomics. An ergonomist, for effective accomplishment of work, tries to integrate the work system (which broadly includes the tasks, working equipment, working conditions, and working space) with the capabilities and requirements of work. In this process, he/she tries to ensure job satisfaction for the workers, which, inter alia, increases their productivity.

> Ergonomics is defined as the application of human biological sciences in conjunction with engineering sciences to the worker and his/her environment so as to obtain maximum satisfaction for the work, which, at the same time, enhances productivity.

Ergonomics can be applied in all schemes of human activity, be it in offices, factories, shops, ships, air, or even space. The following are some of the areas where ergonomics has been successfully applied:

- Design of equipment, power, and hand tools
- Design of displays and warning systems
- Design of furniture, seats, rests, and steps for operators
- Design of tools, jigs, and fixtures
- Plant layout
- Improvement in working conditions and environments
- Computation of relaxation allowances for workers
- Selection, training, and placement of personnel
- Motivation of workers

However, for better understanding, the areas of ergonomic investigations of a work system may be grouped as follows.

Human characteristics Health, physique, anthropometric data, personal background, education, training, experience, age, sex, intelligence, aptitude, reaction time, interest, personality characteristics, temperament, attitude towards work, and motivation

Work Physical loads, perceptual loads, mental loads, displays and warning systems, controls, and compatibility of inputs and outputs

Working conditions Workplace layout, postures, motion and movements, fatigue, monotony and relaxation allowances, comfort, safety and health, working hours, and shift work conditions

Environment Illumination, ventilation, temperature and humidity, colour dynamics, fumes, dust, odour and smoke, landscape, scenery and garden, cleanliness, and sanitation

Many alternative terms such as human engineering, human factors in engineering, engineering psychology, applied experimental psychology, applied and human engineering research, and man–machine system analysis are used to designate the discipline. This subject was developed during World War II as a result of the coordinated efforts of physiologists, psychologists, and design engineers. Its earliest application can be traced to Frederick Winslow Taylor (1856–1915). Taylor's experiments were carried out to mainly arrive at the optimum design of equipment for specific types of work and to also train the workers to suit them for each type of task. Frank Bunker Gilberth (1869–1924) and his wife Lillian elaborated the principles of motion economy and introduced the rest pauses and spacing out of work to reduce fatigue and eliminate stress. Since then, with the advancement of experimental physiology, psychology, and method study, the subject delved deeper into the human make-up for a better and scientific understanding of the effects of the working conditions and environment on the human body and mind.

Impact of Ergonomics on Work Study

Work study, which aims at a scientific analysis of a work system to increase the productivity and satisfaction at work, is dependent on ergonomics for research into the many facets of human reaction to a given work situation. Such input information makes the task of the work study practitioner more scientific and result oriented. This input information or data mostly relates to the following areas:

- Limits of sustained physical endurance, normal speeds of movement, and optimum methods of handling of controls
- Receptivity to sensory inputs and the time required for the perception of deviations
- Reaction time for motion output and time required for evaluation and decision-making
- Anthropometric data to guide the design and layout of equipment, workplace, and furniture
- Effects of different types of environmental conditions on human beings in order to generate improvements
- Effects of working conditions so as to raise the standards of comfort, safety, and health
- Qualitative and quantitative analysis of factors contributing to industrial fatigue for computation of *relaxation allowances*

Practitioner Speak 10.3

Morning Advantage: Your Ergonomic Desk May Be Trying to Hurt You

Sitting at your desk all day isn't healthy. That is why some of us try to mix it up a bit. Take standing desks. A bunch of my colleagues use them, and I totally get the appeal. But if this piece at MarketWatch is any indication, the ergonomic fad—treadmill desks, anyone?—has reached the point of satire.

Read this insightful blog posted by Evers on *HBR Blog Network* by accessing the following link: http://blogs.hbr.org/morning-advantage/2013/02/morning-advantage-your-ergonom.html.

Ergonomics and Management

Ergonomics is a discipline at the service of the management right from the planning and design stage of a work system. In the organization and control of human effort directed to specific ends, the management needs to have an appreciation of the human factors involved in a work system.

The findings of ergonomic research, particularly in the field of perceptual and mental loading, have a special bearing on the work situation confronting the managerial performance in an organization. The aim here will be to eliminate all perceptual and mental loading that may arise from the perusal and evaluation of reports on the normal activities of the organization, thereby highlighting only the deviations from the equilibrium state. This will permit more effective application of the managerial talent to really important problems over a wider span. In other words, ergonomics can help in increasing the productivity of the managerial brainpower. This single improvement, by itself, without any changes in the methods on the shop floor will lead to a spectacular increase in the overall productivity of the organizations.

Exhibit 10.4 discusses the essential considerations and processes in carrying out an ergonomics study at the workplace.

EXHIBIT 10.4 Carrying Out an Ergonomics Study at the Workplace: Essential Considerations and Processes

The use of ergonomics at the workplace has yielded many positive results. The benefits range from checking occupational diseases to reducing work-related musculoskeletal disorders to bettering overall workplace conditions. It also addresses stress-related issues at the workplace. However, ergonomics is a highly technical area and needs specialists to execute the process and monitor its effects.

In this regard, the United States Occupational Safety and Health Administration (OSHA) has set certain guidelines for organizations as well as practitioners of ergonomics to follow, which are as follows:

- Coming up with a written programme on ergonomics
- Identifying ergonomic problems at the workplace
- Carrying out inspections and analyses of the workplace at regular intervals
- Providing training to workers as well as their supervisors

(Contd)

EXHIBIT 10.4 (*Contd*)

- Coming up with practices such as medical management, hazard prevention, and control mechanisms
- Starting a process of documenting all actions at the workplace

Additionally, Larson and Ellexson (2000) have noted that for an effective blueprint for ergonomics, organizations and practitioners should keep in mind certain factors such as workplace temperature, attitudes of workers, seasonal work changes, size of the workforce, corporate philosophy, nature of interaction between labourers and management, and injury management mechanisms in practice.

Again, Moraes and Andrade (2012) have come up with a detailed process for implementing ergonomics management systems in organizations. The steps involved are as follows:

Sensitization

Employees across the organization should be made aware of the ergonomic systems and the benefits these offer in increasing productivity and in ensuring a safe and better workplace. Thus, both senior management and workers should be sensitized about the programme and its benefits.

Ergonomics Policy

Developing an ergonomics policy is as important a step as is establishing an ergonomics committee. The policy should be documented and disseminated across the organization such that all employees have a look at it.

Ergonomics Committee

The establishment of an ergonomics committee intends to identify senior and supervisory level members of the organization who are trained to identify risks at the workplace, suggest changes and improvements, determine the costs the organization has to incur for these, and ascertain the benefits these steps are likely to provide.

Ergonomics Mapping within Organizations

The mapping of ergonomics in the organization is normally done by preparing a checklist of potential areas of risks at the workplace.

Ergonomics Analysis of Work

The ergonomics analysis of work is done by analysing all major work functions and through worker participation. Special attention is given to sections wherein workers exhibit musculoskeletal diseases or suffer from work-related stress. The committee studies and recommends improvements.

Implementation of Ergonomics Improvements

Once the recommendations are made, steps are taken towards implementing them to the best extent possible.

Evaluation of Outcome Indicators

Identifying outcome indicators help in evaluating the results of implementing ergonomics at the workplace. It also helps in identifying areas that require more attention and improvement.

Sources: Larson, B. and T. Ellexson, 'Blueprint for Ergonomics', *Work*, No. 15, 2000, pp. 107–12; Moraes, B. and V.S. Andrade, 'Implantation of an Ergonomics Administration System in a Company: Report of an Occupational Therapist Specialist in Ergonomics', *Work*, No. 41, 2012, pp. 2637–42 (adapted).

Working Areas

The working area of an operator may be categorized into three groups—normal, immediate, and maximum. The normal working area is one that can be reached by the operator using any movement up to and inclusive of class three movements.

Two arcs made by the fingers using the elbow as the pivot bind this area. The immediate working area is the surface immediately in front of the operator where the two arcs of the

Table 10.2 Classes of movements

Class	Pivot	Body member movement
1.	Knuckle (finger joint)	Finger(s)
2.	Wrist	Hand and fingers
3.	Elbow	Forearm, hand, and fingers
4.	Shoulder	Upper arm, forearm, hand, and fingers
5.	Trunk (body apart from limbs)	Torso, upper arm, forearm, hand, and fingers

normal working area overlap. The maximum working area is one that can be reached by the operator using arcs made by the fingers with the shoulders as the pivot.

The space between the normal and the maximum working areas is accessible through a class four movement. Anything beyond the maximum working area may be reached only through a class five movement, including body bending or stretching.

The immediate working area is most suitable for bimanual operation. If the various equipment, materials, and tools are placed within the normal working area, they can be reached without using the upper arm and shoulder muscles. It is not desirable to place anything outside the maximum working area.

The field of vision should also be taken into account while considering the working areas. The normal cone of vision, without head movement, is restricted. Covering the whole perimeter of the normal working area would impose undue eyestrain and sometimes involves excessive head movements. Due care must, therefore, be taken to position all the materials well within this cone of vision. During inspection, as much of the work as possible must take place in front of the operator.

For better understanding, the classes of movements can be grouped under five categories, based on the pivots around which the body members move, as shown in Table 10.2.

A similar classification of the movements of the corresponding members of the leg is available. For economy of motion, the movement should be of the lowest classification possible, compatible with the normal capacity of the body member affected.

MOTION ECONOMY

> Motion economy is the process of minimizing the physical and perceptual loads imposed on people engaged in any type of work, be it in the office, the shop floor, the kitchen, or at the driving wheel.

Motion economy is the process of minimizing the physical and perceptual loads imposed on people engaged in any type of work, be it in the office, the shop floor, the kitchen, or at the driving wheel. It leads to a better designing of equipment, jigs and fixtures, hand tools, furniture, and labour-saving devices. In addition, it facilitates a better layout of offices, warehouses, plants, and operating areas such as office desk, workbench, aircraft, cockpit, and crew compartments of armoured fighting vehicles. Application of the principles of motion economy eliminates or minimizes wasteful and fatiguing movements and increases the productivity of the workers. It minimizes the movements with respect to the following:

- Number of movements
- Length of movements
- Classification
- Number of parts of body used
- Necessity for control
- Muscular force

- Complexity of movements
- Distances between eye fixation
- Time required for eye fixation

For achieving motion economy, the following principles have been evolved by different specialists:

- Principle of minimum movement
- Principle of natural movement
- Principle of simultaneous movement
- Principle of symmetrical movement
- Principle of rhythmic movement
- Principle of habitual movement
- Principle of continuous movement

Simultaneous movements reduce fatigue and increase the rate of output. More fatigue is caused when only one hand is working while the other is idle. Simultaneous movement includes the movements of the feet while both the hands are operating as in driving a car. Application of this principle leads to a better designing of jigs, fixtures, and duplication of tools, so that both the hands simultaneously work at similar tasks.

The principle of symmetrical movements should be applied in conjunction with simultaneous movements. Proper balance is achieved only when the movement of one hand is the 'mirror image' of the movement of the other or eliminates fumbling. When movements of the hands are asymmetrical, there is a tendency on the part of the operators to interpolate additional but non-productive movements in order to achieve a balance.

Rhythm is the regular repetition of a movement pattern. It often incorporates the accentuation of a specific part of a cycle. Rhythm contributes to the speed, elimination of fumbling, and reduction in fatigue. Examples of rhythmic movements are boat rowing, hammering at the smithy, and drawing water from a well using a see-saw lift.

The pattern of movement should be designed so as to facilitate habituation. When a cycle of activities is performed habitually, the movements are executed almost as a reflex action. Habitual movements eliminate hesitations and increase the speed of performance. Rhythm helps in speed habit formation. Tools, materials, displays, and controls must always be located at the same position. The pattern must be standardized for similar types of panels, workplaces, and equipment. Continuous movements, which are smooth and curved, are superior to jerky, straight-line movements, which involve sudden changes of direction and loss of momentum. Materials, tools, and jigs must be so positioned so as to incorporate smooth, curved, and continuous movements and eliminate undue changes of direction.

These principles should be treated merely as guides and not as rigid rules. Quite often, one principle would be in conflict with another and a proper evaluation of the principles, in their totality, would be needed for optimization. Conditions differ from job to job. It may sometimes be necessary to compromise load over the various muscles or to give due weightage to the principle of continuous movement. It is, therefore, essential that the principles are applied with flexibility.

HUMAN ENGINEERING

Method study seeks to determine the effective combination of man, machine, and working environment. In doing so, it is necessary to determine which functions are better performed by man and which are better performed by machine. Both man and machine can surpass each other

> Human engineering is the mechanism for the adaptation of human tasks and working environment to sensory, perceptual, mental, physical, and other attributes of people.

in certain ways. The question of economy, again, influences the man–machine combination. The term human engineering is more appropriately used to solve man–machine problems in the design, operation, and maintenance of plants and machineries, and thus, it broadly comes under the purview of ergonomics. It is therefore not appropriate to designate human engineering as an independent discipline, separating it from ergonomics. However, to understand the context and meaning of human engineering, it is considered necessary to define it in line with Ernest J. McCormick. McCormick defined it as the mechanism for 'the adaptation of human tasks and working environment to sensory, perceptual, mental, physical and other attributes of people'. This adaptation for human use applies to functions such as the design of equipment, instruments, man–machine systems, and consumer products and to the development of optimum work methods and work environment.

Human Engineering and Machine Design

The designer of a machine should know the way a human being functions, his/her body dimensions, his/her physical limitations, and the conditions under which a person performs perfectly. For performing a task, a person normally does the following three activities:

- Receive information (through different sense organs)
- Make decisions (acting on perceived information)
- Take action (which results from decision)

Thus, the basic control cycle for human beings consists of these actions—sense, decide, and act. The ability to reason inductively, exercise judgement, develop concepts, decide, and create methods are unique to human beings. While quickly performing repetitive routine tasks, the ability to perform rapid computations, apply great force, and simultaneously perform many different functions are the characteristic features of machines.

The designer of the machine, therefore, is required to consider all these details before developing a better-designed machine for productive use. Most computer numerically controlled (CNC) machining centres developed by large industrial organizations in India are not performing well as they have been designed without considering the human factor. In fact, the sophisticated machine centres, whenever introduced, have become instrumental in perpetual industrial relations problems as these adversely affect the workers' pay packets. This is because the cycle time printed in the machine literature is considerably less than the actual time taken by the workers. This complicates job correlation with the workers' payment, as technically they are supposed to get payment as per the printed cycle time.

Since a badly designed machine may be responsible for the poor performance of workers, application of ergonomics or human engineering techniques is necessary to design the machines. Modern machines are ergonomically designed to prevent stress and fatigue among workers, to make them work at ease, and at the same time to gain an increased rate of production. Application of human engineering or ergonomic techniques can be found even in designing consumer products, kitchen gadgets, furniture, and so on. For example, recently, Blowplast Ltd, under technical collaboration with Klober of Germany, has ergonomically designed office chairs.

VALUE ANALYSIS

Henry Erlicher of General Electric company, drawing lessons from World War II, observed in 1947 that substitution of materials (as manufacturers were then compelled to go for substitution to encounter shortage of original materials) often led to cost reduction and better functionality. This has prompted further research in the field of alternative materials and processes and L.D. Miles, another top executive of the company, was directed by him to go into the details, which were later called value analysis. By 1949, this approach was used in a more institutionalized form in General Electric and gradually, the US Department of Defense also adopted it. By 1970, the value engineering concept received international attention.

Value engineering is an organized creative technique to analyse the functions of a product, service, or system to achieve the required functions at the lowest cost while ensuring its performance reliability and maintainability. It is also known as value analysis or value management.

Value is the worth of an article, product, or service. It is determined in terms of cost and function. The value of a product can be improved by the following measures:

- Improving function (keeping cost constant)
- Reducing cost (keeping function constant)
- Both by improving function and by reducing cost

There are different types of values of an industrial product, which may be classified as follows:

Use value The properties and attributes that are useful and help in the accomplishment of work, which may be for primary, secondary, or auxiliary use

> Value analysis is an organized creative technique to analyse the functions of a product, service, or system to achieve the required functions at the lowest cost while ensuring its performance reliability and maintainability.

Esteem value The aesthetic features or properties that attract a customer to own it

Cost value The cost required to produce the item

Exchange value The properties that enable the owner to exchange it for anything else, if he/she so desires, in future

However, for all practical purposes, in an industrial situation, we are primarily concerned only with the use value and esteem value.

In the backdrop of this discussion, value analysis can be defined as a method of search, a systematic procedure, resulting in the orderly utilization of alternative materials and processes. It focuses on engineering, manufacturing, and purchasing, with attention on one objective—obtaining equivalent or even better performance at a lower cost.

Steps in Value Analysis

The following steps are carried out during value analysis:

- Collect all the facts and information about the product.
- Obtain details of the cost break-up.
- Determine the function.

- Think creatively.
- Compare and evaluate the alternatives.

To succeed at each step, it is necessary to take the following line of action:

- Eliminate the redundant parts.
- Initiate action of cheaper substitutes without impairing the use value.
- Standardize the parts.
- Develop alternative methods.
- Redesign, if necessary.

Advantages

The following are the advantages gained from value analysis:

- Lowering of cost
- Better quality of product
- Increased efficiency
- High level of morale and team spirit
- Increased customer satisfaction
- Optimum resource utilization
- Improved methods of production
- Increased job satisfaction and motivation to workers through the use of their creative ability

The term value analysis has now been replaced by value engineering in corporate circles. In most organizations, value engineering practices are followed by forming a value engineering team of workers (a small-group activity like quality circles). This, therefore, provides an opportunity for workers to derive creative satisfaction and to also fulfil their intrinsic needs. At the same time, organizations also get active services from the workers.

COMPETENCY-BASED APPROACH IN JOB DESIGN

The competency-based approach has two initial stages—identifying or analysing competencies and assessing competencies. The first is concerned with what competencies are used in the job and the second with measuring the extent to which existing employees (or would be recruits) possess them. This information can be used in making better judgements in selection and recruitment, career development, promotion, and pay. According to Wood and Payne (1998), the most commonly adopted competencies are as follows:

- Communication
- Achievement or result orientation
- Customer focus
- Teamwork
- Leadership
- Planning and organizing

- Commercial or business awareness
- Flexibility and adaptability
- Development of others
- Problem-solving
- Analytical thinking
- Building relationships

As an example, the competency sets and the evidences required for the job of a regional director are given in Annexure 10.3.

While designing jobs, competency mapping is done in the defined job context by collecting inputs from the following:

- Workforce and skills analysis
- Job analysis
- Supply and demand analysis

- Gap analysis
- Situation analysis

Skills analysis describes the skills required to carry out a function. Workforce analysis and job analysis focus on the tasks, responsibilities, and knowledge and skills required for a successful job performance. Supply analysis is done considering workforce demographics (in terms of occupation, structure, race, origin, gender, age, service experience, education, training, health status, retirement time, and similar other information), trends, and present workforce competencies. This, therefore, helps to understand the existing workforce status. Demand analysis, on the other hand, helps identify the workforce for the future in line with the vision, mission, objectives, goals, and strategies of an organization. Critical inputs from demand analysis contribute to the development of competency models for workforces of the future.

With these input reinforcers, organizations undertake gap analysis to understand the differences between the workforce of today and the workforce of the future. After such identification of differences, organizations need to plan to address them.

Addressing of gaps is done through solution analysis, taking into account both the ongoing and the unplanned changes in the workforce. Solution analysis also weighs the options to get the work done, considering either institutional or contractual employment. In this phase, new recruitment, restructuring, training and retraining, redeployment and rightsizing are all done in the light of the new competency model.

Design of jobs using the competency framework can be done on the basis of a model that has been agreed upon and developed for some common categories of employees in one textile manufacturing company, using the aforementioned approach, shown in Table 10.3.

Table 10.3 Competency framework model for some selected employees of a textile manufacturing organization

S. no.	Designation	Business management competencies	Professional competencies	Technical competencies
1.	Assistant Manager (SQC)	Quality assurance Outcome measures and evaluation Planning and scheduling Time management and prioritization Getting unbiased information	Communication Thinking clearly/ analytically Identifying and solving problems Giving clear information Teamwork	Disciplining and counselling Quality testing at lab and shop floor Statistical calculations Computer skills Knowledge of ISO 9000, ISO 14000, SA 8000, OHSAS 18000

(Contd)

Table 10.3 (*Contd*)

S. no.	Designation	Business management competencies	Professional competencies	Technical competencies
2.	Assistant Manager (PM and HR)	Organizational awareness Negotiating skills Planning and scheduling Time management and prioritization Getting unbiased information	Communication Conflict management Interpersonal skills Listening and organizing Teamwork	Pay administration Human resource fundamentals Labour–Management relations Discipline and adverse action Knowledge of ISO 9000, ISO 14000, SA 8000, OHSAS 18000
3.	Assistant Manager (Production) Weaving, Wool Combing, Flax, RSM, Worsted Fabric	Product knowledge Cost–Benefit analysis Planning and scheduling Time management and prioritization Getting unbiased information	Communication Interpersonal skills Identifying and solving problems Listening and organizing Teamwork	Disciplining and counselling Knowledge of machines and production process Knowledge of computers Knowledge of ISO 9000, ISO 14000, SA 8000, OHSAS 18000
4.	Assistant Manager (MIS/Accounts/ Purchase and Stores)	Business awareness Customer relations Financial management Planning and scheduling Time management and prioritization Getting unbiased information	Communication Interpersonal skills Thinking clearly/ analytically Giving clear information Teamwork	Disciplining and counselling Accounting, export–import, taxes knowledge Knowledge of computers Knowledge of ISO 9000, ISO 14000, SA 8000, OHSAS 18000
5.	Assistant Manager (Engineering) Flax SPG, Engineering Department, RSM, Maintenance	Outcome measures and evaluation Organizational awareness Planning and scheduling Time management and prioritization Getting unbiased information	Thinking clearly/ analytically Communication Teamwork Technology application Identifying and solving problems	Detailed technical knowledge regarding machines and process knowledge Computer skills Disciplining and counselling Knowledge of ETP/ ERP/energy conservation as required Knowledge of ISO 9000, ISO 14000, SA 8000, OHSAS 18000

(*Contd*)

Table 10.3 (*Contd*)

S. no.	Designation	Business management competencies	Professional competencies	Technical competencies
6.	Assistant Manager (Sales and Marketing) RSM, Worsted Fabric	Customer relations Negotiating skills Planning and scheduling Time management and prioritization Getting unbiased information	Communication Interpersonal skills Cross-cultural sensitivity/creativity Giving clear information Teamwork	Product/Market knowledge Knowledge of taxes, duties, etc. Computer skills Disciplining and counselling Knowledge of ISO 9000, ISO 14000, SA 8000, OHSAS 18000
7.	Officer (SQC)	Quality assurance Planning and scheduling Time management and prioritization Getting unbiased information	Communication Thinking clearly/analytically Giving clear information Teamwork	Quality testing at lab and shop floor Statistical calculations Computer skills Knowledge of ISO 9000, ISO 14000, SA 8000, OHSAS 18000
8.	Assistant Officer (SQC)	Quality assurance Planning and scheduling Time management and prioritization	Communication Analytical thinking Teamwork	Quality testing Statistical calculations Computer skills
9.	Officer (PM and HR)/Assistant Administrative Officer (Fabric)	Negotiating Time management and prioritization Planning and scheduling Getting unbiased information	Conflict management Communication Interpersonal skills Giving clear information Teamwork	Human resource management fundamentals Labour–Management relations Pay administration Knowledge of ISO 9000, ISO 14000, SA 8000, OHSAS 18000
10.	Officer/Senior Officer (Production) Weaving, Wool Combing, Flax, RSM, Worsted Fabric	Product knowledge Planning and scheduling Time management and prioritization Getting unbiased information	Communication Interpersonal skills Identifying and solving problems Teamwork	Knowledge of machines and production process Computer skills Knowledge of ISO 9000, ISO 14000, SA 8000, OHSAS 18000
11.	Assistant Officer-(Production) Weaving, Wool Combing, Flax, RSM, Worsted Fabric	Product knowledge Planning and scheduling Time management and prioritization	Communication Interpersonal skills Teamwork	Knowledge of machines in production process Knowledge of computers

(*Contd*)

Table 10.3 *(Contd)*

S. no.	Designation	Business management competencies	Professional competencies	Technical competencies
12.	Officer/Senior Officer (MIS, Accounts, Purchase, Stores)	Business awareness Customer relations Planning and scheduling Time management and prioritization Getting unbiased information	Communication Thinking clearly/ analytically Giving clear information Teamwork	Accounting knowledge Knowledge of computers and their application in accounting Knowledge of ISO 9000, ISO 14000, SA 8000, OHSAS 18000
13.	Assistant Officer (MIS, Accounts, Purchase, Stores, MS)	Customer relations Planning and scheduling Time management and prioritization	Communication Thinking clearly/ analytically Teamwork	Accounting knowledge Computer skills
14.	Officer/Assistant Officer (Computers)	Planning and scheduling Time management and prioritization Getting unbiased information	Thinking clearly/ analytically Identifying and solving problems Communication Giving clear information Teamwork	Technical knowledge as required Knowledge of production and commercial system Knowledge of ISO 9000, ISO 14000, SA 8000, OHSAS 18000
15.	Officer/Senior Officer (Engineering) Flax SPG, Engineering Department, RSM, Maintenance	Quality assurance of machines Planning and scheduling Time management and prioritization Getting unbiased information	Thinking clearly/ analytically Communication Teamwork Technology application Listening and organizing	Technical knowledge of machines Computer skills as required Knowledge of ISO 9000, ISO 14000, SA 8000, OHSAS 18000
16.	Assistant Officer (Engineering) Flax SPG, Engineering Department, RSM, Maintenance	Planning and scheduling Time management and prioritization	Thinking clearly/ analytically Teamwork Communication	Technical knowledge of machines Computer skills
17.	Assistant Officer (Guest Relations)	Organizational awareness Negotiating Planning and scheduling Time management and prioritization	Communication Interpersonal relations Pleasing personality/ courteous Thinking clearly	Computer skills Experience in the field (if any)
18.	Officer (Excise)	Business awareness Negotiating skills Customer relations Planning and scheduling Getting unbiased information	Communication Interpersonal skills Decision-making Thinking clearly	Thorough knowledge of excise rules and regulations Knowledge of export and import

(Contd)

Table 10.3 (Contd)

S. no.	Designation	Business management competencies	Professional competencies	Technical competencies
19.	Officer/Senior Officer (Sales and Marketing)	Business awareness Customer relations Negotiating skills Planning and scheduling Time management and prioritization Getting unbiased information	Communication Networking Interpersonal skills Creativity Teamwork	Knowledge of market and product Computer skills Knowledge of ISO 9000, ISO 14000, SA 8000, OHSAS 18000
20.	Assistant Officer (Sales and Marketing) RSM, Worsted Fabric	Customer relations Negotiating skills Planning and scheduling Time management and prioritization	Communication Cross-cultural sensitivity Teamwork Interpersonal skills	Knowledge of market and product Computer skills
21.	Development Officer (RSM)	Planning and scheduling Time management and prioritization Getting unbiased information	Communication Thinking clearly/ analytically Giving clear information Decision-making	Knowledge of old products and new products to be developed Market demand for various products Knowledge of yarns, shades, etc. Computer skills Knowledge of ISO 9000, ISO 14000, SA 8000, OHSAS 18000
22.	Commercial Officer (Warehouse)	Business awareness Planning and scheduling Time management and prioritization Getting unbiased information	Communication Analytical thinking Interpersonal skills Giving clear information	Knowledge of products Accounting knowledge Knowledge of ISO 9000, ISO 14000, SA 8000, OHSAS 18000

SUMMARY

Job design helps in organizing job tasks; it has direct impact on the mental and physical health of the employees as well as on their performance levels. The physical aspects of jobs require organizations to consider ergonomic issues as it helps in reducing physical strain, fatigue, and even, at times, boredom (which occurs due to carrying out repetitive tasks). Mental aspects require organizations to address behavioural issues such as developing work systems and culture, which enables employees to get relief from the dehumanizing effects. Compatibility of both the physical and mental aspects leads to employees' satisfaction and develops a high-performing organization.

In order to properly address the ergonomic and behavioural issues, job design relates to organizational structure and style of management. Appropriate management styles, a structural shift from autocratic to democratic decision-making, delegation, and formation of autonomous work groups reorganize the structure by reducing the number and levels of managers, increase the span of control, and increase the productivity and motivation levels of the employees.

The job design principle focuses on the motivational aspects of jobs to make them more interesting and challenging to employees. In the scientific management era, we have seen that jobs were broken into small independent elements, so that workers could repetitively perform the same task. The argument was that in this process jobs become more scientific and the workers' performance could be easily identified to decide on their financial incentives. However, with the emergence of the human relations school, this argument was negated and the addressing of behavioural issues in job designs started gaining acceptance. Thus, human aspects of job design now receive more importance in organizations to synergize the productivity and employee satisfaction.

For effective management of organizational behaviour, critical inputs related to the jobs are necessary. Although job analysis and job evaluation are considered important techniques for such purposes, we have also discussed other important areas for understanding a job from a holistic point of view. Job design serves to improve performance and motivation. Job design analysis starts by looking at a job with a broad perspective and swiftly moves towards identifying the specific activities required to do the job. It is done for the purpose of identifying and correcting any deficiencies that affect performance and motivation.

KEY DEFINITIONS

Ergonomics   It is a discipline at the service of the management right from the planning and design stage of a work system. In the organization and control of human effort directed to specific ends, the management needs to have an appreciation of the human factors involved in a work system.

Factor comparison   This method is used in job evaluation. It uses five factors, namely mental requirements, skill requirements, physical requirements, responsibility, and working conditions. After job descriptions, key jobs are judged and related to one another. The jobs are considered one by one and reviewed to understand how much of the current wage rate for the job is paid for each factor. Key jobs are arranged on a scale in the order of the values for each factor.

Job rotation   It involves periodic vertical and horizontal movement of a group of employees between a set of jobs or tasks. Job rotation, therefore, provides some relief from boredom and the monotony of repetitively performing the same jobs or tasks. However, this requires organizations to initiate multi-skilling of employees through continuous training and learning activities. In some organizations, we get the opportunity for skill interchangeability because of commonality of tasks or jobs. However, in some other organizations, the scope of skill interchangeability may be very little because of the specialized nature of jobs. Even in the latter case, multi-skilling initiatives can provide the results.

Motion economy   It is the process of minimizing the physical and perceptual loads imposed on people engaged in any type of work, whether it is in the office, the shop floor, the kitchen, or at the driving wheel. It leads to better designing of equipment, jigs and fixtures, hand tools, furniture, and labour-saving devices. In addition, it facilitates a better layout of offices, warehouses, plants, and operating areas such as office desk, workbench, aircraft, cockpit, and crew compartments of armoured fighting vehicles.

Position analysis questionnaire   This was developed in the early 1970s through the efforts of McCormick and others. It consists of 194 job elements of a 'worker-oriented' nature, which are divided into six major categories. The analyst rates the job elements on a scale of 0 to 5. However, administering PAQ is not very easy.

Task identity   Tasks should be fit together to make a complete job since this gives the employee a sense of doing a whole job from beginning to end with a visible output. An important benefit derived from task identity is that it can aid a worker in tracing his/her performance to the overall goals and target achievement of the organization. Workers can cultivate their sense of belongingness and can realize that they are partners in the organizational progress.

Task variety The tasks to be performed should be varied, so that an individual employee can move from one job to another at any point of time, making it possible for employees to move to different job verticals. Such variation provides a change in both the mental activity and the physical well-being of employees.

Value engineering It is an organized creative technique to analyse the functions of a product, service, or system to achieve the required functions at the lowest cost while ensuring its performance reliability and maintainability. It is also known as value analysis or value management.

CONCEPT-REVIEW QUESTIONS

10.1 What are the purposes of job evaluation? Discuss the steps involved in it.

10.2 Discuss the different types of job evaluation techniques. Which type of job evaluation technique do you consider more suitable and why?

10.3 In what ways are job analysis and job assessment different? Select any job and analyse its individual content.

10.4 How is compensation structure linked with job evaluation?

10.5 Define work study. What are its important objectives? Why do trade unions react to work study programmes? How would you combat such a reaction?

10.6 What are the important roles of method study? Identify the important contributions of method study and discuss at least five such contributions in detail.

10.7 Discuss in detail the steps involved in a method study programme.

10.8 Define work measurement. What are its different techniques? Discuss in detail at least three techniques.

10.9 What are the steps involved in a time study programme? How does it help the work measurement programme in an industrial unit?

10.10 What is ergonomics? How does it help in increasing productivity? Discuss with examples.

10.11 What are the basic principles of motion economy? Discuss these principles in relation to a work area with which you are familiar.

10.12 Explain how human engineering techniques influence machine design. Select an advertisement of a furniture item and discuss its ergonomic features.

10.13 What are the steps involved in value analysis? What course of action can you suggest for a successful value analysis study? Elaborate your answer.

10.14 Write short notes on the following:
(a) Job characteristics model
(b) Assessment centres approach in job design
(c) Job assessment methods
(d) Ergonomics
(e) Competency-based approach in job design

CRITICAL THINKING QUESTIONS

10.1 A particular organization gives 80 per cent weightage on strategic areas for a marketing manager. The company is engaged in the lifestyle drugs and cosmetic business. You have been entrusted to help the company in designing a competency-based job description report for the marketing manager. Prepare the report and suggest how your approach will benefit the company in following the competency-based interview of the marketing manager for the company.

10.2 X is the HR manager of your organization. He is unable to appreciate the need for job description when your company restructures its operations and activities, including change of product line at short time intervals. In fact, your company recruits multi-skilled professionals. Critically comment on the HR manager's point of contention.

SELECT BIBLIOGRAPHY

- Bhattacharyya, Dipak Kumar, *Human Resource Planning*, 3rd ed., Excel Books, New Delhi, 2012.
- Bhattacharyya, Dipak Kumar, *Human Resource Research Methods*, Oxford University Press, New Delhi, 2007.
- Brown, R., *Design Jobs that Motivate and Develop People'*, from http://www.media-associates.co.nz/fjobdesign.html, last accessed on 14 February 2004.
- Campion, M.A., 'Interdisciplinary Approaches to Job Design: A Constructive Replication with Extension', *Journal of Applied Psychology*, Vol. 73, 1988, pp. 467–81.
- Campion, M.A. and P.W. Thayer, 'Development and Field Evaluation of an Indisciplinary Measure of Job Design', *Journal of Applied Psychology*, Vol. 70, 1985, pp. 29–43.
- Cunningham, J.B. and Ted Eberle, 'A Guide to Job Enrichment Redesign Personnel', Vol. 67, Issue 2, 1990, pp. 56–60.
- Fleishman, E.A. and M.K. Quaintance, *Taxonomies of Human Performance: The Description of Human Tasks*, Academic Press, Orlando, 1984.
- Hackman, J.R. and G.R. Oldham, 'Motivation through Design of Work: Test of a Theory', *Organisational Behaviour and Human Performance*, Vol. 16, Issue 2, 1976, pp. 250–79.
- Hackman, J.R. and G.R. Oldham, *Work Design*, Pearson Education, New Jersey, 1980.
- Herzberg, F., *Work and the Nature of Man*, World Publishing Co., Cleveland, 1966.
- McCormick, E.J., *Job Analysis: Methods and Applications*, AMACON, New York, 1979.
- Robertson, I. and M. Smith, *Motivation and Job Design: Theory, Research, and Practice*, West Publishing Co., St Paul, 1985.
- Rush, H., *Job Design for Motivation: Experiments in Job Enlargement and Job Enrichment*, The Conference Board, New York, 1971.
- Shaw, James B. and John H. Riskind, 'Predicting Job Stress using Data from the Position Analysis Questionnaire', *Journal of Applied Psychology*, Vol. 68, 1983, pp. 253–61.
- Kotila, O., *Job Enrichment*, 2001, www.academic.empuria.edu/smithwil/001fmg456/eja/kotila456.html.

CASE STUDY
Amrita Sugar—Challenges Ahead

Over the past few years, Amrita Sugar has consistently been recording profits and increasing the productivity of its workforce. After price de-control, the company is facing challenges from many new players in the market. Most new players have started their activities in collaboration with international giants with access to the latest technology, thereby substantially reaping the benefits of cost curtailment. In the past, Amrita was forced to go for backward integration, developing its own plantation to fight the erratic price movements of raw materials, that is, sugar canes. With the development of a new supply source for sugar cane from Cuba and other countries, such exclusive privileges of Amrita did not continue for long. All the new players could substantially divert their funds (which was otherwise diverted by Amrita for backward integration) for a technology-intensive production method.

In the last board meeting, when the secretary was briefing the shareholders on the company's performance, things went out of order and shareholders got extremely annoyed with the company's performance, which indicated the following:

- Profitability of the company increased to zero.
- Productivity of the workmen had come down by 40 per cent.
- Work-in-progress increased by 30 per cent.
- Inventory holding of the company had substantially gone up.

In the light of this information, the board of directors of the company decided to consider the following options:

- Go in for technological changes.
- Reduce manpower by offering a voluntary retirement scheme.
- Sell the captive plantation area and switch over to import of raw materials.
- Strengthen the production planning and control function by separating it from traditional manufacturing activity.

- Develop a strong management information system with simultaneous focus on aggregate planning, developing of master production schedule, capacity and material requirements planning, and so on.

Question for Discussion

What options do you consider most appropriate to turn around Amrita? Write your answer assuming that the company does not face, for the present, any liquidity crisis and can substantially get financial support by capitalizing its reserves.

ANNEXURE 10.1

Job Analysis Data Sheet

FORM NO.1

Job Title _____ CODE _____
Other Titles _____
Suggested Title _____
Department _____ Dept. No. _____ Dept. Head _____
No. on Job _____ Range _____ Supervised By _____
PERSONS INTERVIEWED
ANALYSIS _____ DATE _____ LOCATION OF JOB _____
OTHER IDENTIFICATION _____

JOB SUMMARY (Key phrases that describe job):

RELATION TO OTHERS' JOBS:
PROMOTION FROM:
PROMOTION TO:
TRANSFER TO AND FROM:

WORK PERFORMED: WHAT—HOW—WHY (Use additional sheets if required)
MAJOR DUTIES:
OTHER TASKS:
EQUIPMENT, MACHINES:

SKILLS INVOLVED—PHYSICAL DEMANDS:
Experience (Type and Amount):

Education and Training (Specific skills required):
Responsibility for Product and Material:
Responsibility for Equipment and Machinery:
Responsibility for Work of Others:
Other Jobs Directly Affected:
Resourcefulness:
Monetary:
Visual Efforts:
Physical Efforts:
Surroundings:
Hazards:

ANNEXURE 10.2

Job Description and Specifications

FORM NO. 2

JOB IDENTIFICATION DATA:
PRESENT JOB TITLE:
DEPARTMENT/SECTION:
SUGGESTED JOB TITLE: DATE :
JOB CODE:
EMPLOYEES INTERVIEWED:

JOB SUMMARY

(A) REGULAR TASKS:

1.
2.
3.
4.

(B) CASUAL TASKS:

1.
2.
3.

(C) EQUIPMENT OR MACHINE USED:

(D) WORKING CONDITIONS AND HAZARDS:

JOB SPECIFICATIONS

FORM NO. 3

JOB TITLE (EXISTING):
JOB CODE NO.:
JOB TITLE (suggested):
DEPARTMENT/SECTION

TOTAL POINTS

CLASSIFICATION

1. Education   Points
2. Experience   Points
3. Responsibility for Product or Materials   Points
4. Responsibility for Machinery and Equipment   Points
5. Responsibility for Works of Others   Points
6. Responsibility for Safety of Others   Points
7. Manual Skill   Points
8. Physical Effort   Points
9. Working Condition including Hazards   Points

ANNEXURE 10.3

Competency Sets and the Evidences Required for the Job of Regional Director[1]

Competency Sets Evidence

1. Strategic thinking, innovation, and creativity: Recently I turned around the Centre for Management Education (CME) of All India Management Association (AIMA) within a year and achieved increased revenues, that is, ₹2.5 crore on gross revenue of approximately ₹6 crore. I achieved significant cost control amounting to ₹1 crore (approximately), which again is a record in the last 10 years. I also developed participative work culture by empowering faculty and managers, reduced manpower by restructuring from 44 to 38 in one year, and implemented MIS using in-house talents. In addition, I restructured every area of activity and reduced the cycle time with innovative work simplification. I also developed the competency of people—fitting it to organizational requirements. Furthermore, I aligned CME to market requirements by programme restructuring, introducing new programmes, and collaborating and customizing industry-specific programmes.

Past: I developed institutions, that is, Institute of Management Technology (IMT), Kolkata, and ICFAIAN Business School, Kolkata, from scratch through innovative and strategic thinking. I was the founder director of IMT, Kolkata. Within two years, from a corpus of ₹50,000, I generated a surplus of ₹1.5 crore even after covering huge operational and capital expenditure. In ICFAIAN Business School, Kolkata, I introduced new programmes at the postgraduate level and made it acceptable to the industry even without AICTE recognition. As a trainer in Indian ordnance factories, I was a catalyst for changes in the management and instrumental in introducing the total quality management (TQM)

---

[1] Evidences compiled from an applicant for the position

culture by training more than 5000 employees of different categories. Here too, I have demonstrated strategic, innovative, and creative thinking by playing a crucial role in restructuring and redeployment of manpower.

2. Leadership and teamwork: In recent employments, I have demonstrated this competency by empowering people with key result areas (KRAs) and developing their job process and expected performance quality level. I always practise a nurturing parent attitude with complete transparency. The job environment is based on mutual trust, where all identify with me more as a co-worker than as a boss. While operational decisions are left at an individual employee's level, all strategic decisions, including budget making, are participative. Teamwork culture is reinforced by forming cross-functional teams. Everybody feels that they work in a team and not in isolation. A similar approach was also adopted in the earlier employment, which yielded results as explained in point 1.

3. Financial and resource management: I have been able to manage this well and achieve business growth even in sluggish markets. I go into the details to achieve cost savings and ensure optimal utilization of resources through job simplification. All through I remained frugal, percolating the message 'more savings add to your future'. You remain for an organization and hence organizational viability strengthens your existence. In all earlier employments, I successfully managed financial and other resources ranging from ₹1 crore to ₹6 crore. In all previous employments, I also successfully managed human resources ranging from 10 to 44 (head counts).

4. Ability to get things done: I am extremely good at this. All faculty members were given administrative responsibilities with full empowerment, redesignating them as programme directors. Within the CME, I formed many small business units (SBUs) to sell the concept of job ownership, which again not just ends with addressing the specific job but encompasses coordination with other cross-functional teams up to the point of delivery. Response time to customers (students, companies, regulatory authorities, by and large) and suppliers queries reduced to one working day, even if it required my involvement. A similar approach was also adopted in my earlier employment, which yielded results.

5. Relationship building and customer focus: CME has been made more customer-focused without sacrificing quality. I always try to meet students when they visit AIMA, even if it requires stretching beyond office hours and responding to students' queries over phone. I maintain a harmonious relationship with the nodal centres, which are our delivery points, spread across the country. I am also efficient when it comes to networking with companies, regulatory authorities, and other bodies for reaping the benefits of synergy.

6. Experience of working in an international environment and recent knowledge of UK: I have no direct experience of working in an international environment, but by way of managing international collaborations, I have gained some insights into their way of working. I would like to add that I have recently gained some knowledge of the education, economics, and social life of UK.

Employee Motivation

LEARNING OBJECTIVES

After studying this chapter, the reader will be able to

- define motivation and explain the concepts of motivation
- explain the process of motivating employees
- understand motivation and its relation to employees' morale and productivity
- describe the different theories of motivation

CASE STUDY

Motivating through Ownership

Sharing ownership through an employee stock ownership plan (ESOP) is one of the necessary ingredients to establish a successful ownership culture. However, employee ownership by itself will not increase employee motivation and performance. A combination of employee ownership and employee participation yields a substantial improvement in organizational performance. Only genuine employee partnership can make employees responsible. A high-performance workplace provides its employees with incentives, information, skills, and responsibilities to make decisions essential for innovation, quality improvement, and rapid response to change. Such environments exist in companies that integrate their business, human resources (HR), and technology strategies and have the following common characteristics:

- They give workers a stake in the performance through employee ownership and gain sharing.
- They create employment security strategies, which recognize the value of workers, and long-term economic safety.
- They push responsibility down to the frontline employees by organizing the work into self-managing teams.
- They provide workers with necessary information to exercise a high level of autonomy and discretion.
- They build employee relations on trust, mutual interest, and cooperation.
- They focus on customer satisfaction, both internal and external, by improving quality and building organizations that adapt easily to market change.

- They encourage employees to learn new skills through skill-based pay and pay-for-performance compensation systems.
- They invest in training and retraining to develop their employees as critical business assets, rather than treating them as costs to be minimized.
- They provide employees with safe and supportive work environments.

Therefore, employee ownership along with participation, education, information, and training contributes to higher financial performance. An equally important observation is that companies that reward employees with stock ownership outperform those that reward participation with profit sharing alone.

The transformation of employees into owners requires cultivating a genuine sense of ownership, where the employees take the responsibility of ownership seriously and their actions contribute to the company's success. This process obviously does not occur immediately. Developing an ownership culture among employees means giving them equity, a 'say in how things get done', information, and training. Employees need to understand their company's financial reports and develop their decision-making, communication, and problem-solving skills.

Unlike a person who rents a house, the homeowner has equity in his/her investment and, therefore, will have an incentive to increase the value of that investment. How many renters paint the outside of their residence? Similar to a homeowner, an employee-owner has greater incentive to drive up the value of the stock in his/her company. This could result in reducing scrap, generating creative ideas on how to improve a process, and producing products of a better quality. This ownership could be in the form of stock options, a cooperative, or an ESOP. Although rewards such as profit sharing and bonuses are great supplementary incentives, they do not provide employees with an ownership stake.

When employees have an ownership interest in their company and are valued for their inputs, their jobs become more meaningful. Satisfied employees as well as satisfied customers stay longer with the company. However, ownership is just the first step in creating a successful ownership culture. As mentioned earlier, the remaining ingredients are participation, training, and information.

Motivated employee-owners need the opportunity to express their ideas for improving business to the management. Effective communication requires that managers listen, appreciate dissent, and tolerate opposition. Likewise, supervisors need to lead rather than order, assist rather than discipline, and teach rather than threaten. It is the responsibility of the employees to make suggestions without confrontation, learn basic business concepts, and work cooperatively with others. Open channels for input should be maintained throughout the company. To initiate increased levels of participation, one might consider creating problem-solving teams or shop-floor committees.

Whether a company is employee-owned or not, the goal of participation is to maximize employee involvement in all areas of company decision-making, from the shop floor to the boardroom. It is through participation in decision-making bodies that employees can truly accept greater responsibility.

An owner needs access to financial and other strategic information to make sound business decisions. Responsible employees also need access to company information such as financial reports, scrap rates, customer satisfaction indicators, and on-time delivery records. Of course, information is useful only if it is communicated effectively. This information can be in the form of regularly published newsletters, annual or quarterly meetings to review business issues, and company financial statements. Of course, employees need to understand the information presented. This requires long-term commitment to education and training.

The American Society for Training and Development confirmed that two-thirds of corporate training money goes into conducting training programmes for those who already have college degrees. If one wants to create a successful ownership culture in an organization, just informing employees is not enough. Employees need to understand the information they receive in order to be informed and become involved owners.

Opening books to the employees is meaningless unless employees understand how financial reports are read. Meetings to improve quality lead nowhere if the participants lack effective meeting skills.

Education is a process of learning, and coordinating an effective training programme requires long-term commitment. Training non-managerial employees in problem-solving and group process techniques helps make employee participation programmes work successfully.

It is relatively inexpensive and highly cost effective to undertake some combination of employee participation, training, open-book management, and financial incentives to increase company competitiveness. These foster an environment that allows employees to think and act like owners.

INTRODUCTION

Once employees are hired and trained, it is important to motivate them to get the desired efforts from them in order to achieve organizational objectives. While designing their compensation package, organizations try to meet their expectations at the outset, suitably identifying their extrinsic and intrinsic needs, within the given policies and procedures of the organization. However, this is restricted only in those cases where organizations can afford to become flexible. Such a flexibility in approach can attract and retain talent in key positions and at the same time will help avoid general dissatisfaction among other employees. Major problems in employee motivation become evident when employees of an organization start perceiving that there is a wide mismatch between their expectations and organizational commitments. At times, such perceived expectations of the employees far exceed the organizational commitments, resulting in a significant drop in their perception.

Motivation is a dynamic organizational behaviour issue and there cannot be any organization-specific motivation tool. The subject of motivation, perhaps, has received the highest attention from management thinkers worldwide. Despite this, it is found that organizations are not able to address the problem, as employee demotivation is a perennial issue from the days of the Industrial Revolution. Before the Industrial Revolution, such problems were non-existent, as the owners of labour services and the owners of means of capital had the same identity and the motivation for work was spontaneous in a home-centred production system.

This chapter discusses the different theories of motivation and briefly mentions the different empirical studies on motivation in India and abroad. It also explores other issues such as concepts, objectives, processes, and benefits. It should be noted that motivation is a much-discussed and much-debated subject of organizational behaviour studies.

ELEMENTS

The motivational perceptions of all types of employees throughout the world are fast changing in response to a number of key variables. The conventional motivational reinforcers, either extrinsic or intrinsic, are gradually losing importance. What exactly can cause motivation varies with time and space. In India too, it is not possible to identify and indicate one single motivational tool commonly applicable to various cross sections of employees. Nevertheless, we can try to appreciate the relative importance of a tool for a particular segment of employees belonging to some homogenous organizations.

This chapter discusses the motivational elements in detail, with the support of various leading theoretical and empirical works.

DEFINITION AND CONCEPT

It has been established that motivational factors are the perceived needs of employees, which when satisfied, contribute to the employees' performance and productivity. However, motivation, per se, can be better defined as a process of governing choices. This process may be internal or external to the individual and arouses enthusiasm and persistence to pursue a certain course of action. The motivation process starts with a physiological or psychological deficiency, a need that activates a behaviour, or a drive that is aimed at a goal or an incentive. All the definitions, therefore, authenticate that motivation is a behavioural syndrome, which develops when there is a perceived incongruence in the employees' needs and expectations. With the widening of such perceived gaps, employees feel demotivated and reduce their level of performance and productivity. On the contrary, if the gap is reduced, employees feel motivated and contribute their best for achieving organizational objectives. From the organizational point of view, the motivation process follows certain defined steps, which, as a continuum, need to be periodically reviewed and strategized to ensure its proper renewal. This helps maintain the motivation of employees, which is evident from their behavioural congruence matching the organizational objectives.

In the first stage, it is important to identify the need deficiency of employees, if any. Need deficiency centres on extrinsic and intrinsic needs. Extrinsic needs are the needs related to material and tangible gains. Increased pay, incentives, bonus, better medical facilities, better retirement benefits, and better canteen facilities are a few examples of extrinsic needs. Intrinsic needs, on the other hand, are the needs related to mental satisfaction and are abstract in nature. Increased status, challenges, sense of belonging, scope for growth and creativity, recognition, and sense of achievement are examples of such needs. Identification of need deficiency is possible through direct observation of the employees' behaviour and through a survey using a structured-questionnaire response. However, employees, by and large, are reluctant about giving responses that criticize an organizational policy because of the fear that they might be identified. Confidentiality in survey responses can be ensured through a secret opinion poll, where the questionnaire does not require any employee identity. However, for better results, it is always desirable to integrate survey findings with personal interviews, which can be in the form of open discussions with employees by their respective seniors. Some organizations try to document such information through a 360-degree performance appraisal by incorporating certain items in the appraisal form itself. Need deficiency can also be understood from the trend of the employees' performances, developing a performance index or productivity index.

> The motivation process starts with a physiological or psychological deficiency, a need that activates a behaviour, or a drive that is aimed at a goal or an incentive.

In the second phase of the motivational process, organizations try to identify appropriate strategies to close the perceived need gap of the employees. There are many innovative ways to close such need gaps without much impairment

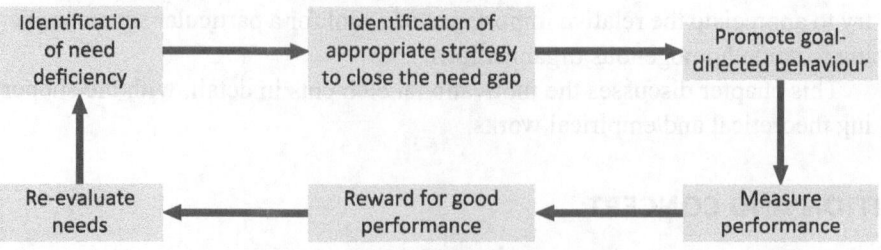

Figure 11.1 Motivation model

to the budget. For example, organizations can increase the employees' pay by reducing their deferred benefits such as non-wage labour cost (NWLC) and adding such reduced amounts to their current pay. This is particularly important for those organizations that mostly employ young people in the exploratory age groups (less than 35 years). Similarly, linking the pay with performance also facilitates the development of a proper compensation structure to reward and motivate good performers. In addition, gaps of intrinsic needs can be reduced by adopting an enabling organization structure, which among others, fosters creativity and growth.

To understand the importance of extrinsic and intrinsic needs, the industrial disputes scenario in India at the macrolevel has been illustrated. Figure 11.1 shows that in terms of percentage share, intrinsic factors are also very significant. However, the severity of extrinsic and intrinsic factors in terms of man-days lost cannot be measured for inherent problems in data collection. The identification of an appropriate strategy to close the need gaps helps an organization develop goal-directed behaviour among its employees to achieve organizational objectives. Thus, in the third phase of the motivational process, organizations enforce goal-directed behaviour. This enhances the performance and productivity of the employees, which further influences compensation strategies and other motivational reinforcers.

Likewise, the cycle continues as an ongoing process in an organization and at the end of the continuum, needs are again re-evaluated to understand the emerging need deficiency, if any. In Fig. 11.1, the model is illustrated as a continuum.

OBJECTIVES

Motivation enhances performance and improves productivity. Therefore, motivation fulfils the following important objectives of an organization:

Ensure productive use of resources Physical, financial, and human resources are the important resource constructs for an organization. Proper utilization of such resources is possible only when people in the organization feel motivated. Motivation leads to goal-directed behaviour, which, in turn, facilitates productive utilization of all such resources. The important measures for productive use of resources are total factor productivity indices (TFPI) and labour productivity indices (LPI).

Ensure efficiency of people The efficiency of motivated people increases, as motivation augments their willingness to work. Increased efficiency also contributes to cost reduction.

Motivation describes the drive that impels an employee to work.

Ensure quality consciousness A motivated employee becomes quality conscious, as behaviourally he/she identifies himself/herself with the organization and always tries to take extra care of his/her job. Motivation, therefore, also strengthens the quality objectives of an organization.

Promote goal-directed behaviour By promoting goal-directed behaviour, motivated employees help realize organizational objectives and strategies.

Promote friendly work culture Motivation promotes friendly work culture, increases morale, and gives employees a sense of responsibility, brings about a feeling of belonging, integrates individual identity with organizational identity, and encourages team work and participative decision-making. All these together create an environment for creativity and growth, which truly empower an organization.

Ensure organizational stability Motivation ensures organizational stability by reducing employee turnover and absenteeism.

MECHANISM

The word motivation is used to describe the drive that impels an employee to work. Therefore, the process starts with physiological (extrinsic) or psychological (intrinsic) needs, satisfaction of which activates the drive to achieve a goal. Thus, the mechanism of motivation starts with a need, which activates the drive towards a goal. This has been illustrated in Fig. 11.2.

At this stage, it is important to understand the basic differences between motive, motivation, and motivating. Motive is the inner state that activates and directs the behaviour of individuals towards certain goals. The inner state of an individual is created out of a perceived need imbalance. The degree of imbalance decides a strong or a weak motive, and accordingly, an individual propels himself/herself into action. Strong motives create drives that energize people into action. The degree of work behaviour decides the level of motivation. If an employee performs well, putting in his/her best efforts, his/her motivation is considered to be high, whereas in the opposite case, it is considered to be low. Motivating implies inducements to energize work behaviour. This is a managerial role, as it satisfies both the individual and the organizational needs. Managers always try to sustain a motivating environment to get work done in an effective and efficient manner. For this purpose, managers need to understand the degree of motive strength of employees. The process of identification of need deficiency has already been explained. Since needs

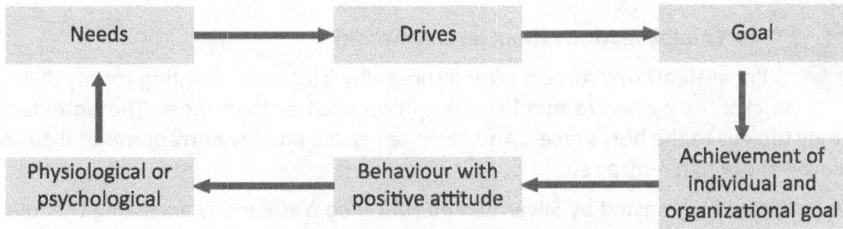

Figure 11.2 Mechanism of motivation

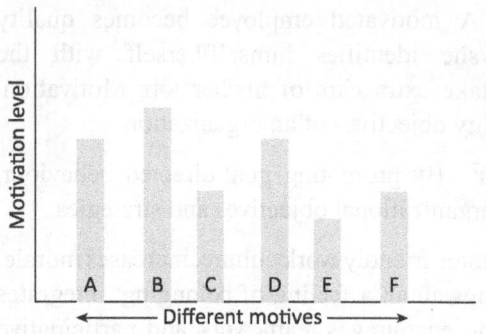

Figure 11.3 Degree of importance of motives

or motives are the reasons for work behaviour, for effective decisions managers need to plot the motives with the degree of importance, which can be done as shown in Fig. 11.3.

A, B, C, D, E, and F denote different motives, which may be compensation, promotional opportunities, functional autonomy, creativity, challenge, and flexibility in policies.

Using the Pareto diagram, a manager can optimize the motive strength, as the Pareto principle suggests that every problem (for us it is the motive strength) is the result of a few causes and all causes are not equally important—'a vital few and trivial many'. Hence, by taking care of 10–15 per cent of the motive strengths, managers can reduce the need gaps in 70–80 per cent of the areas. This is because of the interdependence and interrelationship of motive strengths. A typical Pareto diagram looks as shown in Fig. 11.4.

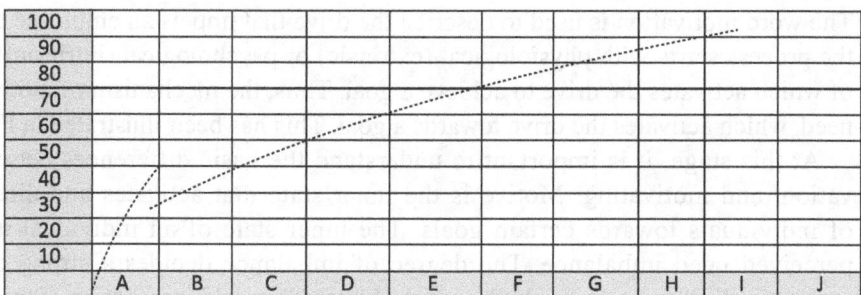

Figure 11.4 Pareto graph

THEORIES OF MOTIVATION

We have already discussed the theories of motivation in brief. Here, we will be discussing the major theories of motivation with some critical notes. The various developments in motivation theory are provided in Fig. 11.5.

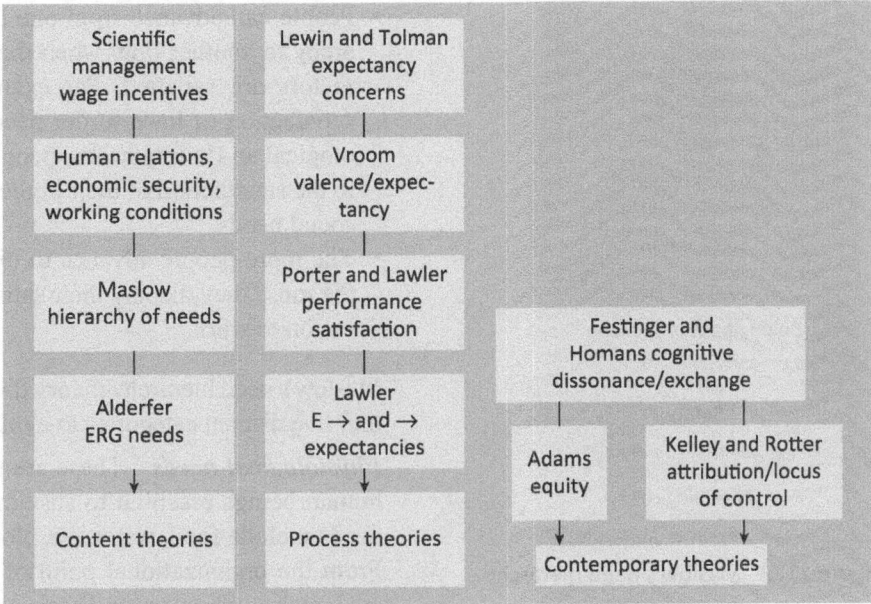

Figure 11.5   Developments in motivation theory
Source: Luthans (1998)

Frederick W. Taylor (1856–1917), the father of scientific management, observed that prosperity of management and workforce are interdependent. People are inherently capable of doing hard work but they show such qualities irregularly. To harness such potentiality, the pay and rewards (incentives) must be linked to the achievement of optimum goals. Good performers get rewards and better pay, whereas bad performers lose out on this count.

Elton W. Mayo (1880–1949) and his associates, through a series of experiments known as Hawthorne Experiments (Western Electric Co., US, 1927–32), established that work satisfaction, and hence performance, is basically not economic. It depends more on the working conditions and attitudes, communications, positive management response and encouragement, working environment, and so on.

Maslow's Need Hierarchy Theory

Abraham Maslow (1908–70), through his need hierarchy theory, established that motivation of people arises from various levels of a hierarchy of needs. We have briefly introduced this earlier. Here, we will elaborate his concepts, examining first the essence of his theory and then critically examining the theory. The essence of his theory can be summarized as follows:

- The wants and desires of human beings influence their behaviour.
- Already satisfied wants and desires do not act as motivators. People are motivated by their desire to fulfil their unsatisfied wants and desires.
- The needs of people are arranged in the order of their perceived priority or hierarchy. The perceived need factors of people vary.

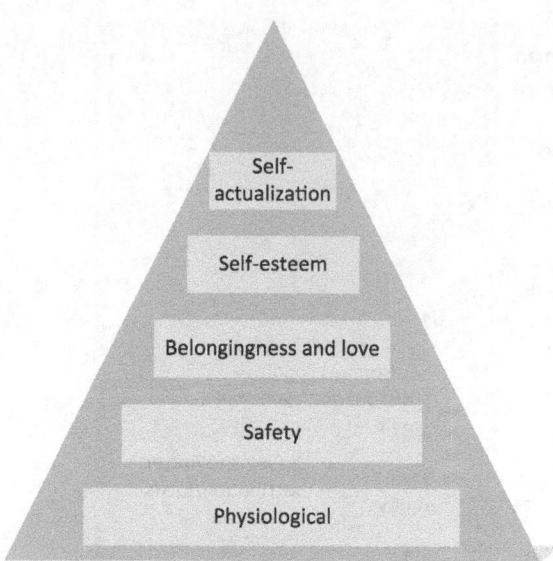

Figure 11.6 Maslow's need hierarchy

- People can advance from one level of need hierarchy to another only when their preceding need factors are satisfied. For example, without the satisfaction of lower-order needs, such as physiological and safety needs, people cannot advance to the satisfaction of their higher needs, including social needs.
- The more people advance to higher-order needs, the more they display their satisfaction and motivation to work.

Maslow's need hierarchy theory divides human needs into five distinct categories as explained in Fig. 11.6.

Physiological needs These are the basic needs of human beings essential to sustain or survive. Such needs include food, water, air, clothing, and shelter. From the organizational point of view, such needs are met through salary and basic working conditions.

Safety needs These needs ensure protection from the economic and physical environments. People expect some reasonableness in their perceived environment, which minimizes the degree of uncertainty. Job security, degree of continuity, order, structure, and predictability are precisely the nature of such needs. Organizations fulfil such needs of their employees by ensuring a protective work environment.

Belongingness and love needs The need for a sense of belonging and love arises after the satisfaction of the earlier two lower-order needs. These needs are also known as social needs. People in this need level develop a strong sense of affiliation and get concerned with love, affection, sense of belonging, acceptance, and friendship. Organizations meet such needs by providing the appropriate work culture to help employees identify themselves with their organizations.

Self-esteem needs At the self-esteem need level, employees look for satisfaction of their esteem or egoistic needs. Esteem needs pertain to self-respect and respect or esteem from others. Self-respect is ensured by achieving competence, confidence, personal strength, adequacy, achievement, independence, and freedom, whereas respect from others comes from prestige, recognition, acceptance, attention, status, reputation, and appreciation. To fulfil such needs of the employees, organizations provide challenging work assignments, performance feedback, performance recognition, a participative work culture, empowerment, participation in decision making, and so on.

> Maslow's theory of hierarchy of needs considers five factors—physiological, safety, belongingness, self-esteem, and self-actualization.

Self-actualization needs At the self-actualization need stage, employees desire to become what they are capable of becoming. They want to create something of their own using their talent, capacities, and potentialities. Organizations try to fulfil such needs of their employees by nurturing an environment that fosters creativity and growth.

Evaluation of Need Hierarchy Theory

The concept of needs helps managers understand human behaviour at work. It also accounts for interpersonal variations in human work. Another important aspect is that it is dynamic, as the model defines motivation as a constantly changing force.

Despite all these advantages, the theory is criticized on the following counts:

- The theory has no empirical support and is not a theory of work motivation. Maslow did not even intend to relate his theory to work motivation. Maslow's theory was, in fact, popularized by others (Douglas McGregor, etc.) as a work motivation theory.
- Needs cannot be placed in strictly defined levels. In fact, the hierarchy of needs is simply a misnomer. Employees who are motivated by the need for self-actualization may still have lower-order needs such as food and shelter.
- The theory is not culturally aligned. It is more western value-laden than eastern culture-specific. To illustrate, work is perceived differently in different cultures. Hence, motivation to work is different in different countries and also varies within a country from one individual work group to another. Therefore, the theory cannot hold good for heterogeneous work groups.
- Maslow's existential philosophy is questioned on the ground that people may like to remain content plateaued with the satisfaction of their lower-order needs. They may not like to move further up in the hierarchy.
- Diagnosing need deficiency for employees following Maslow's approach is time consuming. Even after such diagnosis, it may not help an organization to develop a tailor-made model for employee motivation.

Herzberg's Two-factor Theory or Motivation–Hygiene Theory

Frederick Herzberg (1968), extending the work of Maslow, developed the content theory of motivation. His study is based on the responses of 200 accountants and engineers drawn from 11 industries in the Pittsburgh area. Using critical incident methods, he asked the samples to respond on the following two aspects:

- When did they feel particularly good about their job?
- When did they feel exceptionally bad about their job?

Herzberg found that the samples described different types of conditions for good and bad feelings. The factors responsible for job satisfaction are quite different from the factors they perceive as contributors to job dissatisfaction. Their reported good feelings were found to be associated with job experiences and job content, whereas their reported bad feelings were found to be associated with the peripheral aspects of job, that is, job context. Since his study was based on a two-factor hypothesis, his theory is called the two-factor theory. His study established that the opposite of satisfaction is not dissatisfaction and removing dissatisfying elements from a job does not necessarily make the job satisfying. Herzberg has classified the factors into two categories:

- Motivation factors
- Hygiene or maintenance factors

Hence, the theory is also known as motivation–hygiene theory. Herzberg mentioned the following six motivation factors:

- Recognition
- Advancement
- Responsibility
- Achievement
- Possibility of growth
- Job content or work itself

The presence of these factors in the job creates a motivating environment but its absence does not cause dissatisfaction.

Similarly, Herzberg mentioned 10 hygiene or maintenance factors, which are as follows:

- Company policy and administration
- Technical supervision
- Interpersonal relations with subordinates
- Salary
- Job security
- Personal life
- Working conditions
- Status
- Interpersonal relations with supervisors
- Interpersonal relations with peers

These factors are context factors. Their existence just creates an environment for doing work. However, the factors by themselves cannot motivate people to work. In Herzberg's words, their absence can dissatisfy people but their presence, per se, cannot satisfy people.

The crux of the two-factor theory of motivation, therefore, is that managers should cater to both satisfiers and dissatisfiers. The mere improvement of hygiene factors cannot guarantee a motivating environment. Figure 11.7 presents the essence of Herzberg theory.

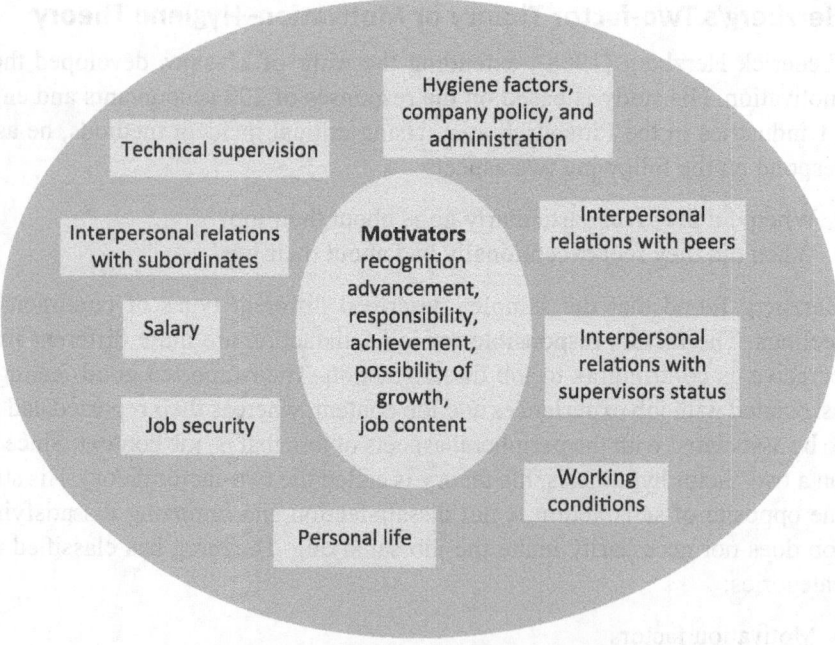

Figure 11.7   Hygiene factors and motivators

Critical Evaluation of Herzberg's Theory

Herzberg's theory is the first of its kind based on field research. Maslow's work was based on clinical observations (laboratory-based findings), whereas Herzberg did his study to understand motivation in the work environment. Secondly, Herzberg's study recommends actions for managers to improve motivation in the work environment. His emphasis on content factors shifts the focus from the traditional money motivators concept, which was earlier viewed as the most potent factor for work motivation. Thirdly, Herzberg has also contributed to the alternative approach to motivation by job enrichment. Finally, Herzberg had double dimensionalized the needs instead of its absolute categorization into five distinct levels as was done by Maslow.

Despite all the listed merits, Herzberg's theory has also been subjected to the following criticisms:

- It is limited by its methodology. When things go well, people tend to take credit for themselves. On the contrary, they attribute failures to the external environment.
- It is also method-bound. We cannot get similar results if we use other methods. The critical incidents method, by its very nature, may cause people to recall only the recent incidents or experiences. However, experiences are always subject to change. Moreover, while narrating a critical incident, respondents get wide flexibility to give vent to their opinions rather than the realities. Thus, survey findings become opinion-laden.
- It talks more about job satisfaction than about job motivation.
- The theory ignores situational variables, as it is not backed by adequate research in different work environments.
- Even though the theory assumes a relationship between job satisfaction and productivity, the methodology applied by Herzberg limits its focus to job satisfaction and does not focus on productivity.

Comparison of Maslow and Herzberg's Models

Herzberg's framework is compatible with Maslow's hierarchy of needs. Maslow referred to the needs or motives, whereas Herzberg dealt with the goals or incentives that tend to satisfy those needs. To illustrate, the hygiene or maintenance factors of Herzberg are satisfied by the physiological, safety, and belongingness needs of Maslow, whereas the motivation factors of Herzberg tend to be satisfied by the self-esteem and self-actualization needs of Maslow. This is why Herzberg's theory is often referred to as an extension of Maslow's need hierarchy theory. Despite such similarities, there are some major differences between the two theories. Maslow's need hierarchy is a sequential arrangement of needs, whereas Herzberg's model does not have any such hierarchical arrangement. Maslow believed that any unsatisfied need, irrespective of its level of hierarchy, could be a potential motivator. On the contrary, Herzberg believed that only the higher-order needs serve as motivators.

Job Characteristic Model

Richard Hackman and Greg Oldham (1975) developed a job characteristic model based on Herzberg's two-factor theory, showing how a good job design can lead to internal motivation of employees and contribute to a better job performance. The theory postulates that five job characteristics lead to three psychological states, which affect the motivation and satisfaction of the employees. The five job characteristics are skill variety, task identity, task significance, autonomy, and feedback.

Skill variety This is the extent or range of skills, abilities, and talents of the employees. The more they are able to utilize their skills in the job, the greater their level of satisfaction. Hence, jobs are to be designed in a way that ensures utilization of a wide variety of individual skills.

Task identity This signifies the extent of involvement of the employees in the total job. This enables an individual to identify himself/herself in the total creation, which gives him/her a sense of pride and satisfaction.

Task significance This denotes the significance of a job on the life of others—both within and outside the organization. A positive significance of a job gives psychological satisfaction to the person who does it.

Autonomy This refers to the freedom given to the employees to perform their jobs. The degree of autonomy depends on the extent of independence given to an employee in deciding about job scheduling, formulating the procedures, and decision-making without interference from others. Job satisfaction and motivation increase with more job autonomy.

Feedback This provides the opportunity to assess the right and wrong in doing a job.

The three psychological states that an individual experiences are skill variety, task identity, and task significance, which provide *experienced meaningfulness*. Autonomy provides *experienced responsibility* and feedback ensures *experienced knowledge of results*.

Once an employee experiences these three psychological states, he/she feels intrinsically rewarded and this results in intrinsic motivation.

Hackman and Oldham developed a Motivating Potential Score (MPS) based on their study. It measures the propensity of a job to become motivating. The formula is presented as follows:

$$MPS = \left[\frac{\text{Skill variety} + \text{Task identity} + \text{Task significance}}{3} \right] \times (\text{Autonomy}) \times (\text{Feedback})$$

ERG Theory

Clayton Alderfer (1972) of Yale University developed the ERG theory based on empirical research. He modified Maslow's five levels of needs to three levels and labelled them as the needs for existence, relatedness, and growth. The name ERG has been derived from the first letter of each need. The ERG theory differs from Maslow's need hierarchy theory in the following ways:

> The ERG theory postulates three levels of needs, namely the needs for existence, relatedness, and growth.

- Instead of five need hierarchies, the ERG theory considers only three need hierarchies.
- The need hierarchy theory postulates rigid progression from one need level to another, whereas the ERG theory assumes that more than one need may be operative simultaneously. Thus, an employee working on the growth need may even remain unsatisfied in relatedness and existence needs.

- The basic postulate of the ERG theory is that it works on the frustration–regression model. If, for any reason, employees continually become frustrated in satisfying their needs at one level, they intensify their desire to satisfy their lower-level needs. It is similar to the failure to get recognition being compensated by the desire to make more money. Contrarily, Maslow suggests that people will stay at a certain need level until they are able to satisfy the same.

Critical Evaluation of ERG Theory

The ERG theory is pragmatic in its approach, as it considers the individual differences among people. Individual differences in terms of education, family background, and culture can alter the motive strength vis-à-vis the perceived need factors. The theory is more appealing, intuitive, and logical than Maslow's need hierarchy theory. Despite such advantages, the theory does not offer any clear-cut guidelines. It just indicates that people will be motivated to behave in a particular way to satisfy one of the three sets of needs, that is, need for existence, need for relatedness, and need for growth. Moreover, the theory is yet to be backed by adequate research.

McClelland's Three Needs Theory or Achievement Motivation Theory

David C. McClelland (1976), through his 20 years of study at Harvard University, documented the differences in the needs of people in the following three important areas:

Achievement need (nAch)   People in this need category strive to excel, to achieve, in relation to a set of standards. They like challenges and they like to succeed in a competitive environment. They willingly work hard and volunteer for work that stretches their ability to the maximum. People in this need category do not get motivated by money. They feel more motivated by a sense of accomplishment and achievement.

Affiliation need (nAff)   This need emerges from the desire for friendly and close interpersonal relationships. People in this need category try to fulfil such needs with satisfying relationships with the organization, peer groups, work teams, and so on. Since people of this need group try to identify them with their organizations, they always prefer to foster a friendly work culture and try to meet their needs through friendly relations.

Power need (nPow)   People in this need group always try to draw satisfaction by controlling others. This need emerges from the drive for superiority. People in this need category obviously look for leadership positions in their organizations.

Evaluation of Three Needs Theory

> McClelland's three needs theory postulates three important need areas of human beings—achievement need, affiliation need, and power need.

McClelland highlighted the importance of matching individuals with jobs. People with high achievement needs always prefer challenging job assignments, whereas those with low achievement needs prefer a job situation that ensures stability, security, and predictability. By manipulating the achievement need, organizations can get their complex jobs accomplished by high achievers. However, McClelland's work is criticized on many important counts such as how a sense of achievement or other associated motives can be inculcated in an adult employee. McClelland contends that this can be taught and thus motives related to achievement can be developed in an adult. This contention is not tenable in the psychological literature. Secondly, McClelland contends that needs can be changed through education and training. However, psychologists contend that needs are acquired permanently. Thirdly, the Thematic Appreciation Test (TAT) used for the study by McClelland is also subject to criticism, as the interpretation of responses using TAT is subject to the researcher's bias.

Theory X and Theory Y

Douglas McGregor (1990) of Massachusetts Institute of Technology (MIT) defined organizations as psychological entities that can be characterized by their assumptions about what motivates people. The basic hypothesis is that managerial decisions and actions are based on certain assumptions about human nature and human behaviour. McGregor proposed two distinct views and assumptions about human behaviour. He categorized negative behaviour group people under theory X and positive behaviour group people under theory Y. Theory X contended that employees dislike work, are lazy, dislike responsibility, and need to be coerced to get work done. Theory Y contended that employees like work, creativity, and responsibility, and they can exercise self-direction. The motivational implications of McGregor's analysis, therefore, can be best analysed in the context of Maslow's need hierarchy theory. According to Theory X, people can be motivated by satisfaction of the lower-order needs, whereas according to Theory Y people can be motivated by satisfaction of the higher-order needs. The different characteristics of people as attributed by Theory X and Theory Y are presented in Table 11.1.

> McGregor's theory X and theory Y postulate two distinct views and assumptions about human behaviour—negative behaviour group called theory X and positive behaviour group called theory Y.

Table 11.1 Theory X and Theory Y attributes

Theory X attributes	Theory Y attributes
The average human being inherently dislikes work and will always try to avoid work.	People of this group exercise self-direction and self-control in achieving objectives to which they have committed.
For such inherent human characteristics, people must be coerced, controlled, directed, and threatened with punishment to get work from them.	Commitment to objectives is a function of rewards associated with their achievements.

(Contd)

Table 11.1 *(Contd)*

Theory X attributes	Theory Y attributes
The average human being prefers to be directed, avoids responsibility, is less ambitious, and likes security above all other things.	The average human being learns (under proper conditions) to not only accept but also seek responsibility.
For motivating this group of people, an organization has to enforce strict control with a stick and restrict the motivational reinforcements only to those areas that fulfil their lower-order needs.	They have the capacity of imagination, intensity, and creativity in the solution of organizational problems.
Organizations are able to only partially utilize their potentials.	People with these attributes need to be developed so that they can use their potential to achieve even common goals. These people, by and large, can be motivated with the satisfaction of their higher-order needs.

Cognitive or Process Theories of Motivation

The content theories of motivation emphasized the importance of inner needs in motivation. On the contrary, cognitive models or process theories of motivation emphasize the idea that people make conscious decisions about their job behaviour. Therefore, process theories suggest that in order to motivate employees, organizations must understand how an individual takes decisions and what efforts he/she makes towards the job. Expectancy theory, equity theory, and performance satisfaction model are important approaches to understand the cognitive or process theories of motivation.

Expectancy Theory

The expectancy theory essentially emphasizes that people feel increasingly motivated if they perceive the following:

> The expectancy theory postulates that people feel motivated if they perceive that their effort will lead to successful performance and this in turn will help them attain their desired goals. It is also called the valence–instrumentality–expectancy theory.

- Their effort will result in successful performance.
- Successful performance will ensure the desired results.

This theory has different names such as instrumentality theory, path–goal theory, and valence–instrumentality–expectancy (VIE) theory. It has its roots in the cognitive concepts of Kurt Lewin and Edward Tolman, and in the choice behaviour and utility concepts from the classical economic theory. However, it was Victor H. Vroom (1964) who formulated the expectancy theory as an alternative to content models for work motivation. The theory identified relationships among the variables that affect individual behaviour in a dynamic environment. It was an attempt to capture how people determine their extent of effort for a job and how their perceived expectation influences such effort. The strength of a tendency to act in a certain way depends on the strength of an expectation of the outcome that is likely to accrue upon accomplishment of the job. Therefore, motivation is the product of the strength of one's desire (valence) and the perceived probability of getting something good (expectancy). The relationship can be shown as follows:

$$\begin{pmatrix} \text{Valence} - \\ \text{strength of one's desire for} \\ \text{something} \end{pmatrix} \times \begin{pmatrix} \text{Expectance} - \\ \text{probability of getting it with a} \\ \text{certain action} \end{pmatrix}$$

$$= \begin{pmatrix} \text{Motivation} - \\ \text{strength of drive towards} \\ \text{an action} \end{pmatrix}$$

$$V \times L = M$$

Valence is the degree of desirability of certain outcomes. It is, therefore, the strength of an individual's preference for a particular outcome, which may be a promotion, pay raise, or recognition, after he/she successfully accomplishes the job. Since people may have positive or negative preferences for an outcome, valence may be negative or positive. Hence, valence may vary from −1 to +1.

Expectancy is the perceived possibility of a particular outcome that would follow an action. It is, therefore, the strength of belief that an act will be followed by a particular outcome. The strength of expectations is based on past experiences. People expect what will happen in the future on the basis of what has occurred in the past. As expectancy is an action–outcome association, it may range from zero to one. If employees perceive no possibility of an outcome from certain acts, their expectancy would be zero, whereas the value of expectancy would be one when they feel (from their experience of action–outcome relationship) that they are likely to achieve something with certainty.

Vroom has used one more term in between expectancy and valence, which is usefulness or instrumentality. It is the belief that the first-level outcome would lead to the second-level outcome. For example, one may be motivated to achieve superior-level performance because of his/her desire to get promoted. Here, the first-level outcome (superior-level performance) is seen as being instrumental for the second-level outcome (promotion).

Therefore, the strength of motivation to perform a certain act will depend on the sum of the products of the valences (including instrumentality) and the expectancies, which can be represented as follows:

$$\text{Motivation strength} = \Sigma V \times I \times E$$

where V stands for valence, I stands for instrumentality, and E stands for expectancies.

Evaluation of expectancy theory   It is believed that the content theories oversimplified the complex process of work motivation. However, Vroom's model highlights the importance of organizational behaviour, clarifying the relationship between the employees and the organizations. His model has generated research interests among the corporate and academic circles. The theory also has a cognitive dimension, as individuals are viewed as thinking and reasoning beings, and they just do not simply act for the satisfaction of their unfulfilled needs.

Despite such unique features in Vroom's approach, his theory was criticized on the following grounds:

- It needs to be adequately tested in different work environments.
- Employees may not always take a conscious decision. It was observed that they are also prone to taking impulsive decisions and would later try to rationalize the action with their own logic.
- Linkages between efforts and performance, and between performance and rewards may not be linear. Organizational policies may further complicate the process. For example, promotion may be based on seniority, educational background, and so on.

The theory is complex, and in real-life situations, managers may face time and resource constraints to implement it.

Equity Theory

The equity theory owes its origin to several contributors such as Festinger, Heider, Homans, Jacques, Patchen, and Weick. However, the contribution of James Stacy Adams (1965) is much discussed in the literature on motivation. The theory proposes that in a work environment, motivation is influenced by one's perception of how equitably one is treated as compared to others. The theory is also known as *social comparison theory* or *inequity theory*. Perceptively, employees try to reduce their inequity through such comparisons or by establishing hypothetical exchange relationships. An individual takes into account the amount of work he/she puts in and the corresponding rewards that he/she gets for it and then compares the efforts and rewards of similarly placed persons in the organization. If equity exists, the individual feels satisfied. In case of inequity, it propels him/her into action to create a condition of equity. Since inequity propels action, it is the motivator. The greater the perceived inequity, the greater the motivation to reduce it. While doing so, individuals can make any of the following choices:

- Change or alter inputs
- Change or alter outcomes
- Distort inputs and outcomes of others (with whom they compare themselves)
- Distort inputs and outcomes
- Select a different referent (to compare)
- Withdraw from the field

Evaluation of equity theory   It is a promising theory of work motivation as well as job satisfaction. Hence, it has generated extensive research. Since the basic theory works on perception in a social comparison process, it is, by default, dynamic, as inequity in perceived perception motivates employees to restore equity.

> The equity theory proposes that at the workplace, motivation is influenced by one's perception of how one is treated as compared to others.

However, the theory is criticized on the following counts:

- It is complex and difficult to apply.
- Perceptions are difficult to measure or assess.
- Choosing a comparison with others may not always be correct.
- A given factor may be an input as well as an outcome.
- The study is based on laboratory experiments rather than real-life situations in organizations.

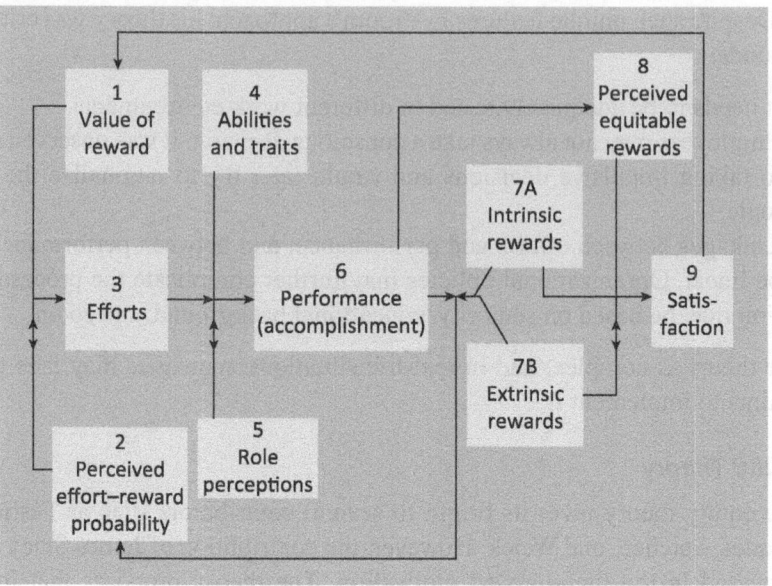

Figure 11.8 Performance satisfaction model

Performance Satisfaction Theory

Layman W. Porter and Edward W. Lawler (1968), based on Vroom's expectancy model, observed that performance leads to satisfaction, contrary to the belief that satisfaction leads to performance. Other interesting observations made by them are that motivation (efforts), performance (accomplishment), and satisfaction are separate variables. This again is in contrast to the belief that motivation leads to performance, which in turn leads to satisfaction. Effort (force or motivation) does not directly lead to performance. It is mediated by abilities, traits, and role perceptions. After performance, the rewards that follow and the way they are perceived determine satisfaction. The theory is illustrated in Fig. 11.8.

Whether an individual will make an effort depends on the interaction between the value of the reward (box 1) and the perceived effort–reward probability (box 2). Effort (box 3) is the motivation. Performance (accomplishment) (box 6) is not the direct consequence of effort. It is the product of effort (box 3), abilities and traits (box 4), and role perceptions (box 5). Performance leads to certain outcomes in the form of intrinsic rewards (box 7A) and extrinsic rewards (box 7B). Both intrinsic and extrinsic rewards provide satisfaction (box 9). However, such a reward–satisfaction relationship is moderated by the perceived equitability of rewards (box 8).

Attribution Theory and Locus of Control

> Performance satisfaction theory postulates that performance leads to satisfaction and not the other way round.

Harold Kelley advocated the attribution theory. It is mainly concerned with the cognitive process by which an individual interprets behaviour, attributing it to certain parts of the relevant environment. Such causal relationships or attributes are interpreted by an individual for his/her own behaviour or for others' behaviour. Fritz Heider contended that both perceived internal forces (ability, efforts, and fatigue) and external forces (others' supervision, machines, methods, climate, rules, and procedures) together determine the behaviour of an individual.

Since the perceived causes are the determinant of work behaviour and the perception differs, people behave differently in a given situation. The concept of locus of control is different from the concept of attribution. The attribution theory is concerned with identifying the causes of one's own as well as others' behaviour, whereas the locus of control theory is applicable only to oneself. Employees may perceive that their own behaviour is internally or externally controlled. Since external control factors (which influence their own behaviour) are beyond their own control, employees believe that their rewards and punishments are dependent on factors such as fate, luck, or chance. As for internal control factors, they feel that they can influence their outcomes through their own ability, skills, or efforts. Julian Rotter (1966) developed a 13-item scale for the measurement of locus of control called the internal–external (I–E) scale.

Employees in organizations perceive that their success or failure can be attributed to three characteristics—internal or external, stable or unstable, and controllable or uncontrollable. When the attribution is internal or external, it can be either controllable or uncontrollable. Internal control requires efforts from the employees, whereas external control requires the employees to opt for alternative options. Internal factors become uncontrollable when the employees fail to change their attitude and the basic intellectual base. Similarly, external factors become uncontrollable when the employees are unable to cope with changes. The level of effort put in by the employees towards performing their jobs depends on their attributions to either internal or external factors. This is why attribution theory is considered important for employees' motivation.

By interpreting the responses to the 13-item questionnaire of Rotter, it is possible to measure the general expectancies of people from internal versus external control reinforcement. A low score is an indicator of internal control, whereas a high score indicates external control. According to Rotter, our behaviour is the function of our expectations and reinforcements.

Goal Setting Theory

Edwin Locke (1968) considered two cognitive determinants of behaviour—values and intentions (goals). Emotions and desires represent a form of values and value judgements. Intentions are goals to satisfy desires or emotions (values). This results in consequences, feedback, and reinforcement. The study suggests that individuals are willing to work hard when they know what is required from them. Setting specific attainable goals is related to high-level performance.

Miscellaneous Theories on Motivation

Apart from the theories of motivation listed in the preceding paragraphs, there are certain other theories which, however, revolve around the core content or process theories. These can be briefly discussed as follows:

Manifest needs theory   H.A. Murray (1938) discussed the manifest needs theory, which is basically a multivariate approach to the structure of needs. The basic difference between Murray's formulation and the formulations of Maslow and Alderfer is that Murray does not suggest a hierarchical order of the various types of needs. Based on several years of clinical observations at the Harvard Psychological clinic, Murray argues that the intensities of various personality-related needs, taken together, represent a central motivating force.

Competence motive theory   This theory (slightly similar to the power motive theory of Adler), advocated by R.W. White (1959), relates motivation to the desire of the employees for mastery over the physical and social environs (Cornell study).

Affiliation motivation theory   S. Schachter (1959) formulated this theory, which relates motivation to the strong need for affiliation.

Maturity–Immaturity theory   This theory of C. Argyris (1957) relates motivation to an environment that serves the needs of both the organization and the members of the organization (Yale study).

Money motivation theory   This theory was advocated by W.F. Whyte (1955). It suggests that people are motivated primarily by the desire to make money. However, Whyte contends that monetary incentives should not be considered in isolation from other non-monetary incentives.

Michigan studies   These were conducted by R. Likert and D. Katz (1948). The studies emphasized the vital point that a productivity-motivated work team is really a function of a particular type of supervisory style. Since productivity has its root in employee motivation, it can be harnessed by carefully designing an organization in which the individual develops a feeling that he/she has some importance in the organization.

For the sake of our convenience, Megginson has classified the leading theories of motivation into the following three groups:

Perspective theories   This group includes Taylor's scientific management approach, various human relations theories, and McGregor's Theory Y and Theory X, which, in reality, advise managements to motivate people.

Content theories   This group includes Maslow's hierarchy of needs theory, Herzberg's two-factor theory, and McClelland's achievement need theory, which try to identify the causes of behaviour.

Process theories   This group includes various behaviouristic theories, which believe in stimulus–response relationship vis-à-vis motivation (e.g., Skinner's behaviour modification theory), and cognitive theories (e.g., Vroom's expectancy theory and Porter–Lawler's future-oriented expectancy theory), which deal with the genesis of behaviour.

The foregoing brief discussions regarding the different motivation theories, studies, and experiments, taken together, reflect our basic understanding of the concept of motivation and its related aspects in a systematic manner.

Practitioner Speak 11.3

Does Money Really Affect Motivation? A Review of the Research

How much should people earn? Even if resources were unlimited, it would be difficult to stipulate your ideal salary. Intuitively, one would think that higher pay should produce better results, but scientific evidence indicates that the link between compensation, motivation and performance is much more complex. In fact, research suggests that even if we let people decide how much they should earn, they would probably not enjoy their job more.

Read this insightful blog posted by Chamorro-Premuzic on *HBR Blog Network* by accessing the following link: http://blogs.hbr.org/cs/2013/04/does_money_really_affect_motiv.html.

MOTIVATION STUDIES IN INDIA

Our next phase of discussion mainly focuses on relevant Indian studies in this field in order to understand the underlying motive forces determining the behaviour and performance of the Indian employees.

In India, not many empirical studies on motivation and its related aspects have been carried out. There are some studies on industrial workers and some on technical personnel, supervisors, and mangers. Most of the studies in India have attempted to identify job satisfaction variables, which have been construed as motivational variables.

The first such study in India was by Bose (1947) on industrial workers; it paved the way for other researchers to investigate the perceived importance of job factors to workers.

Most studies relating to industrial workers, during the period 1951–71, have rated adequate earnings, job security, boss, and personal life as the main factors that determine their behaviour.

Ganguli (1964), who conducted a study on first-line supervisors ($N = 44$), where N denotes the number of persons in the study sample, has ranked incentive, adequate income, promotional opportunities, job security, and sympathetic treatment from superiors as the important job factors with regard to motivation.

The study of Lahiri and Srivastava (1967), on middle-management personnel ($N = 93$), has ranked good organizational policies and administration, better scope for promotion, good salary, good superior–subordinate relationship, and opportunity for growth as the major determinants of satisfaction.

Sawalapurkar and others (1968) performed a study on middle-level managers ($N = 30$) and have ranked nine job factors in the following order of importance:

- Job content
- Opportunity for advancement
- Job security
- Boss
- Company

- Working conditions
- Facilities
- Working hours
- Grievance redressal

The study of Padaki and Dolke (1970), on job attitudes of supervisors ($N = 15$) (based on Herzberg's two-factor theory), has found lack of recognition, unfavourable superior–subordinate relationship, lack of technically competent supervision, unfavourable organizational policies and administration, and inadequate salary as the major causes of dissatisfaction. Another study conducted by them also found more or less the same reasons for these perceived dissatisfactions.

Rao (1970) studied bank managers ($N = 60$), with a view to testing the Herzberg's two-factor theory, and found promotion, company policies, and salary on the dissatisfaction scale.

A study on public sector managers ($N = 1213$) was conducted by Narain (1971); it ranked eight factors in the following order of decreasing importance:

- Feeling of worthwhile accomplishments
- Recognition
- Decision-making authority

- Opportunity for personnel growth and development
- Promotional opportunity

- Prestige of the organization in the community
- Pay and fringe benefits
- Job security

As far as the need deficiencies are concerned, he found that promotion, recognition, and personal growth and development show very high degrees of dissatisfaction in that order.

The study by Bhattacharyya (1972) on managers ($N = 210$) has shown lack of participation in goal setting, inadequacy of pay, inadequacy of job authority, and lack of opportunity given to help people on the dissatisfaction scale.

Pestonjee and Basu (1972) conducted a study on executives ($N = 80$), which showed promotion and growth, recognition, prestige, organizational policies and administration, and autonomy as the major determinants of satisfaction.

The study undertaken by Singhal and Upadhyay (1972) on supervisors ($N = 22$) has found opportunities for promotion, job security, working conditions, work group, opportunities for training, competent and sympathetic supervisors, adequate income, and other facilitates as the major motivational factors.

Agarwal (1976) has sharply criticized the Indian studies on work motivation, alleging that such researches suffer from a number of inconsistencies, mainly because they have been carried out practically as part of the job done for employees with a view to help them reduce production costs. Thus, the measures suggested by such researchers have always proved to be short-term remedies, and their theories on motivation are more like fads than being substantial and lasting. Along the same lines as Pareek (1974), he has developed a stratification model of work motivation with variables such as social system, self-status, and role. Pareek (1974) considered the societal system as a very important variable in the field of motivation as it causes or determines the behaviour of an individual in an organization.

The study by Sharma (1981) on administrators in Delhi ($N = 67$) has found power as the main guiding force for motivation.

Another study by Sharma (1982) on supervisors ($N = 3378$) drawing samples from 50 manufacturing organizations, both in the public sector and the private sector, has obtained score values for different factors that influence motivation as shown in Table 11.2. The study has been carried out on a three-point scale, containing low, medium, and high frequencies.

Neelamegham and Vaid (1986) studied the motivation of the sales force ($N = 116$) and found the highest need deficiencies with respect to prospects of promotion and recognition for good work.

It is important to note that a majority of the Indian studies are on supervisory and managerial personnel. Another important feature is that most of these studies have been carried out with a small sample, using only conventional methods such as ranking and percentage calculation. Some studies have been carried out simply to authenticate Herzberg's two-factor theory, whereas some others are highly opinionated studies without much adherence to the norms of sampling and survey methods. In most

Table 11.2 Motivational factors and their level of influence

Factor	Percentage
Superintendent–Management relations	63.21
Monetary benefits	60.30
Objectivity and rationality	56.00
Recognition and appreciation	51.32
Welfare facilities	48.39
Scope for advancement	47.32
Grievance handling	45.83
Training and education	43.46
Participative management	39.68

cases, even a suitably structured close-ended questionnaire was not administered. They contain simple inferences after informal discussions, with the samples mostly drawn without following proper sampling procedures. Another feature is that most studies are based on the experiences of single industrial units. Representative results are difficult to obtain from a survey based on a small sample drawn from a single unit.

Exhibit 11.1 discusses the factors involved in motivating Indian employees.

MOTIVATION AND MORALE

Edwin Flippo (1961) defined morale as 'a mental condition or attitude of individuals and groups which determines their willingness to cooperate'. Yoder Dale (1972), on the other hand, explained morale as 'the overall tone, climate, or atmosphere of work perhaps regularly sensed by the members. If workers appear to feel enthusiastic and optimistic about group activities, if they have a sense of mission about their jobs, and if they are friendly with each other, they are described as having a good or high morale. If they seem to be dissatisfied, irritated, cranky, critical, restless, and pessimistic, they are described as having poor or low morale'. Elton Mayo

---

EXHIBIT 11.1 Motivating Employees: The Indian Perspective

Motivating employees in an emerging economy like India can be difficult given the increasing opportunities the labour pool has recently been subjected to. Demotivated employees are likely to leave unless proper steps are taken by the management. High attrition rate is one of the most pertinent problems faced by organizations. However, there are solutions to this problem and the most widely accepted solution is focusing on employee motivation.

In this regard, Dr Groznaya has noted that employee motivation cannot be achieved by following the same methods throughout the world. This is one common mistake that multinational companies make while trying to motivate employees. Though certain widely accepted methods such as salary and benefits, name and recognition, and providing opportunities for individual growth are followed all over the world, there are certain culture-specific methods as well that apply exclusively to India.

Dr Groznaya has further noted that since India has a low cost of living, satisfying employees by offering good salaries and monetary benefits is rather easy. However, money is not the only way to motivate them. At least 70 per cent of the Indian employees look at safety and emotional comfort as important determinants of motivation. In addition, charting a proper career path for employees is seen as a crucial motivating factor.

However, other factors also need to be taken into consideration. Employee engagement is said to considerably increase employee motivation. Vision and values also need to be considered. Since employees are different individuals, they need to be motivated in different ways. The work environment should promote employee motivation.

Management acknowledgement and appreciation also helps increase motivation to a large extent. Lastly, leadership makes a huge difference in helping employees who are not willing to seek job changes to stay motivated.

Sources: Groznaya, E., 'Attrition and Motivation: Retaining Staff in India', *tcworld*, July 2009, http://82.165.192.89/initial/index.php?id=63, last accessed on 2 September 2013; SHRM, 'Motivation in Today's Workplace: The Link to Performance', July 2010, http://www.shrmindia.org/motivation-today%E2%80%99s-workplace-link-performance, last accessed on 2 September 2013 (adapted).

> Morale is defined as a mental condition or attitude of individuals and groups which determines their willingness to cooperate.

defined it as 'the maintenance of cooperative living', which means a sense of belonging. Many authors have defined morale as a 'pursuit of a common purpose', attitude, individual and group job satisfaction, participative attitudes, team spirit, and so on. Irrespective of the way of defining, it is evident that morale is a cognitive concept, encompassing feelings, attitudes, and sentiments, which together contribute to a general feeling of satisfaction in the workplace.

Similar to morale, motivation is also a cognitive concept. However, it is different from morale in certain important aspects. Motivation stimulates individuals into action to achieve desired goals. It is, therefore, a function of needs and drives. It mobilizes energy, which enhances the potential for morale. Morale, on the other hand, is the individual or group attitude towards a particular subject. It contributes to a general feeling of satisfaction at the workplace. It is, therefore, the function of freedom or restraint towards some goal. It mobilizes sentiments, which form an important part of the organizational climate. Attitudes and sentiments, that is, morale, per se, affect productivity. High morale is an index of good human relations, which, inter alia, reduces labour turnover, absenteeism, indiscipline, grievances, and so on.

The primary factors that affect morale are the attitude and job satisfaction levels of individual employees. We have discussed attitude and its measurement in Chapter 6. From an organizational point of view, such factors can be delineated into organizational goals, leadership styles, co-workers' attitude, nature of work, work environment, and the employee himself/herself.

High morale is conventionally considered as a contributor to high productivity, but such correlation may not always be true. This is because high productivity may be the outcome of many other organizational initiatives, which may be independent of employee morale. Hence, even with low employee morale, high productivity is achievable. This can be illustrated using the model of Keith Davis, as in Fig. 11.9.

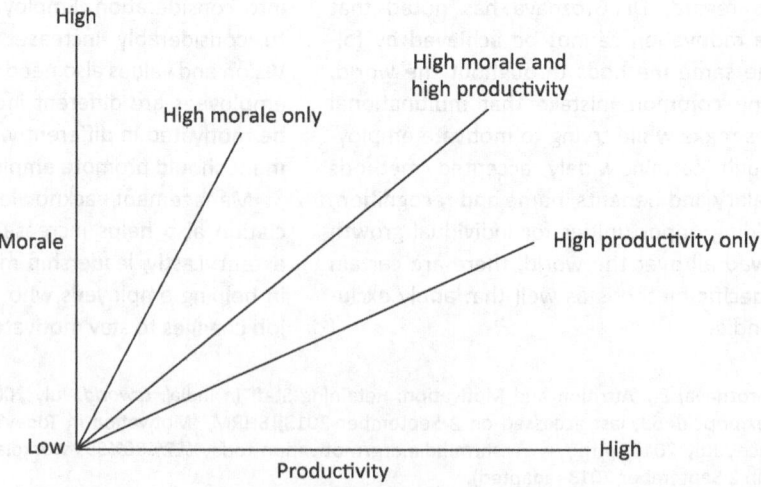

Figure 11.9 Motivation and morale

EMPLOYEE COUNSELLING

Counselling refers to a discussion with an employee having a problem that is emotional in nature. It is intended to help the employee overcome emotional stress, so that he/she can get back to the main track of performance. In organizations, the need for counselling may arise because of several reasons. For example, an employee may fail to achieve the results or performance targets, may have problems with the team leader, or may fail to relate himself/herself to the job as also with the organization (see Table 11.3). As a result of such divergent needs for employee counselling, its characteristics also differ. It may be an exchange of feelings between two people (hence an act of communication), a help to an employee to overcome his/her emotional problems (hence an act of problem solving), or to coach or guide an employee to achieve his/her goals (hence a developmental support).

Table 11.3 Causal factors for industrial disputes

Causes	Years							
	1994		1995		1997		1998	
	No. of disputes	Percentage to total	No. of disputes	Percentage to total	No. of disputes	Percentage to total	No. of disputes	Percentage to total
Wages and allowances	354	29.4	320	30	305	23.4	233	21.2
Personnel	194	16.2	195	18.3	261	20.0	175	16.0
Retrenchment	19	1.6	10	0.9	7	0.5	8	0.7
Lay-off	3	0.2	4	0.4	7	0.5	6	0.6
Indiscipline	185	15.2	145	13.6	246	18.9	225	18.9
Violence	20	1.7	14	1.3	13	1.0	7	0.6
Leave and hours of work/shift working	17	1.4	21	2.0	31	2.4	14	1.3
Bonus	92	7.8	79	7.4	112	86	123	11.2
Gherao	1	0.1	1	0.1	—	—	—	—
Non-implementation of agreements, awards, etc.	37	3.1	43	4.0	43	3.3	32	2.9

(Contd)

Table 11.3 (*Contd*)

Causes	Years							
	1994		1995		1997		1998	
	No. of disputes	Percentage to total	No. of disputes	Percentage to total	No. of disputes	Percentage to total	No. of disputes	Percentage to total
Charter of demands	55	4.6	61	5.7	68	5.2	97	8.8
Workload	10	0.8	10	0.9	9	0.7	6	0.6
Surplus labour	1	0.1	—	—	1	0.1	—	—
Betterment of amenities	16	1.3	18	1.7	34	2.6	12	1.1
Suspension/ Change of manufacturing process	1	0.1	—	—	—	—	1	0.1
Standing orders/ rules/service conditions/safety measures	50	4.2	52	4.9	34	2.6	13	1.2
Others	118	9.8	57	5.4	85	6.5	89	8.1
Not known	21	1.7	29	2.7	37	2.8	49	4.5
Total	**201**	**100**	**1066**	**100**	**1305**	**100**	**109**	**100**

Objectives of Counselling

The objectives or functions of counselling can be categorized into six major areas, which are detailed as follows:

Rendering advice   It is the function of coaching by the counsellor, who may be the immediate boss or a professional. Here, the counsellor listens to the problems of the employees and then guides them in the right direction.

Reassurance   It is the function of restoring the confidence of the employees, helping them to feel courageous, gain strength, and develop positive thinking. In cases where employees are entrusted with challenging assignments, reassuring them is very important to help them realize that they can achieve the results.

Clarifying thinking   It is the function of encouragement to the employees to be rational and realistic. Employees often lose their emotional balance in executing their assignments and jobs and hence commit decisional errors. Helping them be rational by clarifying their way of thinking brings them back to reality and enables them to achieve results.

Release of emotional tension   It is the process of being relieved from frustration and stress. The counsellor allows the employees to share their grief. The process of sharing helps the employees relieve their emotional tensions. This does not lead to a solution by itself, but it breaks the ice, allowing the counsellor to understand the possible ways for solution.

Communication It is the process of sharing information and understanding, through upward and downward communication. Upward communication flows from the employees, who bring their feelings and emotional problems to the notice of the management. Downward communication flows from the counsellors, who help the employees gain insight into the activities of the organization.

Reorientation It is the process of providing encouragement to bring about internal changes in goals, values, and mental models, helping employees to leverage their strengths and guard against their weaknesses.

Types of Counselling

Depending on the reasons for counselling, a counsellor can make use of the following three types of counselling:

Directive counselling In this type of counselling, the counsellor plays the role of an empathetic listener and then takes decisions about the right courses of action for the employees. The counsellor also motivates them to follow the suggested courses of action.

Non-directive counselling The counsellor uses this type of counselling to not only listen, but also urge the employees to explain their problems. On understanding the problems, the counsellor determines the courses of action and then facilitates the employees to identify on their own the possible solutions to those problems. Since finding the solutions to the problems is left to the employees being counselled, this is also called client-centred counselling.

Participative or cooperative counselling It is in between the other two types of counselling. Here, both the counsellor and the person being counselled develop a close emotional relationship and exchange ideas, feelings, knowledge, and information to overcome the problem of the person seeking help. Since possible solution inputs are also collected from the person going through a problem, this is called participative counselling.

In organizations, managers have to adopt a suitable type of counselling depending on the reason for counselling, the type of employees for whom counselling is intended, and the underlying situation that prevails at a particular point of time. Directive counselling is preferred in cases where the employees are unable to decide their course of action. Non-directive counselling is for those who are knowledgeable and capable enough to take a decision once the problems are explained to them. Participative counselling is effective in cases where organizations are trying to change, which may be for mergers and acquisitions, technological changes, business process reengineering, or policy-related changes. Most mergers fail due to emotional blocks from the employees. Videocon's success in transforming a Philips unit, after its acquisition, is attributable to participative counselling. All senior executives were initially told to spend 80 per cent of their time in talking to people and helping them get their doubts and apprehensions clarified. This helped the company empower its people to identify themselves with the transformation process, shedding their age-old legacy-bound thoughts and beliefs. However, another Philips unit, Total Plastics Solutions, acquired by Philips' employees could not be transformed. Hence, a manager as a counsellor has to adopt a contingency view of counselling, irrespective of his/her preferred style.

Steps in Counselling Process

Irrespective of the reasons and the style adopted for counselling, the counsellor has to adopt certain common steps to make the process successful. These are as follows:

Initiating   At this stage, the counsellor establishes a rapport with the employee concerned, developing mutual understanding and promoting openness. This ensures inculcation of confidence in the mind of the person being counselled and in the process, helps gain acceptance from that person.

Exploring   At this stage, the person under counselling is urged to describe in his/her own words the situation, feelings, problems, and needs. Here, the counsellor endeavours to let him/her understand his/her own weaknesses and shortcomings and in the process develop a sense of mutuality. Mutuality is positively relating and interacting with the people. To promote mutuality, the counsellor has to have empathy in his/her communication, negotiation, and mediation skills. In addition, he/she should exhibit a personal attitude of care and respect for the person in need of help and should also show an eagerness to cooperate.

Framing of action plan   To make the counselling process successful, the counsellor has to frame an action plan, duly charting the rules to be followed.

Thus, counselling is used by organizations as a tool to help the employees bring about attitudinal changes in themselves and adjust with the changing situations, duly promoting a sense of mutuality. However, it is also important to understand that counselling, per se, cannot improve the work environment or make the workers productive. Along with other tools, counselling has to be used as a supplemental effort to bring about the required improvements and changes in the behaviour of the employees.

> The steps in a counseling process are initiating, exploring, and framing of action plan.

Exhibit 11.2 examines the process of counselling employees from an Indian perspective.

EXHIBIT 11.2   Counselling Employees: An Indian Perspective

Counselling is an important human resources function and Indian employers are much behind their western counterparts in helping employees better their performances at work through effective counselling processes. However, certain information technology (IT) firms have launched extensive programmes to counsel their employees and help them cope with long and stressful jobs.

TCS has launched 'Maitree'—a counselling programme that aims at counselling 30,000 employees. Launched in 2005, the initiative not only counsels employees but also is instrumental in arranging family get-togethers and other allied activities such as yoga classes and workshops for the performing arts. These initiatives help employees stay healthy and perform better on their jobs.

Wipro Technologies, on the other hand, has launched 'Mitr'—a programme that intends to reduce employee stress from working for long hours. This is an in-house initiative, which was started way back in 2003. The programme has, since then, been useful in helping stressed out employees at the workplace.

Counselling service providers have been upbeat about the moves taken by companies to deal with employee stress and trauma. Employers have realized that employees cannot leave their personal

(Contd)

Exhibit 11.2 (*Contd*)

lives and get to work and thus need emotional care from time to time. Moreover, the trauma faced by individuals varies greatly, and professionally qualified people are required to tackle such situations. Lastly, counselling is no longer considered a taboo in Indian firms.

Sources: Navare, S., 'Counselling at Work Place: A Proactive Human Resource Initiative', *Indian Journal of Occupational and Environmental Medicine*, Vol. 12, Issue 1, 2008, pp. 1–2; Sengupta, D., 'Dealing with Emotional Baggage: Cos Take on Role of Counsellors', *The Economic Times*, 21 June 2010 (adapted).

DESIGNING MOTIVATIONAL STRATEGIES

Motivated employees help organizations survive and become more productive. Hence, it is important that managers understand what motivates employees within the context of their job roles. However, this task is not so simple because the perceived motivational reinforcement of employees changes from time to time. Therefore, managers need to understand the application of motivational theories in designing motivational strategies for their employees, whose needs may be wide and varied. The entire task of designing motivational strategies requires managers, at the outset, to identify the correct reinforcers for employee motivation. This is done primarily through survey-based investigation, using questionnaires, and prioritizing the perceived need factors of the employees. Apart from these, direct observation may also help.

Using either of the needs identification methods, organizations list the employees' perceived rank orders of various motivational reinforcers and then group these into extrinsic and intrinsic factors. Extrinsic needs focus on tangible gains in the form of increased pay, incentives, bonus, better medical benefits, better retirement benefits, better canteen facilities, and so on. Intrinsic needs, on the other hand, are more related to mental satisfaction and are abstract in nature. Increased status, challenge, sense of belonging, scope for growth and creativity, recognition, and sense of achievement are examples of such needs.

Framing appropriate strategies to motivate helps the organization close the perceived need gap of employees. Strategies need to be framed such that the budget is not unnecessarily strained, or else HR costs will rise. For example, the need for increased pay can be ensured by reducing the deferred benefits, that is, NWLC. Various studies indicate the NWLC's share towards the total HR costs vary between 50 per cent and 97 per cent. In countries such as France and Germany, such burden is on the higher side. In India, many organizations need to allocate as high as 57–60 per cent towards deferred benefits. For many organizations, retention of employees in the exploratory age group (usually less than 35 years) is quite difficult, as these employees value their current pay more than future benefits. To motivate such employees, to retain, and to make them more productive, organizations strategically discount the deferred benefits component, limiting it to only the statutory part (provident funds, gratuities, etc.) and increasing their current pay level. This strategy does not strain the budget line and at the same time ensures employees' motivation.

Various motivational theories discussed earlier also focus on a number of intrinsic factors that require a thrust on developing an enabling work culture, giving employees opportunities to learn, grow, and participate in decision-making. Such strategies do not strain the budget line and keeps the HR costs competitive. Organizational practices, therefore, require identifying such motivational strategies to create a win–win situation.

To sum up, organizational motivational strategies depend on first identifying the need gap of employees, then ranking those as per their perceived prioritization, and finally identifying the appropriate motivational reinforcers that address the perceived needs of most employees, using the test of commonality.

SUMMARY

Motivation is a dynamic organizational behaviour issue. The behaviour of people largely stems from their dissatisfied needs. Organizations try to identify these needs and then select appropriate motivational tools that would satisfy the employees' needs and also fit into the organizational purposes. As the needs of the people vary widely, there cannot be any organization-specific motivational tool. The content and process theories on motivation suggest various methods for enhancing employee motivation. Many empirical studies carried out in India and abroad validated such tools, either partially or in their entirety. Motivation, both through intrinsic and extrinsic reinforcers, contributes to employee satisfaction and hence enhances performance and productivity.

For effective management of an organization, managers align aims, purpose, and values between the employee and the organization and in the process nurture a motivating work environment. Organizations with high levels of employee motivation typically enjoy high-level performance from the employees, and thus, sustained motivational reinforcement is considered to be the important strategic intervention for organizational competitiveness. Motivation—being need dependent with human needs never remaining constant—is a complex area of study for managers. However, it is clear that employees can get motivated towards something if they can relate to it and even more if they believe in it. Thus, strategic alignment of people's needs and values with the organizational purpose can best be achieved once employees see themselves as partners in the process.

KEY DEFINITIONS

Attribution theory and locus of control This theory is mainly concerned with the cognitive process by which an individual interprets behaviour, attributing it to certain parts of the relevant environment. An individual interprets such causal relationships or attributes for his/her own behaviour or for others' behaviour.

Equity theory This theory proposes that in a work environment, motivation is influenced by one's perception of how equitably he/she is treated compared to others. The theory is also known as social comparison theory or inequity theory.

Esteem needs This pertains to self-respect and respect or esteem from others. Self-respect is ensured by achieving competence, confidence, personal strength, adequacy, achievement, independence, and freedom, whereas respect from others comes from prestige, recognition, acceptance, attention, status, reputation, and appreciation.

Goal setting theory This theory considers two cognitive determinants of behaviour—values and intentions (goals). Emotions and desires represent the form of values and value judgements. Intentions are goals to satisfy desires or emotions (values). This results in consequences, feedback, and reinforcement. The study suggests that individuals are willing to work hard when they know what is required from them. Setting specific attainable goals is related to high-level performance.

Job characteristic model This is based on the study of Richard Hackman and Greg Oldham (1975) on Herzberg's two-factor theory. The model shows how a good job design can lead to internal motivation of the employees and contribute to better job performance. The five job characteristics that lead to employee motivation are skill variety, task identity, task significance, autonomy, and feedback.

Performance satisfaction theory   This theory postulates that performance leads to satisfaction, contrary to the belief that satisfaction leads to performance.

CONCEPT-REVIEW QUESTIONS

11.1 Define the term motivation. Why is it so important for HR managers?

11.2 What motivational tools would you like to use for knowledge workers? Would your approach be different for operators on a shop floor?

11.3 Critically review the contribution of Maslow and Herzberg on the theories of motivation. Do you think they have any relevance for the new generation workers?

11.4 How would you distinguish between the process theories and content theories of motivation?

11.5 Distinguish between motivation and morale. Discuss how morale can influence productivity.

11.6 Can motivation be defined as perception? What are the circumstances in which perception can influence the motivation strength of a worker?

11.7 Write short notes on the following:
(a) Job satisfaction
(b) Performance satisfaction theory
(c) Motivation and morale
(d) Employee stock options
(e) Theory of expectancy
(f) Motivation and productivity

CRITICAL THINKING QUESTIONS

11.1 Nearly 10,000 people work in a manufacturing organization. They are recruited from different states, have different cultures and different education levels, and belong to different age groups. Studying their family backgrounds, it is evident that 30 per cent are from families classifiable in the higher-income group, whereas 70 per cent are from families in the poor-income group. This organization, being professionally managed, periodically carries out a need analysis of employees. The HR director of the company on going through such an analysis could identify several perceived need factors, which cannot be accommodated by the organization, to derive the motivational benefits of the employees. Suggest what should be the course of action.

11.2 Your company has now started recruiting management trainees from the best business schools. As the HR director, of late you are observing that many of these newly recruited employees have started disliking the existing system of working in the organization, and many even overtly criticize the system. You are apprehending that these bright young people may leave their jobs. From a motivational point of view, what steps can you initiate to turn this situation to your advantage?

SELECT BIBLIOGRAPHY

- Atkinson, John W., *An Introduction to Motivation*, Affiliated East-West Press, New Delhi, 1966.
- Bhattacharyya, Dipak Kumar, *Human Resource Management*, Excel Books, New Delhi, 2006.
- Bhattacharyya, Dipak Kumar, *Human Resource Research Methods*, Oxford University Press, New Delhi, 2007.
- Herzberg, F., 'One More Time: How Do You Motivate Employees?', *Harvard Business Review*, Vol. 46, pp. 53–63.
- Vroom, V.H., *Work and Motivation*, Wiley, New York, 1964.
- Whyte, W.F., *Money and Motivation*, Harper and Row, New York, 1955.

ICBank—Model of Employee Motivation

The chief executive officer (CEO) of a national-level private sector bank, ICBANK India, which is growing at a fast pace, always nurtures the view that HR people themselves are poor in managing the behaviour of the people in his organization. He feels that over the years his HR has been instrumental in demotivating the people, as it failed to retain the result-oriented employees, causing huge manpower-replacement costs to the organization. Besides, employees feel that the performance management system is too complicated and focuses only on the achievement of quantitative targets rather than on the other positive aspects of employees. They largely feel that they are instrumental in taking their organization to new heights, with a focus on customer satisfaction and by developing organizational loyalty. Business target achievement, fixing a stretch goal and forcing employees to accept the key result areas (KRAs), without listening to them, may have helped in achieving the short-term goals, but such achievements far outweighed the losses when good performers left the organization in less than two years. As per policy, immediately after recruitment, the organization has to train new recruits through a month-long induction programme and allow them to understand the jobs for the next two months, without setting for them any specific targets for achievement. All these add to the costs of the company. The CEO laments that every employee replacement directly costs the organization two times the annual salary paid to an employee, and indirectly costs even more, as the value addition differs between the existing individual employees and the replacement employees. Five years earlier, the average value addition potentiality of marketing executives (at current discounted values), as assessed by the organization using the learning curve theory, taking the employment span to be of 10 years, indicated a figure of ₹25 lakh, whereas now the figure is ₹15 lakh. The CEO justifiably argues that what HR is doing is to recruit on a

piece-meal basis rather than considering the long-term effect.

In one of the corporate-level meetings, with all functional heads present, the CEO was blunt in accusing the HR department and said, 'Let us accept that our HR department is an utter failure. It still considers employees as just another input into the process. There is no effort to make our employees a partner in the organization.' The CEO then asked the HR personnel to come up with a detailed performance-driven compensation plan, which would help the organization optimize the compensation cost and, at the same time, reduce the attrition rate, thereby increasing the motivation level of the employees.

The HR manager accordingly prepared the following plan:

Variable pay component in executive compensation in India has now been increased to almost 50 per cent from 20–30 per cent only a few years back. Without linking it to company performance alone, a three-tiered structure has now emerged; that is, the variable pay is linked to company performance, team performance, and individual performance.

Our company's annual turnover today is ₹1000 crore. We have 900 marketing executives, with the current rate of staff turnover at 15 per cent. The number of marketing executives with a tenure of more than five years with the company is 115. The number of marketing executives over 40 years of age is only 60.

The benchmarked annual salary data in comparable private sector banks in the country for marketing executives is ₹6 lakh (considering the cost to the company), whereas our organization today pays ₹6.25 lakh. Our organization believes in pay equity and follows broad banding while designing base pay. The calculated wage cost to annual sales is 20 per cent.

An employee-motivation survey carried out by the HR department of the organization indicated that 30 per cent of the marketing executives feel that they are underpaid, 50 per cent feel that they are getting the competitive benchmarked salary, whereas the remaining 20 per cent feel that they are getting more than the market rate. In response to a questionnaire item requiring executives to point out what should be their perceived percentage of salary rise that they feel will motivate them, the replies suggested that an incentive plan that corroborates with the Scanlon plan needs to be designed.

This Scanlon plan relates compensation cost ratio to the total sales value to measure the effectiveness of performance. As per this plan, an incentive bonus will be payable to marketing executives, based on the percentage reduction in the marketing executive to sales ratio, comparing the base period and assessment period. The formula for computing percentage reduction in the marketing executive to sales ratio is as follows:

$$\frac{\dfrac{L_b}{R_b} - \dfrac{L_a}{R_a}}{\dfrac{L_b}{R_b}} \times 100$$

where L_b = Total wage cost of the marketing executive for the base month

R_b = Total sales value for the base month

L_a = Total wage cost of the marketing executive for the assessment month

R_a = Total sales value for the assessment month

L_b = Standard wage to sales ratio for the base month

$\dfrac{L_a}{R_a}$ = Actual wage to sales ratio for the assessment month

The HR manager believes that following this plan will not only ensure optimization of compensation cost of the marketing executives (whose variable component of compensation is now linked with individual performance achievement) but also foster teamwork and develop a culture of togetherness, which would have an enduring effect on the marketing executives' motivation and retention.

Questions for Discussion

1. Imagine you are the CEO of the bank. Critically review the proposal of the HR manager and give your comments on whether this proposed incentive plan would really ensure motivation and increased retention of marketing executives in the company. Give reasons to support your answer.

2. Based on your understanding of the content and process theories of motivation, explain how the HR department can reduce the rate of attrition in this organization.

Leadership

LEARNING OBJECTIVES

After studying this chapter, the reader will be able to

- understand the theories of leadership
- differentiate between a leader and a manager
- explain the different styles of leadership
- appreciate why leadership is essential for managing organizational behaviour
- understand the process of development of leadership abilities
- discuss various theories of leadership

CASE STUDY
Leadership Crisis

XYZ Corporation holds an annual meeting of its salespeople right at the beginning of every year. Such meetings are used for two purposes—to announce the reward plan for the salespeople and to communicate the strategies and product mix for the coming year. Last year, the company's sales were down due to the increased number of competitors in the same product line and the sudden resignation of their national sales manager, who had an inspirational style of leadership. A new national sales manager was promoted from within the corporation, but he lacked the charisma and showmanship of his predecessor. Another important factor was that the new incumbent was relatively young and rose to this position because of his merit, superseding others. However on

assuming office, the new boss placed emphasis on confidence building of the sales force and devised a participative strategy, comprising a cross-functional management advisory board. He did not talk about the adverse performance of the sales force during the previous year. Instead, the new manager, with a nurturing attitude, discussed the issues at hand, duly focusing on the competitive scenario, with an assurance to the sales force that he would give effect to every recommendation (on the approval of the advisory board) that they suggested to increase the sales of the company. He also reiterated that the company was going to be in business and there was no scope of job loss as of then. His strategy yielded results and the company, within two years, could turn around and achieve increased levels of commitment and motivation from its sales force.

What lessons about leadership do you learn from this case?

INTRODUCTION

The word *leader* first appeared in the English language in the 1300s. It stems from the root *leden*, which means 'to travel' or 'show the way'. The term *leadership* was born some five centuries later. The scientific study on leadership was primarily done in the US. Fields as divergent as political science, psychology, education, history, agriculture, public administration, management, anthropology, biology, military sciences, philosophy, and sociology have all contributed to an understanding of leadership and many of them have established sub-fields in leadership. The earliest literature in almost every culture deals with accounts of heroes and the results of their leadership. Joseph Campbell (1991), in his work on various myths, observes the following in every culture: 'Essentially, there is but one archetypal mythic hero who is the founder of something—a new age, a new religion, a new city, a new way of life. In order to found something new, one has to leave the old and go in quest of a new thing. It involves a journey, abandoning the old and searching for the new.' Leadership arises in response to a need. It essentially derives from the uncertainties and dangers built into the human condition (Bolman and Deal 1991). Conditions that develop leadership vary from situation to situation and from one historical time to another. Therefore, it is difficult to generalize the term leadership. Leadership in a battlefield is different from that in a business organization. Effective leadership at the corporate level (the highest level of an organization) is different from that at the shop floor (operational) level. Hence, a universal model of leadership is unthinkable.

Leadership is the only area in which more than 3000 studies have been carried out so far and more than 2000 definitions have been provided by different management researchers and thinkers. Even then, leadership continues to remain an unexplainable concept.

In any work situation, when two or more people come together to work towards a goal, a structure or a group develops and leadership emerges. The difference between success and failure in business, sports, or any other field can be attributed to leadership. Based on the review of existing literature, leadership can be defined as an activity that influences people to strive willingly for group objectives. It exists only in relationships and only in the imagination and perceptions of the 'followers'. Thus, leadership is what goes with the people and not what is within an individual.

There is vast disagreement over the meaning of leadership. However, there exists a common agreement that leadership makes a substantial difference to organizations. It is typically a solution to most organizational problems.

DEFINITIONS AND CHARACTERISTICS

The complexities involved in defining leadership, a leader, and a follower have already been explained. Here, some definitions are first examined and then the different attributes and traits

> A leader is defined as someone who occupies a position in a group, influences others in accordance with the role expectation of the position, and coordinates and directs the group in maintaining itself and reaching its goal.

of good leadership are identified. Raven (1976) defined a leader as 'someone who occupies a position in a group, influences others in accordance with the role expectation of the position, and coordinates and directs the group in maintaining itself and reaching its goal'. Sears, a retail chain in the UK, has defined a leader as 'the one who initiates action, gives order, makes decisions, settles disputes between group members, offers encouragement, serves as a model, and is in the forefront of group activity'. Therefore, a leader is a person who has the greatest impact on a group's behaviour and beliefs. Avery and Baker (1990) defined leadership, expanding this concept, as a 'process of influence between a leader and his followers to attain group, organizational, and societal goals'.

Let us now consider a few more definitions of leadership. George R. Terry (1960) defined leadership as 'the relationship in which one person, the leader, influences others to work together willingly on related tasks to attain that which the leader desires'. McFarland, et al. (1994) has defined it as 'a process of interpersonal influence by which the executive or manager influences the activities of others in choosing and attaining given ends'. According to Koontz, et al. (2008), leadership is 'the art or process of influencing people so that they will strive willingly and enthusiastically toward the achievement of group goals'. Robert Tannenbaum, I.R. Weschler, and F. Massarick (1979) defined it as 'a process of interpersonal relationships, through which a manager attempts to influence the behaviour of others toward the attainment of pre-determined objective'. Keith Davis (1999), on the other hand, defines it as 'the ability to persuade others to seek defined objectives enthusiastically. It is the human factor which binds group together and motivates it towards goals.'

Based on the foregoing discussion, we can define leadership as a process of influencing people for achieving the intended goals in a given situation. Thus, we can list the characteristics of leadership as follows:

Personal quality   It makes other people follow the leader. The quality of a leader is the aggregation of his/her intelligence, communications skills, emotional balance, inner drive, energy, and other managerial skills (e.g., conceptual, technical, and human relations). To make others follow or to exert others to do the work requires the presence of all these qualities. The degree of requirement of these qualities will, however, depend on the situation.

Process of influencing others   Through the process of influence, a leader makes others work towards achieving goals. People may lack the initiative and the urge to do some work and may feel demotivated. Such behavioural characteristics may seriously impede the achievement of organizational objectives. However, a good leader, through his/her influence, can turn the situation in his/her favour and motivate people to work willingly towards the accomplishment of those objectives.

Process of regulating individual behaviour   Individual behavioural attributes may stand against achieving group goals. A leader through his/her process of influence can regulate individual behaviour and make an individual submit to the group norms. To illustrate, following an approach of discipline without punishment, as advocated by John Huberman, a leader can correct indiscipline and transform him/her into a good performer.

Process of creating relationship between leaders and followers A leader succeeds by developing a relationship with his/her followers. He/She cannot flourish in a vacuum. This is why leadership is also known as followership. In order to develop such a relationship, the leader has to gain the confidence of his/her followers. Developing a two-way relationship, through an effective interpersonal relationship, achieves this confidence, which can also be achieved through participative decision-making, that is, taking decisions by group consensus.

Continuous process Leadership is not a one-time influence on subordinates or followers. In order to be a good leader, a manager should continuously sustain the leadership.

Situational Leadership is exerted in a situation, which varies from time to time. Responding to varying situations requires different leadership approaches. One situation may require taking a lenient view, whereas another may require being tough. Since organizations have to respond to changes in order to remain competitive, leaders also need to change their approach. This requires leaders to develop multi-skills and abilities in order to emerge as winners.

Another way of identifying the characteristics and features of leadership was suggested by Bolman and Deal. They have listed the following four important characteristics of leadership:

- Get others to do what the organization wants (exercise power).
- Motivate people to get things done—mostly through persuasion.
- Provide a vision.
- Empower people to accomplish their tasks.

MANAGEMENT AND LEADERSHIP

A good leader may be a poor manager, and a good manager may not be a good leader. Bennis and Nanus (1997) suggested that 'managers do things right and leaders do the right thing'. Yet, the terms *manager* and *leader* are used interchangeably. However, leadership and managership are not the same. The existence of leadership can be found in unorganized groups as well. However, managership exists only in organized and structured groups. A manager is more than a leader. Due to his/her positional role, a manager has to organize and control the activities of people towards the accomplishment of objectives. As a manager, one has to perform all functions of management, whereas as a leader one is more related to the directing part, that is, influencing people to achieve goals. Therefore, leadership is a part of and not the whole of management. This is why it is often said, 'All managers are leaders, but all leaders are not managers.'

> Managers do things right and leaders do the right thing. However, in the organizational context, a manager is more than a leader.

To stretch the debate further, let us examine the views of the major contributors in this regard. Their main contentions are that leaders and managers vary in their orientation towards goals, conceptions about work, interpersonal styles, and self-perceptions. French (1990), while distinguishing between a leader and a manager, opined the following:

Leaders are often dramatic and unpredictable in style. They tend to create an atmosphere of change, ferment even chaos. They are often obsessed by their ideas, which appear as visionary and consequently excite, stimulate and drive other people to work hard to create reality out of fantasy. Managers are typically hard working, analytical, tolerant and fair-minded. They have a strong sense of belonging to the organization, and take great pride in perpetuating and improving the status quo.

Another opposing view states that leadership is just one aspect of what a manager does. Leaders are involved only in influencing subordinates towards the achievement of the organizational goals.

Vecchio (1988) pointed out that 'leadership can exist on a formal or informal basis'.

John Kotter (1996) summarizes the differences between leadership and managership, and his view is a worthy conclusion to the discussion:

Leadership is different from management, but not for the reason most people think. Leadership isn't mystical and mysterious. It has nothing to do with having 'charisma' or other exotic personality traits. It is not the province of a chosen few. Nor is leadership necessarily better than management or a replacement for it. Rather, leadership and management are two distinctive and complementary activities. Both are necessary for success in an increasingly complex and volatile business environment.

Management functions include planning, organizing, staffing, directing, and controlling. In order to direct the subordinates, a manager must motivate, communicate with, supervise, guide, and lead them. Thus, it is in his/her directing function that a manager becomes responsible for effectively and successfully leading his/her subordinates. Managing can be very effective if those who manage are also leaders because, leadership can substantially influence results. Since a part of a manager's job involves getting things done through the efforts of other people, he/she will be more successful in the job if he/she is also a skilful leader. The following are the important favourable results that may be achieved if managers are also good leaders:

- The leader guides and directs by eliminating uncertainties regarding the action to be taken, and thus, he/she coordinates the individual efforts to make all of them pull in one direction.
- The leader motivates people and integrates the individual needs with the needs of the organization.
- The leader represents the group to the outside world and vice versa. The group looks upon the leader as its source of information and satisfaction.

These three results provided by the leader are also referred to as direction, drive, and representation, respectively, and are sufficient to prove that leadership is an essential part of successful management. It is, however, argued that since managers have the authority to provide incentives, reprimand, fine, deprive, or otherwise punish people in the organization, management leadership has more potential. Discipline and conformity can be maintained through the system of hierarchy and by instilling the fear of loss of employment. However, leadership should not be so emphasized as to make it synonymous with management. If the manager is also a skilful leader, the results are bound to be better. Nevertheless, a leader need not be a good manager, as managing involves more than mere leading and a manager can do reasonably well even when he/she is not a leader. Leadership, therefore, is considered as one of the significant prerequisites of managerial effectiveness.

Practitioner Speak 12.1

Management Is (Still) Not Leadership

A few weeks ago, the BBC asked me to come for a radio interview. They told me they wanted to talk about effective leadership—China had just elevated Xi Jinping to the role of Communist Party leader; General David Petraeus had stepped down from his post at the CIA a few days earlier; the BBC itself was wading through a leadership scandal of its own—but the conversation quickly veered, as these things often do, into a discussion about how individuals can keep large, complex, unwieldy organizations operating reliably and efficiently.

Read this insightful blog posted by Kotter on *HBR Blog Network* by accessing the following link: http://blogs.hbr.org/kotter/2013/01/management-is-still-not-leadership.html.

Table 12.1 Differences between managers and leaders

Managers	Leaders
1. A manager is more than a leader. Hence, management is a wide term.	1. A leader need not be a manager. Leadership is a narrow term.
2. A manager fits well in an organized structure.	2. A leader may also be in an informal group.
3. A manager exercises different functions of management to achieve group goals. Therefore, a manager performs the functions of management in a more holistic manner.	3. A leader exerts influence on people to voluntarily achieve group goals. A leader performs only one aspect of the various management functions, that is, directing.
4. The authority of a manager stems from his/her positional role, that is, it is delegated from the top management.	4. A leader earns his/her authority by virtue of his/her skills, knowledge, and abilities.
5. To be successful as a manager, one has to be a good leader.	5. Leaders need not be managers.

From the preceding discussion, we can differentiate between management and leadership as shown in Table 12.1.

FORMAL AND INFORMAL LEADERS

An organizational structure is characterized by a hierarchy of positions, which are manned by individuals in the scalar chain. Officially, every manager enjoys the power to lead and secure the support of his/her subordinates. Managers, therefore, are leaders because they have the formal authority to direct, motivate, and lead people. This kind of leadership is known as formal or managerial leadership. Informal leaders are not delegated any authority to lead, but rather acquire such authority so as to guide and lead. Informal leadership is spontaneous and is a part of the informal organization. If properly handled, the informal organization offers a good training ground for formal leaders to develop and test their leadership skills.

SIGNIFICANCE OF LEADERSHIP

From the meaning and characteristics of leadership and the differences between leadership and management, one can understand the importance of leadership for an organization. The benefits of leadership can be enumerated as follows:

Improves motivation and morale of employees A successful leader influences the behaviour of individuals. He/She enhances the levels of involvement of the individual employees in their work. The leader creates self-confidence in employees, sustains their enthusiasm and involvement in their work, enhances the motivation and morale of employees, and thus helps greatly in the achievement of organizational goals by the employees. Even in a situation of crisis (e.g., when an organization is facing a bad phase in terms of profitability due to market slowdown or other reasons), a leader can sustain high levels of commitment and motivation from employees, which may ultimately help an organization to turn around. This is why good leaders are considered as turnaround agents in an organization.

Leads to higher performance   Leadership motivates the group to strive for achieving the results, that is, accomplishment of the organizational goals. By increasing the levels of commitment and motivation, a good leader encourages the employees to reach higher levels of performance. This results in increased productivity, which further leads to increased profitability, even in a competitive market.

Acts as an aid to authority   Leadership is a process of influencing others. The mere use of authority by managers may not lead to results. However, when managerial authority is enriched with good leadership, employees start cooperating. Therefore, formal exercise of authority alone may not result in success. Authority when combined with leadership brings success to an organization.

Determines organizational success   In the process of unification of group efforts to achieve organizational goals, leadership enhances organizational efficiency. Good managers alone cannot achieve this.

Helps to respond to change   Organizations today need to quickly respond to changes. A change in the technology, process, methods, and plans (including strategic plans) always encounters resistance from employees. Leadership can play a vital role in implementing change in organizations by creating a conducive environment. People follow leaders, and they like to emulate the examples set by leaders. This makes the change process smooth and successful.

Inculcates values in organization   A value-based organization gets increased commitment and loyalty from its employees. Good leadership being inspirational, also successfully percolates human values, which shape the attitude of employees towards work.

LEADERSHIP QUALITIES

The basic characteristics or qualities of leadership can be grouped as follows:

Being self-aware and continuously seeking self-improvement   To know oneself, one has to understand attributes such as being, knowing, and doing. Seeking self-improvement means continually strengthening these attributes; this can be accomplished through reading, self-study, attending classes, and so on.

Being technically proficient   A leader must know his/her own job and also those of the employees.

Seeking responsibility and taking responsibility for his/her actions   A leader must guide his/her organization to new heights. In the process of guiding, things may, at times, go wrong.

At such times, the leader must not blame others but shoulder the responsibility himself/herself. He/She must analyse the situation, take corrective action, and move on to the next action.

Making sound and timely decisions   Using problem-solving, decision-making, planning, and various controlling tools, a leader must make sound and timely decisions.

Setting example   A leader is a role model for his/her followers. Leaders must practise what they preach.

Knowing people and thinking about their well-being   A leader must know the nature of his/her followers, nurture them, and care for them.

Keeping followers informed   Transparency in information enhances commitment from followers. Hence, a leader must know how to communicate with his/her followers and keep them well informed.

Developing a sense of responsibility among his/her followers   Development orientation requires inculcating good character traits among followers, which will help them to carry out their professional responsibilities.

Ensuring that tasks are understood, supervised, and accomplished   In order to do this, the leader must effectively and transparently communicate with his/her followers the work plans and the important points to be considered while operationalizing the plans.

Training followers to work as team   By inculcating team spirit and a team culture amidst his/her followers, a leader succeeds in accomplishing the goals. Hence, this is also considered one of the important principles of leadership.

Developing full capabilities of organization   By developing team spirit among his/her employees, a leader is able to develop the organization to the level where it works to its maximum capabilities.

Thus, the quality factors of leaders can be categorized into the following four major areas:

Follower   Different people require different styles of leadership. For example, a newly recruited person requires more supervision than an experienced one. Similarly, a follower with poor motivation requires a different approach to one with a high degree of motivation. Thus, the fundamental starting point is having a good understanding of human nature—needs, emotions, and motivation.

Leader   One must have an honest understanding of what one is, what one knows, and what one can do. It is also important to note that it is the followers who determine whether a leader is successful or not. If a follower does not trust or lacks confidence in a leader, he/she remains uninspired. Hence, to be successful, a leader has to convince the followers.

Communication   A leader leads through two-way communication, which need not always be verbal but may also be non-verbal. For instance, through personal selling (i.e., through his/her own behavioural skills) a leader sets the example. While communicating with the followers, a leader should not ask them to do anything that he/she would not be willing to do himself/herself. What and how a leader communicates either builds or harms the relationship between the leader and the followers.

Situation   All situations are not the same. What works in one leadership situation may not work in another situation. Therefore, a leader must use his/her judgement to decide the best course of action and the leadership style needed for each situation. For example, a leader may need to confront an employee for inappropriate behaviour, but if the confrontation is too late or too early, too harsh or too weak, the result may be disastrous.

There are many researches on leadership qualities and characteristics. Hence, it is difficult to come out with some universal qualities and characteristics of leaders, which often tend to vary with organizations. Recently, therefore, a competency-based approach to leadership has been developed, and many organizations follow this approach to identify the qualities and characteristics required of their leaders. For example, NASA's leadership competencies are limited to just three items—making critiques a part of job routine, identifying problems in unlikely places, and creating a problem-solving culture.

ORGANIZATIONAL LEADERSHIP AND ENVIRONMENT

Each organization has a particular work environment that dictates to a considerable degree how its leaders ought to respond to problems and opportunities. This environment is created by the practices followed by the organization's past and present leaders. Leaders exert influence on the organizational environment by establishing the following:

Goals and performance standards   Successful organizations have good leaders who set high standards and goals in terms of strategies, market leadership, plans, presentations, productivity, quality, and reliability.

Values   Values reflect the concern an organization has for its employees, customers, investors, vendors, and the local community. These values define the manner in which business is to be conducted and the type of business the organization will engage in.

Business and people concepts   These define the products or services that the organization will offer and the methods and processes that will be opted for conducting business.

These goals, values, and concepts make up the organization's *personality*. The world at large, as also the employees of the organization, frames its views about the organization on the basis of these goals, values, and concepts. This personality defines the roles, relationships, rewards, and rites of the organization.

Roles are the positions defined by a set of expectations about the behaviour of any newly recruited person. Each role has a set of tasks and responsibilities that may or may not be spelt out. Roles have a powerful effect on behaviour. Since remuneration is paid for the performance of a role, there is prestige attached to it. There is also a sense of challenge and accomplishment.

Relationships are determined by tasks. Some tasks are performed alone, but most are carried out jointly with others. The tasks will determine who the role-holder is required to interact with, how often he/she is required to interact, and towards what end. In addition, greater the interaction, greater would be the liking. This, in turn, leads to more frequent interactions. In general, the tendency of human behaviour is to not like someone with whom one has no contact. People tend to seek out those whom they like. They tend to do what they are rewarded for, and friendship is a powerful reward. Many tasks and behaviours that are associated with a role are brought about by these relationships. Thus, new tasks and behaviours are expected of the present role-holder because a strong relationship was developed in the past, either by the present role-holder or by a past role-holder. Two distinct forces, culture and climate of leadership, dictate how to act within an organization.

Culture and Climate of Leadership

Each organization has its own distinctive culture. It is a combination of the founders, past leadership, current leadership, crises, events, history, and size. This results in the routines, rituals, and the 'way we do things'. These impact individual behaviour regarding what it takes to be in good standing (the norm) and direct the appropriate behaviour for each event.

Culture is the deeply rooted nature of the organization that is a result of long-held formal and informal systems, rules, traditions, and customs. In contrast, climate is a short-term phenomenon created by the current leadership and represents the beliefs about the feel of the organization—the individual and shared perceptions and attitudes of the organization's members. This individual perception of the feel of the organization comes from what people believe about the activities that occur in the organization.

Organizational climate is directly related to the leadership and management style of the leader based on the values, attributes, skills, actions, and priorities of the leader. The ethical climate, then, is the feel of the organization about the activities that have ethical content or those aspects of the work environment that constitute ethical behaviour. It is the feel about whether we do things right or behave the way we ought to behave. The behaviour (character) of the leader is the most important factor that impacts organizational climate.

> Organizational climate is related to the leadership and management style of the leader based on the values, attributes, skills, actions, and priorities of the leader.

On the other hand, culture is a long-term, complex phenomenon. It represents the shared expectations and self-image of the organization, the mature values that create tradition, or the 'way we do things here'. Each organization functions differently. The collective vision that defines the institution is a reflection of its culture. Individual leaders cannot easily create or change culture because it is a part of the organization. It influences the characteristics of the climate by its effect on the actions and thought processes of the leader. Nevertheless, each act of a leader will affect the climate of the organization.

FUNCTIONS OF LEADERSHIP

Leadership is a means of directing; it represents that part of the executive activities by which one guides and influences the behaviour of the subordinates and the group towards some specified goals by personally working with them and understanding their feelings and problems. In recent years, management experts, psychologists, sociologists, and behavioural scientists have tried to identify the functions of leadership in varied ways and from different viewpoints. Hence, it is essential that we not only make ourselves familiar with these viewpoints but also analyse some of the important ones.

Sociological View

Sociologists who want to study in depth the functions of leaders should study the opinion of Selznick (1957). He viewed setting goals, shaping and reshaping organizations, and reconciling internal and external forces as part of the leadership functions. It is the creative function of a leader to view and review the organizational environment and work accomplishments and to determine the short- and long-term goals in such perspective.

A review of the work of other sociologists highlights that a leader is supposed to build goals into the social structure of the enterprise and determine its policies. It is his/her fundamental duty to see that the enterprise not merely survives but also grows in stature. Leaders should be in a position to read the desired changes, movements, and functions of the enterprise to get it placed properly in the industrial complex. Another important function of leaders is to manage and mitigate internal conflicts. It is a fact that conflict is inevitable in big organizations due to diverse opinions, views, beliefs, and values of the people. Therefore, the effectiveness of leaders lies in their endeavour to win the consent of several groups and motivate them to work towards accomplishing the objective and mission of the organization.

Psychological View

In the opinion of psychologists, people will respond best in terms of output if the organization provides them opportunities to appraise and appropriate their basic, social, and ego needs. One of the basic functions of managers and executives is to devise the necessary motivational system to meet the needs of the employees. It should, however, be kept in view that though such an arrangement is sound from the viewpoint of motivation, it is not adequate to precisely outline and specify the scope for the exercise of leadership on the part of the management.

Other Views

Management experts, of late, have given a lot of attention to identifying the exact functions of leadership. According to them, leadership functions can be viewed as (a) directing, (b) responding, and (c) representing.

Directing   The eminent scholar Leonard Sayles viewed directing as the primary function of leadership. In big organizations, where divergent views and several groups exist, it is essentially through the means of directing that all of them are unified and coordinated for a central purpose. In this matter, managers and executives have to take the required initiative, with an intelligent approach and a rational attitude.

Practitioner Speak 12.3

The Most Challenging Leadership Job

If I had to single out the leadership job that's hardest to do, I'd say head of sales. And not just because sales brings in the revenue and tends to feel the friction from the external environment first, though both are certainly true. But because in addition, sales organizations are unique in ways that create singular challenges.

Read this insightful blog posted by Edinger on *HBR Blog Network* by accessing the following link: http://blogs.hbr.org/2012/04/the-most-challenging-leadership.html

Responding   Management experts consider responding as the second function of leadership. It signifies responsiveness to the initiatives of subordinates. It may be remembered that from time to time subordinates ask for guidance, assistance, advice, and help from their superiors. Moreover, subordinates always want to be assured that the services rendered by them are useful. Leadership qualities help superiors to appraise the needs of their subordinates and meet them intelligently.

Representing   The other essential function of leadership is representing. It signifies that superiors would properly and effectively represent the interests of the total group among their peers and to the higher levels in the managerial hierarchy. This aspect of subordinate thinking may commonly be observed where they initiate an action that requires to be accomplished by their superiors or higher-level personnel. In fact, leadership enables executives to represent such group efforts to the superiors and secure positive responses.

Effective leadership undoubtedly creates a comfortable environment among the employees not only by influencing them but also by responding to their problems, feelings, aspirations, and ambitions. In addition, it enhances the image of the organization to the outside world.

From the foregoing discussion, the functions of a leader can be listed as follows:

- To develop teamwork in the organization
- To act as an important change-agent in the organization
- To balance the use of power
- To act as a representative of the subordinates
- To act as a counsellor for the employees
- To help the employees to optimally utilize their time
- To help in achieving organizational effectiveness
- To enhance the levels of motivation and morale of the employees
- To inculcate human values in the organization
- To increase the levels of commitment and loyalty of the employees towards the organization

LEADERSHIP AND POWER

Power, in the case of leadership, is divided into six categories. However, they can be linked with one another, as they are all interrelated. *Expert* and *informational* power are concerned with skills, knowledge, and information, using which the holders of such abilities are able to influence others, that is, technicians and computer personnel. *Reward* and *coercive* power differ from the earlier-mentioned powers because they involve the ability to either reward or punish the persons being influenced to gain compliance. *Legitimate* power is the power that has been confirmed by the role structure of the group or organization and is accepted by all as correct and without dispute, such as in the case of the armed forces or the police force. *Referent* power, on the other hand, involves those being influenced identifying with the leader, for example, rock or film personalities using their image to enter the political arena.

Most leaders make use of a combination of these six types of powers, depending on the leadership style used. Authoritarian leaders, for example, use a mixture of legitimate, coercive, and reward powers to dictate the policies, plans, and activities of a group. In comparison, a democratic or participative leader would mostly use referent power, involving all members of the group in the decision-making process.

LEADERSHIP STYLES

Leadership styles provide an insight into the extent to which a manager should be dictatorial, participative, or consultative. The different leadership styles can be categorized as follows:

- Authoritarian, leader-centred, or autocratic style
- Democratic, participative, consultative, or group-centred style
- Laissez-faire or free rein style
- Paternalistic style

Autocratic

The autocratic style is characterized by centralization of authority and decision-making in the leader and very limited participation by subordinates of the group. The autocratic leader accomplishes the objectives using authority, fear of deprivation, punishment, and other coercive measures. Since the authoritarian approach is negative in character, it will succeed only in the short run and will fail to induce subordinates to perform better in the long run. Resentment, absenteeism, and higher rate of employee turnover are some of the most natural consequences of this approach. Yet, the autocratic style deserves consideration in the following situations:

> Autocratic leadership style is characterized by centralization of authority and decision-making in the leader and limited participation by subordinates in the group.

- There may be very little time for participation, particularly in crises.
- Confidential matters may not permit normal consultation.
- The leader may possess a very high level of knowledge, which may compensate for lack of participation by other members of the group in the decision-making process.

Democratic

The democratic style is characterized by allowing a substantial participation of the members of the group in the management and the decision-making process of the leaders. Subordinates are frequently consulted by the manager on wide-ranging problems and are provided sufficient freedom to communicate with their leader as well as with their fellow subordinates. The democratic style of leadership is based upon positive assumption about human beings. It encourages a cooperative spirit and the development of subordinates for higher responsibility. This style of leadership substantially contributes to the satisfaction of the subordinates.

Laissez-faire

Under the laissez-faire style, the leader largely depends upon the members of the group to establish their own goals and make their own decisions. The leader is passive and assumes the role of just another member of the group. Tasks are assigned in general terms. This approach is meant for selective application. If the subordinate is intelligent, highly qualified, experienced, and desires self-fulfilment, a manager may follow this approach without much risk. This style of leadership is, therefore, confined to a small creative or development group.

Paternalistic

The paternalistic type of leader assumes the role of a father and treats his/her followers as members of his/her family. He/She helps the subordinates do their work, guides and protects them as the head of the family, and keeps them happy so that they work as family members. This type of a leader always tries to provide his/her followers with good working conditions, fringe benefits, and employee services. Due to the differences in style, people working under this style of leadership exert themselves even harder to accomplish the jobs.

A manager is not always free to choose the leadership style most appropriate to him/her under a given situation. Long-cherished feelings and attitudes are difficult to change. Though the democratic style of leadership works better as a general-purpose style, the manager should be able to occasionally switch over to the autocratic style so that people are effectively led. In general, the choice of the pattern or style of leadership depends upon the following factors:

- Skill, personality, and values of the manager
- Forces dominating the subordinates, such as their expectations, aspirations, needs, and values
- Situations such as the type of structure, clarity or ambiguity in defining work and objectives, nature of problems, and pressure of time
- Types of people in the group and the differences in their education, interests, motives, loyalties, and the like

Thus, leadership style varies with different leaders, subordinates, and situations.

LEADERSHIP ATTITUDES

In order to improve a manager's ability to lead, certain attitudes need to be cultivated. These are generally identified as empathy, objectivity, and self-knowledge.

Empathy

Empathy is generally described as the ability of a person to consider things or problems from another person's perspective. It involves projecting oneself into the position of the subordinates who are being directed and led. A manager should not assume that the subordinates would understand issues and problems as he/she perceives them. People differ in their experiences, ability, and understanding of things. Each has his/her own value system and attitudes. Thus, in order to understand their feelings and problems and lead them successfully, a manager must be able to place himself/herself in the position of his/her subordinates.

> The salient leadership traits are empathy, objectivity, and self-knowledge.

Objectivity

In the task of leading, a manager should not be guided by any preconceived notions about the attitude and behaviour of his/her subordinates. Problems and their causes should be evaluated objectively and unemotionally. Thus, instead of getting frustrated with his/her subordinates because results are poor or because changes are resisted, a manager must observe things as they are and objectively analyse the situation. It is only when a manager is unbiased and detached in his/her behaviour towards the members of his/her group that he/she would be able to assess their feelings and problems and guide them. However, this approach needs to be learnt.

Self-awareness

A manager may think himself/herself to be fair and objective, but the subordinates may view him/her otherwise. Managers should, therefore, be aware of how they appear to others and of the effect of their attitude and behaviour on the subordinates. This would help them lead as per the style best liked by their followers. Self-knowledge will help the leader to improve and cultivate those habits and attitudes that evoke a favourable response from the subordinates. For instance, if self-awareness leads a manager to learn that instructions are not properly understood, he/she can attempt to improve his/her ability to communicate.

Exhibit 12.1 discusses a distinctly Indian leadership style.

EXHIBIT 12.1 The Distinct Indian Leadership Style: Putting Subordinates on Top

Studies on leadership have generated volumes of knowledge and insight on how to lead organizations effectively. Studies on organizational culture and leadership have continually highlighted that leadership owes a lot to creating the right organizational culture, which, in turn, is deeply rooted in the culture of the people and the country. Irrespective of these factors, Indian multinational companies, some of the most formidable names in the world today, have exhibited tremendous growth and are poised to grow even more in future. Some obvious factors for such astronomical growth rates coincide with Western companies, whereas certain factors are distinctly Indian.

When it comes to leadership qualities, Indian leaders have, to a large extent, deviated from their Western counterparts. Vineet Nayar, chief executive officer, HCL Technologies, for example, has subverted the way organizations view internal and external customers today. For him, internal customers take precedence over external customers. This U-turn has indeed helped his firm reap the advantages of harnessing the most from a motivated workforce. With over 55,000 employees globally and a turnover of $24 billion, HCL has indeed made a mark in the global informational technology industry.

Nayar has further overseen the process of transparency and employee empowerment through giving employees the opportunity to take decisions when they meet clients. This way he feels the organization will follow an inverted leadership approach, thereby making the top management accountable to the employees and render the position of the chief executive officer irrelevant.

Others, such as B. Muthuraman, managing director, Tata Steel, feel that Indian leaders should be visionaries. By visionary, Muthuraman refers to the qualities of energizing, enthusing, and empowering employees. Typical leadership qualities exhibited by Indian leaders include a preoccupation with the internal management, organizational culture, and long-range planning for the organization. They are not much concerned about financial

(Contd)

EXHIBIT 12.1 *(Contd)*

matters. What rules their list of concerns is motivating employees to improve performance as much as possible and setting examples for others to follow.

Sources: Cappelli, P., H. Singh, J.V. Singh, and M. Useem, 'Leadership Lessons from India', *Harvard Business Review*, March 2010; India Knowledge, 'Are Indian Business Leaders Different', 1 November 2007, http://knowledge.wharton.upenn.edu/india/article.cfm?articleid=4238, last accessed on 3 November 2013 (adapted).

LEADERSHIP SKILLS

A leader has to play many roles to achieve the intended goals and objectives of the organization. It is important to define the skill sets essential for leaders. From a general perspective, we can classify the requirement of such skill sets in the following categories:

Human

In order to win the cooperation of followers, a leader has to successfully resolve more people-oriented issues than job-related issues. He/She must understand human behaviour—know their needs, sentiments, emotions, motivations, and their contemplated actions and reactions to a particular situation. Therefore, without human relations skill, which emphasizes the need to understand people, one cannot be a successful leader. Two essential human skills requirements, namely empathy and objectivity, have already been discussed while explaining leadership attitudes. In addition, a good leader should have communication, teaching, and social skills, which form a part of the human skills. Good communication skills are vital for a leader to be able to persuade, inform, stimulate, direct, and convince the followers. Communication means transfer of information in the form of an understandable message. It helps in establishing and disseminating the goals of the enterprise and enables the leader to create a climate in which people want to perform. Expecting the followers to perform would be futile unless the leader himself/herself successfully demonstrates how to accomplish the tasks. Teaching skills, therefore, also form an important component of human skills. Similarly, to win the confidence and loyalty of followers, leaders should have the requisite social skills; these skills require a leader to understand the followers and be helpful, empathetic, and friendly with them.

Conceptual

Conceptual skill requires sensing the organization from an overall perspective. A leader should have the ability to consider the organization as a whole. He/She should be able to relate to the various functions of the organization and determine how changes affect functions. Having a good understanding of the organization, competitors, financial status of the organization, functional details, and interrelationships between all these skill elements are the essential requirements of conceptual skills.

Technical

Technical skill involves specialized knowledge, analytical skills, and competence (the aggregation of skills, knowledge, and abilities) for performing a job. Moreover, principles, procedures, and operations of a job also add to the technical skills. Therefore, expecting followers to do the jobs without the leaders themselves possessing the requisite technical skills would not be useful.

Personal

To get the best from the followers, a leader should also have the necessary personal skills such as intelligence, emotional maturity, personal motivation, integrity, and flexibility of mind.

LEADERSHIP THEORIES

While discussing the leadership theories, we shall first take a cursory view of the theories and subsequently group them into four major categories.

Contingency Theories

There is a general agreement among the contingency theories that the right or effective leadership style varies according to the context. The Blake and Mouton's managerial grid (1964), which explains this well, has been very influential in organizational development practices.

Instrumental Theories

According to instrumental theories, the leader places emphasis on tasks and person-oriented behaviour (e.g., participation, delegation) to gain effective performance from others.

Inspirational or Transformational Leadership Theories

> The most prominent leadership theories are contingency, instrumental, inspirational or transformational, informal leadership, and path-goal theories.

The inspirational theories include charismatic leaders and transformational leadership. The leader of this category appeals to values and vision and enthuses others by raising their confidence levels and motivating them for change. Such leadership comes from their compelling vision that draws in commitment and acceptance of change and offers a potential for everyone to grow and develop with that vision. The qualities required for a leader are trust, loyalty, devotion, commitment, inspiration, and admiration. House and Shamir (1993) see leadership as the ability of an individual to get an intense moral commitment and a strong identification from subordinates. They list a number of qualities expected of a leader, such as articulating the vision, passion, self-sacrifice, risk-taking, and symbolic behaviours.

Informal Leadership Theory

The informal leadership theory looks at behaviours associated with those who are not appointed by authority but assume leadership in other ways.

Path–Goal Theory

The path–goal theory of Robert House (1991) looks at what leaders must do to motivate people to perform well and to get satisfaction from work. It draws on the expectancy theory of motivation and has four leadership styles—supportive, directive, participative, and achievement-oriented.

Fiedler's Theory

Fiedler (1972) is one of the pioneers of the contingency school. He offered a continuum ranging from task-focused to people-focused leadership. He argued that the most effective style depended on the quality of relationships, relative power position between the leader and the led, and the nature of the task. Fiedler also argued that the style adopted is relatively stable and a feature of a leader's personality and can, therefore, be predicted. He distinguished between tasks-oriented and relation-oriented leaders.

Hersey and Blanchard's Situational Leadership Theory

Hersey and Blanchard's situational leadership dimensions are linked to task and relational behaviours. While task behaviour focuses on defining roles and responsibilities, relational behaviour is more about providing support to teams. The extent to which either is used depends on a person's job maturity and psychological security.

Leadership is a process by which a person influences others to accomplish a mission, task, or objective and directs the organization in a way that makes it more effective. A leader carries this out by applying his/her leadership attributes such as beliefs, values, ethics, character, knowledge, and skills. The authority to accomplish certain tasks and objectives in the organization does not make one a leader. By virtue of power, it simply makes one the boss. Leaders make people achieve goals and objectives, whereas bosses tell people to accomplish a task or an objective.

According to Bass (1989), there are three theories to explain how people become leaders:

Trait theory   Some personality traits may lead people naturally into leadership roles. Good leaders are not born but made. With one's desire and willpower, one can become an effective leader. Good leaders develop through a continuous process of self-study, education, training, and experience.

Great events theory   A crisis or an important event may bring out extraordinary leadership qualities in an ordinary person.

Transformational leadership theory   People can choose to become leaders. They can learn leadership skills. This is the most widely accepted theory today.

The basis of good leadership is honourable character and selfless service to the organization. In the employees' eyes, leadership signifies everything the leader does that affects the organizational objectives and their well-being. A respected leader concentrates on what he/she *is* (beliefs and character), what he/she *knows* (job, tasks, human nature), and what he/she *does* (implement, motivate, provide direction).

What makes a person want to follow a leader? People want to be guided by those they respect and those who have a clear sense of direction. To gain respect, a leader must be ethical. A sense of direction is achieved by conveying a strong vision of the future.

WIDELY ACCLAIMED STUDIES ON LEADERSHIP

The following studies will be discussed in this section.

- Iowa leadership studies (1939)
- Ohio state leadership studies (1945)
- Michigan studies on leadership styles (1961)
- Managerial grid (1978)
- Continuum of leadership behaviour (1973)
- Four framework model (1991)
- Miscellaneous studies

Iowa Leadership Studies

Ronald Lippitt and Ralph K. White conducted the Iowa Leadership studies in 1939 under the supervision of Kurt Lewin at the University of Iowa. Hobby clubs for 10-year-old boys were formed in which the boys were given the tasks of making masks, model airplanes, murals, and soap carvings. Each club was placed under one of the three different styles of leadership—authoritarian, democratic, and laissez-faire. The authoritarian leader was very directive and did not allow any participation. The democratic leader encouraged discussion and participation, and the laissez-faire leader gave complete freedom. Under such experimental conditions, the researchers studied the satisfaction, frustration, and aggression of the boys while they performed their assigned tasks. The study revealed that the boys under the democratic leadership performed better than those who were under the authoritarian and the laissez-faire leadership. However, the study was considered not compatible with formal organizational environments, because preadolescent boys formed the sample and the variables were not adequately controlled. Even so, the study is considered a pioneering attempt and is the first to experimentally determine the effects of leadership styles on groups.

Ohio State Leadership Studies

The Business Research Group of Ohio State University with an interdisciplinary team (psychologists, sociologists, and economists) of researchers analysed the influences of leadership on different groups with the researchers using a structured Leader Behaviour Description Questionnaire (LBDQ). Consideration and initiating structure of leadership, which were formulated in this study, were found to be widely accepted by different heterogeneous groups such as the air force commanders and school superintendents.

Using LBDQ, employees of organizations may map the behaviour of their leaders, which can be either people oriented (consideration type) or task oriented (initiating structure type). Both the types have their own specific advantages and disadvantages. Empirical researches using LBDQ indicate that successful leaders are strong in both people-centric and task-oriented approaches.

Michigan Studies on Leadership Styles

In the Michigan studies, Rensis Likert and his group identified two major styles of leadership—employee participation and production orientation. The employee-centred style resulted in a higher performance compared to the production-centred style. See Fig. 12.1.

Directive, authoritarian, or autocratic style of leadership is based on the assumption that the leader's power is derived from the status and the position that he/she occupies and the subordinate is inherently lazy and unreliable. Democratic or non-directive style of leadership is more concerned with human relationships, and considers that people are basically self-directed and can be made creative at work if properly motivated. In between the two extremes, there is a wide variety of leadership styles.

The third leadership style, that is, the laissez-fair style, permits the members of the group to do whatever they want to do. No policies or procedures are established and everyone is left alone. No one attempts to influence anyone else. Practically, this style develops no leadership at all in the group.

Managerial Grid

Robert R. Blake and Jane S. Mouton have integrated the authoritarian and democratic concepts in a new concept known as the managerial grid. They recognized that leadership style is not either authoritarian or democratic but an admixture of the two philosophies, and the degree of the two components in the mixture will vary according to situations.

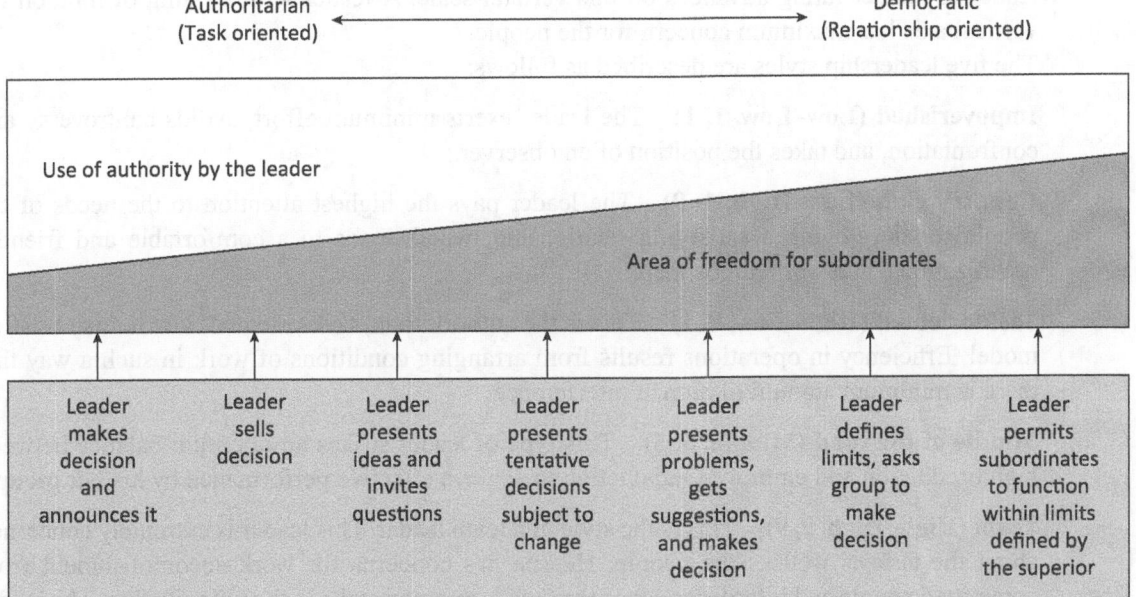

Figure 12.1   Leadership continuum

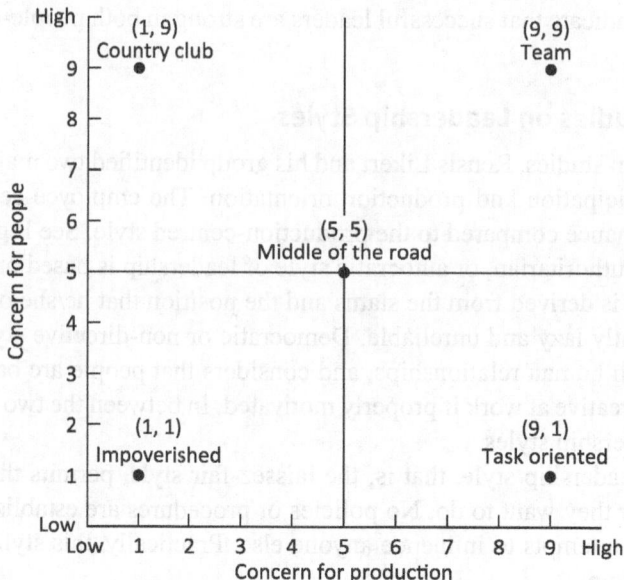

Figure 12.2 Managerial grid

In the managerial grid, five different types of leadership, based on the concern for production (task) and concern for people (relationships), are located in the four quadrants as shown in Fig. 12.2.

Here, concern for production is represented in the horizontal axis. Production becomes more important to the leader as his/her rating advances on this horizontal scale. A leader with a rating of nine on the horizontal axis has maximum concern for production.

Concern for people is illustrated on the vertical axis. People become more important to this leader as his/her rating advances on this vertical scale. A leader with a rating of nine on the vertical axis has maximum concern for the people.

The five leadership styles are described as follows:

Impoverished (Low–Low, 1, 1) The leader exerts minimum effort, avoids controversy and confrontation, and takes the position of an observer.

Country club (Low–High, 1, 9) The leader pays the highest attention to the needs of the people for developing a satisfying relationship, which leads to a comfortable and friendly organizational and work atmosphere.

Task oriented (High–Low, 9, 1) This is the authoritarian, task-oriented, low human relation model. Efficiency in operations results from arranging conditions of work in such a way that there is minimum amount of human interference.

Middle of the road (Middle, 5, 5) This type of leader strikes an optimum balance between high production and employee satisfaction to achieve effective performance by his/her group.

Team (High–High, 9, 9) This is the style of a team leader. This leader is extremely concerned about the task as well as the people. He/She has concerns for work accomplishment from committed people and interdependence through a common stake in the organization. The leader also strives for a relationship of trust and respect.

Theoretically, there are 81 possible positions on the grid and each such position reflects one leadership style. However, the analysis of the grid focuses on the five basic styles listed earlier.

The grid approach is widely accepted in organizations because it helps managers to identify their individual leadership styles, based on which they evolve a framework for the ideal leader and develop suitable training programmes. However, it lacks empirical evidence. Only a few organizations can put them into use due to the wide differences in the prevailing cultures and practices.

An important extension of the managerial grid approach is Reddin's three-dimensional grid (1971), which is also known as three-dimensional management. The three-dimensional axes represent task orientation, relationship orientation, and effectiveness. By adding the effectiveness dimension to task orientation and relationship orientation, Reddin had actually tried to integrate leadership styles with the situational variables. Task orientation is defined as the leader's direction given to followers in connection with the achievement of goals. It is concerned with planning, organizing, and controlling. Relationship orientation is defined as the extent of personal relationships of leaders with followers. It is achieved through mutual trust and respect for the followers' ideas. If the style of a leader is appropriate to a given situation, we call it effective; otherwise, it is ineffective. On the basis of this model, we can explain the four styles of leadership as shown in Fig. 12.3.

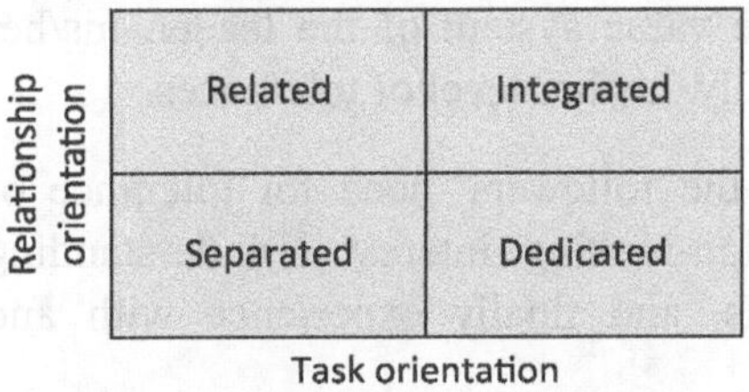

| | Related | Integrated |
| Relationship orientation | Separated | Dedicated |

Task orientation

Figure 12.3 Task and relationship orientation model

These four styles represent the four basic types of behaviour. A separated leader is concerned with correcting deviations. A related leader accepts others, does not bother about time, looks at the organization as a social system, loves to work with others, and receives cooperation from others (followers) by setting examples. A dedicated manager dominates and is interested only in production. He/She never identifies himself/herself with subordinates. He/She only works with power. The integrated leader gets self and followers involved with the organization. He/She emphasizes teamwork. Any of these styles may be effective in one situation but not in another. We can illustrate these styles, categorizing them into two types, namely less effective style and more effective style, as shown in Table 12.2.

Continuum of Leadership Behaviour

Tannenbaum and Schmidt have explained the range of possible leadership styles on a continuum from authoritarian to free rein. Figure 12.4 illustrates a number of leadership behaviours. On the left side of the continuum, leaders enjoy a high degree of control and believe in less delegation of authority. On the extreme right side, leaders give their followers freedom and show

Table 12.2 Leadership styles

Basic style	Less effective style	More effective style
Integrated	Compromiser	Executive
Dedicated	Autocrat	Benevolent autocrat
Related	Missionary	Developer
Separated	Deserter	Bureaucrat

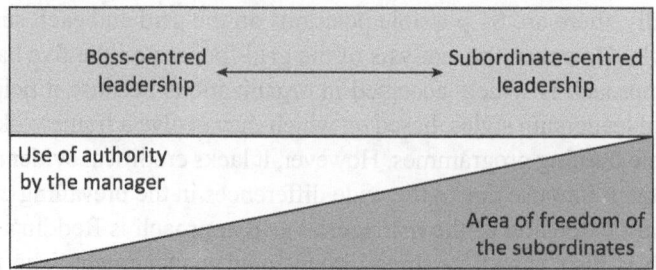

Figure 12.4 Continuum of leadership behaviour

their initiative in work-related matters. A leader moves along the continuum based on three forces, namely forces in the leader, the followers, and the situation.

Forces in leaders These forces are influenced by the value system of the leader, his/her confidence in the followers, his/her inclinations, and finally, his/her level of tolerances.

Forces in followers These forces are influenced by the followers' need for tolerance of ambiguity, readiness to assume responsibility for decision-making, interest in understanding problems, level of understanding organizational goals, and finally experience with and expectations from their leaders.

Forces in situations These forces include the type of organization, its problems, group effectiveness, and time pressure.

The continuum theory provides a wide range of leadership behaviours, and its success depends on the behavioural flexibility of the leader as per the demands of situations. However, the basic difficulty in the theory lies in the fact that it supports unidimensional thinking. Increase or decrease of any particular type of behaviour may decrease or increase the other type of behaviour. Another important aspect of this theory that the researchers have focused on is that employee orientation and task orientation are not the opposite ends on a continuum. It means that if a leader becomes more employee oriented, he/she need not necessarily become less task oriented. The Ohio studies also corroborated this.

Four Framework Model

The four framework model of leadership was suggested by Bolman and Deal, attributing leadership to structural, human relations, political, and symbolic types. Depending on the situation, a leader adopts one style or the other and accordingly varies the behavioural pattern. The effectiveness or otherwise of the behavioural pattern of a leader is highly dependent on his/ her choice of leadership style and analysis of the prevailing situation. These frameworks are briefly illustrated here:

Structural framework Leaders who adopt the structural framework play the role of a social architect; they analyse every situation and act accordingly. They behave like a system- and structure-bound bureaucrat but, at the same time, become adaptable to the environmental needs while drawing their strategy. However, at times, they may be insensitive to the needs of the followers.

Human resource framework   In this case, the leaders act as catalysts, support and empower their followers, repose trust in them, and believe in transparency in decision-making. This type of leader enjoys greater participation from followers who respect such leaders and comply with their directives for achieving the organizational goals and objectives. On the negative side, these leaders may also be manipulators.

Political framework   A political leader with a positive outlook becomes an advocate of and helps in team building. A political leader with a negative outlook is a manipulator. These leaders balance the distribution of power and interest by establishing linkages with various stakeholders. However, at times, they may be coercive and may force followers to comply with their orders.

Symbolic framework   Leaders of this type inspire their followers and captivate their attention by effectively communicating their vision. They help their followers to dream and make an effort to transform their dreams into reality. On the negative side, such leaders may be fanatics and may keep their followers waiting.

The appropriate model of leadership depends on the leaders' selection of style after analysing the given situation. Again, any particular model may not be sufficient to tackle every situation. Here, we can illustrate an organizational example to clarify this point. After acquiring Philips, Videocon adopted the structural model of leadership to effect the transformation process. Thereafter, Videocon quickly shifted to the symbolic framework of leadership to achieve accelerated growth in the highly competitive consumer electronics sector. Thus, the approach that will work better depends on the leader who analyses the situation and then decides the right fit of leadership style.

Miscellaneous Studies on Leadership

Various other studies and theories also discuss leadership. These include the scientific manager's style of F.W. Taylor (1911), contingency theory of leadership by F.E. Fiedler (1967), group and exchange theories of leadership by Hollander and Julian (1969), path–goal theory by R.K. House (1971), trait theory of J. Kelly (1974), social learning theories by A. Bandura (1977), and situational leadership approach by Kenneth Blanchard, Patricia Zigarmi, and Dera Zigarmi (1990). Among all these theories, the situational approach is preferred for its relevance to real-life work situations and more particularly for its applicability in the service sector also. Hence, this has been discussed in detail in this text.

GROUPING OF LEADERSHIP THEORIES

From the preceding discussions on theories, we can group various leadership theories into the following four categories:

- Trait theory
- Behavioural theory
- Situational theory
- Great man theory

These four theories of leadership are discussed in this section.

Trait Theory

The trait theory seeks to determine the personal characteristics of effective leaders. It points out that the personal traits or characteristics of a person make him/her an effective or successful leader. Charles Bird examined 20 lists of traits attributed to leaders in various surveys and found that none of the traits appeared on all lists. Leaders exhibit a wide variety of traits ranging from neatness to nobility. They are presumed to display better judgement and engage themselves in social activities. The study of the lives of successful leaders reveals that they possessed many of these traits. According to the trait theory, successful leaders exhibit the following characteristics:

Good personality Physical characteristics and the level of maturity determine the personality of an individual. The success of a leader depends to a great extent on his/her having a good personality.

Intellectual ability The level of intelligence of a leader should be higher than that of his/her followers. Intellectual ability enables a leader to analyse the situation accurately and take decisions accordingly.

Initiative A leader should take initiative to start activities on time.

> The trait theory of leadership seeks to determine the personal characteristics of effective leaders. These are good personality, intellectual ability, flexibility and adaptability, self-confidence, maturity, objectivity and fairness, and being considerate.

Imagination This is another essential trait for a successful leader. He/She must be able to visualize trends and adopt the right course of action to achieve the result.

Maturity A leader should have emotional maturity and balanced temperament. Maturity is reflected through behavioural tolerance.

Responsibility A leader should accept responsibility for his/her actions (irrespective of the results). This creates a positive impression on the followers.

Self-confidence A leader should be self-confident. His/Her self-confidence will motivate his/her followers and boost their morale.

Flexibility and adaptability To become flexible and adaptable, a leader should have an open mind to accept others' viewpoints. This will foster innovation and creativity in the organization.

Objectivity and fairness   In dealing with followers, a leader should be objective and fair. This trait makes a leader honest, fair, impartial, and unbiased.

Being considerate   A leader who is considerate with the followers is able to win their cooperation, which adds to his/her success.

Limitations of Trait Theory

The trait theory, critics argue, suffers from certain limitations, which are as follows:

- One of the major limitations of this theory is that it assumes leadership as an inborn quality. This is not always correct. Leadership quality can also be developed through training. Even by successful handling of a crisis situation, one can emerge as a leader. This has happened in the case of Russi Mody on 1 May 1947 at the Jamshedpur plant of Tata Iron and Steel Company, where he could pacify the militant workmen who were beating the company's executives and supervisors.
- A particular trait or some traits may help a leader to successfully manage a particular situation. However, he/she may fail in other situations. It is also difficult to find a leader with all such listed traits.
- There is no quantitative tool to measure a trait or traits. The absence or presence of traits could be understood only when a situation occurs and a leader manages or fails to manage the situation.
- The list of personal traits is only indicative and not exhaustive. A successful leader may also have other traits such as foresight, vision, being methodical, and being thorough.
- Personal traits form only a very small part of leadership. In order to be a successful leader, one must have other qualities as well. Hence, measuring leadership quality only in terms of personal traits may not result in accurate inferences.

Behavioural Theory

As per the behavioural theory of leadership, a particular behaviour of a leader provides greater satisfaction to the followers. Such behavioural attribute enables followers to recognize a leader. This theory is based on the premise that a leader plays a role behaviour, using his/her conceptual, human, and technical skills, which influence the behaviour of the followers. Behaviour is not a trait—it sets a particular role pattern. For example, a leader may have a nurturing parent behaviour, which appreciates the problems of followers and even cajoles them when they fail to deliver. A leader may also have a critical parent behaviour, which depicts the critical nature in dealing with such situations. Such leaders never appreciate but only reprimand.

> According to the behavioural theory of leadership, a particular behaviour of a leader provides greater satisfaction to the followers.

Limitations of Behavioural Theory

The limitations suffered by the behavioural theory are listed as follows:

- The behavioural theory cannot justify why a particular leadership behaviour is effective in one case but fails in another case. For example, the nurturing parent behaviour may be effective to stop recurrence of failure on the part of subordinates in one case; however, it may not work in another case, where followers may take advantage of this behaviour of their leader and repeat the mistake committed earlier. Critical parent behaviour could have been better in the second situation.

- This theory does not recognize the traits of leaders. Certain traits, however, may make a successful leader.

Situational or Contingency Theory

Situational or contingency theory holds that leadership emerges from a situation—that is, how a leader performs in a given situation. People tend to follow a leader who is capable of fulfilling their aspirations in a given situation. A leader performs as per the need of the situation. Hence, his/her style may differ from situation to situation. Again, we can cite the example of Russi Mody, who had emerged as a leader because of his proactive way of dealing with the militant workmen.

The trait and behavioural approaches to leadership showed that effective leadership depends on many variables, such as the organizational culture, nature of tasks, and personalities and attributes of leaders as well as followers. However, there is no single common trait for all leaders. Likewise, no single type of leadership can be effective in all situations. This approach assumes that leaders are constructs of situations. A number of studies have been carried out to understand the situational leadership theory. Primarily, this theory focuses on three factors:

> Situational or contingency theory of leadership holds that leadership emerges from a situation—that is, how a leader performs in a given situation.

- Task requirements
- Peers' expectations and behaviours
- Organizational culture and policies

The following are the four popular theories of situational leadership:

- Fiedler's contingency approach
- Path–Goal theory
- Vroom–Yetton model
- Hersey and Blanchard's situational leadership model

Fiedler's Contingency Approach

Fiedler's contingency approach to leadership rests on the premise that people become leaders not only on the strength of their personality attributes but also on the strength of different situational factors and the interactions between them and their followers. To illustrate his assumptions further, Fiedler identified three critical dimensions that determine the style of leadership—position power, task structure, and leader–member relations. Position or the role power being conferred by the organization, a leader with more position power can draw the followers more easily. Similarly, leadership becomes more effective when tasks are well defined, because of which the quality and quantity of performance of people can be easily measured and the responsibility of people for task accomplishment can be easily defined. According to Fiedler, the quality and degree of leader–member relations can also determine the effectiveness of a leader, because good leader–member relations ensure more control over subordinates. Based on his theory, Fiedler identified two major styles of leadership—task oriented and employee centred. To understand whether a leader is task oriented or people centred and also to measure the style of leadership, Fiedler used the scores of two scales—least preferred co-worker (LPC) and assumed similarity between opposites (ASO). Using the results of these two scales, Fiedler proved that people work best with those with whom they can relate to. Fiedler's leadership model suggests that by matching leadership style (based on LPC) with the situation (position power, task structure, leader–member relations) organizations can get the best results.

Path–Goal Theory

Path–Goal theory is mainly the outcome of research by Robert J. House and Terence R. Mitchell. The theory explains that a leader can achieve the best results by showing the subordinates the best path, removing their obstacles, and thus helping them accomplish the organizational goals. Based on this premise, this theory suggests four leadership styles—instrumental, supportive, participative, and achievement-oriented.

Instrumental   This leadership behaviour can provide clear guidelines to subordinates by describing the work methods, schedules, standards, evaluation parameters, and rewards. It corresponds more to task-oriented leadership behaviour.

Supportive   This leadership behaviour creates a pleasant organizational climate, showing concern for the subordinates. In this case, leaders emphasize more on the relationship-oriented behaviour.

Participative   This leadership entails participation of subordinates in decision-making and encourages them to make suggestions. Hence, this style enhances the level of motivation of subordinates. The Hawthorne studies, Kurt Lewin (1947) and Likert (1961, 1967), discuss participative styles of leadership, which lead to increased job satisfaction and higher performance.

Achievement-oriented   This leadership behaviour focuses on setting up goals to help subordinates to perform at their best-possible levels. This style inculcates confidence and makes people develop their capabilities.

Vroom–Yetton Model

This model, pioneered by Victor Vroom and Philip Yetton, suggests the extent to which a manager should involve employees in solving specific problems. It further suggests that the manager should accordingly decide the appropriate style of leadership. The model identifies the following five styles of leadership, based on the subordinates' degree of participation in decision-making:

Autocratic I — AI   This type of leader or manager solves the problem or makes the decision himself/herself, using the available information.

Autocratic II — AII   In this case, leaders or managers obtain information from subordinates and then make their own decisions.

Consultative I — CI   In this case, leaders or managers discuss the problems with the relevant subordinates individually, obtain their ideas and suggestions, and then decide the courses of action, which may or may not have the inputs obtained from the subordinates.

Consultative II — CII   In this case, leaders or managers discuss the problems with the subordinates as a group, obtain their ideas and suggestions, and then take decisions, which again may or may not be influenced by subordinates' views.

Group II — GII   In this approach, managers discuss the problems with the subordinates as a group, generate and analyse alternatives together, reach a consensus, and then take a decision. Here, the leaders or managers do not try to impose their decisions but rather help the subordinates to evolve their own solution models, based on the inputs shared.

Hersey and Blanchard's Situational Leadership Model

The basic premise of Hersey and Blanchard's situational leadership model is that leaders need to alter their behavioural style, in line with the major situational factor and the readiness of the followers. Readiness is the desire for achievement, willingness to accept responsibility, and the ability of the subordinates to handle a particular task. To ensure this, Hersey and Blanchard proposed four different phases.

In phase one, the managers clearly spell out the duties and responsibilities to the group. In phase two, the group members and employees learn their tasks, and if required, they take guidance from the managers. In phase three, employees build their capability and volunteer for increased responsibility. In the fourth and last phase, followers do not require directions from the managers and can take their own decisions.

The basic contention of this model is that the leadership style should be dynamic and flexible to determine which style contributes more in a given situation. An appropriate fit of leadership style not only motivates employees but also increases their capabilities and aids them in their professional development.

Limitations   The following are the limitations of this theory:

* The major limitation of this theory is that it emphasizes the leadership of a leader in a given situation. If the situation changes, there is no mention as to whether a person still continues to be a leader. The best examples are the trade union leaders. Their followers may reject their leadership if they fail to meet their expectations in different situations.
* Since situations change, the same style may not guarantee success in all situations. Further, the style of leadership is also influenced by the particular traits and behavioural roles of a leader.

Great Man Theory

The great man theory emphasizes that leaders are born and not made. Hence, great leaders are natural leaders. It is partly true that some leadership qualities cannot be obtained even through training. For example, commanding personality, charm, courage, intelligence, persuasiveness, and aggressiveness cannot be acquired through training. This theory therefore emphasizes that leadership qualities are inborn, and hence, ordinarily people cannot become leaders. This is the oldest approach and Galton Gas had done some studies on this in the later half of the 19th century.

Limitations   The following are the limitations of this theory:

* This theory is not scientific and has no empirical basis. In many cases, this theory can be easily disproved.
* It also does not explain who leaders are and how they emerge as leaders.

LANGUAGE OF LEADERS

The language used by leaders is a powerful tool they use to motivate people, win people, and turn things their way. A few important examples of the language used by leaders are given here:
    The six most important words: 'I admit I made a mistake.'
    The five most important words: 'You did a good job.'

Boringness: The Secret to Great Leadership

Until recently, I hadn't really known any great leaders. As a writer, the highest-ranking people I deal with are editors, and they're pretty much just writers who have gotten lazy. The only thing an editor has ever led me into is a bar.

Read this insightful blog posted by Stein on *HBR Blog Network* by accessing the following link: http://blogs. hbr.org/cs/2012/05/boringness_the_secret_to_great.html.

The four most important words: 'What is your opinion?'
The three most important words: 'If you please.'
The two most important words: 'Thank you.'
The one most important word: 'We'
The least important word: 'I'
Exhibit 12.2 explains how leadership and innovation are complementary forces.

EXHIBIT 12.2 Leadership and Innovation: Complementary Forces

Leadership and innovation, in the present-day business scenario, go hand in hand. The most relevant example would obviously be Steve Jobs, and he is not the only one. Most business leaders who have made it big owe a lot to their innovation apart from effectively leading their organizations. As for an innovative leader, a study published by Forbes notes five salient characteristic features:

Questioning

This refers to challenging established norms, beliefs, and practices and exploring new possibilities.

Observing

This refers to keeping a track of minute details of the behaviour exhibited by customers, employees, vendors, and other stakeholders.

Networking

This helps innovative leaders to gain exposure from people of diverse backgrounds.

Experimenting

This helps in exploring new possibilities, testing new ideas, and staying ahead of the competition.

Associational Thinking

This helps in correlating problems, ideas, and questions of unrelated fields.

On the other hand, a study conducted by McKinsey has concluded that not many organizations or managers are keen to pursue innovation. Most leaders, despite admitting the need for innovation in the growth of organizations, have only resorted to innovative business practices on an ad hoc basis. The study further suggests that in order to nurture innovative leadership in organizations, management should take the following actions:

- Practise innovation as the foremost priority.
- Transform select managers and leaders of innovation.
- Come up with provisions for managed experimentation and rapid success.

Sources: Upbin, B., 'The Five Habits of Highly Innovative Leaders', 20 July 2011, http://www.forbes.com/sites/bruceupbin/2011/07/20/the-five-habits-of-highly-innovative-leaders/, last accessed on 3 September 2013; Barsh, J., M. Capozzi, and M. Davidson, 'Leadership and Innovation', January 2008, http://www.mckinsey.com/insights/innovation/leadership_and_innovation, last accessed on 3 November 2013 (adapted).

LEADERSHIP COMPETENCIES

Competencies are the desired set of skills, knowledge, attitudes, underlying characteristics, or behaviours that differentiate effective performers from ineffective ones (Boyatzis 1982; McLagan 1996). The competency-based leadership approach requires organizations to identify the appropriate leadership skills and behaviours that enhance the performance of the organizations. Moreover, once the competencies are recognized, organizations can also use them for developing future leaders. Though there are some generic leadership competencies common to every leader in every organization, organizations also need to identify the specific leadership attributes that can enhance their competitive advantages. Such identified leadership attributes are then used to determine the set of competencies required for their leaders.

McCall and Hollenbeck (2002) identified some universal set of leadership competencies as follows:

- Open-mindedness and flexibility in thoughts and tactics
- Cultural interest and sensitivity
- Ability to deal with complexity
- Resilience, resourcefulness, optimism, and energy
- Honesty and integrity
- Stable personal life
- Value-added technical or business skills

ENTREPRENEURIAL LEADERSHIP

Organizations today face mounting pressure due to the competitive environment. To cope with this, they need entrepreneurial leaders, who are different from the other behavioural forms of leaders. Entrepreneurial leaders function like self-employed persons. They have a proactive attitude and take initiatives on their own to improve things in the organization. This type of leader demonstrates entrepreneurial creativity and always explores new opportunities, takes risks, ventures into new areas, and provides strategic direction and inspiration to their personnel. Moreover, this type of leader also takes responsibility for the failures of his/her team members.

> An entrepreneurial leader functions like a self-employed person. They have a proactive attitude and take initiatives on their own to improve things in the organization.

In the new era of rapid changes and knowledge-based enterprises, managerial work is increasingly becoming a leadership task. Leadership is the primary force behind a successful change. Leaders empower employees to act on the organizational vision. They execute through inspiration and develop implementation capacity networks through a complex web of aligned relationships.

CROSS-CULTURAL LEADERSHIP

Globalization has increased the cross-border trades and exchanges, increasing cross-cultural interactions in organizations across the globe. Many leadership researches are currently taking place, acknowledging the importance of cross-cultural leadership. Some of the researchers even came out with a global leadership competency model to guide the organizations to equip their leaders on cross-cultural interactions. The influence of culture on leadership has to be understood in terms of the contributions of Hofstede (1980), who had seen culture as the collective programme of the mind that differentiates one group of people from another. Although there are no agreed definitions on leadership, there is more or less a consensus that leadership is a process of exerting influence on the behaviour of others. Cross-cultural leadership, therefore, exerts influence on the behaviour of culturally different groups of people to achieve some goals. An example of a cross-cultural leader is an expatriate leader. Many organizations require their managers and leaders to manage their activities across several countries. Hence, developing cross-cultural leadership competence has now become important, or else the managers may fail in delivering the desired results. The scope of cross-cultural leadership varies even within a country, because of the differences in regional culture and diversity.

Cross-cultural leadership styles follow either emic or etic approaches. Emic approach considers one culture at a particular time to map the leadership behaviours. For example, an Indian manager understanding the culture of Kazakhstan for effective management of the people there to achieve results is an emic approach. Etic approach, on the contrary, takes into account multiple cultures at the same time to map the leadership behaviours. For example, an Indian leader managing international operations spread across several countries has to develop a cross-cultural leadership competence following an etic approach.

SUMMARY

This chapter discusses the various concepts of leadership, drawing lessons from organizational practices across the globe. Leadership is the art or process of influencing people so that they willingly strive towards achieving the goals of the organization. Organizational effectiveness depends not only on the talent available in the organization but also on the quality of leadership available at its disposal. An organization's success depends on the ability of its leaders to align individual goals to business goals and objectives and to bring out the best out of all the members through resolution of conflict and proper team building. The process of obtaining technical and management skills is comparatively simpler than acquiring the skills and qualities of a true leader, because leadership skills—though inherent in each individual—need self-realization to make one lead or follow. Leaders will have to take greater responsibilities as changes in perceptions, thoughts, optimization processes, and organizational interventions will take place at a fast pace. However, it is important to remember that no particular style may prove successful in all situations. Situational changes determine the leadership style. Today, organizations across the world consider leadership as one of the important training needs required to gain competitive advantage. Hence, building leadership is one of the highest priorities of organizations. It requires a systematic understanding of the existing skills and proficiency of the employees and suitably training them through a methodical approach.

KEY DEFINITION

Conceptual skill This requires sensing the organization from an overall perspective, such as an understanding of the organization, competitors, financial status, functional details, and their interrelationships.

Contingency approach This approach helps ensure the goodness of fit between the prevailing organizational structure and different situational factors.

Entrepreneurial leadership This type of leadership demonstrates entrepreneurial creativity and explores new opportunities, takes risks, ventures into new areas, and provides strategic direction and inspiration to the people. This type of leader also takes responsibility for the failures of his/her team members.

Fiedler's contingency approach This approach rests on the premise that people become leaders on the strength of not only their personality attributes but also different situational factors and the interactions between them and their followers. Fiedler identified three critical dimensions that determine the style of leadership—position power, task structure, and leader–member relations.

Paternalistic leadership This type of leader assumes his/her functions like that of a father. Paternalistic leaders treat their followers as members of their family, guide and protect them, and keep them happy so that they work as family members.

Psychological view of leadership This view believes that leadership is more effective when leaders or managers account for the psychological constructs of employees, which basically emerge from their perceived needs.

Sociological view of leadership This view considers the leadership function to include setting goals, shaping and reshaping organizations, and reconciling internal and external forces. It is a creative function of the leader; it calls for viewing and reviewing the organizational environment and work accomplishments and determining the short- and long-term goals.

CONCEPT-REVIEW QUESTIONS

12.1 Briefly state the history of leadership. Why is leadership so important in organizations today?

12.2 Is leadership different from management? Explain.

12.3 What are the important characteristics of leadership?

12.4 State the significance and principles of leadership.

12.5 How does the environment affect leadership styles? Can the culture and climate of an organization affect the leadership of an organization?

12.6 Write short notes on the following:
(a) Communication and leadership
(b) Laissez-faire style of leadership
(c) Transformational leader
(d) Paternalistic leader
(e) Leadership and empathy

CRITICAL THINKING QUESTIONS

12.1 Is leadership an exertion of power? Explain the relationship between leadership and power in the context of an organization engaged in a protocol-bound manufacturing operation, where time standards are fixed for each operation and any deviation can cause great harm to the entire production chain.

12.2 In a collective bargaining situation, where management and union leaders (as representatives of workers) deliberate on work-related issues and come to a consensus, both the management and the union representatives indulge in a power game. However, the leadership styles are different for the management personnel and the trade union representatives. Enumerate and explain the differences.

SELECT BIBLIOGRAPHY

- Avery, G. and E. Baker, *Psychology at Work*, Prentice-Hall, New York, 1990.
- Bass, Bernard, *Stogdill's Handbook of Leadership: A Survey of Theory and Research*, Free Press, New York, 1989.
- Bass, B.M. and B.J. Avolio, *MLQ Multifactor Leadership Questionnaire for Research: Permission Set*, Mind Garden, Redwood City, 1995.
- Bass, Bernard, 'From Transactional to Transformational Leadership: Learning to Share the

Vision', *Organizational Dynamics*, Vol. 18, Issue 3, 1990, pp. 19–31.

- Bass, Bernard M., *Bass and Stogdill's Hand Book of Leadership*, Free Press, New York, 1990.
- Bennis, Warren and Bert Nanus, *Leaders: Strategies for Taking Charge*, Harper Business, 1997.
- Blake, Robert R. and Jane S. Mouton, *The Managerial Grid*, Gulf Publishing Co., Houston, 1964.
- Bolman, Lee G. and Terrence Deal, *Reframing Organizations: Artistry, Choice, and Leadership*, Jossey-Bass, San Francisco, 1991.
- Boyatzis, R.E., *The Competent Manager: A Model for Effective Performance*, John Wiley, New York, 1982.
- Campbell, Joseph, *The Power of Myth: Interviews with Bill Moyers*, Vol. 6, 2nd ed., Society Series, Basil Blackwell, Oxford, 1991.
- Davis, Keith, *Human Behaviour at Work*, Tata McGraw Hill Publishing Company Limited, New Delhi, 1999.
- French, W.L., *Human Resource Management*, 4th ed., Houghton Miffin, Boston, 1990.
- Haynes, Andy, *'3 Brilliant Leadership Qualities I Learned from NASA'*, http://fullstart.com/knowledge/3-brilliant-leadership-qualities-learned-nasa/, last accessed on 23 January, 2014.
- Hofstede, G., *Culture's Consequences: International Differences in Work-related Values*, Sage, London, 1980.
- Hersey, Paul, Kenneth H. Blanchard, and Dewey E. Johnson, *Management of Organizational Behaviour—Leading Human Resources*, Pearson Education, New Delhi, 2001.
- Koontz, Harold, Cyril O'Donnell, and Heinz Weihrich, *Essentials of Management*, Tata McGraw-Hill Publishing Company Limited, New Delhi, 2008.
- Kouzes, James M. and Barry Z. Posner, *The Leadership Challenge*, Jossey-Bass, San Francisco, 1987.

- Kotter, John P., *Leading Change*, Harvard Business School Press, 1996.
- Lamb, L.F. and K.B. McKee, *Applied Public Relations: Cases in Stakeholder Management*, Lawrence Erlbaum Associates, New Jersey, 2004.
- Lewin, K. 'Frontiers in Group Dynamics', *Human Relations*, Vol. 1, Issue 1, 1947, pp. 5–42.
- Likert, R., *New Patterns of Management*, Harper and Row, New York, 1961.
- Likert, R., *The Human Organization*, McGraw-Hill, New York, 1967.
- McCall, M. and G. Hollenbeck, *Developing Global Executives: The Lessons of International Experience*, Harvard Business School Publishing, Boston, 2002.
- McFarland, Lynne Joy, Larry E. Senn, and John R. Childress, *21st Century Leadership: Dialogues with 100 Top Leaders*, The Leadership Press, New York, 1994.
- McLagan, P., 'Great Ideas Revisited', *Training and Development*, Vol. 50, Issue 1, 1996, pp. 60–6.
- Raven, B. and J. Rubin, *Social Psychology: People in Groups*, John Wiley and Sons, New York, 1976.
- Robbins, Stephen P., *Organizational Behaviour*, Prentice-Hall of India, New Delhi, 2005.
- Selznick, P., *Leadership in Administration: A Sociological Interpretation*, Harper and Row, New York, 1957.
- Tannenbaum, Robert, Irving B. Weschler, and Fred Massarick, *Leadership and Organization*, McGraw Hill, New York, 1979.
- Tannenbaum, Robert and Warren H. Schmidt, 'How to Change a Leadership Pattern, *Harvard Business Review*, Vol. 3, Issue 51, 1973, p. 180.
- Terry, G., *The Principles of Management*, Richard Irwin Inc., Homewood, 1960.
- Vecchio, Robert P., *Organizational Behaviour*, Dryden, Chicago, 1988.

CASE STUDY

A Leadership Case Study—MOVEFAST

The most compelling human resource (HR) issue for today's organizations is leadership. Why do people change jobs? Many feel that the boss factor is responsible for this. The HR director of MOVE-FAST, a new generation management consulting organization, which has grown to the level of a first-tier consulting organization with an annual turnover of $1 billion within a span of five years, also has the same opinion. The company's core business is manpower recruitment for client organizations and providing consultancy support in HR and strategic issues. With 350 seasoned management consultants, the company operates from nine different locations in India, South East Asia, and South Africa. The company's per employee business volume is internationally benchmarked and it now grows at an annual rate of 30 per cent. With globalization and new market opportunities, the company is now poised for expansion of business in three more locations: the US, Canada, and the UK. As part of the company's value systems, people are recruited for consultant positions from premier business schools in India. After induction into its New Delhi-based corporate headquarters, the consultants are posted to different locations, depending on their area of specialization and business requirement.

A major crisis that the company is now facing is an increasing role conflict and lack of tolerance among young management graduates, who always feel that the boss still lives in his/her old school of thoughts in managing MOVEFAST's business. The HR director of the company is based in New Delhi and reviews the performance records of all the management consultants operating from different locations. His current review indicated that the mismatch between self-appraisal and boss rating is unjustifiable in 80 per cent cases. He wonders why they are being perceived differently when, in terms of achievement of business growth, the management graduates deliver. In some of the ratings, even the heads (boss) alleged that their executives lack mannerism and do not always listen to the directives given to them. They work more in isolation.

The HR director is having serious problems in talent retention. Experienced management graduates are now the most sought-after candidates in consulting organizations, including international ones. Realizing this, the HR director recently reframed the people policies and the HR's own delivery system. Supporting organizational effectiveness has been given the main emphasis to measure the performance. In order to function more strategically, the HR department outsourced labour cost management and administration to an HR outsourcing organization. From the confidential exit-interview reports of those who had resigned earlier, the HR director could understand that the major issue is poor interpersonal relations with their superiors. He then subjected all managers and executives to go through a team role exercise, using a standard structured psychometric tool, internationally known as Belbin Team Role Test. Based on the test, the 350 consultants have been categorized as shown in the following table:

Belbin team role type	Contributions	Allowable weaknesses
Plant (40)	Creative, imaginative, unorthodox, solves difficult problems	Ignores incidentals, too preoccupied to communicate effectively
Coordinator (50)	Mature, confident, a good chairperson, clarifies goals, promotes decision-making, delegates well	Can often be seen as manipulative, offloads personal work
Monitor evaluator (50)	Sober, strategic, and discerning, considers all options, judges accurately	Lacks drive and ability to inspire others
Implementer (30)	Disciplined, reliable, conservative, efficient, turns ideas into practical actions	Slightly inflexible, slow to respond to new possibilities
Completer finisher (25)	Painstaking, conscientious, anxious, searches out errors and omissions, delivers on time.	Inclined to worry unduly, reluctant to delegate

(Contd)

Belbin team role type	Contributions	Allowable weaknesses
Resource investigator (35)	Extrovert, enthusiastic, communicative, explores opportunities, develops contacts	Over-optimistic, loses interest once initial enthusiasm has passed
Shaper (25)	Challenging, dynamic, thrives on pressure, has the drive and courage to overcome obstacles	Prone to provocation, offends people's feelings
Teamworker (15)	Cooperative, mild, perceptive, diplomatic, listens, builds, averts friction	Indecisive in crunch situations
Specialist (80)	Single-minded, self-starting, dedicated, provides knowledge and skills in rare supply	Contributes only on a narrow front, dwells on technicalities

The results of the test helped indicate the category to which the various executives belonged.

Questions for Discussion

1. You are now required to suggest what course of action the HR director should take to develop the leadership culture of the organization.

2. Apart from the reasons mentioned in the case, can you identify other reasons for people leaving organizations?

Power and Politics in Organizations

LEARNING OBJECTIVES

After studying this chapter, the reader will be able to

- understand the process of managing power and politics in an organization
- discuss how power can be balanced to create a culture of mutual trust and respect in the organization
- explain the various sources of power
- describe the process of employee empowerment
- understand organizational politics and its dysfunctional effect on organizations

CASE STUDY

Misuse of Power

Thomas, a manager of a large retail chain, believed in applying pressure on newly appointed store sales representatives to get better results from them. He would insult them and also make critical comments about their work. The sales representatives were not appreciated even when they exceeded the expected standards, and would, instead, get the message 'deliver more'. The manager considered his habit of making open as well as behind-the-back derogatory remarks about the subordinates as his core leadership strength. To show his anger, he, at times, even threw items on the sales representatives in front of others and made them cry. Retail chains operate in a very competitive market with new players entering the market almost every month. Sales representatives play an important role in helping the stores survive in the market. Most of the newly recruited sales representatives in Thomas' store were in their teens. They considered his behaviour to be largely like that of a critical father who never understood how to get friendly with them to get the work done. Not everyone could endure such a tormenting work environment. As a result, 90 per cent of the newly recruited sales representatives left their jobs after six months of work, causing tremendous pressure on the rest to ensure customer service. Thomas became even more ferocious and started assaulting the remaining employees, making them take up the responsibilities of even those who had left the organization. One evening, when the store was overcrowded with customers, he suddenly started shouting at his sales personnel, asking them to withdraw from the workstations and report to his office. The issue was 'reduced sales volume in the past week'. One of the boys stated that it was because of the reduced number of salespersons that they could not cater to all customers in person.

Thomas asked this boy to come closer. While he went near, Thomas was about to slap the boy for such remarks. Apprehending his intention, the boy suddenly caught Thomas' hand and twisted it, making Thomas fall on the floor. All the other boys followed suit and attacked him; even some of the girls joined the fray. In no time, Thomas

became unconscious and was rescued by the customers. He was admitted to a hospital after undergoing a massive heart attack. The managing director of the company rushed to the spot. After enquiring into the details, he decided to sack Thomas for his failure to manage the employees and for being responsible for gross misbehaviour at the workplace. Thomas' behaviour threatened the professional status and personal standing of the employees and made them a victim of overwork. All these formed a suitable case for bullying at the workplace. On his recovery, Thomas went to court but the court prima facie rejected his plea for reinstatement, upholding the employer's decision.

Managers often resort to bullying at the workplace to exert power. However, this leads to adverse situations, similar to what was seen in this case.

INTRODUCTION

Power is the potentiality of a person to exert influence over others. In organizations, it principally operates through direct control. The right to command is granted by ownership of the means of production and is typically vested in distinct proprietary knowledge. However, this may not always be the case in all organizations. Some may delegate power from the principal to agents, that is, from the managers, who enjoy the right to command, to the lower levels. Irrespective of the principal–agent, that is, employer–employee relation, personal or impersonal command, by nature, is discursive. Hence, power is often construed as using stress-inducing strategies by organizations (or managers, per se) to achieve conformity with the superordinate preferences. This, however, is a negative connotation of power. There are also many positive aspects of power. An organizational structure shows the reporting relationships of people who are working at different hierarchical levels within the organization. Thus, power in organizations necessarily binds the hierarchical structure and the relationship of organizational members to each other. The design of tasks and their interdependencies relate to the distribution of power. Some tasks may have functional interdependence, whereas some others may be stand-alone functions. The actual power structures in an organization, therefore, conform to the organizational chart. Thus, power need not always be discursive, nor is it necessarily coercive. It can also be used effectively by recognizing the diversity of interests of the members of an organization.

> Power is the potential of a person to exert influence over others.

Politics is another inseparable part of the organizational environment. Unlike power, politics reflects on the decision-making style of managers, emphasizing more on hypocrisy, veil of secrecy, rumours, and cliques. Too much politics destroys the fabric of teamwork culture in an organization. Politics is inbuilt in organizations that represent coalitions of people with diverse interests. Individuals and groups differ in their values, preferences, beliefs, and

> **Practitioner Speak 13.1**
>
> **How to Build (and Use) Thick Power**
>
> He's ba-a-ack! Like a supervillain who's impossible to vanquish, Dick Cheney's moseyed on into town once again.
>
> Read this insightful blog posted by Haque on *HBR Blog Network* by accessing the following link: http://blogs.hbr.org/haque/2009/05/power.html.

perceptions. Hence, they indulge in politics to influence the organizational decisions to their benefit. This is natural, as every organization, for obvious reasons, manages to run its show with limited resource availability. Thus, individuals and groups get involved in politics to bargain for a larger share of the scarce resources.

THEORIES OF POWER

Max Weber (1947), in his classical organization theory, explained power in an organization through the process of control. Weber related authority to legitimacy, implying that managers enjoy it by virtue of their position in the organizational hierarchy. Although legitimate authority itself is a power, an individual member of an organization without authority can also enjoy power. Sources of authority need not always depend on legitimacy. Charismatic authority may be independent of legitimacy, as it is embedded in the outstanding characteristics of an individual. Traditional authority is essentially a respect for custom (e.g., a senior member of an organization is respected by others). Rational–Legal authority is based on the code or set of rules of an organization. According to Weber, rational–legal authority can be efficiently used by an organization through bureaucracy, which restricts managers from arbitrarily resorting to it. Bureaucracy binds organizations by a certain set of rules. A formal set of rules in an organization can command obedience from organizational members, primarily because people obey impersonal orders. Weber's concept of bureaucracy has already been discussed in Chapter 2.

David C. McClelland (1961) identified power as one of the three needs related to management behaviour of an organization, with achievement and affiliation being the other two needs. The need for power is an urge to control others—to make them do things. McClelland identified four stages of power:

> Weber's classical organization theory explains power in an organization through the process of control. Managers enjoy power and authority by virtue of their position in organizational hierarchy.

Drawing inner strength from others This is enjoyed by looking up to and emulating those in power. Organizations ensure this through the process of empowerment.

Strengthening oneself This is done by playing the power game, collecting symbols of status, and dominating situations.

Increasing self-assertiveness This is ensured by becoming more aggressive and manipulating situations.

Acting as an instrument of higher authority People identifying with some system of authority and emulating the methods in stages two and three can claim formal legitimacy.

Blake and Mouton (1964) described the kind of person with this kind of approach as having an authority–obedience style of management, concentrating on result optimization through the exercise of personal authority and power. Managers who belong to this category combine a high concern for production with a low concern for people. They concentrate on maximizing production by exercising power and authority and achieving control over people by dictating what they should do and how they should go about it. Typically, these managers drive themselves and others. They investigate situations to ensure control so that others do not make mistakes. They prefer to defend their own ideas and opinions even though it may mean rejecting those of others. They deal with conflict by either trying to cut it off or winning their own position. Finally, these managers make their own decisions; they are rarely influenced by others and are not afraid to pinpoint other people's weaknesses and failures.

Despite many commonalities among leadership, authority, and power, at this stage, it is very appropriate to clarify these terms to clearly delineate the term *power*. Leadership is the ability to influence people to willingly follow one's guidance or adhere to one's decisions. Obtaining followers and influencing them in setting and achieving objectives makes one a leader. Effective leadership in an organization creates a vision for the future that considers the long-term interests of the parties involved. Leaders use power for influencing group behaviour. Leadership has to cope with politics to make sure that it does not cause disturbances within the organization.

Authority is the right to issue directives and expend resources. It is related to power but is narrower in scope. Basically, authority depends on the amount of coercion, reward, and legitimate power one can exert. An individual can have expert power or referent power without having formal authority.

Power, on the other hand, encompasses both the authority and leadership ability, but the nature of authority is more personal than organizational.

To understand the dynamics of organizational behaviour, both power and authority are important. Leaders exert power over others to get something done by them, which otherwise they would not be able to get done. It means that by wielding power over others, one can get them to act in a way that they may consider being contrary to their own interests. Leaders can do it because their power to exercise control over people has some value, which may be in the form of the power to grant incentives, bonuses, promotions, and so on. This is called the dependency model of power. This model of power can be balanced when both the parties depend on each other. For example, a boss may be dependent on a subordinate's performance to achieve his/her targets. In this case, the subordinate exercises control over something of value (in terms of his/her performance) for the boss. Hence, in a balanced dependency situation, the subordinates may not be completely powerless. In managing the behaviour of people in organizations, managers make a trade-off between their power and the power of the people reporting to them, often attaching a price. Thus, this argument substantiates the statement that there is no one in an organization who is powerless. In addition, power is not the exclusive right of managers. A balanced dependency model of power in organizations thus promotes a work culture of mutual trust, effectively influencing the attitudes and beliefs of people.

ORGANIZATIONAL POWER AND CONTROL

Organizational control through power implies the general ability of managers to direct and organize the efforts of the employees. Organizations use various types of controls such as simple control, technical control, and bureaucratic control.

Simple control   This is enforced by direct supervision and is more evident in a protocol-bound manufacturing process. Such control is the use of powers of supervisors over the jobs of workers.

Technical control   This is imposed by the technology used in a manufacturing process. For example, in an automated assembly line production process, the speed of work may be important; this is because each job remains in a particular workstation for a fixed time and then automatically moves to the next workstation. Supervisors control the process by using their power, imposing timely completion of jobs by each worker within the given time limit.

> Organizational control through power implies the general ability of managers to direct and organize the efforts of the employees.

Bureaucratic control   Managers enforce bureaucratic control through formal rules and regulations. Bureaucratic organizations frame rules on hours of work, entitlement to time off under various circumstances (e.g., annual leave, compassionate leave, and maternity leave), grievance procedures, and so on. There are also rules or standard operating procedures that people must follow in the course of their work. This form of control involves a still more subtle form of power.

POWER AND SYSTEMS OF ORGANIZATIONAL MEMBERSHIP

Amitai Etzioni, in exploring the sources of organizational power, offered a synthesis of systems that organizations adopt to secure member compliance. His interest was in identifying how people in organizations conform to organizational requirements and follow the standards of laid-down behaviour. Goal-oriented, performance-directed organizations require the compliance of members. The problem, however, is that deviance from these standards occurs because of weaknesses in the commitment of the members. Thus, systems of control are exerted by other members of the organization—both managers and other members.

Compliance is ensured by organizational control and authority structures, formal hierarchies of authority, supervision, job definitions, policies, and specified procedures. These—as per the bureaucratic model of Weber—make the organization less dependent on individual variability and whims.

There is a motivation element to this, as these structures shape the involvement of the individual within the organization. The simple proposition is that the more the individual is committed, the less formal is the control needed. Etzioni's typology (classification scheme) includes coercive, calculative, and normative systems. We can thus label organizations or parts of organizations as we see them adopting such systems (e.g., as prevailing cultures).

Coercive   Coercive systems reflect an organization's ability to apply physical, constraining force on people when they fail to meet the expectations. Examples of coercive power in organizations include the ability (implied or real) to fire, demote, transfer to undesirable positions, or strip subordinates of preferred perquisites. Coercive methods nurture dysfunctional group processes with the following typical characteristics:

- Dislike and rejection
- Anger and backlash of conflict
- Conspiracies and coalitions
- Reticence and reduced intrinsic motivation

Calculative   Calculative or instrumental systems of control make use of various kinds of material or non-material rewards to secure member compliance. Organizational membership is based on the member contracting with the organization and bargaining over the desired reward in return for compliance, loyalty, reliability, and performance. Members calculate the benefits accruing to them in the form of overtime, pay raise, promotion, steady income, long-term future, and so on. This involves shades of willingness ranging from the mildly negative orientation to calculation (what is in it for me—akin to McGregor's Theory X stick approach or the Goldthorpe affluent worker) to a positive instrumental orientation (McGregor's stick and carrot theory X and normative theory Y).

Normative   Normative or moral involvement systems of power depend on shared values that are promoted and which the members subscribe to. Organizations consciously generate and maintain these values, which are represented in signs and symbols—visual, verbal, behavioural, and conceptual. Commitment to the organization's ideology brings with it persuasive or suggestive power. Members internalize organizational values, which become their own and naturally guide their behaviour. Individuals within the organization act as one, with a very intensive commitment to the organization and the goals it is trying to achieve.

Modern business organizations invest considerable effort and resource into creating an environment where employees *join as one*—within a unitary, harmonious framework of consensus—to achieve organizational goals. A monastic order is an obvious example of a normative system of organizational control; so is the total quality or continuous quality improvement or learning company culture.

These systems are evident in most organizations. When a large modern organization heavily relies on calculative and normative systems, it can lead to motivational problems. Employees in this organization are calculative, requiring the organization to bargain with them both individually and collectively over the substance of their rewards.

Overall, Etzioni's categories are too simple and broad. Others expand the number of types.

Dependence–Power Relationship

Dependence is created when the things under one's control are very important in nature. Hence, the element of scarcity is embedded with the dependence hypothesis. In many organizations, managers often become dependent on those workers who possess some knowledge, skills, or expertise not possessed by the managers. Such a scarcity–dependence relationship is more evident in some occupational categories. This is evident in tea gardens, where tea labourers can sense the attack of red spiders (that can destroy the garden in a short time) but managers in organizations cannot sense it. In fact, in skilled jobs like business analytics, managers often depend on their subordinates for their specialized knowledge.

In addition, dependence is created because of non-substitutability of the important resources possessed by one or a few members of the organization. The dependence–power relationship, therefore, is understood in terms of its three important constructs—scarcity, importance, and non-substitutability.

SOURCES OF POWER

French and Raven (1959) suggested five sources or types of power, based on Etzioni's power typology. Broadly, the sources of power can be categorized into two types—organizational sources and individual or personal sources.

Organizational Sources

An organization itself can be a potential source for power. However, such powers normally vest with the managers. We'll discuss some of these in this section.

Coercive Power

Leaders exert coercive power to punish those who do not comply with their requests or demands. Individuals exercise this power through reliance upon physical strength, verbal competency, or the ability to grant or withhold emotional support from others. These bases provide the individual with the means to physically harm, bully, humiliate, or deny respect to others.

Managers make use of several tools to effectively manage organizational behaviour by addressing the power issues. Information sharing is construed as the most important tool. The performance of the subordinates can be improved by making them aware of the behaviour expected of them. Information contents in this case can change the cognitive elements and wean people away from indulging in power conflicts in the organizations. Managers and leaders need to develop their expertise. This will create a *halo effect*, thereby making the subordinates realize that the managers not only legitimately enjoy the power because of their role and position, but also deserve it because of their knowledge and expertise.

In addition, managers and leaders make effective use of power to get results through the participation of people using coercion and reward, personality, authority, and an attitude of caring for their people. What is more important here is that people must acknowledge the power of managers and leaders, beyond the legitimacy, and submit to it, accepting their command and control.

Practitioner Speak 13.2

Samsung Scandal Offers Power Lessons for Any Workplace

Samsung's Lee Kun-hee was in power, then out of power, and is now in power again. And that's not making life easy for his former employee Kim Youg-chul. As reported today, the latter is in a form of career exile after accusing his boss and other top executives of corruption. The complaint got results: Lee was removed from Chairmanship of Samsung last year.

Read this insightful blog posted by Kirby on *HBR Blog Network* by accessing the following link: http://blogs.hbr.org/hbr/hbreditors/2010/06/rules_for_political_animals_if.html.

Reward Power

A supervisor has reward power over his/her staff. He/She can—through the staff appraisal process—open up doors to promotion. He/She may allocate overtime or more interesting work. The manager can offer involvement in decision-making and enhanced status (referent power). Students will work hard to complete a project because of the tutor's reward. Such power is effective when employees trust that a direct relationship exists between the effort and the achievement of the reward that they value (expectancy theory). It is important to recognize, however, that in most modern organizations—a corporation, a hospital, a trust, a local authority—managers have little scope to widely vary reward components to employees because reward systems are governed by rules and require consistency in application.

Legitimate Power

Legitimate power reflects Weber's rational–legal authority. The member accepts an authority's legitimate right to require and demand compliance. People comply with the Income Tax Department's request to submit a completed tax form or accept the penalty imposed by the department. This legitimacy depends on the official status of the person exercising it, which may be upheld because of the prevailing cultural values assigning authority. Examples are the respect given to elders and the legitimacy of the monarchy (Weber's traditional authority).

Personal Sources

Personal power vests with the individual, irrespective of their job position. Some of the bases of personal power can be explained as given in this section.

Expert Power

Expert power is derived from the recognition that the power holder has valued skills and abilities in an area critical to the members' success.

Referent or Charismatic Power

Referent power is based on personal identification and respect for a leader figure who is followed or supported because of his/her personal qualities and characteristics.

Exhibit 13.1 maps the outcome of power struggles in organizations.

EXHIBIT 13.1 Mapping the Outcome of Power Struggles in Organizations

Power in the context of organizations can be a very interesting topic to ponder on. While it does not refer to the muscle power a goon may have, it is nevertheless something worth reckoning. To be able to make others listen to one at every beck and call is a skill that most employees would envision attaining at the workplace. However, power is not something that everyone enjoys and thus in most cases,

a struggle ensues. Power struggles can be a big deterrent for organizations—especially in view of the fact that the very nature of such struggles is to outsmart others and is therefore, divisive by nature.

Apart from the core objective of wielding influence over others, power in the organizational context often starts from win–lose objectives and ends up becoming lose–lose affairs. Thus, in a vast majority of

(Contd)

EXHIBIT 13.1 *(Contd)*

instances, people trying to dominate over others ultimately make enemies out of their potential followers.

Though power for most has to be forcibly usurped, natural leaders have the innate ability to gain influence over others without having to get down to power struggles. This, in turn, helps them in being respected and followed by others. With the vision and wisdom they have, true leaders exert influence over others and lead them to attain organizational objectives, ending up in win–win situations, unlike leaders and employees who try to do it through force and sneaky politics.

Source: 'Two Perspectives of Power in Organizations and their Relationship to Conflict', *The Center for Human Systems*, http://www.chumans.com/human-systems-resources/power-diversity-organizations.html, last accessed on 5 September 2013 (adapted).

POWER AND EMPOWERMENT

In general, power is viewed from the perspective of power *over* people. On the contrary, empowerment recognizes and realizes the power *with* the people. Empowerment is not something given to employees by the top management; it is rather the role of the top management to create a culture in which employees can use their full potential to the benefit of the organization. In this process, employees also attain the stage of maturity.

Empowerment—Definitions and Concepts

The word *empowerment* is used in many different contexts by many different organizations. It encompasses the fields of education, social work, psychology, politics, community development, and gender studies. The Human Development Report 1995 stresses that empowerment is about participation. Empowerment must be *by* the people and not *for* them. People must participate fully in the decisions and processes that shape their lives (UNDP 1995:2). Investing in people's capabilities and empowering them to exercise their choices is not only valuable in itself but also the surest way to contribute to economic growth and overall development. For Oxfam (1995), empowerment is about challenging oppression and inequality: 'Empowerment involves challenging the forms of oppression which compel millions of people to play a part in their society on terms which are inequitable, or in ways which deny their human rights.' Gender studies stress that women's empowerment is not about replacing one form of empowerment with another. 'Women's empowerment should lead to the liberation of men from false value systems and ideologies of oppression. It should lead to a situation where each one can become a whole being regardless of gender, and use their fullest potential to construct a more humane society for all' (Batliwala 1994). Jo Rowlands (1995) points out that empowerment is a bottom-up process and cannot be bestowed from the top down.

> Empowerment involves challenging the forms of oppression which compel millions of people to play a part in their society on terms which are inequitable or in ways which deny their human rights.

At its most basic level, empowerment is defined as a process of assumption or transfer of legal power and official authority (Webster's New World Dictionary 1994). Empowerment primarily is a feeling or state of mind (Riger 1993; Tyne 1994), that is, assertiveness. Harp (1994) viewed empowerment of individuals as the possession of the same degree of control over one's own life and the conditions that affect life as is generally possessed by people who are already empowered in a similar context. West and Parent (1992) defined empowerment as the transfer of power and control over decisions, choices, and values. Again, empowerment can be viewed in the context of individuals and groups.

Understanding of Power and Empowerment Implications in Practice

Power conflict is natural in organizations. Power over conflict and direct confrontation between powerful and powerless interest groups in organizations are evident even in professionally managed organizations, not to talk about the non-professionally managed ones. Organizational power for capacity building, supporting individual decision-making, leadership, and so on can be best reinforced through the process of empowerment. Thus, empowerment can also be defined as giving power to the employees. It triggers social mobilization, building of alliances and coalitions, increase in self-esteem, rise in levels of awareness, heightened consciousness, and confidence building among the people so empowered. In organizations, when people fully participate in the decision-making processes, both the organizations and the people themselves stand to benefit and they achieve, in the true sense, the empowerment of people. The Human Development Report (1995) lists empowerment as one of the four essential components of the human development paradigm, the others being productivity, equity, and sustainability.

Process of Empowerment

Empowerment is essentially a bottom-up process rather than something that can be formulated as a top-down strategy. Hence, organizations per se cannot claim that they have empowered people but rather, can only facilitate the process of empowerment. Facilitating empowerment requires an organization to carefully devise coherent policies and programmes, ignoring the traditional concept of power over people. The power over people concept dissuades people from developing their problem-solving capabilities and participating in decision-making. On the contrary, the power with people concept encourages people to be more proactive in addressing the organizational issues and pacing their individual process of development. With the power with approach, organizations encourage people to participate, to acquire skills, to develop their decision-making capability, and to exercise control over resources. The process of empowerment can, therefore, be categorized in the following order:

> Empowerment is essentially a bottom-up process rather than something that can be formulated as a top-down strategy.

Empowering Directly

Individuals can be directly empowered if the management of an organization takes the following steps:

- Allowing people to develop their capability to enforce self-control
- Allowing people to participate in decision-making
- Developing the ability of employees to understand situations and respecting their efforts
- Building a knowledge base, helping in the enhancement of the ability of employees, and allowing them to get access to the knowledge repository
- Encouraging people to autonomously choose their own approach

Practitioner Speak 13.3

Women and Soft Power in Business

The leadership of women in politics, business, and society is becoming evident across the globe. Growing numbers of women are becoming political leaders, the most recent being Dilma Rouseff, who took over as Brazil's first woman president. She follows in the footsteps of other female politicians such as Chile's Michelle Bachelet, Argentina's Cristina Kirchner, and Germany's Angela Merkel. Last year, India even reserved a third of the seats in its legislature for women.

Read this insightful blog posted by Nayar on *HBR Blog Network* by accessing the following link: http://blogs.hbr.org/hbr/nayar/2011/01/women-and-soft-power-in-business.html.

- Allowing participation in the action, development, planning, strategic, and operational processes
- Developing a transparent information-sharing process
- Allowing people to develop their ability to influence
- Making people feel confident about expressing and presenting their viewpoints
- Inculcating a sense of responsibility in people

Empowering by Changing Work Environment

Individuals can also be empowered by making suitable changes in their working environment, by doing the following:

- Removing false assumptions
- Removing oppression or fear
- Creating equality
- Changing practices
- Generating communal goals
- Institutionalizing change
- Enabling dialogue and open communication
- Sharing responsibility
- Making the processes democratic and transparent
- Inculcating a culture of collective action

However, empowerment cannot be defined in terms of specific activities or end results because it involves a process whereby people can freely analyse, develop, and voice their needs and interests, without those being predefined or imposed by the organizations. Organizations working towards an empowerment approach must, therefore, develop ways of enabling people to critically assess their own situation and shape a transformation. This transformation process through empowerment should be an ongoing initiative rather than being a time-bound one.

ORGANIZATIONAL POLITICS

Politics is inseparable from organizations. This is because of the involvement of people in organizations, and the involvement of a large number of people cannot but lead to politics.

> Politics is inseparable from organizations because of the involvement of people in organizations.

Organizations overrun by politics are typically identified by the type of managerial decisions being made; they encourage hypocrisy, secrecy, deal-making, rumours, power brokers, self-interests, image building, self-promotion, and cliques. These organizations lack in effective teamwork. There are five possible reasons for organizational politics taking place, which are as follows:

- Organizations are coalitions composed of varied individuals and groups.
- There are enduring differences among individuals and groups in their values, preferences, beliefs, information, and perceptions of reality.
- The most important decisions in organizations involve the allocation of scarce resources.
- Conflict is central to organizational dynamics, and power is the most important resource.
- Organizational goals and decisions emerge from bargaining, negotiation, and jockeying for position among members of different coalitions.

Besides causing problems for the individuals who work together, the end result of organizational politics can be far more devastating. Employees and managers who must concentrate on the political aspects of work may have less time to pay attention to their jobs. This translates into financial loss, which may in turn translate into job loss.

To reduce organizational politics, managers and leaders make use of several strategies in their people-related decisions. All these may minimize the level of politics, but cannot guarantee its total elimination, because politics is inherent in any social form of togetherness of people. Managers must emphasize performance, making a culture of employee rewards being earned and not granted as favours. Similarly, promotions and pay rise decisions should be aligned to transparent performance management systems, making people believe that the system is impersonal and reliable. A very strong weapon to reduce organizational politics is to nurture transparent communication systems. Everything that affects the workplace should be made transparent to dissuade employees from concocting stories and spreading rumours and to restrain them from deal-making and favouritism.

Thus, organizational politics can be reduced if organizations pursue the following principles:

- Transparently measure performance of its employees.
- Make payments strictly on the basis of the performance so measured.
- Publicize performance data.
- Reveal the reasons for decisions.
- Openly consider all good ideas.
- Shun deal-making.
- Shun secret deals.
- Avoid all political behaviour.

In the corporate world, there are many good examples of leaders who successfully managed workplace politics. Jack Welch, former head of GE, was one of the most impressive political players. His slogan was 'control your destiny or someone else will'. He chose people to push through changes and weed out 'resisters'. He replaced GE's ornate structure with a *cartwheel*—13 spokes of business units radiating from his office, reminiscent of the *kingdoms* model.

Practitioner Speak 13.4

Reinventing Office Politics

I am constantly surprised by the number of executives who say 'I don't do politics.' Regardless of nationality or organisation, they claim that politics plays no part in their work and they flaunt this refusal as a badge of pride.

Read this insightful blog posted by Corkindale on *HBR Blog Network* by accessing the following link: http://blogs.hbr.org/corkindale/2007/10/reinventing_office_politics.html.

EXHIBIT 13.2 Playing Positive Politics at the Workplace

Politics has always been an integral part of our daily interactions with others. It has a crucial role to play whenever anything involves two or more people. Since workplaces involve a large number of people, politics at the workplace is but an inevitable phenomenon. Though many people indulge in guileful, manipulative, and regressive politics, there are some who do politics but not by using mean tactics like some of their peers do.

Politics can indeed be seen in a positive light, if people use it constructively. Since there is no escape from workplace politics, one may resort to certain pointers to benefit from politics without having to degrade themselves or compromising with their ethics:

Forming alliances One may form partnerships with other employees to work better. However, alliances should not be made to disrupt others and only be used to increase work efficiency and productivity.

Performing negotiations One should look for give-and-take relationships with employees at the workplace. Thus, one can do favours to colleagues and get the same in return.

Observing human dynamics One should keenly study the people at the workplace. This helps in understanding people and acting likewise so as not to offend them.

Communicating selectively Communication with others may make or break one's image in the organization. Thus, one should be careful about what to say, whom to say, and when to say. One should refrain from office gossip or at least remain silent when in doubt.

Having ethical considerations One should always think about the ethical considerations attached to indulging in politics. Thus, whatever politicization one indulges in, it should never be at the cost of compromising with one's ethics.

Sources: Addesso, P., 'Using Organizational Politics to your Advantage', *Articles: University of Phoenix*, 28 April 2010, http://www.phoenix.edu/profiles/faculty/patricia-addesso/articles/using-organizational-politics-to-your-advantage.html, last accessed on 5 September 2013; King, D. 'Winning at Organizational Politics without Losing your Soul', 2008, http://www.careerfirm.com/article-politics.htm, last accessed on 5 September 2013 (adapted).

Exhibit 13.2 discusses the art of playing positive politics at the workplace.

Factors

Organizational politics exist in every organization; however, its influence is less in formal organizations, which are bound by documented policies, procedures, and rules. Research studies on organizational politics indicate there are numerous personal and organizational factors responsible for organizational politics. Among personal factors, personality and demographic issues are the important ones. The influence of personality and demographic issues predispose individuals to negative affectivity, because of which they start viewing their workplaces as political. With negative affectivity, individuals try to gain power in organizations through politics to satisfy their personal needs. With positive affectivity, however, their perceptions change.

Organizational factors also influence individuals to play politics to achieve personal gains. Some of the important factors for organizational politics attributable to organizations can be listed as follows:

- Resource limitation, which makes individuals vie for the maximum share
- Decisional uncertainty because of absence of policies, systems, and rules, which makes an individual take advantage through politics
- Unstructured performance management systems, which make individuals play politics to influence their superiors for a better performance rating
- Stringent performance control, which makes individuals exert political pressure on the organization to reduce control

Thus, organizational politics is a natural phenomenon for divergent people with divergent interests. Hardy and Clegg (1996) identified two perspectives of organizational politics—functional and critical. Organizational politics from a functional perspective influence the decision-making process of the organization. From a critical perspective, it is viewed more as a process of resistance to the power exerted by the management.

Defensive Behaviour

Defensive behaviour of people is embedded in their unsatisfied needs, an inferiority complex, guilt, and even a sense of unworthiness. Such negativity makes them build their defences to meet their needs. It is important for managers to understand the defensive behaviour of their employees and provide guidance as to how they can meet their needs by suitably addressing their problems. For example, if the knowledge and skills of the employees are deterrents to their getting promoted, managers need to extend appropriate career development support through mentoring and coaching and by encouraging the employees to enrol themselves in some skill development programmes. With the shift to alternative pursuits to satisfy their needs, their propensity to defensive behaviours decreases. Some of the defensive behaviours of employees can be categorized as follows:

Aggression   It is an extreme nature of defensive behaviour to release the inner fear of employees. To manage such aggressive defensive behaviour, managers need to confront the employees' way of doing things and then explain how meaningless their suggestions are.

Day dreaming   This is a typical characteristic of adolescence, as newly-recruited employees are far from reality. Managers in such cases guide employees to understand the results. Moreover, to prevent any disaster, they help the employees set achievable short-term goals. Success in achieving the short-term goals can gradually propel the employees to the world of adulthood, that is, more pragmatism and action.

Repression This is an extreme state of feeling inferior with total destruction of the self-image of employees. Such employees often indulge in self-criticism. Managers need to boost the morale of such employees by praising their strong points and reminding them of the success they achieved in the past.

Rationalization Employees with this behaviour try to legitimize their failures with some excuses. They never admit their faults but rather attribute it to organizational problems. Curing this syndrome requires managers to provide positive as well as corrective feedback, so that employees can understand their weaknesses and change their behavioural pattern.

Compartmentalization This is a conscious defensive behavioural syndrome when employees, despite knowing it is wrong, indulge in such behaviour. A good example is saying 'as my salary is low, I work less'. It is difficult to manage such people; however, appealing to their emotions often leads to positive results.

Whatever may be the nature of defensive behaviour, it is always better to recognize those at the outset and then design therapeutic action plans to transform employees from defensiveness to cooperation.

SUMMARY

Power is the potentiality of a person to exert influence on others, primarily through direct control. In organizations, the right to command is granted by ownership of the means of production. However, organizations may delegate the power down to the lower levels as well. Power in organizations, whether personal or impersonal, is, by its very nature, discursive. Managers and leaders often use power as stress strategies to get work done. However, power can also be used effectively, recognizing the diversity of interests of the members of an organization.

Similar to power, politics is also an inseparable part of the organizational environment. Organizational politics reflect on the decision-making styles of managers, emphasizing more on hypocrisy, veil of secrecy, rumours, and cliques. Too much politics destroys the fabric of teamwork culture in an organization.

Leaders and managers derive their power by virtue of not only their position (based on principles of legitimacy) but also their personal characteristics, knowledge, and expertise. The balanced dependency model of power recognizes the power of the subordinates as well and accordingly creates a culture of mutual trust and respect at the workplace, making people feel empowered and encouraged to participate in decision-making. Employee empowerment involves a process whereby people can freely analyse, develop, and voice their needs and interests, without those being predefined or imposed by the organizations.

KEY DEFINITIONS

Charismatic authority Authority that is independent of legitimate authority and primarily drawn from the outstanding characteristics of an individual

Employee empowerment Essentially a bottom-up strategy to facilitate people down the line to feel themselves to be a part of the organization, thus making them more responsible for their jobs

Etzioni's typology Classification of the systems of power—coercive, calculative, and normative—which shape the culture of an organization

Stress strategies Strategies adopted by using the personal powers of managers and leaders to achieve results from their employees

CONCEPT-REVIEW QUESTIONS

13.1 Discuss the role of power and politics in organizational behaviour.

13.2 Discuss the various sources of organizational power.

13.3 What is the dependency model of power? How

is it different from the power over syndrome? How does it benefit an organization?

13.4 Explain the term *employee empowerment*. How is employee empowerment ensured in an organization?

CRITICAL THINKING QUESTIONS

13.1 In a highly unionized workplace, you as a human resource (HR) manager introduced the participative management culture, making it possible for workers to share their views in management committees on strategic decisional areas. However, workers started alleging that their inputs do not get reflected in the ultimate decision of the management. Critically review this situation and then comment upon where you went wrong in truly empowering the employees. What could be your possible move to alleviate this problem?

13.2 In the introductory case study of this chapter, we have projected a character, Thomas, whose excessive administration of power led to his ultimate dismissal from service. In the case study at the end of the chapter, however, we have painted the character of Bose who, without even using his personal power as vice-president—HR, had to face a crisis. As a manager, analyse both the situations and critically comment on how you can achieve synergy by nurturing a win–win model of power sharing.

SELECT BIBLIOGRAPHY

- Batliwala, Srilatha, 'The Means of Women's Empowerment: New Concepts from Action', in Gita Sen, Andrienne Germain, and Lincoln, C. Chan (eds), *Population Policies Reconsidered, Health, Empowerment and Rights*, Harvard University Press, Boston, 1994.
- Bhattacharyya, Dipak Kumar, *Human Resource Research Methods*, Oxford University Press, New Delhi, 2007.
- Blake, R. and J. Mouton, *The Managerial Grid*, Gulf Publishing, Houston, 1964.
- Blanchard, K., J. Carlos, and W.A. Randolph, *Empowerment Takes More Than a Minute*, Berrett-Koehler Publishers, San Francisco, 1998.
- Block, Peter, *Stewardship: Choosing Service over Self-interest*, Berrett-Koehler Publishers, San Francisco, 1993.
- French, J.R.P. and B.H. Raven, 'The Bases of Social Power', in D. Cartwright (ed.), *Studies in Social Power*, University of Michigan Press, Ann Arbor, 1959.
- Hardy, C. and Clegg, S.R., 'Some Dare Call it Power,' in S.R. Clegg, C. Hardy, and W.R. Nord (eds),

Handbook of Organization Studies, Sage, London, 1996.
- Harp, H.T., 'Empowerment of Mental Health Consumers in Vocational Rehabilitation', *Psychological Rehabilitation Journal*, Vol. 17, 1994, pp. 83–90.
- McClelland, David, C., *The Achieving Society*, Van Nostrand Co. Inc., Princeton, 1961.
- McClelland, D.C. and D.H. Burnhan, 'Power is the Great Motivator', *Harvard Business Review*, Vol. 54, Issue 2, 1976, pp. 100–10.
- Oxfam, *The Oxfam Handbook of Relief and Development*, Oxfam, Oxford, 1995.
- Recognizing Defensive Behaviour, http://www.businessconsultantsreno.com/business-articles/business-articles/supervisory-management/recognizing-defensive-behaviors/, last accessed on 02 December 2013.
- Riger, S., 'What's Wrong with Empowerment', *American Journal of Community Psychology*, Vol. 21, 1993, pp. 279–92.
- Rowlands, J., 'Empowerment Examined: Development in Practice', *Oxfam*, Vol. 5, Issue 2, 1995.

- Tyne, A., 'Taking Responsibility and Giving Power', *Disability and Society*, Vol. 9, 1994, pp. 249–54.
- UNDP, *Human Development Report*, Oxford University Press, Oxford, 1995.
- Weber, Max, *The Theory of Social and Economic Organization*, translated by A.M. Henderson and Talcott Parsons, The Free Press, New York, 1947.
- West, M. and W. Parent, 'Consumer Choice and Empowerment in Supported Employment Services: Issues and Strategies', *Journal of Association for Persons with Handicaps*, Vol. 7, 1992, pp. 47–52.

CASE STUDY

The Fall of Sona Computers

Vinod Chopra, chief executive officer (CEO), heads Sona Computers, a leader in the global computer hardware market, with the largest market share in servers and desktops. Chopra is a hardworking person, and he nurtures the vision of taking Sona to new heights, by doubling the business turnover in five years' time. The computer hardware market is very competitive with the presence of Dell and HP–Compaq as international majors and many large, medium, and small players in India. Sona's value-added desktops and servers have made them reach their peak in sales in India, far exceeding the market share than the other competitors. With respect to product quality and price, Sona still remains a market leader. However, Chopra, in furthering his vision to double the turnover, faced some inter-organizational crisis. Once known as the best workplace and even having bagged the best employer award from various national and international agencies, Sona suddenly started decaying. Political infighting, cynicism, gender bias, and labour law violations riddled Sona with frequent work stoppages, workplace violence, and loss of productivity.

Bose is the vice-president of Sona's HR department. Both Chopra and Bose had worked together earlier and had a good understanding and mutual respect. Bose joined Sona five years after Chopra became the CEO of the company. Bose leveraged his earlier ties with Chopra and started restructuring the entire organization in line with Chopra's vision. Restructuring followed manpower rationalization decisions, rendering many people surplus in their jobs and their redeployment in different areas of the organization. Bose did the entire task very diligently in the best interest of the organization and with a view to further Chopra's vision.

One morning, PC assemblers at the shop floor level, with their union leaders, stormed into Chopra's office along with a weeping middle-aged woman, who alleged outrageous behaviour by Bose. This woman had been working with Sona since its inception. She was known for her clout with the unions and the management, being the only woman member who joined Sona in the 1980s. Chopra asked them to cool down, and after listening to their allegations against Bose, pacified them saying, 'I will talk to Bose and then get back to you.' After their departure, Chopra asked Bose to meet him in his office and narrated the incident to him. Bose told him that he had identified the woman as surplus and had asked her to report to the packaging shop floor. To that effect, he had also issued a note to the supervisors of the assembly and packaging shop floors, with a copy to the woman concerned.

Chopra, being extra sensitive about the business and success of Sona, requested Bose to withdraw the order and allow the woman to remain with her earlier job. Bose immediately resented this decision, stating that it will give a wrong signal to the entire organization and things will go out of control. He politely requested Chopra to bear with this for some time and allow him to sort out the issue.

Bose asked the woman to see him. The woman demanded she must be allowed to come with her colleagues. Bose emphasized that since the issue pertains to her, it would be preferable for her to come alone. The woman entered Bose's office; without even seeking his permission, she sat on a chair and started asking why he had called her. Bose could sense that the woman was not in a mood to compromise. He feared that she might further muddle the issue. Hence, he asked her to sit and allow him a few minutes to finish some important work. He then asked his secretary, a woman, to come into his chamber and in her presence started speaking to the woman employee. He informed her in no uncertain terms that she must report to the packaging department and failure to do so will make her liable for disciplinary action. The woman left Bose's room with tears rolling down her cheeks. The mob waiting outside Bose's room suddenly started shouting alleging that he had sexually harassed her. In no time, the entire workforce rushed to the site, leaving their jobs, and demanded the immediate removal of Bose.

They threatened to stop work if their demand was not immediately met.

Chopra was out of the country at the time of this incident. On getting the news, he asked Bose to immediately leave the office, asking Sharma, the chief financial officer of the company, to take charge in his absence. On return, Chopra was briefed by the union leaders and others about Bose's outrageous behaviour. The workers now also demanded that all their interdepartmental transfer orders be scrapped because these were all ill-intentioned moves of Bose, who hardly understood the company's needs.

Questions for Discussion

1. Study the power dynamics here, putting yourself in the role of Bose, and analyse where things went wrong. In addition, critically evaluate Chopra's role as a CEO.
2. Can you find out from the case a few limitations of empowerment?

Communication and Negotiation in Organizations

CASE STUDY

Managing without Control

Chevron Corporation, a leader in the petroleum industry, has been practising *direct participation* as an efficient process of designing and implementing change. This has helped the company develop a response capability for the workforce (using their collective wisdom) to outmanoeuvre competitors. The working of the system involves taking the following steps in the order described herein:

- Organizing large-scale conferences (two–three days) involving a variety of stakeholders
- Discussing issues that require change
- Bringing multiple perspectives for action
- Selecting the line of action

- Communicating it throughout the organization
- Implementing identified changes

Excited by the results of Chevron, a large automobile manufacturer in India, which employs mostly engineers even in their shop floors, decided to emulate its practices. Being a professional organization with the employees highly educated, this Indian organization followed a matrix structure, creating a number of positions for project heads, who had been given the task of managing work independently after the finalization and implementation of participative plans. The system started with much enthusiasm, hoping that results would be better in a sluggish, competitive market. However, the annual review indicated that the company could achieve only up to 70 per cent of its targets. There was no system of midterm review by the top management. The company had to drop its new system and revert to the old hierarchical structure. What is the lesson that you draw from this case?

INTRODUCTION

The word *communication* has many interpretations. Communication is the process of interacting with people and their environment. Through such interactions, two or more individuals influence the ideas, beliefs, and attitudes of each other. These interactions take place through the exchange of information by means of words, gestures, signs, symbols, and expressions. In organizations, communication is a continuous process of giving and receiving information and building business relationships. The word *communication* is derived from the Latin word *communis*, which means common. Commonness of understanding is an essential component of all kinds of communication, more particularly in organizational communication. Without a common understanding, communication in organizations creates misunderstanding and people may become directionless. Today, organizations talk about having a shared vision. To develop a shared vision, effective communication mechanisms are needed. Communication plays an important role even in day-to-day operational issues, such as in clarifying doubts and in making the efforts of the people result-oriented. Our ancient texts have sufficient references to non-verbal communication among man, nature, and animals. Communication with nature and animals was considered the best way to reinforce learning in the Indian *gurukul* system of learning. Thus, communication is as old as our civilization. Even in pre-civilization days, non-verbal communication was in existence among man, nature, and animals.

In organizations, however, language-based or verbal communication is more important. With language, communication within and outside the organizations has become much more effective and global. With market globalization, English has been accepted as a medium of communication even by countries such as China, Japan, Russia, France, and Germany; these countries earlier followed the policy of communicating—even while trading with the various countries of the world—in their own languages, but that did not work well. Thus, language has made communication in organizations much more simple and meaningful.

DEFINITIONS AND CONCEPTS

An all-inclusive definition of communication is difficult to develop because of its all-encompassing nature. Hence, in this text, to the extent possible, the definition of communication is restricted to the organizational context. Denis McQuail defined communication as 'a process which increases commonality'. Hovland, however, defined it as 'a process by which an individual communicator transmits to modify the behaviour of other individuals'. Warner Weaver considers communication as 'the procedure by which one mind can affect another'. According to the *American College Dictionary*, 'Communication is the imparting or interchange of thoughts,

> Communication is defined as the imparting or interchange of thoughts, opinions, or information by speech, writing, or signs.

opinions, or information by speech, writing, or signs.' From an organizational point of view, therefore, communication has the attributes of interaction, interchange, sharing, and commonness.

From these definitions, the following can be stated to be the features of communication:

- Communication is a two-way process. It involves a sender and a receiver. The sender or receiver can be an individual or a group.
- All communication carries a message, which can be some information, a directive, an enquiry, a feeling, an opinion, an idea, or in any other form.
- Communication can occur only when there is commonness of understanding between the sender and the receiver. The commonness includes factors such as common culture, common language, and common environment. Words, phrases, idioms, proverbs, gestures, and expressions are deeply culturized and possess high communicative potential for people from similar backgrounds.
- Communication must be able to evoke a response from the receiver, which would be evident in the form of some behavioural changes.
- The method of communication can be verbal, that is, through words, or non-verbal, that is, through signs, gestures, expressions, and so on.

Thus, the elements of communication, also called the process of communication, involves the following—sender, message, method, receiver, and response of receiver.

NATURE OF COMMUNICATION

Communication can be broadly divided into the following two categories:

Verbal Verbal communication is the use of words and languages for interaction between two or more individuals. It can either be oral or written. Hence, speaking, listening, reading, and writing are all classified under verbal communication. Since it elicits immediate feedback, organizations make extensive use of verbal communication.

Non-verbal Non-verbal communication can occur without the use of words. This type of communication sensitizes the senses, thereby evoking responses depending on the way a particular cue is interpreted. It is often referred to as body language, that is, any non-flexile or re-flexile body movements of the communicator that carry some meaning. Gestures, facial expressions, glancing, staring, smiling, and raising of finger are some examples of body language that carry some meaning. In organizations, non-verbal communication is very important for interpersonal relations.

Based on organizational practices, communication can be further divided into the following:

- Internal and external
- Formal and informal
- Downward and upward
- Horizontal and diagonal
- Grapevine

The flow of information within the organization is known as *internal* communication, which may be either formal or informal in nature. *External* communication takes place between two entities, that is, between two organizations or between an organization and others outside the organization. *Formal* communication is official communication, whereas *informal* communication takes place between the members within the formal organization. Communication that flows from superiors to subordinates is *downward* communication, whereas communication that flows from subordinates to superiors is *upward* communication. *Horizontal* communication takes place between two equals, that is, between persons working at the same level. *Diagonal* communication cuts across the hierarchical barriers. However, this is formal in nature. For example, direct communication from a field sales person to the vice-president of the human resources (HR) department is diagonal in nature. It may be noted that they are not only functionally apart but also hierarchically different. Apart from these types, globally dispersed organizations have the system of network communication.

EFFECTIVE COMMUNICATION

Effective communication is the basic need of an organization. Since it develops commonness of understanding about organizational issues, managers need to understand the dynamics of communication. Some of the important features of effective communication are as follows:

Common frame of reference   The sender and the receiver should interact at a common level of understanding. If managers communicate with their subordinates in their (managers') own perceived languages, they will never be able to achieve the results. They need to communicate in such a manner that the receivers of their communication understand it. This basic requirement can be understood from the way communication happens in a family. A parent interacts with his/her children in their perceived languages and symbols. It can also be observed that excellent corporate leaders prefer to talk to workers in their (workers') perceived way. Without a common frame of reference, it is quite unlikely to develop a common level of understanding. To understand the common frame of reference, managers first need to understand the people around them and their behavioural patterns, interpersonal skills, and knowledge base.

Mutual congruence   The contents of any communication in organizations should be of mutual congruence—it should be of common interest to both the senders and the receivers. Many organizational problems are now resolved by adopting the goal congruence model. The erring workers will not listen to managers unless the managers communicate keeping in view the workers' interest areas. In dealing with the collective bargaining issues, unions are usually reluctant to understand the financial rationale for comprehending the company's financial health. They would instead, be more interested in receiving the information in simple factual terms.

Compatibility in communicating language   In a training session, delivering a lecture in English to workers who are not comfortable with the language serves no purpose. To make the training message clear, the trainer has to communicate with them in the language that they understand. Dr Ishikawa of Japan carried the message of quality by adopting the statistical process control tools of Deming and Juran of the US and developing the fishbone diagram.

> **Practitioner Speak 14.1**
>
> **Three Elements of Great Communication, according to Aristotle**
>
> In my nearly 20 years of work in organization development, I've never heard anyone say that a leader communicated too much or too well. On the contrary, the most common improvement suggestion I've seen offered up on the thousands of 360 evaluations I've reviewed over the years is that it would be better if the subject in question learned to communicate more effectively.
>
> Read this insightful blog posted by Edinger on *HBR Blog Network* by accessing the following link: http://blogs.hbr.org/cs/2013/01/three_elements_of_great_communication_according.html.

Successfully cascading the message of quality to the workers' level in their perceived style helped Japan excel in quality.

Compatible environment   Compatibility in environment, that is, communicating with people of similar backgrounds, ensures effectiveness of organizational communication. A common environmental premise for communication develops in organizations when both the sender and the receiver of communication are alike—culturally, economically, professionally, demographically, and interest-wise. In case of incompatibility in the organizational communication environment, managers always try to synchronize the premise with the goal congruence model. Selling the threat of globalization and competition to workers would be more effective when managers try to draw them to common interest areas, for example, informing them that all are at risk unless they together try to achieve the best.

ORGANIZATIONAL COMMUNICATION

Communication is a means by which people are linked together in an organization to achieve a common purpose. No group activity is possible without communication. In organizations, managers may be skilled, but lack the ability to communicate. Thus, they will not be able to build a proper chain of authority and improve relationships. It must be noted that interpersonal communication and organizational communication are different in nature. However, interpersonal communication skill is the base. With this, managers should be able to communicate well in the organization, by adopting some common frames of reference, assessing individuals, and building relationships. In all types of communication, one not only transfers information but also provides behavioural inputs. Hence, organizational communication is considered a unified activity, making the process productive to achieve some specific goals. Organizational communication provides social inputs into a social (organizational) system by which managers try to modify the behaviour of the employees to effect change. High integrity of the sender and consistency in verbal and non-verbal messages increase the probability of acceptance of communication by the receiver.

> Organizational communication provides social inputs into a social (organizational) system by which managers try to modify the behaviour to effect change.

Managers communicate internally at different hierarchical levels, groups, and departments in the organization and externally with customers, suppliers, and other external stakeholders. They must be efficient in all such communication. Oral communication skill is very important for managers. While a manager gives an oral presentation, it is important to understand the purpose and the audience, and then frame the style of delivery.

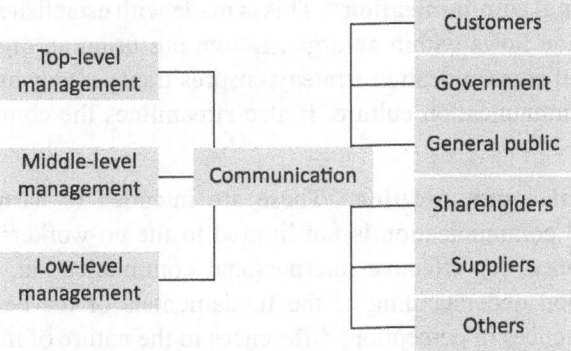

Figure 14.1   Organizational communication model

Thus, organizational communication is basically intended to influence action in a positive way to achieve organizational goals. Such purposes of organizations can be listed as follows:

- To establish the objectives
- To establish a link between plans and actions
- To organize HR so that the goals can be achieved
- To create a climate conducive to lead, direct, and motivate people
- To enforce effective control

The organizational model is illustrated in Fig. 14.1.

TYPES OF ORGANIZATIONAL COMMUNICATION

Organizations make use of various types of communication. Although it is difficult to distinguish between the different types of organizational communication, a general understanding will, at least, enable managers to adopt the right approach. For example, a business communication approach is different from a communication that is intended for team building. Depending on the organizational requirements, managers make use of the following different types of communication:

Business communication   This includes all forms of communication taking place in the business context. Effective business communication requires an understanding of both the business and the style of communication. The use of common business English and the style of business correspondence are important requisites. In business communication, organizations also need to focus on various other aspects such as psychological, sociological, special effects design, management, marketing, and information technology (IT).

Managerial communication   This lays emphasis on the achievement of specific organizational objectives by adopting suitable communication strategies. For example, for disciplining an erring worker, who is otherwise a good performer, the organization may be required to develop a warning letter, without hurting the sentiments but arguing logically, to sensitize the conscience of the worker. Similarly, writing a letter to a customer who has defaulted in making payment, but who otherwise has a good record of meeting payment commitments, requires one to be strategic in communication.

Organizational communication   This is made with established communication networks and communication flows within an organization, nurturing an organizational climate. A suitable organizational communication strategy ensures transparency and makes people adaptable to a particular communication culture. It also streamlines the communication systems within the organization.

Interpersonal communication   These are intended to harmonize interpersonal relations. Interpersonal communication is not limited to the co-workers but extends even to customer relations. Hence, for effective interpersonal communication, it is essential that one should possess a good understanding of the fundamentals of the behavioural dynamics of people, such as differences in perception, differences in the nature of motivation, common behavioural strategies, establishing rapport, developing mutual respect, and reaching a consensus.

Sales communication   This is designed to achieve sales objectives and encompasses advertising, telephone etiquette, and face-to-face communication. Without effective sales communication, organizations cannot improve their sales and revenue (top line). Hence, developing a sales communication that elicits a positive response from the target customers is an art. Marketing managers get special training on sales communication to make their efforts more result-oriented.

Report writing   This type of communication focuses on written reports that are analytical in nature. A company's product literature design, standard operating procedures, policy manuals, and customer information brochures are all developed in this style. Since a report clarifies queries, which may be raised by the users, it has to be written in simple and understandable language.

Electronic communication   IT-enabled communication systems or electronic communication modes have drastically changed with the advancement of technology. E-business now facilitates better customer reach, cutting across national boundaries. With increasing computerization, organizations worldwide now make use of this type of communication to spread their customer reach.

International communication   This requires customization of the communication systems of organizations, duly accounting for the cultural differences. With globalization, organizations now need to live up to the cross-cultural expectations and behaviour of people while entering into verbal and non-verbal communication with their international clients.

   The specific type of communication suitable in a particular case depends on the organizational choice, keeping in view the intent or the purpose. Thus, managers should be professional in their communication and need to acquire the requisite technical skills; otherwise, poor communication will prove detrimental to the organization, rendering it inefficient in responding to the needs and expectations of various stakeholders.

Communication Process

Communication is a process that is limited not only to some units in an organization but rather encompasses various psychological, behavioural, and group influences. Thus, to understand the communication process, one has to think beyond the traditional ambit of source, target, message, and medium, that is, the several units of communication.

Practitioner Speak 14.2

Your Communications May Not Be Communicating

Have you ever been in an organization where communication was not an issue? If so, you're the exception rather than the rule.

Read this insightful blog posted by Ashkenas on *HBR Blog Network* by accessing the following link: http://blogs.hbr.org/ashkenas/2011/02/your-communications-may-not-be.html.

PSYCHOLOGICAL AND BEHAVIOURAL INFLUENCES ON COMMUNICATION

The basic intent of communication is to develop a common understanding. Through communication, one tries to develop relationships based on shared mental maps. These maps follow a structure and understanding that enriches the managers' subjective experience, which they relate with the external reality for a trade-off with the perceptual incongruence between the sender and the receiver of communication. Perception is the use of senses to construct mental maps that are congruent with an individual's beliefs and the environment. Cross-cultural differences make perceptions less than perfect in three different ways—deletion, distortion, and generalization.

Deletion   This occurs due to the limitation of the physical senses. Development of the senses takes place as a natural process of an individual's experience of responding to the environment. Thus, the beliefs and values develop in a gradual process, which are then used in communication. For example, Douglas McGregor's Theory X and Theory Y, categorizing people as bad or good, are the reflections of the beliefs and values that might have developed through the process of deletion.

Distortion   Similar to deletion, distortion in communication also takes place due to the inability to correctly observe the external environment. It alters people's perceptions because it influences them to perceive things in a way that supports their existing beliefs and values. Describing a strange flying object as an unidentified flying object (UFO) from another planet or attributing the failure of a business to the ill luck of its chief executive officer are good examples of distortion.

Generalization   Many beliefs, which are based on one's perceptions and generalizations, are used in communication. The quality of any product made by TATA is good, whereas that made by others will be questionable, is an example of generalization-based perception. The generalization of the environment develops through the process of experience. Similar to a situational leader, one generalizes the environment to decide one's style of communication according to what yielded results in the past. Some generalizations in communication may be good, whereas some may be bad.

An organization may find it difficult to change its communication strategies because of the dynamics of human behaviour. An effective communication strategy should match the mental maps of both the communicators so that it evokes the desired response.

GROUP COMMUNICATION

Communication in organizations takes place both individually (interpersonal communication) and in groups. To manage the business complexity, organizations form groups to pool knowledge and resources. People in a group jointly solve problems; hence, they need to communicate to coordinate their activities. Exchange of information and communication takes place both between groups and within groups. The nature and type of group communication depends largely on the intent or purpose of the group. Communication within a self-directed group is different from that within a focus group. The factors essential for ensuring the effectiveness of interpersonal communication also apply for group communication. However, non-verbal communication and listening skills are more important for groups.

In general, small groups are formed to achieve a specific task. Hence, unlike most interpersonal communication, communication in a small group is primarily task-oriented. It is important to adopt a blend and motivational approach of communication to make the group members feel comfortable. This helps in quickly reaching a group consensus. The blend approach resolves differences of opinion, and motivation makes members follow through. Hence, group communication requires managers to have special skills such as an understanding of the group characteristics, group dynamics, specific influence over group members, and role of leadership. There are no specific guidelines for the size, type, and purpose of small groups, and they vary from one organization to the other. The size of a small group may be anything between two and twenty members if the goal or purpose remains the same. A strategic group may represent members in the top level of the organization, whereas a task group may involve people at the operational level. Hence, the style of communication varies according to the members constituting the group.

Groups can be primary, formal, or informal. *Primary groups* are formed for the self-satisfaction of its members. *Informal groups* are formed to improve interpersonal relations rather than for achieving any specific task or objective. *Formal groups*, however, are formed to achieve a specific goal or objective, that is, they are by nature more task-oriented. Again, depending on the goals or objectives, formal groups can be informational, educational, related to training, or problem-solving. *Informational groups* are formed in conferences, meetings, and briefings. In communications among this type of formal group, information sharing is ensured by adopting consistency in approach. Members in such groups can raise questions and participate in discussions. *Educational and training groups*, such as the employee induction, training, and development departments, facilitate the development of employees. *Problem-solving groups* can be either formal or informal and are formed to attain a specific objective.

Depending on the degree of group influence, organizational communication styles differ. A strong group influence makes the group members subscribe to certain assumptions and behavioural norms, which may either be explicit or implicit. Group influence can result in conformity, resistance, competition, or conflict. A manager's role is to communicate in a manner that develops group cohesiveness; however, intragroup conflicts spark higher levels of competition. Organizations need to enhance their competitive advantage by developing collaborative capabilities and increasing their spread globally. This requires organizations to revisit their communication strategies, focusing on virtual teams to cope with uncertainty, ambiguity, and many cross-cultural issues. The problem further mounts in cross-border mergers and acquisitions. With geographically dispersed virtual teams, communication now largely depends on electronic media. Group communication influenced by the opinion of the majority may vitiate the ultimate purpose, as culturally different minority groups may not be able to participate in decision-making. To ensure cohesiveness in group communication, therefore, organizations need to share information and provide opportunities to everyone to contribute their viewpoints.

Managers thus need to study cross-cultural dynamics to avoid confrontation, misunderstanding, and conflict in group communication.

COMMUNICATION BARRIERS

Communication in organizations is one of the biggest challenges today. Whenever there is an interaction between two individuals, each brings up divergent values, beliefs, expectations, goals, personality types, communication styles, and feelings. Better communication in an organizational relationship is possible only when one recognizes these differences and becomes flexible in accepting and understanding the other person's views, opinions, or communication styles; otherwise, it gives rise to communication barriers.

> Communication barriers are the results of several inadequacies that tend to distort communication and affect the success of managers in achieving organizational goals.

Communication barriers, therefore, are the results of several inadequacies that tend to distort communication and affect the success of managers in achieving organizational goals. The important communication barriers can be listed as follows:

- Distortion due to superior–subordinate relationship
- Semantic distortion
- Distortion due to premature evaluation by the recipient of communication
- Distortion due to perfunctory attention
- Distortion due to failure to communicate
- Distortion due to resistance to change

Exhibit 14.1 explains how communication barriers impede organizational effectiveness.

EXHIBIT 14.1 How Communication Barriers Impede Organizational Effectiveness

Communication barriers can prove to be a great deterrent for organizations. They can create numerous problems and ultimately be an obstacle to organizational effectiveness. Communication barriers impede organizational effectiveness because of the following reasons:

Ambiguous Messages

The message delivered often lacks clarity. This leads to confusion and the message is often misinterpreted. In order to reduce such ambiguities, the sender should keenly consider the words and technical jargon used as well as the overall message being sent.

Differences in Value Sets and Culture

Differences in value sets and other cultural considerations create many problems in organizational communication. One culture may not perceive something to be offensive, whereas others may have reservations about it. Again, value sets may vary from individual to individual within the same culture. Thus, the sender of the message has to take into consideration words and jargon that may offend others.

Stress at Workplace

Stress at the workplace may also impede the message from achieving its desired level of effectiveness. In today's world, people are always in a hurry to complete tasks and meet deadlines; hence, the sender of a message should ideally send important messages when the level of activities of the receivers is relatively low.

(Contd)

EXHIBIT 14.1 (*Contd*)

Faulty Listening Skills

Faulty listening skills can entirely mar the message. The effectiveness of any message depends on both the sender and receiver; though most of the times the sender is at fault, at times, the receiver also misses out on important messages due to poor listening skills. Many times, managers put across their points without giving others a chance to speak. This can create a barrier in achieving organizational effectiveness.

Faulty Mode of Communication

At times, the desired effect of a message is not obtained because of adopting a wrong mode of communication. Some messages, for example, official orders, are best delivered through mail, whereas others, like feedback, through verbal communication. The wrong mode of communication can create a wrong impression and the receiver is likely to take offence.

Assumptions Made during Communication

Certain assumptions underlie messages. Among these, the most prominent one is the assumption of the sender that the receiver will understand the message and react in a logical manner. However, very often it is seen that people react to messages in ways that the sender did not think of. This gap can lead to conflicts between individuals and thus becomes a barrier for attaining organizational effectiveness.

Sources: Joseph, C., Barriers to Communication that Detract from Organizational Effectiveness', http://smallbusiness.chron.com/barriers-communication-detract-organizational-effectiveness-693.html, last accessed on 6 September 2013; Liraz, M., 'Overcoming Communication Barriers', http://www.bizmove.com/skills/m8k.htm, last accessed on 6 September 2013 (adapted).

Yet, in another way, communication barriers can be broadly classified into external, organizational, and personal barriers.

External Barriers

The external barriers are further classified into two categories—semantic barriers and psychological or emotional barriers.

Semantic barriers   Semantics is the study of the meanings of words and phrases in a language. Semantic barriers are caused in the process of receiving or understanding a message by coding and decoding ideas and words. Communication primarily uses words and each word has several meanings. Therefore, the linguistic capacity of either the sender or the receiver, or both, may lead to a misunderstanding of the message. *The Oxford English Dictionary* mentions about 25 different meanings for the most commonly used 500 English words. Similar problems exist in other languages as well. Therefore, words may fail to accurately convey the meanings if they are not properly used. Semantic barriers may result due to the following reasons:

- Badly expressed message
- Faulty translation
- Unqualified assumptions
- Use of technical language

Psychological or emotional barriers   Barriers of this type arise in interpersonal communication. The interpretation of a message largely depends on the psychological and emotional states of the parties involved. These barriers arise due to the following reasons:

- Premature evaluation
- Lack of attention
- Loss of information in transmission
- Poor retention

- Lack of reliance
- Distrust of communicator

- Failure to communicate

Organizational Barriers

Organizational barriers are also known as structural barriers. Organizations are designed on the basis of formal hierarchical structures. They are created to attain certain identified objectives, which require that the day-to-day activities be regulated by developing performance standards and framing rules, regulations, procedures, policies, and behavioural norms. All these affect the free flow of communication in organizations, unless suitably managed. Superior–Subordinate relationships in a formal organizational structure inhibit the free flow of communication. Certain managers believe in keeping their subordinates at a distance. In such instances, communication often loses its very essence of being two-way. The causes of organizational barriers can be listed as follows:

Hierarchy Several hierarchical levels result in transmission losses and communication may get delayed or distorted. This particularly happens in upward communication, that is, in communication from subordinates to superiors.

Status relationships Superior–Subordinate relationships, found in a formal organizational structure, also block the flow of communication due to status incongruence.

Functional specialization Fragmenting organizations in accordance with specialization develops departmental interest and thereby, affects the free flow of communication.

Organizational policies, rules, and regulations These also stand against effective communication within an organization.

Organizational facilities Communication among the people in organizations requires certain facilities such as meetings, conferences, complaint boxes, suggestion boxes, open-door systems, and social and cultural gatherings. Unless such facilities are adequate, communication fails.

Personal Barriers

Factors internal to the communicator and the communicatee, that is, the sender and the receiver, that exert influence on the processes are known as personal or interpersonal barriers. These barriers can be broadly categorized into two types—barriers in superiors and barriers in subordinates.

Superiors act as barriers in communication in the following ways:

Nurturing of typical attitude A favourable attitude of superiors fosters effective communication, whereas an unfavourable attitude inhibits communication.

Fear of challenge to authority Such fear often causes superiors to withhold information, which dissuades them from communicating effectively.

Insistence on proper channel Superiors often insist on the flow of communication through appropriate channels, which blocks communication.

Lack of confidence in subordinates   Superiors often consider subordinates as less competent. Such perception stands against the free flow of communication.

Conscious ignorance of communication   Some superiors consciously ignore communication, which discourages subordinates from communicating.

Lack of time   Superiors think that they have no time to talk to their subordinates, which results in loss of communication.

Lack of awareness   Some superiors lack awareness about the importance and effectiveness of communication, which affects the superior–subordinate communication process.

Similarly, subordinates also act as barriers to communication in the following ways:

Unwillingness to communicate   Such unwillingness may be the result of past unpleasant experiences.

Lack of incentive   The prevailing reward and punishment system of the organization is largely responsible for this. If suggestions or any other communication from subordinates do not evoke any response from the superiors, they lose interest in communicating upward.

Methods of Overcoming Communication Barriers

The effectiveness of communication greatly contributes to the success of an organization and the performance of its managers. Therefore, it is imperative for an organization to improve the free flow of communication, overcoming the possible barriers. Some communication barriers cannot be eliminated altogether but can be controlled. To overcome communication barriers, the following methods may be carried out by organizations:

Employee orientation   If employees are given orientation about organizational objectives, policies, procedures, programmes, authority relations, and so on, communication barriers stand significantly minimized. In addition, employees need to be communicated about the organizational vision, mission, goals, objectives, and strategies, in the development of which, if required, they should be involved. Such participation enhances commitment from the employees and transparency keeps them informed. Unfortunately, organizations neglect this aspect, which culminates in conflict and creates organizational barriers. There are many examples in the corporate world where employee orientation helped the organizations achieve even more than the planned rate of growth. Wal-Mart is an example that could be emulated.

Improving interpersonal relations   Improved interpersonal relations develop mutuality in organizations, with employees becoming more cooperative and working together to accomplish organizational goals. This requires superiors to respect the dignity and authority of their subordinates, which in turn develops the subordinates' trust towards their superiors and eliminates status differences. Such an environment in an organization makes it possible for managers to communicate freely even with their personal contacts and makes communication a two-way process.

Practitioner Speak 14.3

How Leaders Refine the Message

In HBR's April issue you'll find an interview with Doris Kearns Goodwin about the lessons executives can learn about leadership from Abraham Lincoln. Goodwin is, of course, the author of the one book President Obama said he took with him to the White House (apart from the Bible), the Lincoln biography, *Team of Rivals*.

Read this insightful blog posted by Ovans on *HBR Blog Network* by accessing the following link: http://blogs.hbr.org/hbr/hbreditors/2009/03/how_leaders_refine_their_message.html.

Lack of empathetic listening Due to typical managerial attitudes, quite frequently, upward communication is greatly distorted. Managers often use their status and tend to dominate during discussions with subordinates, not allowing the subordinates to express their feelings and emotions. Such lack of listening creates barriers in communication, as managers evaluate information without getting the free and frank response from the subordinates.

Using proper language Barriers in communication are often created due to semantic distortions. This can be avoided using direct and simple language in communication. Avoiding technical terms, words with more than one meaning, difficult symbols, and so on makes it possible to eliminate communication barriers.

Communication through actions Actions speak louder than words. When subordinates communicate and superiors do not act upon them, it sends back the wrong message, which dissuades future communication. The same thing happens when the actions of superiors differ from what they say. It leads to a situation in which subordinates listen but do not act. Such barriers need to be eliminated through actions and deeds.

Judicious use of grapevine Grapevine is important for communication. However, at times, managers depend too much on the grapevine, ignoring official channels of communication. This develops a culture of informal communication, thereby creating barriers in communication. Hence, grapevine needs to be judiciously used.

Lack of information feedback Communication is essentially a two-way process. Hence, feedback is very important. When there is no information feedback, it creates barriers in communication. Even in face-to-face communication, body language may provide a successful feedback.

TRANSACTIONAL ANALYSIS

Transactional analysis (TA) was founded by Eric Berne (1961). It is now widely applied in organizational communication. The basic premise of Eric Berne's transaction analysis is Sigmund Freud's contribution to human psyche, which has already been discussed in Chapter 5. Berne advocated that during communication, one reflects one's state of mind, which translates to child ego, adult ego, or parent ego. It is also possible for a person to simultaneously reflect on all the three ego states while communicating with others.

> The basic premise of transactional analysis in organizational communication is based on the fact that during communication, people reflect their state of mind.

Every ego state carries a different meaning. For example, a communication from a child ego may be either destructive or happy. When communicating from the destructive child ego, a person reflects an uncompromising attitude and does not listen to the information provided by others. Such a person can even decide to go wrong, knowing fully well that it is going to be wrong. In contrast, a communication from the happy child ego is more accommodative, reposing confidence in others and stating that things are going to happen as desired. An adult ego communication—being formal and between two mature minds who understand the environment—is effective and contributes to organizational effectiveness. However, it can be possible only between two similar mindsets.

Communication from a parent ego can either be critical or nurturing. Critical parent ego communication shows uncompromising attitude and often becomes very unrealistic. While communicating with their subordinates, corporate leaders often become critical, further damaging the spirit and morale of the people. Nurturing parent ego communication is, however, understanding, accommodative, and more facilitating, Yet, in another way, the nurturing parent ego can be defined as nurturing (positive) or spoiling (negative), and the critical parent ego as structuring (positive) or critical (negative). Similarly, a child ego can also be classified as adapted, which may be either cooperative (positive) or compliant/resistant (negative), and free, which again may be either spontaneous (positive) or immature (negative). According to Berne, it is important for every manager to understand the communication dynamics in the context of TA.

Parent ego is the ingrained voice of authority, absorbed conditioning, learning, and attitudes, which are developed right from childhood. It is formed by external events and what influences a person as he/she grows through childhood. Child ego develops through internal reactions and feelings to external events from a person's childhood. This mental imprint represents the seeing, hearing, and feeling experiences. Adult ego, being the reflection of mature minds, embodies the experience of dealing with a situation. Thus, in a nutshell, it can be said that parent is one's taught concept and adult is one's thought concept.

Berne (1972) defined ego states as 'coherent systems of thought and feeling, manifested by corresponding patterns of behaviour'. Some authors, however, prefer the term *body language* to the word *behaviour*, because behavioural impulses may not always be evident but rather are internally felt experiences. According to Berne, each ego state is a distinct system of interacting feelings, thoughts, and potential behaviour. TA is extensively used in organizational development to create the right change premise, eliminating dysfunctional organizational behaviours.

Alternatively, TA can also be defined as a language within a language that is used to reflect the true meaning, feeling, and motive of the communicator. It helps understand the environment and then decide the choice of ego states while communicating with others. Due to its all-encompassing effects, TA is used in the theories of personality and communication; it provides a framework for understanding the behavioural pattern of the people.

As a subject, TA has developed beyond Berne's original theories. Subsequent to his death in 1970, many of his followers further extended the concepts. Wagner, Jones, and Mountain (1980) subdivided the three ego states into a seven-element model. Their model is illustrated in Fig. 14.2.

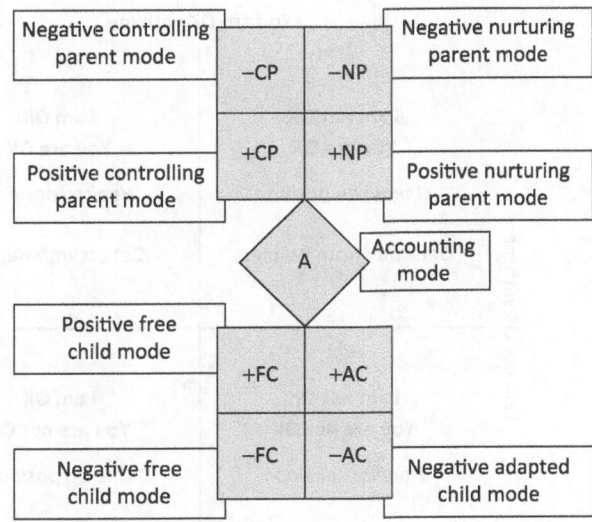

Figure 14.2 Seven-element model of transaction analysis

Parent Ego State

Nurturing   Nurturing (positive) and spoiling (negative)

Controlling   Structuring (positive) and critical (negative)

Adult Ego State

Single entity

Child Ego State

Adapted   Cooperative (positive) and compliant/resistant (negative)

Free   Spontaneous (positive) and immature (negative)

Franklin Ernst (1971) developed the OK corral matrix, which is also called corralogram, to diagram the life positions in quadrants. In this quadrant (Fig. 14.3), except for the 'I am OK–You are OK' situation, the rest are not healthy situations.

Thus, TA helps effectively communicate, duly understanding the ego states of the communicator and the communicatee. It is used to assess the ego state from which the sender is communicating the message and the ego state from which the receiver is replying to the message. One can effectively plan the transactions, analysing the ego state of the communicatee, and get the desired results. A useful technique that can be followed in transactions to make communication effective is inviting the communicatee to move into the adult ego state or the nurturing parent ego state. One can move the communicatee to the adult ego state by asking him/her questions, narrating facts, and soliciting his/her opinions, views, and preferences. Similarly, one can move the communicatee to the nurturing parent state by asking him/her for help, advice, or opinions. Often transactions from the happy, natural, or free child ego state yield better results. This is possible by showing enthusiasm, looking unconventionally at issues, or even by highlighting the lighter side of the situation.

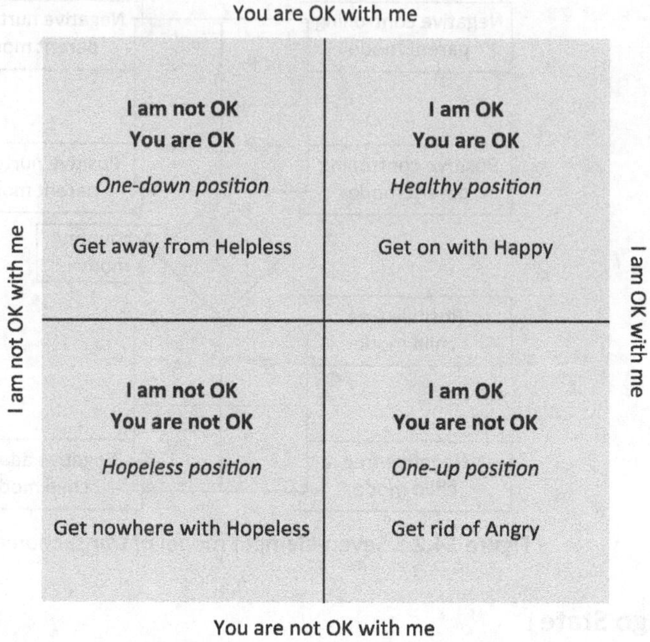

You are OK with me

I am not OK **You are OK** *One-down position* Get away from Helpless	**I am OK** **You are OK** *Healthy position* Get on with Happy
I am not OK **You are not OK** *Hopeless position* Get nowhere with Hopeless	**I am OK** **You are not OK** *One-up position* Get rid of Angry

I am not OK with me   I am OK with me

You are not OK with me

Figure 14.3 OK corral matrix

Therefore, TA can help alter the unfavourable behavioural syndrome in communication to one's advantage. Managers can model their interactions or communication with others for effective results in meetings, interpersonal relationships, negotiations, and so on.

NEGOTIATION

> *Without communication there is no negotiation. Negotiation is a process of communicating back and forth for the purpose of reaching a joint decision.*
>
> —Roger Fisher and William Ury (1981)

This quote clarifies the importance of communication for successful negotiation. In work situations, people negotiate in different forms with different stakeholders. Most of the negotiation initiatives fail due to miscommunication, poor listening skills, and misinterpretation of body language. Hence, mastering communication for effective negotiation is essential for managers. Many empirical researches on communication and negotiation observed that these two terms are intertwined.

Negotiation is a decision-making process that takes place between two parties having opposing interests. In conflict resolution, negotiation is mostly used to settle differences between the management and the unions through the collective bargaining machinery. Collective bargaining has been explained in Chapter 9. This chapter is more concerned with the communication perspectives of negotiation. In any negotiation process, two goals are considered—substantive and relationship. *Substantive goals* are those that help settle some

> Negotiation is a decision-making process that takes place between two parties having opposing interests.

claims, involving either receiving or giving some benefits. A negotiation for wage increase is an example of a substantive goal. *Relationship goals* deal with the outcome of decisions that make the two negotiating parties work together subsequent to the negotiation reached. These are very important in managing resistance to change. We not only negotiate with the employees to gain their acceptance to change issues, but also ensure they become a party to change for greater commitment and participation. Effective negotiation, therefore, requires resolving the substance issues while nurturing the harmonious relationships between the two negotiating parties. Whatever may be the process for negotiation, two approaches are followed—distributive and integrative. *Distributive approach* is a win–lose or a zero-sum game approach, whereas *integrative approach* is a collaborative approach, where both the negotiating parties try to expand the outcomes of their decisions by sharing the benefits.

A distributive negotiation approach is taken in those cases where the negotiating parties aim to settle their differences with mutually exclusive goals. Hence, both the parties intend to withhold as much information as possible and try to obtain maximum information from the other. Hence, in distributive negotiation, it often becomes difficult to take an informed decision, as the agreement is reached between the parties without adequate information backup. In contrast, in integrative negotiation, the goals of the negotiating parties are not mutually exclusive. Hence, neither of the negotiating parties gains at the expense of the other. Both the parties work together to optimize the resources in the best possible manner to gain mutual benefit. In substantive negotiation, one always tries to gain tangible benefits, whereas in integrative negotiation, one tries to gain both tangible and intrinsic satisfaction. Hence, in integrative negotiation, the negotiating parties adopt a supportive attitude, show empathy, and take informed decisions.

In some negotiations, third-party intervention is required to reach a conclusive settlement. The involvement of an arbitrator and a mediator is often required in organizational conflicts, particularly in wage-related matters.

Thus, negotiation is a process by which two parties seek to reach an agreement through bargaining. A win–win situation is possible in negotiation when each party is prepared to give up something to achieve something that the other party has. During negotiation, an organization needs to understand the following:

- What does it want?
- What can it bargain?
- What are the demands it can agree to?

It is possible to follow these steps with the help of a list of objectives, such as what the organization intends to get and what it must get. While negotiating, one must listen carefully, ask questions whenever necessary, and get clarifications whenever required. In addition, one must try to summarize the discussion. During negotiation, one must avoid arguments, interruptions, and assumptions, and even one's concerns must be expressed in a controlled manner. The negotiation can be made effective by searching for areas of common interest and by making use of positive body language. The most-commonly accepted model of negotiation involves preparing (which includes setting objectives, defining strategy, and gathering data), opening, bargaining, and closing.

Conducting negotiations in one area or the other is a part of a manager's routine work. To succeed in negotiations, managers must have analytical ability, empathy, planning ability, interactive skills, and communication skills. Such skills can be developed only through experience. Some theoretical understanding may help, but putting the learned theories into practice requires a manager to be a part of a negotiation, initially as only an observer to watch how the seniors play their role in negotiation. Negotiation skills help a manager in the following important areas:

- Optimizing time, scope, costs, and quality
- Successfully managing change in the organization
- Optimizing resource allocation
- Managing contractors and vendors
- Managing industrial relations
- Settling industrial disputes

As already mentioned, negotiation in organization involves an interaction between two conflicting groups to reach a solution acceptable to both the groups. Thus, effective negotiation intends to resolve conflicting situations by striking a win–win solution (acceptable to both the conflicting parties). Depending on the situation, the style of negotiation may differ. For successful negotiation, managers need to prepare beforehand. They must understand the scale of disagreement. For major disagreements, thorough preparation is necessary, preferably using a worksheet. For minor disagreements, such preparation may not be necessary, as it may turn out to be manipulative. While preparing to negotiate for disagreements, managers (negotiators) must try to understand the following:

- Goals—what they intend to achieve through negotiation—and the trades—the extent to which they can stretch (in terms of accepting the conditions, involving financial benefits or otherwise)
- Alternatives—possible ways to reach a decision when the original line of action fails
- Relationships—account for the history of relationships and how it may impact the negotiation
- Expected outcome—understand in advance the possible expectations of people from the negotiation
- Consequences—analyse the possible consequences (winning or losing) of the negotiation
- Power—analyse the power in the relationship, resource control, etc.

In addition, a manager must assess the possible solutions of the negotiation.

It is important for both the negotiating parties to feel positive and to control their emotional reactions. Managers, at the outset, try to unfreeze in order to ensure that the negotiating

Practitioner Speak 14.5

How to Size Up a Negotiation

In one of my posts last year, I shared a framework for more effective negotiations. The first step of the framework described the need for pre-negotiation homework with an emphasis on understanding the specific interests and positions of the opposing side. Making a list of these points is the right starting place as it helps show where the biggest gaps might be.

Read this insightful blog posted by Tjan on *HBR Blog Network* by accessing the following link: http://blogs.hbr.org/tjan/2010/02/how-to-size-up-a-negotiation.html.

group members feel at ease to break the deadlock. The entire negotiation should be so conducted that everyone commits to the issues of differences and agrees to the line of solution.

Exhibit 14.2 discusses the deterrents to an effective negotiation process.

EXHIBIT 14.2   Deterrents to an Effective Negotiation

Negotiation is not everyone's favourite activity. Some people get it right almost every time they are into it, whereas others find it hard to come out with a favourable bargain. Negotiating can be an art for many; for others, it is a typically stressful activity. However difficult negotiations might pose to be for managers, there are some obvious rules that set things right for them to haggle on. Even before one gets the premise for negotiations right, one should be aware of the deterrents that do not let managers negotiate properly.

Fear can be a major hurdle for many managers. Managers often panic while negotiating and this deters them from settling for the best outcome. Panic obviously leads to apprehension and fear and this in turn to a less favourable outcome in the negotiation. There are three major types of fears that individuals face while negotiating:

- Fear that the negotiation will end up as a futile exercise
- Fear that dragging the negotiation beyond a point may end up proving the individual incompetent
- Fear that one's knowledge base may not be taken seriously by the opponent

While these fears are rampant in organizational negotiations, one must also set the basic premise of the negotiation right. This refers to the basic rules of the game or the basic points on which the negotiation is supposed to take place. Many times, both parties in a negotiation keep discussing different terms and thus a consensus may not be reached. Even if there is consensus, the resulting deal is an uneasy equilibrium and never a win–win situation for the parties involved. Thus, the first step in any negotiation is to ensure that both parties are playing the same game, that is, negotiating on the same points.

Establishing common grounds for any negotiation helps managers fall back on their preparedness and thus favourable outcomes are likely for both parties.

Sources: Camp, J. 'How Fear Can Derail a Negotiation', 9 March 2013, http://www.forbes.com/sites/jimcamp/2013/09/03/how-fear-can-derail-a-negotiation/, last accessed on 6 September 2013; Jensen, K. 'You Can't "Win" Negotiations without Rules of the Game', 9 March 2013, http://www.forbes.com/sites/keldjensen/2013/09/03/you-cant-win-negotiations-without-rules-of-the-game/#, last accessed on 6 September 2013 (adapted).

SUMMARY

Communication is a process involving interaction, interchange, sharing, and common understanding. In business, most of one's working time is spent on communication. Communication follows a definite process involving the sender, receiver, message, channel, feedback, and situation. It essentially follows a two-way channel. Communication plays an important role in all managerial functions. It serves the purpose of information, command and instruction, influence and persuasion, and integration. There are certain barriers in communication. An organization has to control such barriers for more productive and efficient use of communication.

There is a difference of opinion about the term *communication*, more specifically about the usage of the word as *communication* or *communications*. Hence, managers need to understand the contextual differences. The plural of communication refers to a system for communicating or a system of routes. Communication per se is a process through which exchange of information takes place between individuals, using some system, symbol, or behaviour.

The total process of communication attempts to activate the human senses. Thus, perceptual congruity between the sender and the receiver is very important to get the desired result through communication in organizations.

Negotiation is a decision-making process that takes place between two parties having opposing interests. In conflict resolution, negotiation is mostly used to settle differences between the management and the unions through the collective bargaining machinery. Effective negotiation, therefore, requires resolving the substance issues while nurturing the harmonious relationships between the two negotiating parties.

Transactional analysis was founded by Eric Berne. It is now widely applied in organizational communication. Berne advocated that during communication one reflects one's state of mind, which translates to child ego, adult ego, or parent ego. It is possible for a person to simultaneously reflect all the three ego states while communicating with others.

KEY DEFINITIONS

Diagonal communication Interactions that cut across the hierarchical barriers, such as a communication between the chairman and a worker of an organization

Downward communication Interactions between the superiors and subordinates wherein the superiors communicate with the subordinates

External communication Interactions between two organizations or between an organization and others outside the organization

Horizontal communication Interactions between two equals, that is, between persons working at the same level in organizations

Human relations and team building Communication that harmonizes interpersonal relations, which extends even to customer relations

International communication Interactions that cut across international boundaries and require customization of communication systems of organizations, duly accounting for the cultural differences

Non-verbal communication A form of communication that occurs without the use of words

Sales communication A form of communication designed to achieve sales objectives and encompasses advertising, telephone etiquette, and face-to-face communication

Upward communication Interactions between the subordinates and the superiors where the subordinates communicate with the superiors

Verbal communication A form of communication that uses words and languages for interaction, which can be either oral or written, and is extensively used in organizations

CONCEPT-REVIEW QUESTIONS

14.1 Define the term *communication* and list out its important characteristics.

14.2 Explain the process of communication.

14.3 What is a two-way communication channel? What are its features?

14.4 What are the important features of communication?

14.5 List out the important objectives of communication.

14.6 Describe the essential elements of business communication.

14.7 What are the different types of communication? Explain their relative merits and demerits.

14.8 Discuss the barriers to communication in an organization. How do they affect organizational efficiency?

14.9 How can we overcome barriers to communication?

14.10 Write short notes on the following:
 (a) Formal and informal communication
 (b) Verbal and non-verbal communication
 (c) Upward and downward communication
 (d) Horizontal and diagonal communication
 (e) Grapevine
 (f) Body language

CRITICAL THINKING QUESTION

14.1 You have been called by your boss to attend your annual performance review meeting. During the last two quarters, your performance level was below 50 per cent of your target, whereas in the first two quarters, you could achieve more than 120 per cent of the targets assigned. In your organization, performance targets are decided in a participative manner. Your boss appears to be quite concerned about your performance. In such a situation, how will you communicate to your boss when he asks the reasons for your poor performance? Frame your answer in the form of a conversation.

SELECT BIBLIOGRAPHY

- Berne, E., *Transactional Analysis in Psychotherapy*, Grove Press, New York, 1961.
- Berne, E., *What Do You Say after You Say Hello?* Grove Press, New York, 1972.
- Berne, E., *The Mind in Action*, Simon and Schuster, New York, 1947.
- Berne, E., *The Structure and Dynamics of Organizations and Groups*, Grove Press, New York, 1963.
- Berne, E., *Games People Play*, Grove Press, New York, 1964.
- Bhattacharyya, Dipak Kumar, *Human Resource Management*, Excel Books, New Delhi, 2006.
- Ernst, Franklin, 'The OK Corral: The Grid for Get-on-with', *TAJ*, Vol. 1, Issue 4, 1971, p. 23.
- Fisher, Roger and William Ury, *Getting to Yes: Negotiating Agreement without Giving in*, Houghton Mifflin, Boston, 1981.
- Novey, T. 'Measuring the Effectiveness of Transactional Analysis—An International Study', *Transactional Analysis Journal*, Vol. 32, 2002, pp. 8–24.
- Usunier, J.C., *International and Cross-cultural Management Research*, Sage, London, 1998.

CASE STUDY

Failed Communication

Vachani is the quality controller for the four divisions of a family-owned manufacturing organization in which the functional heads enjoy a large measure of autonomy. Bose is the production superintendent of one of the four divisions. By and large, both these senior executives, who report to the general manager (works), get along well as colleagues though they have their usual differences and disagreements over issues concerning quality.

One day, Bose stormed into Vachani's office and shouted, 'Your senior inspector, Sundaram, has misbehaved with me and I will not tolerate it. You must take immediate action against him.' Vachani asked Bose to cool down and explain what exactly had happened, giving the facts. Narrating the incident, Bose said that in the morning he had observed one of his workers carrying out a job out of routine. On being asked to explain why this was so, the worker said that he was working on the job as per the advice of Sundaram. On returning to his office, he called Sundaram to enquire about the matter. The latter did not respond at first but, on being sent for once again, appeared before him. Asked why he had assigned the out-of-routine job to the worker, Sundaram did not give a satisfactory answer. He was asked to leave after being advised not to confuse the workers. However, Sundaram reacted by making rude remarks and misbehaving.

Vachani patiently listened to Bose and advised him not to get agitated, adding that he (Vachani) would talk to Sundaram about the matter. On Bose's attempts to again tell Vachani as to what he wanted to be done, the latter said he would himself decide the best course of action, though of course, Bose was free to take any alternative action he felt necessary.

After some time, Sundaram came to see Vachani in his office. The latter did not indicate that he was aware of the incident with Bose. After discussing various matters, Sundaram told Vachani, 'Today I had a fight with Bose.' He proceeded to narrate the whole incident. His account of the meeting with Bose was as follows: 'I went to Bose's office a little after I was called in. He harshly asked me to explain why I did not respond immediately on being sent for. I politely replied that when I arrived, he was immersed in some work and I did not want to disturb him. When he continued to press the issue, I told him to discuss with you (Vachani) if I was required to respond immediately to his calls even if some work suffers in the process. About the out-of-routine job, I tried to explain that this became necessary in view of the important inspection on Monday (about which Bose was also aware) and that I had taken the initiative in the interest of work. Anyway, Bose rudely told me not to instruct his men directly and to get out. This infuriated me and I angrily told Bose that it was he who had called me. He then used foul language and as a result hot words were exchanged, so much so that I felt like hitting him.' Sundaram further added that he was nowhere at fault and that Bose's behaviour, especially in asking him to 'get out', really provoked him. He said though he always gave Bose due regard as a senior, the latter had no right to be as rude and insulting as he was.

It needs to be mentioned here that Sundaram had been working to the complete satisfaction of Vachani and at times carried out his own liaison with Bose and his department, whenever required to do so. After thinking over the incident for a few minutes, Vachani advised Sundaram to go to Bose some time later and talk to him reminding him (Bose) politely about the use of strong words like 'get out' and admitting that he (Sundaram) had lost his temper. In this way, he felt that Bose would not take offence to what Sundaram had said. After some persuasion, Sundaram agreed to do so and went back. About an hour later, Vachani received a call from Sundaram saying that he had information that Bose had reported the matter to the personnel manager, and as such, there was no need for him now to talk to Bose as suggested by Vachani. He also said that he would rather let the matter be decided otherwise, since he was not at fault.

Questions for Discussion

1. Was Vachani's suggestion to Sundaram to talk out the matter with Bose correct under the circumstances?

2. Was Bose justified in reporting the incident to the personnel manager soon after he had apprised Vachani of it?

3. What action, if any, should the personnel manager take in this regard once this is reported to him?

4. If Bose is found to be guilty in implicating Sundaram without any substantial reason, what remedy do you think the personnel manager should suggest to avoid recurrence of such incidents in the future?

Globalization and Organizational Behaviour

LEARNING OBJECTIVES

After studying this chapter, the reader will be able to

- understand the definition and context of globalization
- discuss the role of transnational corporations
- realize the impact of technology in the context of globalization
- describe the role of governments in the context of globalization
- understand the challenges of globalization for managers
- explain organizational purposes, values, core processes, and decentralized authority
- describe leadership, globalization, and changing business practices in India
- determine the future of career planning and development in India in the context of globalization
- examine public sector reforms in the context of globalization

CASE STUDY

Globalization and Organizational Change in Fortune Furnitech

Globalization is perceived as an economic imperative in today's organizations. Economic issues often overshadow the internal organizational changes in the corporate sector; these changes are aimed at preparing the organization's defence mechanism in the global economic integration process. Major changes in the restructuring processes of organizations (which also includes the firms' behaviour) due to globalization necessitate changes in the production and distribution processes as well. Firms become part of global supply chains with widespread global networking. All these require new management strategies, such as outsourcing and encompassing people-related issues. To cut costs and achieve economies of scale, companies are now creating networked organizational structures, outsourcing their production and service facilities and even manpower requirements, by opting for cross-border recruitment.

Fortune Furnitech has to source its furniture upholstery from China to achieve price efficiency. However, the Chinese manufacturers refused to customize the upholstery items, catering to the design requirements of Fortune Furnitech, which they source from Italian designers. The company performs the final crafting in India and then sells its finished furniture items in domestic and global markets.

In the first year, the operational results of the company saw its net worth depleted to the extent of 50 per cent. This resulted in immediate restructuring and a re-look at the company's strategies and business plans. A board-level review committee emphasized the need for a quick solution to improve the cash flow. It suggested the introduction of low-price furniture items for the domestic market, duplicating the Italian designs, to avoid royalty payment obligations to the designers. The committee felt that after two years of such operations in the domestic market, the company would be able to stabilize its business globally. However, the implementation of this plan led to serious problems, because the local designers refused to copy the Italian designs on grounds of professional ethics. When they were forced, many of them resigned and joined its rival companies, making the company's strategies openly known in the market.

INTRODUCTION

The importance of organizational behaviour (OB) has accentuated subsequent to globalization and the consequent changes in business practices. Since the term *globalization* has many ramifications, one needs to first understand its different dimensions and then attempt a compact definition. In the economic context, globalization is interpreted as a worldwide phenomenon or process. Some economic and monetary policies together facilitate the process of globalization. Some of the economic dimensions of globalization include expansion of international trade, cross-border labour migration, and cross-border flow of investments. From the OB point of view, the biggest concern of globalization is the impact and influence of multinational and transnational companies. Participation of these companies in trade, investment, and production expanded international communication and created various cross-cultural issues. Nowadays, even to operate locally, Indian organizations need to track these issues and renew their business practices regularly, changing the mindsets of their people.

Globalization has many dimensions. The most general is the economic globalization. OB studies are now increasingly becoming complex due to the effect of globalization. Some of the important areas of concern are the changing technologies with a sharp increase in cross-border technology transfers, the mobility of organizations and people in the global world, and the competition for markets and customers on a global scale. Globalization can be considered as the increasing trend to interact beyond physical boundaries. The consequence of globalization includes deregulation and privatization of public sectors in certain countries, technological convergence, and increased competition. Furthermore, globalization has taken many forms such as foreign investment and international partnerships. From the perspective of business organizations, there are three different types of globalization—multinationals, global, and international companies. The cascading effect of globalization transcends even to the task or operational environment of business organizations. Changes in the operational environment require focus not only on the new product or service development but also on the skills and competency sets, attitudes, values, and cultures of the people. These changes are primarily attributable to the shift in the expectations of customers and the behaviour of competitors.

The consequential effect of globalization on organizations is an increase in alliances and partnerships rather than authority and control. This is characterized by the breakdown of tall hierarchies, increase in the use of teams, reorganization of functional departments into cross-functional groups, reduction in centralized control, and enhancement of local autonomy. Another key aspect, from the perspective of a business organization, is the harvesting of the knowledge of the people. This is facilitated by knowledge management practices, using various tools, techniques, and values. Through knowledge management, organizations can acquire, develop, measure, distribute, and earn a return on their intellectual assets.

Globalization has also changed the nature of managerial work, requiring managers in the globalized era to increase their judgemental power, use persuasion and influence, shape the behaviour of people, and so on.

DEFINITION AND CONCEPTS

Globalization implies the integration of world economies. It includes a rapid increase in the movement of goods, services, and capital across national borders. Globalization is related to the increase in the significance of individual businesses that operate in a range of countries. Increasingly, these businesses are considering the world as a single market. One of the key drivers in globalization is the role of transnational corporations (TNCs). The United Nations defines TNC as 'an association which possesses and controls the means of production of goods and services outside the country in which they were established'. Activities are dispersed worldwide but are specialized in locations that are best suited to these particular activities. TNCs usually have their headquarters in one country but have complex networks servicing their worldwide activities. Examples of TNCs include General Motors, Shell, Nestle, and Sony.

For OB, globalization means changes in the way the organizations work. It is characterized by unprecedented increases in international trade (Legrain 2002). It is difficult to isolate any single reason for the globalization of an organization. A series of structural changes in the markets and societies succeeds globalization. Some of these are the behaviour and performance of firms that operate across several countries, relationships between firms across national boundaries, increasing ability of consumers to access international suppliers, and international exploitation of intangible assets within firms, which are also accessible to consumers. As a result of globalization, there is decreasing importance of geography in the choices firms make regarding where to conduct specific parts of their operations, how much of their operations they choose to do themselves, and how they finance them. Yip (1992) documented the effect of globalization on a firm's behaviour and strategy. The investment strategy of a firm can be either horizontal or vertical. Organizations that follow the horizontal investment strategy reproduce their own business models in foreign countries. The vertical investment strategy, on the other hand, requires an organization to create a production chain even in foreign countries for reaping the advantages of integration.

> Globalization implies the integration of world economies. For organizational behaviour, globalization means changes in the way organizations work.

Outsourcing is the most visible outcome of globalization that impacts industry structures, wages, and income distribution (Feenstra 1998). Globalization has made it possible for individual consumers to access international markets and make an informed choice. Customers are now able to internationally benchmark price, quality, and services, and then take informed decisions. Globalization, thus, increases the incidence of international trade with appropriate trade integration in a borderless market and accentuates cross-border transactions. Inevitably, all these have impact on the organizational activities.

Issues concerning OB now require more emphasis on making people adaptable to change by enabling them to understand the competition. Partnering people in the change process evokes a positive response from the workers. For many organizations, labour cost is the most significant component of the total cost. With globalization, cost competitiveness is now achieved by organizations through outsourcing and the relocation of their manufacturing operations to countries with low labour cost. The lowering of inter-country trade barriers has made it possible for organizations to internationally source their requirements.

Role of Transnational Companies

Organizations such as BP and Coca-Cola provide the framework and motivation for globalization. To maximize profits, these organizations locate their manufacturing activities in countries with low-wage cost and globally sell their products. This ensures cost competitiveness and a wide market reach across the globe. Nike, for example, produces much of its output in low-wage countries like Indonesia, using contract labour.

Role of Global Consumers

Cultural differences have traditionally created a great variety of distinctive markets. Increased interaction through travel, television, and the Internet has reduced the preference for local products. McDonald's, for example, is now able to market a reasonably uniform product in diverse places such as Russia and China, and more recently even in India.

Impact of Technology

Globalization has brought the world closer in terms of economic activities, thereby reducing distances and time. All these have become possible due to revolutionary advancements in the technologies of transport and communications. Technology has now extended the market reach, ensuring the free flow of goods and services. With the easy transferability of technology, today even low-technology third-world countries can reap the advantages of globalization and make themselves globally competitive.

Role of Governments and Deregulation of Financial Markets

Globalization has also induced the governments of many countries to deregulate their economies through a series of economic reforms and restructuring programmes. For example, India has reduced the trade barriers, allowing free flow of foreign capital in a number of areas. It has also initiated a few institutional changes, such as delicensing, price decontrol, financial sector reforms, virtual scrapping of the Monopolies and Restrictive Trade Practices Act, and partial rupee convertibility.

The deregulated financial markets are now encouraging foreign direct investment and foreign institutional investment, taking the Indian economy to a new regime of openness,

> **Practitioner Speak 15.1**
>
> **Globalization Myths versus Reality**
>
> I still remember a TV interview a year ago in Mumbai where the first question I was asked—quite seriously or, should I say, flatly?—was why I still thought the world was round. Spouting such attitudes—the flattening of the world, the death of distance and the disappearance of differences across countries—seems to be considered a hallmark of global thinking. But I prefer to think of it as 'globaloney'.
>
> Read this insightful blog posted by Ghemawat on *HBR Blog Network* by accessing the following link: http://blogs.hbr.org/ghemawat/2007/09/globalization_myths_versus_rea_1.html.

globalization, and efficiency and achieving an almost double-digit growth in the gross domestic product (GDP). Many countries have also actively encouraged TNCs by offering concessions and making special exceptions to their environmental laws. Earlier, South Korea was engaged in the environmentally hazardous commercial activity of wrecking the ships of developed countries in its territory. In the early phase of its response to globalization, India also allowed the entry of low-technology manufacturers (e.g., companies such as Coca-Cola and Pepsi) to set up their manufacturing facilities in India, even though it hurt the interests of the domestic companies.

GLOBALIZATION CHALLENGES FOR MANAGING ORGANIZATIONAL BEHAVIOUR

A key management challenge is to balance the short- and long-term strategies, with investment in people as a long-term strategy while simultaneously managing short-term finances. This includes the long-term development of people through the creation of new jobs within the organizations. Within this context, the key management challenges are to focus on the customer rather than the product and services, integration and management of the resources required to provide this focus, open systems encouraging the sharing of information, and new forms of customer–supplier relationships and organizational structures. Another management challenge is to develop the ability to encourage loyalty and to motivate employees. Both these aspects have a direct impact on the way managers deliberate in managing the human, technical, and business dimensions of an organization and strategically manage intellectual capital.

With such challenges before the management, change can be viewed from multiple perspectives, such as the level of change (global, societal, organizational, individual), the significance of change (deep-rooted, superficial), and the implications of change (social, management), to mention a few possibilities. One of the most significant issues facing business organizations is developing a sense of the fundamental changes. The increasing need for business transformation to position oneself for the new business contexts represents a fundamental shift in the relationship of corporations to individuals and to the society as a whole. The most important question raised by globalization is how to deal with this shift at the level of the individuals affected by such changes.

The first challenge for an organization is the complexity in managing it, more particularly the behaviour of the people. In managing diversity, global organizations face a complex set of challenges characterized by diversity inside and outside the organization—across every aspect of the business and its strategy drivers. Inside the organization, executives must manage and respond to more diversity in the (internationalizing) human resource (HR) pool, more variety in the management systems, more variation in the means and ends ranging from simple financial goals to a more comprehensive view, and different business models for different types of business units. Outside the organization, there is higher diversity; heterogeneous customer needs; differing cultural values; a plethora of stakeholders with different claims (investors, customers, employees, regulators, etc.); various political, economic, and legal environments; and finally, the competitors' differing strategies. Most firms today increasingly face each of these types of diversity.

The second challenge of globalization for an organization is interdependence. Organizations need to manage the effect of global interdependence to an unprecedented degree. Everything is related to everything else, and the impact is felt more rapidly and pervasively. Value webs have replaced traditional value chains. Reputation, financial flows, value chain flows, and top management and corporate governance issues have reached advanced levels of interdependence. The less clear-cut the boundaries of a company become, the more it is exposed to impacts on the value chain flow through mistakes, frictions, reverse trends, or even shocks. Interdependence creates opportunities for globalization but also raises challenges.

The third challenge faced by the organizations in a globalized era is that of managing ambiguity. The business world today is characterized by too much information with very little clarity on how to interpret and apply insights. A diversity of accounting standards renders financial figures ambiguous. Studies, scenarios, survey results, and reports become less reliable due to an ever-increasing uncertainty. Many businesses find it more and more difficult to discover what their clear value drivers are. Are these their image, price, related services, privileged relationships, speed, knowledge, or something else? The cause–effect relationships become blurred.

As if these complexity drivers are not enough, managers have to face yet another one—the flux. Even if they figure out temporary solutions for the challenges of interdependence, diversity, and ambiguity for their specific company, industry, and personal situation, the situation can change the very next day. Today's solutions may be outdated tomorrow.

Organizational Preparedness to Cope with Challenges of Globalization

Global companies first reacted to the complex business environment by creating complex organizations. The law of requisite variety suggests that the internal complexity of an organization must match the complexity of its external environment. There are multiple axes of management—along product lines, geography, customers, functions, and projects. For example, ABB had a six-dimensional matrix structure (for a short time, at least, before they simplified the structure dramatically in their turnaround). The simple relation between the headquarters as the strategic decision-makers and the subsidiaries as the implementers is blurred by the centres of excellence or competence, market responsibilities, joint ventures, and so on.

> The law of requisite variety suggests that the internal complexity of an organization must match the complexity of its external environment.

However, structures and policies alone are not the solution. The more complex the structures and policies, the more complex they are to manage. Eventually, the organization implodes upon itself, spending more time managing the internal complexity than interacting with the environment, where real value is created. Some organizations, therefore, believe in simplification. In managing complexity, organizations should focus on the professional quality of decision-making. They should encourage the simplification of the organizational processes in specific ways rather than predicting the outcome and simplifying one's picture of the environment. Four key issues are identified around which companies must simplify—purpose and values, core processes and decentralization, early awareness systems, and leadership. Once these are clear and consistent, managers in different areas of the company can respond to complexity according to their own needs and realities.

Purpose and Values

Globalization requires organizations to review their vision and mission. Organizations should develop a framework for prioritizing goals. Managers should clearly and thoroughly understand the factors that drive the business, the fundamentals of the business's profitability, and the reasons for the company being in business. This might be difficult for a diversified multinational, but it has to be achieved at least at the level of a division or strategic business unit. Once this is understood, it leads to the values—the business *should and ought to* focus on—to determine the priorities in dilemmas, to help focus on actions, and to provide consistent patterns of behaviour over time. Companies that are the best in dealing with complexities never have more than three or four core values. These values should never be compromised and, therefore, should be consistent with the compelling business logic. A long list of values is confusing at best, and at worst provides a rationale for any action. At the same time, it is helpful to have a few behavioural values beyond the core, which guide the *how* of the execution. Behavioural values can be compromised but explanations must be provided. A clearly defined and well-accepted set of core values and a guiding set of behavioural values therefore allow diversity at the periphery, local empowerment for adaptation, learning and experimentation, and the existence of additional values per region, unit, and profession—as long as they do not contradict the core values.

Core Processes and Decentralization

Core processes are the processes used by the entire company. These vary from business to business. For a manufacturing unit, the core processes might be capital budgeting and logistics. In a pharmaceuticals firm, they might be research and development and go-to-market strategy. In a consulting firm, they might be knowledge sharing and recruitment. A firm's core processes should always be standardized (not necessarily centralized) and should be based on comprehensive and accessible information platforms. As this imposes cost, one has to be very clear about what is needed as the core.

Such processes might change over time and also more frequently than the changes in the business model or the core values. It is, therefore, important to erase the old processes when introducing new ones. However, only standardized processes generate the transparency key for accountability on the levels further down the organization. With such transparency and accountability, decentralization is possible. Decentralization consistent with the core processes allows local managers to handle complexity in the way that is most effective for them.

Early Awareness Systems

To cope with unpredictable situations, organizations develop their early awareness systems to track the dysfunctional activities. Such tracking is possible when organizations use tools like tracking signals, design or structure in line with the viable systems model, or change some of their metrics. Tracking signals can help in understanding the deviation from plans, and therefore, can alert or send signals when the degree of deviation reaches its danger level. Viable systems model, pioneered by Stafford Beer (1979), suggests continuous interface or organization with the external environment, and accordingly calibrates the organization, pacing with the changing needs. Metrics are designed by the organizations to interpret the functions and assess their changes in quantitative terms.

Leadership

Leading a complex organization requires an entirely different mindset. Hierarchy works if every level is doing something distinct and specific. However, due to the interdependence and complexity, this is impossible in today's organizations. By simplifying and clarifying the purpose, values, and core processes and through decentralization and early awareness systems, hierarchy can be supplemented by *heterarchy*—the interdependent, networked organization in which every part reflects a different perspective of the whole, which is needed in today's global business world. The boss no longer tells the team members what exactly to do but rather depends on their initiative, creativity, and competence for the success of the organization.

Leadership in a networked organization not only means managing complexity in global organizations by providing different leadership roles and styles depending on the situation (but always consistent with the purpose, values, and core processes). It also means leading different parts of a networked organization to work together to create value. The leader of a complex organization must create and communicate an understanding of the different roles the managers, teams, business units, and bosses play in the interdependent structure; otherwise, the confusion might get intensified. Leadership must not be repetitive; however it should be predictable. Permanent communication is, therefore, a leadership survival tool in complex organizations, but much more in terms of storytelling, interpreting context and meaning, and investing in relationships than in transferring dry facts or ultimatums. It is difficult to achieve global complexity by following corporate practices.

It is very difficult to come across a company that has mastered global complexity—perhaps there never was and there never will be any. The decade-long difficulties of General Motors (GM)—and, to a lesser degree, Ford—clearly have their roots in the long traditional control mode, leading to GM's vast bureaucracy and a typical outcome—mediocre products due to risk aversion, mistrust of management (reflected in the high degree of unionization), high transaction costs, and slow response. An opposite example is Toyota, with a very clear value set (which is now challenged, as it becomes a truly global

> By clarifying the purpose, values, and core processes and through decentralization and awareness systems, hierarchy can be complemented by *heterarchy*—the interdependent, networked organization in which every part reflects a different perspective of the whole.

company, a simpler model of core business processes, and standardized processes throughout the world. The famous notion that every engineer at Toyota can work in every Toyota factory of the world without having adaptation problems is probably slightly exaggerated). A similar set of elements is found in many other global companies, family-managed businesses, and luxury goods businesses (due to the identification with the product). DuPont is known for its strong values on safety. Industries driven by research and development, such as the pharmaceutical industry, are known for focused business models (if they have not overcompensated this by seize-through mergers). Energy companies, especially Exxon Mobile, are driven by standardized global processes. On the contrary, the fast-moving consumer goods industry and the food industry are known for strong regional decentralization, but they have shared processes bound together across business lines. Although no company may ever completely master complexity, it is possible, using these principles, to at least navigate through complexity and even take advantage of it.

Exhibit 15.1 discusses the challenges that leaders face because of globalization.

EXHIBIT 15.1 How Globalization is All Set to Change Leadership

Globalization has left its imprint on all major areas of business including the way it is managed. Since globalization has helped the business community integrate like never before, leadership has also changed accordingly to accommodate the changes in the macroenvironment. In this regard, given the changed business environment under which leaders have to work, quite a few fundamental changes have to be brought forth in leadership to sustain and lead effectively. These are as follows:

Managing Workplace Diversity

Globalization has brought the global business community closer. This has led to the proliferation of transnational organizations wherein employees from different cultures, backgrounds, and value sets work together. A key leadership challenge would be to manage the increasingly diverse kinds of employees who work together to meet the organizational objectives under the same roof.

Managing and Coping with Demographic Changes

As all major nations adopting globalization abound with opportunities, an increasingly migrant workforce has to be taken care of. This may lead to a shortfall of skilled personnel in some areas, whereas its excess in other areas. This issue may have to be tackled by the leaders of tomorrow.

Digitization of Business

Business is rapidly aligning towards a more and more digitized format. This necessitates future leaders to cope with this new format of business and encourage a more transparent operational format to sustain under virtual workplaces and other offshoots of digitization at the workplace.

Constantly Maximizing Opportunities in Changing Business Environments

Future leaders should always be on the lookout for opportunities. Globalization has already ushered in a host of opportunities for all major globalized firms. However, more is in the offing and successful leaders would only be those who can take advantage of these opportunities and help their businesses grow.

Sources: Taggart, J., 'Management Innovation and Globalization: The Leadership Challenge', 29 January 2011, http://deltapartners.ca/blog/management-innovation-and-globalization-the-leadership-challenge, last accessed on 8 September 2013; CIO New Zealand, '"Globalization 2.0" Leads Trends Impacting Leadership', 19 September 2011, http://www.cio.co.nz/article/467477/_globalisation_2_0_leads_trends_impacting_leadership/, last accessed on 8 September 2013 (adapted).

IMPACT OF GLOBALIZATION ON ORGANIZATIONAL BEHAVIOUR

Globalization has changed the business landscape of the world. Among others, it now requires organizations to make major changes in their strategies, culture, cross-cultural issues, and structure and also in the redesigning of work and processes. All of these have a cascading effect on OB. Understanding OB in the era of globalization requires managers to equip themselves to cope with these issues. Understanding culture and cross-cultural issues helps managers develop desirable social behaviour for managing the organizations. Many researchers have observed that globalization has significantly altered business practices, which, among others, influence the behavioural issues in organizations. Many organizations have to bring about changes in their HR management (HRM) practices with diversity inclusion to ensure that their business processes and practices demonstrate a global perspective. To understand the issues of OB in a globalized age, managers need to embrace certain core values and then try to understand how those core values are reflected in different cultures. For example, honesty, as a value, is differently interpreted in different cultures. Being fair is seen as honesty in some cultures, whereas being direct and speaking one's mind is considered as honesty in some other cultures. Hence, modelling the OB based on those identified as core values across different cultures is important. OB in a globalized world also requires managers to relook their comfort zones. It means more tolerance to other cultures, accommodating even issues that may be beyond the comfort zone. For example, one culture may appreciate someone taking quick decisions, whereas in another culture patience may be more valued.

GLOBALIZATION AND CHANGING BUSINESS PRACTICES IN INDIA

To respond to the worldwide trend in globalization, the Government of India has gone in for a major economic restructuring with a view to consolidating its position in the world market and achieving internal economic balance and growth. Liberalization, in terms of major changes in the industrial policy and as part of economic restructuring programmes, has brought in much competition for the over-protected Indian industrial organizations in general. Allowing the free flow of foreign capital and the direct participation of multinational organizations in the corporate sector has exposed the Indian industrial organizations to intense competition.

The effects of such liberalization in the domestic front on Indian industrial organizations have been multiplied by certain developments at the international level, which are more in the form of global trade restrictions. Certification of the products of Indian industrial organizations as per the quality system standards developed by the International Organizations for Standardization (ISO) is now almost essential for going global. Total quality management (TQM) is also a widely discussed issue in the corporate world.

The major economic restructuring at the macro level and the global changes taken together have prompted the Government of India to start a National Renewal Fund (NRF) to give effect to the exit policy on the one hand and to upgrade the skills of the retained employees through intensive training on the other. Organizations, in order to trim their employees, will henceforth have to implement voluntary retirement schemes (VRS) by making extra payments in the form of compensation (exit incentive) in addition to the normal statutory payments. The remaining employees (who do not opt for VRS) will have to be trained vigorously to enable them to adapt to the changed job requirements—upgradation of technology, modernization, and restructuring of jobs.

Training the employees on the TQM strategy at a time when the Indian economy is undergoing major restructuring has assumed much importance primarily because today a corporate organization in India cannot expect to survive merely by developing a strategic plan based solely on the extrapolation of production and profit figures. It has to survive in a highly competitive environment at both the domestic and global fronts. Thus, restructuring of the production process in an organization based on technological dynamism has become imperative. The economic restructuring at the macro level has an inevitable impact on the production process in an organization at the micro level. Restructuring of a production process, as a natural consequence of economic restructuring, necessitates restructuring of manpower in organizations. Since trimming of surplus employees in an organization, by offering them golden handshakes under the VRS, is restricted only to those who opt for that scheme, the only other effective way open is to redeploy the surplus employees after intensive need-based training.

Keeping in mind the important performance areas in TQM strategy in the corporate sector, training programmes are arranged for all categories of employees. Such training programmes are usually imparted in the following areas:

- TQM
- Product familiarization
- Process familiarization
- Multiple-skill development
- Simple problem-solving techniques
- Statistical process control
- Quality circle concepts
- Total productive maintenance

The duration of each training programme varies from one week to two weeks depending on the participant's level and power of understanding.

For managers and executives, TQM techniques, inter alia, calls for appreciating the following issues:

- Formal education and age are really not the factors that determine the effectiveness or otherwise of learning the TQM techniques. These techniques essentially have their roots in basic humanism. The conceptual and technical aspects of TQM can be appreciated at a deeper level only if training programmes on TQM genuinely have the humanistic tone.
- Attitudinal changes at the top are important to operationalize TQM in an organization. Unless the top-level personnel change their attitudes—accepting a flatter organization structure, following an egalitarian approach, becoming receptive to change on a continuous basis, encouraging participative management, and supporting group performance—it is not possible to inculcate the TQM culture in an organization.

The emerging issues in designing training programmes in India, therefore, can be listed as follows:

Developing culture-specific management programmes to appreciate humanistic tone of TQM techniques This dimension of the TQM techniques was incorporated with rare precision and clarity in a number of ancient Indian texts, which are grossly misunderstood as ethico-religious.

Teachings of the Ramayana have, inter alia, underscored the role of enthusiasm as the driving force in all human endeavours. Similarly, the Srimad Bhagwat Gita has emphasized the significance of mutuality and cooperation in all spheres of human life. One of the important messages of the Srimad Bhagwat Gita is that the imminent role of man in the work environment can be effective provided it continues to be guided in the light of a transcendental perspective about work. The importance of group performance and participative management has also been emphasized in the Ramayana and the Mahabharata. Indian psycho-philosophy recognizes that each human being is spontaneously bestowed with perfection within.

Appreciating corporate practices and social systems while designing training programmes Jobs in Indian industrial organizations are not specialized and fractionized to replace the intuition and ingenuity of the employees in general. Employees, in their limited spheres, always make use of their craftsmanship to resolve technical problems in different activity areas. On tracing history, it can be found that the Indian social system had a definite orientation towards developing and maintaining different social groups in terms of certain crafts. The quality elements in a particular craft and the skills necessary were the deciding factors for ranking the craft along with others in order of importance. There was a time when goldsmiths, carpenters, and weavers were the craftsmen groups who enjoyed the highest status in India. In the later years, however, the human aspects of social functioning gradually lost importance.

The future training programmes in India, therefore, cannot merely sustain on traditional skill upgradation and conceptual or technical issues. Most of the other general, culture-specific, and human issues will also be required to translate the challenges of change into reality. This is the only reason why many training programmes now emphasize human dimensions.

Future of Career Planning and Development in India

In India, there are no significant empirical studies on career planning and development. New challenges such as competition, market globalization, deregulation, and TQM have now made it imperative for organizations to restructure their career planning and development programmes to retain the best talents. Companies such as Bajaj Auto, Arvind Mills, Gujarat Ambuja, Essar Gujarat, Reliance Industries, Bombay Dyeing, Hindustan Unilever, Crompton Greaves, and Tata have now brought in many perceptive changes, which can be listed as follows:

- Most companies now consider employees as their important assets. The concept of TQM considers every employee as a customer (internal) of the organization. In order to empower the employees and make them work as entrepreneurs for the organization, companies are redesigning career progression tracks to attract and retain the best talent. Making people psychologically prepared for ownership, some organizations are also experimenting with a flatter organizational structure with adequate decentralization.
- While appointing people for managing senior executive positions, organizations are now placing more emphasis on the knowledge of the person than on the functional skills. This, perhaps, is the only reason for selecting people who are just in their early thirties for senior managerial posts.
- Organizations are now keen to get rid of those employees who have been rendered redundant due to changing requirements, by offering them golden handshakes, rather than developing these persons for better redeployment.

- Merit is now receiving overriding priority over seniority. This, therefore, renders career progression paths less important. Many, however, feel that even with greater priority to merit over seniority, career progression paths do not become completely meaningless. This is because even for promotion by merit, the lines of progression paths are relevant. For any succession planning or promotion planning, these are still important.

In addition, organizational restructuring programmes are now rendering many employees surplus, and it has become a major problem for organizations to redeploy employees in restructured jobs. Career panic has now become a global issue. Most organizations, fearing employee turnover, are now working on designing jobs that can offer employees recognition, creativity (by lateral transfers, etc.), challenges, and empowerment.

Many Indian organizations have now been exposed to the problem of major restructuring as a consequence of the economic liberalization programmes of the government. Such programmes of the government are now compelling the Indian managers to face the challenge of competition, survive under economic uncertainty, take decisions, move quickly, shoulder the risks, improve the quality of work-life, make organizations socially more responsive and transparent, and so on. Market globalization is also compelling Indian organizations to update their technology. Management philosophies are also constantly changing, particularly in the context of the development of the TQM concept, which inter alia calls for employee empowerment, total participation, small group activities like quality circles, and attitudinal change of the managers cutting across structural barriers. Change in public policies, increased consumer awareness, increased social and institutional requirements (like pollution control), labour relations, and other such factors are also compelling organizations to introduce management development programmes for their managers and executives to renew their knowledge and skills. The primary objective of the management development programmes, therefore, is to make executives and managers as well as the organizations socially responsive and managerially competent to survive in an atmosphere of uncertainty.

All these, therefore, now require Indian organizations to focus on the following important issues with respect to their managers and senior executives:

- To recruit managers and executives with requisite knowledge and skills to meet the present and anticipated future needs of organizations
- To encourage managers to develop their full potentiality for handling greater responsibility
- To improve the functional competence of managers, making them more transparent and responsive to the changing needs of the organization
- To sustain the good performance of the managers throughout their career and to prevent them from developing managerial obsolescence
- To develop managers for higher assignments, duly replacing elderly executives

Irrespective of managerial levels and the nature of organizations, there is an emphasis on the following aspects in managing people:

- Attitudinal change
- Behavioural change
- Change in knowledge and skills
- Change in performance
- Change in desired operational results

The personal characteristics, level of intelligence, and learning efforts of people at different managerial levels being different for each level, there exists different sets of objectives, which an organization should strive to achieve.

Labour Market and Work Processes

Economic adjustment and restructuring of processes and policy tools in the developing and transitional countries have had a profound impact on various aspects of labour markets—employment structure and terms, work organization, productivity, human capital and training, and acquisition of technological capability. People (social groups) and organizations (enterprises and labour market institutions) have thus been exposed to new realities and challenges in a way hitherto not experienced.

The key issue, which remains a challenge, is no longer creating employment (as provided by the informal sector in many countries) but creating quality employment—which means fostering patterns of higher productivity leading to higher earnings. Hence, enterprise reform and restructuring emerge as the central issues in combating the negative outcomes of adjustment and in meeting the new economic challenges that have developed from both adjustment and the globalization process. In the enterprise reform and restructuring processes, the development of human resources, aimed at improving productivity and efficiency, takes an important place.

Changes in the organization of the work processes (e.g., flexible specialization) require a different (increasingly more general than specific) skill profile of the workforce. Adaptable production systems require more discretion and intellectual activity from production workers than was required by the simplified tasks characteristic of mass production. Similarly, a team-based work organization requires a multi-skilled workforce capable of understanding the whole production process. As a result of these changing skill needs, when compared to any earlier period, enterprise-level training and HR development are now in need of more coordination at the meso levels and more interaction with the institutional supply of training and education as well as with external private training systems. In the era of restructuring, this wider firm environment demands utmost attention, because enterprises—whether large, medium, or modernizing small ones—need sectoral support (government- and/or business-initiated) in training and skill upgrading or retooling.

The ability of an enterprise to respond to the changing skill needs, to acquire appropriate technological capabilities, and to introduce modern HRM practices explains the relatively wide differences in the firm-level productivity that characterizes the restructuring economies.

> The key issues, which remains a challenge, is no longer creating employment but creating quality employment, which means fostering patterns of higher productivity leading to higher earnings.

At the same time, it is realized that the shift away from mass production to flexible specialization and the concomitant introduction of HRM practices is neither universal nor complete. A heterogeneous pattern has emerged from the total absence of innovative HRM practices, low levels of worker involvement, and enhanced labour management communication to systems that include intensive skill training and high levels of worker involvement in teams, individual incentive systems, and flexible and rotating job assignments.

It is obvious then that this heterogeneous praxis of labour relations is mirrored by an equally varied labour response. On the one hand, the process of industrial restructuring has complex gender implications that go beyond the confines of the enterprise. On the other hand, organized labour is also rather ambiguous about the managerial embrace of the concept of employee empowerment. With empowerment becoming a euphemism for work intensification, workers and their unions have become sceptical about the process. Trade unions have responded in ways that were sometimes quite adversarial but supportive at other times. The understanding of, and the response to, the interface between industrial relations and HRM is not the only challenge that organized labour is facing.

Economic and labour market restructuring has led to a process of informalization of employment (with a profound gender dimension—i.e., women are more adversely affected than men). The latter not only means that the base of the organized labour has been eroding, but also that trade unions have been facing new challenges, including the need to build in the gender dimension in their strategies and to move more from the national-level to the sectoral-level coordination of strategies and actions.

It is interesting to note that the process of labour market restructuring is leading to a stronger focus on the meso level (sectoral organizations and coordination) from both the enterprise and organized labour. However, the role of the sectoral organizations and sectoral-level coordination can be appreciated and positively utilized only on the basis of a profound understanding of the new micro dynamics of the enterprise and of the macro-level processes of political, socio-economic, and institutional changes resulting from the restructuring processes.

Disinvestment of shares of select public sector undertakings in India, which was declared on 24 July 1991 as a government policy, and which as a process started in 1991–92, has now become a socio-economic and political issue. It is being debated almost every day by all cross sections of people of the society. With the frequent changes (more political) of power at the national level, the government is trying to handle this issue very cautiously, in line with the sentiments of the people, fearing that its action should not otherwise widen the gap between the people and the government.

Before discussing further, it is necessary to study the public sector units and disinvestment scenario in the global context.

Participation of the government in the industry (economic activity), which began in India right at the beginning of the planned economy (1951 onwards), was initially envisaged as a necessity for strategic reasons and for the development of infrastructural facilities. In other words, either as a departmental undertaking or as an enterprise, the government should restrict its participation only to Schedule A and Schedule B industries. All these mean that the government should play a direct role in bringing about macroeconomic changes through its participation in the economic activity. This model by and large holds well for many countries of the world such as Brazil, Argentina, Mexico, China, Hungary, Malaysia, Poland, and Peru.

Over the years, however, the Indian government had to take over a number of sick private sector units as part of the nationalization move, primarily to check socio-economic imbalances.

The first form of participation was a necessity, whereas the second form (presumably out of political compulsions) made the government an unnecessary competitor to the private sector, more particularly in low-technology areas.

Over the years, the Indian economy started responding to the changes in the global economic environment, primarily out of economic compulsion, which necessitated changes in the institutional policy, making it more open and global in line with the others.

Two major global changes—new policy resolutions of the European Economic Community (EEC), which have been made effective from 1 January 1993, and successive resolutions of the World Trade Organization (WTO), of which India is a member/signatory—followed by major political reforms of the erstwhile socialist countries created a tremendous impact on the Indian macro and microeconomic environment.

The policy resolutions of the EEC, inter alia, eliminated the non-price competition among member countries and abolished preferential country-specific export quota (like Multi-fibre Agreement for India). They also made it compulsory for organizations to have ISO certification to facilitate trade with the EEC member countries. The WTO, on the other hand, through its successive resolutions, attempted to strengthen the economic ties with the member countries, urging them to make their markets open and global. Annexure 15.1 provides a brief on the WTO.

While it is not the purpose of this text to debate whether or not India is succumbing to global pressure, to liberalize the economic environment, it is important to analyse its relative merits or otherwise, more particularly in the backdrop of disinvestment, through a scientific approach, judging different parameters and using various scientific and quantitative tools.

Exhibit 15.2 discusses the effect of globalization on the labour market.

EXHIBIT 15.2   Globalization and Labour Market Changes

Globalization has increased business manifold. With the growth in business, various emerging economies have seen huge GDP growth in the recent past. Many of these economies such as the BRICS nations are still growing at an astronomical pace. However, rapid industrialization has put forth many daunting questions for these economies to answer, and many of these questions have been left unanswered. One such very pertinent question is that of labour market problems that globalization has given rise to.

If the latest statistics are to be believed, within a span of three decades, the global workforce has increased from 1.7 billion to 2.9 billion, that is, more than 70 per cent. Furthermore, at least 0.9 billion workers have been added in sectors other than agriculture. However, there is also a highly skewed growth in the numbers since 0.4 billion of the 0.9 billion labourers are from either India or China. Moreover, there is a rising shortfall of skilled labourers in developed nations, given the way organizations there have invested in the latest technologies.

This shortfall of skilled labourers in developed nations is likely to continue. Though emerging economies such as China and India are fast becoming the global hub for skilled manpower, the condition of education in these countries is not encouraging with only 30 per cent and 70 per cent, respectively, of the workers having primary education.

Manpower migration is also on the rise. In a globalized economy, employees rapidly migrate to other nations in search of work and better payment. This phenomenon is likely to continue and even increase in the near future. Though there are many barriers for such migration of workers to the developed world, eliminating these barriers can also help economies reap huge benefits and make nations truly global, both in letter and in spirit.

Sources: The Economist, 'United Workers of the World', *The Economist*, 16 June 2012, http://www.economist.com/node/21556974, last accessed on 10 September 2013; Rodrik, D., 'Labour Markets: The Unexploited Frontier of Globalization', *The Globalist*, 31 May 2011, http://www.theglobalist.com/labor-markets-the-unexploited-frontier-of-globalization/, last accessed on 10 September 2013 (adapted).

Public Sector Reforms

Public sector reforms as an ongoing process started in India in the 1970s with focus on the following five points in the agenda:

Increased efficiency   This is aimed at improving the input–output ratio by controlling the huge wasteful expenditure and reducing the inefficiency of many of the public sector's processes.

Decentralization   This aims at creating more flexible and responsive decision-making by transferring the decision-making power down the line and reducing the cost at the central level.

Increased accountability   This is the process of making the staff members accountable for their decisions and actions to reduce inefficient and corrupt practices.

Improved resource management   This aims at effective utilization of human, financial, and other resources.

Marketization   The aim here is to achieve cost efficiency (increasing the use of market forces to cover relationships within public sector undertakings) and to increase the efficiency and/or effectiveness of the service delivery mechanism.

The reform agenda was silent over the integration of information technology with the reform process, that is, delivering the ongoing reform components with greater use of information technology.

Trade unions, not only in India but also globally, are finding it difficult to cope with the economic globalization. As already mentioned, globalization effect changes in the organization and necessitates changes in the work systems and procedures. Organizational changes lead to behavioural changes among the people working in them. Hence, from the OB point of view, the study of the impact of globalization assumes importance.

The three important drivers for this phenomenon are technology, structural change in the economy, and increased competition.

Technology   The introduction of new technology changes the expectations of the customers. Organizations cannot retain their customers without changing in accordance with the changes in technology. All public sector banks in India had to initiate technology changes to extend value-added services to their customers at par with new-generation private banks. In the consumer electronics industry as well, liquid crystal display (LCD) and plasma televisions are now preferred over the conventional colour televisions. In automobiles, Hindustan Motors had to fall behind because of its failure to change with the new designs and technologies in the automobile sector.

Public sector reforms as an ongoing process focus on a five-point agenda—increased efficiency, decentralization, increased accountability, improved resource management, and marketization.

Structural changes   Structural changes in the economy have intensified competition, as today's organizations need to think globally even for their local customer base. Opening up of the economy has invited many new players and hence destroyed the level playing field for the local players. For organizations, saving cost and improving quality are now important priorities, which they ensure by redefining the employment relationship—increasing

> **Practitioner Speak 15.3**
>
> **Globalization Myths versus Reality, Continued**
>
> Some of the commentary on my last post took issue with my focus on levels of globalization, as embodied in my '10% presumption' chart—and suggested that I focus on trends instead. This is actually very useful to do because one of the standard evasions glommed on to by the purveyors of globaloney is that even if the world isn't quite flat today, it will be tomorrow. In fact, I just heard Colin Powell say exactly that at an after-dinner talk.
>
> Read this insightful blog posted by Ghemawat on *HBR Blog Network* by accessing the following link: http://blogs.hbr.org/ghemawat/2007/09/globalization_myths_versus_rea.html.

outsourcing, sub-contracting, and casualization of labour. The effect of the structural changes of the economy is visible within the industries as well. Some of the low-end industries are now relocating their manufacturing bases to countries with cheaper labour costs. This is what the newly industrializing countries (NIC) in Asia—such as Hong Kong, Taiwan, and South Korea—did in the 1980s and 1990s by concentrating on global marketing and relocating low-end production processes to Indonesia, the Philippines, Vietnam, Cambodia, and China.

Increased competition The pressure of competition also forces organizations to match the situation. Businesses have to constantly adjust to the reality of global competition—in both domestic markets (which were liberalized by free traders) and export markets (also opened up by free traders). In this globalized competition, success is measured in terms of expansion in the export market as well as in the globalized domestic market. Smaller, undercapitalized, and less-prepared industries need to upgrade themselves to survive and grow. Otherwise, they will be destroyed by the big global players or the TNCs, as is happening in many areas of the economy. The merger mania that has swept the big corporate world, including Asian TNCs, is due to the efforts of the TNCs to position themselves in the most strategic manner in the key industries of the world.

In the less-developed economies of Asia, China is seen as a major threat even by cheap-labour countries. There are widespread complaints that the repression of labour rights in China is partly responsible for its competitiveness. Without free and democratic trade unions, Chinese workers cannot effectively bargain for a fair share of their efforts.

All these challenges of the global economy even now require the government to reform the public sector enterprises, strengthening those that are viable and eliminating the non-performers.

SIX SIGMA, GLOBALIZATION, AND TECHNOLOGICAL CHANGE

To leapfrog ahead of competition in this world of uncertainty, the corporate world is experimenting with one process after another. From *conformance* to *standards* to *achieving total quality*, the focus has now shifted to adding economic value and practical utility to both the organization and the customer. Realizing value entitlement by both the customers and the organizations is now the determinant of business relationships. It is now a win–win situation for both. While for customers, it is their rightful expectation to buy quality products at competitive costs, for organizations, it is to produce at the highest possible profit. This synergy is what everybody tries to achieve in the corporate world. Rejection allowance and unavoidable rejection are now forbidden words. Six sigma, as a business process, is now allowing organizations to improve their bottom line by designing and monitoring business activities in a way that minimizes waste of resources without compromising on customer satisfaction. The Six sigma process is broader than TQM programmes. TQM focuses on detecting and correcting defects, whereas six sigma recreates the processes to ensure that defects never arise, right from the beginning. From an organization's perspective, it provides maximum value in the form of increased profits, and from the customer's perspective, it provides maximum value in terms of high-quality products and services at competitive costs.

Sigma is a letter in the Greek alphabet and is used to denote the standard deviation of a process. As a concept, it was first developed by a consortium—including Motorola—in the mid-1980s and was adopted by many major manufacturing organizations including General Electric (GE). Now, however, it is applied in other organizations as well. For example, GE Capital, the world's first service transaction-based company, introduced it in 1996.

Broadly, six sigma is the statistical application of TQM to achieve a new paradigm in customer quality. Sigma quality level describes the output of a process. Six sigma goes beyond defect reduction to emphasize improvement of business processes, which includes cost, cycle time, customer satisfaction, and any other metric important to the company. Six sigma can now imply a whole culture of strategies, tools, and statistical methodologies to improve the bottom line of the companies.

An objective of six sigma is to eliminate every molecule of waste that can be found in an organization's processes. Substantial bottom line benefits can be achieved by organizations practising the six sigma breakthrough strategy through the improvement of cycle time, reduction of defects, reduction of costs, and so on. Quite often, organizations are perplexed at having to adopt yet another strategy and wonder why they should consider six sigma. The answer to this is simple—today's organizations are customer-centric. Customers form the base of today's world market and companies want to send to them a clear message—they produce high-quality products at lower costs with greater responsiveness. Six sigma helps an organization achieve these objectives when aligned with other initiatives as part of a business strategy.

Higher sigma values indicate better quality products and lower sigma values represent lower quality products. At the six sigma level, products are almost defect-free, that is, it allows for only 3.4 defects per million opportunities (DPMO).

INTERNATIONAL ORGANIZATIONAL BEHAVIOUR

International OB issues encompass the OB concepts from intercultural perspectives. In this era of globalization, organizations are required to align their culture with that of the countries where they decide to expand their business. Lack of knowledge of the international issues concerning OB forced Mazda Motors of Japan to withdraw from their US operations even though it was the first company from Japan to enter the US market. Mazda's failure is attributed to its poor understanding of the teamwork culture of the US workers. Much later, Toyota and Honda of Japan entered the US market, and they could establish their businesses by aligning the Japanese culture with that of the US. Country-specific culture has its impact on the work environment; hence, in international OB, it is important to study the cultural differences in motivation, communication, and leadership. It also impacts country-specific cultural norms on ethics, values, and business practices. Cross-cultural issues have been adequately dealt with in Chapter 18.

SUMMARY

Technological change and globalization issues nowadays greatly influence the functions of the HR department in any organization. It has become important for corporate leaders to hone the skills of their available manpower to avoid their obsolescence, and to make the best use of them, focusing on the technical and various process-related skills. Talent management is now a top priority. Nurturing and developing talent not only requires training and development but also enforces change in the organizational cultures and practices. Playing the role of an effective change agent in technology transfer, corporate leaders now balance their organizations by aligning people, business plans, and resources. A sustained performance management does not allow people to feel alienated from the organizations. They partner them with the change process. In India, the effects of globalization and technological change cascaded into the organizational practices, in nurturing both new skills and new processes. This has made Indian organizations competitive in the world and they are experiencing impressive growth rates. With such adjustments with technologies and the environment, Indian organizations are likely to leapfrog in competition, benchmarking their human resources with global organizations.

KEY DEFINITIONS

Heterarchy A system of organization replete with overlap, multiplicity, mixed ascendancy, and/or divergent but consistent patterns of relations

Networking The establishing of links between people with similar professional interests

Six sigma A business process that allows an organization to improve its bottom line by designing and monitoring business activities in a way that minimizes waste of resources without compromising customer satisfaction

Talent management The process that ensures achievement of performance targets by managing employees' talents and skills

Total quality management A strategy for organizational improvement that is aimed at creating quality consciousness in all organizational processes

CONCEPT-REVIEW QUESTIONS

15.1 Discuss how technology and globalization issues exert influence on organizational HR department practices.

15.2 Explain the concept of change agent. What qualities should an organizational leader possess to become an effective change agent in technology transfer?

15.3 How is the changing technology now affecting OB activities in Indian organizations? What response mechanisms have the Indian organizations created to remain competitive in the global market?

15.4 Write short notes on the following:
(a) Organizational restructuring
(b) Six sigma
(c) Total quality management
(d) Networking
(e) Change agent
(f) Talent management

CRITICAL THINKING QUESTION

15.1 Many Indian organizations claim that they have achieved the six sigma level of quality. Visit any such organization and study the processes that have six sigma compliance. Detail their processes, with specific focus on behavioural issues (like competencies).

SELECT BIBLIOGRAPHY

- Beer, S., *Heart of the Enterprise*, John Wiley and Sons, Chichester, 1979.
- Bhattacharyya, D.K., 'Competency Mapping and Manpower Redundancy—A Macro Level Study of Indian Organizations', *Management and Accounting Research*, Vol. 4, Issue 2, 2000, pp. 97–105.
- Bhattacharyya, D.K., *Human Resource Management*, Excel Books, New Delhi, 2006.
- Bhattacharyya, D.K., *Human Resource Research Methods*, Oxford University Press, New Delhi, 2007.
- Criscuolo C. and Martin R. Ceriba, *Multinationals, Foreign Ownership and US Productivity Leadership—Evidence from the UK*, 2003, http://www.ceriba.org.uk, last accessed on 28 Jan 2014.
- Eckes, George, *The Six Sigma Revolution*, John Wiley and Sons, Inc., New York, 2001.
- Feenstra, R., 'Integration of Trade and Disintegration of Production in the Global Economy', *Journal of Economic Perspectives*, Vol. 12, Issue 4, 1998, pp. 31–50.
- Kristine, Ellis, 'Mastering Six Sigma', *Training*, Vol. 38, 2001, pp. 30–5.
- Legrain, Philippe, *The Truth about Globalisation*, Abacus, London, 2002.
- OECD, 'Measuring Globalisation', *The Role of Multinationals in OECD Economies*, 2001.
- Yip, G., *Total Global Strategy—Managing for Worldwide Competitive Advantage*, Prentice Hall, New York, 1992.

CASE STUDY
Korean Management

The Korean economy came to be widely regarded as a possible role model to be followed by other newly industrializing economies. However, the 1997 Asian Crisis shattered this image. The economy faced a competitive squeeze between lower cost and rapidly growing economies such as China on the one hand and higher knowledge- or technology-based economies such as Japan on the other hand. Such a situation results from structural economic problems, such as high cost but rigid systems and widespread bureaucratic intervention. It is believed that there is a need to build a new economic paradigm, one based on market-led, global, and transparent systems, providing it the potential to combine the best of both the worlds. It is argued that the principal reason for the financial collapse was the failure of the Korean management to adjust to the changing business conditions. As Korean firms grew in size and scope, many of the entrepreneurial characteristics that supported their early successes were replaced by bureaucratic, non-responsive management structures, which were unable to cope with the emerging external opportunities and threats.

The central question here is this: What must the Korean firms do to reinvent themselves in ways that will enhance their competitive edge in the future? Since the mid-1980s, many Korean companies have adopted a unique approach in managing their organizational culture, that is, the so-called *culture change campaign*. This case study examines how effective the campaigning approach to managing organizational culture was in Korea. Although many Korean companies made substantial investments in their campaigning efforts, empirical data indicates that the campaigning approach was not, on the whole, successful. The possible reasons for the failure were identified and suggestions for improvements made. Lessons on culture change management were learnt from the Korean experiences. A review of the foregoing research was done to summarize the critical success and failure factors of corporate culture change. The government—the majority stockholder and a major institutional force—played a critical role as an initiator of the change but turned into an inertial force in the later phases of change. The change of organizational structure, which was strongly supported by the top management, was successful; however, the momentum for HRM change, without such support, was not enough to overcome trade union opposition and employee resistance.

The Korean business management has a tendency for individualism in comparison to the Japanese social collectivism, where employees forget their family. It is also described as *family egoism*. Korean people are said to find their identities in their family groups. In other words, their individualism can possibly run on their family egoism. In every factory or office, people work with a strong sense of responsibility. However, the Korean style of production in their workshops is open for everything, but it cannot do well because they work with rough spirits. The concepts of business management in Korean companies are almost similar to the companies in Japan and the US.

Question for Discussion

Study this case carefully. In India, we have two major Korean consumer electronics conglomerates. Though both the companies have achieved tremendous market growth, they have started encountering the problem of attrition of their key people. Track such reasons to the typical Korean culture and suggest how such Korean companies can best adopt the theory Z model.

ANNEXURE 15.1
World Trade Organization Brief

1.0 Introduction

The World Trade Organization (WTO) was established on 1 January 1995 as a successor to the General Agreement on Tariffs and Trades (GATT). The implementation problems of the WTO agreements are partly linked with the organizational structure and partly due to the specific features of the agreements. The main differences between the WTO and GATT are as follows:

- The GATT was a set of agreements and not an organization. The role of the GATT was in the area of the export and import of goods, in particular the reduction of tariff and elimination of non-tariff barriers. Agriculture was under a very soft discipline in the GATT and textile was under a special regime in the derogation of the normal GATT rules.

   The WTO, on the other hand, is a full-fledged organization with a permanent secretariat and well-defined structure. Besides the trade in goods, its area of operation extends to the intellectual property rights and services. It includes enhanced disciplines in the areas of agriculture and textiles.
- The dispute settlement mechanism of the GATT was relatively weak to deal with the effective implementation of the decisions.

   The dispute settlement mechanism of the WTO is much more efficient and comprehensive than that of the GATT. It has a better mechanism for the enforcement of rights and obligations as well as for ensuring acceptance of the decisions. The dispute settlement process has several problems for India.

2.0 WTO Agreements

WTO agreements cover the following 12 subjects in the area of trade in goods:

- Agriculture
- Textiles and clothing
- Trade-related investment measures (TRIMS)
- Sanitary and phytosanitary measures (SPS)
- Technical barriers to trade (TBT)
- Anti-dumping
- Customs valuation
- Pre-shipment inspection
- Rules of origin
- Import licensing
- Subsidies and countervailing measures
- Safeguards

It also covers agreements in the following specific areas:

- The General Agreement on Trade in Services (GATS)
- The Agreement on Trade-related Aspects of Intellectual Property Rights (TRIPS)
- The Trade Policy Review Mechanism (TPRM)
- Agreement on the Dispute Settlement Undertaking

The WTO has 150 member countries. The Ministerial Conference, the top policy-making body of the WTO, has met several times. The first meeting took place in Singapore (1996), the second in Geneva (1998), the third in Seattle (1999), the fourth in Doha (2001), the fifth in Cancun (2003), and the sixth in Hong Kong (2005). The seventh meeting was scheduled to take place in Germany (2007), which, however, did not materialize.

Ethics and Organizational Behaviour

LEARNING OBJECTIVES

After studying this chapter, the reader will be able to

- understand the meaning and concept of ethics
- explain the process of framing a code of ethics
- describe the benefits of ethical practices in organizations
- differentiate between perception and behavioural issues and ethics
- understand the various dimensions of corporate ethics

CASE STUDY

Market Penetration and the Question of Business Ethics

In its second spell in India, an international soft drink major was very aggressive in its product-positioning strategy, thereby eliminating the local soft drink bottlers. With the traditional perception that Indians like to get more for lower prices, the international brand initially introduced 300 ml bottles against the conventional local bottlers' 250 ml bottles at the same price band. However, taste mismatch did not give it the opportunity to successfully position its product in the market. It tried sweetening the taste and reintroduced its brand; however, there was no major change in its market position.

The company then tried to understand the major weaknesses of the local bottlers. A careful study indicated that the same bottles were repeatedly being refilled. The lead time to procure these bottles was high, as they were not a standard saleable item. Hence, if the empty bottles did not reach the bottling plant, local bottlers would not be able to refill them and make the filled bottles available in the market.

Soft drinks are usually bought on impulse. People ask for it as and when they see it. The international major started procuring the bottles of the local bottlers and destroying them. By the time the local bottlers could understand the game plan, the company had positioned its brands in the market. In no time, the local bottlers' bottling process came to a grinding halt.

The international major then proposed that they bottle its brands as its franchisee. For survival, the local bottlers had to go ahead with it, and this helped the international major successfully position its brands, making the local varieties almost unavailable.

INTRODUCTION

An ethical organization can achieve better business results. This maxim is now making more and more corporate leaders accept their social responsibilities and adopt ethical practices. Organizations indulging in unethical business practices or even in unethical dealings with their employees are quickly identified and globally exposed in this era of technology-intensive communication systems. Organizational activities require redesigning and updating, keeping pace with public expectations and ever-rising standards. With the negative aspects of organizational behaviour (OB)—injustice, corporate dishonesty, exploitation, and negligence—becoming more visible and attracting public opinion and criticism, corporate organizations are going the extra mile to ensure that ethical violations are avoided. An example is the case of City Toys in China, which used child labour to manufacture toys that were offered as gift items to the customers of McDonald's. It was internationally subjected to criticism to such an extent that McDonald's had to withdraw the practice. The Indian carpet industry and the Bangladesh garment industry faced a similar predicament in terms of export restrictions for using child labour. Even suppressing facts on products and services become an ethical violation from the customers' point of view.

Organizations have realized that every citizen of the world has to be dealt with ethically. The definition of a stakeholder is no longer limited to shareholders, investors, and partners. A stakeholder is any group that is affected by, contributes to, has an interest in, an involvement with, or dependence on the organization. A stakeholder is any individual or group who could lose or gain something because of the actions of the organization.

Unethical corporate practices are categorized as 'immoral', that is, a deliberate violation of ethical issues to harm the stakeholders. Apart from this, there may be unknowing violations of ethics by an organization, which can be categorized into the amoral type. The negative consequences of an unethical corporate culture in human resource (HR) management or OB pervade selection and staffing, performance appraisal, compensation, and retention decisions. Thus, HR systems and ethical corporate cultures should be considered partners in the process of creating competitive advantages for organizations.

DEFINITIONS AND CONCEPTS

Ethics are moral principles—about what is good, defensible, and right. They are often treated as an afterthought. Ethics and ethical reflection need to be integrated with OB. A common philosophical definition of ethics considers them as the science of conduct or values of management. Moral values such as respect, honesty, fairness, and responsibility are important constructs of ethics. Organizations ensure the implementation of ethics by adopting a code of ethics. Ethics include fundamental ground rules that organizations provide to the employees.

Practitioner Speak 16.1

Corporate Ethics Isn't about Rules; It's about Honesty

Somewhere along the way, as we chase our goals, deadlines, targets or simply our daily to-do lists, we tend to forget the real issues in the world outside our windows. This post may seem a tad more emotional than my previous ones. I am emotional. Recent developments impel me to cut across all boundaries and appeal to leadership to shake off the 'bigger-larger-higher' stupor that has consumed business.

Read this insightful blog posted by Nayar on *HBR Blog Network* by accessing the following link: http://blogs.hbr.org/hbr/nayar/2009/01/corporate-ethics-isnt-about-ru.html.

> Ethics are moral principles about what is good, defensible, and right.

As a result, employees can take informed decisions and understand whether something is right. Ethics, therefore, provide the framework of values for moral behaviour. They act as a social glue to ensure that an organized society prospers and everybody's interests are served. The Ten Commandments for the Christians and the teachings of the Bhagwad Gita for the Hindus are sources of direction for ethical behaviour in life.

Today, ethics are of utmost importance with regards to business and profession. While businesses represent the entrepreneurs, professions represent those who are employed in an organization or who work for an employer. In other words, ethics are equally applicable for the employers and the employees. In India, references to ethics can be found in the *Bhagwad Gita*, which emphasizes the need for internalization of the ethical codes by individuals, so that these can be reflected in their behaviour. Organizations can reap maximum benefits when they make their people internalize the ethical codes and values. The traditional guild systems laid down the ethics of business and profession. However, now, external forces also compel organizations to comply with ethical issues. The external forces need not always be the regulatory authorities; they could even be stakeholders, whose changing expectations require organizations to step up their ethical standards and conduct. In the case of a profession, the external forces could be the professional association or the guild, and in the case of a society where there is a government, they are the government agencies, which ensure that the laws are obeyed. In fact, in a secular society, it is the law that lays down what is acceptable conduct and what is not. Acceptable conduct would be encouraged, and unacceptable conduct would be considered illegal and a punishment meted out.

CODE OF ETHICS AND CODE OF CONDUCT

Code of ethics and code of conduct specify the ethical standards that individuals (e.g., the staff or a professional group) should follow in order to continue as a member of the group. They are generally formally stated and members are required to accept them as part of being a member of the group while accepting employment or membership.

Values vary between individuals and across cultures. Hofstede's four value dimensions (1980) help us understand cultural value clashes. Long-term versus short-term values affect many aspects of organizational life. The four key ethical principles are egalitarianism, utilitarianism, individual right, and distributive justice. Organizations following the utilitarianism approach in ethics take decisions based on their outcomes and consequences. Ethical behaviour is influenced by moral intensity, ethical sensitivity, and the situation. A code of ethics serves a number of key roles.

A code of ethics is different from a code of conduct. The code of ethics for an organization or a profession is developed in the form of a statement of values and beliefs that define an organization or a group. Value statements are aspirational, whereas rules or principles are beliefs that individual members of an organization should subscribe to in order to continue as members of the organization. These are listed in different sections in the code, regarding specific relationships with employees, customers, shareholders, suppliers, and competitors, as well as the society in general. Owing to the increasing importance of ethical compliance, professional organizations lay emphasis on imparting training on ethics.

The code of conduct, on the other hand, translates the values (documented in the code of ethics) into specific behavioural standards, keeping in mind the possible reflection on the stakeholders' interest. According to *Ethics Today*, an online publication of the Ethics Resource Centre, a code of conduct 'outlines a fundamental set of principles'. It helps to explain why members of an organization should behave in a certain way, what actions are prohibited, and how to determine which action is ethical or unethical. Therefore, codes of ethics are general guides to operational values and decisions, whereas codes of conduct are more specific or formal statements of the values and practices of a business. The code of conduct of any organization is better understood through the mission statement of the organization.

A common philosophical definition of ethics considers them as the science of conducts or values of management. Moral values include respect, honesty, fairness, and responsibility, and these values are translated into a code of ethics, according to Carter McNamara (2002), a Minneapolis consultant specializing in leadership development and strategic planning. Doug Wallace and John Pekel, of the Twin Cities-based Fulcrum Consulting Group, state that ethics 'include the fundamental ground rules by which we live our lives'. As regards business, ethics are generally considered the act of learning what is right and what is wrong at the workplace and taking the right action.

> Code of ethics and code of conduct specify the ethical standards that one should follow in order to continue as a member of the group to which he/she currently belongs.

> A common philosophical definition of ethics considers them as the science of conducts or values of management.

Benefits of Code of Ethics

Merely having a code of ethics or conduct will not solve the ethical problems of an organization. However, having a developed code of ethics will certainly be beneficial to the organization and to the society as a whole. For the organization, a clear code of ethics or standards provides concrete guidelines necessary to deal with situations both within the company and in external relations. Internal ethical dilemmas need not always be straight and simple; they may be complex, requiring well-defined policies to facilitate fairness and moral management. In external relations with suppliers, customers, and shareholders, a solid code is the best way to avoid decisions that can lead, in extreme cases, to governmental intervention and prosecution.

A clear statement of the ethics policy of an organization also helps employees to align their personal values with those of the organization, creating a stronger workplace bond with both fellow workers and company leaders. In addition, a code of ethics provides individual workers with security, which protects them from a possible violation of ethical practices by unscrupulous

A clear statement of the ethics policy of an organization also helps employees to align their personal values with those of the organization, creating a stronger workplace bond with fellow workers and company leaders.

organizations. Society also benefits when the organizations comply with the ethical codes. For example, an organization may decide to cope with environmental hazards or improve the quality of work life (apart from the benefit to the people who work with the organization, such decisions also benefit the society through improved infrastructure facilities). Moreover, a code of ethics benefits future corporate leaders, as it can improve their moral standards right from the beginning, helping them rise to the future expectations of ethical standards in their higher role positions.

Hence, a developed code of ethics benefits all types of organizations and businesses, irrespective of their size and nature of activities. Such a code not only transcends business practices but also encourages employees to be upfront about problems that they may encounter at the workplace.

Process of Framing Code of Ethics

Once a decision is made to develop a code of ethics or a code of conduct for an organization, the next step is to decide what it will include, what it will aim at, and who will prepare it. Carter McNamara, in the guidebook *The Ethics Toolkit for Managers*, points out that 'codes should not be developed out of the human resource or legal departments alone, as is too often done'. Rather, he says, 'All staff must see the ethics programme being driven by top management.'

The Institute of Business Ethics recommends the following general steps to be carried out in the initial planning phase:

- Find a champion—preferably a very senior level management person.
- Get endorsement from the chairman and the board.
- Find out what bothers people—talk to both employees and management to identify topics that are sensitive issues or require guidance.
- Pick a well-tested model, looking at other organizations' codes to develop ideas and to understand what could be appropriate for meeting one's own organizational needs.
- Develop the organization's code of conduct and document it with due care to customization, in order to deal with the problems that are likely to arise in all areas of organizational relations.
- Pilot test it both within and outside the organization to understand its suitability.
- Issue the code—publish the code and make sure it is directly sent to all employees, shareholders, suppliers, and customers. It is also a good idea to post it on the company's website.
- Introduce examples of the code in action at the company's training programmes.
- Enforce the code and regularly review it to assess whether it continues to remain a good fit for the organization's needs.

Ben and Jerry's (1978) code begins with its mission statement. The code goes on to state the company's mission, relating to product quality, economic mission, and the social mission of the organization. Similarly, the code of Gap Inc. (1978) contains specific statements for each group with whom the company has a relationship, such as commitment to ethical sourcing, code of vendor conduct, and code for the global compliance team. The company feels that such elaborate codes for specific groups are necessary because of its globally expanded operations, including outsourcing from factories located in Malaysia, Guatemala, and Italy. It has developed codes even for many of its internal activities like training.

Implementation

The next step after writing the code is to provide training to the staff members. McNamara offers suggestions that include practices such as reviewing the code during management training, incorporating the code in the new employee training programme, and including ethical categories in performance evaluations. The best training method of all, McNamara suggests, is education through setting examples by the company's leaders.

It needs to be noted that employees generally respond better to training programmes that customize examples of ethical problems they may have to deal with as part of their particular job or function within the organization. Therefore, though packaged training programmes are available for companies in use, the one-size-fits-all approach is not very effective for all organizations. Hence, customization of ethical training programmes may be necessary as per the organizational needs.

Even after ethics training, organizations face the challenge of implementation. Some organizations prefer the incentives and rewards approach, whereas some others make ethical violation a disciplinary issue. However, both the practices are not advisable, as in both the cases, employees are forced into complying with ethics. What is important is to make the employees volunteer to comply with the ethical practices. Initially, volunteerism may not be achieved. It requires a systemic ethics audit, monitoring by an ethics committee, and time-to-time counselling of employees.

Thus, the process of implementation of ethics in the workplace needs to be structured, keeping in mind all the issues discussed until now to derive the benefit.

Benefits of Ethical Practices

By behaving ethically, organizations can derive huge advantages. Even though the primary constructs of ethical practices are humanity and compassion for the stakeholders, it can provide the following advantages to organizations:

Competitive advantage   Customers favour those organizations that are known for their ethical practices. Hence, ethical violation reduces a company's market share, reduces its sales and revenues, and ultimately adversely affects its bottom line.

Better staff attraction and retention   Ethics-compliant organizations develop their brand image. Such employer branding helps them attract and retain the best people, which eventually contributes to their sustainable competitive advantage. On the contrary, ethical violation means a high attrition rate of employees, recruitment of average performers, and overall cost inefficiency.

Investment   Ethics-compliant organizations attract investors, as people repose their confidence only on those who show integrity, a sense of responsibility, and are trustworthy.

Morale and culture   Ethics-compliant organizations also create a workplace where employees want to work. Ethical organizations develop high integrity and become socially responsible and globally considerate. All these make such organizations less prone to stress, attrition, and dissatisfaction. Therefore, by complying with ethics, organizations develop a work culture free from stress, which makes employees feel happier and become more productive.

Reputation   Building organizational reputation takes years of effort, but ruining it requires only one violation. Ethically responsible organizations are less prone to scandals and disasters.

In addition, they become more sensitive to any practice that may adversely affect the reputation of the organization.

Legal and regulatory reasons   Even though compliance with ethics is still voluntary and organizations comply with these for their long-term business interests, globally, ethical issues are likely to come under legal and regulatory norms, making it compulsory for organizations to comply with them. Hence, early preparedness of the organizations will benefit them in the long run, when ethical issues become legally enforceable.

Legacy   It is human nature to be good. Ethical consideration is changing the precept of legacy, which believes in not earning profits at the cost of others' sufferings but making decisions and following business practices that are beneficial to mankind. Hence, organizations believe that the real test of legacy is ethical decision-making.

TEST OF ETHICAL DECISION-MAKING

The UK Institute of Business Ethics suggests a simple test for ethical decision-making in business. Some of the tests, which are applicable to all types of decisions in organizations, can be illustrated as follows:

Transparency   Am I happy to make my decision public, especially to the people affected by it?

Effect   Have I fully considered the harmful effects of my decision and the ways to avoid them?

Fairness   Would my decision be considered fair by everyone affected by it (consider all stakeholders—the effects of decisions can be far-reaching)?

An honest *yes* to each of these questions will ensure an ethical decision.

STAKEHOLDERS AND ETHICAL ORGANIZATIONS

Any ethical organization first tries to identify its stakeholders. Although it is not altogether wrong to identify stakeholders on the basis of relationship, it is, however, difficult to measure the degree of importance of the stakeholders' relationship. Whenever a group is affected by an organization, it becomes a stakeholder, and the organization then must acknowledge its full responsibilities towards that group.

A stakeholder model or analysis recognizes all the stakeholders, identifies a relationship (needs and interests, etc.), and shows a degree of impact for each stakeholder. While doing so, sometimes the level of impact might be small, whereas in other cases it might be large, and

A stakeholder model recognizes all the stakeholders, identifies a relationship, and shows a degree of impact for each stakeholder.

organizations accordingly recognize their responsibility towards that group. Some examples of stakeholder groups are presented in Table 16.1. However, the degree of their relationship with organizations may vary with the nature of activities of the organizations.

As it may be difficult for any organization to establish linkages with such diverse stakeholder groups, weighted analysis is used to assess, analyse, compile, and prioritize stakeholder needs from the organizational point of view. A basic stakeholder analysis template shown in Table 16.2 can help perform this task.

Table 16.1 Stakeholders group

Shareholders	Trustees; guarantors; investors; funding bodies; distribution partners; marketing partners; licensors; licensees; approving bodies; humankind
Regulatory authorities	Endorsers and recommenders; advisors and consultants; employees—staff, managers, directors, non-executive directors; customers; suppliers; the local population (community); the regional general public; national general public; international communities

Table 16.2 Stakeholder analysis template

Stakeholder group	Effect/Interest/Expectation/ Needs/Rights/Quantification	Percentage significance or weighting	Priority or ranking
Shareholders			
Trustees			
Guarantors			
Investors			
Funding bodies			
Distribution			
Marketing partners			
Licensors			
Licensees			
Approving bodies			
Regulatory authorities			
Endorsers and recommenders			
Advisors and consultants			
Employees—staff, managers, directors, non-executive directors			
Customers			
Suppliers			
Local population (community)			
Regional general public			

Table 16.2   (*Contd*)

Stakeholder group	Effect/Interest/Expectation/Needs/Rights/Quantification	Percentage significance or weighting	Priority or ranking
National general public			
International communities			
Humankind			

A survey among 22,480 managers of UK organizations, conducted by the Chartered Management Institute and Remuneration Economics and published on 28 June 2006, indicated that the organizations are unable to retain their key staff. The reason attributed for such failure is the lack of corporate social responsibility.

It has been indicated that UK organizations fail to meet the needs of their staff, who are frustrated by their company's pay structures and a lack of job satisfaction. This apart, recruitment problems, adverse environments, lack of job security, relocation plan, lack of facilities at the workplace, inequitable distribution of pay, and truncated training (not aligned with their career development plans) are some major sources of employee dissatisfaction and attrition. All these problems centre around ethical issues and values.

Ethical values are those by which individuals or a group of employees represent a company and undertake business. It is found that organizations in their practices and individual employees in their professions do not consider ethical values on issues such as honesty, transparency, integrity, openness, trust, respect, fairness, truth, or responsibility. Even in matters of diversity, which require respect and fairness, organizations lack ethical values. Many organizations in their code of ethics make conformance with the diversity issues explicit. They are emphatic about fair employment practices with an explicit code of fairness and ethics in matters such as race, religion, origin, gender, marital status, and disability. They also believe in considering merit in their promotion decisions, but fail to practise them, making the code of ethics available only on paper. In a true sense, ethical practices require active employee involvement and systematic awareness programmes to translate ethics into practice.

BUILDING ETHICAL CULTURE IN ORGANIZATIONS

The ethical values and culture of an organization are critical to its performance. Ethical culture can be measured, understood, and changed. Measuring and understanding an organization's ethical culture is the first critical step towards improving it. Ethical tone or culture has traditionally been considered a difficult aspect of an organization to understand or measure. It could be argued that the decision to behave unethically is an individual one, upon which the organization has little bearing. However, research findings suggest that the 'ability to see and respond ethically may be related more to attributes of corporate culture than to attributes of individual employees' (Chen, et al. 1997, p. 856). The organization is, therefore, a very powerful influence; it has the potential to make an ethical person act unethically or an unethical person behave ethically.

> Measuring and understanding an organization's ethical culture is the first critical step towards improving it.

International research has found the ethical tone of an organization to be an integral part of an organization's functioning. For example, organizational culture and ethical research has shown that the ethical tone of an organization has an impact upon the following:

- Efficiency and effectiveness
- Decision-making processes
- Staff commitment and job satisfaction
- Staff stress
- Staff turnover

Making ethical practices a priority is not just about functioning with integrity or being seen to be functioning with integrity, nor is it just about being credible and competitive. It is also about optimizing the efficient functioning of the organization. Organizations are, therefore, urged to improve their ethical cultures on priority, because focusing on ethics is a fundamental aspect of good management practices. The terms honesty, integrity, and right and wrong behaviour are often used interchangeably with the term ethics, but all of these are the outcomes of ethical practices.

PERCEPTION VS BEHAVIOURAL ISSUES AND ETHICS

The perception of individual employees helps them understand the organizational environment. The degree of their perception is instrumental in shaping their behavioural response. Thus, perception per se does not constitute an actual measure of behaviour. It offers an indication of how a person may behave in his/her environment, given certain perceptions. According to sociologist W.I. Thomas (cited in Coser 1977, p. 521), if men define situations as real, they are real in their consequences, suggesting that the meaning ascribed to a situation, more than the situational variables alone, determines the consequent behaviour. The challenge then is to create a situation in which employees feel safe to indicate their true beliefs rather than what they think the favourable response should be. To establish the key areas that managements need to focus on, in order to build an ethical workplace, factors such as job satisfaction and attitude to workplace, leadership and management behaviour, and communication about ethics need to be considered by the organization. If ethical issues are rightly perceived by the employees, they will stress on ethics in their behaviour, show trust and respect towards leadership, ensure team dynamics, show commitment to the organization, and honour values in the organization.

Employees develop their perceptions by observing the behaviour of their leaders. Some of the leadership behaviours closely observed by the employees are direct supervision, honest practices (matching what they do with what they preach), encouraging and emphasizing honest behaviour at the workplace, encouraging new ideas from the staff, and practising principles of fairness and equity in the organization. Therefore, leaders wishing to build and maintain an ethical culture in an organization must comply with the following requirements:

- Communicate about ethics through clearly stated values, codes, policies, and procedures and state the importance of ethical work practices.
- Recognize and utilize the behaviour of leaders as a critical part of setting the ethical tone of the organization.
- Follow good people management practices.
- Deal appropriately and effectively with violations.

Practitioner Speak 16.3

Why Ethics Matter in a Downturn

When times get tough, many companies reflexively play everything close to the vest. Executives often stop sharing information with anyone, fearing that any tidbit of data that show weakness may cause employees to leave, customers to flee, and investors to sell. These fears distort thinking, damage relationships, and lead some managers down the slippery slope of white lies and deception.

Read this insightful blog posted by Korver on *HBR Blog Network* by accessing the following link: http://blogs.hbr.org/korver/2008/08/in-a-downturn-you-should-show.html

Exhibit 16.1 discusses how moral disengagement is a deterrent for ethical behaviour at organizations.

EXHIBIT 16.1   Moral Disengagement: A Deterrent for Ethical Behaviour at Organizations

Moral disengagement in employees occurs when individuals indulge in unethical practices without being restrained by self-censure. The cognitive links that deter such transgressive behaviour are disabled and thus individuals fail to prevent unethical actions. The theory of moral disengagement makes an important contribution towards the understanding of unethical behaviour such as wrongdoings and corruption at organizations. Thus, in order to envisage an organization free from corrupt and dishonest practices, organizations should take a re-look at the cognitive mechanisms that lead to such deviant behaviour.

According to Bandura (1986), the three salient cognitive mechanisms that lead to moral disengagement are as follows:

Moral Justification

Moral justification is the act of trying to justify that unethical actions are being done for the cause of the greater good. Examples of moral justification include organizations indulging in unfair business practices to save their friends who are facing a loss in their businesses, thereby creating a nexus between firms through unethical practices.

Euphemistic Labelling

Euphemistic labelling is the process of making unethical actions sound more benign than they actually are through the use of sanitized language. Examples of euphemistic labelling include colluding employees being termed as *team players*.

Advantageous Comparison

Advantageous comparison is the process of referring to heinous acts to alleviate the response to some unethical behaviour under consideration. Trying to prove that some action in the past is far more reproachable than unethical acts committed recently is an example of how employees use comparison to their advantage.

Annually, trillions of dollars are lost by organizations and society owing to unethical business practices. Thus, an understanding of factors that propel individuals to resort to unethical behaviour is likely to help curb such deviant behaviour at organizations and lead to a cleaner and fairer workplace.

Sources: Moore, C., J. Detert, L. Trevino, V. Baker, and D. Mayer, 'Why Employees Do Bad Things: Moral Disengagement and Unethical Organizational Behaviour', *Personnel Psychology*, Vol. 65, 2012, pp. 1–48; White, J and A. Bandura, 'Moral Disengagement in the Corporate World', *Accountability in Research*, Vol. 16, 2009, pp. 41–74 (adapted).

VALUES

Values are the enduring beliefs of people that shape their specific code of conduct in both their personal and social lives. However, values cannot be said to be totally stable. They can change with personal and social maturity. One develops one's own value system, which determines the course of one's life. The individual value system of a person reflects attributes such as ambition, competency, integrity, sense of responsibility, dedication, loyalty, credibility, teamwork, sense

> Values are the enduring beliefs of people that shape their specific mode of conduct in both their personal and social lives.

of accountability, and innovativeness. Depending on the requirement, during the process of recruitment, organizations try to map a particular attribute or attributes from the value precepts of individuals. Again, attributes could be content attributes (values that are important) or intensity attributes (the degree of requirement). It is for this reason that every organization nurtures some core values to provide some fundamental purpose and direction to its employees. When employees subscribe to the organizational core values, the organization can achieve the desired goals and objectives.

Organizational Values

Organizational values determine the way people are treated as well as shape the basic work ethics. A systematic approach to build organizational values enables an organization to develop an effective and strong work culture to bind the behaviour of people. Theoretically, values can be categorized as terminal and instrumental. Terminal values are developed during the process of an individual's upbringing with cues that emerge from his/her experiences of happiness, freedom, and friendship. However, in the process of upbringing, people may not always experience happiness. To sustain this, they develop instrumental values to shape their values, which guide them on the ways to be cheerful and responsible and to maintain self-control.

Cultural differences also lead to major differences in people's values. Americans want everything immediately, have little patience when it comes to waiting, and are pushy. Japanese workers tend to be more patient in waiting for job promotions and are willing to stay with the company for a long period. Germans believe more in analytical decision-making, with less interest in brainstorming and quick decision-making. Indians are influenced by a conservative decision-making style, hedging the risk of uncertainty. They believe in, and are used to, taking decisions with emphasis on constraint—the reason being they have survived the ages of scarcity and been brought up in a social system that requires them to accommodate and adjust with a high degree of tolerance.

Attitude is the way people reflect their values. An optimistic employee always tends to look at the brighter side of an organization and is always positive in his/her approach.

Value systems are largely developed through education. The cognitive part is developed through knowledge—recognizing what is right and what is wrong. The affective part, being the emotional side, is developed through experience. The behavioural part is a blend of knowledge and emotions.

Management of Values

Managing the value systems of employees is important. Mismatch between the value systems of the employees with those of the organization affects their efficiency and performance, which, therefore, causes the organization to experience a competitive disadvantage. Some of the reflections of values at work are listed as follows:

Job satisfaction—overall positive or negative   This refers to an individual's general attitude towards his/her job. This is most often looked at in terms of work in the long run. For example, one may be having a bad day (or even week), but that does not mean that one is not satisfied with one's job.

Job involvement   This is not about being involved in decision-making on the job but rather about how important the job or work is to an individual. Does it help to define him/her? If losing one's job would make one feel less of a person, one has a high degree of job involvement. Job involvement measures the degree to which a person identifies psychologically with his/her job and considers his/her perceived performance level important to self-worth.

Organizational commitment   This refers to how committed one is to the goals of the company for which one works. Most of McDonald's employees are committed to the quality of its burgers. Similarly, most of the EMC (US) employees are committed to customer service. Thus, the degree to which the employees of an organization identify with it and its goals and wish to maintain membership in the organization decides their attitude towards organizational commitment.

Mapping Value Systems of Employees

As value systems largely influence the behaviour of individual employees, companies always try to check these aspects of a person before their recruitment, primarily through reference checking and during interview.

- Values are measured using scenario analysis (with ethical bent), in-basket exercises, role-playing, and degree of fit, keeping in view the organizational requirement. The focus of all these exercises is to predict the response and behavioural pattern of employees on the job.
- A value change exercise used by organizations is modelling the desired behavioural standards with instructions to employees to emulate those standards. For example, a good customer relationship model can be developed and shown to the employees so that it would help them in their dealing with customers. This is particularly important for knowledge management practices in organizations, showcasing some of the best roles in the organization (inside) and outside.
- The degree of information transparency and the degree of building of mutual trust are also used to map organizational value systems. Accordingly, on matching these with the employees' perceived values, one can identify the gap and initiate necessary corrective action.

Examples of Some Organizational Value Systems

To inculcate value systems, organizations may document their value statements to provide a sense of direction to their employees. All employees shape their pattern of behaviour based on such espoused value statements of the organization. The model value systems of the Tata Group, Infosys, and SAIL are discussed here.[1]

---

[1] The information on Tata, Infosys, and SAIL has been extracted from the websites of the respective companies, last accessed on 24 September 2008.

Tata Group   The Tata Group's core value system is the improvement of quality of life of the communities. The group believes in the following five core values:

Integrity   We must conduct our business fairly, with honesty and transparency. Everything we do must stand the test of public scrutiny.

Understanding   We must be caring towards and show respect, compassion, and humanity for our colleagues and customers around the world and always work for the benefit of the communities we serve.

Excellence   We must constantly strive to achieve the highest possible standards in our day-to-day work and in the quality of the goods and services we provide.

Unity   We must work cohesively with our colleagues across the group and with our customers and partners around the world, building strong relationships based on tolerance, understanding, and mutual cooperation.

Responsibility   We must continue to be responsible and sensitive to the countries, communities, and environments in which we work, always ensuring that what comes from the people goes back to the people many times over.

Infosys Technologies   The value systems of Infosys Technologies are empowered by C-Life, which is explained as follows:

Customer's delight   A commitment to surpass our customers' expectations

Leadership by example   A commitment to set standards in our business and transactions and be an exemplar for the industry and our own teams

Integrity and transparency   A commitment to be ethical, sincere, and open in our dealings

Fairness   A commitment to be objective and transaction-oriented, thereby earning trust and respect

Pursuit of excellence   A commitment to strive relentlessly to constantly improve ourselves, our teams, our services and products so as to become the best

Steel Authority of India Limited   Similarly, SAIL, the PSU major in steel manufacturing, also subscribes to strong value systems, which are built into its credo:

- We uphold the highest ethical standards in the conduct of our business.
- We create and nurture a culture that supports flexibility and learning and is proactive to change.
- We chart a challenging career for employees, with opportunities for advancement and rewards.
- We value the opportunity and responsibility to make a meaningful difference to people's lives.

Importance of Values at Work

Globalization is increasing the awareness of, and sensitivity to, different values across cultures. It poses major challenges in relation to communication styles, incentive and reward structures, recruitment procedures, and so on. Replacing direct supervision potentially aligns the employees' decisions and actions with corporate goals. Globalization has increased the pressure to engage in ethical practices.

ETHICS OF PRODUCTION

Ethics of production deals with the duties of a company to ensure that its products and production processes do not cause harm. Some of the more acute dilemmas in this area arise because there is usually a degree of danger in any product or production process and it is difficult to define a degree of permissibility or the degree of permissibility may depend on the changing state of preventive technologies or changing social perceptions of acceptable risk. Various dimensions of production ethics encompass areas such as the following:

> Ethics of production is concerned with the duties of a company to ensure that its products and production processes do not cause harm.

- Defective, addictive, and inherently dangerous products and services such as tobacco, alcohol, weapons, motor vehicles, chemical manufacturing, and bungee jumping
- Ethical relations between the company and the environment such as pollution, environmental ethics, and carbon emissions trading
- Ethical problems arising out of new technologies such as the effect of genetically modified food and mobile phone radiation on health
- Product testing ethics such as animal rights and animal testing, and use of economically disadvantaged groups (say, students) as test objects

ETHICS OF INTELLECTUAL PROPERTY RIGHTS, KNOWLEDGE, AND SKILLS

Knowledge and skills are valuable but not easily ownable objects. Moreover, it is not clear as to who has the greater rights to an idea—the company who trained the employee or the employee himself/herself. As a result, attempts to assert ownership and ethical disputes over ownership arise. Patent infringement, copyright infringement, and trademark infringement are some of the areas of ethical violation in issues related to intellectual property rights (IPR). Misuse of intellectual property systems weakens the competitive strength of the organizations who own it. Some organizations even practise employee raiding, that is, the practice of attracting key employees away from a competitor to take unfair advantage of their knowledge or skills. Apart from these, some organizations also employ the most talented people in a specific field, regardless of need, to prevent competitors from employing them. Hence, ethical issues in IPR-related areas can manifest themselves into various dimensions, which may not necessarily be restricted to IPR infringement alone.

INTERNATIONAL BUSINESS ETHICS

The concept of international business ethics emerged in the late 1990s. Theoretically, cultural relativity of ethical values receives more emphasis in international business ethics. It primarily focuses on the search for universal values as the basis for international commercial behaviour and the comparison of country-specific and religion-specific business ethical traditions. Some of the ethical issues in international business are biopiracy (in the pharmaceutical industry), transfer pricing, cultural imperialism, varying global standards, and use of child labour.

DIMENSIONS OF BUSINESS ETHICS

The ethical organization theory can be understood better in the context of moral philosophy, which again is classified into many different dimensions, such as egoism, utilitarianism,

The ethical organization theory can be understood better in the context of moral philosophy, which is again classified into egotism, utilitarianism, deontology, rights, and relativism.

deontology, rights, and relativism. The deontological approach relies upon individualistic application of abstract philosophical theories, whereas the utilitarian approach focuses upon the pragmatic organizational concern for the outcome. Another potential way of understanding organizational ethics could be in the context of role theory. All these dimensions can again be grouped into two approaches, namely consequentialist and non-consequentialist. The consequentialist approach to ethics focuses on the outcomes of the situation, whereas the non-consequentialist approach focuses on the process or means to those outcomes. Egoism and utilitarianism are examples of consequentialist approach, and deontology, rights, and relativism are examples of non-consequentialist approach. The deontological approach, advocated by Immanuel Kant (translated in 1964), is associated with the moral rights and duties of an individual. Kant emphasized that each person has both the right to expect to be treated according to universal moral laws and the corresponding duty to behave according to that law. This is what is called *categorical imperative* or the golden rule: 'Do unto others as you would have them do unto you.'

Any study on theories of organizational ethics, therefore, must recognize the complexity and disorder of real-life management practices rather than depending solely on abstract philosophical concepts. In OB, it is necessary to consider intervening in the psychological processes to address the issue of workplace ethics. Some of these issues are discussed in Exhibit 16.2, which shows the sample code of ethics of Infosys.

EXHIBIT 16.2 Sample Code of Ethics on Corporate Governance of Infosys

We believe that sound corporate governance is critical to enhance and retain investor trust. Accordingly, we always seek to ensure that we attain our performance rules with integrity. Our Board exercises its fiduciary responsibilities in the widest sense of the term. Our disclosures always seek to attain the best practices in international corporate governance. We also endeavour to enhance long-term shareholder values and respect minority rights in all our business decisions.

Our corporate governance philosophy is based on the following principles:

- Satisfy the spirit of the law and not just the letter of the law. Corporate governance standards should go beyond the law.
- Be transparent and maintain a high degree of disclosure levels. When in doubt, disclose.
- Make a clear distinction between personal conveniences and corporate resources.
- Communicate externally, in a truthful manner, about how the Company is run internally.

- Comply with the laws in all the countries in which the Company operates.
- Have a simple and transparent corporate structure driven solely by business needs.
- Management is the trustee of the shareholders' capital and not the owner.

At the core of our corporate governance practice is the Board, which oversees how the management serves and protects the long-term interests of all stakeholders of the company. We believe that an active, well-informed, and independent Board is necessary to ensure the highest standards of corporate governance. The majority of the Board, eight out of fifteen, are independent members. Further, we have audit, compensation, investor grievance, nominations, and risk management committees, which comprise independent directors.

As a part of our commitment to follow global best practices, we comply with the Euro shareholders Corporate Governance Guidelines 2000 and the recommendations of the Conference Board

(Contd)

EXHIBIT 16.2 (*Contd*)

Commission on Public Trusts and Private Enterprises in the US. We also adhere to the UN Global Compact Programme. Further, a note on Infosys' compliance with the corporate governance guidelines of six countries—in their national languages—is presented in the section *Additional information to shareholders*.

Source: http://www.infosys.com/investor/corporategovernance.asp, last accessed on 16 August 2007.

Practitioner Speak 16.4

Sleep-deprived People Are More Likely to Cheat

Good managers focus not only on bottom-line performance, but on the means by which their people achieve that high performance. Unethical behaviors can be damaging to a broad variety of stakeholders, and are often the cause of organizational crises. Ethical behavior not only keeps consciences clean; it can boost the reputation and performance of your firm. More than ever, ethics must be a primary management concern.

Read this insightful blog posted by Barnes on *HBR Blog Network* by accessing the following link: http://blogs.hbr.org/cs/2013/05/sleep_deprived_people_are_more_likely_to_cheat.html.

CONFLICTING INTERESTS

Business ethics can be examined from various perspectives, including the perspective of the employee, of the commercial enterprise, and of the society as a whole. Very often, situations arise during a conflict in which serving the interest of one party is detrimental to the interest of the other(s). For example, a particular outcome might be good for the employee, whereas it would be bad for the company or society, or vice versa. Some ethicists (e.g., Henry Sidgwick) see the principal role of ethics as the harmonization and reconciliation of conflicting interests.

SUMMARY

Social and environmental responsibilities are vital components of a business strategy. They are the cornerstones of successful sustainable businesses. While addressing ethical issues, organizations worldwide base strategic decision-making on respected social and environmental principles. Ethical consideration starts with senior managers and is carried right down to the grass-roots level of the organization.

Organizations adopting a code of ethics make practical sense from two very important perspectives—first, through assuring people and governments that organizational activities will be pursued in a thoughtful, careful, and ethical manner, eliminating all potential harmful barriers, and second, by adopting an ethical approach to conducting business.

Ethical issues have become increasingly important to the modern business community. Respected professional organizations as well as successful companies have already adopted formalized codes of ethics and standards. Within these professional organizations, all members and employees adhere to their respective corporate ethical codes. A successful code of ethics should not only be voluntary, but also facilitate the work and expansion of individual businesses rather than hinder their efforts towards providing products and services. A properly designed code of ethics ensures the development of space for commerce unfettered by government-created barriers. It encourages and supports businesses. Consideration of this code should begin the process of critical thinking to move decision-makers beyond the bottom line or short-sighted technical and engineering concerns. Though the bottom line is extremely important to all businesses, it should not be the sole focus of the company. By paying attention to the other equally important aspects of the business, including personnel, management, ethics, and strategy, the company helps ensure a bottom line that draws strength from all of its business operations.

KEY DEFINITIONS

Code of ethics   A specific set of ethical standards that one (such as staff or a professional group) should follow in order to stay as a member of the group to which they currently belong

Ethical culture   The ethical environment of an organization that influences ethical or unethical behaviour of the members of an organization

Ethics of intellectual property, knowledge, and skills   A system of principles that organizations need to comply with while doing business in order to avoid ethical violation in the form of patent infringement, copyright infringement, and trademark infringement

Ethical decision-making   Decision-making in compliance with the ethical issues, providing transparency, effect, and fairness

CONCEPT-REVIEW QUESTIONS

16.1 Explain the meaning and importance of corporate ethics. Do you think compliance with ethics will deter achieving the business goals of an organization? Justify your answer.

16.2 In designing ethical guidelines for managing the behaviour of people in an organization, what are the important areas one should consider? Illustrate your answer, selecting any such area (e.g., discipline, promotion, transfer), with a suitable description of the concerned ethical issues.

16.3 Explain how ethical cultures can be built in organizations.

16.4 Write short notes on the following:
 (a) Code of ethics
 (b) Ethical decision-making
 (c) Ethics in production
 (d) International business ethics

CRITICAL THINKING QUESTIONS

16.1 Review some recent press reports on ethical violation in organizations. Critically examine those and suggest what could be the possible course of action for your chosen organization to avoid such ethical violation.

16.2 Study any ethical compliance report of an Indian organization. Relate their degree of compliance with their business achievement along with your comments and observations.

SELECT BIBLIOGRAPHY

- Andrews, K.R. 'Ethics in Practice', *Harvard Business Review*, Vol. 67, Issue 5, 1989, pp. 99–104.
- Badenhorst, J.A. 'Unethical Behaviour in Procurement: A Perspective on Causes and Solutions', *Journal of Business Ethics*, Vol. 13, 1994, pp. 739–45.
- Bailey, J.E., J.R. Schermerhorn, J.G. Hunt, and R.N. Osborn, *Managing Organisational Behaviour*, John Wiley and Sons, Brisbane, 1991.
- Chen, A.Y.S., R.B. Sawyer, and P.F. Williams, 'Reinforcing Ethical Decisions through Corporate Culture', Journal of Business Ethics, Vol. 16, 1997, pp. 855–65.

- Chonko, L.B. and S.D. Hunt, 'Ethics and Marketing Management: An Empirical Examination', *Journal of Business Research*, Vol. 13, 1985, pp. 339–59.
- Coser, L.A., *Masters of Sociological Thought: Ideas in Historical and Social Context*, 2nd ed., Harcourt Brace Jovanovich, New York, 1977.
- Ferrell, O.C. and S.J. Skinner 'Ethical Behavior and Bureaucratic Structure in Marketing Research Organizations', *Journal of Marketing Research*, Vol. 25, 1988, pp. 103–09.
- Gap Inc., *Code of Ethics*, 1978, www.gapinc.com, last accessed on 7 July 2007.
- Hegarty, W.H. and H.P. Sims, Jr. 'Some Determinants of Unethical Behaviour: An Experiment', *Journal of Applied Psychology*, Vol. 63, Issue 4, 1978, pp. 451–7.
- Hegarty, W.H. and H.P. Sims, Jr., 'Organizational Philosophy, Policies and Objectives Related to Unethical Decision Behaviour: A Laboratory Experiment', *Journal of Applied Psychology*, Vol. 64, Issue 3, 1979, pp. 331–8.
- Himan, Lawrance M. and Immanuel Kant, 'The Ethics of Duty' in W.D. Ross (ed), *Kant's Ethical Theory*, Clarendon Press, Oxford, 1964.
- Hofstede, G., *Cultural Consequences: International Differences in Work-related Values*, Sage, Beverly Hills, 1980.
- Laczniak, G.R. and E.J. Inderrieden, 'The Influence of Stated Organizational Concern upon Ethical Decision Making', *Journal of Business Ethics*, Vol. 6, 1987, pp. 297–307.
- McNamara, Carter, 'An Ethical Toolkit for Managers', *Journal of Business Ethics*, Vol. 35, Issue 1, 2002, pp. 35–49.
- Neck, C.P. and G. Moorhead, 'Groupthink Remodelled: The Importance of Leadership, Time Pressure, and Methodical Decision-making Procedures', *Human Relations*, Vol. 48, Issue 5, 1995, pp. 537–57.
- Rich, A.J., C.S. Smith, and P.H. Mihalek, 'Are Corporate Codes of Conduct Effective', *Management Accounting*, Vol. 72, 1990, pp. 34–35.
- White, Jerry, *Honesty, Morality and Conscience*, NavPress, Colorado Springs, 1978.
- Zey-Ferrell, M. 'Predicting Unethical Behaviour among Marketing Practitioners', *Human Relations*, Vol. 32, Issue 7, 1979, pp. 557–69.

CASE STUDY

Ethics of Leadership

Jagdish Nair is the chairman and chief executive of a large diversified business group, having presence in various industries such as two-wheelers, hotels, finance, fertilizers, and fine blanks. The company was a closely held, family-managed business until 2005. To reap the advantages of the diversified and globally expanded market, the company made its initial public offer (IPO) in January 2006. As the company was making high profits and was having a consistent track record of performance, the issue was oversubscribed even with a premium price of 500 per cent over the face value. The company is headquartered in Chennai with units and offices scattered over the country and abroad. However, Jagdish continued to manage the business in the same way as the company's founding father, Avilash, with a traditional pyramidal structure. The family

stake after the IPO reduced to 40 per cent, making Jagdish the largest stakeholder with the highest voting power. Immediately after the successful IPO, Jagdish called for an extraordinary general meeting to transact important issues related to business policy. One of the points on the agenda was to get the consensus of the shareholders to transfer the company reserves to other sister companies for better fund management and business efficiency. The second issue was to switch over from the pyramidal structure to strategic business unit (SBU) structure. The minority shareholders' representation in the extraordinary general meeting was very poor, although it was enough for forming the quorum. Both the issues were smoothly passed and Jagdish was authorized to transact these two issues in the best interest of the organization.

Jagdish transferred the reserves to some of the family-managed units, which continued to be closely held ones. In fact, these units were not within the IPO, although in the IPO offer, Jagdish had given the name of the company as Swarasati Group of Industries. Jagdish then deployed some of the trusted family members in such units as the heads of the SBUs. As per Indian law, any business transacted at the extraordinary general meeting needs to be vetted in the next annual general meeting. The annual general meeting of Swarasati Group was long overdue. Finally, it was convened on 1 July 2007.

While transacting the business of getting the shareholders' approval for the annual reports, some of the shareholders raised their objection, pointing out that the entire process of transferring the company reserves to other units made the group suffer losses. All these beneficiary units eroded the fund, incurring huge losses, because of which the Swarasati Group had to face uncertainties in coping with the changing business scenario. Some of the shareholders even alleged that Jagdish, as the chairman of the group, unduly influenced the shareholders present in the earlier extraordinary general meeting and had in fact diverted the company reserves by such transfer to other units (which still continue to remain family-managed) for his own personal gain. The number of dissenting shareholders increased and they wanted to put this matter to vote. Jagdish had no other choice but to agree for the proposed voting, and accordingly, a secret ballot was conducted. After counting the votes, it transpired that the dissenting shareholders lost the case.

These shareholders then went to the Company Law Board and framed ethical violation charges against the chairman of the company. The Company Law Board on going through the papers could not uphold the charge and communicated to the shareholders that the process, being in compliance with the legal provisions, does not merit review on ethical grounds. These shareholders then decided to contest the case in court and accordingly mobilized the opinion of other shareholders. The court, on reviewing the case, upheld the charge against the company, citing it, prima facie, as a case of gross ethical violation in terms of both suppression of facts and misuse of company's funds for personal interests.

With renewed thrust and vigour, the victorious shareholders made a request to the company to convene an extraordinary general meeting to propose the removal of the chairman on grounds of having followed unethical business practices.

Questions for Discussion

1. Review the case and suggest how Jagdish could have avoided such an ethical violation.
2. What actions of the chairman can be termed as unethical or unprofessional?

Learning Organizations

LEARNING OBJECTIVES

After studying this chapter, the reader will be able to

- understand the concept of learning organization
- discuss the importance of a learning organization
- identify the characteristics of a learning organization
- explain the steps necessary for developing a learning organization
- describe the implementation strategies for developing a learning organization
- understand the need for behavioural changes for developing a learning organization
- comprehend the process of learning orientation
- explain the basics of a learning curve

CASE STUDY

Motorola University—A Learning Organization

Forming a corporate university to cater to the needs of continuous organizational learning is not something new in the business world. There are many such examples in the corporate world. One such corporate initiative is the formation of Motorola University in 1981. The university acts as Motorola's training and education centre to meet the company's training needs. It is a separate corporate department of Motorola. The primary objective of Motorola University is to promote a quality culture through an internal training system. With the global expansion of its business, Motorola further reinforced its pledge to be a learning organization,

setting up the Galvin Centre for Continuing Education in 1986 and the Singapore Training Design Centre in 1989. Today, many managers, supervisors, and employees from all locations of Motorola attend various training and learning programmes to achieve their full potential and meet the ever-rising needs of a learning organization like Motorola, which recruits about 20,000 associates every year. Hence, the task of Motorola University has become further challenging. The University transforms Motorola's new recruits into productive team members, disseminating consistent messages about the company's business and core values.

INTRODUCTION

In a competitive world, organizations need to transform the workplace into a dynamic and effective place to optimize the talent of the employees and to align them with the business goals. However, the process is not simple. Organizations are a configuration of complex systems and strategies; hence, the learning imperatives for different domains are different. However, the objective is the same, that is, to maximize performance by using the learning principles. Hence, organizational emphasis should be on supporting and maximizing long-term effective and sustainable learning. At the same time, the technical or task-related skills cannot be made redundant. These are essential but not the absolutes in the new-age economy. To sustain itself in a competitive global market, an organization has to adapt to the changing environment and make its people capable of undertaking new tasks and responsibilities. Continuous capacity building of the people in organizations will be possible only when organizations follow the learning management principles. Thus, in the true sense, a learning organization should support the development process skills and attitudes to improve performance in a competitive business situation. Learning develops organizational intellectual capital, which is the only sustainable competitive strength for any organization.

Organizational learning involves individual learning, and those who make the shift from traditional organization thinking to learning organizations develop the ability to think critically and creatively. These skills transfer to the values and assumptions of the organizational development (OD). OD is a continuous, long-term effort to effect improvement in all spheres of organizational activities and to set the premise for organizational change. Organizational learning is the most important intervention tool for OD. Learning reinforcement develops people and makes them capable of solving problems. Thus, a learning organization evolves by developing the organizational capability to respond to changes.

Theoretically, a learning organization has two dimensions. The first dimension perceives it as a process for individual and collective learning within an organization. The second dimension, on the other hand, considers it as a specific diagnostic and evaluative tool to identify, promote, and evaluate the quality of learning processes inside organizations. The goal of both these dimensions being the same, that is, to transform the organization into an ideal learning organization, this text does not debate their individual merits and demerits but rather concentrates more on the nature of the activities and processes involved.

DEFINITIONS AND CONCEPTS

A learning organization learns and encourages learning among its people, promotes exchange of information, and makes people adaptable to new ideas and changes through a shared vision. Historically, references to such learning organizations can be found even in the work of the Chinese philosopher Confucius (551–479 BC). Confucius believed that everyone should benefit from learning: 'Without learning, the wise become foolish; by learning, the foolish become wise.' Hence, organizations need to be aware of both the company as a whole and the individuals within the company. Before the introduction of this concept, companies used to concentrate on their own needs and not on the needs of their workers. The systems approach to management suggested that organizations should also include the ambitions of the individual workers rather

A learning organization learns and encourages learning among its people, promotes exchange of information, and makes people adaptable to new ideas and changes through a shared vision.

than focusing solely on the business goals. For example, corporate executives use a decision support system (DSS) to help them take decisions for the future. The benefit of a DSS is that it makes implicit knowledge explicit. This makes extra knowledge available to the organization and allows the organization to learn better because explicit knowledge tends to spread faster through an organization.

In the 1970s, this idea was renamed *organizational learning*. Two of the early researchers in this field were Chris Arygris and D. Schön (1978) from Harvard University. Despite Argyris's pioneering work, it was hardly accepted by any organization to bring about changes in the style of functioning. In the 1980s, however, organizations worldwide recognized the importance of capability-based learning to derive competitive advantages. Thereafter, because of Peter Senge's work (1990), the learning organization concept gained worldwide popularity. The true definition of a learning organization, however, still remains elusive. Some of the best possible definitions of a learning organization that could be identified from the review of literature are provided here.

Senge considered learning organizations to be those organizations where people continually expand their capacity to create the results they truly desire, where new and expansive patterns of thinking are nurtured, where collective aspiration is set free, and where people are continually learning to see the whole together.

Pedler, et al. (1991) saw a learning organization as a vision and not simply as a training of people. It facilitates transformation of all members of the organization and the organization per se through continuous learning. It is essentially a top-down approach.

Watkins and Marsick (1992), on the other hand, characterized a learning organization as a process of total employee involvement to introduce collective accountability and change through the principles of shared values. It is characterized by a bottom-up approach.

Easterby-Smith and Araujo (1999) made a distinction between the technical and social variants of a learning organization. The technical variant looks at the problems of a learning organization as a technical option. Here, organizational interventions are based on measures like the learning curve, which analyses historical data on production costs against the cumulative output of a particular product. Therefore, this approach essentially focuses on outcomes rather than on the process of learning. On the other hand, the social view considers a learning organization as an interaction and a process. This approach considers organizational behaviour aspects and now dominates the literature available on learning organizations.

Some of the common identifiable problems that compel an organization to become a learning organization are listed as follows:

- Increase in the number of unmotivated or uninterested workforce
- Lack of skill and knowledge of workers to adjust to new jobs
- Incapability of workers to come up with new ideas
- Preference of workers to only follow orders
- Lack of teamwork and real productivity
- Lack of communication among employees

Practitioner Speak 17.1   **The New Organization Model: Learning at Scale**

In recent posts we've described a massive institutional transformation that will occur as part of the big shift: the move from institutions designed for scalable efficiency to institutions designed for scalable learning. The core questions we all need to address are: who will drive this transformation? Who will be the agents of change? Will it be institutional leaders from above or individuals from below and from the outside of our current institutions?

Read this insightful blog posted by Hagel, Brown, and Davison on *HBR Blog Network* by accessing the following link: http://blogs.hbr.org/bigshift/2009/03/can-your-company-scale-its-lea.html.

> The steps necessary to create a learning organization are awareness, environment, leadership, empowerment, and learning.

- Lack of responsibility and accountability on the part of the workers, especially in the absence of the boss
- Lack of ability or interest on the part of the boss to rectify problems
- Regular occurrence of customer complaints
- Recurrence of similar problems

If such problems persist, organizations can adopt the learning organization philosophy to solve them and truly become an enabling organization that can respond to a situation.

CHARACTERISTICS

According to Sandra Kerka (1997), most conceptualizations of learning organizations seem to work on the assumption that 'learning is valuable, continuous, and most effective when shared, and that every experience is an opportunity to learn'. Kerka has identified the following six characteristics of learning organizations.

- They provide continuous learning opportunities.
- They use learning to reach their goals.
- They link individual performance with organizational performance.
- They foster enquiry and dialogue, making it safe for people to openly share and take risks.
- They embrace creative tension as a source of energy and renewal.
- They are continuously aware of and interact with their environment.

Greatly influenced by Senge's fifth discipline concept, Kerka echoed that personal mastery, mental models, shared vision, team learning, and systems thinking are the keys to building a learning organization.

STEPS FOR DEVELOPMENT

The following steps are necessary to build a learning organization:

Awareness   To start with, organizations must appreciate that learning is necessary at all levels and is not just limited to the managerial levels. Moreover, the need for change must also be accepted as the only way to survive. Such awareness at organization levels can be created only if organizations believe in emulating the success stories of those who have leapfrogged their growth by truly developing the learning organization culture.

Environment Creating a learning environment requires sharing with all members of the organization a comprehensive picture of the whole organization and its goals. This requires creating a more flexible organic structure. An organic structure is a flatter structure, which encourages innovations. It also promotes transparency of information between members of the organization, thereby developing a more informed workforce. The desired environment for a learning organization encourages openness and reflectivity and accepts error and uncertainty. Members of the organization should be able to question decisions without fear.

Leadership Leaders should activate learning, which enables an organization to gain a competitive advantage. However, to obtain the results, the leader should sell the concept and encourage learning to help both the individuals and the organization. It is the leader's responsibility to help mould the individual views of team members. The management should provide commitment for long-term learning with resource support.

Empowerment The real testing tool for learning is the degree of empowerment, which requires involving workers in decision-making. Empowerment makes workers more responsible for their actions, without bringing down the managerial involvement. Managers still need to encourage, enthuse, and coordinate the workers. Empowerment must be allowed at all levels so that members can simultaneously learn from one another.

Learning Learning systems need to replicate real-life situations through a series of simulation games. This facilitates learning from mistakes to make the future learning more effective. The learning environment needs to be open, flexible, and motivating. To facilitate continuous learning, some organizations also make extensive use of the electronic media, for example, e-learning, duly providing a track to measure the learning progresses. However, its acceptance largely depends on the workers' urge to learn. This can be ensured by linking learning with various incentive packages and human resource decisions.

IMPLEMENTATION STRATEGIES

To implement the learning organization philosophy in an organization, an overall strategy with clear, well-defined goals is required. Once the goals and the overall strategy are identified, specific action plans are required to implement them. Senge focused on certain initiatives required at organization levels to implement the learning organization concept. However, there are three generic strategies to develop a learning organization, which are as follows:

Accidental Sometimes, the implementation of the learning organization philosophy is more accidental than preconceived in some organizations. For achieving business goals, organizations often unknowingly develop a framework, which, at times, corroborates with the philosophy of the learning organizations. Therefore, organizations are seen to follow the learning organization philosophy to gain a competitive advantage, even while remaining unaware that they are following the principles of this philosophy.

> Implementation strategies for learning organizations are accidental, subversive, or declared.

Subversive Subversive strategy encapsulates the dissidence by exploiting the ideas and techniques of people working in the organization. It requires an open endorsement of the learning organization ideal so that people can express their ideas.

EXHIBIT 17.1   How Successful Organizations Transform into Learning Organizations

Learning organizations, in recent days, have been highly successful. The concept of continuous improvement has complemented the age of rapid change and advancement in the business fraternity all over the world. However, what many organizations, in their attempts to change continuously, forget is that one cannot really change for the better without having learnt anything new. Changes without learning new things are rather cosmetic and do not turn out to be truly meaningful.

Most multinational organizations (MNCs) have included the learning organization concept in their management philosophy. However, the way they have integrated it into their working varies widely. In addition, successful adaptation of the philosophy of a learning organization is based on the idea of lending it true meaning and must be actionable, that is, easy to apply. In this regard, one may like to see how some MNCs have successfully adopted the learning organization concept at their workplaces.

Toyota

The key elements in Toyota's learning organization are as follows:

- Identifying root causes and taking steps accordingly
- Utilizing responsibility, self-reflection, and the concepts of organizational learning
- Using policy deployment

Xerox

The following are the key points of Xerox's learning organization:

- Identification of problem
- Analysis of problem
- Generation of potential solutions
- Choosing and planning of solution
- Implementation of solution
- Evaluation of solution

It is important to note that both organizations considerably vary in their approach to building a learning organization and yet have become successful in doing it.

Sources: Garvin, D., 'Building a Learning Organization', *HBR Magazine*, 1993, http://hbr.org/1993/07/building-a-learning-organization/ar/4, last accessed on 16 September 2013; Dolcemascolo, D., 'A Look into Toyota's Learning Organization', http://www.reliableplant.com/Read/13439/toyota-learning-organization, last accessed on 16 September 2013 (adapted).

Declared   The third option is the declared approach. This is a clear promotion of the principles of learning organizations as part of the company ethos and is manifested openly in all company initiatives.

Exhibit 17.1 discusses how successful organizations get transformed into learning organizations.

LEARNING ORGANIZATION MODEL

A typical learning organization model normally follows a three-dimensional approach—individual, team, and organizational learning. Investors in people approach are designed to support action plans for OD for maximizing human resources. This complies with the belief that organizations can improve by increasing human talent and potentials. The model is based on the integration of strategies in the domains of individual, team, and organizational learning. Figure 17.1 shows a three-dimensional model of a learning organization. The emphasis here is on learning rather than

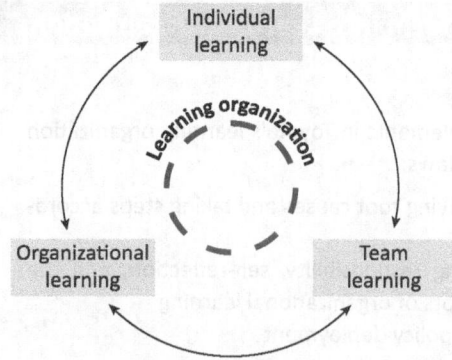

Figure 17.1 Three-dimensional model of a learning organization

on training. The primary focus is on the key constituents of the learning process and the way they are facilitated.

Individual learning

It is essential that all organizations aspiring to become learning organizations must support and sustain the learning of all its employees. Personal development plans serve as excellent platforms for creating environments in which all members of the staff strive for their own growth through learning. These initiatives should also involve an increased responsibility for managing the individuals' learning and act as a key success criterion for aspiring learning organizations. Traditional education and training programmes, when organizations use them, often play an important part in the individual learning dimension. An informal learning environment integrated with responsibilities promotes individual learning. However, the most significant aspect of individual learning lies with formal teaching and training. Thus, to promote individual learning, organizations train their manpower to understand new roles and acquire new skills, with a sustainable long-term approach to stay competitive in the market.

Team learning

Teams are a collection of individuals who are driven by common goals. Thus, teams are separate entities of individuals with collective goals to achieve. Today's organizations highly depend on teamwork. Team learning requires organizations to ensure transfer of learning experiences between the team members and also between various teams. The only difference between team learning and individual learning is the influence of social effects. Pooling knowledge, understanding the limits of the team's knowledge for any given situation, and sharing possible solutions to any given problem are all key components in team learning environments. In team learning, one must also recognize the importance of minority views (wherever applicable) and develop alternative perspectives and options.

Organizational learning

Organizational learning has four components, which are explained as follows:

New systems and structures New systems and structures influence the learning of individuals and teams. Systematic thinking with information technology-enabled communication ensures free and lateral flow of information within the organization to nurture the learning environment. Good internal communication in an organization increases the interface between the people, the systems, and the structures, building their capabilities to understand the changing requirements. With technology backup, organizations can also facilitate sharing of their knowledge repository with all the members, making it possible to document, store, and retrieve information (at times of necessity). Employees can access learning materials on a real-time basis to enhance their understanding.

New processes Learning organizations support the learning of individuals and teams and assess how they have learnt the new tasks and responsibilities. Similar to an open organization with boundary-spanning subsystems, learning organizations emulate the best practices from other comparable organizations, understanding how market and other economic factors have been successfully incorporated by them and what new practices have been adopted to satisfy the needs of the customers and suppliers. In this way, a learning organization understands the requirements of the new processes. Adoption of any new process alters the interface between the organization and the environment. In addition, a successful adoption requires practising the philosophy of learning organizations.

New values   New systems, structures, and processes create new values. Members of learning organizations need to commit themselves to these new values, exploiting the learning opportunities. Adopting new values also requires behavioural modifications and the development of mutual trust among the members and between the members and the organization. Allowing employees to commit mistakes and encouraging them to learn from their mistakes is the most important aspect of a learning organization. Without such relaxations, people will not be able to endorse their new values and will shy away from risk taking and experimentation.

New roles   A changing environment requires shift from control to empowerment, requiring managers to be more proactive, developmental, and facilitating. Managers and team leaders have to develop leadership and coaching skills to exploit the learning opportunities. Appreciating such new roles will, thus, be a precursor to organizational learning.

LEARNING CYCLE

A typical learning cycle for an organization shows the learning process, which involves having an experience, reviewing it, drawing required inputs, adopting it, and finally planning the next step, as shown in Fig. 17.2.

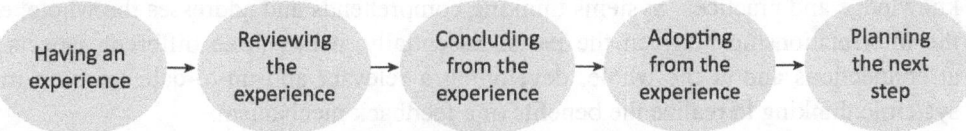

Figure 17.2   Learning cycle

DESIRED BEHAVIOURAL CHANGES

Senge described the following five disciplines as essential for learning organizations to effect behavioural changes:

Team learning   Team learning focuses on the learning ability of the group. Adults learn best from each other, by reflecting on how others are addressing problems, questioning assumptions, and receiving feedback from their teams as well as the outcome of their efforts. With team learning, the learning ability of the group becomes greater than the learning ability of any individual in the group.

Shared vision   To create a shared vision, all members of an organization must be involved and empowered to create a single image of the future. They must understand, share, and contribute to make the organizational vision a reality. With a shared vision, people will do things because they want to and not because they have to.

Mental models   Each individual has an internal mind with deeply ingrained assumptions. Individuals act according to their mental models and not according to the theories they learn. By challenging each other's ideas and assumptions, individuals can study each other's mental models. They can even voluntarily change their own ideas to create a shared mental model for the team. This is very important, or else an individual's mental model may stand in the way of the organization transforming into a learning one.

Personal mastery   Personal mastery is the process of continually self-clarifying and deepening an individual's personal vision. It activates individuals to continuously assess the gap between their current and desired proficiencies in an objective manner and practise and refine the skills to internalize. It develops self-esteem and creates the confidence to tackle new challenges.

Systems thinking   Systems thinking is the conceptual framework of Peter Senge's fifth discipline approach. The approach integrates different theories to develop a coherent body of knowledge and practices. Systems thinking comprehends and addresses the whole, examining the interrelationship between the parts. Essentially, it has three different aspects—looking at connections and at the whole, developing a relevant and up-to-date learning model, and systemic thinking to realize the benefits of a feedback mechanism.

The first aspect looks at the connections within the system and then the system as a whole. Here, people look beyond the immediate context to appreciate the impact of their actions on others and vice versa. This develops a more holistic understanding of organizational requirements. The second aspect requires organizations to be more dynamic and develop an up-to-date learning model, shifting the focus from the parts to the whole. Parts are micromanagement issues at the organization level. Organizations often lose sight of the whole picture while giving more attention to the parts. The third aspect primarily focuses on a long-term view, recognizing the importance of feedback, so that organizations can initiate desired changes in their learning process. Sometimes, organizations concentrate only on achieving the immediate short-term goals. However, without feedback and regular corrective intervention, this may not be sustainable in the long run.

According to Senge, systems thinking is critical to a learning organization, because it represents a new perception of the individual and his/her world.

> The five disciplines that are essential for learning organizations to effect behavioural changes are team learning, shared vision, mental models, personal mastery, and systems thinking.

| Conversation or dialogue is a process of understanding and questioning each other's beliefs and assumptions. | At the heart of a learning organization is a shift of mind—from seeing oneself as separate from the world to seeing oneself as connected to the world; from seeing problems as caused by someone or something *out there* to seeing how one's own actions create the problems one experiences. A learning organization is a place where people are continually discovering how they create their reality and how they can change it. However, systems thinking requires skills and tools, which can be developed only through lifelong commitment. Moreover, it requires that not just one member but many organizational members acquire them. Thus, some |

authors refer to learning organizations as *communities of commitment*.

Skills and Tools for Systems Thinking

The core of systems thinking is the identification of circles of causality or feedback loops. These can be reinforcing or balancing and may contain delays. Nevertheless, they still provide a long-term sustainable direction to the organization, building its capability through learning reinforcement. Senge argues that organizations often fail to appreciate this aspect and get involved only in micromanagement issues. Hence, it is important that organizations should understand what animates them by questioning their practices and culture and using critical analysis. Although it is not possible to transform a bureaucratic organization by learning initiatives alone, they can at least minimize the risk of failure by bringing organizational change and acceptance of people. The learning organization concept primarily focuses on the culture, structures, processes, and work systems to transform an organization. Thus, for promoting the philosophy of a learning organization, micro level focus on training activities alone will not yield any result. Training can develop individual and collective learning but it cannot connect to an organization's strategic intent. Dixon (1994), therefore, suggested a model of organizational learning, establishing a link between individual and collective learning and the organization's strategic objectives.

DIALOGUE AND LEARNING ORGANIZATIONS

For effective team learning, Senge emphasizes the need for dialogue in organizations. Conversation or dialogue is a process of understanding and questioning each other's beliefs and assumptions. Gadamer (1975) stresses the importance of dialogue for objective understanding of each other on any issue or subject. Dialogue is necessary not to win arguments but to promote mutual understanding. It entails virtues and emotions in social relationships and hence, as per Habermas (1984), an attempt to reach at a common conviction. Dialogue is emphasized in a learning organization since in a team learning process, members can suspend their assumptions and can genuinely think together. Dialogue can also promote shared vision and can thus help organizations reach their intended goals and objectives.

WHY LEARNING ORGANIZATIONS WORK

A learning organization tends to work because of the following reasons:

People development A learning organization facilitates learning, which improves the personal skills and qualities of the members of an organization. They gain benefits not only from their own experiences but also from sharing the experiences of others.

Greater motivation   As people tend to voluntarily participate to improve their skills, values, and work, they become more mature in their roles and feel motivated to contribute their best. Opportunities for innovation, creativity, and freethinking help them develop their self and make them feel satisfied in their job roles.

Workforce flexibility   Learning organizations make workers more flexible. Workers can move freely within the organization in between jobs and thereby develop their capability to deal with a rapidly changing environment to survive competition.

Greater creativity   People get more opportunities to become creative in a learning organization. They can try out new ideas without bothering about mistakes. They get recognized for their creative contributions, which provides opportunities for new ideas to flourish.

Improved social interaction   Learning improves social interaction and develops interpersonal communication skills. This encourages teamwork, which, in turn, makes organizations work better.

High-performing teams and groups   A learning organization develops high-performing teams. They learn, grow, and perform efficiently for the organization to deliver better results.

Knowledge sharing   Sharing of common knowledge is important for completing a job. In a learning environment, information and knowledge freely flow around. Intra- and inter-team sharing of knowledge also helps develop mutual trust and makes an organization a high-performing one.

Interdependency   A culture of interdependency increases awareness of an organization's members and improves relations between them at a personal level. By understanding each other and appreciating their roles, needs, and tasks, members can learn to manage their time better and plan their work more efficiently. With the increased rate of learning, members can manage on their own and plan their jobs better without relying on others.

Apart from these, a learning organization facilitates the breaking down of traditional communication barriers, improves customer relations, develops knowledge resources, fosters innovation and creativity, and hedges against risk in decision-making.

LEARNING ORIENTATIONS

Learning orientation is defined as a process of individual learning, which makes one different from the others. With the help of a multidimensional learning orientation construct (LOC), it is possible to understand the factors that contribute to differences in individual learning. Thus, LOC provides a learning success model by making available the factors that significantly impact individual learning. There are three important domains of LOC—conative and affective learning, learning independence, and learning effort.

> Learning orientation is defined as a process of individual learning, which makes one different from the others.

Conation   The conative (i.e., the desire to learn) domain examines the learner's will, commitment, intent, drive, or passion for improving, transforming, setting, and achieving goals, taking risks, and meeting challenges. Learning becomes intentional and people enjoy the learning process.

Learning independence The learning independence domain focuses on assessing an individual learner's desire and ability to take responsibility, make choices, control, manage, improve, and feel self-motivated in achieving both the learning and his/her personal goals.

Learning effort The learning effort (also referred to as committed strategic planning) domain examines the learners' degree of persistence and commitment to accomplish results (including the learning results).

Based on the LOC, learners can be characterized as transforming, performing, conforming, and resistant.

Transforming Transforming learners are passionate and committed learners. They are aggressive in achieving their learning needs. They take serious efforts to learn and achieve their transformation goals. They are, by nature, very creative and innovative and hence discard protocol-bound learning or instructional initiatives.

Performing Performing learners are self-motivated and they learn for their perceived extrinsic rewards. They are systematic and partially protocol-bound, and recognize the need for implementation of systems and structures.

Conforming Conforming learners believe in routine, structured, and supportive relationships and stability. They play the role of compliant learners to programmed instructions and thus remain a passive recipient of learning. They prefer to be less sophisticated and hence show less desire to control, manage, take risks, and initiate change in jobs; they remain focused on supportive relationships.

Resistant Resistant learners do not believe in academic learning and achievement. People of this type are mostly unskilled labourers and they dislike any type of formal learning. Organizations face problems in training and reskilling these people, even though skill renewal through systematic training or learning initiatives is very important for them.

LEARNING CURVE

It is a common belief that people and organizations become more efficient over time. Such difference in efficiency rate over time has a major impact on business decisions. To illustrate, an organization may estimate the production rate of a given product and determine from it the time and money resources required for future production. Such effect of increased efficiency with production volume is known as the *learning curve* effect. A learning curve displays the relationship between production time per unit and the number of units produced.

> Learning curve refers to the idea that if the production time per unit is plotted over time, the amount will curve down.

There are three major assumptions in the learning curve effect:

- The time required to complete a given task will decrease with increase in the number of times the task is performed.
- The unit time will decrease at a decreasing rate.
- The decrease will follow a predictable pattern.

Calculation

The most common form of learning curve calculation is an exponential decay function (i.e., production rates decay—or decrease—following an exponential curve). The standard equation is as follows:

$$T_n = T_1 n^b$$

where

n = unit number (1 for the first unit, 2 for the second unit, etc.)
T_1 = Time required to produce the first unit
T_n = Time required to produce the nth unit
b = Learning curve factor, calculated as $\ln(p)/\ln(2)$, where $\ln(x)$ is the natural logarithm of x
p = Learning percentage

The learning percentage, p, is interpreted as follows:

Every time the cumulative production quantity doubles, the unit production rate will decrease by percentage p. This is shown in the following calculation:

Imagine that $T_1 = 10$ hours and $p = 90\% = 0.90$. The production time for the first 10 units can be calculated as follows:

$b = \ln(0.90)/\ln(2) = -0.152$
$T_1 = 10(1^{-0.152}) = 10$
$T_2 = 10(2^{-0.152}) = 9$
$T_3 = 10(3^{-0.152}) = 8.46$ (rounded to two decimal places)
$T_4 = 10(4^{-0.152}) = 8.10$
$T_5 = 10(5^{-0.152}) = 7.83$
$T_6 = 10(6^{-0.152}) = 7.62$
$T_7 = 10(7^{-0.152}) = 7.44$
$T_8 = 10(8^{-0.152}) = 7.29$
$T_9 = 10(9^{-0.152}) = 7.16$
$T_{10} = 10(10^{-0.152}) = 7.05$

This shows that even though the first unit will take 10 hours, the tenth unit will take only 7.05 hours. While the improvement from the first unit to the second was $10 - 9 = 1$ hour, the ninth unit to the tenth showed only $7.16 - 7.05 = 0.11$ hours of improvement. Thus, a decreasing improvement rate is observed. Moreover, when production doubles, the unit production time is reduced by $p = 90\%$.

T_2 is 90 per cent of T_1, T_4 is 90 per cent of T_2 (i.e., $8.10 = 9 \times 0.90$), T_8 is 90 per cent of T_4 (i.e., $7.29 = 8.10 \times 0.90$), and so on.

Thus, it can also be observed that the 2,00,000th unit will take 90 per cent of the time it takes to produce the 1,00,000th unit. Let us consider an example to calculate the learning curve factor. A former construction company executive has just started a new company called Cookie-Cutter Homes. The company makes homes of only one type to maximize the learning

Practitioner Speak 17.3

Does the Experience Curve Matter Today?

In the 1920s a group of analysts at a U.S. Air Force base outside Dayton, Ohio, were following an intriguing trend. Wright-Patterson AFB, where they worked, was the manufacturing center for a number of iconic World War I era airplanes—including the ninety horsepower Curtiss 'Jenny' that a generation of barnstorming daredevils made famous after the war.

Read this insightful blog posted by Hagel, Brown, and Davison on *HBR Blog Network* by accessing the following link: http://blogs.hbr.org/bigshift/2009/04/does-the-experience-curve-matt.html.

curve effect. The entrepreneur assumes that his company will realize a 75 per cent learning percentage. The first home took 200 days to complete. How long will it take to produce the fifth home? What is the time taken to produce the 10th, 100th, and 104th homes?

First, calculate the learning curve factor.

$$b = \ln(p)/\ln(2) = \ln(0.75)/\ln(2) = -0.415.$$

$$T_1 = 200$$
$$T_5 = 200(5^{-0.415}) = 102.56 \text{ or about } 103 \text{ days}$$
$$T_{10} = 200(10^{-0.415}) = 76.92 \text{ or about } 77 \text{ days}$$
$$T_{100} = 200(100^{-0.415}) = 29.58 \text{ or about } 30 \text{ days}$$
$$T_{104} = 200(104^{-0.415}) = 29.10 \text{ or about } 29 \text{ days}$$

Thus, it can be seen that Cookie-Cutter Homes will realize dramatic learning curve benefits for the early homes but reduced incremental benefits later on.

Exhibit 17.2 talks about the commitment of Indian MNCs towards imparting quality education in rural areas.

EXHIBIT 17.2 India's Learning Curve: Indian MNCs' Commitment towards Imparting Quality Education in Rural Areas

The learning curve when related to school-going children in rural India falls flat too early. Though, in recent years, the Indian government has wooed back millions of students to school through free education and midday meals, there is much to be done to delay the flattening of the learning curve.

Azim Premji Foundation (APF) and Bharti Foundation have vowed to change the existing scenario of Indian rural education. Though various schemes launched by the Government of India have seen large footfall of students, the focus has largely been on quantity and not quality. In contrast, these two foundations are poised to bring quality in education.

APF has envisioned changing the education system by working parallelly with the state education departments across the country. They focus on the following aspects:

Training teachers so that classrooms become livelier than before This will lead to more students

(Contd)

EXHIBIT 17.2 (*Contd*)

flocking to the classrooms and completing their education.

Inculcating leadership skills among education officers This will help in better utilization of the resources provided by the government for rural education.

Inculcating critical thinking among students This will help in developing their independent thought processes.

The programme of APF opines that students in rural areas usually learn by rote. However, what should be developed in them is the critical thinking ability, and APF will ensure that its endeavours are directed towards harbouring critical thinking skills in rural pupils.

In contrast, Bharti Foundation has started its own chain of schools, namely Satya Bharti Schools. These schools envision setting examples for the rural areas as to how education should be imparted. They focus on taking land from local authorities and building schools where education is imparted free.

With such attempts as these, and other leading MNCs joining in, the learning curve of rural education in India is all set to steepen before falling flat. We can obviously expect better quality of education in rural areas in the coming days.

Sources: Goyal, M. and M. Jayashankar, 'Learning Curve: Two Ways to Educate India', 1 July 2010, http://forbesindia.com/article/big-bet/learning-curve-two-ways-to-educate-india/14642/1, last accessed on 16 September 2013; Woodman, A. and M. Jamwal, 'India's Education Sector: Learning Curve', *Asian Venture Capital Journal*, 2 May 2013, http://www.avcj.com/avcj/analysis/2265569/indias-education-sector-learning-curve, last accessed on 16 September 2013 (adapted).

SUMMARY

The learning organization concept arises out of ideas long held by leaders in OD and systems dynamics. One of the specific contributions of OD is its focus on the humanistic side of organizations. To make the learning a reality, it is important to ensure that strategies and actions of the organizations support the process of development of the learning organizations. The model of the learning organization, with its three-dimensional approach, proposes strategies within the domains of individual, team, and organizational learning. This model enhances the improved performances necessary for competitiveness and offers individuals the capacity to adapt more rapidly to change. A true learning organization even allows individuals to grow independently in a changing work environment. With the concept of learning organizations in the new millennium, organizational behaviour studies are now becoming more challenging. The notion of the learning organization provides managers and others with a picture of how things could be within an organization. Along the way, writers like Peter Senge introduced a number of interesting dimensions that could aid personal development and increase organizational effectiveness—especially where the enterprise is firmly rooted in the *knowledge economy*. Learning organizations support collaboration, commitment, ready access to knowledge and talent, and coherent organizational behaviour. They are considered as the appropriate organizational investments to provide people with adequate space and time to connect, demonstrate trust, communicate their aims and beliefs, and offer equitable opportunities and rewards through genuine participation in building their capabilities. The corporate world largely embraces the idea of a learning organization to meet the demands of the global economy.

KEY DEFINITIONS

Affective The factor that describes the influences resulting from emotions such as passion, frustration, satisfaction, distress, joy, fulfilment, gratitude, comfort, arrogance, or disinterest

Conative The factor that describes one's basic strivings, intentions, motives, and will as expressed in behaviour and actions

Learning orientation model The model that identifies the distinct characteristics or aggregate learning patterns for four learning orientations, namely transforming, performing, conforming, and resistant.

CONCEPT-REVIEW QUESTIONS

17.1 Briefly discuss the steps necessary for creating a learning organization.

17.2 Explain briefly why learning organizations work.

17.3 For reinforcing behavioural changes, what are the strategies of learning organizations that can be adopted by an organization? Explain how such selected strategies help in behavioural changes.

17.4 Explain the learning orientation model. How can this model help an organization nurture the learning organization concept?

17.5 Write short notes on the following:
   (a) Learning cycle
   (b) Systems thinking
   (c) Learning curve
   (d) Learning orientation model

CRITICAL THINKING QUESTION

17.1 Read the following text and answer the question given at the end. It is about learning from doing, performing, and taking action. A classification of objectives that focus on the development of attitudes, beliefs, and values shows the following stages of learning in any typical organization:

Receiving: Aware of passively attending to certain stimuli
Responding: Complies with given expectations by reacting to stimuli
Valuing: Displays behaviour consistent with a belief or attitude
Organizing: Committed to a set of values as displayed by the behaviour

Characterizing: Total behaviour consistent with internalized values

Learning encompasses any activity (either overt or covert) that is observable and measurable. It is the primary component of an objective and an individual's preference for using one's cognitive abilities. There are two styles of thinking—right brain (intuitive, spontaneous, and qualitative) and left brain (factual, analytical, and quantitative).

From the foregoing discussion, identify any organization that you feel is a learning organization, detail the organization's strategies and actions, and critically evaluate them.

SELECT BIBLIOGRAPHY

- Argyris, C. and D. Schön, *Organizational Learning: A Theory of Action Perspective*, Addison Wesley, Reading, 1978.
- Argyris, C. and D. Schön, *Organizational Learning II: Theory, Method and Practice*, Addison Wesley, Reading, 1996.

- Dixon, N., *The Organizational Learning Cycles: How We Learn Collectively*, McGraw-Hill, New York, 1994.
- Easterby-Smith, M. and L. Araujo, 'Current Debates and Opportunities,' in M. Easterby-Smith, L. Araujo, and J. Burgoyne (eds), *Organizational Learning and the Learning Organization*, Sage, London, 1999.

- Gadamer, H., *Truth and Method*, 2nd ed., Continuum, New York, 1975.
- Garvin, D.A., *Learning in Action. A Guide to Putting the Learning Organization to Work*, Harvard Business School Press, Boston, 2000.
- Habermas, J., *The Theory of Communicative Action, Vol. 1, Reason and the Rationalization of Society*, Beacon Press, Boston, 1984.
- Kerka, S., *Constructivism, Workplace Learning, and Vocational Education*, ERIC Digest No. 181, ERIC Clearinghouse on Adult, Career, and Vocational Education, Columbus, 1997.
- Marquardt, M.J., *Building the Learning Organization*, McGraw-Hill, New York, 1996.
- Marquardt, M. and A. Reynolds, *The Global Learning Organization*, Irwin Professional Publishing, New York, 1994.
- Pedler, M., J. Burgoyne, and T. Boydell, *The Learning Company: A Strategy for Sustainable Development*, McGraw-Hill, London, 1991.
- Senge, P., *The Fifth Discipline: The Art and Practice of the Learning Organizations*, Doubleday, London, 1990.
- Senge, P., A. Kleiner, C. Roberts, R. Ross, G. Roth, and B. Smith, *The Dance of Change: The Challenges of Sustaining Momentum in Learning Organizations*, Doubleday/Currency, New York, 1999.
- Senge, P., N. Cambron-McCabe, T. Lucas, B. Smith, J. Dutton, and A. Kleiner, *Schools That Learn: A Fifth Discipline Fieldbook for Educators, Parents, and Everyone Who Cares about Education*, Doubleday/Currency, New York, 2000.
- Tsang, E., 'Organizational Learning and the Learning Organization: A Dichotomy between Descriptive and Prescriptive Research', *Human Relations*, Vol. 50, Issue 1, 1997, pp. 57–70.
- Watkins, K.E. and V.J. Marsick, 'Towards a Theory of Informal and Incidental Learning in Organizations,' *International Journal of Lifelong Education*, Vol. 11, Issue 4, 1992, pp. 287–300.
- Watkins, K.E. and V.J. Marsick (eds), *Sculpting the Learning Organization: Lessons in the Art and Science of Systematic Change*, Jossey-Bass, San Francisco, 1993.

CASE STUDY

T-Mobile—Intensifying the Learning Gain

T-Mobile US is part of T-Mobile International, one of the top three global wireless carriers and a proud subsidiary of Deutsche Telekom AG. This is what T-Mobile believes: 'In a world full of busy and fragmented lives ... wireless communication can help.'

Headquartered at Bellevue, Washington, T-Mobile reaches 268 million Americans, with the support of a 29,000-strong workforce. In 2006, T-Mobile introduced smartphones with solutions and received the highest ranking in wireless customer care by J.D. Power and Associates. It continued to receive such high ranking in wireless customer care for several consecutive years. With the backup of learning organizations, principles, and practices, T-Mobile is truly emerging as a world-class wireless communication organization for others to emulate.

T-Mobile's customer service division is a compelling place to work in. People enjoy their work and get continuous opportunities to learn and develop. The focus on customer services at T-Mobile is not limited to sharing information but also extends to adding value for customers through knowledge acquisition. The company's philosophy is to support the learning of its employees not only by training and development programmes but also by creating a mutually supportive and happy work environment.

T-Mobile's customer contact centres are standardized and have cybercafé and free Internet service for all staff members, learning development centres, relaxation and recreation rooms with tabletop football, video game consoles, vending machines, air conditioning, vibrant colour schemes, space-age design, ample room for each employee, and a subsidized cafe/restaurant. T-Mobile encourages its staff members to make use of both the learning development centres and the cybercafes for their personal development and recreation.

With such backup, training, and development support, T-Mobile could excel in its customer services. It believes that learning can take place in formal and informal technology-based, self-managed methods.

The learning process at T-Mobile starts with seminars and workshops for team managers to refresh their managerial skills and concepts. Then they extend it to the next stage, partnering with the *mind gym*, to offer high-impact, 90-minute sessions in over 60 topic areas. Each face-to-face session involves up to 20 people learning and practising new techniques and ways of thinking. After the session, the delegates receive weekly e-prompts that remind, refresh, and entertain. Individuals also receive open learning workbooks to back up the programmes and to promote self-development and accountability.

The workouts received excellent feedback. A wide variety is now offered to each contact centre so that their management team can plan for the key development requirements of its managers. Interestingly, middle to senior managers who have experienced the courses have welcomed the approach and managers outside the customer services directorate (e.g., technology managers) have submitted requests for being allowed to join the future sessions.

Further development has concentrated on the design of seminars and workouts for customer service advisors, both to refresh and to implement toolkits for new items as required. The toolkit concept has been developed further so that rather than the training advisors leading all sessions (which are no longer than two hours), team managers can use the material and integrate them into their team briefings or in development sessions. This has helped to develop the team managers' skills and devolve responsibility, freeing the training team to facilitate and design future programmes.

Issues and Developments

The following are the issues and developments:

Design concepts

Delivering shorter sessions means that the trainer (or team manager) has to engage and involve the participants more quickly, in order to ensure that they cover the objectives of the session and the delegates reach the desired outcomes. This means a review of design techniques and an increasing focus on accelerated learning techniques and neuro-linguistic programming (NLP) methodology.

E-learning

A key project is now underway for developing modules for the customer service advisors that will make induction training more effective. This form of training can be delivered in short modules of 10, 20, and 30 minutes. E-learning also supports information communication technology (ICT) skills development.

Skills development

T-Mobile has also been a key partner in the Tyne and Wear DfES Skills for Life Pathfinder, led by the Tyne and Wear Learning and Skills Council. A week-long in-company event to promote skills development and learning among staff consisted of events such as a T-Mobile directors *Desert Island Booklist* hosted on the intranet, a book swapping scheme, and a national T-Mobile intranet literacy competition for the entire staff.

Ongoing evaluation

The new approach will continue to be evaluated to ensure that it successfully meets the company's needs, develops new skills, and enhances performance, while motivating the staff to learn.

Questions for Discussion

1. Discuss critically the T-Mobile case and explain the learning culture prevalent in the organization.
2. Can you outline the learning model in T-Mobile? Highlight the various learning organization qualities in any Indian corporate office.

Organizational Culture

LEARNING OBJECTIVES

After studying this chapter, the reader will be able to

- understand organizational culture and how it influences the function of an organization
- explain cultural change
- discuss different diagnostic mechanisms for identifying the cultural constructs of an organization
- understand the appropriate interventions strategy to cultural change
- appreciate how cultural change influences behavioural issues in an organization
- understand the use of organizational development tools for effecting cultural changes in organizations

CASE STUDY

Managing Insidious Culture—The AMD Way

Global research indicates that most of the acquisitions lower the shareholder value. Cultural mismatch is identified as the single most important factor responsible for this. Internationally, organizations experience difficulties in making different nationals work together. However, in some cases (e.g., in the HP–Compaq merger), it has been seen that organizations can take advantage of the best of the various cultures involved.

A good example from an international perspective is Advanced Micro Devices (AMD). AMD is located in Dresden, Germany, and is a composite of three cultures—American, West German, and East German. The Americans are ambitious; they believe in shooting first and aiming later. The West Germans are analytical, thorough, and correct, whereas the East Germans have mastered the art of innovation with limited resources. The Dresden start-up team designed a meeting format that opened with American-style brainstorming sessions. During these meetings, the Americans learnt the art of deliberation and the Germans off-the-cuff dynamism. As a result, this multicultural style provided AMD with the much-needed competitive edge. AMD's case has led to the development of the dilemma theory (Trompenaars and Hampden-Turner 1998), now a much-discussed theory worldwide and commonly known as the THT theory. According to this theory, insidious culture clashes and most management problems are a result of the human habit of viewing life in terms of all-or-nothing choices. It is always winning versus losing strategies, right versus wrong answers, and good versus bad values. Business issues must not be approached as a contest between good and evil, or the potential benefits might be lost. It is better to interpret clashes as a reconcilable dilemma.

AMD reaped the advantages of the multicultural style. It could gain competitive edge by breaking production records in less than three years and could come out with redesigned third-generation chips with product innovation. Thus, the AMD dilemma suggests that success depends on the willingness of employees to overcome their defences and talk about ethnic and national personalities and the way they can learn from each other.

The THT theory of cultural dilemmas has its roots in the Japanese culture—*shukanteki* and *kyakkanteki*. *Shukanteki* means subjectivity or the host's point of view, whereas *kyakkanteki* is the ability to perceive oneself as a stranger or the guest's point of view. Thus, the essence of THT is this: 'Learn to adopt the guest's point of view about the host's point of view.' Only through such awareness of reasons for the differences between guest and host can the cultural barriers between the two be overcome.

INTRODUCTION

In this era of globalization and multinational and transnational corporations, a question that the new generation of knowledge workers often ask organizations is this: What is your culture? Culture is the moral, social, and behavioural norms of an organization. It creates impacts on the beliefs, attitudes, and priorities of organizational members. Building culture through continuous learning is now a global practice. This is primarily more important for globalization and cross-border mergers and acquisitions. The movement of people from one country to another has renewed the attention on building organization-specific corporate cultures to bring order in behaviour and attitudes. To build a corporate culture of their own, many global organizations have now started their own universities. These universities not only focus on competency building through renewal of knowledge and skill, but also ensure that their culture is deeply etched in the minds of their people. However, in India, only a few organizations focus on building a corporate culture of their own.

Indian organizations limit their efforts to general induction programmes at the time of recruitment. A few have also extended their period of induction by three to six months to orient their employees. However, they restrict it to job-specific or function-specific domain knowledge. Every organization has its own unique culture or value set. For some it may be consciously created through induction, whereas for others it may be unconsciously created, primarily based on the value systems of the people at the top level or the promoter.

> Culture is the moral, social, and behavioural norms of an organization.

'When in Rome, do as the Romans do'—this adage has been reinforced by Geert Hofstede (1980). Hofstede, after surveying more than 1,00,000 employees of IBM with operations in 50 countries, proposed five continuums of culture, which organizations around the world translate as their own culture. The five continuums are individualism versus collectivism, uncertainty avoidance (low and high), power distance (low and high), masculine versus feminine, and long-term versus short-term orientation. Whether the focus should be on individualism, collectivism, or power-distance approach depends on the organizational value system. Globally, collectivism is the more-desired practice because it promotes team culture by developing common and consistent goals, organizational commitment, mutual accountability, team leadership, and, above all, shared rewards. Power distance focuses on distribution of power and adherence to formal channels. The uncertainty avoidance culture, on the other hand, emphasizes to the employees the relative importance of rules, long-term employment, and steady progression through well-defined career ladders. Dominant values focus on the quality of relationships, job satisfaction, and flexibility, whereas short-term versus long-term culture gets reflected in the organizational employment relations.

DEFINITIONS AND CONCEPTS

An organization does not operate in isolation. In fact, every organization continuously interacts with its environment. This, therefore, requires an organization to strike a balance between the internal features and the characteristics of the external environment, which is part of the contingency theory in organizational science. The theory suggests that an organization has to understand the dynamics of its environment to be able to adapt to the changing internal or external demands of the organization. There are different ways of scanning the organizational environment. Once the scanning is done, it is imperative to implement organizational development (OD) to match the requirements and stay updated in a competitive environment. However, to understand OD, it is important to understand various other issues.

The concept of organizational culture became popular in the early 1980s. There is no consensus on its definition, but most authors agree that it is something holistic, historically determined, related to the object or article, socially constructed, soft, and difficult to change. It is something an organization has, but it can also be seen as something an organization is.

> The contingency theory in organizational science states that an organization has to understand the dynamics of its environment in order to be able to adapt to the changing internal and external demands of the organization.

Organizational cultures should be distinguished from national cultures. Cultures manifest themselves, from superficial to deep, in symbols, heroes, rituals, and values. National cultures mostly differ on the value levels, but organizational cultures mostly differ at the levels of symbols, heroes, and rituals. These together translate into organizational practices.

Research into organizational cultures identified six independent dimensions of practices—process-orientated versus results-orientated; job-orientated versus employee-orientated; professional versus parochial; open systems versus closed systems; tightly controlled versus loosely controlled; and pragmatic versus normative. The position of an organization on these dimensions is determined in part by the respective business or industry that the organization belongs to. Scores on the dimensions are also related to a number of other *hard* characteristics of the organizations. These lead to conclusions about how organizational cultures can be or cannot be managed.

Managing international business means handling both national and organizational culture differences at the same time. Organizational cultures are manageable to some extent whereas national cultures are given facts for the management; common organizational cultures across borders are what keep multinationals together.

Thus, the concept of organizational culture developed from the early studies of organizational climate, intertwined with human resources and various sociological disciplines. The true definition is more a matter of perspective. Some authors believe that the organization itself is a culture (Bate 1994). This considers organizational culture more as a metaphor for study through which meanings are constructed and expressed.

More modern views, however, consider organizational culture as a variable rather than a metaphor (Wilson 2001). The variables are different organizational practices such as performance management (Deal and Kennedy 1982), mechanism for effectiveness and control (Peters and Waterman 1982), recruitment and selection (Guest 1997), training and development (Schein 1968, 1990; O'Reilly 1989), knowledge management practices (Brown 1995), reward systems (Kerr and Slocum 1987), and overall human resource management practices.

ORGANIZATIONAL CULTURE AND ORGANIZATIONAL BEHAVIOURAL PRACTICES

The word culture has many dimensions; hence, defining it requires us to consider the term from different perspectives. Anthropologist James P. Spradley (1972), however, provided the best definition: 'Culture is the acquired knowledge people use to interpret experience and generate behaviour.' Culture is the abstract miniscule that moves the organization. It is an ongoing process of reality construction, providing a pattern of understanding that helps members of the organizations to interpret events and provide meaning to their working worlds. It is a shared understanding of the people (Schein 1990; Schneider 1988; Kotter and Heskett 1992), and it frames the interactions and processes that make up everyday society and, therefore, the organizational environment. If context frames the situation, then culture frames the context. Understanding and predicting behaviour and human processes within a given environmental context can be best done based on the cultural constructs of an organization. For managing organizational behaviour, one can use psychological concepts and theories to influence employees and improve the dynamics of the organization. However, for understanding how these are affected by culture, managers need to study the employees' behaviour in the cultural context. From organizational contexts, culture can be defined in terms of the following:

> Culture is the acquired knowledge people use to interpret experience and generate behaviour.

- Overt organizational behaviour
- Organizational ideology and philosophy

> Organizational culture refers to the shared meanings, beliefs, and understandings held by a particular group or organization about its problems, practices, and goals.

- Group and organizational norms
- Espoused organizational values
- Policies, procedures, and rules of socialization
- Climate

Similar to the term *culture*, there is no single universally accepted definition of the term *organizational culture*. However, organizational culture is generally accepted as referring to the shared meanings, beliefs, and understandings held by a particular group or organization about its problems, practices, and goals. The concept of organizational culture is often misunderstood and confused with the related concepts of climate, ideology, and style. Organizational culture evolves from the social practices of members of organizations and is, therefore, the socially created realities that exist in the heads and minds of organizational members as well as in the formal rules, policies, and procedures of organizational structures.

Though the terms *organizational culture* and *corporate culture* are interchangeably used, corporate culture refers to a company's values, beliefs, business principles, traditions, ways of operating, and internal work environment. It is developed from a complex combination of sociological forces operating within organizational boundaries. An organization's culture is either an important contributor or an obstacle to successful strategy execution. A strong organizational culture promotes good strategy execution. However, this would be possible only when there is a cultural fit. Good organizations endeavour to match culture with their strategy. Organizations with strong cultural bonds cannot eliminate the deep-seated values and behavioural norms of people.

A strong culture is a valuable asset when it matches strategy but a liability when it does not. When organizations go in for mergers and acquisitions, redefining the cultural aspects becomes necessary. Many mergers and acquisitions fail due to mismatch of cultures between the parent unit and the acquired unit. Organizations try to achieve a match through sustained reinforcement. In some cases of mergers and acquisitions, it is also evident that organizations try to develop adaptive culture models to adjust with the changing environment. The HP–Compaq merger is one such example. Once a culture is established, it is difficult to change it. Organizations use awards ceremonies, role models, and symbols for shaping and reshaping the culture. An ethical corporate culture has a positive impact on a company's long-term strategic success, whereas an unethical culture can undermine it. Values and ethical standards must not only be explicitly stated but also be embedded into the corporate culture. A result-oriented culture that

---

Practitioner Speak 18.2   **Six Components of Great Corporate Culture**

The benefits of a strong corporate culture are both intuitive and supported by social science. According to James L. Heskett, culture 'can account for 20–30% of the differential in corporate performance when compared with "culturally unremarkable" competitors'. And HBR writers have offered advice on navigating different geographic cultures, selecting jobs based on culture, changing cultures, and offering feedback across cultures, among other topics.

Read this insightful blog posted by Coleman on *HBR Blog Network* by accessing the following link: http://blogs.hbr.org/cs/2013/05/six_components_of_culture.html.

inspires people to do their best is conducive to superior strategy execution. Organizational culture, therefore, emerges from values and beliefs, ethical standards, philosophy, key policies, and traditions. Thus, organizational culture is what the organization espouses, which transcends into the ways things are being done.

MANAGING CORPORATE CULTURE CHANGES

The need for culture change in an organization is not always necessitated because of mergers and acquisitions. It may also be for developing organizational capabilities to respond to changing environments. Both Toyota and Honda Motors of Japan had to undergo a change in their corporate culture to suit the US conditions. However, another major Japanese automobile company, Mazda, had to withdraw from the US because of its failure to adapt to the US culture, despite the fact that it entered the US market much before Toyota and Honda. India also experienced a cultural mismatch between the Honda and Hero groups, whereas Suzuki and Maruti is a successful case of adaptive corporate culture. Many Indian organizations had to redefine their culture to keep pace with globalization.

Cultural changes in organizations have to be personally led by the top management and cannot be delegated to people down the line. This is primarily due to the top management's power to exert influence to bring about necessary changes. Culture change requires dynamic leadership, the understanding of people's behaviour, and the changing environmental cue. For restructuring, organizations may often go for changes in the skills and attitudes of their people. These changes succeed cultural changes. They encounter resistance and non-cooperation from the people but can be achieved with sustained intervention from the top management. Cultural changes also succeed changes in internal practices. Making people innovative, empowered to take decisions, and capable of troubleshooting the problems is not so easy. Top managements need to lead the show with their teams, identifying change agents to further the process of cultural transformation.

Organizational culture change is a constant organization-building challenge to broaden, deepen, or modify organization capabilities and resource strengths in response to ongoing customer and market changes. Focus on customer relationship management (CRM) and

> Organizational culture change is a constant organization-building challenge to broaden, deepen, or modify organization capabilities and resource strengths in response to ongoing customer and market changes.

development of people capabilities requires organizations to undergo perceptive cultural changes. Managers play the role of a teacher in cultural transformation; they send signals through practices, which people down the line emulate.

Building a strategy-fit corporate culture is important for successful strategy execution, which facilitates a performing work environment and develops esprit de corps, as propounded by Henry Fayol (1949).

Since culture sets the work climate, any change in corporate culture always encounters resistance. Organizations in a changing business environment are always required to take an adaptive culture, which, among others, necessitates being receptive to new ideas, experimentation, innovation, new strategies, and new operating practices. Changing prevailing organizational cultures, therefore, requires competent leadership at the top. Apart from symbolic actions from the top leadership, substantive actions that demonstrate the degree of commitment

> Bringing about a cultural change in organizations requires strong corporate ethics and values. Another important enabler for cultural change is the top leadership.

from them are also essential. With symbolic and substantive actions from the top management, the behaviour of the people down the line will be changed automatically.

Bringing about a cultural change in organizations also requires strong corporate ethics and values. Ethical norms develop business principles and moral values of people, which enhance their capabilities to take socially responsive decisions. Ethical standards denote integrity, doing the right thing, and showing genuine concern for stakeholders. To ensure practice of ethical standards, organizations conduct training programmes on ethics and values, form ethics committees, develop code of ethics, and periodically conduct ethics audits. Above all, however, it is important for the top management to comply with those ethical norms that they expect their people to comply with.

As already mentioned, an important enabler for cultural change is the top leadership. Leaders need to understand organizational pulses through active listening and talking to people, coaching and mentoring, ensuring transparency in information sharing, and encouraging people to be creative and innovative in their work. Since influence needs to be exerted to elicit voluntary participation from organizational members, it is imperative that leaders (top management) be more proactive in their practices so that people down the line can emulate them. Adopting a participative approach in planning and decision-making, developing the problem-solving capability, and assisting people to mature are also important perquisites for successful leadership to bring about cultural changes in organizations.

Thus, implementing cultural change in organizations requires a series of actions, without, however, any universally accepted sacrosanct practices. What actually leads to this change, therefore, depends on specific organizational constructs. In India as also in other countries, there are many cases of successful cultural transformation. When Videocon, a traditional Indian organization, acquired a legacy-bound multinational like Philips, it undertook difficult successive stages of cultural transformation. However, with the sustained efforts of the top management, mostly in line with the aforementioned courses of action, it could successfully achieve the results. In their initial phases of cultural transformation, the top management of Videocon spent about 80 per cent of their time listening to the people, playing a supportive role, in order to infuse confidence in the apprehensive minds of the people. Organizational cultural change, therefore, is more situation-specific.

Exhibit 18.1 discusses the changing organizational culture at Hewlett-Packard (HP).

Practitioner Speak 18.3

You Can't Dictate Culture—but You Can Influence It

There's an old joke about a CEO who attended a presentation on corporate culture and then asked his head of HR to 'get me one of those things'. Of course it sounds ludicrous—but like most jokes, this story is based in truth. Many organizations treat the creation, maintenance, and periodic updating of their cultures in a cavalier manner. Either they pay lip service to the kind of culture they want, but don't do much about it—or worse, ignore culture completely.

Read this insightful blog posted by Coleman on *HBR Blog Network* by accessing the following link: http://blogs.hbr.org/ashkenas/2011/06/you-cant-dictate-culture-but-y.html.

EXHIBIT 18.1 **Changing Organizational Culture at Hewlett-Packard**

Changing the organizational culture can be an uphill task, and many times, it does not yield the desired outcome. In most cases, changing the organizational culture would mean injecting an alien culture from outside the organization and the management trying to defend it using all its might. However, this is least likely to work, and in most cases it does not. Kotter (1996) has noted that for changing organizational culture the management must believe in what they profess and practise. For HP, the world-famous computing giant, successfully changing its organizational culture meant even more than that. It not only developed a new culture in-house—the managers let the employees devise it themselves.

Cheng and Anderson, two seasoned managers at HP, were wondering how to keep pace with the fast-changing business environment and offer prompt services. HP's systems seemed laggardly and processes needed to be changed. This also necessitated a change in managerial style and organizational culture. After having discussed various probable solutions to the problem, they hit on the idea of not having any structure at all. This would give employees space to go about things the way they wanted and realize their individual goals. However, giving liberty to employees implied running the risk of ending up in a mess.

With no manager and a system sans hierarchy, each employee would have to manage oneself and come up with ideas to do one's part in a project.

When they tried this plan for a specific client, the two managers were successful in reducing their delivery time from 26 days to 8 days. Though initially things did not seem to go anywhere and some employees wanted to be instructed, the plan slowly picked up pace and each member contributed wholeheartedly towards reaching the goal.

The basic premise behind this model is that when people are free to define their jobs and roles at work, their commitment to work accentuates, and the task becomes personally meaningful. Anderson and Cheng introduced two basic ideas to the team—the value of considering multiple viewpoints and the importance of learning skills and viewing the situation in its entirety and not just the part one is responsible for.

The resulting culture that set forth has indeed shown results. More than the tangible outcome of reducing delivery time by almost 70 per cent, the motivation with which employees worked, the way they sorted out problems related to the project, and the sense of personal ownership they showed on their jobs were exemplary. It is indeed true that great organizational culture is rooted in great concepts and HP's culture is just an example of this.

Sources: Sherman, S., 'Secret of HP's "Muddled" Team Two Managers at a Great High-tech Company Developed a New Way to Lead', *Fortune*, 18 March 1996, 116–120; Kotter, J., 'Leading Change', Harvard Business School Press, Harvard, 1996 (adapted).

ORGANIZATIONAL CULTURE AND ORGANIZATIONAL CLIMATE

In its evolution within the academic and managerial literature, organizational culture has increasingly become a mechanism for effectiveness and control (Peters and Waterman 1982). Hence, organizational culture sets the organizational climate.

Whether it is a metaphor or a variable, organizational culture translates into organizational climate, which decides the organizational practices. Organizational practices on people-related issues are classified under human resource (HR) management, which governs issues concerning organizational behaviour. Hence, culture issues encompass recruitment, selection, training, appraisal, reward systems, and so on.

> Organizational culture translates into organizational climate, which decides the organizational practices.

Recruitment and selection is the method by which an organization generates and sorts its applicants for employment. It plays a major role as it directly controls the types of people that enter the organization (Guest 1997). In managing the cultural environment, the aim of the recruitment and selection processes would be to generate a pool of people who have some familiarity with the organization and its culture (Harrison and Carrol 1991). Although an organization may not be able to pick and choose its applicants, it can advertise a realistic and comprehensive description of what is required from their employees, both in terms of culture and performance (Brown 1995). This would then indicate to potential applicants the desired state of the organization they are planning to join and provide them the opportunity to judge whether they suit the requirement. An applied psychologist would be able to offer an accurate job analysis, which would highlight the key aspects of the job in terms of what is required from the person performing it. This could include performance goals and cultural aspects of the employment and therefore paint a good picture for any potential applicant.

The training and development taking place within the organization can also have cultural implications, particularly for the newer recruits. Many authors think of these processes as formal socializations. Training programmes can demonstrate the ways in which an organization would like its employees to think and, therefore, indicate the aspects with which they must be compatible with. They can also add direction to the desired cultural state (Schein 1968, 1991; O'Reilly 1989). Training can be used to orientate appropriate beliefs, values, and assumptions in employees, setting their cultural framework in their working environment (Wilson 2001). Although this method is seen as valid, a study by Silvester, et al. (1999) of a training scheme designed to bring about a change in the organizational culture found that senior managers and trainers were less optimistic about the success of the programme than the trainees themselves. This indicates the level of scepticism surrounding such formal cultural management practices.

The appraisal systems implemented by any organization can also impact its culture at several levels (Fletcher and Williams 1992). Organizations that choose to implement appraisal systems are implying that the areas that are appraised are more important to them. An applied psychologist looking to put together an appraisal system for an organization would want to consider the implications of the system on the culture of the organization. This consideration needs to occur at a number of levels, including not only what to appraise but also who should do the appraising and even how feedback on the appraisal is to be given. For example, organizations that aim for an open and relaxed culture might want managers to give one-to-one feedback rather than a written report delivered impersonally (Brown 1995). Indeed, 360-degree appraisal systems are often implemented as an attempt at optimizing fairness within organizations, as these systems gather their data from a range of sources (London and Smither 1995). Yet, this may not suit an organization desiring a culture that only respects management views.

Appraisal systems often (but not always) lead to reward systems, which are frequently thought to be a mechanism for controlling the behaviours and, to some extent, the cognitions of employees. This is because they set the guidelines as to what the employees need to achieve in order to receive pay rises, bonuses, and other rewards that organizations believe are valuable to their staff (Kerr and Slocum 1987). This, then, is thought to be the organization's statement of its beliefs, values, and assumptions inherent in its everyday life. It is important to note that

Practitioner Speak 18.4

A Good Way to Change a Corporate Culture

'I'd like to talk to you about a big project,' the woman told me on the phone. 'We need to change our culture.'

Read this insightful blog posted by Bregman on *HBR Blog Network* by accessing the following link: http://blogs.hbr.org/bregman/2009/06/the-best-way-to-change-a-corpo.html.

many organizations have different reward settings for different areas of their business, representing different values in different business settings (Brown 1995). For an applied psychologist intending to design a reward system, there is a range of theories relating to what motivates employees in the workplace. However, the choice that is made and the structures for reward that are put in place must combine motivational qualities with the goals and beliefs of the organization, alongside a consideration as to how the culture will be manipulated by the values the system introduces.

Interestingly, Clark (1996) suggests that the success or failure of performance-related pay (PRP) systems should not be judged solely on their motivational qualities. Such schemes can be used to manipulate the prevalent culture to make it more individualistic (if that is what the management wants to achieve). He also notes that these reward schemes should be introduced sensitively in an attempt to conserve any team spirit that may already exist. This seems contradictory to the overruling idea of PRP, yet the aim is one of balance where individual goals take precedence over collectivist goals without scrapping team communication all together (Clark 1994).

In HR practices and personnel management in general, the management of organizational culture can play a large part in the type of decisions made and strategic directions taken by practitioners. From the perspective of an applied psychologist assisting an organization with the design and implementation of its various HR programmes, the culture and climate of the organization should play a role in the preparation and design stages. A thought should be given to the current and future cultures of the organization and the impact that any intervention may have (in whatever shape or form). The possibility of objective assessment is appealing from a psychological perspective, and there is no reason why thinking about psychology and its relation to cultural change and management might not become more prominent in the future.

ORGANIZATIONAL CULTURE FROM GLOBAL PERSPECTIVE

A dictionary definition of corporate culture is 'the act of developing intellectual and moral faculties, especially through education'. Another definition of culture is that it is 'the moral, social, and behavioural norms of an organization based on the beliefs, attitudes, and priorities of its members'. Even though the first definition dwells on building culture through the act of education, its relevance is largely found in those corporations having a unique system that lays emphasis on continuous learning. Many of them have their own universities, such as the Sears University, the Hamburger University of McDonald's, and the Motorola University.

The corporate culture of HP can be taken as an example. HP has been successful in creating a conscious corporate culture, which is called 'The HP Way'. It is based on (a) respect for others, (b) a sense of community, and (c) plain hard work (Fortune, 15 May 1995). HP has developed this conscious culture and is sustaining it through extensive training of managers and all cross sections of employees. Today, HP's growth and success may be traced to its conscious corporate culture, which is reviewed here.

HP's culture is commitment to diversity, inclusion, and non-discrimination. Since its formation, the company has demonstrated an ongoing commitment to its people and to fair employment practices. As it has grown and expanded throughout the world, its workforce has become more diverse. HP believes that this diverse workforce helps the company realize its full potential. Recognizing and developing the talents of each individual brings new ideas. The company benefits from the creativity and innovation that result when its people with different experiences, perspectives, and cultures work together. This is what drives invention and high performance at HP. The company believes that a well-managed, diverse workforce expands its base of knowledge, skills, and cross-cultural understanding, which, in turn, enables them to understand, relate, and respond to diverse and changing customers throughout the world, connecting them to the power of technology. HP's overall commitment is reflected in its diversity and inclusion philosophy, which is listed as follows:

- A diverse, high-achieving workforce is the sustainable competitive advantage that sets HP apart. It is essential to win in the marketplaces, workplaces, and communities around the world.
- HP has an inclusive, flexible work environment that values differences and motivates employees to contribute their best.
- To better serve customers, HP attracts, develops, promotes, and retains a diverse workforce.
- Trust, mutual respect, and dignity are the fundamental beliefs that are reflected in HP's behaviour and actions.
- Accountability for diversity and inclusion goals drive HP's success.

Similarly, Jack Welch, chief executive officer (CEO), General Electric (GE), created a new corporate culture for the organization. The key elements of GE's corporate culture are as follows:

- Redesigning the role of the leader in the new economy and creating followers through communicating a vision and establishing open, caring relations with every employee
- Creating an open, collaborative workplace where everyone's opinion is welcome
- Empowering senior executives to run far-flung businesses in entrepreneurial fashion
- Liberating the workforce and making everybody a participant by improving vertical communication and employee empowerment

Another illustration of corporate culture is that of Southwest Airlines. It is one of the most profitable airlines in the US. Its CEO, Herb Kelleher, defines the Southwest culture as follows:

> Well, first of all, it starts with hiring. We are zealous about hiring. We are looking for a particular type of person, regardless of which job category it is. We are looking for attitudes that are positive and for people who can lend themselves to causes. We want folks who have a good sense of humour and people who are interested in performing as a team and take joy in team results instead of individual accomplishments. ... If you start with the type of person you want to hire, presumably you can build a workforce that is prepared for the culture you desire. ...

Another important thing is to spend a lot of time with your people and to communicate with them in a variety of ways. And a large part of it is demeanour. Sometimes we tend to lose sight of the fact that demeanour—the way you appear and the way you act—is a form of communication. We want our people to feel fulfilled and to be happy, and we want our management to radiate the demeanour that we are proud of our people, we are interested in them as individuals, and we are interested in them outside the workforce, including the good and bad things that happen to them as individuals.

An example of a down-to-earth corporate culture can be that of Sears, the second-largest retail chain in the world. Sears emphasizes the three Cs—compelling place to work, compelling place to shop, and compelling place to invest. It believes that these cultures when practised take into account the overall growth and prosperity of the organization. Incidentally, Sears also aligns its performance management system with the three Cs. Similarly, Wal-Mart, the largest retail chain of the world, also believes that all its employees are its associates; hence, as part of its corporate culture and practice, it shares all strategic information with its employees to get the benefit of empowerment and motivation. It should be noted that Wal-Mart achieves a significant rate of growth every year.

IMPACT OF MERGERS AND ACQUISITIONS ON CORPORATE CULTURE

Mergers and acquisitions also bring about major changes in the corporate culture. Many examples are found across the globe. However, certain cultural issues were experienced by organizations throughout the world during the post-merger phase, such as the following:

- There is a disintegration of organizational value systems (e.g., rent-to-own stores).
- Low employee morale results in poor productivity and conflicts (e.g., rent-to-own stores and Dell).
- Benefits of synergy require time to materialize. An example is the merger of Indian Oil Corporation (IOC) and Indo-Burma Petroleum Company (IBP). IOC's market share is 54 per cent in petroleum, oil, and lubricant (POL) products, but in the retail business, its share is 40 per cent. With IBP, IOC gets 1540 outlets to its existing 7750 outlets (IBP's market share is 8 per cent).
- There will be threat from emerging new organizations. For example, Hindustan Petroleum Corporation Limited and Bharat Petroleum Corporation Limited (together now enjoy 20 per cent) face competition from Reliance.
- Rationalization and relocation of manpower creates problems (e.g., Blue Star).
- Generation gap may create conflict (e.g., merger of Computer Maintenance Corporation (CMC)–Tata Consultancy Services (TCS) and merger of Bank of Madura and ICICI Bank).
- There will be loss of talents.
- There will be problems due to differing cultures, including cross-country culture (e.g., AMD discussed in the Introduction section).
- Rigidity of the blue-collar employees to learn new things may create difficulties.
- Sentimental attachment to the old culture may inhibit change.

- There is anxiety about lay-offs, as merger follows manpower rationalization.
- Difference in HR style can lead to issues in adjustment (e.g. Blue Star).
- There is loss of faith in management due to the veil of secrecy in a merger (e.g., acquisition of India Foils by Sterlite).
- There is stalemate in managerial positions, as one has to leave or compromise for the new group that is taking over.
- Employee enthusiasm will be reduced.
- There will be cost control to get a synergy of 'two plus two is greater than four', which may affect the executive pay.

Effective Mergers from Organizational Behaviour Perspectives

In order to make mergers effective, addressing the people-related issues, organizations need to consider the following aspects, which largely encompass interventions in streamlining organizational behaviour:

- Ascertain the differences in basic culture and procedures.
- Pre-assess the cost implication to integrate the manpower of the merging organization.
- Plan for adopting voluntary retirement scheme (VRS) for people who are rendered surplus.
- Make provisions for increased HR cost for training and redeployment, relocation, and VRS benefits.
- Accommodate employees (including executives) of the merging organization in the new environment. For example, this was followed in the Tata and Videsh Sanchar Nigam Limited (VSNL) merger.
- Develop an integrated culture with inputs from two organizations (which was again followed in the Tata and VSNL merger).
- Focus on the training and learning process. For example, in the CMC–TCS merger, TCS executives mostly handle international projects whereas CMC executives mostly handle domestic projects, thus maintaining their individual identity even after merger.
- Develop a new organization chart and make it transparent.
- Align the compensation package, if required even by redesigning, as done in the International Business Machines Corporation (IBM)–PricewaterhouseCoopers (PwC) merger.

All these examples illustrate how developing and sustaining a conscious culture in the organization can contribute to its growth and prosperity. Corporate culture as a separate branch has received priority due to globalization, consequent mobility of people, and cross-cultural influence, more particularly for multinational and transnational organizations.

HOFSTEDE'S CULTURAL ORIENTATION MODEL

Hofstede's cultural orientation model is considered one of the best models that help appreciate cultural diversity. Prof. Geert Hofstede is a Dutch researcher and the author of *Culture's Consequences*. In his book, Dr Hofstede elaborates his pioneering study of IBM affiliates in 50 countries. His work laid the foundation for the field of comparative management. The cultural orientation model has five continuums:

Individual vs collective orientation   At this level, behaviour is appropriately regulated.

Power distance orientation   It explains the extent to which less powerful parties accept the existing distribution of power and the degree to which adherence to formal channels is maintained.

Uncertainty avoidance orientation   It is the degree to which employees are threatened by ambiguity and the relative importance of rules, long-term employment, and steady progression through well-defined career ladders to employees.

Dominant values orientation   Dominant values such as assertiveness, monetary focus, well-defined gender roles, formal structure, focus on quality of relationships and job satisfaction, and flexibility are covered in this continuum.

Short-term vs long-term orientation   Through this continuum, it is possible to understand the time frame used, that is, short term (involving more inclination towards consumption, saving face by keeping up, etc.) versus long term (involving preserving status-based relationships, thrift, deferred gratifications, etc.).

People quite often debate on how cross-cultural influence may persuade an organization to redesign its HR policies and reward systems. Such trends influence an organization to re-engineer, more particularly in its approach to team orientation. For example, the theory Z management combines American and Japanese management philosophies.

The following characteristics are necessary for a company to change to a team culture:

- Common and consistent goals
- Organizational commitment
- Role clarity among team members
- Team leadership
- Mutual accountability within the team
- Complementary knowledge and skills
- Reinforcement of required behavioural competencies
- Power (real and perceived)
- Shared rewards

Cultural Issues across Nations

Differences in national cultures have been studied in over 50 countries. They show five independent dimensions of values—power distance, individualism versus collectivism, masculinity versus femininity, uncertainty avoidance, and long-term versus short-term orientation (Fig. 18.1). National culture differences are reflected not only in solutions to organizational problems in different countries but also in the validity of management theories in these countries. Different national cultures have different preferred ways of structuring

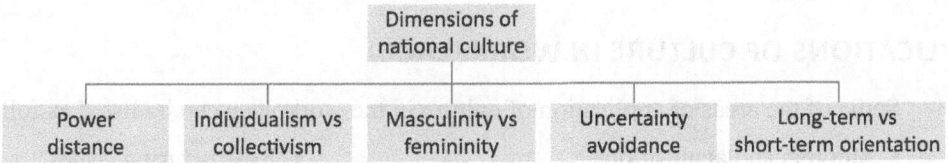

Figure 18.1   Hofstede's cultural orientation model

Practitioner Speak 18.5

Beyond the American Model of Leadership

I have always been intrigued by one sentence in Bill George's bio since I first saw it: 'Under his leadership, Medtronic's market capitalization grew from $1.1 billion to $60 billion, averaging 35% per year.' Always in his bio and clearly something he is very proud of, it raised two questions that have haunted me ever since and finally led me to a cultural interpretation.

Read this insightful blog posted by Liu on *HBR Blog Network* by accessing the following link: http://blogs.hbr.org/imagining-the-future-of-leadership/2010/05/beyond-the-american-model-of-l.html.

organizations and different patterns of employee motivation. For example, they limit the options for performance appraisal, management by objectives, strategic management, and humanization of work.

A study by Laurent (1983) established that internationally experienced executives display major differences, by nationality, in their beliefs about how to manage effectively. Though such a pattern of differences is partly attributable to biographical characteristics such as age, education, job, professional experience, hierarchical level, and company type, a more important reason for such a change, as indicated by Laurent, is attributable to international ethos. Thus, nationality is a potent factor to explain psychological attributes and behaviour of people across the nations. There are four important characteristics of differences in nationality—values, cognitive scheme, demeanour, and language.

Hofstede (1980) has already established that nationality affects one's values. A cross-national study by England (1975), which compared managers from the US, Japan, Australia, Korea, and India, found that nationality accounted for 30 to 45 per cent of the variation in the managers' values. Cognitive schemes are the knowledge of facts, events and trends, and knowledge about future events, alternatives, consequences for the alternatives, etc. Hence, the perception of people across the nations largely stems from the nationality constructs (Lord and Foti 1986). The difference in the cognitive scheme of people across the nations is the primary reason for recruitment of people of different countries by multinational organizations. Demeanour is the outward physical behaviour of people.

Values also affect demeanour. Differences in eye contact, punctuality, conversational style, interruption patterns, physiological reactions to emotional stimuli, and other types of behaviour are characterized as demeanour and associated with nationality (Frijda 1992). Finally, nationality has implications on the language of people. Not only the language that people know but also the propensity to know other languages varies from nation to nation.

Therefore, managing organizational behaviour in a cross-cultural set-up assumes importance. In order to achieve efficiency, managers need to understand the characteristic differences of people across nations.

APPLICATIONS OF CULTURE IN WORKPLACE

Some of the areas of application of culture in the workplace can be listed as follows:

- Mergers and acquisitions
- Strategic alliances and partnerships
- Restructuring issues
- Change management

- Self-development processes
- People management skills
- Executive coaching
- Negotiation skills
- Multinational virtual team building
- Facilitating top teams
- Project teams

- Expatriate/Inpatriate coaching/Briefings
- Sales and marketing skills
- General management training and education
- Counselling
- Leadership
- Organizational influencing

ORGANIZATIONAL STRUCTURE

Similar to organizational culture, organizational structure is one of the central issues in organizational theory in the 20th century. Three main theories of organizational structure have emerged—the archetypical bureaucracy; the stakeholder model; and newer ways of thinking, especially reflexive theories.

The archetypical bureaucracy theory stems ultimately from the theories of Max Weber. Its features are rationality, task specialization, hierarchy, and regularity, and there is a strong emphasis on structure as a controlling force. In the stakeholder model, on the other hand, rationality is abandoned and structure becomes the framework in which the various stakeholders—leaders, internal parties, and external parties—seek to achieve their own goals.

However, new research on organizational structure has focused on variables such as culture, metaphors, learning forms, and dynamic organizational variants and fields such as total quality management, six sigma, lean production, and the related paradigm shift. Both organizational theory and organizational practice reflect on the significance and use of the concept of structure. Details of organization structure have already been discussed in Chapter 4; hence, the discussion is not repeated here.

Managing Cultural Change

Cultural change can be managed either through organizational diagnostics or organizational development.

Organizational diagnostics Before initiating cultural changes in organizations, it is important to gauge the morale of the workforce to determine the nature of intended interventions. This is done using organizational diagnostic tools. Although several diagnostic tools are available, Table 18.1 examines some of the diagnostic tools and measures, elaborating the issues of concern and the possible questionnaire items.

Organizational development Organizational development is understood to mean planned change based on the paradigm of action research. It can thus be described as a learning process. The active development of an organization towards its desired corporate identity succeeds only if this change process is undertaken holistically. From a behavioural perspective, this means that the behavioural conditions that lie within the person (qualifications, motivation) as well as those lying outside the person (organizational structure, technology) must be modified. The process of change is also described as a political process, that is, characterization of change as the result of a clash. Lastly, the change process is often examined in terms of whether,

Table 18.1 Diagnostic tools and measures

Diagnostic areas	Issues of concern	Sample question items
Attitudes towards work		
Job satisfaction	Degree of workers' satisfaction	I feel satisfied with my nature of job.
Role clarity	Knowledge about behavioural expectations from the assigned job	I know my job responsibilities.
Role conflict	Degree of job pressure (simultaneously trying to achieve too many things)	I need to go beyond policies to achieve my goal.
Autonomy	Degree of employees' freedom in scheduling their work	I enjoy autonomy in accomplishing my tasks.
Participation in decision-making	Degree of employees' involvement in setting goals, objectives, and policies of the organization	I participate in decision-making, particularly in my work areas.
Job involvement	Degree of employees' commitment to the job	I do not become a clock watcher in accomplishing my task.
Organizational commitment		
Job security	Degree of stability in current job	My company believes in good work; hence, I do not feel threatened about losing my job as I am a good worker.
Loyalty	Degree of attachment towards the organization	My primary motivation for a job change is the scope of earning more in the same field of work.
Trust in management	Degree of confidence in actions and work of the management	I believe in my management's task and actions.
Identification	Degree of sense of belonging to the organization	I consider organizational problems as my problems.
Alienation	Degree of employees' disappointment in achieving their career goals and objectives	I lack a sense of pride in my current job.
Helplessness	Degree of feeling helpless in the organizations	I hardly have any option to leave the organization.
Issue for management to verify		
Organizational climate		
Fairness	The extent to which employees perceive their workplace to be equitable and free of bias	Employees in my workplace are treated fairly, regardless of race.
Safety	The extent to which employees perceive their workplace to be safe and free from physical dangers	I am often in situations at work where I can easily get physically hurt.
Support	The amount of perceived emotional support employees feel from their organization	Management here is interested in the welfare of its people.

(Contd)

Table 18.1 (*Contd*)

Diagnostic areas	Issues of concern	Sample question items
Communication	The accuracy and openness of information exchange	I am kept informed about changes that affect my work.
Tolerance for risk	The degree to which the organization encourages bold actions, risks, and independence of thought from employees	Risk taking is a value supported by our corporate culture.
Flexibility	The degree of adaptability and tolerance for ambiguity in an organization	My organization adapts quickly to changes.
Continuous learning	Perceptions of training and development opportunities in one's organization	There are adequate opportunities to pursue professional development activities beyond the scope of my immediate job.

and how, basic assumptions within an organization can be decoded through the analysis of symbols.

The types of organizational change intervention include the person-centred approach, the structural approach, and the relationship approach. The person-centred approach requires the development of both a social competence that fosters cooperation and a general intellectual competence that promotes innovation. The structural approach requires moves to reintegrate hitherto segregated work sequences and attempts to decentralize decision-making. The relationship approach requires team development, role negotiations, and survey feedback methods.

On the whole, evaluations of OD highlight the potential fruitfulness of its key approaches. However, follow-up studies have so far shown the outcomes to be widely variable, meaning that the degree of success or failure cannot be precisely forecast in each case. Accordingly, the conditions on which OD measures depend upon for their success are discussed later in the chapter.

A new approach to organizational transformation is beginning to gain acceptance in literature. Organizational transformation is a *harder* concept, often associated with re-engineering, and there is some concern that this could be used as a replacement for OD rather than as a contingency measure. Clearly, there are dangers in the widespread adoption of such an approach.

Process of Organizational Development

Organizational development is a strategy or an effort that is planned and managed from the top to bring about planned changes for increasing organizational effectiveness through planned interventions based on social philosophy.

Ever-changing market and compulsion for new product development to remain competitive are instrumental for organizational change. In this globalized era, an organization unprepared for such a change is likely to face extinction. Thus, continuous change is an organizational imperative, and only OD can facilitate such change.

Characteristics of Organizational Development

The following can be laid down as the characteristics of OD:

Planned organizational change It involves identifying the problem, diagnosing the problem, and developing strategies for improvement. The variables considered by OD programmes are values, attitudes, organizational culture, and team development.

Planned intervention It helps an existing organization become more viable. It, therefore, examines the present working norms, values, and possible areas of conflict in the organization and develops alternatives for better health. The interventionist needs to diagnose the different subsystems of the organization and develop alternatives accordingly. The important areas of intervention are planning and decision-making processes, goal setting, team development, organizational structure, values and culture, and upgrading employees' skills and abilities.

Top management commitment Top management should be interested in the OD programme and its outcome and effectively support efforts in this direction. Unless mutual trust and collaborative relationships are developed between the change agents (which in most of the cases are consultants or professionals) and the management, OD efforts may not succeed.

Social philosophy as norm for change The bureaucratic model of an organization ignores the basic human factors and thereby reduces organizational effectiveness. The interventionist, therefore, requires using the behavioural science knowledge and developing a system that is more humane and democratic.

Important Goals of Organizational Development

Organizational development emphasizes the need for transformation from a closed system to an open system by inculcating various changes in the organization. Such changes, inter alia, also include the introduction of concepts of social philosophy in the organization, which makes the organization socially more responsible and transparent.

To supplement authority and hierarchical roles with knowledge and skills and to replace the traditional authority-assigned role, which creates a more congenial work environment (the ultimate goals of OD), the following steps are necessary:

- Build mutual trust and confidence in the organization for man management and conflict reduction.
- Change the structure and roles consistent with the accomplishment of goals.
- Encourage a sense of ownership and pride in the organization.
- Decentralize decision-making, moving it close to the source of activity.
- Emphasize feedback, self-control, and self-direction.
- Promote a spirit of cooperation, mutual trust, and confidence.
- Develop a reward system based on the achievement of goals and employee development.

It is apparent from this discussion that the goal of OD is to basically change the attitudes of the people in the organization so as to enable them to identify the change areas and implement the desired organizational changes on their own.

Steps in Organizational Development

Robert Blake and Jane S. Mouton (1964) suggested a six-phase approach to OD as follows:

- Investigation of own managerial style by each member of the organization
- Examination of boss–subordinate relationship
- Analysis of work team action
- Exploration of coordination issues of interrelated terms
- Identification and definition of major organizational problem areas
- Planning for executing agreed-upon solutions that will result in changes in the organization

However, OD effort progresses through a series of well-defined stages, which can be enumerated as follows:

Identifying and diagnosing problems   Required changes in relation to various units in the organization should be identified and diagnosed, duly examining the feedback from employees. Effective identification and diagnosis of the problem should be preceded by an employee survey.

Developing strategies   While developing an appropriate strategy, it is necessary to study the people, subsystems, and organization as a total system. Strategy is formulating the direction and scope of an organization in the long run, in accordance with the resources and the changing environment.

Implementing organizational development programmes   An OD programme should be implemented in a phased manner. At first, it should be tried only in a small part of the organization. Only on receiving positive results should it gradually be implemented in the total organization. Since total organizational change precedes attitudinal changes and changes in values and beliefs of the people, the initial thrust should be given to training employees, improving their skills, developing self-awareness, improving interpersonal relationships, reducing conflict, and so on.

Reviewing progress   A qualified person who is not involved in the design and development of the OD programme should preferably review it to provide an unbiased opinion.

Leadership and Organizational Culture

According to Edgar H. Schein, culture is a phenomenon that surrounds us all and defines leadership. One can understand an organization by understanding its culture.

Schein defined organizational culture as customs and rights. It implies structural stability, patterning, and integration; hence, organizational culture is the accumulated shared learning from the shared history. Based on Schein's study, culture can be defined as a pattern of shared basic assumptions that the group learns through external adaptation and internal integration. On the basis of Schein's classification, the elements of culture can be listed as follows:

> Culture is a phenomenon that surrounds us all and defines leadership.

- Culture explains the incomprehensible and the irrational.
- Any organization with a history has a culture.
- Not every group develops a culture.

- Once culture exists, it determines the criteria of leadership.
- Leaders should be conscious of the organizational culture; otherwise, the culture will manage them.

SUMMARY

The word *culture* has many dimensions. Hence, in this chapter, it has been defined from different perspectives. Culture is an ongoing process of reality construction, providing a pattern of understanding that helps members of an organization to interpret events and provide meaning to their working worlds. It is a shared understanding of the people (Schein 1990; Schneider 1988; Kotter and Heskett 1992), and it frames the interactions and processes that make up everyday society and therefore the organizational environment. Understanding and predicting behaviour and human processes within a given environmental context can be best done based on the cultural constructs of an organization. For managing OB, one can use psychological concepts and theories to influence employees and improve the dynamics of the organization, but understanding how these are affected by culture requires managers to study the employees' behaviour in the cultural context.

Likewise, there is no single universally accepted definition for the term *organizational culture*. However, it is generally accepted as referring to the shared meanings, beliefs, and understandings held by a particular group or organization about its problems, practices, and goals. The concept of organizational culture is often misunderstood and confused with the related concepts of climate, ideology, and style. Organizational culture evolves from the social practices of the members of an organization and is, therefore, the socially created realities that exist in the heads and minds of organizational members as well as in the formal rules, policies, and procedures of organizational structures.

In general, the terms *corporate culture* and *organizational culture* are interchangeably used. However, corporate culture refers to a company's values, beliefs, business principles, traditions, ways of operating, and internal work environment. It is developed from a complex combination of sociological forces operating within the organizational boundaries. An organization's culture is either an important contributor or an obstacle to successful strategy execution. Strong organizational culture promotes good strategy execution. However, this would be possible only when there is a cultural fit. Good organizations endeavour to match culture with their strategies. Organizations with strong cultural bonds cannot eliminate the deep-seated values and behavioural norms of the people. A strong culture is a valuable asset when it matches strategy but a liability when it does not. When organizations go for mergers and acquisitions, redefining the cultural aspects becomes necessary. Many cases of mergers and acquisitions fail due to the mismatch of cultures between the parent unit and the acquired unit. Through sustained reinforcements, organizations attempt to achieve the required match. In some cases of mergers and acquisitions, it is also evident that organizations try to develop adaptive culture models to adjust to the changing environment.

KEY DEFINITIONS

Archetypical bureaucracy theory Its features are rationality, task specialization, hierarchy, and regularity and there is a strong emphasis on structure as a controlling force.

Dilemma theory It is commonly known as the THT theory. According to this theory, insidious culture clashes and most management problems are a result of the human habit of viewing life in terms of all-or-nothing choices.

Hofstede's cultural orientation model It identifies five independent dimensions of values—power distance, individualism versus collectivism, masculinity versus femininity, uncertainty avoidance, and long-term versus short-term orientation.

Organizational commitment It emphasizes the emotional bonding between employees and their organization.

Organizational development It is a planned change based on the paradigm of understanding the environment, benchmarking, and action research.

Organizational diagnostics It is the assessment of organizational environment through a structured approach.

Social This factor describes social and cultural communication, interaction, and relationships between individuals and environments.

CONCEPT-REVIEW QUESTIONS

18.1 Define corporate culture. Why do organizations across the globe try to create their own culture?

18.2 Provide a detailed account of the cultures of HP and Sears. You may download information from their websites.

18.3 Explain Hofstede's cultural orientation model.

18.4 Discuss how an organization can create a team culture. What are the areas that an organization should change while endeavouring for a team culture?

18.5 Write a short note on culture-specific management.

18.6 What are the important differences in work-related values? Support your answer with corporate examples.

18.7 What is OD? What are its important characteristics? How does it differ from management development?

18.8 Write short notes on the following:
   (a) Individual versus collective orientation
   (b) Power distance
   (c) Uncertainty avoidance
   (d) Dominant values orientation
   (e) Masculinity and femininity
   (f) OD intervention

CRITICAL THINKING QUESTIONS

18.1 Study the corporate culture of one Indian company that is operating globally. Understand the differences in people management practices in different nations. Attribute such differences to cultural constructs of the respective nations. You must use information from the relevant websites to develop your answer.

18.2 It is a normal practice for organizations to undergo a cultural transformation after mergers and acquisitions. In India, there are many examples of cross-border mergers and acquisitions. Identify one such unit and critically study its cultural transformation process.

18.3 You have been retained by an organization to help them develop OD interventions. The organization feels this is necessary to bring about attitudinal changes in their employees, as they are now operating in a globally competitive market. Draw your action plan.

SELECT BIBLIOGRAPHY

- Albert, M. and M. Silverman, 'Making Management Philosophy a Cultural Reality, Part 1: Getting Started', *Personnel*, Vol. 61, 1984, pp. 12–21.
- Bate, P., *Strategies For Cultural Change*, Butterworth Heinemann, London, 1994.
- Bhattacharyya, Dipak Kumar, *Human Resource Research Methods*, Oxford University Press, New Delhi, 2007.
- Blake, Robert P. and Jane S. Mouton, *The Managerial Grid*, Gulf Publishing, Houston, 1964.
- Brown, A., *Organisational Culture*, Pitman Publishing, London, 1995.
- Carr, C., *Choice, Chance and Organizational Change*, Amacom, New York, 1996.

- Clark, T. (ed.), *European Human Resource Management*, Blackwell, Oxford, 1996.
- Deal, T. and A. Kennedy, *Corporate Cultures*, Addison–Wesley, Reading, 1982.
- Fayol, H., *General and Industrial Management*, Pitman, London, 1949.
- Fletcher, C. and R. Williams, *Performance Management in the UK: An Analysis of the Issues, Part II*, IPM (now IPD), London, 1992.
- Guest, D.E., 'Human Resource Management and Performance: A Review and Research Agenda,' *The International Journal of Human Resource Management*, Vol. 6, Issue 3, 1997, pp. 263–76.
- Guest, D.E. 'Right Enough to Be Dangerously Wrong: An Analysis of the "In Search of Excellence Phenomenon"', in G. Salaman (ed.), *Human Resources Strategies*, Sage, London, 1992.
- Hampden-Turner, C. and F. Trompenaars, *Building Cross-cultural Competence: How to Create Wealth from Conflicting Values*, Yale University Press, New Haven, 2000.
- Harrison, J.R. and G.P. Carrol, 'Keeping the Faith: A Model of Cultural Transformation in Formal Organizations,' *Administrative Science Quarterly*, Vol. 36, 1991, pp. 552–82.
- Hofstede, G., *Cultural Consequence: International Differences in Work-related Values*, Sage, Beverly Hills, 1980.
- Kerr, J. and J.W. Slocum, 'Managing Corporate Culture through Reward Systems', *Academy of Management Executive*, 1987, pp. 99–108.
- Kleiner, A., 'The Dilemma Doctors', Journal of Strategy Business, May 2001.
- Kotter, J.P. and J.L. Heskett, *Corporate Culture and Performance*, Free Press, New York, 1992.
- O'Reilly, C., 'Corporations, Culture and Commitment: Motivation and Social Control in Organizations', *California Management Review*, Vol. 314, 1989, pp. 9–25.
- Peters, T. and R. Waterman, *In Search of Excellence*, Harper and Row, New York, 1982.
- Schein, E.H., 'Organizational Culture', *American Psychologist*, Vol. 45, 1990, pp. 109–19.
- Schein, E.H., *Process Consultation: Its Role in Organizational Development*, Addison–Wesley, Reading, 1969.
- Spradley, James P., *Culture Cognition: Rules, Maps and Plans*, Chandler, San Francisco, 1972.
- Trompenaars, F. and C. Hampden-Turner, Riding the Waves of Culture: Understanding Diversity in Global Business, 2nd ed., McGraw-Hill, 1998 (adapted).

CASE STUDY

Managing Change in Tata Consultancy Services Ltd

Tata Consultancy Services Ltd, a part of Asia's largest conglomerate—the Tata Group, is a leading global information technology (IT) consulting, services, business process outsourcing, and engineering services organization of India. The company commenced its operations in 1968; today, it has a presence in 44 countries across six continents and provides a comprehensive range of services across diverse industries. TCS is Tata's business offshoot, leveraging its century-old business experience in diverse fields. The global business reputation of TCS is visible from the fact that seven of the top ten companies in the Fortune Global 500 list are its clients. By creating and perfecting the *global delivery model*, the company is able to provide high-quality, value added services and products in IT consulting and business process outsourcing. It is an example to be emulated by the Indian IT industry. Known for reliability, passion, creativity, and uniqueness to cater to a wide range of IT needs with more than 2,76,000 of the world's best-trained IT professionals, TCS is rated very high in the customer satisfaction index (about 95 per cent). Its consolidated revenue was 11.6 billion US dollars in the fiscal year 2012–13. The pace of growth will certainly take TCS further. However, what is important for us is to watch their business practices and more specifically how they manage their people-related issues. Being essentially a knowledge intensive organization, TCS needs to pioneer the art of leveraging its human resources for business gain.

Mission, Vision, and Values

TCS's mission statement articulates its reason for existence, its vision reflects its aspirations to improve continuously, and its values guide its actions; these are provided in the following table:

Mission	Vision	Values
• To help customers achieve their business objectives by providing innovative, best-in-class consulting, IT solutions and services • To make it a joy for all stakeholders to work with us.	To decouple business growth and ecological footprint from its operations to address the environment bottom-line	• Leading change • Integrity • Respect for the individual • Excellence • Learning and sharing

A close assessment of its organizational practices will help understand how committed TCS is today to achieve its strategic intent. Some of its people-related practices can be benchmarked against the world's best organizations. These have made the organization truly innovative to cater to a wide range of industry verticals, placing almost every aspect of IT under its product or service lines and mix.

Industry Practices of TCS

The TCS industry verticals are structured into 11 industry practices, under the entire IT domain. Its products are globally popular and are known for their user-friendliness, flexibility, and comprehensiveness. Its industry areas and services and solutions spectrum are listed in the following table:

Industry areas	Services and solutions
Banking	Consulting
Financial services	IT services
Insurance	Business process outsourcing
Telecom	IT infrastructure services
Manufacturing	Engineering and industrial services
Media and entertainment	Application Development and Maintenance
Retail and consumer goods	Business intelligence
Healthcare and life sciences	Enterprise solutions
Energy and utilities e-Governance	Assurance services
High Tech Construction	Asset-leveraged solutions
Metals and Mining	
Travel, Transportation, and Hospitality	

Organizational Practices

TCS believes that innovation, dynamism, and creativity are its key drivers for growth. All these being people-centred, they show that the company believes in peoples' power and has made its HR an integral partner for organizational success. This required it to reinvent its HR with increased emphasis on dynamism. Truly speaking, TCS, in this respect, set the benchmark for others to emulate. Realizing the need for strategic focus on HR as its business imperative, it adopted incremental and collaborative practices to develop the people. Focus on development and growth, retention, and motivation and alignment of its people to business goals are its HR's strategic challenges.

Attractive benefits, competitive pay, and a work environment conducive to growth and competent management help TCS gain an edge over others in attracting and retaining talent.

The company does all these through value creation, extending the concept from business and organization to its employees. It creates value through strong, positive company cultures that foster happy, engaged employees who feel empowered to make decisions and thus feel connected with the company.

TCS accentuates the pace of employee development and growth, even extending its scope beyond the organizational boundaries, by introducing Academic Interface Programme (AIP). Launched in 2002, AIP facilitates robust, high-quality, and long-term relationship with academia, leading to a win–win situation for both. It enables TCS in identifying, engaging, and attracting talent.

Transformation of TCS

To make employees responsive to internal and external factors and to persuade them to change their mindsets and build capabilities, TCS always focuses on empowered decision-making and inculcates a sense of ownership among its people. The company views change as an ongoing process and quickly responds to changes to remain globally competitive, revisiting its organizational structure, practices, and decision-making practices. Adjustments against industry practice (IP), service practice (SP), and geography matrix (GM) always continue as ongoing exercises. In fact, the company always senses these in advance. Perhaps for this reason, TCS, for the first time in India, envisaged the need to designate a chief transformation officer (CTO). Through its learning programme, TCS always ensures development of its people's capabilities, which facilitates continuous mutation of organizational structure, meeting both the changing employee aspirations and customer delight. Its concern about the organizational structure is evident from its recent change to the matrix structure, only to keep pace with the external front. Organizational changes often cannot succeed with internal initiatives alone. TCS engaged an outsider who acted as a change agent, bringing about fresh perspectives in the organization.

Involvement of everyone in the process of transformation, clearly making the key concerns (why change, why now, what it means, where it will take the company, and what it means to everyone) transparent provides a cascading effect and makes the process a great success through voluntary participation of employees. TCS's organizational transformation model encompasses strategic planning, change management, and alignment with project management to create business value. A performance measurement system with an economic value added (EVA) approach provides a framework to align corporate values with the performance of the constituent business units and the individual employees attached therewith.

The HR group of TCS operates with technical experts to create a synergy that is enviable. The HR evidently plays the role of a facilitator—a catalyst—to initiate and institutionalize processes. The following figure shows the role of HR at TCS.

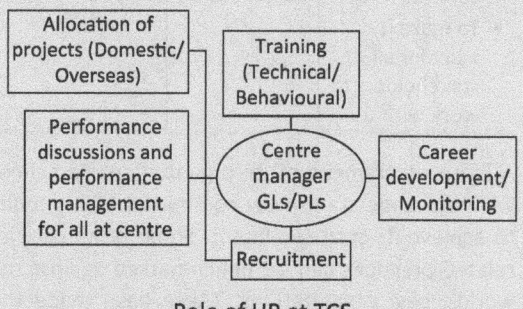

Role of HR at TCS

The following figure illustrates that the HR head at each region has a sufficient degree of authority to perform relevant functions, and yet, the corporate is easily accessible for advice and guidance. Such a structure promotes sharing of best practices across the regions and their institutionalization across the regions.

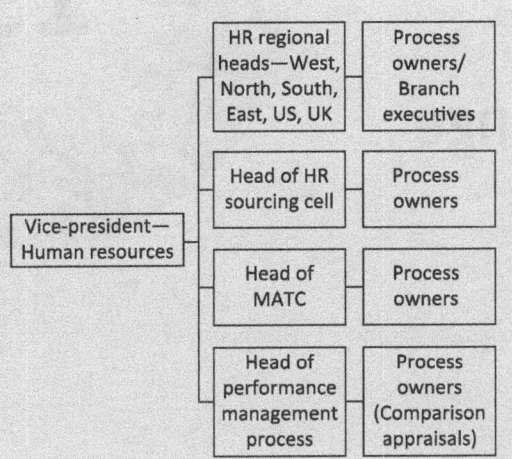

The HR group at TCS

Achieving High Maturity Level of Employees

Adopting People Capability Maturity Model (P-CMM) by integrating HR with the software engineering process, TCS could achieve synergy and thus a sustainable high maturity level of its people. This again proves the company's capability to leapfrog in the competitive global market. Periodic HR audit further ensures quality of people. Using cutting-edge HR technology, TCS continues with its efforts to develop HR capabilities through its Tata Management Training Centre (TMTC) and by exposing employees to various labs and conferences. Thus, the HR team in TCS truly transcends its developmental role.

Question for Discussion

Critically evaluate this case and justify if TCS can sustain in the long run with its people-friendly approach. What else do you recommend to TCS to think about people-related issues, benchmarking with the best practices of world-class competing organizations?

Introduction to Organizational Change

LEARNING OBJECTIVES

After studying this chapter, the reader will be able to

- understand the concept and theories of organizational change
- explain the motive behind organizational change
- describe the philosophy behind organizational change
- enumerate the steps to successful organizational change
- explain organizational transition
- distinguish between organizational change, transformation, and renewal
- identify organizational change triggers
- list the elements of success in organizational change
- provide various organizational change tips
- define the role of training, development, and motivation in organizational change
- analyse the various models of organizational transition
- classify the types of organizational change
- elucidate systems thinking and organizational change
- explain the various strategies of organizational change
- describe personal construct psychology and organizational change
- understand management of resistance to organizational change

CASE STUDY

Kick-start Your Change Initiative by Questioning and Storytelling

In change management, it is important to break the ice to make the start more effective and acceptable to workers. They feel relaxed even though the news about the change might distress them. Any activity other than the traditional activity-centric tasks can be used for this purpose. In many cases, particularly when people are tense (usually because of change), activity-based ice breaking will not succeed but rather prove to be counterproductive. An effective way to help workers relax is to ask them questions.

A change agent must talk to his/her employers. He/She must understand the job process first and then ask questions that relate to the jobs. Change agents must ask many questions, so as to get as many details as they can from the employees. It is like a role reversal from teacher to student. The employees must be given the role of a teacher, and the change agent must be the student. People like teaching what they know. A change agent must be a good listener when workers talk. Questions must be asked only to clarify doubts. The experiences shared must be recorded. Employees must feel that their views are valued. Then, the change agent must slowly change the pattern of questioning. Workers must be given the more empowered role of a mentor. They can be asked for suggestions to build the competitive strength of their company. Such questions make them open up. It must be remembered that the more the people are allowed to talk, the more the information is obtained about their weaknesses. This understanding will later help the change agents to sell their points.

Questioning as an art of ice breaking can be used to get positive results. In general, change resistance is high in people who are in a protected employment and are unionized. Making them change requires this unfreezing exercise of questioning.

Other than questioning, change agents can also use storytelling as a tool to break the ice. The agent has to especially construct a story specific to the organization and must know how to tell stories. Here, in addition to the actual stories, the agent's art of narrating the stories is also important. The body language, the emotion—everything should be fine-tuned with the narration. The story should give the impression that the agent has personified himself/herself as well as the workers with the story. It is important to identify some of the great achievements of the organization in the past and the people behind it—not just the managers and executives but also the workers—and a story must be developed based on them. People easily relate with stories, they feel engaged, narrow their differences, and feel like a part of a family. Increased sense of togetherness dilutes their differences, which can be used by the change agent as the trump card for subsequent change reinforcement.

INTRODUCTION

Change in organizations is a continuous process. Once a change effort becomes successful, an organization will have to bring about further changes. Depending on its nature and scope, organizational change can be categorized into two types—transactional and transformational. Transactional changes are specific to some issues, such as change in performance management systems, change in a particular work process or system, and change in compensation policies. Transformational changes are more holistic as they may require considerable changes in the organization. One may not face major problems while managing a transactional change issue or issues, when it is rational or legitimate. However, a transformational change issue requires one to make effective use of change strategies, aligning with the people and organization, and is more a long-term project. Issues related to organizational change are grouped into content, contextual, process, and criterion issues. Content issues are the substance of change. Contextual issues centre on external and internal environmental forces that trigger change. Process issues relate to the actions that one intends to take to bring about change. Criterion issues map the outcomes of the intended change actions. As a change management leader, one has to understand all these issues and accordingly frame the change strategies.

There are various factors that prompt an organization to change. Radical change in the business environment subsequent to globalization, among others, intensified the competition, changed the expectations of customers, and significantly changed the landscape of the national and international economy. Organizations need to make suitable calibrations to make them adept at managing those issues that influence business in one way or the other. One needs to understand the triggers, which may even be unknown to an organization. Nobody anticipated that Microsoft's introduction of Encarta CD-ROM would liquidate the print edition of Encyclopaedia Britannica, which was in publication for more than 200 years. And then, Microsoft itself had to withdraw Encarta later. Hence, it is difficult for an organization to visualize what could be a remote trigger for organizational change. It requires one's business intelligence function to collect, compile, and monitor the information, map the environment, and make internal adjustments in one's organization through changes on an ongoing basis (Bhattacharyya 2014).

DEFINITIONS AND CONCEPTS

As mentioned earlier, issues related to organizational change are divided into four major areas—content issues, contextual issues, process issues, and criterion issues. Content issues focus on the substance of contemporary organizational changes. Contextual issues centre on the forces or conditions present in the external and internal environments of organizations. Process issues concentrate on the actions undertaken during the establishment of the intended change. Criterion issues, on the other hand, tackle outcomes usually evaluated in organizational change. In the available literature, the terms *organizational change* and *organizational development* (OD) are used interchangeably. In fact, one encompasses the other. To effect organizational change, it is important to go for OD. Organizational change is unavoidable for organizations that want to keep pace with the changing business scenario. Globalization has further increased the spate of change. Increased competition, changing customers' expectations, economic uncertainty, and many such factors are now damaging age-old organizational systems and practices. Every now and then, organizations need to focus on internal business processes as well as account for the external environmental issues to stay competitive in the market.

Sashkin and Burke (1987), while discussing the prospects of OD and organizational change, had identified five contemporary trends:

- High integration of task and process aspects of OD (as in networked organizations)
- Increased attention to develop OD theory
- Increased interest to manage conflict (particularly in cases of mergers and acquisitions)
- Increased thrust on OD research to identify improved methodology for organizational change
- Increased focus to design organizational culture to manage change

Similarly, Woodman (1989), after summarizing the recent developments in OD and organizational change, recommended seven such trends, four of which match the trends suggested by Sashkin and Burke. The other three trends of Woodman are as follows:

> To make organizational change successful, it is important to bring in OD.

- Increased interest in high-performance and high-commitment work systems
- Application of change management research outcome to internal organizational processes
- Application of change research outcome to social movements

Apart from the aforementioned scholars, others like Pasmore and Fagans (1992) identified and explored issues in OD and organizational change. Their main focus was on increasing the participation of all employees in OD and organizational change; for this, they had taken historical and philosophical perspectives, which dates back to Plato, as the basis. Participation in OD and organizational change accentuates individual development as well. Successful participation in the change process precedes knowledge and focused preparation of people. Pasmore and Fagans have delineated the required knowledge as well as the steps required for the preparation of individuals for participation in the OD and change process. All these, therefore, suggest that OD and organizational change is essentially a participative process.

THEORIES ON ORGANIZATIONAL CHANGE

The success or failure of organizational change processes can be attributed to several factors. Such factors, once identified, help organizations develop the right strategy mix, suitable structures, overall mission (to get a sense of direction), and organizational long-term relationship to the environment; they also help delineate the organizational scope of activities. Contextual theory of organizational change emphasizes the identification of forces and conditions in organizational internal and external environments. The external conditions or forces are governmental regulations, technological advances, and various competitive forces that augment market competition. The internal conditions or forces are the degree of specialization (technology specific), level of organizational slack, and lessons of previous change issues. Contextual issues or elements of organizational change, therefore, relate to the success or failure of organizational responses to internal and external environments.

Process theories of organizational change deal with various process issues, addressing the actions taken by organizations in their change initiative. Such organizational actions may be taken to tackle the external environment or the internal environment and may be taken even at the individual level. External environmental issues such as rules and regulations of various central and state governments and local bodies influence the organizational employment practices, consumption of energy, production processes, health and safety of workers, environmental pollution, outputs, product safety regulations, and so on. In the process of responding to changes in the external environment, organizations need to bring about changes in the operating environment and change the behaviour of employees to achieve the desired goals and objectives. The process theory of organizational change, therefore, focuses on the actions or organizational responses to implement changes within the organizations and the employees' reactions to such organizational responses. Hence, organizations adopting a process theory approach of organizational change are basically concerned with developing suitable response mechanisms to external environment components that affect the internal activities of organizations so as to optimize employees' responses.

Content theory of organizational change deals with causes (conditions of organizations) and the resultant effect based on the change in individual and organizational performance data. Hence, it identifies inbuilt transformational and transactional dynamics of a successful organizational change. Transformational change factors identify areas that require employees to change their behaviour as a consequence of external and internal environmental pressures. These factors are leadership, culture, mission, and strategy. On the contrary, transactional factors deal with the psychological and organizational variables that predict and control the motivational and performance consequences of a work group's climate. These variables include management practices, structure, systems (policies and procedures), task requirements, and individual skills or abilities.

NEEDS FOR ORGANIZATIONAL CHANGE

It is difficult to track the necessity for organizational change in a given organization, as such needs vary widely. Organizational change is basically organic adjustment, and it is needed for different reasons. Some of the important motives behind organizational change can be listed as follows:

To set right situations   Organizations often need to correct a situation that they feel requires some adjustments or changes. For example, an existing human resource (HR) policy on variable pay, in a recessionary market, may seem to be incorrect when such pay is based on the value of total sales. An organization may amend this with a fixed performance incentive until the market situation improves.

To fix things that are needed   Organizations orchestrate change often through external interventions to set right poor performance areas. This may require alignment of some activities to derive strategic advantages. For example, to derive the benefits of strategic location, an organization located at a distance from its market may need to set up its marketing office near the market and relocate some of its marketing officials there. For example, Asian Paints and Dabur, two Indian multinationals, had to set up their manufacturing units across the nation and also abroad to derive the advantage of market proximity and to optimize the cost of distribution and supply chain.

To grab opportunities to grow   New market opportunities may motivate an organization to build new capabilities through expansion of its activities or through strategic alliances, identifying business partners, and so on. This requires increasing the manpower and investing in building new resources. For example, when political pressure mounted in the US to stop outsourcing to India, Infosys had to set up units at Canada to get the jobs outsourced from the US and then route those jobs to its Indian units.

To emerge as different entities   Organizations often change to enjoy flexibility. While adaptability to a new situation is essential, flexibility in operation or functions may be the necessity in special circumstances, like developing strategic business units based on product mix or type to make each product type an independent profit centre. For example, to give a competitive edge to each of its products, Kodak formed 34 strategic business units, restructuring its organization to get an edge over Fuji Photo Film.

Besides these, many other needs prompt an organization to change. These are elaborated in separate sections, while explaining the change triggers.

PHILOSOPHY OF ORGANIZATIONAL CHANGE

Philosophies are the value systems and the guiding force for organizational change. It is difficult to provide the philosophy and value systems of individual organizations. However, in most cases, it is observed that change in organizations is motivated by the following core philosophies:

- Being adaptable
- Being flexible
- Being strategic
- Focusing on behavioural issues

- Following participative change processes
- Being ethical
- Balancing the stakeholders' interests

STEPS TO SUCCESSFUL CHANGE

To understand and manage the process of organizational change, John Kotter (1995, 2002) suggested an eight-step model. Each step relates the responses of people to the change process, where people see, feel, and then change. The following is a summary of the eight-step change model:

Developing sense of urgency This is done by duly activating people through inspiration, so that people move and appreciate the relevance of change objectives.

Creating team to manage organizational change The team members will ensure placing the right people in the right place, addressing the issues of emotional commitment, right skill mix, and hierarchical levels. This process will ensure the success of any organizational change initiatives.

Developing right vision The vision should be simple, understandable, and shared by all members of the change team. The real effectiveness of a right vision is determined by how far it becomes a shared vision and the extent to which people can relate with the vision of the organization. With a shared vision, people can draw the right strategy, matching their emotional and creative needs to successfully drive the organizational change process.

Communicating vision The vision is communicated more from the selling perspective to increase the involvement of all cross sections of people in the organization, especially those who are being affected by the change process, so that they can positively respond to the change process. This would be possible only when change initiatives of the organization respond to people's needs.

Empowering people It is essential to make them become active in the change action. This would be possible only when obstacles in the participation of people in the change process are removed, when people are given constant feedback and support, and when they are recognized and rewarded for their progress and achievements.

Using incremental approach A step-by-step approach is essential to bring about change and short-term goals need to be set. People will be happy to taste victory early in the change process. Each such win will further motivate people. To ensure this, organizations need to set aims that are easy to achieve and manageable, and for which results are traceable. Strategically, organizations drive the change process with the mantra to do the first thing first, before starting the next stage of change.

Practitioner Speak 19.1

Change Management Needs to Change

As a recognized discipline, change management has been in existence for over half a century. Yet despite the huge investment that companies have made in tools, training, and thousands of books (over 83,000 on Amazon), most studies still show a 60–70% failure rate for organizational change projects—a statistic that has stayed constant from the 1970's to the present.

Read this insightful blog posted by Ashkenas on *HBR Blog Network* by accessing the following link: http://blogs.hbr.org/2013/04/change-management-needs-to-cha/.

Building on change   Organizational change requirements never cease to exist; hence, Kotter suggests not giving up change initiatives, as change is an ongoing process. A dynamic organization always encourages change and highlights what it could and what it intends to achieve in the future.

Reinforcing success   It is important to reinforce the success of change with new values and culture and with more proactive policies in recruitment, promotion, motivation, and so on. This will ensure sustaining the change process in organizations and help them truly excel in this competitive world.

ORGANIZATIONAL TRANSITION

The term *organizational transition* has been used by many scholars on organizational change, indicating that by implementing change, organizations reach a transition state as they move through the desired conditions and activities to reach the future. In another way, one can differentiate between organizational change and organizational transition by stating that organizational transition succeeds organizational change. Beckhard and Harris (1987), however, consider transition as a distinct phase of organizational change, which precedes the other two distinct conditions, namely the present state and the future state. Organizational transition process starts when organizations feel the need or desire for a new future. Such needs emerge from the following three important sources:

- Changes in the external environment, which compels organizations to find faster, cheaper, and better ways to meet the changing needs of the customers and other stakeholders
- Technological changes that requires introduction of new processes, which, in turn, requires skill renewal and competency development of existing manpower
- Top-down change initiatives of managers and executives who prefer to emulate the best practices of the industry

Organizational transition succeeds organizational change.

The first two needs unfreeze organizations and introduce new work methods. This is a reactive approach, as organizations go for transition or change only after a change in circumstances. The last approach is proactive, as organizations on their own volunteer to change to remain competitive in the market.

Another model of organizational transformation, pioneered by Healthcare Transformation Institute (HTI) in the 1990s, suggests the following steps:

- Understanding the opportunities to change
- Designing a guiding vision for change
- Measuring the organizational energy (strength) for change
- Developing a comprehensive plan and commitment to change
- Developing partnerships (specific working relationships) to implement the change plan
- Developing leadership to initiate, manage, and sustain the desired change

To understand the degree of change preparedness, HTI further suggests that organizations should measure their degree of preparedness on a five-point scale; if an organization secures the highest value, say four to five, in all these areas, one can understand that transformation is possible. HTI is a US-based professional body and a pioneer in initiating organizational transformation.

Irrespective of the nature of needs for organizational change, a clear perspective on the present state and the desired future state of the organizations in the post-change phase facilitates better management of the organizational transition.

DIFFERENCES AMONG ORGANIZATIONAL CHANGE, TRANSFORMATION, AND RENEWAL

Organizational change alters the way an organization functions. Hence, organizational change encompasses change, transformation and renewal. Change may vary in degree from one organization to another. Whatever may be the degree of change, it is necessary for the organizations to survive. Change introduces new ways of doing work in organizations and assigns new goals to the employees. If the change process continues, organizations can derive strategic advantages.

Organizational transformation is called a metamorphosis, as the structure, functions, organizational activities, and attitudes of the people radically change with the process of transformation. The word *transformation* in organizational context is more appropriate in cases of mergers, acquisitions, corporate gobbling, and so on, when the culture change in organizations becomes imminent. In such cases, due to the change in the management and the way of work, employees of the merged entity undergo a cultural shock. To set them in the right direction, organizations need to transform. Among others, such organizational transformation results in employee rightsizing, hiving off businesses, redundancies, process changes, and so on. Hence, the term *metamorphosis*, which means change or transformation, is used in such instances.

CHANGE TRIGGERS

Organizational change is necessary to enable organizations to remain competitive, productive, and profitable. The change process is initiated from the top and is then cascaded down through the workforce. It continues until it is integrated with the organization. In the process of integration or implementation, many organizations unsuccessfully adopt a negative approach, that is, persuade people to change without sharing with them the information. Such a negative approach puts organizations in a tight spot, as change resistance percolates to all areas of the organization, resulting in loss of productivity and fall in the bottom line (profitability). However, positive change initiatives lead to successful integration and implementation of the change, as people voluntarily accept the change. Although there are many reasons for organizational change, the following are some of the common reasons:

- Mergers and acquisitions
- Management restructure
- Introduction of new technology
- Relocation of business premises

All these issues have been discussed in subsequent chapters; hence, they are not elaborated at this stage. As of now, it is imperative to understand that the impact of change can be striking and has an effect on all cross sections of employees in an organization. In some cases, such as partial technological change or process changes, activities of only certain departments, more particularly people who are involved with those departments, might be influenced. Whether it is a partial change initiative or an all-encompassing change, for its success, it is important to reinforce the organizational change through required cultural change, new strategies, business plans, process design, training and development, and effective performance management systems. Hence, change management must first take stock of the current situation, including the quality of people, and then design a tailor-made change management programme to ensure success in the organizational change process.

It is difficult to state why organizations need to change and to list the controllable or uncontrollable change triggers (both internal and external to the organizations). Hence, some of the important change triggers, which are common for all organizations, are discussed here.

Business Development-driven

Changes driven by business development encompass every factor in the organization that exerts potential influence in organizational business expansion. Change precedes a well-crafted business plan, which spells out the mission, goals and objectives, and framing of strategies and action plans. Some of the potential areas of organizational change driven by the business development are as follows:

- Sales development
- New product development
- New market development
- Organizational structure, systems, and processes
- Tools, equipment, plant, logistics, and supply chain
- Attitude of people
- Style of management
- Way of communications
- Training and development activities
- Strategic collaboration and partnerships
- Distribution network
- Market focus
- Disposal process

In most organizations, changes driven by business development take place in the vision of the people at the top, corporate, or strategic level. They envision the change imperatives in various areas (a tentative list of which has been drawn here) and accordingly initiate the change process to make their organizations competitive in the market. Strictly speaking, business development-driven change process is more an art than science, as many change initiatives are based on the hunches and intuitions of the top management. Some of their actions are difficult to interpret and analyse, because of which it is difficult to emulate the best practices in changes driven by business development. Most chief executive officers (CEOs) of India Inc. still base their decisions concerning change related to business development on intuition. Although there are many structured theories on managerial decision-making such as rational, bounded-rational, incremental, and garbage-can models, managers in their real-life situation often make a trade-off between risk return and short-term (incremental) view. Not everyone is a Dick Fuld, CEO of Lehman Brothers, a Fortune 500 company, who could risk over-borrowing hoping for better returns and profitability for the company (a garbage-can model of decision-making) and ultimately leading the company to bankruptcy. CEOs of India Inc. cannot afford to gamble, as attitudinally they are risk-aversive; however, they often indulge in intuition-based decision-making with a bounded rationality approach (non-rational model of decision-making).

Environment-driven

The environment of an organization has a wide canvas. In a global economy, even recessionary trend in one country (with whom one may not have business relations) may require an organization to prepare for change. Thus, adapting to the environmental change is an imperative for today's organizations. Environment-driven change requires an organization to review its structure, relationships with its stakeholders, organizational dependence on environment linked with its important activities, such as buying and selling, that is, customers and suppliers, and compliance with the changing government policies and programmes. The degree of dependence decides the extent of adaptability of an organization. Environmental factors being exogenous to the organizations, and environment being continuously changing, organizations need to be dynamic to respond to even the slightest change cues. Changing tastes and preferences of the customers ultimately forced many Indian organizations to come out with value-added products. Hindustan Unilever's (HUL) brand extension strategy of Lifebuoy soap with Lifebuoy Plus and Lifebuoy Gold and adding moisturizers is a fine example of customer-centric change in the product mix. Similar change can be observed in companies that address customers' complaints with a 24×7 helpline or structured customer relationship packages.

Culture-driven

Many organizations undergo cultural change to make their organizational change process successful. Developing the desired culture enables organizations to focus on their changing goals and objectives, which, among others, may require people to take a re-look at their attitudes and revisit their perceptions about the customers and market situation. Corporate culture also develops shared values and beliefs, addressing diversity issues, which become more important in cases of mergers and acquisitions. Once people start subscribing to the corporate culture, organizations can implement their vision and values while drawing their strategies and action plans. A successful cultural change initiative of organizations slowly exerts a rippling effect on all functional areas, including operation-level activities. With the increasing diversity of the workforce and the pursuit of organizations to sustain in a competitive market, cultural fit with the changing systems and processes becomes almost a regular necessity. Finally, organizational change initiative becomes successful when it precedes cultural change of the organizations.

Strategy-driven

Strategy provides direction to an organization to achieve its goals and objectives. When goals and objectives change, strategy also needs to change. A strategy to achieve the objective of increased sales in the domestic market will not hold good for achieving the objective of increased sales in the international market. Many Indian companies differentiate their products and services, which they also sell in the domestic market, to cater to the needs of the international market. Organizational change, being all-encompassing, requires change of strategy. The question of which comes first—strategy change or organizational change—can be answered in both ways. A change in strategy requires organizational change; similarly, organizational change may require change in strategy. For example, a product differentiation strategy through a value-added approach, which is often adopted by organizations to remain competitive in the market, necessarily requires organizational change. Similarly, organizational change enforced through organizational restructuring requires change in organizational strategy. A term that is often used now is *strategic organizational change*, which indicates strategically pursuing the organizational change process to sustain a competitive advantage. Strategic organizational change can again be understood in a different way—an organizational change initiative taken by the strategic, corporate, or top level of organizational members. However, strategy again being all-pervasive, strategic organizational change holds good for business level as well as operation level when it addresses the strategic issues, that is, anything pertaining to the enhancement of competitive advantage of an organization.

To sum up, organizational strategy requires organizational change. Simple framing of strategy without effecting organizational change may not help an organization achieve the strategic intent. Strategic organizational change indicates the initiative of an organization to change, meeting the needs of stakeholders, responding to environmental threats, developing the capability of the organization and the people with a new set of competencies, and developing shared values and vision, all to grab new market opportunities.

Business Plan-driven

As mentioned earlier, strategic organizational change plans for an organization are usually drawn at the strategic, corporate, or top level of an organization. A business plan, usually drawn at the business or middle level of an organization, translates strategies into specific tactics to facilitate the process of achieving the desired results through desired change in the organizations. A strategy to achieve increased market share through customer retention can be translated into tactics of ensuring customer retention through increased level of discounts on successive buying or through visiting the customers from time to time to ensure that the company is with them. In India, this is hardly done by the manufacturers or service providers. Implementation of this tactic requires change in the organizational policies on discounts, if any. A business plan drawn after the strategic plan of the organization also induces organizational change.

A business plan also provides direction to the members of the organization to pursue the organizational objectives. In addition, it may be drawn to raise funds for the organization. Among others, a business plan should contain details of organizational change and development and strategies for marketing, operations, HR, and financial management functions.

Process-driven

Organizations are often required to undergo process redesign to optimize resource utilization. Process redesign may also be essential for achieving an increased level of productivity and performance. Any technological change may lead to process redesign. Moreover, changing market requirements may require change in the way the jobs are done. Whatever may be the reasons, process redesign calls for organizational change. Effective process redesigns aligned with the organizational change strategies help the organization transform.

Competency-driven

Competencies are the aggregation of knowledge, skills, and abilities of the people that together build the capabilities for the organization to stay competitive in the market. A systematic competency mapping identifies the competency gap, and accordingly, organizations initiate training and development activities to reduce the gap and to extend support for the organizational change. Competencies for an organization cannot remain fixed. With the changing technology, business environment, and degree of competition, organizations need to revisit the available competencies of the people and the organization as a whole and appropriately initiate organizational change.

Performance-driven

With the changing market requirements, organizations need to review their objectives and accordingly alter the performance standards, changing the key result areas (KRAs) or key performance areas (KPAs) for the employees. Such a change in the performance levels requires organizational change. Alignment of performance management systems with organizational change initiatives yields better results. Managers ready to take on organizational change missions will be experienced in integrating performance management with business planning. This integration is achieved by first establishing the common organizational change goals that will drive business plans and then linking the organizational change goals to the roles, competencies, and performance improvement measures needed to achieve them.

Individual performance development plans include assessment of role requirements and competencies needed to achieve organizational change goals, mapping of career and linking to developmental plans, establishment of performance improvement actions, and agreement on organizational resources and support requirements.

A performance management system will be effective in supporting organizational change only if it is objective, valued by both employees and managers, judged to be fair and realistic, and proven to make a positive contribution to personal and organizational development.

Innovation-driven

In order to give the message of change to the employees, William Ford Jr, Chairman and CEO of Ford Motor Co., said that henceforth 'innovation will be the compass' that sets the direction for Ford. He adopted innovation as Ford's core business strategy. In the same line, Jeffrey Immelt, Chairman and CEO of General Electric Co., believed that innovation is central to the success of GE and the company's change should be driven by innovation. He used the term *innovation imperative*. GE pursued 100 innovation breakthrough projects to drive the change in the organization. Steve Ballmer, CEO, Microsoft, moving one-step forward, said that Microsoft can make customers happy and keep competitors at bay.

Use of innovation as a tool for organizational change is often misconstrued as new product development or simple research and development work. A new framework called the *innovation radar* was developed by Sawhney, et al. (2006). Dell Inc., for example, could become the most successful personal computer manufacturer in the world through user-friendly computers, quick market positioning, and process changes in supply chain management, manufacturing, and direct selling. For many companies, therefore, creating value for the customers in the true sense is the innovation and not just creating new things. Innovation radar considers 12 dimensions, of which two are explained here:

Offerings It means the company's products and services. By introducing new products and services that are valued by the customers, companies can strengthen their offerings and consolidate their market position. For example, Procter & Gamble's customer-friendly Crest Spin Brush (electric toothbrush) with disposable batteries received wide acceptance in the market for its simple usability, portability, and affordability.

Platform In the innovation radar, platform indicates various components, assembly methods, and technologies that are used for products and services offerings. Platform innovation helps in new products and services making use of the power of commonality. Nissan Motor Co., with a common set of components, could develop markedly different cars and consolidate its market position.

Apart from these, brand offerings (what), customers (who), processes (how), presence (where), solutions, customer experience, value capture, organization, supply chain, and networking are the other areas of innovation radar.

Setting the pace for change with the innovation radar benefits both the company and stakeholders. For the company, successful change, keeping pace with the market and changing tastes and preferences of customers, benefits in the form of enhanced competitive advantage. For the customers, it gives value for their money.

KEY ELEMENTS FOR SUCCESS IN ORGANIZATIONAL CHANGE

An effective organizational change is not easily possible. It requires sustainable efforts from all members of the organization, with strategic focus on people-related issues. Drawing a road map for successful organizational change, therefore, may not be quickly possible. What organizations can do is to focus on some key elements, which are largely drawn from the best practices in change management, emulating the examples of successful organizations. Such elements can be listed as follows:

Planning long-term A sound strategic vision, not a specific detailed plan, can help an organization make reliable predictions. This is because a detailed five-year plan becomes outdated within a short time frame, because of change in the planning premises (on which such plans are drawn). Hence, a long-term plan broadly drawn with sound strategic vision and with the provision to revisit planning premises (periodic review) can ultimately benefit an organization to initiate change in the desired direction.

Establishing forums to communicate methods to review and implement change All members of the organization (not just limited to change agents) should be urged to participate in such forums. Such participation will benefit the organization to get their inputs, approval, and commitment and automatically enhance their cooperation to the change process. The process may not be that simple, unless it precedes sharing of change information with the people.

Empowering people to make decisions at operation level This is done through the delegation of power and responsibility. Encouraging people to participate in decision-making will make the organizational change process much simpler, because with their increased ability of problem-solving, employees will volunteer for change for improving the organizational efficiency.

Making strategic change process free from autocracy and interference Managers and executives who do not subscribe to such mindsets or attitudes should be carefully removed from the change team, or they may mar the change process.

Encouraging, enabling, and developing people to be active in change process This will enable the organization to form virtual teams and practise the matrix organization structure, where matrix bosses will play a more proactive role in initiating the change in the organization.

Making effective use of information systems This is essential for effective management of change-related information with real-time sharing.

Using workshops These are used for all cross sections of employees to review priorities and to agree on broad medium to long-term vision and aims and short-term action plans, implementation methods, and accountabilities.

Making adjustment in recruitment, training, and development This is required to accelerate the pace of development of people to enable them to contribute positively to a culture of empowerment.

All the aforementioned change constructs can be grouped under either external or internal forces of organizational change.

ORGANIZATIONAL CHANGE TIPS

Based on the earlier-listed key elements, the following tips for organizational change may be used as guidance:

- Use a team approach that involves many stakeholders in the change management process.
- Recognize that organizational change can be achieved only through people and therefore the change management team must address their emotional needs.

- Recognize that organizational change takes time and resources, and results should not be expected too soon.
- Appreciate that organizational change requires skills and business awareness training. Any cost-cutting on this count is not correct.
- Understand that organizational change plans are critical but should not be made too rigid to realize the results, because in the process of change, organizations may have to alter the plans to adapt to changing situations or circumstances.
- Be systematic while establishing and implementing organizational change.
- Educate and train organizational change agents. Help change agents develop intelligent understanding of new work practices.
- Remember that results from the change management may not always be up to the level of expectation in the short run; in some cases, it may even be negative. Hence, cajole the stakeholders, reassuring that such phenomena is natural. They should continue to support the change and provide their best efforts to improve the situation. The May 2002 merger of Hewlett-Packard (HP) and Compaq Computer Corporation and the subsequent change process under their ex-CEO Carly Fiorina did not give immediate results. Shareholders of HP were very critical about the CEO's change initiative. However, today the situation has changed for HP-Compaq in terms of revenue, growth, and profitability.
- Share power and empower others to implement organizational change.
- Identify people who are interested in making substantial changes in working practice and make them the champions of organizational change.

Despite following such success tips, it may not always be possible for an organization to achieve the desired results.

Exhibit 19.1 discusses the reasons for employees' resistance to change.

EXHIBIT 19.1 Resistance to Organizational Change: Why and Why Not

Resistance to organizational change is one of the inevitable problems faced by managements. Though employees normally resist change, there are reasons for it. Other than the reasons widely accepted in the academia, practitioners have their own tales to tell.

Renowned Harvard professor Rosabeth Kanter believes that there are 10 basic reasons why employees are averse to change, which are as follows:

- Fear of loss of control
- Uncertainty associated with change
- Inherent surprise factor in change
- Difference change brings in the schemes of things
- Fear of being unsuccessful

- Rise in anxiety regarding one's competence
- Fear of increased work pressure
- Ripple effects associated with change
- Bad experiences from the past
- Fear that anxiety over change may actually come true

On the other hand, mentor Lisa Quast opines that there are five major reasons why employees resist change. Though some points echo the concerns raised by Prof. Kanter, there are points of departure as well. The reasons are as follows:

- Fear of what is awaiting them post-change
- Lack of trust in the management

(Contd)

EXHIBIT 19.1 (*Contd*)

- Reduced job security and control over scheme of things
- Inappropriate timing of introducing change
- An individual's outlook towards change

Again, Christine Comaford, mentor and eminent management consultant, feels that resistance to change should not always be looked down upon. In fact, in resistance to change lies the potential for an immensely successful change. Her model for successful change involves the following five stages:

- Resisting the change
- Mocking the change
- Discovering usefulness in the change
- Change becoming a habit for employees
- Change becoming the new standard that employees abide by

Sources: *Kanter*, R., 'Ten Reasons People Resist Change', *HBR Blog*, 25 September 2012, http://blogs.hbr.org/2012/09/ten-reasons-people-resist-chang/, last accessed on 10 October 2013; Quast, L., 'Overcome the Five Main Reasons People Resist Change', 26 November 2012, http://www.forbes.com/sites/lisaquast/2012/11/26/overcome-the-5-main-reasons-people-resist-change/, last accessed on 10 October 2013; Comaford, C., 'Why Resisting Change isn't a Bad Thing: The Social Change Adoption Path', 9 April 2012, http://www.forbes.com/sites/christinecomaford/2012/09/04/what-to-expect-when-youre-expecting-change-the-social-change-adoption-path/, last accessed on 10 October 2013 (adapted).

TROUBLESHOOTING TIPS FOR ORGANIZATIONAL CHANGE

Some of the troubleshooting tips to avert poor performance of organizational change are listed as follows:

- Ensure that the change facilitator is helpful and cooperative.
- Ensure that initiatives to overcome the challenge of change do not get deterred despite resistance and defensiveness to the change process.
- Compare the results of change based on organizational plans. Change results will be evident from the mission, values, goals, priorities, targets, key performance indicators, processes, and measures. In addition, measure the change impact on people, particularly the employee turnover, retention, morale, attitudes, and so on, and also its impact on other stakeholders such as customers, suppliers, and the society as a whole.
- Observe change protocols diligently, properly communicating to the people the change actions, asking for their help and cooperation, clarifying their doubts, and so on. Politeness, courtesy, and sensitivity to people are very important.
- Adopt a facilitation style and approach rather than imposing the change actions.
- Prefer to be led by the people rather than lead the people.
- Act more like an enabler rather than a problem solver.
- Help people to raise questions and prefer to get their answers to such questions to improve the things.
- Avoid using 'why', else the employees will become defensive.
- Respect people.

ORGANIZATIONAL CHANGE THROUGH TRAINING AND DEVELOPMENT

It is widely believed that organizational change, irrespective of the nature of organization, encompasses training, development, and motivation. All these are primarily required to help people understand the need for change. Irrespective of the ranks of the individual employees, it is important to make them understand that without change, they will lose their competitive advantage and the company's drop in the market share will eventually lead to the loss of their jobs. It is possible to gain people's acceptance to change once they are properly educated through training and development.

This can be illustrated with the help of two real-life situations. In the first case, 44 operators of a public sector unit (PSU) petroleum, oil, and lubricants (POL) major were trained on the change imperatives, which ultimately made them agree to redeployed job positions. All these operators were in the technical grade and were entrusted with the filling of POL products in barrels and loading the barrels in trucks for distribution. The PSU, as part of its restructuring plan, went for automatic filling and loading of barrels, rendering these 44 employees redundant. The company did not have any voluntary retirement scheme. It could identify two possible areas for their redeployment—canteen and security jobs. Both these jobs were outsourced by the company then. Asking workers to accept these jobs immediately had an adverse impact, as they considered those jobs as demeaning and disgraceful to their present official positions. In a two-day training programme, the workers were made to understand the need for change. They were also made to realize that canteen and security jobs are not demeaning, as both are critical service areas for the organization. This exercise was not so simple. First, ice breaking was done by making them believe that they should also change. This was possible when they were asked about the type of school in which they had admitted their children. Almost 40 employees had put their wards in the best English medium schools, despite the fact that their average education level was much below secondary school. On enquiring the reason for their action, they answered that they want to give their children the best education to help them compete in future. This was the cue that indicated that mentally they are not averse to change. Subsequent training reinforcement could help them understand the necessity to accept their redeployment in the canteen and security jobs.

In the second case, militant trade union leaders were made to understand the process of job pricing, which subsequently helped them realize that their company was not cheating them on incentive payouts.

Training and development are integral to organizational change since these help employees understand the need for change.

The thrust of training and development programmes to introduce change in organizations should be to help people align their personal aims, wishes, and needs with those of the organization.

GENERIC CHANGE OR TRANSITION MODELS

Generic change or transition models provide the basic direction for organizational change programmes.

Lewis–Parker Model of Transition

Ralph Lewis and Chris Parker described a change concept, also called the *transition curve*, in their paper 'Beyond the Peter Principle—Managing Successful Transitions', published in the *Journal of European Industrial Training* in 1981. The Lewis–Parker transition curve model approaches personal change from a different perspective to the Fisher model. The transition is represented in a seven-stage graph, based on the original work by Adams, Hayes, and Hopkins in their 1976 book *Transition, Understanding and Managing Personal Change*. The seven stages of the Lewis–Parker transition curve are summarized as follows:

Immobilization   Shock, overwhelmed mismatch, expectations versus reality

Denial of change   Temporary retreat, false competence

Incompetence   Awareness and frustration

Acceptance of reality   Letting go

Testing   New ways to deal with new reality

Search for meaning   Internalization and seeking to understand

Integration   Incorporation of meanings within behaviours

The Lewis–Parker transition curve contains interesting parallels at certain stages with the conscious competence learning model, which is another helpful perspective for understanding change and personal development.

John Fisher's Personal Transition Curve

John Fisher's personal transition curve has several stages; these transform an individual to the ultimate stage of acceptance of organizational change. The stages are briefly stated here as per their order:

Anxiety

At this stage, individuals are unable to adequately visualize their future. This is primarily because they do not have enough information to construe the organizational change in the right perspective.

Happiness

At this stage, awareness is increased and the viewpoint of one is shared with others. Members of the organization get a sense of relief, as their feeling of anticipation matures and they can predict what is going to happen. At this stage, the organization needs to manage nurturing of unrealistic expectations by its members and help them correctly perceive the change implications with increased psychological contract. Information about change makes many people feel alienated. Organizations should avoid this, or else resistance to change will increase.

Fear

Once the awareness of change implications increases, people might suffer from a sense of fear, as they need to act in a different manner in the changed situation.

Threat

Threat arises when members of the organization perceive a major lifestyle change, which generally comes from radical alteration of their future choices and an increased feeling of uncertainty as to how they will be able to act or react in a new and alien environment.

Guilt

Guilt occurs with the awareness of dislodgement of self from one's core self-perception, when members of the organization recognize the inappropriateness of their earlier decisions.

Depression

In this phase, members of the organization suffer from general lack of motivation and confusion. With the increased sense of uncertainty, they undermine their core sense of self and lose their identity. There is no clear vision.

Disillusionment

Disillusionment occurs when the members of the organization understand that their values, beliefs, and goals are not compatible with those of the changed organization. As a result, employees become unmotivated, unfocussed, and dissatisfied, and they gradually withdraw themselves both mentally and physically.

Hostility

Hostility is a typical syndrome that occurs when the members of the organization are sure about the failure of the change initiatives, based on their past experience. They continue to operate processes that have repeatedly failed to achieve successful outcomes and are no longer a part of the new process.

Denial

At this stage, people refuse to accept the change and deny that there will be any impact on the individual. They behave as if the change has not happened and continue with their old practices and processes. They even ignore any evidence or information contrary to their belief systems.

It can be seen from the transition curve that it is important for employees to understand the impact that the change will have on their own personal construct systems; it is also important for them to be able to work through the implications for their self-perception. Any change, no matter how small, has the potential to impact an individual and may generate conflict between existing values and beliefs and anticipated altered ones.

One danger for the individual, team, and organization occurs when an individual persists in operating a set of practices that have been consistently shown to fail (or result in an undesirable consequence) in the past and that do not help extend and elaborate his/her world view. Another danger area is that of denial where people continue operating as they always have, denying that there is any change at all. Both of these can have a detrimental impact on an organization trying to change the culture and focus of its people.

TYPES OF CHANGE

Depending on the nature of the change trigger, organizations adopt their change initiatives, which can be classified into various types of change.

Planned vs Emergent Change

When the organizational change is deliberate, based on conscious reasoning and actions, it is called a planned change. On the contrary, at times, organizations need to go for emergent change for many reasons. This type of change is known as unplanned change. These two types of change can be illustrated using two different situations:

Planned change To optimize cost, a manufacturing organization changes from job shop to assembly line. A job shop manufacturing process requires multiple skill sets of people, as it has the flexibility to accommodate customer specified designs and specifications, as customers' requirements vary. However, the process is slow because of frequent job changeovers and often causes a problem due to skill mismatch of available manpower. Hence, the cost of production becomes high and the firm cannot enjoy economies of scale. Assembly line system, on the contrary, standardizes the manufacturing process, breaking the total job into a number of operations, assigning each operation to a specific workstation, and assigning people to perform a specific task with specific plant and machineries. Although the initial investment for setting up an assembly line is very high, the firm can enjoy economies of scale and hence can optimize cost when it goes for bulk production. An organization had to go for such a change in the manufacturing process, as it had decided to manufacture auto spares for a major global automobile company.

A decision on this type of change can be categorized as a planned change, which requires the firm to make people adaptable to perform a specific repeated task, whereas they were earlier doing multiple jobs, making effective use of their multi-skills.

Unplanned change Any change decision based on unspoken and unconscious assumptions, external environment, and the future of the organization is categorized as an unplanned change (Mintzberg 1989). Mintzberg categorized it as a change process by drift rather than by design. This type of change can be influenced by both external and internal factors. External factors are economic situation, competitors' behaviour, political situation, legislative changes, and so on. Internal factors may be the sudden power of different stakeholders or interest groups, knowledge management practices, building the capability of people, and so on.

> Planned change is deliberate whereas unplanned change is known as emergent change.

After the collapse of the two-century-old Encyclopaedia Britannica, the new promoter had to go for product differentiation, introducing both the CD version and single-volume encyclopaedia to sustain in the competitive market.

While explaining unplanned change, Dawson (1996) stated that although a change process requires planned perceptive analysis, at times the change process cannot be isolated from the effects of coincidence, uncertainty, and chance. Thus, organizational change need not always be planned, fixed, or linear; it may be unplanned for an emergent element.

Episodic vs Continuous Change

Episodic change is infrequent, discontinuous, intentional, and radical in nature (Weick and Quinn 1999). Replacement of a strategy or a programme on a new product launch can be categorized under this type of change. Continuous change, on the other hand, is ongoing, evolving, and cumulative. Weick and Quinn termed episodic change as second order and continuous change as a first order change process. Organizations often go for continuous change as part of their incremental or short-term strategy.

Developmental, Transitional, and Transformational Change

In terms of the extent and scope, Ackerman (1986) distinguished between the three types of organizational change—developmental, transitional, and transformational.

Developmental change   This can be planned or emergent, that is, it could be first order or incremental organizational change. Developmental change enhances or corrects the existing aspects of an organization, primarily focusing on skill or process improvement.

Transitional change   Transitional change is the process of shifting from the present state of the organization to the new state, using a step-by-step processes. Organizational journey to the new state requires change in the attitude of people, process, systems, designs, etc. This process tries to achieve a known desired state, different from the existing one. It is episodic, planned, and a second order or radical change process. Most of the organizational change models are of a transitional type (Kanter 1983; Beckhard and Harris 1987; Nadler and Tushman 1989). However, it originated from the work of the three-stage process of Lewin (1951), which is illustrated as follows:

- Unfreezing the existing organizational equilibrium
- Moving to a new position
- Refreezing in the new equilibrium position

Schein (1992) further explored these three stages, suggesting that the unfreezing stage encompasses the disconfirmation of expectations, creation of guilt or anxiety, and provision of psychological safety (to convert anxiety into motivation) to change. Similarly, the moving stage, which is achieved through cognitive restructuring, encompasses the identification of a new role model or mentor and scanning of environment for new and relevant information. Schein further suggested that the refreezing stage requires the integration of the new point of view with the total personality and self-concept and with significant relationships.

Transformational change   This is radical and second order in nature. It requires a shift in the assumptions made by an organization and its members. Transformation can result in an organization that significantly differs in terms of structure, processes, culture, and strategy. It may, therefore, result in the creation of an organization that operates in the developmental mode—one that continuously learns, adapts, and improves.

To sum up the various forms of change, developmental change emphasizes improvement of the existing situation. Transitional change implements a known new state within a time-bound schedule. Transformational change focuses on the emergence of a new state, which is unknown until it takes shape.

SYSTEMS THINKING AND CHANGE

Organizational change is generally supposed to be a rational, controlled, and an orderly process. However, in reality, it is more chaotic. Pursuing organizational change involves shifting of goals and often discontinuity and surprise with unexpected change outcomes (Cummings and Worley 2005; Dawson 1996). Hence, change can be understood in the context of complex dynamic systems. The concept of systems thinking originated in the 1920s, primarily from biology and engineering. To explain the concept of systems thinking, Popper (1972) introduced the concept of the three R's, namely reduction, repeatability, and refutation. Systems thinking enhances one's knowledge and understanding by breaking things to manage the change.

A system is a set of elements connected together to form a whole, thereby possessing properties of the whole rather than of its component parts (Checkland 1981). Activity within a system is a result of the influence of one element on another. This influence is called feedback and can be positive (amplifying) or negative (balancing) in nature. Systems are not chains of linear cause-and-effect relationships but complex networks of interrelationships (Senge 1990). They are described as closed or open. Closed systems are completely autonomous and independent of what is going on around them. Open systems exchange materials, energy, and information with their environment. The systems of interest in managing change can all be characterized as open systems.

In terms of understanding organizations, systems thinking suggests that issues, events, forces, and incidents should not be viewed as isolated phenomena but seen as interconnected, interdependent components of a complex entity. Applied to change management, systems theory highlights the following points:

- A system is made up of related and interdependent parts, so that any system must be viewed as a whole.
- A system cannot be considered in isolation from its environment.
- A system in equilibrium will change only if some type of energy is applied.
- Players within a system have a view of that system's function and purpose, and their views may be very different from one another.

From a typical organization point of view, holistic systems thinking may be understood from the following perspectives:

- Awareness of the multi-factorial issues involved in organizational activities; for example, employees of a typical rectified spirit processing unit (rectified spirit is the core raw material for the liquor industry and is processed out of industrial molasses) should not only understand the operational process but also be aware of the extent of carbon deposition, which sparks environmental pollution.
- Interest in designing, planning, and managing organizations as living, interdependent systems committed to providing seamless attention to the customers

- Recognition of the need to develop shared values, purposes, and practices within the organization and between organizations
- Use of large group interventions to bring together the perspectives of a wide range of stakeholders across a wider system

CHANGE MANAGEMENT STRATEGIES

Different strategies and procedures are used to categorize the change environment. In organizations, change strategies are adopted on the basic premise or assumption that people will volunteer to engage themselves in the change process. Normally, four types of change strategies are adopted by any organization. These strategies are not mutually exclusive, but rather work and support the effective implementation plan at different stages of the change process.

Normative-reeducative strategy This strategy believes that changing the norms, attitudes, and values of individuals will lead to changes in their behaviours. This strategy is based upon the core beliefs, values, and attitudes. It assumes that change will occur when individuals change their attitudes as it makes them want to behave differently.

Rational-empirical strategy This type of change management believes in the rationality of people to embrace change for their own self-interest. However, this could be possible only after persuasion and detailed communication. Change intents need to be made clear to them, and they must understand the extent of benefits of change.

Power-coercive strategy Organizational change often requires application of power. Employees tend to become change compliant when change is enforced from the top echelons of management. Hence, power-coercive strategy often works to achieve the change intents by the organization.

Action-centred strategy Action-centred strategy in managing organizational change is developed based on the focus on problem-solving. It not only helps in troubleshooting the problem, but also effectively manages the change implications, particularly during the post-change phase.

Exhibit 19.2 talks about how information technology (IT) companies manage organizational change.

EXHIBIT 19.2 Organizational Change: The Case of IT Companies

Organizational change is one of those topics that has caught the fancy of many management gurus. Organizations, practitioners, and academicians have come up with various models for effective and successful organizational change in recent times. However, what many of these models and individuals behind these models are not able to foresee is that organizational change, for the most part, rather than being a huge one-time activity, involves constant activities that help companies and individuals evolve every now and then. Given the very nature of organizational change in modern times, IT companies have come up with ways to build capacities for adapting to new internal as well as external environments and changes at any moment.

Accenture, one of the foremost IT consulting companies operating all over the world, focuses

(Contd)

EXHIBIT 19.2 (*Contd*)

more on being *change capable*. This is in direct contrast with the set notion of making organizational change an event in itself. Huge transformations are time consuming, and the rapidly changing environment in which companies work does not offer scope for such time-consuming activities. Thus, change management at Accenture is concerned with truly adaptive change capabilities that ensure the organization's competitiveness in the face of changes in the operating environment of the company.

On the other hand, CISCO, another IT major, envisages organizational change as the process of meeting organizational objectives such as increased operational efficiency and profitability. In its point of view, organizational change should help attain certain short-term as well as long-term objectives, which it would otherwise not have attained. Thus, the solutions that it was looking forward to through organizational change were rather permanent in nature. CISCO wanted to focus more on its activities along with increased efficiency in its turnaround time and ultimately build a more effective organizational structure.

Given the vast difference in orientations in the two IT companies, it is clear that organizational change is one concept whose meaning lies in its use. Both companies have been successful in their endeavours and have used organizational change to stay competitive and focused and to continue as leaders in their respective business areas.

Sources: Gossage, W., Y. Silverstone, and A. Leach, 'The Change-capable Organization', www.accenture.com, 10 October 2010, http://www.accenture.com/us-en/outlook/Pages/outlook-journal-2010-change-capable-organization.aspx, last accessed on 6 October 2013; CISCO IT case study, 'How Cisco IT Implemented Organizational Change and Advanced Services for Operational Success', www.cisco.com, http://www.cisco.com/web/about/ciscoitatwork/downloads/ciscoitatwork/pdf/NDCS_Restructuring_AdvSvcs_Case_study.pdf, last accessed on 6 October 2013 (adapted).

PERSONAL CONSTRUCT PSYCHOLOGY AND ORGANIZATIONAL CHANGE

Personal construct psychology (PCP) or personal construct theory (PCT) is a concept pioneered by George Kelly. The PCP theory proposes that one must understand how others see their world and what meaning they attribute to things in order to effectively communicate and connect with them. This theory is extremely relevant to developing personal emotional maturity and awareness in oneself and others, and for understanding the behaviour of others. Hence, the concepts of PCP augment and support many of the behavioural models and methodology.

> PCP postulates that one must understand how others see their world and what meaning they attribute to things in order to effectively communicate and connect with them.

The PCP theory provides a very useful and accessible additional perspective to the world and the manner in which one relates to it. PCP places the individual at its central focal point. It is based on understanding the individual from within his/her own world view, that is, understanding how others see the world and not how one interprets their picture of the world. Every individual interacts with the world from a unique perspective—his/her own; this interaction is built from all the past and potential future experiences of the individual and dictates how he/she approaches situations.

In general, psychological theory purports that one observes other people's behaviour and actions and places one's own interpretations on them, attributing meaning based on one's own past (childhood) experiences. PCP is a more liberating theory, allowing the individual to develop and grow throughout his/her life, constantly observing, assimilating, and developing actions and reactions as well as experimenting and testing beliefs. Kelly (1955/1991) used the phrase *man the scientist* (sic) to explain how one interacts with the world.

Due to the constantly changing tendency of an individual's nature, one is not the victim of one's biography, but has the choice (although sometimes it may not appear as such) to adopt a new way of interacting.

How an individual interacts with others is the result of his/her past experiences and an assessment of the current situation, which is then mapped onto possible alternative courses of action; the individual can then choose that course of action that he/she thinks will best suit his/her needs. Kelly (1955/1991) proposed that all are scientists; by this, he meant that people are constantly experimenting with their world, generating hypothesis about what will happen, acting, and testing the resulting outcome against their prediction. It can be seen from this that the behaviour of people is not static.

Personal construct psychology is a free and empowering psychology. People are not seen as victims of circumstances. They have the power to change and grow. They are only limited in their vision of themselves and their future by their own internal blinkers—these limit the possible futures people can see for themselves and hence restrict their ability to develop. One of the fundamental tenets of PCP is that of *constructive alternativism*. In simple terms, this means that there are as many different interpretations of any situation and possible future outcomes as one can think of—how many different uses can one think of for a paper clip?

For example, one might define people by the way they act in the company of others and decide that some people are extroverts and others introverts; other constructs may be physical—tall or small, fat or thin. Objects can fall into more than one category, so there can be small, thin extroverted people. Within Klienian psychology, one example of a construct would be 'good breast/bad breast'. It should be noted here that the opposite of introvert might not be extrovert for some people; it could be loud or aggressive. Hence, just because one individual likes being associated with another, it does not mean that everybody does. This is why some understanding of other people's construct system is needed to be able to effectively communicate with them.

To be able to interact with each other, people need to have some understanding of how others perceive their world. What do they mean when they call someone extroverted? Are they the life and soul of the party? Or are they loud and overbearing? How an individual treats the extrovert depends on whether it is viewed as a positive or negative character trait.

Kelly defined his theory in a formal structured way by devising what he called his *fundamental postulate*—basically a stylish term for a statement that underpins the whole of PCP. A further eleven corollaries (or clarifying statements) were also developed, which extended the theory and added more elaboration to how the theory impacts and is used. These eleven have over time, been expanded and added to, as the range of the theory developed (e.g., Dallos 1991; Procter 1981; Balnaves and Caputi 1993). However, it must be said that these additions have not been universally acclaimed and many people recognize only the original eleven.

From the organization point of view, some constructs are more important than others. The most important constructs are those that are core to one's sense of being. These are very resistant to change and include things such as moral code and religious beliefs. They cause significant psychological impact if they are threatened in any way. The other constructs are called *peripheral* constructs and a change to them does not have the same impact. It also follows that some constructs will actually subsume other constructs as one moves up the hierarchy. The constructs are categorized into three types.

Pre-emptive constructs These are constructs that are applied in an all-or-nothing manner. If something is a ball, then it is nothing else but a ball, which is a very black-and-white way of thinking.

Constellate constructs These constructs are the stereotyping constructs. If something is a ball, then it must be round, made of leather, and used in football matches.

Propositional constructs This one carries no implications or additional labels and is the most open form of construct. It should be noted that constructs do not have to have words attached to them. There can be, and are, constructs that were formed before one could speak or have a non-verbal symbol identifying it. Something like the 'gut feeling' or 'it feels right' would be a non-verbal construct. Kelly originally called these *preverbal* constructs, but others (notably Tom Ravenette 1977) prefer the term *non-verbal*.

Kelly also proposed a form of drama therapy for use by the organizations. In his version, which he called the *fixed-role therapy*, in conjunction with the client organization, he drew up a new character (including a new name and history) and encouraged the client organization to act as if it was this new character. This allowed his client organization to try out new ways of looking at the world in a safe environment. (If it did not work, it just became itself again.) Hypnotherapy has also been used to loosen (and tighten) constructs.

ABC TECHNIQUE AND ORGANIZATIONAL CHANGE

One powerful tool for understanding why people are not willing to change is the ABC technique (Tschudi 1977). Here, A is the desired change with constructs B1 and B2 elicited. B1 represents the disadvantages of the present state and B2 the advantages of moving to the new state. However, it is possible (if not probable) that the current situation has some advantages, which may outweigh the disadvantages. Therefore, C1 is a construct that shows the negative side of moving whereas C2 shows the positive aspects of staying the same. However, by looking at the pay-offs for not changing, one can identify the barriers and introduce measures in place to overcome them (if necessary).

CHANGE EQUATION

Paul Elrich has designed a change model with an equation, which clarifies the magnitude of change requirement. Although his model is more appropriate at the macroeconomic level, that is, for the nation as a whole, it can also be used by an organization. The equation is presented as follows:

$$I = P \times C \times T \text{ (originally } I = P \times A \times T, \text{ where } A \text{ stands for affluence)}$$

Here, I = impact, P = number of people, C = consumption per capita (GDP per capita), and T = technology. Reducing population in the short run is not possible for a country and so is the case with the consumption. However, technological change is feasible, and with efficient use of resources (according to Elrich, 90 per cent more efficiency), society can ensure change. A similar analogy is also applicable for organizations.

INTEGRATIVE APPROACH TO ORGANIZATIONAL CHANGE

To ensure successful organizational change, the most desirable method is to adopt the integrative approach. Integrative approach aligns behavioural, structural, and technical strategies with OD strategies and accordingly develops new behaviours, relationships, and processes. Figure 19.1 illustrates the integrative model of organizational change.

ROLE OF ORGANIZATIONAL CHANGE CONSULTANTS

For organizational change to work, it must be a unique solution developed either by the organization itself or by an outsider who plays the role of a consultant. Consultants specializing in organizational change can fill a number of needs. First, they can acquire useful information from customers, suppliers, employees, and managers. Second, they can provide and generate insight into organizational change issues not previously known, or understood, by the senior management. Third, they can facilitate organizational change decision-making sessions that lead to clear change management action. Finally, they can provide specialized organizational change expertise in a new procedure, technique, or way of thinking that is unknown to the organization.

COMMON DRAWBACKS IN IMPLEMENTING ORGANIZATIONAL CHANGE

All organizational change initiatives, across the organizations, do not become successful. The failure rate of organizational change initiatives is very high. There are many reasons why organizational change fails, some of which are as follows:

- Inappropriate approach of the management, which is not suitable for organizational change requirements
- Inappropriate and often unrealistic expectations from organizational change
- Absence of sustained efforts over a period of time to introduce organizational change
- Incompatibility between declared change objectives and actual behaviour and actions

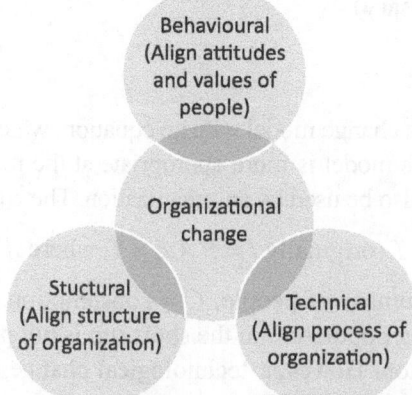

Figure 19.1   Integrative approach to organizational change

Practitioner Speak 19.4

In a Change Effort, Start with the Last Mile

One problem that constantly recurs in changing organizations is what we might call the last mile dilemma. The term comes from the telecommunications industry, which struggled for many years with how to efficiently extend their networks to the 'last mile', or into individual homes. In large organizations the analogous challenge is how to make sure that important changes actually reach the most remote stakeholders, whether they be front-line workers or customers.

Read this insightful blog posted by Ashkenas on *HBR Blog Network* by accessing the following link: http://blogs.hbr.org/2012/12/in-a-change-effort-start-with/.

- Poor understanding of organizational change, like systematic training being construed as a part of organizational change by some organizations
- Lack of support and systems.
- Lack of commitment to organizational change plans

Addressing all these drawbacks can ease the process of organizational change.

SUMMARY

The basics of organizational change have been discussed in this chapter. Organizational change encompasses four major issues, namely content, contextual, process, and criterion. Content issues deal with substance, contextual issues focus on external and internal environmental conditions, process issues account for actions taken, and criterion issues tackle the outcome of organizational change. OD is now an imperative for every organization to sustain a competitive environment. Organizational change precedes the OD initiative of any organization. Although it is difficult to enumerate possible reasons for organizational change, this chapter has highlighted some of the motives such as setting right something that is not in order, fixing things that are needed, grabbing opportunities to derive strategic advantage, and driving the organization with a structured vision. The steps to successful change, the differences between organizational change, transformation, and renewal, and the different change triggers have been enumerated in this chapter. In addition, the different organizational change tips and the mechanism of organizational change through training and development and employee motivation have been provided. Various models of organizational change such as Lewis–Parker model and John Fisher's model have also been discussed. The chapter has also outlined various types of change, role of systems thinking in organizational change, various change management strategies, and methods of managing resistance to change.

KEY DEFINITIONS

Organizational transition It starts when organizations feel the need or desire for a new future.

Environment-driven organizational change It is a change in the structure with respect to the environment.

Competency-driven organizational change Initiate organizational change based on identified competancy gap.

Lewis–Parker model The model helps in understanding change and personal development.

Transformational change This radical model requires a shift in the assumptions made by an organization and its members.

Normative-reeductive strategy This approach believes that changing the norms, attitudes, and values of individuals will lead to changes in their behaviours.

ABC technique   This is a tool to understand why people are not willing to change.

Transitional change   This seeks to achieve a known desired state using a three-step change process.

CONCEPT-REVIEW QUESTIONS

19.1 Explain why organizations need to change. What are the important theories of organizational change?

19.2 Explain John Kotter's model of successful change.

19.3 What is organizational transition? How does organizational transition differ from organizational change and renewal?

19.4 Identify some of the organizational change triggers. How can a new strategy act as an organizational change trigger?

19.5 What are the key elements for successful organizational change? What are the troubleshooting exercises necessary for organizational change?

19.6 Explain Lewis–Parker model and John Fisher's model of organizational transition.

19.7 What are the different types of changes? How does planned change differ from emergent change?

19.8 Explain the concept of systems thinking in organizational change. How does systems thinking influence change management strategy in an organization?

19.9 Write short notes on the following:
 (a) ABC technique
 (b) Normative-reeducative strategy
 (c) Episodic change
 (d) Generic change

CRITICAL THINKING QUESTION

19.1 One Indian multinational company (MNC) has recently acquired a US-based company, consolidating its stake by more than 51 per cent. During the acquisition, the Indian MNC agreed to ensure that there would be no lay-offs or downsizing in the acquired US unit. At the stage of consolidation, the Indian MNC restructured some of the job positions in the US unit, due to which some employees were rendered surplus.

However, the surplus employees were asked to get redeployed in some newly identified job positions after retraining. This action of the Indian MNC was viewed as a violation of the initial agreement of acquisition, as US employees considered such a move as an attempt to future retrenchment. Discuss this scenario in the context of personal construct psychology of George Kelly.

SELECT BIBLIOGRAPHY

* Ackerman, L.S., 'Development, Transition or Transformation: The Question of Change in Organizations', *Organizational Development Practitioner*, December 1986, pp. 1–8.
* Balnaves M. and P. Caputi, 'Corporate Constructs: To What Extent are Personal Constructs Personal?', *International Journal of Personal Construct Psychology*, Vol. 6, Issue 2, 1993, pp. 119–39.
* Beckhard, R. and R.T. Harris, *Organizational Transitions*, Addison-Wesley OD Series, Reading, 1987.
* Bhattacharyya, Dipak Kumar, *Human Resource Research Methods*, Oxford University Press, New Delhi, 2007.
* Bhattacharyya, Dipak Kumar, Managing change with a Time-tested Organic Model, Compensation and Benefits Review, Sage, DOI: 10.1177/0886368714525011., 2014.
* Checkland, P., *Systems Thinking: Systems Practices*, Wiley, New York, 1981.
* Cummings, T.G. and C.G. Worley, *Organization Development and Change*, 8th ed., South-Western Publishing, Mason, 2005.

- Dallos R., *Family Belief Systems, Therapy and Change*, Open University Press, Milton Keynes, 1991.
- Dawson, S.J.N.D., *Analysing Organizations*, Macmillan, Hampshire, 1996.
- Fisher, John and Dr David Savage (eds), *Beyond Experimentation into Meaning*, EPCA Publications, Farnborough, 1999.
- http://media.ford.com, *Bill Ford: Innovation Key to Ford's Future; Commitment to Hybrids to Grow*, last accessed on 21 September 2005.
- Immelt, J., *The Innovation Imperative*, Robert S. Hatfield Fellow in Economic Education lecture at Cornell University, Ithaca, 15 April 2004.
- Kanter, R.M., *Evolve! Succeeding in the Digital Culture of Tomorrow*, Harvard Business School, Boston, 2001.
- Kanter, R.M., *The Change Masters: Innovation and Entrepreneurship in the American Corporation*, Simon and Schuster, New York, 1983.
- Kanter, R.M., *When Giants Learn to Dance*, Simon and Schuster, New York, 1989.
- Kanter, R.M., *World Class: Thriving Locally in the Global Economy*, Simon and Schuster, New York, 1995.
- Kelly G.A., *The Psychology of Personal Constructs*, Routledge, London, 1955/1991.
- Kotter, J., 'Leading Change: Why Transformation Efforts Fail', *Harvard Business Review*, Vol. 73, Issue 2, 1995, pp. 59–67.
- Lewin, K., *Field Theory in Social Science*, Harper and Row, New York, 1951.
- Mintzberg, H., *Mintzberg on Management: Inside Our Strange World of Organizations*, Free Press, Chicago, 1989.
- Nadler, D.A., 'Concepts for the Management of Organizational Change', in C. Mabey and B. Mayon-White (eds), *Managing Change*, 2nd ed., Paul Chapman, London, 1993, pp. 85–98.
- Nadler, D. and M. Tushman, 'Organizational Frame Bending', *Academy of Management Executive*, Vol. 13, 1989, pp. 194–202.
- Nobel, C., *Ballmer: Microsoft's Priority Is Innovation*, 19 October 2005, www.eweek.com.
- Pasmore, W. and M. Fagans, 'Participation, Individual Development, and Organizational Change: A Review and Synthesis', *Journal of Management*, Vol. 18, Issue 2, 1992, pp. 375–97.
- Popper, K., *Objective Knowledge*, Oxford University Press, Oxford, 1972.
- Procter H. 'Family Construct Psychology', in S. Walrond-Skinner (ed.), *Family Therapy and Approaches*, Routledge and Kegan Paul, London, 1981.
- Ravenette T., *Selected Papers: Personal Construct Psychology and the Practice of an Educational Psychologist*, EPCA Publications, Farnborough, 1977.
- Sashkin, M. and W. Burke, 'Organization Development in the Nineteen-eighties', *Journal of Management*, Vol. 13, 1987, pp. 393–417.
- Sawhney, Mohanbir, Robert C. Wolcott, and Inigo Arroniz, 'The 12 Different Ways for Companies to Innovate', *MIT Sloan Management Review*, Vol. 47, Issue 3, 2006, pp. 74–82.
- Schein, E.H., *Organizational Culture and Leadership*, Jossey Bass Publishers, 1992.
- Senge, P.M., 'The Leader's New York: Building Learning Organizations', *Sloan Management Review*, Fall 1990, pp. 7–23.
- Tschudi F., 'Loaded and Honest Questions', in D. Bannister (ed.), *New Perspectives in Personal Construct Theory*, Academic Press, London, 1977.
- Weick, K.E. and R.E. Quinn, 'Organizational Change and Development', *Annual Review of Psychology*, Vol. 50, 1999, pp. 361–86.
- Woodman, R. 'Organization Change and Development: New Arenas for Inquiry and Action', *Journal of Management*, Vol. 15, 1989, pp. 205–228.
- Woodward, N.H., 'To Make Changes, Manage Them', *HR Magazine*, Vol. 52, Issue 5, 2007, pp. 63–7.

CASE STUDY

Navigating Change: Lessons from HUL

'We help people feel good, look good, and get more out of life with brands and services that are good for them and good for others. We will inspire people to take small, everyday actions that can add up to a big difference for the world. We will develop new ways of doing business with the aim of doubling the size of our company while reducing our environmental impact.' This is what Hindustan Unilever Limited (HUL) professes. HUL is India's largest fast-moving consumer goods (FMCG) company. It is present in the home and personal care as well as the foods and beverages categories. HUL has over 16,500 employees, including over 1500 managers. Incorporated in 1933, its current business turnover is ₹21,736 crore. HUL is part of the €44.3 billion Unilever Group. Today, every two out of three Indians use HUL products daily.

Around 450 of India Inc.'s CEOs today are HUL alumni. Many Levers alumni attribute the flight of talented top performers to restrictive career movements and non-competitive compensation structures. Some even say that Levers is too big to change. HUL always struggled for incremental growth rather than consolidate its market growth with some robust and sustainable long-term growth strategy. The perennial margin-focused attitude of the company even forced it to lose market share to competitors such as Godrej Consumer Products, Reckitt & Benckiser, and Wipro. The cascading effect of global slowdown in 2008 and 2009 made HUL a second choice to many graduating students of top business schools.

With Nitin Paranjpe, Managing Director of HUL, the change wave is on. The change philosophy of Paranjpe is 'inside out'. In 2010, about two years after he took over the top job in April 2008, he made HUL accounts, production, and HR people go out and meet consumers in villages across India, just as he did himself—and there was learning. Today, Hemant Bakshi, the company's executive director for sales and distribution, says the company will not cede any space to competition even if it means cutting prices and allowing a higher share of margin to retailers. Today HUL executives systematically visit 6.4 million retail outlets.

Powered by project Shakti, HUL is back to market with an excellent track record of growth. HUL's Shakti Entrepreneurial Programme helps women in rural India set up small businesses as direct-to-consumer retailers. The scheme equips women with business skills and provides a way out of poverty as well as creating a crucial new distribution channel for HUL's products in the large and fast-growing global market of low-spending consumers. By 2010, the Shakti network had reached 600 million consumers. Today, project Shakti, which was initially a Shakti Amma programme for women more for door-to-door sales in rural India, extends to Shaktiman, which gives the village men bicycles to sell HUL's products to beyond their village boundaries. This was HUL's coverage expansion strategy.

The 'inside out' change wave has further been strengthened by HUL through a series of internal restructuring programmes in all areas of activities.

HUL is back as a dream employer again. Setting goals, assessing performance, and providing merit-based rewards—its three clear steps in annual performance cycle—along with clarity and consistency helped it institutionalize the performance-driven work culture. The company now aligns its change strategy with the growth of the people, which makes every employee of HUL proud to be a member of a successful and caring organization.

Paranjpe also initiated a couple of new strategies to bring about change in HUL. The Perfect Stores programme ensures better visibility of HUL's products. Today, 1.1 million Perfect Stores account for 90 per cent of HUL's turnover in retail outlets. Joint Business Planning (JBP) for distributive trade further strengthened its market share.

HUL makes point of presence critical for its business expansion, as 70 per cent of the decisions regarding buying are made because of the quality of presence at the point of purchase. This is also aligned to the performance indicators of HUL's associates. Similarly, for institutional sales, HUL has embraced the modern trade strategy creating joint marketing plans with leading customers such as Wal-Mart, Metro, and Tesco.

Among the internal changes, HUL's initiatives are continuous improvement, lean, responsive, and customer-led strategies, better service, better quality, flawless execution, cost reduction, management of cash, collaboration with suppliers, and sustainable growth. All these substantially increased the market spread and share of HUL, bringing about positive change outcomes in the company.

No market- and customer-driven change can be successful without change within the people. HUL was successful in winning the market, reaching out to the hearts of their customers; however, it had to go for similar changes internally as well. People-centric changes in HUL are evident in HUL's focus on its employees. Best talents, high-performing teams, and perpetuation of the winning organizational culture were strengthened by a series of HR initiatives. HUL's Future Leaders Programme (UFLP) for the management trainees for global leadership positions across Unilever excites new talents to vie for the position. Young age is no bar for top positions if one is a performer. The performance culture along with clear goal setting is also powered by continuous learning for building the capabilities of the employees. Annual organizational health check-up survey tracks employees' feedback for internal changes and better employee engagement programmes.

Paranjpe's change navigation to put HUL back on track has proved to be successful. However, the years ahead are more challenging with competitors such as Godrej and Wipro gaining market strength at the regional levels. HUL's future strategies for sustainable ongoing change need to be seen.

Today Unilever wants to become leaner and meaner—focus on the big products (those that get Euro 1 billion plus in sales) for growth, reduce its stock-keeping units (SKUs), improve the working capital management, cut the headcount, and focus on margins rather than on sales growth alone. SKUs represent the total unique units of all brands (i.e., all sizes and variants). Unilever also wants to change the way it operates, removing layers to speed up decision making. With Sanjiv Mehta as the new CEO and MD of HUL (India), a finance professional (former CEO Nitin Paranjpe had a marketing background and was more of an innovator), it is expected that the company will experience a lot of changes.

Question for Discussion

As a change management specialist, develop a sustainable change model for HUL.

ANNEXURE 19.1

Organizational Change Guidelines

This guideline is prepared based on different organizational practices, where the author was also instrumental as an external change consultant. Before we spell out the tentative guidelines, first let us list out the possible action plans that are commonly adopted by organizations seeking change.

- Greater employee participation
- Greater understanding of the change

- Flexibility for informed decision-making power to people
- Inculcating trust in people throughout the change process
- Allowing employees to influence the decision-maker through a consultative process

The guidelines suggested based on these principles are presented here.

Step 1.0 Identification of organizational change

| Step 1.1 The work area identifies organizational change may be required. | To identify the need for organizational change, at the outset, have dialogues with the employees irrespective of their rank and shortlist the work areas where change is imminent. At this stage, focus should be more on assimilating employees' thoughts. A good approach should precede such exercises with sharing of information about company's present status in terms of productivity, cost, profitability, competition, and some macroeconomic information. Presentation should be in their level of understanding. For example, in one of the cases, 42 semi-skilled workers of a PSU POL major had to be redeployed in some jobs outside their job family (from operator to security and canteen staff) due to technological change (automatic |

loading of oil barrels). The author first sold to them the need to change, by enquiring the reasons for their desire to see their children study in the best schools. The employees replied that they wanted their children to survive in the competitive job market and to get decent and stable employment opportunities. This cue helped the author to subsequently make them understand why it is so important to their employer to redeploy with some lessons that canteen and security jobs are not demeaning.

Step 2.0 Determination of significant effects

Step 2.1 The work area determines whether organizational change will have significant effects on their employees.

With the identification of work area(s) that need change, in the next stage, the organization should study the possible effects of such change in terms of existing work process and practices, working conditions, employment practices, and so on. A detailed listing of significant effects is difficult, but they can be tentatively listed under the general category of redundancy. Organizational change is followed by change in the job composition, scale of company's operation (which may increase or decrease), size of the workforce, skill and knowledge obsolescence, and so on. In some cases, it even leads to reduction of job opportunities and career prospects of existing employees, alteration of working hours, relocation of employees, and total restructure of jobs.

All these are categorized under significant effects, which evoke immediate response from the employees. With such possible listing, it is important for the organizations to seek people's mandate through collective bargaining and signing of agreements.

With the employees' consensus, the organization can move to the next stage of change implementation.

This process is not so easy. It requires sustained efforts from the organization to cajole the employees, restoring their confidence that change is for a better tomorrow. In one case of acquisition of an MNC consumer electronics major by an Indian company, the author was involved in the process of cajoling the deadwoods (chronically change-opposing employees and non-performers) who were not prepared to believe in the positive effects of change. This cross section of employees with politically tutored lessons, although a minority (small in number), opposed the change, verbalizing that everything is for the worst. The author faced them with a detailed listing of tabulated cost–benefit analysis of change, with emphasis on what it costs to them in the short and also in the long run if the change is not implemented. Strategically, the company assured job guarantee for all, provided they feel mentally prepared for redeployment in restructured jobs and ensure benchmarked performance targets (against the competing organizations). All employees were taken through a compulsory skill-change programme (wherever necessary). With sustained training workshops, ultimately 90 per cent of the deadwoods agreed on the change imperatives, whereas the remaining 10 per cent decided to withdraw by resigning.

Step 2.2 The work area documents the likely significant effects.	At this stage, detailed listing of significant effects in work areas is done. Such detailed documentation is made available for everyone to inspect to ensure that nothing deviates from the agreed conditions in the collective bargaining. The documents should summarize the details of the proposed organizational change, background, and reasons for the organizational change, nature and extent of change, objectives to be achieved through the change, likely significant effects on the relevant employees for the change, new direction, structure and staffing pattern, process and methods of change implementation, information sharing or communication methods of change, resources made available for the change, and so on.

Step 3.0 Meeting with the employees

Step 3.1 Formal and informal meetings take place with the employees, particularly with those who are affected by the proposed change.	Depending on the nature of the proposed change, it may be necessary to invite all employees within the relevant work area. The employees are entitled to invite their employee representatives to attend the meeting and any future meetings. This meeting should be held at the earliest possible time after recognizing a need for change. This meeting is important as it emphasizes participation and communication and assists in minimizing employees' uncertainty. The purpose of this meeting is to outline the extent and nature of the proposed change, reasons for the change, aim of the change, and proposed timeframe. Employees attending the meeting should receive a copy of the document. In subsequent meetings, employees should be given opportunity to discuss their issues, and necessary feedback on the proposed organizational change should be obtained from all of them. Based on the feedback, necessary amendments to organizational change documents can be made.

Step 4.0 Finalization of change decision and implementation

Step 4.1 Review the amended change proposal drawn based on employees' feedback and implement the change.	At this stage, a review of initial change proposal is done in the context of amended change documents, based on employees' feedback, and the change document is finalized. The finalized change document is communicated in subsequent employee meetings and is then implemented in the organization.

It is important to remember to sustain the change process, periodic review of change outcome is necessary and if required necessary amendments to the change documents can be made, keeping employees informed about the move.

Knowledge Management

LEARNING OBJECTIVES

After studying this chapter, the reader will be able to

- understand the concept of knowledge management (KM)
- explain the concepts of data, information, knowledge, and intelligence
- enumerate the benefits of KM
- understand the strategies of KM
- describe the KM practices in Indian organizations
- understand how KM provides resource-based competitive advantages to an organization
- explain the relationship between KM and the organizational behaviour

CASE STUDY

NTPC Knowledge Management System

In 2001, National Thermal Power Corporation Limited (NTPC), the largest thermal power generating company in India, took a major initiative towards organizational transformation under Project DISHA. This ambitious project started with reviewing goals and strategies, formulating action plans, and finally implementing them at various plant levels. The company's core businesses are engineering, construction, and operation of power generating plants and providing consultancy to power utilities in India and abroad. In the near future, NTPC aims to diversify into related businesses through horizontal and vertical integration, which is also one of its corporate objectives.

The company's broad strategy for realizing its overall objectives is to build upon the four building blocks, namely competency, commitment, culture, and systems, derived from its human resource (HR) vision of enabling its people to become a family of world-class professionals and making NTPC a learning organization. For implementing this model, a knowledge management process has been initiated throughout the organization as competency and systems-building measures. It's knowledge management imperatives are derived from its strategic objectives and HR vision of becoming a learning organization. It also realized that to facilitate the implementation of business as well as HR strategies, there is a need for an integrated knowledge management system so that employees can transfer or share their knowledge and expertise for rapid growth and development.

INTRODUCTION

Knowledge is reinforced through learning. Therefore, before defining knowledge, it is essential to understand the meaning of learning. Learning is a process of acquiring new skills, which results in new behaviour. Though learning can take place through multiple ways, the best way to promote learning in organizations is through exposure to new experiences. Knowledge is the ability and wisdom to use the learned experiences for the achievement of individual and organizational objectives. Knowledge management (KM), therefore, is the process of systematically and actively managing and leveraging the store of knowledge in an organization.

At this stage, it is important to understand the basic differences between skills, multi-skills, competencies, and knowledge. Skills are operational attributes to attain some goal or accomplish a particular task. They can be either generic or technical, entry level or advanced. Operationally, skill enrichment is initiated to meet the present requirement. Multi-skilling is the process to train employees on varied skills, cutting across trade-specific and craft-specific skill sets. This initiative enables employees to perform more jobs within the same job family or to do the entire job from a holistic perspective. Thus, multi-skilling optimizes manpower utilization through job enlargement and job enrichment. However, both skill enrichment and multi-skilling are intended to address the present organizational requirements. Competencies, on the other hand, encompass skills, knowledge, abilities, and attributes that are observable and measurable and change over the passage of time. Organizations undertake competency mapping in the defined job context to understand the extent of its alignment with the organizational vision and mission, and based on such competency mapping, they define an ideal workforce. Knowledge is a more holistic approach, which is identified, acquired, and developed for achieving organizational objectives. The Indian *gurukul* system of learning all along emphasized the importance of holistic learning. Knowledge acquired through holistic learning helps employees to think independently and to understand the interdependence among various situations, factors, and so on, which never get obsolete. It becomes self-perpetuating and dynamic to address the changing objectives of the organizations.

From the foregoing discussion, it is evident that 'knowledge is a fluid mix of framed experiences, values, contextual information, and expert insight that provides a framework for evaluating and incorporating new experiences and information. It originates and is applied in the minds of the knower. In organizations, it often becomes embedded not only in documents or repositories but also in organizational routines, processes, practices and norms' (Davenport and Prusak 1997). In general, however, intellectual and knowledge-based assets fall into one of the two categories—explicit and tacit. Tacit knowledge refers to knowledge that is often used but cannot be articulated or externalized and hence cannot be easily diffused. Explicit knowledge consists of knowledge that can be codified and presented in books, manuals, and so on and as a consequence can be easily transferred to others. Included among explicit knowledge are assets such as patents, trademarks, business plans, marketing research, and customer lists.

Thus, from the organizational point of view, KM is a concept in which an enterprise gathers, organizes, shares, and analyses its knowledge in terms of resources and documents and periodically retires the redundant knowledge.

DEFINITIONS AND CONCEPTS

> *...the truly revolutionary impact of the Information Revolution is not artificial intelligence, information, or the effect of computers and data processing on decision-making, policy-making or strategy. The key to continued growth and leadership in the New Economy is not electronics of computers but the cognitive skills of the 'knowledge workers'.*
>
> —Peter Drucker

To understand the concept of KM, it is imperative to know what knowledge is all about. In daily parlance it might sound very simple, but, in fact, it is not easy to define knowledge.

Knowledge is the fact or condition of knowing something with familiarity gained through experience or association. There is no universal definition of KM, just as there is no agreement as to what constitutes knowledge in the first place. Hence, it is best to think of KM in the broadest context. Succinctly put, KM is the process through which organizations generate value from their intellectual and knowledge-based assets. Most often, generating value from such assets involves sharing them with employees, departments, and even with other companies in an effort to devise best practices. It is important to note that the definition says nothing about technology; though KM is often facilitated by information technology (IT), technology by itself is not KM.

In general, KM is a concept in which an enterprise gathers, organizes, shares, and analyses its knowledge in terms of resources, documents, and people skills. It helps an organization to gain insight and understanding from its own experience. It is the process through which an organization generates value from its intellectual and knowledge-based assets. A knowledge manager takes the responsibility of facilitating the ongoing process of knowledge sharing and knowledge renewal. It is important to understand how knowledge is formed and how people and organizations learn to use it wisely. Once the best advice is collected, the knowledge manager publishes the information in books and distributes them to all the concerned employees. The end result of a well-designed KM programme is that everyone wins. Knowledge management is a newly emerging, interdisciplinary business model dealing with all aspects of knowledge within the context of the company. It encompasses both technological tools and organizational routines in overlapping parts to include knowledge creation, knowledge codification, and knowledge sharing to promote learning and innovation.

> Knowledge management is a concept in which an enterprise gathers, organizes, shares, and analyses its knowledge in terms of resources, documents, and people skills.

Before discussing KM in the organizational context, it is important to clarify certain wrong assumptions about it. It is often believed that KM is about technology, but this is not correct. Technology merely acts as an enabler in KM functions. Knowledge is about people who collaborate and share their experiences to help the organization develop its HR. Knowledge is innovative use of information.

> Knowledge is defined as the condition of knowing something gained through experience or the condition of apprehending the truth or fact through reasoning.

It is the fact or condition of knowing something with familiarity gained through experience or association. From the perspective of organizational behaviour, knowledge may also be described as a set of models that describe various properties and behaviours within a domain. It may be recorded in the individual brain or stored in the organizational process, products, facilities, systems, and documents (Webster's dictionary). Knowledge is the capacity to act. It is a product of learning, related to human action, and is more than just a piece of information.

Knowledge assets refer to the knowledge regarding markets, products, technologies, and organizations that a business owns or needs to own and that enable its business process to generate profits. Knowledge management involves identification and analysis of the available and required knowledge and the subsequent planning and control of actions to develop knowledge assets so as to fulfil organizational objectives.

Knowledge management is a discipline that promotes an integrated approach to identifying, capturing, retrieving, sharing, and evaluating an enterprise's information assets. The information assets may include databases, documents, policies, and procedures as well as the uncaptured tacit expertise and expertise resident in individual workers. Corporate knowledge is the sum of the *justified beliefs* of the employees, which diminishes with the departure of employees. It is the major source of competitive advantage and can never be static. Knowledge management is important because of increasing competition in the marketplace. To fight competition, organizations need to be innovative. They should focus on the creation of customer values and reduction in the size of the workforce.

To manage knowledge, it is important to first identify organizational knowledge assets, understand how knowledge can add value, specify what actions are necessary to achieve better usability and added value, and finally review the use of knowledge to ensure added value.

Knowledge management encompasses human capital, innovation capital, process capital and customer capital. Human capital which consists of organizational learning, educational levels, employee empowerment, management experience, and time in training. Innovation capital consists of copyrights and trademarks, patents (legally protected intellectual assets), new market, and research leadership. Process capital includes strategy, decisions, cycle time, and IT capacity. Customer capital includes market growth and share, customer size and contact, and image enhancing customers.

Data, Information, Knowledge, and Intelligence

Data may be defined as factual information, whereas information is useful data communication or receipt of knowledge. Knowledge may be defined as the condition of knowing something gained through experience or the condition of apprehending truth or fact through reasoning. Knowledge may be tacit or explicit. Tacit knowledge is the hidden knowledge that is impossible to imitate or co-opt in its entirety and hence provides a unique and inherently protected commodity to its possessor. Explicit knowledge can be shared, codified, or structured and conscious and can be stored for reuse. Intelligence is the ability to understand and apply knowledge for any business solution.

Practitioner Speak 20.1

Knowledge Management below the Radar

How can we improve how organizations learn and adapt in fast-moving industries? I recently spoke to a group of Silicon Valley HR leaders and this question came up, along with the related matter of how to do knowledge management better. They asked how we do knowledge management at frog design, since we have studios spread all over the world and work in a diverse range of industries. Frog does relatively little formal knowledge management, but as we talked I realized that there are many things we do to support learning but don't get recognized as knowledge management. I suspect the same is true at many organizations.

Read this insightful blog posted by Richardson on *HBR Blog Network* by accessing the following link: http://blogs.hbr.org/2011/01/knowledge-management-below-the/.

INTEGRAL COMPONENTS OF KNOWLEDGE MANAGEMENT

From the definitions and concepts of KM detailed earlier, its integral components can be listed as follows:

- Generating new knowledge
- Accessing valuable knowledge from outside sources
- Using accessible knowledge in decision-making
- Embedding knowledge in processes, products, and/or services
- Representing knowledge in documents, databases, and software
- Facilitating knowledge growth through culture and incentives
- Transferring existing knowledge to other parts of the organization
- Measuring the value of knowledge assets and/or impact of KM

Exhibit 20.1 discusses how personal KM helps to prepare knowledge workers.

EXHIBIT 20.1 Personal Knowledge Management: Preparing Knowledge Workers Better

Personal knowledge management (PKM), as the name suggests, is the management of knowledge of individual knowledge workers in an organization. Given that PKM leads to better organizational KM, organizations are inclining more and more towards using PKM for their knowledge workers.

Personal knowledge management refers to an approach that complements organizational KM by zeroing in on ways to improve the productivity of individual knowledge workers in an organization (Efimova 2006). It equips knowledge workers with the tools and skills necessary to manage their individual knowledge. However, the question still remains as to how individual knowledge can be aligned to organizational knowledge to serve organizational objectives better.

As far as developing PKM is concerned, the most well-known framework is the seven-point PKM framework (Barth 2003):

- Accessing information and ideas
- Evaluating the information and ideas one has
- Organizing the information and ideas one has

(*Contd*)

EXHIBIT 20.1 (*Contd*)

- Analysing the information and ideas one has
- Conveying the information and ideas to others

- Collaborating with the help of the information and ideas one has
- Securing information and ideas

Sources: Barth, S. 'Personal Toolkit: A Framework for Personal Knowledge Management Tools', 2003, http://www.kmworld.com/Articles/Editorial/Features/Personal-toolkit-A-framework-for-personal-knowledge-management-tools-9416.aspx, last accessed on 29 September 2013; Efimova, L. 'Understanding Personal Knowledge Management: A Weblog Case', 2006, in: Jain, P. 'Personal Knowledge Management: The Foundation of Organizational Knowledge Management' *South African Journal of Libraries and Information Science*, Vol. 77, Issue 1, 2011, pp. 1–14 (adapted).

BENEFITS OF KNOWLEDGE MANAGEMENT

Some benefits of KM correlate directly to bottom-line savings whereas others are more difficult to quantify. In today's information-driven economy, companies uncover the most opportunities—and ultimately derive the most value—from intellectual rather than physical assets. Today, both knowledge and information are the main inputs of HR. In fact, the knowledge officers are all from the field of HR. To derive maximum value from a company's intellectual assets, KM practitioners maintain that knowledge must be shared and must serve as the foundation for collaboration. Yet, better collaboration is not an end in itself; without an overarching business context, KM is meaningless at best and harmful at worst. Consequently, an effective KM programme should help a company perform one or more of the following:

- Foster innovation by encouraging free flow of ideas.
- Improve customer service by streamlining response time.
- Boost revenues by delivering products and services to market faster.
- Enhance employee retention rates by recognizing the value of employees' knowledge and rewarding them for it.
- Streamline operations and reduce costs by eliminating redundant or unnecessary processes.

A creative approach to KM can result in improved efficiency, higher productivity, and increased revenues in practically any business function.

Knowledge is impossible to imitate or co-opt and so it provides a unique and inherently protected commodity to its possessor. This lends an increasing importance to the intellectual or knowledge assets (70 per cent of the market value of a company) in the market value of a firm. In this context, tacit knowledge plays a more crucial role in controlling competitive positions in the global business. With the emergence of a knowledge-based economy, a new type of executive will surface in many organizations—the chief knowledge officer (CKO)—who will implement the practice of KM. As a change agent, the CKO will promote and encourage knowledge sharing to build a cultural climate that rewards the sharing behaviour of the employees of an organization.

BUILDING KNOWLEDGE ORGANIZATIONS

Since knowledge and information are the main inputs of HR, it is justified that the KM efforts be led by the HR department. One can define a knowledge organization as one in which knowledge is the key resource that provides it the competitive advantage.

The first step in building a knowledge organization is to understand where knowledge is located in the organization. Who possesses the knowledge that provides the organization its competitive advantage? Knowledge is essentially created and possessed by individuals but within the context of organizational interactions that allow them to use and renew knowledge. There may be very dynamic industries in which individuals may possess knowledge that may be more important than that embedded in the organizational context. However, it is not possible for individuals to possess all the knowledge that is required nor is it possible for others to substitute for the knowledge of the missing individuals. In such situations, the individuals and the organization can jointly possess utilizable knowledge.

Organizational knowledge consists of a combination of the knowledge of all individuals in an organization. Organization learning or knowledge acquisition can take place in three broad ways:

- When individual members within organizations learn
- When individuals who learn have the potential of changing the stock of knowledge in the organization, thus leading to a change in organizational knowledge; and with the new knowledge coming in with new members joining the organization and old knowledge going out with those leaving the organization (if there is a change in the structure and system of an organization)
- When there are significant organizational changes due to which some previously neglected knowledge may come into prominence whereas some of the previously dominant knowledge may lose its importance

KNOWLEDGE MANAGEMENT STRATEGY

Effective KM helps an organization overcome market uncertainties and the ever-rising competition. To make the organization a knowledge-enabled one, it is important to strategically manage KM functions. A KM strategy identifies the key needs and issues within an organization and provides a framework for addressing them. Needs analysis ensures the consideration of those activities and initiatives that pose challenges to the organization. However, the approach depends largely on organization-specific requirements. For a call centre, the most important need factor is real-time answering to the callers' needs. Other usual challenges faced by the call centres are

> Knowledge management strategy identifies the key needs and issues within an organization and provides a framework for addressing them.

high job pressure, closely monitored environment, high employee turnover rate, and high training costs of the new recruits. Hence, the KM strategy for a call centre should address these aspects while making a needs analysis. Similarly, in customer relations jobs, it is important to ensure consistency, accuracy, and repeatability. Hence, the KM strategy should address these needs and issues. Likewise, a business manager needs to support business decisions based on key information. He/She has to bring about organizational changes keeping pace with the market requirements. Hence, understanding accurate, complete, and relevant information and acquiring people management skills, mentoring skills, and coaching skills are very important for designing an appropriate KM strategy.

While formulating a KM strategy at the macrolevel, an organization has to consider innovation as well as its operating environment. Although the KM strategy is organization specific, all organizations follow two holistic approaches—top-down and bottom-up. The top-down approach considers the overall strategy of the organization, whereas the bottom-up approach focuses on key business processes, which are understood based on an analysis of the business areas that deliver the highest business value and the people involved in it.

Many strategic KM tools are available. An important tool from the organizational behaviour perspective is the needs analysis, which managers perform using techniques such as facilitated discussions, focus groups, surveys, interviews, observation, contextual enquiry, and formal task analysis. These techniques will help managers acquire the required strategic inputs that can be used while formulating the KM strategy.

Developing a KM strategy provides a unique opportunity to gain a greater understanding of the way the organization operates and the challenges that confront it. By focusing on identifying staff needs and issues, activities and initiatives can be recommended with the confidence that these will have a clear and measurable impact upon the organization. Supplementing this bottom-up research with a strategic focus then ensures that the KM initiative is aligned with broader organizational directions. Taking this approach to the development of a KM strategy allows limited resources to be targeted to the key needs within the organization, delivering the greatest business benefits while positioning the organization for long-term growth and stability.

Many companies today consider KM as a new process similar to total quality management (TQM) or customer relationship management (CRM). TQM and CRM were earlier thought to be engineering concepts, but later the importance of HR in both these systems was recognized. Owing to the growing importance of HR, the Shingho Prize Model considers employee empowerment as a major component to achieve business results. Research has shown that KM and the transfer of best practices happen best in a business when the process is value-driven.

Another dimension along which the KM strategy needs to be planned, is the degree of codification and personalization. All organizations need to dynamically align their knowledge requirements based on their competitive positions and capabilities. They need to maintain a balance between creating and exploiting knowledge as well as between internal generation and bringing in knowledge from outside the organization. A company's KM strategy will also be influenced by the strategies of other companies in the industry. In knowledge-intensive industries, firms that have a more aggressive (externally oriented) knowledge strategy tend to perform better.

As the basis of value creation increasingly depends on the leverage of the intangible assets of firms, KM is emerging as a powerful source of competitive advantage. However, the general recognition of the importance of KM seems to be accompanied by a technology-induced drive to implement KM with inadequate consideration of the firm's strategic objectives. The case study given at the beginning of this chapter discusses how NTPC has integrated KM with its corporate objectives and the way it is implementing the system in practice.

Knowledge management thus creates, structures, and leverages collective know-how, experiences, and wisdom of the organization for improved business performances. It is considered as the firm's important source of competitive advantage, which rests in its superior adaptation of business conditions by effectively coordinating its internal resources. It is believed that every firm has unique knowledge-based capabilities, which may not be economically feasible

Practitioner Speak 20.2

Forget IP. Mine Strategic Knowledge Instead

While seeking intellectual property rights (IPR) is entirely appropriate for your well-structured knowledge, putting serious effort into mapping the deep, implicit knowledge within your organization can prove equally valuable.

Read this insightful blog posted by Ihrig, Boisot, and MacMillan on *HBR Blog Network* by accessing the following link: http://blogs.hbr.org/2011/05/stop-obsessing-with-ip-rights/.

to replicate. Hence, growth must be based on the coordination of these resources to develop and maintain advantages gained from a superior use of knowledge and competency.

A recent McKinsey survey of 40 companies in the US, Europe, and south-east Asia showed that many executives think that KM 'begins and ends with sophisticated IT systems' (Hauschild, et al. 2001). Knowledge management efforts have been primarily focused on developing new applications of IT. The link between an organization's knowledge and business strategy, while often talked about, has been widely ignored in practice (Davenport and Prusak 1997). If KM is to take root rather than merely become a passing fad, it will have to be effectively linked with the creation of economic values and competitive advantages. This can be accomplished by grounding KM within the context of the business strategy.

A Northeastern University research (Zack 1999) with more than 25 US firms has found that the most important context for guiding KM is the firm's strategy. An organization's strategic context helps to identify KM initiatives that support its purpose or mission, strengthen its competitive position, and create shareholder value. Naturally, it makes sense that the firm that knows more about its customers, products, technologies, markets, and their linkages should perform better. Knowledge strategy requires, in the first place, a proper understanding of the business needs as technology is expensive and bad choices hurt productivity and often eliminate further chances for deploying a better programme (Zack 1999).

Knowledge strategy can be distinguished as aligning organizational knowledge to define business strategy. This approach, therefore, considers KM as a process that optimizes the creation and sharing of market-usable knowledge assets and core capabilities.

The creation of unique strategic knowledge takes time, forcing organizations to balance their short-term and long-term strategic resource decisions. Hence, organizations must determine whether they should focus on knowledge creation, exploitation, or both. Only then should they accordingly balance their knowledge resources and efforts. They must determine those properties of knowledge that other firms cannot easily imitate and for which they enjoy competitive advantage in the processes of knowledge creation, transfer, and utilization.

KNOWLEDGE–STRATEGY LINK

In the strengths, weaknesses, opportunities, and threats (SWOT) framework, a link is established between knowledge and strategy. Based on the strategic opportunities, organizations map their knowledge resources, leveraging their strengths and guarding against the weaknesses (internal) and threats (external). Knowledge, similar to information, is now considered an essential resource input for organizations. Hence, while exploiting new opportunities, organizations need to strategically use their knowledge resources to gain a competitive edge

Based on strategic opportunities, organizations map their knowledge resources, leveraging their strengths and guarding against weaknesses and threats. Moreover, knowledge, similar to information, is considered an essential resource input for organizations.

over others. To illustrate, after acquiring a government-managed food-processing unit, Videocon transformed it into a computer assembly shop, redeploying its traditional workers into computer assembly jobs. For this exercise, Videocon exploited its existing knowledge base for manufacturing liquid crystal display (LCD) televisions. Changing market environments now require every organization to innovate. Hence, the development of a new product or service is a great challenge. Strategic use of knowledge resources helps in a great way in this respect. Organizations need to make many such strategic choices, leveraging their knowledge resources. This may extend to selection of technologies, design of the manufacturing processes, differentiation of the products and services, and so on. Internationally, Wal-Mart is an example of an organization making strategic use of its knowledge resources. It leverages the focused knowledge of its vendors, asking them to share their perceived consumption habits, needs, and practices with the retailers. Its retail shops act as knowledge integrators to meet the expectations of the customers in a better way. However, Wal-Mart is now experiencing difficulty, as there is increased competition from two major rivals—Target and Costco, and is trying hard to reinvent its strategies, with the backup of knowledge resources.

Mentzas (2003) suggested a knowledge-gap analysis model as shown in Fig. 20.1. This analysis model tracks what an organization can do with its available knowledge resources and what it cannot do because of the absence of knowledge resources. Hence, the model is useful for developing strategic knowledge maps to align organizational strategies. Organizations that pursue aggressive KM strategies can outperform their rivals.

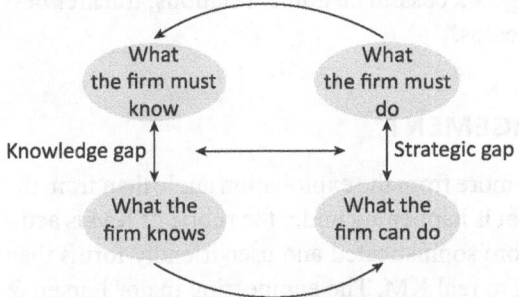

Figure 20.1 Knowledge-gap analysis model

Figure 20.2 illustrates a knowledge strategy integration, based on exploitation versus exploration orientation (Snowden 1999).

In cases where organizational knowledge significantly lags its competitors or the organization is defending a knowledge position, an aggressive knowledge strategy will be required to remain competitive in the market.

For example, Lehman Brothers (before their collapse) had superior knowledge of risky short-term and mid-term capital markets and cut-throat pricing. In addition, it had knowledge of how to integrate multiple services into innovative and comprehensive risk management solutions as well as how to put in place an aggressive knowledge strategy to maintain this competitive differentiation.

	Exploiter	Explorer	Innovator
Unbounded			Aggressive
External			
Internal		Conservative	

Figure 20.2 Knowledge strategy with exploitation vs exploration orientation

STRATEGIC KNOWLEDGE MANAGEMENT IN INDIAN ORGANIZATIONS

An Indian company with an evolving KM strategy that reflects the concerns discussed until now is Samtel, a picture tube manufacturer. After the deregulation of the economy in the early 1990s, Samtel realized that it could not be a long-term competitor in the display technology business without having a strong technological capability of its own.

Tata Steel, another Indian company, is also making extensive use of the KM process to remain globally competitive in steel manufacturing. The central theme of KM in Tata Steel is to leverage and reuse knowledge resources that already exist in the organization so that people will adopt the best practices rather than reinvent the wheel. It benefits the company by making expertise available throughout the organization, reducing loss of intellectual capital from people leaving the company, minimizing redundancy of knowledge-based activities, increasing knowledge productivity by disseminations, and gaining competitive advantage in the market place by turning intellectual capital into values through innovation.

In Bharat Heavy Electricals Limited (BHEL), KM helped the company achieve process improvement, increase employee capabilities, leverage intellectual capital, obtain customer market information, develop new products, manage successful customer relations, transfer best practices, open new markets, and start new businesses.

INDIAN COMPANIES AND KNOWLEDGE MANAGEMENT

Indian companies have so far tended to look at KM more from the exploitation angle than from the perspective of exploration and creation. Part of what is happening under the rubric of KM is actually information storage and retrieval, albeit in more sophisticated and user-friendly forms than before. Some companies are, however, graduating to real KM. The engineering major Larsen & Toubro (L&T) is creating a knowledge base of major projects undertaken by it with technical and managerial learning from each other. To ensure the reliability of this effort, the company has instituted processes for the verification and validation of such learning before it is available to the rest of the organization as best practices. The importance of this step cannot be overemphasized, for true knowledge is created only through such a process of verification and validation. Once such knowledge is created, IT can play a very useful role in allowing it to be catalogued, searched, and accessed in different forms. Organizations such as non-governmental organizations, which provide funding for development activities, and venture capital firms, which achieve their objectives through the performance of other organizations, are also looking towards KM as a way to learn from success stories, identify best practices, and transfer them to other organizations within their networks.

> Indian companies have so far tended to look at KM more from the exploitation angle than from the perspective of exploration and creation. However, this perspective is fast changing.

A strategy needs to be aligned with the structure and systems of an organization for it to be effective. Therefore, the KM strategy also needs some organizational conditions if it is to succeed. Functional or divisional silos, hoarding of information, and poor communication are anathema to KM. In general, KM is associated with decentralized decision-making and a belief in specialization and the value of deep expertise. Many Indian organizations would, therefore, have to change their entire ways of thinking, structure, and culture to make KM work to their benefit.

EXHIBIT 20.2 Knowledge Management in Indian Organizations

Knowledge management, being one of the primary concerns of organizations in today's world, has prompted both HR and IT departments to take proactive measures all over the world. Given the rapidly changing dynamics of business, Indian companies are not left behind. Various measures have been initiated in this regard to ensure that knowledge within organizations is managed properly and used effectively.

Given the importance KM has gained over the years, volumes of research have come up, some including data and statistics on Indian organizations as well. Endeavours to capture knowledge by organizations include Know Net, the web portal of L&T dedicated to gathering knowledge and solving construction and engineering problems at their sites, and Infosys, trying to capture its learning from projects and template it permanently for future use.

Nevertheless, all companies trying to effectively use KM, at least in India, face certain challenges. The first challenge is to understand what various stakeholders know. In this regard, both employees and customers can prove to be equally insightful. The next challenge is to brainstorm how the organization can effectively share the knowledge with others. The act of making the knowledge explicit and understandable as well as useable by all is yet another hurdle that KM specialists have to cross while dealing with Indian companies.

In this regard, Infosys uses a 'learn once, use anywhere' model. However, the universality of the learning may be a problem in trying to apply any learning to all similar situations. Still a bigger challenge for Infosys is to come up with a direct sharing mechanism between all employees.

In order to combat the challenge of knowledge sharing, researchers such as Singh and Soltani (2010) have come up with the solution of recognizing and rewarding the sharing of knowledge within organizations. In addition, knowledge gap quests may be conducted at regular intervals to reduce the gap, seeking best practices as solutions to these problems. Lastly, companies should think of aligning knowledge with their organizational objectives to make KM quests fruitful.

Sources: Goswami, C. 'Knowledge Management in India: A Case Study of an Indian Bank', *The Journal of Nepalese Business Studies*, Vol. 5, Issue 1, 2008, pp. 37–49; Singh, A. and E. Soltani, 'Knowledge Management Practices in Indian Information Technology Companies', *Total Quality Management*, Vol. 21, Issue 2, 2010, pp. 145–57 (adapted).

Today, when firms in India are subject to competition from the best companies in the world on their home turf, paying greater attention to knowledge and its management is inevitable.

Exhibit 20.2 discusses how knowledge management is handled in Indian organizations.

KNOWLEDGE MANAGEMENT AND RESOURCE-BASED COMPETITIVE ADVANTAGE

Organizational resources can be tangible such as land, buildings, plants, and machinery or intangible such as brands and reputations. Tangible resources are unlikely to be the basis for competitive advantage for the simple reason that they can often be duplicated easily by anyone who has financial resources. Intangible resources are much more likely to meet the tests of inimitability, slow depreciation, difficulty of substitution, and competitive superiority. Organizational capabilities are perhaps the strongest intangible resources. Reliance's legendary capability to conceive and implement mega projects based on its ability to think on a global scale, its skills in project management, and its resource mobilization abilities meets all the tests listed earlier.

Practitioner Speak 20.3

A Better Way to Manage Knowledge

We give a lot of talks and presentations about the ways and places companies and their employees learn the fastest. We call these learning environments creation spaces—places where individuals and teams interact and collaborate within a broader learning ecology so that performance accelerates.

Read this insightful blog posted by Hagel III, Brown, and Davison on *HBR Blog Network* by accessing the following link: http://blogs.hbr.org/2010/01/a-better-way-to-manage-knowled/.

> Intangible assets are highly likely to meet the tests of inimitability, slow depreciation, difficulty of substitution, and competitive superiority. Organizational capabilities are perhaps the strongest intangible resources.

Understanding the capabilities that need to be created and initiating the necessary steps to create such capabilities is again an exercise in KM. For example, the tractor and utility automobile manufacturer Mahindra and Mahindra (M&M) realized that to compete effectively it should be able to create a stream of new products on a continuous basis. Given its limited resources and global ambitions, it identified good project management skills as a key ingredient and initiated an organization-wide process, guided by external consultants, to create a robust project management capability.

Another company that has taken a conscious approach to create organizational capabilities is the two-wheeler manufacturer TVS Motor Company. Similar to M&M, the TVS Motor Company realized that a strong product development capability was essential for its survival and growth. However, it considered the essential requirements as being the ability to match user needs to product concepts and the ability to seamlessly transfer designs. It is useful to note that a single resource, however strong, is often not a good basis for strategy. Hindustan Unilever's (HUL) sustained performance is the result of not only strong brands but also leveraging its collective knowledge of brand management, logistics, and distribution management as well as the collective expertise and research skills of its scientists and engineers.

CATALYSTS FOR KNOWLEDGE-MANAGEMENT PRACTICES IN ORGANIZATIONS

To introduce KM practices, organizations make use of many catalysts. A CKO is responsible for enterprise-wide coordination of all knowledge leadership. The CKO may be a part of the IT department (but not always). A knowledge analyst collects, organizes, and disseminates knowledge usually on demand. A knowledge engineer converts explicit knowledge to instructions and programmes, systems, and codified applications. A knowledge manager coordinates the efforts of engineers, architects, and analysts. A knowledge manager is most often required in large organizations where the number of discrete knowledge-sharing processes risk fragmentation and isolation.

A knowledge worker embodies experience, innovation, creativity, and transformation of experience into knowledge for leveraging products or services. He/She transforms business and personal experience into knowledge through capturing, assessing, applying, sharing, and disseminating it within the organization to solve specific problems or to create value. Knowledge workers have the following professional attributes and personalities:

- They hold unique values.
- They align personal and professional growth with corporate vision.
- They adopt an attitude of collaboration and sharing.
- They have innovative capacity and a creative mind.
- They have a clear understanding of the business they are a part of.
- They are willing to learn, unlearn, and adopt new ways that result in better ways of doing a job.
- They possess self-control and self-learning abilities.
- They are willing to grow with the company.

The following are the core competencies of knowledge workers:

Thinking skills   They have a vision of how the product or the company can be made better.

Continuous learning   They are capable of unlearning and relearning in tune with fast-changing conditions.

Innovative teams and teamwork   They are able to make teams work via collaboration, cooperation, and coordination.

Innovation and creativity   They can dream of new ways to advance the firm.

Risk-taking and potential success   They make joint decisions with calculated risks.

Decisively taking action   They are willing to embrace professional discipline, patience, and determination.

Culture of responsibility towards knowledge   They show loyalty and commitment to their manager or leader.

KNOWLEDGE MANAGEMENT AND ORGANIZATIONAL BEHAVIOUR

Knowledge management in organizations emphasizes the creation, administration, and dissemination of knowledge. All the theoretical dimensions, such as organizational learning (Senge 1990), resource-based approach (Prahalad and Hamel 1990; Williamson 1997), and knowledge creation theory (Polanyi 1966; Nonaka and Takeuchi 1995; Davenport and Prusak 1997), consider that KM needs to focus on organizational knowledge to enhance the effectiveness of human capital and organizational capability to innovate and change. However, individual behavioural issues have not been discussed in the KM principles. Individual behaviour of people in organizations manifest from their preferences of cooperation and non-cooperation. Organizational environment influences individual behaviour and it is defined by rules, standards, or traditions, which give stability and security. An individual's adaptation towards organizational change depends on his/her experience. In organizations, people behave rationally to maximize their gains within the constraints

> Knowledge management needs to focus on organizational knowledge to enhance the effectiveness of human capital and organizational capability to innovate and change.

of organizational norms and rules. Hence, the behaviour of people regarding whether to cooperate or not depends on their own economic rationality. Knowledge management can modify this approach or rationality, thereby helping people understand the need to behave within the social context.

Organizational change raises a conflict because of its potentiality to imbalance the existing relationship between the employers and the employees. According to Kubr (1993), employees can cope with organizational change when they are aware of the benefit and purpose in doing so. Knowledge management as a tool can reduce resistance through identifying and analysing both the definable and indefinable parameters of individual behaviour. According to Hayek (1952), the way something is perceived depends on a process of cognitive reflection and involvement. The essential components of this process are interpretation, which is based on personal interests, and categorization, which puts the decision object into a contextual framework. The important point is that decisions are defined not only by the result of rational choice behaviour but also by procedural rule behaviour. Rule behaviour means identifying the context in which something happens and connecting the actual event with the environmental configuration. In this sense, decision-making is a holistic process of perception, interpretation, and evaluation within a framework of rules.

Chandler (1991) indicated that individual competence is configured by knowledge and motivation. Hence, knowledge has to be managed in a way that both the individuals and the organization can derive the benefit of synergy. Hence, the aim of KM is not to motivate people but to awaken individual motivation by nurturing an environment that enables people to relate themselves to the organization. For individual employees, KM defines individual performance through the analysis of specialization and work experience, which can be subsequently measured in terms of observed abilities such as professional, communicative, and social competences. When organizational change (due to the changing environment) is imperative, the individual employees' knowledge becomes the critical success factor for organizations. Management of knowledge, therefore, is crucial to successfully implementing changes in organizations to sustain in a globally competitive economy.

Practitioner Speak 20.4

Are You Wasting Money on Useless Knowledge Management

Is your company investing in expensive knowledge management systems that are useless for making big, strategy decisions? Most companies recognize the need for knowledge management, but often delegate it to the IT and HR departments without linking it to corporate strategy, often thereby wasting both resources and the strategic options their firm's knowledge could generate. The problem is that most current knowledge management efforts merely inventory the company's knowledge, without parsing out the knowledge that is strategically relevant. Strategic management of knowledge focuses only on those knowledge assets that are critical to your firm's competitive performance-from the tacit expertise of key individuals right through to explicit company-wide general principles.

Read this insightful blog posted by Hagel III, Brown, and Davison on *HBR Blog Network* by accessing the following link: http://blogs.hbr.org/2011/01/are-you-wasting-money-on-usele/.

SUMMARY

Knowledge management is a strategy practised globally. The HR department of an organization plays an integral role in creating a learning organization. Knowledge begins and ends at a personal level. Without human understanding, personal context, and immediate utility, all we have is data. Knowledge management is all about people and providing them with an environment that will contribute to enhancing their existing knowledge base and help them develop. Why is there so much stress on human resources? The reason is that competitive advantage is linked to possessing the *right* resources—resources that are difficult to copy or imitate, slow to depreciate, appropriable, difficult to substitute, and competitively unique. An important function of the HR department is not only to recruit the best but to retain them and to help them grow within the organization. Knowledge management is not just about collecting information but also about sharing it with the people. Sharing of knowledge leads to better, creative, and workable ideas and better ways of doing business. The connotations may have changed from learning organizations to KM organizations, but the crux of the matter continues to be related to information and growing with it.

Knowledge is the fundamental basis of competition. Competing successfully on knowledge requires either aligning strategy to what the organization knows or developing the knowledge and capabilities needed to support a desired strategy. An organization's knowledge strategy must be translated into its organizational and technical architecture to support knowledge creation, management, and utilization processes for closing the knowledge gaps.

KEY DEFINITIONS

Cognitive The factor that describes thinking processes and use of knowledge such as knowing, perceiving, recognizing, remembering, associating, discriminating, conceiving, judging, analysing, reasoning, synthesizing, problem-solving, and evaluating

Gap analysis Identifying the gap between what a firm must do to compete and what it is actually doing

Knowledge analyst A person who collects, organizes, and disseminates knowledge, usually on demand

Knowledge engineers People who convert explicit knowledge to instructions and programmes, systems, and codified applications

Knowledge management strategy The strategy that identifies the key needs and issues within an organization and provides a framework for addressing them

Thinking skills Ability to have a vision of how the product or the company can be made better

CONCEPT-REVIEW QUESTIONS

20.1 Define KM and indicate its benefits.

20.2 Explain how a knowledge organization can be created.

20.3 Explain how KM is strategically important for an organization.

20.4 What are the important challenges faced in a KM initiative? How can such barriers be overcome?

20.5 Provide a brief outline of KM initiatives in some Indian and foreign organizations.

20.6 Write short notes on the following:
  (a) CKO
  (b) Strategic KM
  (c) Knowledge-gap analysis
  (d) Resource-based competitive strategy
  (e) Catalysts for KM practices

CRITICAL THINKING QUESTION

20.1 A large consumer electronics major would like to introduce new product lines, starting a new vertical altogether. The company is known for being a low-cost manufacturer of conventional colour televisions (CTVs) in the country. Recently, the company has acquired the global manufacturing facilities of the world's number one television manufacturing company. The strategy behind the acquisition is to reap the cost advantage, as the acquired company has world-class picture tube manufacturing facilities. The company believes that this will ensure its low-cost manufacturing identity, as picture tubes are the most important and costly components in the manufacture of CTVs. The company has now ventured into new product lines, that is, manufacture of desktops. The chief executive officer firmly believes that the synergy between LCD televisions (its new product mix) and desktops will provide the company a competitive edge over others. Explain how the KM strategy can help the company in its new product positioning.

SELECT BIBLIOGRAPHY

- Argyris, C., *On Organizational Learning*, Blackwell, Cambridge, 1994.
- Bhattacharyya, D.K., 'Corporate Body Builder: The Emerging Role of HRD Professional', *Indian Journal of Training and Development*, April–June 1995.
- Bhattacharyya, D.K., 'Manpower Obsolescence: A Study in Indian Ordnance Factories', *International Congress on Economic Transition with Human Face*, Indian Industrial Relations Association, 3–6 September 1995, New Delhi.
- Chandler, M., 'Alternative Readings of the Competence Performance Relation', in M. Chandler and M. Chapman (eds), *Criteria for Competence*, Lawrence Erlbaum Associates, New Jersey, 1991.
- Davenport, T., S. Jarvenpaa, and M. Beers, 'Improving Knowledge Work Processes', *Sloan Management Review*, Vol. 37, Issue 4, 1996, pp. 53–66.
- Davenport, T.H. and L. Prusak, *Working Knowledge: How Organizations Manage What They Know*, Harvard Business School Press, Boston, 1997.
- Hariharan, Arun, 'Knowledge Management', *Journal of Knowledge Management Practice*, December 2002.
- Hauschild, S., T. Licht, and W. Stein, 'Creating a Knowledge Culture', *McKinsey Quarterly*, No. 4, 2001.
- Hayek, F.A., *The Sensory Order: An Inquiry into the Foundations of Theoretical Psychology*, Routledge and Kegan Paul, London, 1952.
- Kubr, M., *How to Use and to Select Consultants*, International Labour Office, Geneva, 1993.
- Mentzas, G., 'Research Directions for Knowledge Management in e-Government', *Issues and Experiences from KM in Business Settings*, 4th International Conference on KM in Electronic Government, Rhodes Island (Greece), 26–28 May 2003.
- Nonaka, I. and H. Takeuchi, *The Knowledge Creating Company*, Oxford University Press, New York, 1995.
- Prahalad, C.K. and G. Hamel, 'The Core Competence of the Corporation', *Harvard Business Review*, Vol. 68, Issue 3, 1990, pp. 79–91.
- Senge, P.M., *The Fifth Discipline: Art and Practice of the Learning Organization*, Doubleday Currency, New York, 1990.
- Snowden, D., 'Storytelling: An Old Skill in a New Context', *Business Information Review*, Vol. 16, Issue 1, 1999, pp. 30–7.
- Williamson, N.J., 'Knowledge Structures and the Internet', *Knowledge Organisation for Information Retrieva: Proceedings of the 6th International Study Conference on the Classification Research*, The Hague, FID, 1997, pp. 23–7.
- Zack, M.H., 'Developing a Knowledge Strategy', *California Management Review*, Vol. 41, Issue 3, 1999, pp. 125–45.

CASE STUDY

Re-engineering AIMA through Knowledge Management

The All India Management Association (AIMA) is an apex body for management professionals in the country. The educational activities of AIMA are the most important among its activities and contribute more than 60 per cent of the total revenue. An AICTE-approved postgraduate level programme, which is widely acknowledged, is offered through a flexible learning mode (through personal contact programmes) at 39 regular nodal centres at widely dispersed locations across the country. More than 60 per cent of AIMA's students are working executives. The rest are students, a good percentage of whom are, however, pursuing AIMA's programmes as dual qualification, that is, simultaneously with some other programme, in an attempt to develop multi-skills for gaining an edge over others in the competitive job market. Any flexible learning programme, by default, encounters several problems in terms of programme delivery, evaluation, and student services. This is a global phenomenon and AIMA is no exception to this. Increased focus on students' services reduces time for other developmental work, which is a continuous process in a competitive environment. Therefore, an initial listing of students' complaints was done, and it was observed that most of the problems centred around the following:

- Non-receipt of registration confirmation
- Non-receipt of identity cards
- Non-receipt of assignments
- Non-receipt of evaluated assignments
- Non-receipt of grade cards
- Error in grade cards
- Non-receipt of coursepacks
- Non-receipt of certificates
- Delay in receiving replies
- General anxiety
- Fear of missing important announcements

From the faculty and other programme managers' side as well, service deficiency is mostly considered as the outcome of information overload and insufficient technology-enabled services. AIMA employs professionals and distinguished academicians for running such programmes. It has no dearth of creative and innovative people, who are always bubbling with ideas. The education division employs 44 people with an average age of 35 years, which is almost the settlement age group from the employees' perspective. At this age, people do not normally leave their job and try to identify themselves with the organization. Though there were a few cases of separation in the past, exit interviews established the fact that they left AIMA more due to personal reasons than for career development elsewhere. The educational profile analysis of the faculty members indicates that except for two cases all are either graduates or professionally qualified (postgraduate level, such as PGDM/PGDITM). All members have considerable experience in teaching, research, and industry. This biographical sketch will help appreciate the profile of AIMA's human resources in the Centre for Management Education (CME) division. Using KM processes during the last seven months, AIMA has succeeded in eliminating students' (customers') problems to a great extent. At the same time, it has also succeeded in elevating its brand image, increasing enrolment (market share), ensuring quality services, reducing cycle time for response, reducing overall time requirement in major student-related services, and finally reducing the cost substantially (almost 25 per cent from the present level). Having such a track record with the KM process, AIMA believes in the philosophy of sharing this experience with others to help them emulate the experience. How did the KM process work?

The basic approach to the KM process in AIMA was initially to collect information from the students' (customers') interaction. Students' interaction with AIMA takes place in the following ways:

- Direct interactions at the information counter
- Direct interactions with programme directors and programme managers
- Direct interactions with the examination department
- Interactions at the nodal centres
- Interactions during seminars, conferences, and workshops
- Interactions through e-mail, letters, fax messages, and phone calls

In the pre-implementation phase of KM techniques, maximum efforts were made to record inputs from interactions, which were later analysed and categorized. A list of such response categories has already been illustrated earlier.

Such inputs from students were further integrated with the in-house perceptions through repeated brainstorming sessions.

In the second phase, analysis of the available systems was done in the context of students' requirements, matching them with AIMA's philosophies (vision), mission, goals, objectives, and strategies. While doing so, it followed the KM process, that is, identification of the nature and kind of knowledge required to improve the services.

Mapping of available knowledge in the defined job context was done following the competency mapping strategy as follows:

- Workforce skills analysis
- Job analysis
- Supply analysis
- Demand analysis
- Gap analysis
- Solution analysis

Workforce skills analysis This helped to describe the skills required to perform a function. This is a dynamic approach as it also considers the changes in the nature of work in AIMA-CME (Centre for Management Education).

Job analysis This focused on tasks, responsibilities, knowledge, and skill requirements, which are required for successful job performance.

Both the workforce skills analysis and job analysis were carried out from inputs collected from survey (through questionnaire responses), interviews with managers and employees, and benchmarking information with successful organizations. For technology intensive and machine-enabled jobs, skill set requirements and cycle time for jobs (as printed in the literatures) also contributed as critical input information.

Supply analysis This was performed considering workforce demographic (in terms of occupations, grades, structure, race, origin, gender, age, service experience, education, training, health status, retirement time, and other similar information) trends and the present workforce competencies.

This helped in understanding the existing workforce status.

Demand analysis This helped identify the workforce of the future in line with the vision, mission, objectives, goals, and strategies of AIMA-CME. Critical inputs from demand analysis contributed to the development of the competency model for the workforce of the future.

Gap analysis With the input reinforcers obtained from the other analyses, AIMA-CME undertook a gap analysis to understand the differences between the workforce of today and the workforce of the future. After such identification of differences, it planned to address those differences.

Solution analysis The gaps were addressed through solution analysis, taking into account both the ongoing as well as planned changes in the workforce. Solution analysis also weighed the different options to get the work done, considering either institutional or contractual employment. In this phase, new recruitment, restructuring, training and retraining, redeployment, and rightsizing were all done in the light of a new competency model.

While doing so, levels two and three of the Capability Maturity Model of Carnegie Mellon University were referred to structure the process in a scientific manner. The mapping process helped in the identification of the availability of relevant knowledge for the re-engineering processes. The knowledge or skills inventory was quantified along with the skill sets to understand the knowledge and skill gaps in the existing manpower. Such quantification was done using a five-point Likert-type scale with discretionary weights (based on experience) for skill or knowledge attributes. The initial skill or knowledge inventory with gaps in each knowledge group was as given in the following table:

Skill/Knowledge group	Nature	Measured gap in percentages
Technical	Related to specific concepts, methods, and tools	10

Skill/Knowledge group	Nature	Measured gap in percentages
Supervisory	Related to effective supervision of others	5
Interpersonal	Related to communication and effective interaction	10
Business	Related to general understanding of educational support and infrastructure	20

After the measurement of knowledge gaps for the re-engineered processes, in-house training plans were scheduled in identified areas such as the following:

- Process and systems familiarization
- Students' relationship management
- Basic computer operation skills
- Interpersonal and communication skills
- Problem-solving, analytical skills, etc.

As mentioned earlier, AIMA, being a knowledge-driven organization, has no dearth of in-house talent. Hence, searching for such talents and aligning with strategic plans were the requirements in the *capturing* phase of KM, and there was no need to outsource such knowledge requirements in the acquiring phase. Hence, *acquiring* of knowledge was addressed through the in-house knowledge bank. *Storing* of required knowledge reinforced the knowledge inventory, matching the requirement of the charted re-engineered processes. Some examples of re-engineered processes in comparison with old processes are illustrated in the following table:

Re-engineered process	Old process
Single-point student interactions at programme managers' level	Multi-point student interactions

Re-engineered process	Old process
Single-channel services to students with proper internal integration within the organization over the intranet	Multi-channel services to students
Centralized evaluation system at AIMA	Decentralized evaluation system
Administrative and managerial responsibilities to the faculty members	Administrative and managerial responsibilities to registrars
Charted cycle time for every operation and adhering to time schedules	Uncharted cycle time and flexibility resulting in delay in some major operations like delivery of course-packs, evaluation, and declaration of end-term results

In the subsequent process of KM, that is, *sharing* of knowledge, intranet services were strengthened through well-designed management information system, (MIS) making it possible for the employees to reinforce their knowledge on a continuous basis.

In the *application* phase, various aspects were monitored by the programme directors (faculty members) and divisional heads to ensure the following:

- People regularly retrieve knowledge.
- People use knowledge in all their actions or phases of activity.
- People become used to collecting information and data through MIS and intranet newswires.

The KM process cycle of AIMA-CME is a continuum for periodic retiring and renewing of knowledge through directed innovation and creativity. Learning from mistakes is encouraged, provided these are judgemental and not mala fide. To ensure optimal utilization of innovation and creativity, AIMA-CME adheres to the following principles:

- Innovate and become creative within the documented policy guidelines, that is, generate ideas in relation to current and future students' requirements, benchmark ideas with competitors, search for ideas that reduce cycle time and costs

- Try to generate focused and need-based ideas.
- Identify ideas through brainstorming.
- Align ideas with AIMA's vision, mission, and strategies.
- Make the ideas more participative through interaction among peer groups.
- Risk hedge ideas through benchmarking.
- Calculate return on investment (ROI) on implementation of ideas.
- Institutionalize ideas by proper documentation and implementation.

Problems and benefits of the KM-reinforced re-engineering process at AIMA could be tested in one complete operation cycle, that is, in the first quarter (April–June 2001).

Problems

The problems faced in this regard can be listed as follows:

- Deficiency in one workstation affected the whole service channel.
- Backup support was required as absenteeism rate was more than 20 per cent, which was mostly among female employees. This necessitated accommodating more manpower than the optimum level.
- There was wide variation in the efficiency level of employees.
- There was increased dependency on technology-enabled services.

- It required close monitoring and at times even employee snooping.
- There was increased job pressure.

Benefits

However, it had led to a number of benefits, which are as follows:

- Reduced students' complaints by 80 per cent
- Increased enrolment by 20 per cent
- Reduced response time to 24 hours (if queries were received within the working hours and on the working days)
- Reduced operational costs by 25 per cent
- Increased knowledge repositories, as indicated by knowledge inventory

Re-engineering of AIMA-CME through the KM process yielded better results in the first quarter. However, this requires longitudinal study to further authenticate the success. Another important aspect is that it is not possible to sign off at any stage of implementation of the KM process. Periodic retiring and renewal of knowledge is extremely important. For better accounting of the results, it is essential to practise the changed systems at least in three–four cycles. Replicating the practices of one organization may not guarantee success in another. Every organization has to adopt KM processes based on its own requirements.

Questions for Discussion

1. Read this case very carefully and illustrate a similar KM initiative in any organization of your choice.
2. Suggest the path forward for AIMA with higher efficiency of KM in future years.

Organizational Behaviour Research

LEARNING OBJECTIVES

After studying this chapter, the reader will be able to

- understand the various types of organizational behaviour (OB) research
- appreciate the ethical issues in OB research
- analyse the various quantitative and qualitative OB research tools and techniques
- recognize the various sources of data collection
- understand the concept of data analysis—reliability and validity
- explain hypotheses framing and testing
- describe the various statistical tools

CASE STUDY

Managing with Minimum Dissension

Workplace diversity issues, more particularly discriminatory employment practices in terms of gender, are now getting more attention from the corporate world. Although diversity issues encompass many areas, gender bias is still one of the more visible issues. A more recent case on workplace diversity is the one against Wal-Mart, in which the US government even went to the extent of appointing a diversity specialist to report on compliance from time to time. Rosabeth Moss Kanter, an American sociologist and professor of business administration in Harvard, in her famous book *Men and Women of the Corporation* (1977), elaborated on the underutilization of women and minorities in businesses, managing change, empowering individuals within the organization, and bringing about synergy between organizations. Her other landmark publication is *When Giants Learn to Dance* (1989). Kanter suggests management 'should be opened up to promotion from a wider range of candidates, including women and hitherto powerless individuals like clerical workers. Changes in certain areas, such as systems of appraisal and career development, would be needed to achieve this.' For this, she suggested that intermediate jobs should be created by the organization.

Empowerment leads to a flatter hierarchy and decentralized authority and develops autonomous work groups. With workplace diversity, it is possible to best assure a culture that is non-discriminatory, motivating, and self-satisfying.

Assume you need to study the workplace diversity scenario in a particular organization. Elaborate on how you will be framing your study plan.

INTRODUCTION

In the study of organizational behaviour (OB), it is essential to study the psychology of people as well as their sociology. The former helps understand their personal behaviour (microphenomena) and the latter their behaviour in aggregates—when they work together in a group in an organization (macrophenomena). Research issues in each of these areas do have some inherent set of theoretical precepts in social science, which are cross-disciplinary and complex. To understand the micro–macro interplay better, organizational research needs to be performed regularly, making use of these complex analyses. Experimental and correlational methods, which are typically used in OB research, may not always be right because of epistemological considerations. This aspect encompasses OB studies to an extent where one clearly finds differences in views in many areas of thought. All the chapters of this book have shown such differences in precepts and theories, stretching the challenge to a holistic understanding through research. This often calls for adopting complex computational methods like simulation, for OB research. The problem in non-linearity in behavioural issues again challenges this assumption. The problem of replication (because of ambiguity, gaps, and erroneous description), the generalizability of research outcomes, the problem of prediction, the problem of data availability, and the problem of validation (confirmation of functional equivalence) are some of the challenges faced during OB research.

Nevertheless, students at this stage need to understand the basic research process of OB studies by going through the elementary statistical tools and restrict their focus to using those tools that may fit in their specific research requirements.

BASIC CONCEPTS

Research is the discovery and description of regularities in the universe, in the world, and in living organisms. Research helps in the development of theories to explain these regularities. OB research helps study the behavioural context of individuals and groups in organizations. Research in OB requires understanding of the variables. A variable is any attribute or property in which organisms vary and it must have at least two values.

> Organizational behaviour research helps study the behavioural context of individuals and groups in organizations.

Variance

The common goals of OB research are to understand behavioural variability, that is, the why and how of behaviour—how behaviour varies across situations, how it differs among individuals, and how it changes over time. It analyses the behaviour, using descriptive statistics, and summarizes and describes the behaviour of subjects using inferential statistics. Such analysis helps understand how likely are the findings due to random extraneous factors and how representative are the findings for the population from which the samples are drawn. Variance studies are carried out measuring the dispersion, range, and standard deviation. Total variance is the sum of systematic variance and error variance. Systematic variance occurs when the sum of total variability relates in a systematic fashion to variability in another variable. Error variance is that portion of the total variance that is unrelated to the variables under investigation in a study. It is computed by dividing systematic variance by total variance.

Since understanding variance is the most important priority in OB research, it needs to be studied in greater detail. The following steps are used to calculate variance:

- Calculate the mean of the terms.
- Subtract the mean from each subject's score to obtain the deviation score.
- Square each participant's deviation score.
- Add the squared deviation scores.
- Add the squares.
- Divide the number of scores minus one.

Another goal of OB research is to study the internal validity, which establishes the consistency of the results. A suitable experimental design helps minimize extraneous variation and makes the research internally valid. Experimental design measures variation both between and within the samples. Different scales of measurement are used in OB research. Moreover, it is essential to distinguish between experimental and non-experimental research and recognize the variables in the design. Experimental and non-experimental researches are distinguished by the degree of control that the researcher has over the subjects and conditions in the study. An experiment is an investigation in which the researcher manipulates at least one variable.

While carrying out research in OB areas, investigators want to make sure that they choose reliable and valid measures. They like to do the same thing to evaluate published studies, a central component of which is whether the investigators used measures with good reliability and validity. Research in the OB context involves many important decisions that affect people's lives, such as studying whether the people are really depressed or not, whether the organizational structure of the company influences worker morale, or whether work culture is leading to employees' dissatisfaction. It is important to have reliable and valid measures to answer each of these questions. Hence, understanding reliability and validity is very important for OB research. Moreover, some of the behavioural issues in organizations cannot be seen or observed but there is a belief that they exist, for example, morale. To support this belief, reliable and valid measures are used in such cases.

ETHICAL ISSUES IN ORGANIZATIONAL BEHAVIOUR RESEARCH

When employee engagement combines with the moral treatment of employees, it denotes an ethical activity. The International Labour Organization (ILO) (2004) provides for fundamental rights of employees to liberty and safety at the workplace, including freedom of association, right to organize, collective bargaining, abolition of forced labour, and equality of opportunity and treatment. Unethical OB practices do not further the interests of the employee group but help the interests

Ethical issues in OB are either macroissues dealing with issues in the OB system or microissues dealing with the assessment of individual practices.

of the shareholders alone. In such organizations, employees are dealt with strategically. The ethical issues on OB research have started gaining importance with decrease in regulation in the workplace and the dwindling power of trade unions. As a result, employees and the employment relationship have now become a high priority. Ethical issues in OB have two dimensions—macrolevel and microlevel. The ethical issues of the OB system are considered at the macrolevel. Here, all strategic OB initiatives and their implications on practices at the organizational level are reviewed. At the microlevel, ethical assessment of individual practices ranging from interpersonal to group behavioural issues is made.

Owing to the ethical issues in OB, public sensitivity to the ethics of human experimentation is also high. All research involving human subjects (even if only interviews or questionnaires are used) falls within the jurisdiction of ethics. To ensure that ethical principles are not violated while doing research on OB, most organizations develop their own ethical guidelines. Some of the important points that are commonly covered in the ethical guidelines for OB research are as follows:

Informed consent Employees can be selected as research subjects only if they give their consent for participation in the research. To help the employees volunteer for participation, it is necessary to accurately provide all possible information, so that they can make an informed choice.

Maintenance of confidentiality Employees must have the right to privacy and confidentiality. Hence, all OB research must ensure that individuals are not identified in the reports.

Some organizations also form an ethics committee to review the compliance of ethical guidelines. For research on OB in general (other than research at specific organizational levels) as well, it is desirable to comply with the aforementioned two points, which by default guard against problems concerning ethical aspects.

TOOLS AND TECHNIQUES OF ORGANIZATIONAL BEHAVIOUR RESEARCH

In order to carry out OB research, it is essential to understand the various tools and techniques of data collection and its analysis. OB research can either be quantitative or qualitative. Quantitative research is descriptive and requires the collection of numerical data to explain, predict, and control phenomena. Hence, statistical knowledge is imperative for analysis of quantitative OB research. Correlational, causal–comparative, and experimental researches fall under this category. Quantitative data collection methods require random sampling and structured data collection instruments to fit the samples into predetermined response categories and produce results for subsequent summarization, comparison, and generalization. Moreover, framing and testing of hypotheses is essential for the correct estimation of the phenomenon of interest. Hypotheses are pre-assumptions and are derived from existing theories on the research premises. Based on the research issue, samples can be randomly subjected to different treatments to draw inferences. Where that is not possible, the researcher may collect data on sample characteristics and other situational variables and statistically analyse the influence on the dependent, outcome, or variable. The researcher should employ probability sampling to select the samples if the observations on the samples are to hold good for the population (for the whole organization).

Typical quantitative data gathering strategies include the following:

- Conducting experimental or clinical trials
- Observing and recording events
- Obtaining relevant data from enterprise resource planning (ERP)/management information system (MIS)
- Administering surveys with structured closed-ended questions

Qualitative research includes historical research. It collects narrative data to understand phenomena by verbal synthesis. Qualitative data collection methods play an important role in impact evaluation and assess changes in the employees' perceptions. These methods can also be used to improve the quality of quantitative evaluations by generating hypothesis and clarifying quantitative evaluation results. Qualitative research has the following attributes:

- It is open-ended and less structured. Being flexible, researchers can change the data collection strategy to suit the research purpose.
- It is primarily based on interactive interviews. Thus, to clarify a concept and ensure the reliability of data, the same respondents may be interviewed several times for a particular issue.
- It helps in checking the authenticity of the evaluations, as the researcher, being flexible, can make use of multiple data collection methods. Thus, it enhances the credibility of the evaluations.
- Qualitative research findings are not generalizable. Hence, each research produces unique results, which the researcher makes use of to understand a general pattern.

Irrespective of the data collection methods, qualitative research is time-consuming. The researcher needs to make use of potential sources—projective instruments (sketches, audiotapes, and photographs) and field notes conforming to ethical principles of research.

Types of Quantitative Research

There are various types of quantitative research. It is for the organization to select a particular type keeping in view its specific requirements.

Descriptive Descriptive research involves data collection and testing of hypothesis to determine and report the current phenomena. For example, to measure the employee satisfaction level, descriptive research requires the collection of employee responses on a structured questionnaire and analysis of the hypothesis to draw inferences on the degree of satisfaction or dissatisfaction.

Correlational Correlational research determines the degree of relationship using a correlation coefficient (which varies between 0.00 and 1.00) between two or more quantifiable variables. However, it should not be construed as a tool to establish cause–effect relationship, which researchers often try to infer through correlational research. For example, a researcher may be interested to measure the correlation coefficient between the value of incentives and the performance output of employees.

Causal–Comparative Causal–Comparative research establishes the cause–effect relationship, comparing two relationships. However, in this type of research it is not possible to manipulate the cause. For example, if one wants to establish a cause–effect relationship between the number of women employees and absenteeism, it is not possible to manipulate the gender (i.e., cause), but one can certainly manipulate the effect (absenteeism) by extending some organizational support to women employees (e.g., crèche and flexible working hours).

Experimental In experimental research, the cause–effect relationship is established by comparison, and in this case, the cause can also be manipulated. Here, cause, that is, the independent variable, makes the difference and effect is dependent on the cause. In the earlier example, if the organization decides to change its policy on the recruitment of female employees (cause) to contain absenteeism (effect variable), then it is known as experimental research.

Conducting Quantitative Organizational Behaviour Research

Before conducting a quantitative OB research, it is essential to understand the following aspects.

Drawing Research Plans

A research plan should be developed before starting the research. This becomes the blueprint for the research and helps in giving guidance to and evaluating the research. The following are the components of a specific research plan:

Introduction This part introduces the problem, developing a suitable statement. To do this, it is important to focus on the relevance of the problem (i.e., selling the problem). A review of existing literature is also done to establish the research premise and finally the introduction part ends with the statement of a hypothesis.

Method This part explains how the research is carried out by detailing the subjects (samples), instruments, and research design.

Data analysis This part mentions how the collected responses, observations, and so on are analysed using various statistical tools and techniques.

Time schedule Time schedule sets the deadline for research completion and also lists the various activities involved in various phases of the research. This ensures control at different stages, particularly in organizations. As most of the OB-related researches are intended to adopt strategic decisions, time-bound research is very essential.

Budget For OB research in organizations, it is important to draw a tentative budget, detailing all the expenses involved, and obtain approval to ensure that research pursuits do not get affected at any stage because of paucity of fund allocation. For academic research, such budgets may be necessary in cases where funding agencies are prepared to provide resources for the research.

There are three major ways to collect quantitative data:

- Administrate a standardized instrument.
- Administrate a self-developed instrument.
- Record naturally available data.

Standardized instruments may be some existing validated instruments, such as FIRO-B, Belbin's team role self-perception inventory, and change management survey of Rosabeth Moss Kanter. Self-developed instruments are designed by researchers to address research problems, whereas naturally available data may be performance records, absenteeism data, and so on.

Exhibit 21.1 discusses whether the developments in OB research methods are all truly progressive.

EXHIBIT 21.1   Hypotheses Creation Vs Hypotheses Testing: Are All Developments in Organizational Behaviour Research Methods Truly Progressive?

Organizational behaviour research has come a long way. During the past six decades, considerable developments have been made in OB research through the inclusion of various research methods, both quantitative and qualitative, and also by adding various subjects related to social sciences under its purview. However, these developments have led to a paradigm shift in the way research is done in OB. Keeping in mind the way the branch of study has grown over the years, it is imperative that research must make room for new methods for a keener analysis of topics. However, one question that plagues researchers is whether anything has gone amiss during this shift in research methods.

Initial research in OB took hypotheses creation or generation into consideration. Gradually, this was replaced by hypotheses testing. Though both methods are concerned with hypothesizing, the differences in the two are fundamental and cannot be bridged.

Early research in OB meant spending a considerable time *on the field*. This gave researchers the opportunity to observe actively. After having gained substantial grounding into the research problem, the researcher was able to apply rigorous methods. This process ensured the creation of hypotheses, meaning that it came out of active observation and field as well as clinical research. Moreover, research largely depended on ideas, and in most cases, these ideas got translated into new questions and therefore hypotheses.

Contemporary research, on the other hand, depends more on passive observation. Hypothesis testing refers to a statistical procedure that involves using data from a sample to judge the credibility of a hypothesis regarding the population (Gravetter and Forzano 2009). There is more emphasis on the accuracy of calculations and precision of analysis. However, given that OB research is becoming more and more complex by the day, focusing only on the precision of measurements and analyses may not suffice. What is more important is bringing in new ideas, mapping how extensive the variables in the research are, and not losing track of the phenomenon.

Sources: Gravetter, F. and L. Forzano, *Research Methods for the Behavioural Sciences*, Wadsworth Cengage Learning, California, 2009; Lundberg, C., 'Hypothesis Creation in Organizational Behaviour Research', *Academy of Management Review*, April 1976, pp. 5–12.

Practitioner Speak 21.1

Smaller, More-homogeneous Research Groups Are More Productive per Researcher

Research organizations like to increase team size to bring in new ideas, but a study of 549 research groups shows that in teams consisting of people from multiple disciplines, the published output per researcher in 13-person groups was 42% lower, on average, than in five-person groups, says a team led by Jonathan N. Cummings of Duke University. The greater the heterogeneity in disciplines, the less effective it was for groups to increase their size. In interviews, team members in large, heterogeneous groups complained of lack of familiarity and personal chemistry with colleagues and problems in communication, the researchers say.

Read this insightful blog posted by O'Connell on *HBR Blog Network* by accessing the following link: http://blogs.hbr.org/2013/07/smaller-more-homogeneous-resea/.

Testing Reliability and Validity

The two most important aspects of precision in OB research are reliability and validity. Reliability refers to the reproducibility of a measurement. It is quantified by taking several measurements on the same subjects. Poor reliability questions the level of precision of measurement and reduces the ability to track changes in subsequent measurements in future studies. Validity refers to the agreement between the value of a measurement and its true value. It is quantified by comparing the measurements with values that are as close to the true values as possible. Poor validity also degrades the precision of a single measurement, and reduces the researcher's ability to characterize relationships between variables in descriptive studies.

The concepts of reliability and validity are related. However, because it is difficult to mathematically put these two concepts together, most of the researchers study these concepts separately. Whatever may be the ways for data collection, it is always desirable to test their validity and reliability. Validity means the degree to which a test measures what it intends to measure and thus, allows appropriate interpretation of results. A test design is measured keeping in view the specific purposes. Therefore, validity can be evaluated only in terms of the test purpose. For example, one may be interested in knowing how the measures on the samples hold good on the population on a specific issue, how the scores predict the success in a future task, or how a particular instrument measures a characteristic. These are examples of content, predictive, and construct validity. In addition, there is also concurrent validity. All these are explained with the following specific examples:

Content validity Content validity is the degree to which a test measures an intended content area. It involves two aspects—item validity and sampling validity. Item validity determines whether the test items represent measurement in the intended content area, and sampling validity determines how well the tests sample the total content area. Content validity is determined by expert judgement, whereas sampling validity is judged in the context of statistical tests. To illustrate, assume that a structured, close-ended questionnaire has been developed for measuring employees' satisfaction levels. The item validity test will establish how far the questionnaire items are valid for measuring the employees' satisfaction levels. In other words, it will establish whether the questionnaire items are valid or not for understanding employees' satisfaction. Similarly, sampling validity will help understand whether the samples drawn correctly represent the population or whether there is any sampling error.

> Two very important aspects of precision in OB research are reliability and validity. Reliability refers to the reproducibility of a measurement. Validity, on the other hand, refers to the agreement between the value of a measurement and its true value.

Construct validity Construct validity measures the degree of a test in the context of a hypothetical construct. To process a test of construct validity, one needs to carry out a series of independent studies to establish credibility. The process is not so simple. It requires a thorough understanding of the various statistical tests and matching the tests in the context of hypothesis constructs. Suppose one wants to determine whether samples are indifferent to incentive schemes, then a hypothesis is formed accordingly and the degree of concordance is measured using Kendall's test of concordance. Similarly, measuring the degree of indifference in the context of analysis of variance (ANOVA) measures the degree with reference to biographical characteristics of samples.

Concurrent validity   It measures simultaneous validity to understand how the degree of a test score relates to another. The other test scores may be already established, they may be the scores obtained on tests administered simultaneously, or they may be an existing valid criterion. It is ascertained by determining a validity coefficient. When the validity coefficient is high, the test is said to have good concurrent validity. For example, one may be interested in measuring how a particular training programme enhances the technical as well as the human relations skills. Technical skill enhancement gets translated to increased performance on jobs, whereas human relations skill develops better interpersonal relations. In this situation, both dependent variables are simultaneously measured, that is, technical skill enhancement and change in interpersonal relations, in relation to training.

Predictive validity   Predictive validity indicates the degree of a test measure in predicting the success of individual samples in a future situation. It is determined with a validity coefficient by establishing the relationship between the test scores and some measures of success in some situations of interest in the future. When the validity coefficient is high, predictive validity is said to be good. For example, one may assess the employees' general capability to learn to predict their on-the-job performance success.

Reliability   It measures the dependability or trustworthiness of an assessment instrument. It is the degree to which a test consistently measures whatever it intends to measure. Reliability is expressed numerically in terms of a coefficient. A high coefficient indicates high reliability, which, in turn, indicates minimum error variance. Reliability is easier to measure than validity. Test-retest, equivalent forms, and split-half reliability are all determined through correlation. Test-retest reliability is the degree to which scores are consistent over time. Reliability can also be expressed in terms of the standard error of measurement (degree of variance), which is an estimate of how often one can expect errors of a given size. A small standard error of measurement indicates high reliability and a large standard error of measurement indicates low reliability. How employees' performance scores are affected by the presence of a human resource (HR) audit team, which do not relate to the characteristic, is measured by test-retest reliability. Similarly, in a multi-rating system, how the different raters score employees' performance is determined by scorer reliability or inter-rater reliability. Finally, how different parts of a single assessment instrument lead to similar conclusions about employees' achievement is measured by internal consistency reliability.

FRAMING OF HYPOTHESES

Hypotheses are assumptions that have to be validated through some testing measures. Proving or disproving a hypothesis requires a formal statement on research assumptions and the use of appropriate statistical tools. There may be a number of null or alternative hypotheses, depending on the research objectives. This can be comprehended better with the help of an illustration. A particular scholar would like to study the determinants of savings behaviour in India. In this case, the formal statement of hypothesis may read as follows: Savings in India is functionally related to the growth rate of income, per capita gross domestic product (GDP), and the expected rate of inflation. After developing the hypothesis, the

> Hypotheses are assumptions that are to be validated through some testing measures.

researcher has to first define the variables, (growth rate of income, per capita GDP, and expected rate of inflation) and then specify the suitable forms of estimation by developing suitable equations.

When doing research in OB areas, the testing of hypothesis plays a very crucial role. To illustrate, a manager may frame a hypothesis like 'increased productivity raises employees' expectation to get higher incentives'. There may be two possibilities:

- Nothing happened—This is called the null hypothesis (H_0).
- Something happened—This is called the alternative hypothesis (H_i).

When a statistical hypothesis is tested, one tries to see if something happened and compares it against the possibility that nothing happened.

To elaborate, null hypothesis (H_0) means *null = nothing = zero*, that is, no effect was observed. In other words, it was not found that increased productivity and employees' expectation to get higher incentives are related.

Alternative hypothesis means *alternative = something = more than zero*, that is, an effect was observed. It was found that increased productivity and employees' expectation to get higher incentives are related.

In hypothesis testing, the logic is to think backward—one tries to disprove the null hypothesis, which means one tries to disprove that nothing has happened. If one disproves that nothing has happened, then it can be concluded that something has happened.

DATA TYPES AND PREPARATION FOR ANALYSIS

> There are four types of measurement scales—nominal, ordinal, interval, and ratio.

Different kinds of data results represent different scales of measurement. There are four types of measurement scales, namely nominal, ordinal, interval, and ratio. It is important to know the type of scale or data one collects for research and the statistical method that is appropriate for the analysis of that data. Table 21.1 explains the typical usage of the various types of measurement scales and the corresponding statistics used for them. However, for a detailed discussion, it is recommended that readers refer to the book *Human*

Table 21.1 Types of measurement

Type	Basic empirical operations	Typical usage	Typical statistics	
			Descriptive	Inferential
Nominal	Determination of equality	Classification of male–female, smoker–non-smoker, team	Percentage mode	Chi-square, binomial
Ordinal	Determination of greater or less	Rankings: preference data, market position, attitude measurement, many other psychological measures, etc.	Median	Rank-order correlation
Interval	Determination of equality of intervals	Index numbers, attitude measurement	Mean, range, standard deviation	Product moment correlation, T-test, factor analysis
Ratio	Determination of equality of ratios	Sales, units produced, number of customers, costs, age, etc.	Geometric mean	Coefficient of variation

Table 21.2 Scaling for univariate data

Measurement level	Statistical technique
Nominal	Frequencies, proportions
Ordinal	Median, mode, range
Preference	Ranking
Interval scale	Mean, standard deviation, Gini

Table 21.3 Scaling for bivariate data

Variables	Measurement scale	Distinction between dependent and independent variables	Statistical technique
X Y	Interval interval	No distinction	Pearson's correlation
X Y	Ordinal ordinal	No distinction	Kendall's Tau Spearman's Rho Wilcoxon Signed Test Mann–Whitney test
X Y	Nominal nominal	No distinction	Chi-square lambda test
X Y	Interval interval	Distinction	Simple linear regression
X Y	Nominal interval	Distinction: Y is dependent	Regression with dummy variables; one-one way ANOVA

Resource Research Methods (Bhattacharyya 2007) published by the Oxford University Press, New Delhi. Similarly, depending on the nature of data (bivariate, univariate, and multivariate), the various statistical techniques used will vary, as explained in Tables 21.2 and 21.3.

SOME UNCOMMON DATA COLLECTION METHODS FOR ORGANIZATIONAL BEHAVIOUR RESEARCH

This part deliberates on those data collection methods that are very unconventional, yet may be necessary for effective OB research.

Unobtrusive data collection This type of data is collected from the existing database of the organization. It is called unobtrusive because one is not required to ask any question or interview samples to collect such data. The following are some examples of such a type of data collection:

- Absenteeism, lateness, and other behaviour records
- Turnover, accident, and grievance statistics
- Performance information such as productivity, costs, reworks, and complaints
- Past survey information
- Letters and memos

Unobtrusive data has both advantages and disadvantages. An advantage is that, in this case, samples cannot change their answer, as answers are inbuilt with the data collected from the

Table 21.4   Sources of unconventional data collection methods

Recorded data	Observable data	Opportunistic data
Annual report and accounts	Pricing and price lists	Data collected by interacting with the suppliers of the competitors
Press releases	Advertisements	Trade shows of the competitors
Published articles	Sales promotions	Sales force meetings of the competitors
Analysts reports		Seminars and Conferences organized by the competitors
Regulatory reports	Published tender documents	Recruitment of ex-employees of competitors
Government reports		Discussion with shared distributors
Presentations/Speeches	Patent Applications	Social contacts with competitors

aforementioned sources. A disadvantage may be the inability of the researcher to collate the information due to ignorance. Table 21.4 lists other possible sources of unconventional data collection methods.

Depending on the nature of OB research, the researcher may select the possible unconventional sources of data collection.

Once the survey is over, the OB researcher has to organize and summarize the data, and the best way to do that is by constructing a frequency distribution table. The number of times a particular value of a variable occurs is recorded.

PROCESSING AND CODING OF DATA

For scoring, the researcher consistently and accurately measures the administered instruments, following the same procedures and criteria followed in each subject's test. Except for objective-type items, there must be more than one scorer for reliability check. For objective-type items, the correctness and accuracy of the score must be ensured. Coding requires developing a system of data identification for subsequent analysis. This is important when the researcher is required to manage a large number of subjects and variables. The entire data of variables and subjects is converted into numerical values and then entered into a selected database programme for subsequent manipulations. Coding is essentially required for the analysis of data, making use of computerized research packages, as software protocols may not permit long entries. Various statistical packages such as SPSS, SAS, WINKS, and STATISCA 7 can be used for OB research.

ANALYSIS AND INTERPRETATION OF DATA

After the collection of data, it is important for the researcher to understand how to make use of the collected data. In analysing data involving a single variable, the univariate analysis technique is used. This analysis focuses on the level (average) and distribution (variance) of the phenomena. Bivariate analysis, on the contrary, helps examine the relationship between two or more variables. Statistical tools such as chi-square, correlation, rank correlation, regression analysis, and ANOVA are used for bivariate analysis. Table 20.2 shows the scaling for univariate data and Table 20.3 shows that for bivariate data. Multivariate analysis, on the other hand, examines simultaneous relationships among three or more phenomena. Multiple linear regression, non-linear regression, and discriminant analysis are some of the tools used for multivariate analysis. At fairly advanced levels, multivariate analysis makes use of factor analysis, cluster analysis, canonical analysis, conjoint measurement, and latent structure analysis. The nature of data and the importance of statistical analysis are reiterated here to simplify the understanding of these concepts.

Statistical theories and methods are used for analysing quantitative data. This helps study and compare the sources of variance of phenomena, based on which the researcher decides to accept or reject hypothetical relations between the phenomena. In the process, it is possible to draw reliable inferences from any empirical research study. Similar to any other research, in HR research too, the researcher can make use of different statistical tools, depending on the nature of data and information compilation.

Univariate analysis Analysis of variation of single variable

$$R = f(X)$$ Organizational awareness (OA)

Bivariate analysis Analysis of variation of two variables

$$R = f(X, Y)$$ Age OA

Multivariate analysis Simultaneous analysis of more than two variables or multiple measurements on each individual or object under investigation

$$R = f(X, Y, Z \dots n)$$

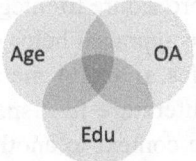

Use of multivariate statistics in OB research is very important. This can be illustrated with the use of the following equation:

$R = f(a, b, c, d, \dots, n, \dots, t, \dots, x, y, z)$
R = Response
a, b, c, d = Aspects of the stimulus
n = Number of times the stimulus is applied to the organism
x, y, z = Internal conditions of set, motivation, and so on

Research Discussion

In this part, researchers detail their interpretations of the results and generalize the implications through discussions. When the interpretation of results supports the hypotheses, it is quite simple to discuss. However, when the results do not support the hypotheses, researchers need to justify it detailing the reasons for such variation. When null hypotheses are accepted, it indicates that the research hypotheses are supported but not necessarily proven. Conversely, when null hypotheses are rejected, research hypotheses are not supported. It, however, does not make the research wrong, as the null hypotheses may be true. Hypotheses may not be framed in all HR research; it may not be possible as well. However, some apparent relationships may exist. It is the researcher's duty to analyse such relationships and present the results, without bothering about the reasons as to why hypotheses were not framed earlier.

It is also important for a researcher to understand that when the results are statistically significant by default, it does not establish a hypothesis. Statistical significance largely depends on the sample size. When the sample size is very large, even a small correlation coefficient may be construed as significant but it may not be considered. Similarly, with a large sample size, the *t* ratio tends to increase even with a small mean difference. Small samples always increase the chance of rejecting null hypotheses, whereas it may not be so with large samples. Large samples, in fact, help better determine some important relationships.

While interpreting results, it is also important to assess how far the results can be replicated. Replication means that it is possible to repeat the study. Validity and reliability are established when the same results are obtained in subsequent studies. Replication may be essential when some unusual relationship is found in the course of research.

Conclusions and recommendations emanate from the detailed analysis of results, that is, from the research findings. Summarizing the results, the researcher draws conclusions. Recommendations are given in a chronological form, addressing the research objectives, whereas both the conclusion and recommendations should follow logic and must have some practical significance.

META-ANALYSIS

Meta-analysis is a statistical procedure to integrate the results of several combinable independent studies. Such an objective appraisal helps explain the heterogeneity between the results of combinable independent studies, if any. A meta-analysis is a quantitative approach to reviewing research literature in a specific area. In OB research, many factors may vary from one context to another, thus making it difficult to design definitive experiments to determine whether a given approach affects a given behaviour. A meta-analysis combines a number of studies (usually conducted by a number of different researchers in a variety of contexts) to quantify the effect of a given approach on a given outcome. By broadening the pool of data to include many different contexts (and increasing sample sizes), a better quantitative estimate can be made of how much a given organizational practice affects the employees.

> Meta-analysis is a statistical procedure to integrate the results of several combinable independent studies.

Most of the literature on meta-analysis concludes that there are three generic steps for conducting any research making use of meta-analysis, which are as follows:

- Clarify the independent variables and outcome variables of interest.
- Perform quantitative research on the independent and outcome variables of interest.
- Compile quantitative information from each selected study to indicate the effect of the independent variable on the outcome variable.

The effect size is the difference between the means of the outcome scores of the experimental and control groups divided by the standard deviation of the scores. A positive effect on the outcome variable is indicated by a mean effect size across the studies that is greater than zero.

Similar to any other research, for OB research as well, use of meta-analysis involves formulating the problem, collecting and analysing the data, and reporting the results.

The researcher is required to write a detailed research report, clearly stating the objectives, hypotheses, and methodology. A standardized record form is needed for data collection. It is better if two independent observers extract the data so as to avoid errors. At this stage, the quality of the studies may be rated according to one of several specially designed scales. Blinding observers to the names of the authors and their institutions, names of the journals, sources of funding, and acknowledgements can lead to more consistent scores.

Individual results have to be expressed in a standardized format to allow for comparison between studies. If the end point is continuous, the mean difference between the treatment and control groups is used. The size of a difference, however, is influenced by the underlying population value. Thus, the differences are presented in units of standard deviation. If the end point is binary—for example, disease versus no disease, or dead versus alive—then the odds ratios or relative risks are often calculated. The odds ratio has convenient mathematical properties, which allow for ease in combining data and testing the overall effect for significance. Absolute measures, such as the absolute risk reduction or the number of patients to be treated to prevent one event, are more helpful when applying results.

The last step consists of calculating the overall effect by combining the data. A simple arithmetic average of the results from all the trials would give misleading results. The results from small studies are more subject to the play of chance and should, therefore, be given less weight. The methods used for meta-analysis use a weighted average of the results, in which larger trials have more influence than the smaller ones. The statistical techniques to do this can be broadly classified into two models, which differ in the way the variability of the results between the studies is treated. The *fixed effects* model considers, often unreasonably, that this variability is exclusively due to random variation. Therefore, if all the studies were infinitely large, they would give identical results. The *random effects* model assumes a different underlying effect for each study and considers this as an additional source of variation, which leads to somewhat wider confidence intervals than the fixed effects model. Effects are randomly distributed, and the central point of this distribution is the focus of the combined effect estimate. Although neither model can be said to be correct, a substantial difference in the combined effect calculated by the fixed and random effects models will be seen only if the studies are markedly heterogeneous.

Practitioner Speak 21.2

Can You Get Better at Research?

It's pretty widely accepted that people's innate intelligence doesn't change much. Youth, health, and a positive environment can help people make better use of their brains, but they can't do much to make the brains significantly better—at least on the weight of the evidence so far.

Read this insightful blog posted by Knott on *HBR Blog Network* by accessing the following link: http://blogs.hbr.org/2012/05/can-you-get-better-at-research/.

The value of an empirical OB research can be enhanced when it is possible for subsequent researchers to generalize the findings. Generalizations require replication and this can be best done through meta-analyses. Glass (1976) first coined the term meta-analysis to mean the analysis of analyses. Subsequently, researchers such as Jack Hunter and Frank Schmidt (Hunter 1979; Hunter and Schmidt 1990) enriched the research literature by synthesizing research findings across studies. In OB, meta-analysis is used for quantitative synthesis of research findings.

QUALITATIVE RESEARCH CONSIDERATIONS

Sources of data collection for qualitative research include formal and informal focus groups, round tables, feedback forms, seminars, usability studies, and so on. It involves a small number of samples. These meetings can include internal participants, such as sales, management, customer service, and engineering, or external participants, such as analyst, press, existing customers, prospects, and governing committees. Qualitative research is a study involving a small number of individuals and hence, in-depth one-on-one interviews are also used. Though the primary tool in qualitative research is the focus group, it can also include modern variations on the focus group idea, such as online focus groups and teleconferences. Finally, qualitative researchers can use one-on-one interviews to delve deep into various topics.

Focus group   These are used for qualitative OB research. A focus group is a round table discussion session. It usually consists of six to ten individuals who come to a central location to sit around a table to answer questions from a trained moderator or facilitator. Here, the respondents are the participants. Focus groups are usually done in pairs, in a series. For example, a study could consist of two or more groups in one unit of an organization followed by another two in some other unit of the organization. Research conclusions made using multiple focus groups are more relevant.

> Sources of data collection for qualitative research include formal and informal focus groups, round tables, feedback forms, seminars, usability studies, and so on. It involves a small number of samples.

One-on-one interviews   Instead of bringing 10 people together in a two-hour focus group, researchers can spend about 20 minutes with each respondent individually interviewing them. Participants are likely to provide more inputs during in-depth interviews than in the group environment. The interviews also provide individual comments uninfluenced by group reactions. Such interviews can also be conducted over the phone.

> Interviews are mainly of two types—structured, which are conducted with a set of specific questions, and unstructured, which are not controlled.

Observational research In this method, rather than verbally interacting with respondents, researchers simply observe how employees make decisions about strategic issues or perform some actions. This often yields better results, as researchers can draw conclusions purely based on their observations. Observational research is an important source of qualitative data collection. The major advantages of observational research are that it guards against inadvertent omission, helps in getting a comprehensive view, and helps in leveraging the knowledge and experience of the researcher.

Document review The researcher here looks for contents to authenticate his/her research. This method is often used to supplement observational fieldwork through documentary evidences. An OB researcher may be interested in performance records, attendance records, HR reports, various compliance reports pertaining to rules and regulations, and so on. These are the important sources for information collection and compilation.

Interview techniques Two main types of interviews—structured and unstructured—are used for conducting research. The unstructured or informal interview is mostly conducted on a pilot basis for framing a hypothesis. However, this type of informal interview may also be used for certain types of research, like understanding the quick response of employees on a changed HR policy (change in attendance system, transfer, relocation, etc.). This is done primarily where there is a constraint of time or money, or if there is a need to have a quick feel of the people working in the organization. Unstructured interviews are not controlled. Certain pre-assumptions to map the reactions of people on certain issues guide the researcher here. The major problem, here, is to consolidate the responses of the respondents. However, at times, it helps in critical management decisions. Focus group interview is an example. Whatever may be the purpose, unstructured interview inputs ultimately help in framing the structured interview questionnaire and also in refining the thought process.

Structured interview is conducted with a set of specific questions. In most of the quantitative research, the primary source for collecting information is this type of interview. The process requires administering a structured set of question items in an orderly manner to samples and then drawing the necessary inferences as per the hypotheses. During the interview process, respondents are asked questions of a uniform type and their responses are recorded in the questionnaire itself for subsequent quantitative analysis. Since respondents do not have the flexibility to add, remove, or alter questionnaire items, the interview process becomes structured.

In-depth Interviews

In-depth interviews are face-to-face encounters. Normally, for this type of interview, the interviewer uses an unstructured or semi-structured approach to unearth innate sentiments, emotions, and attitudes. In general, respondents often try to evade sensitive issues when they are required to give direct answers against structured questionnaire items. At times, their responses may even be misleading. The success of this type of interview largely depends on the skills of the interviewer, specifically on psychometric tools and psychoanalysis.

Telephone Interviews

Telephone interviews are mostly conducted in marketing research. They may be done to assess the success or failure of a new product launch, to map the customers' satisfaction level, or for some other critical marketing issues such as pricing, quality level, and expectations from product or services. This type of interview is more often used in the developed world. However, its success is questionable as the response rate may be very poor, sampling is difficult, and samples may not represent the population. Moreover, the interviews tend to be unstructured, as respondents may not like to answer all the questions raised by the interviewer.

> **Focus group interviews emphasize the collection and compilation of information from a target group of people. The interviewer acts as the moderator and tries to ensure that the group never loses focus on the topic of discussion.**

Focus Group Interviews

Focus group interviews are very powerful survey research instruments in qualitative research. Avoiding the one-to-one interview approach, the focus group emphasizes the collection and compilation of information from a target group of people. The interviewer acts as a moderator and always tries to keep the group focused on the issues of concern. As a moderator, the interviewer plays the role of a psychotherapist to generate more and more information by raising brief provocative statements. The interviewer is more a listener than a talker. Exhibit 21.2 shows a sample questionnaire.

EXHIBIT 21.2   Sample Questionnaire of a Focus Group for Human Resource Research

Focus group for assessing problem of absenteeism

Moderator (HR manager): Hello, you are all here today because the company has shortlisted you. I will now ask you a few questions.

1. Did you remain absent from duties without prior approval of your leave in the last one year?
   Yes   Continue
   No   Exclude
2. Did you participate in a group discussion or survey on absenteeism by us in the last six months?
   Yes   Exclude
   No   Continue
3. Did you remain absent for more than 10 days without prior approval during the last six months?
   Yes   Continue
   No   Exclude
4. Are you currently under any medical treatment that prevents you from being regular at work?
   Yes   Exclude
   No   Continue
5. Now, I will give you some statements on possible

causes of absenteeism. Select the statements as per your perceived priority giving the order of rank in a five-point scale.
   (a) I remain absent due to frequent illness.
   (b) I remain absent because of my household priorities.
   (c) I remain absent because I am doing advanced level studies.
   (d) I remain absent because I have to visit my native place.
   (e) I remain absent because of poor job satisfaction.
6. (For moderator): Please classify the age group of your participants as per the following:
   Above 60   Exclude
   51–60
   41–50
   31–40
   20–30
   Less than 20   Exclude
7. Sex (please record it by observation only):
   Male
   Female

Even though the questionnaire is structured to help the focus group moderator facilitate the discussions, the moderator can also think of following some unstructured approaches, provoking discussions, and then check out points of interest to understand the cause of absenteeism. However, to start with, it is always desirable to follow a structured approach, developing a structured questionnaire to set the pace of discussion.

Evaluation Designs

Evaluation designs are intended to identify the non-participants in a particular research project. They can be experimental, quasi-experimental, or non-experimental.

Experimental An experimental design gathers a group of willing individuals and then randomly divides them into a treatment group and a control group. The treatment group receives some intervention, whereas the control group does not receive any intervention. Since division or grouping is randomly done, it is a more powerful evaluation methodology. It helps in simple interpretation of results, as the difference between the means of the control and treatments group itself forms the primary basis of inference. Experimental designs help in the assessment of the impact of any policy change issues or any new project initiated by the organization.

Quasi-experimental Quasi-experimental evaluation design performs group comparison using the matching or reflexive methods. Matching requires grouping of participants based on some comparable characteristics, keeping in view the possible influence of the research issues on the participants. After the matching of participants in the research, they are divided into prospective and retrospective types. Prospective types are those who represent the group not exposed to the research issue, whereas retrospective types are those who are exposed to the research issue. It is relatively simple, cost effective, and less time-consuming. However, the research results may not be reliable because of the obvious selection bias. It even requires complex statistical analysis. Reflexive comparison groups are formed both before and after treatment comparison groups, and are selected before the research programme. However, the problem lies in the fact that participants before and after intervention may change due to a number of external or even internal factors, which again makes reliability questionable.

> Evaluation designs are intended to identify the non-participants in a particular research project. They are experimental, quasi-experimental, or non-experimental.

Non-experimental Non-experimental evaluation design is formed by randomly selecting a control group through matching or reflexive methods. Similar to the quasi-experimental method, this method is also relatively cheaper but not free from bias. Thus, reliability is a problem in this method as well. It also requires complex statistical analysis to draw inferences.

Estimation Methods

The appropriate estimation method is decided based on the evaluation design. For experimental evaluation design, comparison of means between the treatment and control groups is the preferred method. For non-experimental evaluation design, multivariate regression analysis is used to assess the distinguishing observable characteristics between two groups. Apart from these, instrumental variable methods can also be used for statistical analysis to control the sampling bias. Double difference or difference-in-difference methods are useful for both experimental and quasi-experimental evaluation design. It requires estimating the mean difference between groups and estimating the impact of the research issue.

Experiments and Quasi-experiments in Organizational Behaviour Research

In empirical OB research, inferences are drawn on the basis of four basic kinds of tests—formal experiments, quasi-experiments, matched comparisons, and case studies. A formal experiment depends on experimenter domination over the test conditions and random assignment of observations to the experimental and control groups. Using examples, it examines the value of experimental design in both the real world and the laboratory. In quasi-experiments, the assignment of values among observations is not under the control of the experimenter. The concepts of central tendency, strength, and significance of a relationship are introduced.

Formal experiment   It involves the maximum mastery over test conditions. It uses a moderately large number of randomly selected sample observations. The size makes it sufficiently easy to identify patterns in the data, providing a relatively clear picture regarding what share of cases co-vary or fail to co-vary in expected ways and permitting relatively sure generalizations from the sample data to the wider population. The sample is then subdivided by the researcher, using random selection, into experimental and control groups. The various groups, if not identical, most likely have all the characteristics extraneous to the test accidentally distributed, minimizing the probable effect of spurious influences. Physical isolation can further protect the test against distortions from outside interference. Finally, the researcher consciously affects the groups by the differential application of the independent variable. As a consequence of researcher mastery over the experimental situation, the researcher guarantees the desired range of variation on that independent variable. Comparison of results on the dependent variable across the groups establishes the grounds for a conclusion. Thus, the formal experiment does maximize researcher leverage over the data and therefore is sometimes claimed to be scientific testing in its purest version.

Quasi-experiment   This is the form of testing most commonly found in the social sciences. It begins with the world, as it already exists, in which people have chosen their own behaviour and thus have selected their own values for the independent variable. The researcher does not get to randomly assign them to the experimental and control groups. For example, it is usually not possible to convince the leaders in a set of arbitrarily selected cities to increase the level of police repression just to help research the causes of citizen resentment and resistance. The identification for certain real factors of the value v on the variable X_1 might be influenced by their identification of the value w on the variable X_2. This entails difficulties in controlling possible extraneous causal influences. However, sound modelling and the careful application of multivariate techniques can reduce it.

Matched comparison   This is a testing method that is useful when there are a limited number of appropriate observations in the world or when practical restrictions prevent the examination of more than a few such appropriate observations. As in a quasi-experiment, values on the independent variable occur naturally, but the small size of the sample does not ensure high probability that one has captured the full variation on the independent variable. In this case, the researcher has the responsibility to intentionally select cases in order to produce the anticipated

Practitioner Speak 21.3

Does Money Really Affect Motivation? A Review of the Research

How much should people earn? Even if resources were limited, it would be difficult to stipulate your ideal salary. Intuitively, one would think that higher pay should produce better results, but scientific evidence indicates that the link between compensation, motivation and performance is much more complex. In fact, research suggests that even if we let people decide how much they should earn, they would probably not enjoy their job more.

Read this insightful blog posted by Chamorro-Premuzic on *HBR Blog Network* by accessing the following link: http://blogs.hbr.org/2013/04/does-money-really-affect-motiv/.

range of variation. Moreover, the small sample size makes it somewhat difficult to identify stable patterns within the data and to make generalized inferences with confidence.

Case study   A case study depends upon one observation alone. By itself, it is not a test since there is no variation to be recorded. From a single case study, one cannot determine whether the values adopted by the dependent variable are affected in any systematic manner by the values on the independent variable. It is impossible to distinguish random from systematic effects. It is impossible to control the impact of exogenous variables. Yet, with proper design, there are empirical uses for case studies.

To summarize, there is a hierarchy of methods—from experiments to quasi-experiments to matched comparisons to case studies. The list begins with the most rigorous form of test and descends to the least rigorous form. The formal experiment is a large sample study based on randomly distributed group characteristics and the researcher's mastery over the test environment. The quasi-experiment by necessity accepts the assignment of values existing in the world and therefore infers significance by logical calculation. The matched comparison, because it is a small sample study using intentional selection, is more limited in its ability to assert systematic patterns. The case study examines only a single observation, operating without explicit controls and without perceived variation on the independent variable.

SUMMARY

Organizational behaviour research knowledge enhances the employment opportunities of management students and even benefits HR professionals in developing their scientific decision-making capabilities. Basic OB research helps appreciate the interrelationship between various OB variables, whereas applied OB research helps solve organizational people-related problems. Today, at the organization level, the scope of OB research encompasses even line functions, and in many organizations, even the line managers get involved in the research. It is important to note that the researcher has to comply with many ethical issues. The ethical requirements may

vary from organization to organization. However, all OB researchers must comply with at least two generic requirements—informed consent and maintenance of confidentiality.

It is important to understand the various tools and techniques involved in both qualitative and quantitative OB researches. Quantitative tools require data collection from various experimental or clinical trials, observation and recording of events, ERP/MIS, and questionnaire responses. Qualitative data, on the other hand, requires collection of narrative data through historical research, focus group discussions, and so on. Depending on the nature of research, quantitative OB research may be descriptive, correlational, causal–comparative, or experimental. Similarly, qualitative OB research may be formal or informal and use focus groups, round tables, feedback forms, seminars, usability studies, and so on. A structured approach is required for both quantitative and qualitative OB researches.

Reliability and validity testing is yet another important aspect for authenticating OB research. The researcher has to validate his/her findings by testing the degree of agreement between the value of a measurement and its true value. Again, the extent of reproducibility of a measurement has to be tested to understand the reliability. All these aspects have been extensively discussed in this chapter. The framing of hypotheses and the use of various data analysis techniques, introducing several statistical tools, have also been explained.

KEY DEFINITIONS

Conjoint analysis   This is also called multi-attribute compositional model. It is a statistical technique that originated in mathematical psychology. Today, it is used in many of the social sciences and applied sciences including marketing, product management, and operations research.

Informed consent   Employees can be selected as research subjects only if they give their consent for participation in the research. For helping the employees to volunteer for participation, it is necessary to accurately provide all possible information, so that they can make an informed choice.

Interval scale   An interval scale has all the characteristics of a nominal and ordinal scale. It is based upon predetermined equal intervals.

Nominal scale   This scale represents the lowest level of measurement and classifies persons or objects into two or more categories.

Ordinal scale   This scale puts the subjects in order from the highest to the lowest or from the most to the least.

Quartile deviation   This is one-half of the difference between the upper quartile and the lower quartile in a data set.

Ratio scale   This scale represents the highest and the most precise level of measurement. In addition to having all the advantages of the other types of scales, it has a meaningful true zero point.

Reliability   This refers to the reproducibility of a measurement and is quantified by taking several measurements on the same subjects.

Semantic differential scale   When bipolar adjectives are used at the end points of the scale, it is called a semantic differential scale.

Thurston scale   This scale attempts to represent the attitudes of a group on a specified issue in the form of a frequency distribution.

Unobtrusive data collection   This type of data is collected from the existing database of the organization. It is called unobtrusive because the researcher is not required to ask any question or interview samples to collect such data.

Validity   It refers to the agreement between the value of a measurement and its true value. It is quantified by comparing the measurements with values that are as close to the true values as possible. Poor validity degrades the precision of a single measurement, and reduces the researcher's ability to characterize relationships in variables.

CONCEPT-REVIEW QUESTIONS

21.1   What are the various types of data collection? Which method would you recommend for collection of data relating to employee satisfaction? Justify your recommendation.

21.2   Develop a questionnaire using a five-point scale for measuring the attitudes of workers. In addition, explain how you will analyse the collected responses to define the attitudes of the workers.

CRITICAL THINKING QUESTION

21.1 Conduct a focus group interview with some selected identified issues and suggest how you are going to interpret the outcome of your discussions.

SELECT BIBLIOGRAPHY

- Austin, J.T. and P. Villanova, 'The Criterion Problem: 1917–1992', *Journal of Applied Psychology*, Vol. 77, 1992, pp. 836–74.
- Bhattacharyya, Dipak Kumar, *Human Resource Research Methods*, Oxford University Press, New Delhi, 2007.
- Bhattacharyya, Dipak Kumar, *Research Methodology*, Excel Books, New Delhi, 2006.
- Dutta Roy, D., 'Organizational Health and Life Satisfaction: A Path-analytic Model', *Managerial Psychology*, 1992, pp. 51–62.
- Kanter, R.M., *Men and Women of the Corporation*, Basic Books, New York, 1977.
- Kanter, R.M., *When Giants Learn to Dance*, Simon and Schuster, New York, 1989.
- Schwab, D.P., *Research Methods for Organizational Studies*, Lawrence Erlbaum Associates, Mahwah, 1999.
- Tabachnick, B.G. and L.S. Fidell, *Using Multivariate Statistics*, Allyn and Bacon, Boston, 2001.

CASE STUDY

RichOvernight Financial Services

RichOvernight Financial Services Ltd has grown considerably during the last five years. The company, which was started by Nilesh Dattari with two employees, has gradually reached an annual business of ₹6,00,000 in gross sales. The company now employs 200 people and is expected to have business for ₹6,00,00,000 this year. During the early years, what was expected from each employee was always clear. Everyone knew how to do everything and was often called upon to do exactly that. This is no longer true, and it is apparent to Dattari that each employee must be given a clear set of general guidelines as to what duties he/she must perform.

A number of new players in the financial services sector are closely competing with Dattari's company. The service mix for RichOvernight has also significantly changed to keep pace with the changing customers' expectations. The company, therefore, has to change its operational strategy.

In addition, it is becoming increasingly difficult to hire employees without having a clear understanding of what the individual will exactly be doing. Applicants seem reluctant to join the firm without some information about their probable job profile, and it is difficult to know exactly what skills prospective applicants should have without knowing what roles they will be assigned to.

Dattari decided to write job descriptions and job specifications for his employees. It is his belief that such documents will clear any misunderstanding among employees regarding responsibilities and will help them organize work better. Informing prospective employees about their probable job duties will help orient new employees and help them take better decisions.

You have been retained by Dattari to determine whose responsibility it would be to gather the data and write the descriptions and specifications, how the data should be gathered (observation, questionnaire, or interview), and how detailed the descriptions and specifications should be.

Dattari is currently considering these job analysis issues but has a number of questions about how each will affect the final results.

Questions for Discussion

1. What recommendations would you make to him regarding the most appropriate individuals and methods to be used for data collection?

2. What approach should you consider regarding the design of jobs and why?

3. Keeping in mind the recent trends in financial services companies, design the job roles pertaining to different hierarchical levels for at least four operational areas with supporting background information such as job analysis and job description.

Total Quality Management and Organizational Behaviour

LEARNING OBJECTIVES

After studying this chapter, the reader will be able to

- understand the basics of quality management practices
- explain how quality management practices impact an organization
- relate quality management to organizational culture
- relate people-centred issues to organizations that support quality management practices
- understand six sigma and the need for organizational change
- appreciate the importance of innovation and creativity

CASE STUDY

Change Requires Resource Support

In the new paradigm of quality management, organizations are required to nurture a proactive manufacturing culture as it prevents defects before they occur. It never slows down the process of improvement and establishes a culture of continuous development. Employees of such organizations get trained in process development, statistics, problem-solving, project management, and design for manufacturability (DFM). There is increased focus on understanding customers and adopting customer-desired practices to achieve the highest level of satisfaction.

A traditional family-managed organization in India suddenly decided to adopt proactive manufacturing management practices. The company

first streamlined its manufacturing activities, documenting the process in line with the International Organization for Standardization (ISO) requirements, and then went about developing the appropriate culture to align people with the changing requirements. As a manager, however, you find that the company is yet to appreciate the need for investment in training. No serious efforts are made for helping the employees understand the critical operation parameters, statistical process controls, process of identifying non-value adding activity, and so on. Yet you have been asked to play the important role of a facilitator in this change process. Draw your charted action plans.

INTRODUCTION

The philosophy of total quality management (TQM) has now changed the business paradigm. It is a customer-centric approach and requires all members of the organizations to manage the overall improvement of the organization through systematic participation in problem-solving, cutting across the functional and hierarchical barriers.

The process-centric approach to TQM focuses on product quality, process control, quality assurance, and quality improvement, which by default satisfy the customer needs in the most cost-effective way. The human dimension of quality reinforces this process-centric approach, cascading problem-solving and decision-making down to the lowest levels in the organization and thus allowing people to feel empowered to take corrective action on their own to meet the customers' needs.

There are three opposing views on the effective implementation of TQM in organizations. The first view considers it as a customer-driven organizational improvement strategy. The second view argues that it is achieved by strengthening internal efficiency and cost improvement, whereas the third view considers it as a means to introduce participative management.

Managers and experts disagree about how to effectively apply TQM to their organizations. Some advise that customer satisfaction is the driving force behind quality improvement; others suggest that internal productivity or cost improvement programmes achieve quality management. In other applications, TQM is considered as a means to introduce participative management. For example, Japan considers TQM as a process for addressing the issue of customer satisfaction, meeting their needs and expectations. In the US, however, TQM is considered as the process of saving the cost of non-conformance (cost of quality) by making employees meet the agreed-upon standards. In this context, it is also important to understand that processes and tasks cannot, by default, lead to the desired quality and meet customer requirements. It requires the involvement of employees, change of systems and cultures of the organizations, and total participation.

Further understanding of the TQM philosophy is possible by differentiating quality improvement from quality assurance. Quality assurance activities ensure the meeting of protocol-bound standards in production. Here, the customer is satisfied because products are manufactured conforming to the specification requirements. Quality improvement, on the other hand, refers to the effective and efficient efforts of the members of the organization in meeting customers' expectations. Thus, quality improvement, in fact, emphasizes the people-centric approach to TQM.

TOTAL QUALITY MANAGEMENT AND OPERATING ENVIRONMENT OF ORGANIZATIONS

With increased competition and market globalization, TQM practices are now becoming important for the leadership and management of all organizations. However, with TQM, ISO certification is often confusing—ISO enables an organization to streamline its quality assurance systems in line with ISO systems and standards, whereas TQM practices, which succeed ISO, ensure quality improvement in an organization. According to ISO TC176, which spells out quality management and quality assurance, quality management is a comprehensive and fundamental rule or belief for leading and operating an organization. It is aimed at continually improving performance over the long term, focusing on customers while addressing the needs of all other stakeholders as well. The following eight quality management principles have been spelt out by this standard, which are followed in promoting TQM cultures in organizations.

Principle 1—Customer-focused Organization

Organizations depend on their customers and should, therefore, understand current and future customer needs, meet customer requirements, and strive to exceed customer expectations.

Principle 2—Leadership

Leaders establish unity of purpose and direction of organizations. They should create and maintain the internal environment in which people can become fully involved in achieving the organization's objectives.

Principle 3—Involvement of People

People are the essence of an organization, irrespective of their levels, and their full involvement enables their abilities to be used for the organization's benefit.

Principle 4—Process Approach

The desired result is achieved more efficiently when related resources and activities are managed as a process.

Principle 5—System Approach to Management

Identifying, understanding, and managing a system of interrelated processes for a given objective improve the organization's effectiveness and efficiency.

Principle 6—Continual Improvement

Continual improvement should be a permanent objective of an organization.

Principle 7—Factual Approach to Decision-making

Effective decisions and actions are based on the analysis of data and information.

Principle 8—Mutually Beneficial Supplier Relationships

An organization and its suppliers are independent, and a mutually beneficial relationship enhances the ability to create value.

Successful TQM requires both behavioural and cultural changes to fulfil the commitments of an organization towards achieving customer satisfaction. Hence, TQM principles themselves become a management system, which can be categorized into the following three types:

- Organization management systems
- Human resource (HR) management systems
- TQM systems

Successful implementation of TQM in organizations, therefore, requires the integration of organizational behaviour (OB), HR development, and organizational development issues with quality management practices.

INTERNATIONAL ORGANIZATION FOR STANDARDIZATION AND TOTAL QUALITY MANAGEMENT SYSTEMS

The ISO is a worldwide federation of national standards bodies from more than 161 countries (one from each country). ISO standards are documented quality systems and activities that are used as the basis for the adoption of uniform quality systems norms for international exchange of goods and services. In fact, ISO is a word derived from the Greek word *iso*, meaning *equal*, which is the root of the prefix *iso*. *Iso* occurs in terms such as isometric (of equal measure or dimensions) and isonomy (equality of laws or of people before the law). From *equal* to *standard*, the line of thinking that led to the choice of ISO as the name of the organization is easy to follow. The name ISO is used around the world to denote the organization, thus avoiding a plethora of acronyms resulting from the translation of the *International Organization for Standardization* into the different national languages of members, such as IOS in English and OIN in French.

Selection and Use of ISO 9000:2005 Family of Standards

The ISO 9000 family has many standards, encompassing all areas of quality management systems. The most prominent standards are ISO 9000:2005, ISO 9001:2008, and ISO 9004:2009. ISO 9000 introduces quality management systems, their fundamentals, and vocabulary. It is the starting point of the standards and basically introduces the concepts. ISO 9001 introduces the requirements of quality management systems to address customer satisfaction. Certificates are issued to organizations based on this standard. ISO 9004 provides the guidelines for continuous performance improvements.

ISO 9001:2008 is an integration of three standards—ISO 9001, ISO 9002, and ISO 9003. It specifies the requirements of a quality management system for any organization that needs to demonstrate its ability to consistently provide products that meet customer specifications and applicable regulatory requirements. It aims to enhance customer satisfaction. ISO 9001:2008 has been organized in a user-friendly format with terms that are easily recognized by all business sectors. The standard is used for certification or registration as well as contractual purposes by organizations seeking recognition for their quality management system.

ISO 9001 provides the conformance norms for an organization seeking to establish quality systems. As per this standard, products include services, processed materials, hardware, and software required by the customer. ISO 9001 has five sections, which set the standards for the production of quality products and services. These five sections are quality management systems, management responsibility, resource management, production realization, and measurement, analysis, and improvement. Organizations document all these areas in their quality manual to demonstrate their concerns for quality and for meeting customers' requirements.

Objectives of ISO 9001:2008 Quality Management Systems

The following are the objectives of ISO 9001:2008 quality management systems for an organization:

- To identify the goals that the organization intends to achieve (e.g., efficiency and profitability)
- To consistently meet customer requirements

- To achieve customer satisfaction
- To enhance market share
- To sustain market share
- To improve communications and morale in the organization
- To reduce costs and liabilities
- To increase confidence in the production system

Organizations meeting the expectations of the various stakeholders, such as customers, suppliers, shareholders, employees, and the society, achieve all these objectives.

Optimizing Cost of Quality

The ISO documentation provides an opportunity for organizations to achieve internal efficiency by influencing the attitudinal changes of the people. It helps identify the cost of quality and substantially reduces this cost. This ultimately helps an organization achieve cost efficiency in terms of increased profitability. In order to help analyse the cost of quality, the nature of cost can be classified under the following three categories:

Cost of failure   Quality may fail either internally or externally, that is, either within the organization or in the customers' premises. Hence, failure cost can be grouped as either internal or external. Internal failure costs include the cost of rework, cost for additional raw materials, additional payments required to be made to workmen, and creation of eventual scrap. External failure costs consider the cost incurred for re-transportation, re-packaging, servicing, handling of customers' complaints, and loss of goodwill, in addition to the cost to be incurred for internal failure. Experience shows that the cost of failure accounts for about 70 per cent of the total cost of quality.

Cost of appraisal   Organizations have to incur expenses for verification of quality and for maintaining an inspection team. There is also a requirement of specific gadgets and tools for undertaking inspection. All the expenses incurred on this account are considered as cost of appraisal. Usually, organizations spend between 28 and 29 per cent of the total quality cost on this account.

Cost of prevention   This is the cost incurred to reduce the foregoing two quality costs, including the amounts spent for research and development (R&D) and HR development. This usually varies between 1 and 2 per cent of the total cost.

There is no serious study computing the cost of quality in Indian organizations. From an international perspective, it can be seen that such costs, even though not accounted for under any separate head, are as high as 40 per cent of the production cost. Indian organizations typically assume that in the normal manufacturing process, there will be some natural rejection. This may be as high as 22 per cent (in some cases) and is termed as the unavoidable rejection rate. The philosophy subscribed to by other developed countries, especially Japan, is diametrically opposite—the philosophy of zero defects.

A mere 1–2 per cent more expenditure on the cost of prevention can substantially help reduce the expenditure on the other two divisions of cost of quality. The rate of such incremental cost benefit is as high as 70–80 per cent.

> **Practitioner Speak 22.1** **Keep Your Eye on Process Improvement**
>
> In my consulting and research I've seen many companies launch process improvement programs such as Total Quality Management, Business Reengineering, Lean, and Six Sigma. Many got significant benefits, including lower costs, faster time-to-market, and better customer experiences. But after one round of improvement, they gave up and let their organization get flabby again. Organizations, like people, need to stay fit and make improvement a habit to be competitive. So why don't they? Why is sustained process improvement so rare?
>
> Read this insightful blog posted by Power on *HBR Blog Network* by accessing the following link: http://blogs.hbr.org/2010/08/in-my-consulting-and-research/.

Therefore, though not apparent from the books of accounts, cost of quality is an important wasteful cost factor, which can be significantly reduced to increase the profitability of an organization. The ISO documentation process helps prune the cost of quality in addition to augmenting the internal efficiency of an organization. It also helps in achieving TQM in a phased manner.

TEAMS AND TEAMWORK

When TQM is successful, employees at every level participate in decisions affecting their work. The most common vehicle for employee participation is a team. Teams range in scope and responsibility from problem-solving groups to self-managed work teams that schedule work, assign jobs, hire members, and set the standards and volume of output. A participative work culture is encouraged when quality becomes everybody's responsibility.

Employee involvement practices in organizations may differ in terms of organizational policies and strategies. Common employment practices include the formation of the following:

- Suggestion system
- Survey feedback
- Quality circles (QCs)
- Quality of work life (QWL) teams
- Job redesign
- Self-managed teams
- TQM teams

Participative management is the most important approach used for introducing TQM culture in an organization. According to *Yajurveda* (an ancient Indian scripture), people tend to live together in love and amity. A more organized or institutionalized approach to workers' participation in management dates back to 1920, when Mahatma Gandhi advocated the principles of trusteeship in industry. This idea was further concretized during the plan era through enactments of various legislations and policy decisions. Though the benefits of participative management were successfully used for many years by organizations across the world, India was a little late in institutionalizing the approach. Statutory support has now made it mandatory for Indian industries to introduce the culture. Participation in some form or the other has now become virtually unavoidable for many organizations.

In the new economy, total participation of workers, as opposed to statutory participation, is a must. Participation may be through committees, departmental councils, and other representative forums. One way to enforce total participation is to form QCs or small group forums.

A QC is an important managerial tool and can be related to increased employee motivation and productivity. Total knowledge, skill, creative abilities, talents, and aptitudes together with values, attitudes, and beliefs of the workers and/or individuals can represent an organization's effective HR inventory. The total involvement of employees is ensured by QCs through a number of small group forums. Organizations have succeeded in improving their productivity by QC activities that increase employee motivation. This result can be guaranteed more by QCs than by any other method, such as complex planning and rigorous execution.

Organizations in India have now started training their workers and employees on QC concepts for its successful implementation. They are systematic about follow-up activities in connection with setting up the QC forums involving all workers. Homogeneous groups of 8–12 employees are formed, who regularly meet once a week for at least an hour to deliberate on work-related problems and to identify possible solutions to those problems. The benefits to organizations have been in the form of cost minimization, changing methods of production, work simplification, and so on. The top management supports the QCs without getting directly involved in the process. Other members in the structure play their specific roles, as illustrated in Fig. 22.1.

The basic philosophy of the QCs is to involve all employees in an organization, as total involvement enhances the productivity of the organization. Studies carried out both in India and abroad indicate that successful implementation of QCs is directly related to the following areas of improvement in an organization: productivity, quality, house-keeping, cost minimization,

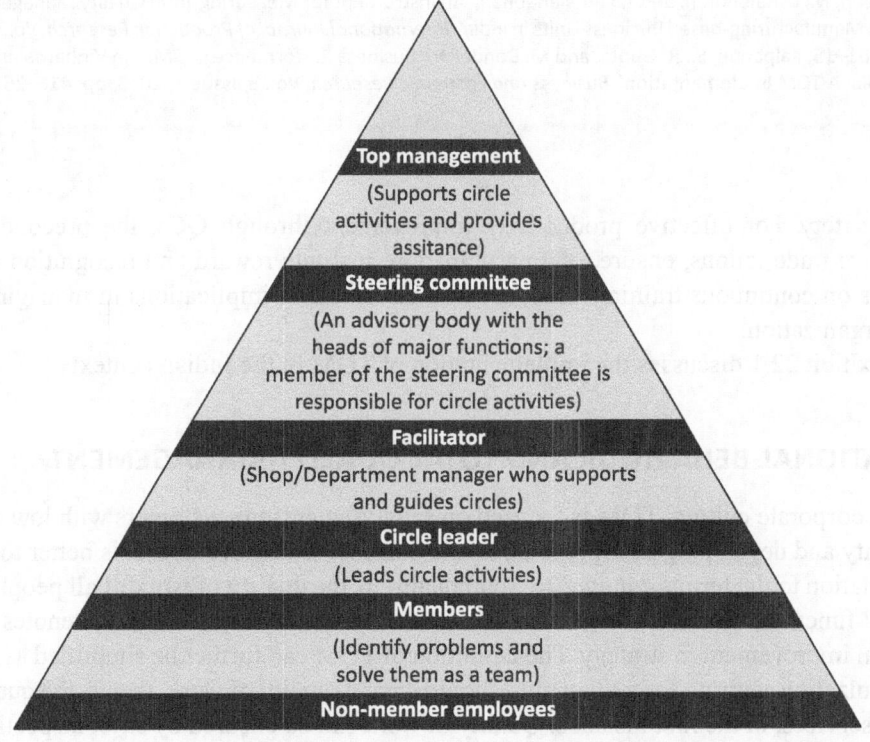

Figure 22.1   Structure of quality circle

EXHIBIT 22.1 Successful TQM Implementation: The Indian Context

The concept of TQM has revolutionized industries all over the world. Volumes of literature have been published on the ways in which TQM can be successfully implemented. However, since business contexts change with markets, people, and cultures, it is better to understand whether the widely accepted steps for successful TQM implementation are valid for specific markets as well.

The critical factors for successful TQM implementation, as discussed by Joseph, et al. (1999), are as follows:

- Role of divisional top management leadership
- Role of the department looking after quality
- Nature of training provided
- Design reviews and coordination with quality department for product design
- Proper supplier quality management, leading to low but dependable suppliers and expounding a purchase policy focusing on quality rather than price

- Process management, focusing on infallible process designs, use of statistical process control mechanisms, and selective automation among others
- Quality data and reporting
- Employee relations, focusing on active participation of employees in quality decisions

India, being a culturally diverse country, offers unique challenges for quality gurus. Though most researchers have stressed on the role of organizational culture, Kalpande, et al. (2013) have concluded that successful TQM implementation necessitates the following:

- Extensive transformation of organizational and operational structure
- Increased focus on the needs of customers
- More emphasis on organizational culture
- Participatory culture

Sources: Joseph, N., C. Rajendran, and T. Kamalanabhan, 'An Instrument for Measuring Total Quality Management Implementation in Manufacturing-based Business Units in India', *International Journal of Production Research*, Vol. 37, Issue 10, 1999, pp. 2201–15; Kalpande, S., R. Gupta, and M. Dandekar, 'Business Performance of SMEs in Vidharba and Khandesh region of India: A TQM Implementation', *Business and Economic Research*, Vol. 3, Issue 1, 2013, pp. 416–26 (adapted).

and safety. For effective productivity improvement through QCs, the preconditions are to involve trade unions, ensure total participation, institute reward and recognition systems, and focus on continuous training. Hence, it has far-reaching implications in managing the OB of an organization.

Exhibit 22.1 discusses the implementation of TQM in the Indian context.

ORGANIZATIONAL BEHAVIOUR AND TOTAL QUALITY MANAGEMENT

As a corporate culture, TQM is focused on satisfying current customers with low cost and high quality and developing new procedures and controls to achieve this. It is better to define TQM in relation to the term *total quality*. Total quality is the quality of work of all people at all levels in all functional areas. Management in relation to total quality, therefore, denotes an organizational improvement in strategy. The definition of TQM can further be simplified as follows: Any organization aspiring for total quality should ensure quality of work, that is, the quality of goods and services, in the first instance. Quality of work can be ensured by strict inspection or quality control, without taking cognizance of other areas. However, that does not serve the purpose of the TQM philosophy. TQM lays emphasis on achieving the quality of work by enriching the quality of all people directly or indirectly related to that work, irrespective of their hierarchical levels and functional areas. Thus, broadly speaking, TQM is an organizational improvement strategy that enforces desired behavioural changes in the employees.

TQM can also be defined as the value addition activities that focus on the following four key performance areas in an organization:

- Quality
- Process
- Equipment
- People

Looking back, it can be found that the Japanese concept of total quality control has actually been renamed TQM. Though the definition of TQM is derived from the ISO specification series, TQM per se is not a standard. It is based on total quality principles.

On observing organizations that have successfully practised TQM, it is evident that the most commonly used TQM technique is the formation of a short-term problem-solving group for simplifying and streamlining work practices, and the second most commonly used one is training. The third common practice is to have a top-down approach (quality is ultimately the responsibility of the top management). The other two practices call for developing relationships with the suppliers and obtaining data about customers. The first three techniques of TQM are, in fact, part of OB and HR management activities in an organization. OB and HR management practices are now laying emphasis on small group activities with a view to not only enhance the problem-solving abilities of the employees but to also provide intrinsic motivation, which culminates in increased satisfaction and enhanced productivity.

Employee Empowerment

Employee empowerment is to confer legitimate rights on employees, irrespective of their nature of jobs and hierarchical levels, to make judgements and take decisions on their own. Hence, employee empowerment can facilitate the development of problem-solving abilities in employees. Operationally, organizations empower employees first by developing their capabilities and second by giving them the freedom to commit mistakes. Unlike other quality

Practitioner Speak 22.2

For Startups, How Much Process Is Too Much?

Whether they're found in a garage or inside an established enterprise, startups struggle with decisions about processes and infrastructure. The speed at which a startup can learn is its competitive advantage and the defining factor in its success. But startups can't rely on the processes and infrastructure that their established competitors use, because those 'best practices' tend to kill disruptive innovation.

Read this insightful blog posted by Ries on *HBR Blog Network* by accessing the following link: http://blogs.hbr.org/2010/02/how-much-process-is-too-much/.

Employee empowerment refers to conferring legitimate rights on employees, irrespective of their nature of jobs and hierarchical levels, to make judgements and take decisions on their own.

management approaches, empowerment not only calls for employee participation in the operational areas but also allows them to participate in corporate-level decision-making. In other words, an empowered employee is not a mere seller of his/her time and labour for a contracted sum of money. He/She acquires the necessary skill and authority to own, that is, a sense of ownership and relatedness with the organization. Employee empowerment, involvement, and participative management as important corporate practices have been experimented in several multinational and national organizations. In all these cases, employee ownership and commitment (which is possible through employee empowerment) were identified to be the two ingredients that help achieve efficiency and productivity. Some organizations are empowering their employees even at the strategic level rather than confining their involvement to limited operational activities alone.

Quality of Work Life

Quality of work (QWL) life is most conventionally defined as those perceived important personal needs that an individual tries to satisfy by working in an organization. Its conceptual foundation, though laid by a host of behavioural scientists, was, in reality, advocated by Chris Argyris (1975) in his famous work on personality and organization. The socio-technical systems theory, pioneered by Tavistock Institute of Human Relations, London, during the 1960s, is considered an important QWL construct. The basic conceptual criteria for QWL incorporates growth and security as important personal needs of an individual. The possibility of furthering one's career within the organization, has, therefore, been identified as one of the important criteria for QWL. Although common QWL strategists lay more emphasis on job redesign, formation of autonomous work groups, and worker participation in management, wide differences exist among the pioneers in this area as to what should be construed as the QWL factors. The process of QWL can be explained with the help of the following criteria:

- Adequate and fair compensation
- Safe and healthy working conditions
- Immediate opportunity to use and develop human capacities
- Future opportunity for continued growth and security
- Social integration in the work organization
- Work and total life space
- Social relevance of working life

Quality of work life is defined as those perceived important personal needs that an individual tries to satisfy by working in an organization.

From studies carried out both in India and abroad, it is evident that the essence of QWL is the opportunity for employees, at all levels, to have substantial influence over their work environment. This is a result of their participating in the decision-making process related to their work, thereby enhancing their self-esteem and obtaining overall satisfaction from their work. Hence, QWL calls for an open style of management, that is, sharing of information and genuinely encouraging the efforts relating to the improvement of the organization. Thus, QWL is an important managerial activity to develop the potential of the employees of an organization.

Thus, the success of TQM programmes largely depends on appropriate OB/HR interventions such as the following:

- Emphasizing continuous training and development activities
- Encouraging participation in management through small group forums
- Increasing employees' motivation
- Looking after the career development of employees
- Empowering employees
- Infusing attitudinal changes at the top (e.g., accepting a flatter organizational structure, following a democratic approach, becoming receptive to changes on a continuous basis, and supporting group performance).

ORGANIZATIONAL BEHAVIOUR AND SIX SIGMA PRACTICES

To add economic value and practical utility to the customers and the organizations, companies globally are now looking beyond TQM practices. The corporate world now accepts the rightful expectation of the customers to buy quality products at competitive costs. However, organizations also strive to improve the bottom line (profit). Synergy between these two can be achieved through six sigma practices. Six sigma, as a business process, allows organizations to improve their bottom line by designing and monitoring business activities in a way that minimizes waste of resources without, however, compromising with customer satisfaction. The six sigma process is broader than the TQM programmes. TQM focuses on detecting and correcting defects, whereas six sigma recreates the processes to ensure that defects never arise at all. From an organization's point of view, it provides the maximum value in the form of increased profits, and from the customers' point of view, it provides the maximum value in terms of high-quality products and services at competitive costs.

Higher Sigma values indicate high quality products and lower Sigma values represent inferior quality products. At the six sigma level, products are virtually defect-free, that is, only 3.4 defects per million opportunities (DPMO).

Similar to TQM, six sigma also requires thorough changes in the culture and practices of organizations. Essentially, all the tools mentioned in TQM are applicable to six sigma as well. However, additionally six sigma requires the organization to make people more creative and innovative, as it recreates processes to ensure that defects never arise.

ORGANIZATIONAL BEHAVIOUR, INNOVATION, AND CREATIVITY

Innovation is a new technique or idea encompassing products or services, processes, managerial styles, and even organizational structures. It may be caused by technology-push, demand-pull, or even a combination of both. R&D activities of an organization are examples of such innovation. The need for innovation is primarily felt when an organization wants to keep pace with the competition. It has to be essentially customer-focused as this backward linkage facilitates process-centred innovative changes. Whether it is just-in-time (JIT) inventory control, supply chain management (SCM), business process outsourcing (BPO), flexible manufacturing systems (FMS), product/service customization, strategic backward or forward integration, synergy through merger or acquisition, alliances or collaboration, organizational re-engineering through TQM or six sigma practices, new work culture as facilitator of organizational change, or any R&D initiative for value addition, which broadly encompasses innovation, it all stems from the customers' explicit or implicit needs. Mapping customers' needs and aligning the innovation initiative to those needs are the imperatives of the corporate world. Innovation is enabled by proactive OB practices. It calls for the creation of a work environment that recognizes creativity, inter-organizational cooperation (rather than competition and working as cross-functional teams), productive meetings for innovative results, introduction of formal innovation programmes, and the organization's receptivity to new ideas and perspectives. Fostering innovation requires a structured approach. It has to broadly be in the given context, leadership, values, and culture. Contextual analysis helps in building the required innovation teams. Leaders facilitate the teams. Values enable the adoption of principles that foster innovation, and culture provides the playing field.

At this stage, it is pertinent to define creativity because innovation and creativity are often used interchangeably in the workplace. The Webster Dictionary defines creativity as 'the ability or power to create, to bring into existence, to invest with a new form, to produce through imaginative skill, to make or bring into existence something new'. Creativity is, therefore, the core competence. It is the talent of the employees of an organization. Competitors can replicate the strategies of an organization but not the creative talents of its employees. To encourage creativity, an organization should first create the right environment where employees feel safe even to come up with ideas that might be termed silly or not sensible. Creativity is often not encouraged in organizations, as creative people spend more time in getting ready for the action. They are also very difficult to manage. Organizations, therefore, often see them as major time and money wasters and inhibit their creative thoughts. A review of creativity literature helps capture creative patterns in the following ways:

- A creative process is a balance of imagination and analysis. It involves idea generation, analysis, and evaluation.
- Creativity does not stem from a subconscious process, as traditionally believed by the classical school of thought. It is a purposeful or directed attempt to generate new ideas under a controlled situation to help an organization leapfrog in competition. Paul E. Plsek (1997) used the term more appropriately as *directed creativity*. It is the useful generation of creative ideas with the seriousness that these will be implemented, whenever they match organizational requirements. Non-implementation of at least some ideas (that fit the purpose) will inhibit creativity.

Innovation is the implementation of creative ideas. Therefore, creativity is the subset of innovation. Being a holistic concept, innovation, here, is used interchangeably with creativity.

Competencies, on the other hand, are sets of behaviours that encompass skills, knowledge, abilities, and attributes. Competencies are measurable and they change over time. Hamel and Prahalad (1990) attributed business success to innovative creativity, knowledge resources, and the expertise, which together create the critical potential of an organization, that is, the core competencies. Other proponents of core competencies, such as Quinn (1992), Drucker (1992), Porter (1995), Waterman (1983), Peter (1988), Nonaka and Takeuchi (1955), and Senge (1990), also showed that developing the core competencies helps an organization build its strategic power. The core competencies are difficult to duplicate by the competitors because of their distinctiveness and are, therefore, critical success factors for any organization. Although

Practitioner Speak 22.3

It's Time to Rethink Continuous Improvement

Six Sigma, Kaizen, Lean, and other variations on continuous improvement can be hazardous to your organization's health. While it may be heresy to say this, recent evidence from Japan and elsewhere suggests that it's time to question these methods.

Read this insightful blog posted by Ashkenas on *HBR Blog Network* by accessing the following link: http://blogs.hbr.org/2012/05/its-time-to-rethink-continuous/.

widespread differences exist regarding the constituents of core competencies and their relation to knowledge, skill, abilities, and attributes of employees, there is agreement among the proponents about how these are created by linking the organization's goals, structures, and cultures. Innovation and creativity help develop the core competencies, supplementing knowledge and skill base for the employees. In this respect, directed creativity, that is, purposeful generation of new ideas matching organizational requirements, is more relevant.

Innovation, creativity, and competencies are important facilitators for organizational change. The imperatives for organizational change basically stem from redefining the business focus, restructuring, and customer orientation—all for competitive advantages.

Exhibit 22.2 talks about the need for organizations to look beyond TQM as a way for growth and success.

EXHIBIT 22.2   The Way beyond TQM

For the past five decades, TQM has been the most potent force leading organizations to the helm of corporate success all over the world. Japanese companies, for example, have shot to fame because of their lean processes and continuous learning programmes. However, with changing times, there is a pressing need to take a re-look at whether these paradigms for success hold their erstwhile efficacy.

In recent years, Japanese companies have been losing out badly to their Chinese and South Korean counterparts. In 2012, the total loss accrued by Japanese electronics companies has been reported to be about $17 billion. Even Western companies such as Motorola and 3M have faced similar fates. Managements should take this loss as a cue to see whether their TQM initiatives are in place. The points they may ponder over are as follows:

- Rethink whether continuous improvement can be applied to all areas of the organization.
- Decide what needs to be done to particular

processes, that is, whether they can be improved, eliminated, or disrupted.
- Find whether TQM is adversely affecting the company culture.

Simultaneously, management gurus are now encouraging thinking beyond lean processes and TQM. They lay emphasis on rethinking the concept of learning within the organization. What most organizations fail to understand is that the word *lean* should not be restricted to only processes. Recent data has revealed that only two per cent of the organizations following lean processes have been able to achieve their desired results. One may take the case of Toyota as an exception. It has been the forerunner of lean processes and is still going strong. This is not because it is continually improving its processes in all areas of management but because it is carefully auditing the proposals of improvement before implementing them. Thus, these improvements are gradually turned into best practices. Another problem associated with TQM is

(Contd)

EXHIBIT 22.2 (*Contd*)

that in many cases, though there is stress on continuous improvement, there is no set goal as to what to achieve and TQM becomes a routine activity. Thus, employees should learn good habits; they

should identify the problems first and then work towards solving them. This new way of learning can be crucial to success when all major firms have wholeheartedly embraced TQM practices.

Sources: Ashkenas, R., 'Why Continuous Improvement May Need to be Discontinued', 24 July 2013, http://www.forbes.com/sites/ronashkenas/2013/07/24/why-continuous-improvement-may-need-to-be-discontinued/, last accessed on 10 October 2013; Denning, S., 'Why Lean Programs Fail—Where Toyota Succeeds: A New Culture of Learning', 5 February 2011, http://www.forbes.com/sites/stevedenning/2011/02/05/why-lean-programs-fail-where-toyota-succeeds-a-new-culture-of-learning/, last accessed on 10 October 2013 (adapted).

SUMMARY

Total quality management plays a crucial role in OB studies, because adopting total quality management (TQM) practices requires organizations to change their employees' attitudes and behaviours and achieve complete cultural transformation. Even though some proponents of TQM believe in the process improvement aspect alone to develop the quality of the products and services, TQM also has a human dimension. TQM is a complete organizational transformation process, which uses both process-centric and people-centric approaches. Understanding TQM is not possible without a brief appreciation of ISO quality standards. Although the international organization for standardization (ISO), per se, is not TQM,

ISO certification (through internal changes) can pave the way for organizations to achieve TQM. In the process of adopting the TQM culture, organizations can transform the behaviour of their people by introducing several employee involvement programmes, such as QCs, self-managed teams, and employee empowerment. Once TQM is achieved, organizations strive for further improvement by adopting six sigma practices. However, this requires developing the problem-solving, innovative, and creative abilities of people. Quality management, TQM, and six sigma practices adequately explain how an organization can sustain in a globally competitive market, leveraging the positive behaviour of its people.

KEY DEFINITIONS

ISO This stands for International Organization for Standardization, which ensures common quality systems standards and introduces series of specifications.

Participative management This refers to the involvement of all cross sections of employees in

organizational functions.

TQM This refers to total quality management, which, from an HR point of view, focuses on adopting organizational improvement strategies through the development of HR.

CONCEPT-REVIEW QUESTIONS

22.1 What is the role of a quality management programme in OB studies?

22.2 Explain as an HR manager how quality management principles are important areas of consideration.

22.3 Explain the concepts of employee empowerment

and QWL. In addition, discuss how these two concepts support the introduction of quality management systems in an organization.

22.4 In what ways do the six sigma practices bring about changes in an organization?

22.5 In what ways can innovation and creativity be

nurtured in an organization? How do innovation and creativity support the introduction of quality management systems in an organization?

22.6 Write short notes on the following:
   (a) ISO 9001:2008

(b) Cost of prevention
(c) QCs
(d) Employee empowerment
(e) QWL
(f) Directed creativity

CRITICAL THINKING QUESTION

22.1 Grasim and Marico are two Indian companies having a vibrant presence in the international market. They have also collaborated outside India for some of their manufacturing facilities. Both the companies adjudge innovation as their key driver for growth. Visit their websites and illustrate some of their innovative practices that you think support both the companies' growth strategy in the international market.

SELECT BIBLIOGRAPHY

- Bhattacharyya, D.K., 'Competency Mapping and Manpower Redundancy: Macro Level Study of Indian Organisations', *Management and Accounting Research*, Vol. 4, Issue 2, 2000, pp. 97–105.
- Bhattacharyya, D.K., 'Corporate Body-builder: The Emerging Role of HRD Professional—A Prescriptive Model for Success', *Indian Journal for Training and Development*, April–June 1995.
- Bhattacharyya, D.K., *Human Resource Research Methods*, Oxford University Press, New Delhi, 2007.
- Bhattacharyya, D.K., 'Manpower Obsolescence—A Study in Indian Ordnance Factories', *International Congress on Economic Transition with Human Face*, Indian Industrial Relations Association, New Delhi, 3–6 September 1995.
- Christiansen, James A., *Competitive Innovation Management*, Macmillan Business, London, 2000.
- Gordon, Edward E., *Skill Wars, Winning the Battle for Productivity and Profit*, Butterworth–Heinemann, Boston, 2000.
- Hamel, G. and C.K. Prahalad, 'The Core Competence of the Corporation', *Harvard Business Review*, Vol. 15, Issue 1, 1990, pp. 47–71.
- Jonne, Ceserani and Peter Greatwood, *Innovation and Creativity*, Crest Publishing House, New Delhi, 2001.
- Nonaka, Ikujiro and Hirotaka Takeuchi, *The Knowledge Creating Company*, Oxford University Press, New York, 1995.
- Plsek, Paul E., *Creativity, Innovation and Quality*, ASQ Quality Press, Milwaukee, 1997.
- Senge, P.M., *The Fifth Discipline: Art and Practice of the Learning Organization*, Doubleday Currency, New York, 1990.
- Stolovitch, H.D. and J.G. Maurice, 'Calculating the Return on Investment in Training: A Critical Analysis and Case Study', *Performance Improvement*, Vol. 37, Issue 8, 1998, pp. 9–20.

CASE STUDY

Innovative Customer Service at EMC Corporation[1]

When customers believe in you ... they'll stick with you almost no matter what.

   —Mike Ruettgers, EMC Corp.

EMC was founded in 1979 at Hopkinton, Massachusetts. Today, it is recognized as the world leader in customer service. Mike Ruettgers, after

[1] The case has been adopted from the author's book on *Human Resource Development for Technological Change*, Excel Books, New Delhi, 2007.

joining the EMC Group as vice-president (operations and customer service), found that the company's product performance failure was virtually leading the company to bankruptcy. Disk drive, one of their core product lines, was witnessing a huge challenge as customers were against accepting it, although the company enjoyed visible market reputation in product quality and customer services. The company's business had witnessed a serious drop due to product unreliability. As part of the comeback strategy, Mike decided to provide options to customers to either receive a new EMC storage system or take an IBM one at EMC rate (the price band of IBM was higher). IBM is its biggest competitor. EMC's customers understood that they were buying an IBM product at EMC price.

This move of Mike was criticized at EMC's corporate level, but Mike was convinced that this was the only way to restore the customers' confidence. His assumption was correct. EMC's customers recognized such an extraordinary move and took it as EMC's commitment to its customers. They decided to continue with EMC. With Mike, EMC could turn around. Technology companies such as CISCO Systems, Sun Microsystems, and Oracle reposed their confidence in EMC data archival products.

The company is now filled with capable technologists who systematically phase out obsolete products and develop new ones to peg competition for others and to retain and expand their customer base. This initiative of new product development, further reinforced by the do-or-die sales culture, improved the company's top line and helped it recover from a deadlock situation. With 99 per cent customer retention, EMC could set an example for others to emulate. This was highly acclaimed by the corporate world and researchers. EMC is convinced that developing world-class problem-solvers does not require heroes; instead, it requires team players to pool the collective wisdom and solve the problem on a real-time basis. Customer service requires people to be in the field and understand the real-time needs of the customers. 'Face the irate customers and dispel their apprehension'—this is the mantra of EMC. To bundle all these activities under the direct control of the top management, Mike centralized the customer and dispatch activities. To EMC, customer service runs like any other business unit; it is implanted in the company's DNA and is a continuous innovation.

Questions for Discussion

1. Read this case and suggest as an OB professional the type of managerial interventions that can ease the problem of customer service in a competitive, technology-intensive market.
2. Relate the TQM concept in this case to customer retention.

Index

Related Titles

Human Resource Management, 2e
(9780198074113)

P. Jyothi, Reader, School of Management Studies, University of Hyderabad

D.N. Venkatesh, Human Resource and Organizational Development Consultant

The second edition of *Human Resource Management*, designed to cater to the syllabi requirements of management students, is now interspersed with additions that make the title even more exhaustive. The text also covers related areas of human resource management (HRM), such as leadership and HR accounting and audit. With its comprehensive coverage of all the basic aspects of HRM, this new edition would also be useful for working professionals.

Key Features:

- Explores emerging areas of HRM such as strategic HRM, knowledge management, HRM in international organizations, and corporate social responsibility
- Provides examples and exhibits for illustrating the key concepts of HRM
- Includes classroom-tested case studies from Indian and international organizations
- Provides objective-type questions in the end-chapter exercises

Organizational Change and Development
(9780198066460)

Dipak Kumar Bhattacharyya, Xavier Institute of Management, Bhubaneswar

Organizational Change and Development is aimed at postgraduate students specializing in human resources (HR) and strategy. Providing a strong conceptual foundation of the subject, the book takes the readers through all the processes and stages of change, as seen and experienced worldwide. It also explains the strategies and the related implementation aspects of various concepts. It provides a detailed coverage of the economic, psychological, political, and sociological perspectives of organizational development (OD). In addition, it provides guidelines for change management.

Key Features:

- Includes exhibits and examples to explain OD and change management practices
- Discusses OD experiences in several Indian and international organizations such as Wal-Mart, Lehman Brothers, Godrej, and Indian Ordnance Factories
- Provides appendices on guidelines for organizational change, sample of a dashboard, and organizational health survey

Industrial Relations (9780195671087)

C.S. Venkata Ratnam, Former Director, International Management Institute, New Delhi

Industrial Relations is a textbook specially designed to meet the requirements of management students specializing in human resource management. The text provides an in-depth coverage of the four key components of industrial relations: the conceptual foundations, the institutional structure and policy framework, the role of government, and industrial relations in unionized organizations.

Key Features:

- Explores the emerging issues in industrial relations, such as labour law reform, employment security and management of redundancies, and technological change and industrial relations
- Examines the challenges faced by business organizations in industrial relations
- Contains classroom-tested case studies of Indian and international organizations
- Includes relevant labour procedures, codes, and recommendations of the national labour commissions
- Provides concept-review questions, critical thinking exercises, and classroom and field projects, such as group discussions and analytical reporting, at the end of the chapters

Cross-cultural Management
(9780198066293)

Shobhana Madhavan, Associate Professor, Amrita School of Business, Amrita Vishwa Vidyapeetham, Coimbatore

Cross-cultural Management—Concepts and Cases is a comprehensive textbook designed for postgraduate degree/diploma students of business management and practising managers. It explains how culture impacts international management in the areas of communication, negotiations, organizational behaviour, and human resource management.

Key Features:

- Discusses cross-cultural management in today's corporate India with a wide variety of Indian/Asian examples, making this text relevant to today's global India
- Includes classroom-tested original cases, providing exposure to a wide range of management contexts in countries such as Japan, Finland, Algeria, Canada, China, US, Mexico, UK, Germany, and India
- Provides important tips on business etiquette and key information regarding doing business in several countries, ranging from Brazil to Nigeria
- Includes mini cases and games to enhance students' interest and learning

Other Related Titles

9780195683592 Agarwala: *Strategic Human Resource Management*
9780195698718 Haldar: *Human Resource Development*
9780195693379 Deb & Kohli: *Performance Management*
9780195698374 Bhattacharyya: *Compensation Management*